Canadian Business and Society

ETHICS, RESPONSIBILITIES, AND SUSTAINABILITY

W9-CRA-206

Fifth Edition

ROBERT W. SEXTY

Professor Emeritus, Faculty of Business Administration
Memorial University of Newfoundland

Mc
Graw
Hill

Canadian Business and Society

Ethics, Responsibilities, and Sustainability

Fifth Edition

ISBN-13: 978-1-26-006591-6
ISBN-10: 1-26-006591-X

1 2 3 4 5 6 7 8 9 M 23 22 21 20

Printed and bound in Canada.

Product Director: *Rhondda McNabb*

Portfolio Managers: *Amy Clarke-Spencley & Mark Grzeskowiak*

Marketing Manager: *Emily Park*

Content Developer: *Krisha Escobar*

Portfolio Associate: *Tatiana Sevciuc*

Senior Supervising Editor: *Jessica Barnoski*

Photo/Permissions Editor: *Alison Lloyd Baker*

Copy Editor: *Sheila Craig*

Plant Production Coordinator: *Heitor Moura*

Manufacturing Production Coordinator: *Jason Stubner*

Cover Design: *Dianne Reynolds*

Cover Image: © *canadastock/Shutterstock*

Interior Design: *Michelle Losier*

Page Layout: *MPS Limited*

Printer: *Marquis*

Dedication

To Suzanne, who has travelled with me through five books including many editions—and to more than 70 countries on seven continents!

About the Author

Dr. Robert Sexty was a Professor of Business Administration at the Faculty of Business Administration at Memorial University of Newfoundland for 39 years, and was awarded a *Professor Emeritus* title in 2008. He holds bachelor, masters, and doctoral degrees in Business Administration from the University of Alberta, Queen's University, and the University of Colorado, respectively. Sabbatical years have been spent at the Harvard Business School, Boston, and the University of Auckland, New Zealand. He was awarded one of the "2001–2002 Leaders in Management Education Awards" sponsored by the *National Post* and PricewaterhouseCoopers.

At Memorial, Robert Sexty taught Business Policy (Strategic Management), Introduction to Business, and Business and Society (Business Ethics) courses at the undergraduate and graduate levels. He developed, and has taught, the strategy and business and society courses in Athabasca University's Electronic MBA Program. He has taught numerous management development seminars and workshops on many management topics, including strategic management and the ethics of business.

Robert Sexty is the author of *Issues in Canadian Business,* the fourth edition of which was published in 1998 as *Canadian Business in the New Stakeholder Economy.* He is also the co-author of *Exploring Strategic Management,* published in 1989, and *Contemporary Management in Canada,* published in 1992, 1995, and 1998. A fourth book, *Canadian Business and Society: Understanding the Social and Ethical Challenges,* was published in January 1995.

Robert Sexty is a past President of the Administrative Sciences Association of Canada, and is a member of, and active in, many academic and professional associations. He consults in the area of strategic planning and management for business, government, and non-profit organizations, and acts as a facilitator in sessions for management groups and boards of directors. He has served on the Boards of Directors of the Egg Farmers of Canada, East Coast Trail Association, and Anglican Homes Inc.

Brief Contents

Contents

Preface

The Philosophy of the Book

Ethics is all the rage throughout society these days; the ethics of business is no exception. Today, integrity is important to business performance and acceptance by society. Society expects business' adherence to moral standards such as honesty, fairness, and justice. This book provides a broad overview of the Canadian business system and society's expectations of it.

The book's title emphasizes "business and society" in addition to three key words: ethics, responsibilities, and sustainability. The ethics of business refers to the rules, standards, codes, values, or principles that provide guidance for morally appropriate behaviour in managerial decision-making relating to the operation of businesses and business's relationship with society. Business is accepted by society as long as it recognizes the responsibilities in its operations and considers the needs and desires of society. The result has been increasing obligations with business agreeing to do more. Sustainability represents a management approach that integrates economic, ethical, and environmental responsibilities into all management systems for the present and future benefit of society.

The corporation—the main business institution—accepts the necessity for integrity in business and recognizes the accompanying responsibilities. Throughout the book, the term *corporation* is used to represent business enterprises. The formal and legal entity of the corporation does not supply all the goods and services to society, but it is by far the principal business institution.

The ethics and responsibilities of business in society are connected to the concept of *stakeholders,* individuals or organizations that influence the corporation and/or that are influenced by the corporation. This concept will be described fully in the book and is key to the connection to or linkage between business and society.

Enhanced Fifth Edition Content

Several concepts and topics relevant to business and society are receiving new or expanded coverage. The ethics of artificial intelligence is examined in Chapter 1, Everyday Ethics 1.4 Artificial Intelligence (AI) and Ethical Issues, and Chapter 5, Everyday Ethics 5.3 The Ethics of Robots. The role of social media is discussed in more detail in Chapter 13, Learning Outcome (LO) 13.2 The Media Stakeholder.

Indigenous Peoples are identified as a stakeholder and discussed in Chapter 2, Everyday Ethics 2.2 Indigenous Peoples and Property Rights; Chapter 8, LO 8.5 CSR and Indigenous Peoples; Chapter 8, Everyday Ethics 8.7 Examples of Corporate Indigenous Community Investment; Chapter 11, LO 11.3 Responsible Investment; Chapter 12, Responsibility for Ethics 12.9 Canadian Aboriginal and Minority Supplier Council (CAMSC); and Chapter 13, Case 13.1 Pipelines, NGOs, and First Nations.

It is appropriate to recognize the role of business students and business schools in society. Relevant content is in Chapter 1, LO 1.2 Integrity of Business Students; Chapter 9, LO 9.8 Business Schools and Sustainability Reporting; and Chapter 16, LO 16.5 Socialization of Capitalism and Business School Programs.

In Chapter 7, a new section has been included in LO 7.2 The Corporate Social Responsibility Debate describing an ethical basis for CSR. LO 9.5 Corporate Social Reporting Guidelines has been revised with more detail on the Global Reporting Initiative. Chapter 10 has been reorganized with LO 10.1 Types of Regulation now covering government, self-regulation, private or civil, and market regulation. Employees as stakeholders in Chapter 12, LO 12.1 has been reorganized and now includes discussion on business' relationship to the LGBTQ+ and #MeToo movements. Chapter 16 defines several variations on capitalism, including clean, moral, and progressive capitalism, that focus on the corporation's social purpose.

In addition, new concepts and topics introduced include: Chapter 1, social contract; Chapter 2, boycott; Chapter 4, issue materiality; Chapter 5, ethical dilemmas; Chapter 6, corporate culture and ethical corporate culture; Chapter 8, redwashing; Chapter 10, third-party certification; Chapter 12, gig economy, localism, ethical consumption, supplier diversity, and lifecycle thinking; Chapter 14, circular economy; Chapter 15, sweatshop production and slowbalisation; and Chapter 16, social intrapreneurship, extrapreneurship, and social purpose.

Two new "Ethics, Responsibilities, and Sustainability" cases are included. "The Bread Scandal and Loblaw's Ethical Culture" examines how an ethical crisis occurred and the appropriateness of the corporation's response, and "'Here's to Our Next 100 Years' and the Closing of a Plant" questions the decision to close a plant and the responsibilities involved.

Overview of the Book's Contents

The topics covered in the book represent a consensus on the current subjects making up the business and society field. Business and the corporation operate within various societal environments,[1] and these environments provide a basis for the book's organization.

- **Business Environment**—The description of the business environment is given in Chapters 1, 2, and 16. Chapter 1, "The Relationship between Business and Society," provides an overview to the book and describes the concept of *business and society.* Other topics covered in this chapter include an outline of the Canadian business system, the role of the corporation, the stakeholders responsible for operating corporations, a brief introduction to ethical thinking, and society's acceptance of business. Chapter 2, "Ethics and Capitalism," describes the fundamentals of capitalism upon which the Canadian business system is based. It is important to understand these fundamentals, as the ethical implications associated with them reappear throughout the book. Finally, Chapter 16, focuses on new developments in the relationship between business and society.

- **Stakeholder Environment**—Chapters 3, 4, 11, 12, and 13 focus on stakeholders and their relationships with business and the corporation. Chapter 3, "Identifying Stakeholders and Issues," gives a detailed list of a corporation's stakeholders and the rationale for the stakeholder concept. The following chapter, "Stakeholder and Issue Analysis," advances the discussion of stakeholders by presenting approaches to the corporation's interrelationships with stakeholders. Although stakeholders are referred to throughout the textbook, some are studied in more detail. Owners and directors in Chapter 11, "Responsible Ownership and Governance"; employees, consumers, competitors, and suppliers in Chapter 12, "Ethics and Responsibilities in the Workplace and Marketplace"; and non-governmental organizations, media, think tanks, religious organizations and education institutions in Chapter 13, "Civil Society Stakeholders."

- **Ethical Environment**—The ethical environment is addressed in two chapters: Chapter 5, "Ethics of Business: The Theoretical Basis," and Chapter 6, "Ethics of Business: Management and Leadership." The former chapter outlines several theoretical ethical principles that will assist in understanding and analyzing moral dilemmas and integrity issues confronting business and the corporation. The latter chapter takes a pragmatic approach to outlining the managerial techniques or methodologies of ethics programs in corporations.

- **Social Environment**—Similar to the approach taken with the ethical environment, the social environment is discussed from theoretical and practical perspectives. Chapter 7, "Corporate Social Responsibility: The Concept," describes the various theories of social responsibility that can be used when analyzing issues and cases throughout the book. In Chapter 8, "Corporate Social Responsibility: In Practice," the approaches taken by corporations to implement their social responsibilities are outlined.

- **Regulatory Environment**—Business and the corporation are accountable to stakeholders as they are influenced by them in various ways. In effect, this is a form of regulation of the corporation. Chapter 9, "Measuring, Reporting, and Communicating CSR," identifies auditing processes used by corporations in reporting how they respond to their economic, stakeholder, ethical, and social environments. Chapter 10, "Regulating Business' Ethics and Responsibilities," identifies the range of regulation—from government legislation and policies through to self-regulation performed by industry associations and the corporation itself. Corporate governance is, in effect, the regulation or oversight of the corporation's activities provided by the board of directors. Corporate governance has been reformed in recent years, with emphasis placed on the corporation's ethics and responsibilities.

- **Ecological Environment**—The natural or ecological environment is considered in Chapter 14, "The Environment and Business Responsibilities." Ecology is a major issue involving many responsibilities and thus is discussed as a separate chapter.

- **International Environment**—The international environment, also referred to as *globalization*, involves many ethical issues and responsibilities. Chapter 15, "Globalization and Business Responsibilities," outlines how globalization is impacting almost every business and identifies how corporations are responding.

The topics covered relate to those addressed by two leading business and society organizations. The contents are consistent with the new domain statement for the Academy of Management's Social Issues in Management Division which "studies the social issues, institutions, interactions, and impacts of management." In particular, the Division addresses: individual and organizational ethics; organizational and systemic governance; and stakeholder behaviours, relationships, and systems.[2] The International Association of Business and Society "focuses on developmental work in the relationships between business, government and society." Some of the subjects covered are corporate social responsibility and performance, emerging social issues for business, business ethics, environmental affairs, and business and government relations.[3]

The frameworks are covered throughout the book and, with the environments described above, provide a comprehensive and contemporary view of the ethics, responsibilities, and sustainability of business.

Features and Benefits of the Book

- **A unique approach.** Each chapter offers unique materials or extensive descriptions of various topics as they relate to the ethics, responsibilities, and sustainability of business. Ethics refers to the fairness and integrity with which business functions in society; responsibilities refers to the increasing obligations that business is agreeing to undertake in society; and sustainability represents a management approach that integrates economic, ethical, and environmental responsibilities into all management systems.

- **A building approach.** The sequence of the chapters and the concepts covered enable students to learn about business and society incrementally. Thus, concepts relating to capitalism and the economic responsibilities of the corporation are introduced early, followed by the stakeholder concept. This body of knowledge is key to understanding the subsequent chapters. Similarly, theoretical material is followed by managerial practice in the social and ethical environments and becomes the basis for understanding the discussions in parts IV and V.

- **A focus on Canadian content.** The material in the book emphasizes Canadian content; it is Canadian ground-up, rather than a conversion of an American or European text.

- **Business and managerial perspectives.** The book is written from the perspective of business and managers, as they have to cope with social, ethical, and environmental responsibilities while also having to meet economic responsibilities. The materials are not intended to make judgments about business behaviour, but instead to increase the understanding of businesspersons and managers of their influence on society and of society's influence on business. Both good and undesirable examples of business behaviour are presented.

- **Non-profit sector included.** Non-profit organizations also play a role in business and society. This sector is represented by stakeholders such as non-governmental organizations, educational institutions, religious groups, and charities. These stakeholders are important in social responsibility initiatives described throughout the book but particularly in Chapters 7, 8, and 9. Most of Chapter 13, "Civil Society Stakeholders," is devoted to non-profit stakeholders. Chapter 16 includes a discussion of the interaction between business and the non-profit sector.

- **A student perspective.** Efforts have been made to present materials, vignettes, example inserts, and cases to which students can relate. Students are the future business leaders and managers and must understand the dynamic relationship between business and society and the ethics and responsibilities involved. More emphasis has been put on the ethics, responsibilities, and sustainability of students, in business programs, and at educational institutions.

Encouraging Critical Thinking

Critical thinking is a higher-order intellectual, purposeful thought and action process. It integrates inquiry, reflection, and deliberation to facilitate more thorough and meaningful learning. This book enables students to accomplish this in several ways: by introducing new ideas and concepts, linking ideas to illustrations, addressing issues from different perspectives, and exposing readers to new sources of information. The concepts, theories, and illustrations allow students to use their skills to clarify facts, assess information, formulate and defend their own intellectual positions, and develop appropriate courses of action. The pedagogical approaches listed below encourage student critical thinking. The Instructor's Manual provides teachers with additional materials that will enhance this process.

Pedagogy: User Approach

- **Learning Outcomes.** At the beginning of each chapter, numbered Learning Outcomes are listed. These tie in with the numbered section headings in each chapter.

LEARNING OUTCOMES

After studying this chapter, you will be able to:

LO 1.1   Describe the complexity of the interrelationships between business and society.

LO 1.2   Define the terminology relating to the integrity of business management and students.

LO 1.3   Differentiate between the three main approaches to ethical thinking.

LO 1.4   Provide a brief description of the Canadian business system.

LO 1.5   Explain the role of the corporation as the main economic institution in the business system.

LO 1.6   Recognize that business operates with the consent of society.

LO 1.7   Summarize factors that influence society's attitudes toward business that lead to criticisms of the system.

LO 1.8   Identify the groups that are mainly responsible for the operation of Canadian businesses.

LO 1.9   Describe the integration of business and society.

- **In-depth examples.** Instead of inserting numerous but short one- or two-sentence examples in the text, this book takes a different approach. Lengthier boxed inserts allow for more discussion of the examples. The two types of boxes are Everyday Ethics and Responsibility for Ethics.

- **Everyday Ethics** boxes provide examples not only of best practices, but also of inappropriate or questionable practices. More than 20 new Everyday Ethics boxes have been included and all the remaining ones updated. Instructors are provided with additional information to facilitate classroom discussion in the Instructor's Manual and online.

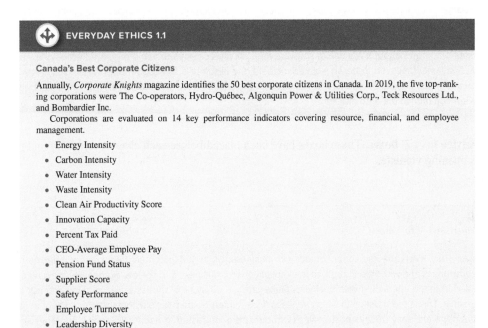

EVERYDAY ETHICS 1.1

Canada's Best Corporate Citizens

Annually, *Corporate Knights* magazine identifies the 50 best corporate citizens in Canada. In 2019, the five top-ranking corporations were The Co-operators, Hydro-Québec, Algonquin Power & Utilities Corp., Teck Resources Ltd., and Bombardier Inc.

Corporations are evaluated on 14 key performance indicators covering resource, financial, and employee management.

- Energy Intensity
- Carbon Intensity
- Water Intensity
- Waste Intensity
- Clean Air Productivity Score
- Innovation Capacity
- Percent Tax Paid
- CEO-Average Employee Pay
- Pension Fund Status
- Supplier Score
- Safety Performance
- Employee Turnover
- Leadership Diversity
- Sustainability Pay Link

- **Responsibility for Ethics** boxes refer to or describe individuals, organizations, practices, or concepts that affect or influence the behaviour of business leaders, managers, or corporations. Most describe the roles or influence of stakeholders. Five new Responsibility for Ethics boxes have been included and the remaining ones updated.

 RESPONSIBILITY FOR ETHICS 1.1

Adam Smith, the "Father of Capitalism"

Adam Smith, 1723–90, was a Scottish philosopher and economist whose ideas have had a major impact on capitalist economic systems worldwide. He wrote extensively, but two books have been the most influential: *The Theory of Moral Sentiments*, published in 1759, and *An Inquiry into the Nature and Causes of the Wealth of Nations*, published in 1776.

Smith proposed a different view of morality than was prevalent at the time. One view was that moral principles could rationally identify right versus wrong, while the other view believed that governments and the laws they created established a standard of morality. Smith believed that people were born with a moral sense, or conscience, that told them what was right or wrong. For Smith, morality was a product of nature, not of reason. In any event, Smith believed that economic man and moral man had to co-exist.

The "invisible hand" concept was originated by Smith. He believed that well-functioning, competitive markets efficiently distributed society's scarce resources without the guiding hand of government or economic planners. Pursuit of individual self-interest through consumption and the achievement of profits resulted in economic growth that benefited everyone.

Smith's writings continue to influence morality in capitalist economies, even though they are still being challenged by some in society.

- **Opening vignettes.** All vignettes are original and based on Canadian materials and examples. Each chapter begins with a real-world situation that introduces the chapter content. All require an individual to respond to an issue or dilemma. Four new vignettes are included in this edition and several others have been revised.

What would you do if...?

··

George Lafontaine had always been an enthusiastic Volkswagen (VW) customer. As a young man, he drove a Beetle, then as he got older he purchased a Golf, then a Jetta, and most recently a Passat. It was time for George to purchase a new car, but he was hesitating at buying another Volkswagen. He had heard some disturbing news about VW's use of software manipulation devices to avoid regulated emissions standards. At first it was believed to be an isolated incident, the result of a few rogue employees. But, investigations by the media and others found that this was not the case. In fact, some believed that unethical behaviours were common in the auto industry.

- **"Your Advice to . . ." boxes.** These boxes have been placed before each chapter summary and relate back to the chapter's opening vignette.

Your advice to Vanessa . . .

··

Every day, everyone has some contact with business. Usually, this contact takes place under normal circumstances and with little thought to the implications for business and society. Sometimes, however, issues arise from the interaction with business. Quite often, the nature of the issues is complex and not easy to resolve. This is the situation in which Vanessa finds herself. Some possible courses of action are suggested but none are easy. Today, most business students are interested in economic, social, and environmental sustainability. In a course focusing on business and society, an understanding of the ethics of business and the responsibilities involved prepares students to answer questions like those posed in the vignette.

- **End-of-chapter cases.** Cases relevant to the chapter content can be found in the end-of-chapter material. The cases are of two types: (1) descriptive of an issue in business and society to which management must respond and can be used as a basis for discussion; and (2) decision making in that the student faces a dilemma that must be addressed. Sixteen new cases are included in this edition, and many others have been altered and updated.

Cases

1.1 SEARS CANADA'S BANKRUPTCY AND PENSIONERS

Most Canadians expect employers to provide pensions as one benefit of the employment contract. The expectations include not only coverage but also adequate funds to maintain a desired retirement lifestyle and security for the longevity of the pension. Government officials and financial industry spokespersons are warning of a crisis in the pension system, especially pensions in the private or business sector. Some claim that the crisis in pensions will have a negative impact on overall economic efficiency.

The two most common types of pension plans are defined benefit and defined contribution. Defined benefit plans guarantee a retirement payment based on income level and years of service. The risk of return and longevity is assumed by the employer; that is, the employer is responsible for deficits in the plan. The defined benefit type is the most common, but this type is experiencing a major problem: there are insufficient assets to support the payment of pension obligations to retired employees. The deficits in the plans have resulted from lower interest rates reducing earnings, stricter standards imposed by government regulations, and higher costs or payouts.

- **"Learn more" boxes.** Boxed features directing readers who want to know more about certain chapter topics to Connect are included where applicable. Several new ones are included.

  Chapter 1
  - Academic integrity
  - Adam Smith
  - Corporate wrongdoing in Canada
  - Artificial intelligence and ethics

  Want to learn more about academic integrity?

- **Critical Thinking and Discussion Questions.** Every chapter ends with a set of questions that challenge the students to apply the concepts they have learned in each chapter. Some questions require students to think on their own to understand and evaluate concepts and, in some instances, to apply them appropriately. Other questions are designed to generate discussion and the articulation of different points of view.

Critical Thinking and Discussion Questions

1. Do most Canadians understand the workings of the Canadian business system or capitalism? Do you? Give reasons to support your answer.
2. Do you agree with the position that the frequency of wrongdoing by business is about the same as for individuals or any other institutions in society?
3. Why do people disagree on what is morally appropriate behaviour? Which approach to ethical thinking do you practise?
4. How would you describe the Canadian business system?
5. Which two factors influence the integrity of Canadian business the most?
6. Should corporations be formed only with the permission of society as represented by government, or should they be allowed to form freely without much government oversight?
7. What is the connection between the type of approach to incorporation and society's expectations of the corporation?
8. Why should the members of the board of directors have any interest in the relationship between business and society?
9. What most influences your attitude toward business?
10. Should businesspersons be concerned about how they and business are portrayed in the media?
11. What are the integrity or ethical challenges you confront as a student?

- **Ethics, Responsibilities, and Sustainability Cases.** Longer cases are included that allow for more in-depth discussion of issues and dilemmas relating to the ethics, responsibilities and sustainability of business. The cases are of two types: (1) descriptive of an issue in business and society to which management must respond and can be used as a basis for discussion of the issue; and (2) decision making in that the student faces a dilemma that must be addressed. Two new cases are provided.

Ethics, Responsibilities, and Sustainability Cases

 Energy Drinks at Prairie Pharmacy[1]

Victor Lukasik has just taken over the operation of the family drug store, Prairie Pharmacy. The pharmacy was started by his grandfather and carried on by his father, who now is semi-retired working as a relief or part-time pharmacist. The pharmacy was located in a Western Canada community of about 5,200 that was also served by a large retail drugstore chain. Despite the competition, Prairie Pharmacy continued to prosper because the loyalty of long-time customers and its personalized service. The pharmacy had started as a prescription filling outlet and sold a few over the counter medications. Over the years, the pharmacy had grown and now sold a large variety of over-the-counter medications, snack food, candies and soft drinks, cosmetics, greeting cards, magazines, and personal care products. It had a Canada Post franchise outlet.

The book's contents have been developed and designed to make the study of Canadian business and society attractive and challenging. The capitalist business system exists in Canada and the ethics, responsibilities, and sustainability of business must be studied in this context. Ethical challenges do exist, and corporations should be held accountable for the responsibilities they have to Canadians. Increasingly, Canadian business is moving toward corporate sustainability strategies. It is hoped this book will increase students' understanding of Canadian business and society.

Acknowledgement

The author and McGraw-Hill appreciate the review of Indigenous content by David Newhouse, Professor and Director, Chanie Wenjack School for Indigenous Studies, Trent University. His recommendations led to appropriately worded references to the Indigenous community.

Award-Winning Technology

McGraw-Hill Connect® is an award-winning digital teaching and learning solution that empowers students to achieve better outcomes and enables instructors to improve efficiency with course management. Within Connect, students have access to SmartBook®, McGraw-Hill's adaptive learning and reading resource. SmartBook prompts students with questions based on the material they are studying. By assessing individual answers, SmartBook learns what each student knows and identifies which topics they need to practise, giving each student a personalized learning experience and path to success.

Connect's key features include analytics and reporting, simple assignment management, smart grading, the opportunity to post your own resources, and the Connect Instructor Library, a repository for additional resources to improve student engagement in and out of the classroom.

Instructor resources for *Canadian Business and Society* 5th Edition:

- Instructor's Manual
- Test Bank
- Microsoft® PowerPoint® Presentations
- Manager's Hot Seat Videos

INSTRUCTOR RESOURCES

- **Instructor's Manual:** Includes comments on each chapter's opening vignette, material by section with the objective for each section, additional notes/materials/suggestions for instructors, responses to discussion questions, analysis of cases, additional resources such as references to case studies relevant for each chapter, video resources, and assignments/questions.

  The IM also provides additional information on the **Everyday Ethics** and **Responsibility for Ethics** boxes. The boxes are considered a key aspect of the text. Rather than give hundreds of one-line examples, the examples/illustrations in the boxes give more detailed information, and are constructed so that instructors can use them for discussion purposes or assignments. Features found throughout the boxes include:

  - Discussion questions
  - Additional material
  - Suggested assignments for students
  - Updated information
  - Internet links and related sites

- **Computerized Test Bank:** Within Connect, instructors can easily create automatically graded assessments from a comprehensive test bank featuring multiple question types and randomized question order. The Test Bank for the 5th Edition was created by John Amendola of George Brown College.

- **PowerPoint® Presentation Slides:** These visually stimulating slides provide an overview using illustrations, defini-tions, and examples, focusing on the primary concepts in each chapter. The PowerPoint Presentation Slides for the 5th Edition was prepared by Renee Majeau from Northern Alberta Institute of Technology.
- **Manager's Hot Seat Videos:** This resource allows students to watch real managers apply their years of experience to management and organizational behaviour issues. Students assume the role of the manager as they watch the video and then answer multiple-choice questions following the segment. The Manager's Hot Seat Videos are ideal for group or classroom discussions.

Effective. Efficient. Easy to Use.

McGraw-Hill Connect is an award-winning digital teaching and learning solution that empowers students to achieve better outcomes and enables instructors to improve course-management efficiency.

Personalized & Adaptive Learning

Connect's integrated SmartBook helps students study more efficiently, highlighting where in the text to focus and asking review questions to give each student a personalized learning experience and path to success.

High-Quality Course Material

Our trusted solutions are designed to help students actively engage in course content and develop critical higher-level thinking skills, while offering you the flexibility to tailor your course to meet your needs.

Analytics & Reporting

Monitor progress and improve focus with Connect's visual and actionable dashboards. Reporting features empower instructors and students with real-time performance analytics.

Seamless Integration

Link your Learning Management System with Connect for single sign-on and gradebook synchronization, with all-in-one ease for you and your students.

Impact of Connect on Pass Rates

72.5%

Without Connect

85.2%

With Connect

SMARTBOOK®

NEW SmartBook 2.0 builds on our market-leading adaptive technology with enhanced capabilities and a streamlined interface that deliver a more usable, accessible, and mobile learning experience for both students and instructors.

Available on mobile smart devices—with both online and offline access—the ReadAnywhere app lets students study anywhere, anytime.

SUPPORT AT EVERY STEP

McGraw-Hill ensures you are supported every step of the way. From course design and set-up, to instructor training, LMS integration and ongoing support, your Digital Success Consultant is there to make your course as effective as possible.

Learn more about Connect at mheducation.ca

Business provides most of the goods and services required by society.
Used © Big Cheese Photo/SuperStock

CHAPTER 1

The Relationship between Business and Society

LEARNING OUTCOMES

After studying this chapter, you will be able to:

LO 1.1   Describe the complexity of the interrelationships between business and society.

LO 1.2   Define the terminology relating to the integrity of business management and students.

LO 1.3   Differentiate between the three main approaches to ethical thinking.

LO 1.4   Provide a brief description of the Canadian business system.

LO 1.5   Explain the role of the corporation as the main economic institution in the business system.

LO 1.6   Recognize that business operates with the consent of society.

LO 1.7   Summarize factors that influence society's attitudes toward business that lead to criticisms of the system.

LO 1.8   Identify the groups that are mainly responsible for the operation of Canadian businesses.

LO 1.9   Describe the integration of business and society.

What would you do if...?

Vanessa Nugent was amazed, overwhelmed, fascinated, and a little upset. These feelings resulted from reading a long article in the student newspaper on "fast fashion," which was defined as an approach used in the apparel industry to design, create, manufacture, and market on-trend, high-fashion-style, inexpensive clothing. A key feature of the approach was to shorten the time between design and delivery, or purchase by consumers. Critics claimed this led to a clothing craze as there was a constant arrival of new designs, enticing consumers to continually purchase newly designed clothing. Vanessa recognized her connection to the issue, as she purchased this type of clothing herself and had been a sales clerk in two stores that sold fast fashions.

The article stated that this approach to clothing was made possible by innovations in the supply chain. Manufacturers in developing countries in Asia used modern technology and hired low-cost employees. Designs could be transmitted electronically and quick factory conversion for the production of new designs was possible. Transportation was inexpensive by sea and even possible by air. Retailers and manufacturers were able to frequently match production with demand.

Vanessa realized that the low prices and constantly changing fashions made possible by supply chain innovations came at the expense of other stakeholders. The fashion and apparel industry was the world's second largest polluting sector after fossil fuels. Large workforces, 80 percent of which were women, were necessary and there was alleged forced labour. Unsafe and poor working conditions existed in many factories. This was highlighted by the 2013 Rana Plaza garment factory disaster in Bangladesh, which killed over 1,000 workers. Many retailers and non-governmental organizations have pressured the factory owners for improvements in working conditions. This occurred at the same time factory owners were being asked to reduce costs and to deliver faster. There was also an issue with intellectual property, as manufacturers copied each other's designs.

There were several retailers that relied on the fast-fashion approach, including Zara, H&M, The Gap, and Forever 21, as well as many department stores. No longer was fashion based on fall and spring changes; instead, there was a constant introduction of new products encouraging consumers to purchase. As small amounts could be ordered, there were fewer markdowns for retailers, and rather than replenishing a product, it was simply replaced with another new fashion product.

The advantage to consumers was that they were able to purchase trendy clothing at affordable prices. The continual purchasing of new styles encouraged a throw-away attitude—that is, the approach had built-in product obsolescence. Many consumers recycled old clothing via charities, thrift stores, or bins provided by some fashion retailers. Some of the surplus clothing was actually returned to developing countries as donations, but in many cases this disrupted local clothing markets. Consumers have become used to low prices and their purchasing of fast fashions will be difficult to break.

Vanessa did find that some retailers were attempting to break the fast-fashion cycle. She found one website of particular interest, Fashion Takes Action (https://fashiontakesaction.com/), which claims to be Canada's only non-profit fashion industry organization focusing on sustainability by changing the way the industry creates and consumes fashion. She was relieved to find that not everyone in the apparel industry was committed to fast fashions.

After learning about the fast-fashion clothing industry, Vanessa wondered what she could or should do. She never appreciated how complex the interrelationship between business and society was. The ethical, social, and environmental issues involved were difficult to resolve. Of course, she could stop purchasing so much clothing and encourage others to follow suit. She could join anti-poverty or charitable organizations to help familiarize them with the issue. She might approach the Students' Union to address the issue.

What is your advice to Vanessa?

Ethical implications are present in all facets of life, and business and society is no exception. The ethics of business receives more attention, as everyone in society is affected. For this reason, students of business should learn about ethics in the relationship between business and society. This chapter gives some background on the setting for understanding the complexity of the relationship. The factors influencing morality in Canadian business are identified. The role of the corporation is outlined, as it is the principal institution in the business system along with the three main stakeholders in the governance and management of the corporation—owners, boards of directors, and managers. Society has expectations of business, and various factors influence society's attitudes toward business. The relationship between business and society is complicated since each depends on the other.

LO 1.1   The Business and Society Relationship

Canadian business and society is a fascinating topic. It involves studying the history and background of the Canadian business system in addition to examining the contemporary issues confronting business. It is very important to obtain all the viewpoints that contribute, or should contribute, to what business' role will be in society. Canadian society comprises many institutions and groups that interact, including governments, labour unions, minority groups, environmentalists, consumers, the communications media, business organizations, and a variety of interest groups or non-governmental organizations. All have an important role to play, and all, in some way, influence business decision making. This book emphasizes several things about the Canadian business system, with certain goals in particular:

1. To increase awareness of the system by describing Canadian capitalism, the stakeholders involved, and society's attitudes toward business;

2. To identify business' response to its role in society by examining who owns and runs business corporations, how business has incorporated ethics and responsibilities into its operations, and how business manages its role;

3. To learn how business corporations have responded to many challenges in their environment; and

4. To address the above from the perspective of the manager or owner of a corporation to emphasize the dynamic nature of the environment in which they manage.

Rather than focusing on what is right or wrong beyond any doubt, the emphasis in this text is on the appropriate analysis of problems and issues using information from a variety of sources, including the conflicting and maybe erroneous perceptions of various parties as to the motives, strategies, and tactics of others. Since we are dealing with so many individuals and organizations, perceptions of business vary—from the very negative attitudes held by some political parties and non-governmental organizations to the very positive attitudes held by business-oriented groups.

The issues that arise as a result of these differing perceptions and points of view are not easily resolved. Solutions are not always straightforward or simple, and tend to be less than optimum for all involved. Trade-offs are a factor, and what is an appropriate solution for one group is not as appropriate for another. An optimum solution is still sought, but it is certainly realized that each group in society will not benefit to the maximum.

A shift has occurred in what society believes business responsibilities should be, and at the same time many corporations are recognizing that they must respond to this belief if they are to survive and continue to be profitable. As a result, corporations are considering the following in their relationship to society:

- Business corporations should meet humanity's needs without harming future generations.

- Social responsibility or corporate sustainability reports published should move beyond the public relations exercises they may have been in the past.

- Increasing numbers of stakeholders are demanding corporations account for more than economic responsibilities.

- Progressive and innovative responses to social, ethical, and environmental responsibilities constitute a valuable intangible asset.

- Executives must have the skills and competencies to manage these additional responsibilities successfully.

- Responses to these responsibilities will determine the corporations that will survive.[1]

One attempt at measuring the responsiveness of corporations is the *Corporate Knights* Magazine's annual ranking of the best corporations in Canada described in Everyday Ethics 1.1.

Canada's Best Corporate Citizens

Annually, *Corporate Knights* magazine identifies the 50 best corporate citizens in Canada. In 2019, the five top-ranking corporations were The Co-operators, Hydro-Québec, Algonquin Power & Utilities Corp., Teck Resources Ltd., and Bombardier Inc.

Corporations are evaluated on 14 key performance indicators covering resource, financial, and employee management.

- Energy Intensity
- Carbon Intensity
- Water Intensity
- Waste Intensity
- Clean Air Productivity Score
- Innovation Capacity
- Percent Tax Paid
- CEO-Average Employee Pay
- Pension Fund Status
- Supplier Score
- Safety Performance
- Employee Turnover
- Leadership Diversity
- Sustainability Pay Link

Source: For indicator details refer to "2019 Best 50 Methodology," Corporate Knights website at https://www.corporateknights.com/reports/2019-best-50 /2019-best-50-methodology-15526619/ accessed June 6, 2019, and "2019 Best 50 Results," Corporate Knights website at https://www.corporateknights.com /reports/2019-best-50/2019-best-50-results-15596280/ accessed June 6, 2019. Also available in *Corporate Knights,* Summer 2019, Vol. 18, Issue 3, 32-33, 35-37. Used with permission of Corporate Knights.

Most business academics and practitioners would agree that the business system is progressing in the right direction. However, other stakeholders would suggest that business is changing too slowly or not at all. The next section, "Integrity in Business," discusses the appropriateness of the business relationship to society.

LO 1.2   Integrity in Business

In the business environment, **integrity** refers to the appropriateness of a corporation's behaviour and its adherence to moral guidelines acceptable to society such as honesty, fairness, and justice. Integrity is the same as acting ethically, but without the negative connotation, the moralizing tone, or the sense of naiveté. According to De George, "Acting with integrity means both acting in accordance with one's highest self-accepted norms of behaviour and imposing on oneself the norms demanded by ethics and morality."[2] Managing with integrity means that business leaders behave in a manner consistent with their own highest values and norms of behaviour, which are self-imposed but at the same time not arbitrary or self-serving. De George states behaviour need not be perfect either: "The imperative to act with integrity cannot insist on moral perfection. It can and does demand taking ethical considerations seriously."[3] Throughout this book, how business enterprises accomplish integrity is discussed and evaluated.

Some fundamental points are to be made about integrity in business. Ethics exist throughout society and are not unique to business. When referring to *business ethics,* what is meant is the ethics that apply to business. It does not mean there is a special kind of ethics peculiar to business and not applicable elsewhere in life. Thus, the phrase "ethics of business" is used in this book unless referring to another work or spokesperson.

Key terminologies relating to integrity in business are listed in Table 1.1. Many definitions for these terms exist; the table provides the basics to assist in understanding their usage prior to reading about them in more detail in the chapters identified within square brackets.

TABLE 1.1	Key Terminology Relating to Integrity in Business

Ethics of business: The rules, standards, codes, or principles that provide guidance for morally appropriate behaviour in managerial decision making relating to the operation of the business enterprise's and business' relationship with society. [Chapters 5 and 6] It is broadly defined to include corporate social responsibility (CSR), corporate sustainability (CS), triple bottom line, corporate citizenship, corporate governance, accountability, and environmental stewardship. [Chapters 7, 8, 9, 11, 14]

Stakeholder: An individual or group who can influence and/or is influenced by the achievement of an organization's purpose. [Chapters 3 and 4]

Corporate social responsibility (CSR): The way a corporation achieves a balance among its economic, social, and environmental responsibilities in its operations so as to address stakeholder expectations. [Chapter 7]

Corporate sustainability (CS): Corporate activities demonstrating the inclusion of social and environmental as well as economic responsibilities in business operations as they impact all stakeholders to ensure the long-term survival of the corporation. The term *sustainability* was first used in the context of environmental sustainability, but corporate sustainability has the wider meaning and includes economic, ethical, and social responsibilities as well. The difference from CSR is that the responsibilities are completely integrated to the structure, policies, and operations of the corporation. [Chapters 7, 16]

Triple bottom line: The triple-E bottom line (3E) is the evaluation of a corporation's performance according to a summary of the economic, social or ethical, and environmental value the corporation adds or destroys. A variation is the triple-P bottom line (3P), which is an evaluation of the corporation's performance according to people, planet, and profits. [Chapter 7]

Corporate citizenship: A corporation demonstrating that it takes into account its role in and complete impact on society and the environment as well as its economic influence. [Chapter 7]

In this book, some assumptions are made about the integrity of business:

- Ethics apply to business in the same manner as they do in any other institution in society, for example public administration, politics, religious organizations, the professions, and the legal, health, and educational systems. There are no ethics unique to business; it is only the issues and settings that are different.
- The appropriateness of behaviour is examined in terms of the ethical implications of addressing issues or decisions and of the distribution of harms and benefits to the relevant stakeholders.
- Integrity results in the **responsible corporation**, a business undertaking that responds to social, ethical, and environmental responsibilities in addition to its economic obligations. Everyday Ethics 1.2 illustrates how some Canadian corporations describe how they are responsible.

 EVERYDAY ETHICS 1.2

Responsible Corporations

Corporations that consider themselves responsible will describe it in different ways as illustrated below. They may also use the terms *social responsibility, community,* and *sustainability.* All terms indicate an effort to operate with integrity in society.

AltaGas Ltd.: "AltaGas operates in a safe, reliable manner in close partnership with First Nations and communities. AltaGas has three guiding principles for developing energy infrastructure: respect the land, share the benefits, and nurture long-term relationships." Source: "Responsibility," AltaGas Ltd. website at https://www.altagas.ca/responsibility.

BlackBerry Limited: "BlackBerry's business is based on trust, a trust maintained and grown by requiring our people, our suppliers and our vendors to conduct business in an ethical, socially responsible manner that meets and exceeds our customers' expectations. We are committed to strengthening our communities and protecting our environment." Source: "Responsibility," BlackBerry Limited website at https://www.blackberry.com/us/en/company/corporate-responsibility/responsibility.

Connect First Credit Union: "Community is all of our responsibility. When you're a member, you can be proud your money is making a difference – a genuine and lasting contribution to the financial success of your local community." Source: "Community," Connect First Credit Union website at https://www.connectfirstcu.com/community.

Gibson Energy Inc.: "Our responsibility begins with the health and safety of our employees, contractors and communities." Source: "Our Responsibility," Gibson Energy Inc. website at https://www.gibsonenergy.com/our-responsibility/.

Lundin Mining Corporation: "Lundin Mining is committed to responsible mining. Our reputation as a good corporate citizen is central to our values and vital to the long-term success of our business. We seek to create enduring relationships and shared values with our local communities and our stakeholders." Source: "Responsible Mining," Lundin Mining Corporation website at https://www.lundinmining.com/responsible-mining/overview/.

Methanex Corporation: "At Methanex we adhere to the highest principles of health, safety, environmental stewardship and social responsibility." Source: "Responsible Care," Methanex Corporation website at https://www.methanex.com/responsible-care.

These assumptions do not mean that business is not involved in wrongdoing or in inappropriate behaviour, as will be pointed out throughout the book. The responses to the issues created relating to the ethics of business and society are usually complex, with implications for many stakeholders. Sometimes the actions, solutions, or outcomes are unsatisfactory to society, in which case business may be required to change its behaviour or may voluntarily change its behaviour.

Integrity of Business Students

The integrity of business has been discussed, but the integrity of *future* business entrepreneurs, managers, and employees must also be examined while they are in academic programs.

At issue is whether the lack of academic integrity will have an influence on business integrity. College and university business programs are facing demands from society and the business community to better prepare their graduates to identify and address ethical implications in business. Until recently, business schools had largely neglected ethics and emphasized functional areas, some of which have focused on the financial rather than the social responsibilities of business. Corporate corruption practices have increased awareness of ethical practice in business. Graduates who will be managers and businesspersons need a moral compass and sensitivity to integrity issues. In other words, graduates must be prepared to face the reality of moral dilemmas.

The focus must not only be on graduates and their future behaviour but also on the practices internal to business schools. Numerous ethical issues arise during the educational experience within the business school. These issues involve not only students but also faculty members. The business school itself must become aware of and address moral dilemmas in the teaching and administrative processes. Processes must be put in place to detect moral deviation and to develop remedies. Many behaviours by students—for example, cheating on examinations, allowing others to cheat, plagiarism, false sources, signing attendance sheets for others, vandalizing school property, and failing to contribute appropriately to group work—have ethical implications; a list of ethical issues facing students is given in Table 1.2. Likewise, the behaviours of faculty members—for example, letting students get away with cheating, improper approaches to grading and examinations, favouritism and bias, one-sided presentation of concepts and theoretical materials, excessive workload, talking about students, and inappropriate relationships with students—have ethical implications.

TABLE 1.2	Ethical Issues for Students

Students are no different from any other group in society, and provide numerous examples of questionable behaviour or academic offences. Examples of such behaviour include the following:

- Plagiarism or copying without giving proper credit or acknowledgement from any printed or electronic source; in other words, theft of intellectual property.

- Copying from another student's paper or exam, or allowing another student to copy one's own.
- Cheating on examinations or any other tests, assignments, and projects, including copying from another student's work.
- Bringing unauthorized materials or electronic devices into the classroom or examination room.
- Having communications or discussions with others during an examination, including through electronic means.
- Turning in the same work for two or more different courses, or turning in the work of others as one's own.
- Giving false reasons for not attending class or handing in an assignment.
- Taking an examination for another student.
- Changing answers after a test or assignment has been graded and asking that it be graded again.
- Engaging in disrespectful and disruptive behaviour in class.
- Harassing others.
- Stealing or defacing the property of the school or others.
- Posting unfair, false, or exaggerated comments on RateYourProfessor.

Want to learn more about **academic integrity**?

In order to assess the integrity of business corporations and business students, a brief overview of some approaches to ethical thinking is presented.

LO 1.3   Main Approaches to Ethical Thinking

Not everyone understands or interprets ethics in the same way, and thus disagreement exists as to the appropriate behaviour by business in society. Many decisions involving ethics are made automatically without thinking, based on individual value standards and judgments and not ethical principles. Unfortunately, automatic decisions cannot be relied upon. Different countries, cultures, and religions may define right and wrong differently. More complexity results in situations where no option is clearly right, giving rise to dilemmas where effort is required to sort out right versus wrong. For some dilemmas, the choice might be between what some would consider two wrongs. Sometimes, because of the challenges presented, it is preferable to have different views of what is right or wrong.

Throughout history, ethicists have described various theories and principles to help understand the ethics of decision making. The difficulty is that numerous theories exist and some even have multiple interpretations. This section describes the three dominant approaches to normative theories of ethics: deontological, teleological, and virtue ethics.

In **deontological ethics**, or rule-based theories of ethics, actions are ethical if done for the sake of what is good without regard for the consequences of the act. Decisions are based upon duty and adherence to universal principles. In other words, individuals have a duty to do the right thing even if the consequences of another action are preferable. It is most important to act in a way in which one would like to see others act in the same or similar circumstances. A variation of deontology is broadened to the societal level, where individuals are born with natural rights possessed equally. But it is difficult to determine the rights to possess. Another variation is based on the principles of justice used to meet a "veil of ignorance" test. That is to say, a rule is just if everyone agrees to it is made ignorant of their position in society, thereby eliminating personal bias and guaranteeing fairness. A universal rule would result that could be used in similar circumstances and treating everyone with respect.

Teleological ethics, or consequential theories of ethics, focus on the outcomes or results of actions. A well-known variation is utilitarianism, which is based on utility or usefulness. The approach looks to the end results and individuals make decisions based on the consequences of the action. The decision is believed to be good if the end result is good. A decision is to result in the greatest good or happiness for the greatest number, and allows for bad consequences or harms. This approach is used every day by individuals and in business to view the relative outcomes; that is, the distribution of harms and benefits. Thus, moral character depends upon the practical matter relating to the extent to which actions benefit or harm those involved.

The third approach is **virtue ethics**, which emphasizes the character or identity of the individual and focuses upon *being* rather than *doing*. Morality is based on the development of good character traits or virtues and assumes that a good person will perform ethically. There are dozens of desirable traits; nine were listed by Aristotle—wisdom, prudence, justice, fortitude, courage, liberality, magnificence, magnanimity, and temperance. Virtue ethics acknowledges that absolute rules are unlikely to apply in all situations. Dozens of possible virtues exist, and the approach does not focus on which sorts of actions are morally permitted and which ones are not. An illustration is provided by responses to the question, "What virtues make a good businessperson or leader?" Possible answers include foresight, courage, commitment, compassion, respectfulness, and honesty. Table 1.3 compares the three approaches, all of which are applicable to the ethics of business as any other facet of life and society. In Chapter 5, these and other approaches to assessing ethical implications will be described.

TABLE 1.3	Comparison of Approaches to Ethical Thinking		
Deontological or Rule-Based Theories	**Teleological or Consequential Theories**	**Virtue Ethics**
Description: • Focus on moral obligations, duties, and rights • Rules should guide decision making and behaviour • More individualistic focus, as individuals should be treated with respect and dignity **Limitation:** • Allows individuals to avoid responsibility as they are following rules or orders **Example: Categorical Imperative** • Respect for individuals, treating them as ends, not as means to ends • Test: Would you do the same thing in similar circumstances? **Ethicists:** • Immanuel Kant • John Locke • John Rawls	**Description:** • Focus on goals, outcomes, or results • Emphasizes maximum benefit and minimum harm • Considers all stakeholders impacted **Limitation:** • Difficult to calculate benefits and harms and apply weights to each **Example: Utilitarianism** • Greatest good for the greatest number • Aims to produce the most net utility; that is, benefits versus harms • Provides a group or societal perspective **Ethicists:** • John Stuart Mill • Jeremy Bentham	**Description:** • Based on character of individual • If individual has good traits or virtues, decisions will be good or ethical • Virtuous characteristics come into play when resolving ethical dilemmas **Limitation:** • Disagreement over what are virtues; that is, how a virtue is defined **Examples:** • Trustworthiness • Honesty • Integrity • Responsibility • Caring **Ethicists:** • Plato • Aristotle • Revived recently by several ethicists including Robert Solomon

This brief introduction to theoretical approaches to understanding ethics can be used to assess the behaviour of Canadian business, corporations, and managers. Ethical dilemmas often exist where the choice is between what those involved consider two right responses—or, put in the negative, two wrong responses. Different approaches can result in two responses where benefits are bestowed on some stakeholders and harms to others. Thus, no matter which choice is made, some stakeholders will consider it "wrong."

LO 1.4   Business as an Economic System

Every country has an **economic system** defined as an arrangement using land, labour, and capital to produce, distribute, and exchange goods and services to meet the needs and wants of people in society. The objective of an economic system is to use a society's resources to meet the society's needs. The Canadian business system produces, markets, distributes, and exchanges goods and services to satisfy society's needs and wants. The majority of goods and services demanded by Canadians are provided by a private-sector economic system or capitalism. Most Canadians feel it is desirable to allow individual business-persons and corporations—rather than some centralized government agency—to provide the goods and services they require. Business institutions have a history in Canada of more than 450 years, and their role in our economic and social development has been substantial. But, it is a role in a continuous state of change.

Terminology is a problem in discussing a business enterprise system. The following list provides definitions of some frequently mentioned terms:

- **Capitalism**—An economic system that allows for private ownership of the means of production (land, labour, and capital) and assumes that economic decision making is in the hands of individuals or enterprises who make decisions expecting to earn a profit. An early advocate of capitalism was Adam Smith, whose views are still influential as described in Responsibility for Ethics 1.1.

- **Free enterprise system**—An economic system characterized by ownership of private property by individuals and enterprises, the profit motive, a competitive market system, and a limited involvement by government. Also referred to as the *private enterprise system*.

- **Laissez-faire capitalism**—An economic system operating with absolute minimum interference by the government in the affairs of business. Government involvement is strictly limited to providing essential services such as police and fire protection. Laissez-faire stems from a French term that means "allow to do."

- **Responsible enterprise system**—An economic system operating as a free enterprise system but incorporating the element of accountability. This definition implies that business enterprises are responsible to society for their actions and are answerable or accountable for being the cause, agent, or source of something.

 RESPONSIBILITY FOR ETHICS 1.1

Adam Smith, the "Father of Capitalism"

Adam Smith, 1723–90, was a Scottish philosopher and economist whose ideas have had a major impact on capitalist economic systems worldwide. He wrote extensively, but two books have been the most influential: *The Theory of Moral Sentiments*, published in 1759, and *An Inquiry into the Nature and Causes of the Wealth of Nations*, published in 1776.

Smith proposed a different view of morality than was prevalent at the time. One view was that moral principles could rationally identify right versus wrong, while the other view believed that governments and the laws they created established a standard of morality. Smith believed that people were born with a moral sense, or conscience, that told them what was right or wrong. For Smith, morality was a product of nature, not of reason. In any event, Smith believed that economic man and moral man had to co-exist.

The "invisible hand" concept was originated by Smith. He believed that well-functioning, competitive markets efficiently distributed society's scarce resources without the guiding hand of government or economic planners. Pursuit of individual self-interest through consumption and the achievement of profits resulted in economic growth that benefited everyone.

Smith's writings continue to influence morality in capitalist economies, even though they are still being challenged by some in society.

Want to learn more about Adam Smith?

Our economic system has changed over time from a relatively "free" system with limited government involvement to one where government involvement became more intensive during most of the twentieth century. Although government involvement has declined recently, business is now expected to account to other stakeholders in society. Even with these changes, the economic system of Canada is still based on such fundamentals as individualism and economic freedom, the right to private property, the importance of competition, and the profit motive. Thus, the economic system is not laissez-faire, but is a capitalist system. The principal advantage of this business system is that it decentralizes decision making from a central authority to many individual enterprises. The system also provides freedom of choice to workers, consumers, and entrepreneurs. High productivity and a high standard of living have resulted.

However, problems have occurred with the system throughout the history of business in Canada. Business provided appalling working conditions for labour in the nineteenth century and has sold unsafe products to consumers. Monopolistic behaviour has been evident in the operation of some business corporations, as witnessed by price fixing and supplier discrimination. Other problems include stock manipulation, misleading advertising, misrepresentation of financial information, and regional disparity. Business is blamed by some for failing to solve many social problems, for example inadequate housing, workplace discrimination against women and minorities, and the impact of business operations on the environment

Although capitalism is the economic system that provides most of the goods and services in society, two other sectors are involved: public and non-profit. The public or government sector is responsible for providing many services in society including the infrastructure that business uses. Government-owned corporations provide some transportation, insurance, pensions, and health and education systems. The non-profit sector, also known as the third sector or plural sector, is a part of the economic system. Examples of organizations in this sector are charities, cooperatives, and non-profit social enterprises.

The result is a business system that has changed over time, and today is quite different from 50 to 75 years ago. It is important to appreciate the fundamentals upon which the system is based, and how the system has changed to accommodate the demands of society. Chapter 2 examines in more detail how the capitalist business system works.

LO 1.5 The Corporation and the Business System

The Canadian business system comprises business enterprises varying from sole or single proprietorships to partnerships and incorporated entities. A business can be established and operated by an individual under very few legal requirements. Any individual may operate a business provided they are capable of entering into a binding agreement, that the business activity is lawful, and that the individual respects the general legal principles governing persons, property, and obligations. For larger undertakings, or where two or more persons wish to share in ownership, a partnership is formed. In proprietorships or partnerships, the business is identified only with the person or persons involved. The owners take all responsibility for success or failure, receive all profits and assume all losses, and can be held directly responsible for business wrongdoing. Today, most business enterprises are incorporated and so holding the owners, or shareholders, responsible is more complicated. Business enterprises are referred to as corporations in this book, but it is recognized that not all enterprises are incorporated, and that most businesses in Canada are small- and medium-sized enterprises.

The corporate form of business enterprise is quite unique. When a business incorporates, a separate legal entity is created. This entity is an "artificial being": invisible, intangible, existing only in contemplation of law, and with limited liability for owners. There are two doctrines of incorporation that represent two distinct views of the relationship of the corporation to society.

The privilege of incorporation was traditionally viewed as a concession granted by the sovereign. The first corporations were granted by British sovereigns to nobility, allowing them to explore, colonize, or commercially exploit some geographical area. It is often suggested that the Hudson's Bay Company, with a charter granted in 1617, was one of the first corporations formed in this manner. The "concession" doctrine held that incorporation was conferred by public act and could not be generated merely by private agreements among several persons to associate together for business purposes. The concession was not followed to the letter, especially as monarchies lost their power to legislatures. There were obvious dangers to individual or group freedoms in the concession approach as the sovereign, and then the state, had the authority to grant the privilege of existence to a corporation. An alternative doctrine of incorporation evolved, and the relationship between business and society has changed.

The second doctrine of incorporation is based on the right to "freedom of association." The association of individuals coming together for some purpose is fundamental to forming a corporation. The argument is that it takes more than a formal agreement among incorporators, between the state and the corporation, and between the state and the shareholders to create and maintain a corporation. The entity, a "going concern," is given life by real people and exhibits collective behaviour unique to it and governed by rules of its own making. Thus, the corporation can be thought of as a "state within a state" and is the most highly developed and useful means of voluntary cooperation as it provides an easy way for people to join and leave. Therefore, incorporation is a right, not a privilege as it is in the "concession" doctrine.

These two doctrines, and others, underlie the statutes that determine how to incorporate a business activity, and who may do so. With the freedom of association doctrine, the privilege of incorporation is freely available with a minimum of special conditions and limitations being imposed by government. Legislative safeguards have been interposed at critical junctures where experience indicates difficulties may arise. These safeguards exist to protect investors and creditors, and to create and preserve the atmosphere of public confidence necessary for the legitimacy of the business system. In the past few decades, additional obligations have been placed on the modern corporation to function for the benefit of the broader society in addition to the benefit of investors, creditors, employees, and customers.

The modern corporation is not the state-created entity of the concession doctrine, nor the uncontrolled free association of owners. But it is more appropriately described by the freedom of association doctrine—and this requires greater responsibility and accountability to society. Incorporation doctrines are one approach to viewing the relationship to society, but contemporary views include the business' legitimacy in society and whether or not business has a social license to undertake operations in society.

LO 1.6   Society's Permission for Business

The business system and corporations do not function in isolation to society and must receive some form of permission to operate. Two concepts that illustrate this relationship are legitimacy and social licence. Trust in business is also a factor.

The attitudes toward business and the criticisms of it present challenges to its legitimacy as an economic system. **Legitimacy** is the belief in the rightness of an institution, in this case the appropriateness of our business system to supply the goods and services wanted by Canadian society. Society must believe in the business system, which involves trust and confidence and the perception that the system operates in the public interest.

The legitimacy of business is questioned by some in society who are suspicious of materialism and excessive consumption. They argue that there are nobler goals than the pursuit of wealth or material things in society. The hypocritical attitudes business has taken toward government lead society to question the legitimacy of the system. Businesses ask for government assistance in a great variety of ways—through tax concessions, grants, and tariff protection, for example—and have requested that the free enterprise system be rescued from particular difficulties in such areas as the automobile, textile, aircraft, and fishing industries. Although businesspersons speak highly of the free enterprise system and competition, many are reluctant to live in an unregulated competitive environment. Lastly, many in society simply do not understand how business works and are concerned by the poor examples set by some businesspeople.

The legitimacy of business is increasingly being shaped by a broader sense of values that includes the treatment of employees, respect for the environment, commitment to product safety and public health, perceived openness and honesty, enlightened recognition of all stakeholder interests, and overall contribution to community, society, and the quality of life. The conclusion is that, to be legitimate, the business enterprise system must respond to the changing values and expectations in society.

Two observations are important from the discussion of society's attitudes toward business: (1) the attitudes—in particular the criticisms—must be monitored by management; and (2) where justified and feasible, management should take actions to counter the negative views of business.

Social licence is the privilege of operating in society with minimal formalized restrictions—that is, legislation, regulation, or market requirements—based on maintaining public trust by doing what is acceptable to stakeholders in the business and society relationship. It has emerged as a concept to explain the relationship between business and society and is mentioned in several contexts, all attempting to explain the relationship between business and society in a general sense, between businesses or corporations and society within an industry, and between a corporation and society related to a particular project. The concept is sometimes referred to as a social licence to operate, which is particularly relevant to the latter relationship.[4]

A social licence must be earned and maintained—it is non-permanent because society's beliefs, perceptions, and opinions change, as do the influential stakeholders. There must be an acceptance and approval of the project by stakeholders, which is accomplished when the corporation establishes its legitimacy and credibility and ultimately gains their trust. A key point to make is that a general or project social licence is not granted by a government, but instead by the acceptance received from the stakeholders involved.

One approach to assessing society's permission is to measure the trust Canadians have in the business enterprise system. According to the 2019 Proof Inc. CanTrust Index based on a poll of 1,543 Canadians, trust in large corporations declined from 28 percent to 20 percent between 2016 and 2019. Comparable figures for small/medium-sized businesses were 44 and 36 percent.[5] The 2019 Edelman Trust Barometer found that trust in business rose from 49 percent in the general population to 56 percent in 2019. The research found that Canadians expected corporations and business leaders to act with purpose and be advocates of social change. The trust in business must be compared to that of other societal institutions. The Barometer found that trust in non-governmental organizations rose from 50 to 59 percent; trust in government increased from 46 to 53 percent; and trust in the media increased from 49 to 57 percent.[6]

Society's permission for business varies. The following section discusses factors that influence how society views business.

LO 1.7   Attitudes toward Business

Occasionally, Canadians are surveyed about their attitudes toward business. The attitudes are constantly shifting and the reasons for this are a reflection of how Canadians are influenced by various factors in business and society.

Factors Influencing Attitudes toward Business

Many factors influence these attitudes toward Canadian business. The following list discusses some of the more commonly identified factors that can lead to positive or negative attitudes.

Standard of living—A prominent argument used in justifying or supporting the business enterprise system is the standard of living that it provides. As living standards increase, it is more likely society will view business in a positive manner.

Decentralized decision making—Another factor of the business system considered desirable is the decentralized decision-making process involved. Millions of businesses make decisions independently of one another, ensuring that a wide variety of goods and services are available. This choice is viewed favourably by consumers.

Allocation of resources—Some argue that the efficient allocation of resources is more likely to occur with a business system, as allocation is based on the price and availability of resources. However, critics of the business system challenge the efficiency claim. They argue that enterprises control prices, for example in oligopolistic industries, or that business enterprises control the availability of resources, creating artificial scarcities.

Self-interest—In a business enterprise system, the individual can behave in their own self-interest. Self-interest acts as a motivator and provides the drive for profit that encourages individuals to get things done. In a competitive business enterprise system, consumers choose among businesses that provide basically the same goods and services. Everyone working in their own self-interest provides a stimulus to the operation of the economy, even though it is referred to by some as greed. Positive self-interest is intended to produce intelligent and informed pursuit of wealth. However, some claim that self-interest sometimes becomes cruel and malicious—and, at other times, dumb and hysterical—and that this is appropriately referred to as greed. Self-interest appeals to many as a motivating force, but to others it is a source of negative attitudes toward the business system.

Business cycle—Business cycles are natural in a market system, and probably are more accentuated in a business enterprise system than in a centralized economy. With periods of prosperity followed by recessions, the business enterprise system is vulnerable to criticisms because of the hardships imposed upon particular individuals and types of businesses at various times. The instability created by business cycles is resented by society.

Business wrongdoing—Corporate misdeeds also influence society's attitudes. Some of the most common examples of corporate wrongdoing are in the financial area, and include misleading financial statements, insider trading, stock manipulation, bid rigging, embezzlement, and bankruptcy fraud. Members of society were particularly annoyed at bank and corporate bailouts in 2008–09, when governments loaned or gave corporations billions of dollars and executives still received high salaries. Some other recent criticism of business has related to workplace health and safety violations, bribery in international markets, weak or absent food safety practices, pollution of the environment, the plundering of natural resources, and excessively high profits and executive compensation. Everyday Ethics 1.3 gives examples of corporate wrongdoing. Corporations are sometimes punished for wrongdoing as stock prices decline, sales drop, and criminal charges are laid, but this is not always the case.

 EVERYDAY ETHICS 1.3

Examples of Business Wrongdoing

The following are examples of business wrongdoing.

- Volkswagen AG: In September 2015, it was disclosed that VW had rigged the emissions tests on vehicles with diesel engines. Environmental emissions testing agencies did not notice the deception, which was revealed by West Virginia University and an environmental non-governmental organization. The VW CEO was fired and the company was fined hundreds of millions.

- SNC-Lavalin: Since 2012, SNC-Lavalin has faced corruption scandals including fraud, bribery, and money laundering in Algeria, Bangladesh, Libya, and Montréal. Former managers face criminal charges relating to corruption of Libyan officials. The perpetrators and SNC-Lavalin's CEO were fired as a result. The Canadian government has laid criminal charges.

- Ponzi Schemes: These schemes promise high returns to investors. Instead of investors being paid from earnings, they are paid from the contributions made by new investors. A key to the success of the scheme is to continuously attract ever-increasing numbers of new investors to pay the previous ones. The schemes eventually collapse as the inflow of money cannot be sustained. They occur regularly.

- Montréal, Maine and Atlantic Railway derailment: An inappropriately secured train of tank cars containing crude oil derailed in Lac-Mégantic, Quebec killing 47 people, forced 2,000 from their homes and destroyed much of the town's downtown core.
- Algo Centre Mall, Elliot Lake, Ontario: On June 23, 2012, a part of the mall collapsed killing two and injuring 20 persons. An inquiry found that decades of incompetence, neglect, greed, and dishonesty by a succession of owners, engineers, and municipal officials lead to the collapse. The mall has been demolished.

Want to learn more about **corporate wrongdoing in Canada**?

Globalization—Business is being increasingly conducted on a worldwide or global scale. This trend applies to large as well as small businesses, and has led to several challenges. Increased competition comes from foreign producers, job loss occurs as production is outsourced to other countries, and businesses must respond to the demands of customers in other nations. Corporations operating globally are faced with ethical, social, and environmental issues relevant to local areas. As an example, Canadian mining corporations have had to respond to complaints about pollution and poor working conditions in their international operations. Chapter 15 will discuss the implications and challenges of globalization.

Unemployment—Employment is associated with a country's economic performance, business cycles, and productivity. How well the country's major industries are performing and the levels of consumer spending determine employment levels. Unemployment occurs when business lays off or fails to hire employees as business activity declines. Declining productivity of Canadian business may result in goods and services being provided from other countries.

Technological innovation—The business enterprise system is designed to constantly seek innovation. A large portion of technological development has been the result of the efforts of business enterprises. Some people criticize continuous and accelerating technology and social change while conceding that technology has improved their material well-being. A problem associated with rapid technological change is alienation, particularly alienation in the workplace. The ethical issues associated with artificial intelligence have become prominent in business and society. Everyday Ethics 1.4 lists some of the current issues. As artificial intelligence is a developing and expanding area, there will be increasing discussion of the ethics involved.

 EVERYDAY ETHICS 1.4

Artificial Intelligence (AI) and Ethical Issues

Artificial intelligence is the ability of machines to exhibit intelligent human-like behaviour to solve problems or make predictions without the hard-coded software that computers need. Terminology associated with AI includes *robotics, data science, machine* and *deep learning*, and *facial recognition*. The issues that business and society will need to address include the following:

- There are challenges of programming AI tools to make decisions involving ethics and social responsibility.
- The social and economic impact of robots and other AI tools must be understood and planned for, particularly the possible loss of jobs.
- There will be changes in skills and expertise; workers will require reskilling training throughout their careers. This may have begun already in the "gig" economy, in which temporary positions are common and organizations contract with independent workers for short-term engagements.
- Greater inequality may occur, as some corporations and individuals may benefit more than others.
- As employment will be scarcer and career changes more frequent, there will need to be changes to society's safety nets; that is, current unemployment and retraining programs may be insufficient.
- Systems must be in place to guard against mistakes, bias, and discrimination.
- Laws must be designed to hold robots accountable for their actions and to ensure their judgments will benefit the humans affected.

- Ethicists, government, and engineers will need to cooperate in formulating appropriate laws.
- The collection, compilation, and use of data gathered by AI tools will make more information available, but, on the other hand, is a threat to privacy.
- The security of data collected by AI tools must be assured.
- Managers will need to understand the capabilities of AI tools and determine the best way to deploy them and to identify what they can and cannot do.

Want to learn more about **artificial intelligence and ethics**?

Media coverage—The media influences society's views of business. Traditional media—that is, books, magazines, newspapers, television, film documentaries, and movies—describes the activities of business and the implications for society. Some of the portrayals are positive, but many are negative and receive a lot of attention—for example, Michael Moore's documentaries *Roger & Me, The Big One*, and *Capitalism: A Love Story*. The extent to which the popular media influence attitudes toward business is not known for certain. More recently. social media has had a dynamic influence on the relationship between business and society. One definition of **social media** is the various forms of interaction or communication enabled by technology-based tools, most of which are Internet based. Both types of media will be discussed further in Chapter 13.

Government—Government is always involved in business and the relationship between business and society. Governments often identify what is unacceptable corporate behaviour and their influence is always changing, at times increasing while at other times declining. Government influence is described throughout the book, and particularly in Chapter 10.

At any time, one or a combination of the above factors influences attitudes. Even though the factors can be listed, it is unlikely consensus will occur on which factors are the most influential. Nevertheless, society's attitudes toward business change through time and businesspersons must always be aware of these changes. Monitoring attitudes toward business is important as it operates as the consent or permission of society.

LO 1.8   The People Who Run Canadian Business

Three groups of persons are primarily responsible for the operation of Canadian business: owners, boards of directors, and managers. Each has some influence on the morality of the business system, overseeing the corporation's ethical behaviour and responsibilities to society.

Owners

A variety of owners exist, categorized as direct and indirect. Direct individual owners are shareholders or investors and entrepreneurs. Also, sometimes employees participate in ownership through stock-purchase and grant programs, and customers and producers participate in ownership through cooperatives. There are other direct owners, including corporations that own shares in other corporations, venture capitalists that finance growing businesses by purchasing shares, and governments that use corporations to deliver some goods and services to citizens.

A growing form of ownership is the indirect category, which occurs when consumers invest in mutual funds, or when employees contribute to pension plans. The managers of these funds have become much more active recently and are influencing corporate decisions frequently now.

Through direct and indirect ownership possibilities, most Canadians participate in the ownership of business, a fact that is often overlooked. The influence of these owners varies and will be discussed in Chapter 11.

Boards of Directors

Owners are represented by a board of directors, which, according to section 97(1) of the *Canada Business Corporations Act*, "shall manage the business and affairs of a corporation"—a process referred to as corporate governance. The board members are elected by shareholders—that is, the direct owners—and thus are concerned with the shareholders' primary objective, return on investment, though in recent years there has been increasing interest in corporate social responsibility. The board's main tasks are to:

- Select, evaluate, and terminate employment of top management, including planning executive succession.

- Provide shareholders with financial statements and an external auditor's report on the financial affairs of the corporation presented in an annual corporate report.

- Direct and evaluate strategic planning, including formulating plans, keeping management accountable for implementation, and assessing performance.

- Represent shareholders by participating in any major decisions impacting the corporation's operations relating to ownership, investments, acquisitions, divestments, takeovers, or insolvency.

- Fulfill the fiduciary and legal requirements as outlined in the *Canada Business Corporations Act*.

Recently, many boards have been active in overseeing the ethics of the corporation and its social and environmental responsibility. The role of the board will be examined in Chapter 11.

Managers

Managers require a variety of skills to oversee the operations of corporations in today's dynamic business environment. Managers must know how to direct the corporation's affairs in an increasingly competitive environment and how to cope with large-scale change in their corporations. Technological developments and the globalization of business present additional challenges. In addition, managing relationships with stakeholders has become increasingly important, and knowledge of the ethics of business and social and environmental responsibility is necessary.

Everyday Ethics 1.5 describes one corporation's approach to corporate responsibility or sustainability. The report outlined highlights management's attention to its relationship with society.

In Chapters 7 and 8 other examples will be presented that describe the roles and responsibilities of managers in implementing morally acceptable behaviour and social responsibility in their corporations.

 EVERYDAY ETHICS 1.5

Suncor Energy Inc.'s Commitment to Society

Suncor Energy Inc. (Suncor) is an integrated energy company involved in the Alberta oil sands and offshore petroleum development, petroleum refining, and marketing of petroleum products through Petro-Canada. As an energy corporation, Suncor is subject to greater scrutiny than corporations in other industries. As a result, the corporation is particularly aware of its relationship to society.

Suncor has summarized its approach to society in a comprehensive 155-page *Report on Sustainability*. The report includes a CEO message emphasizing Suncor's long-term view of its impact on society. Details are provided on its mission and values, corporate governance, and sustainability goals.

Its business operations are described, including economic impact, ethical business conduct, and approach to diversity and inclusion. Suncor's approach to climate change is discussed in detail with topics such as GHG performance, low-carbon innovation, carbon risk, and carbon policy and regulation.

The environment receives attention including information on water stewardship, tailing management, air quality, land reclamation, land biodiversity, and caribou conservation.

Stakeholder relations, community investment, and social goals are outlined. Emphasis is given to Aboriginal relations with descriptions of efforts to strengthen relationships and partner with Aboriginal youth, businesses, and communities.

Suncor's involvement in innovation in all aspects of its operations is identified, and appendices provide details on sustainability performance, an independent assurance statement, and scoring on the Global Reporting Initiative standards.

It has been argued that integrity is now at the top of the list of essential qualities of a good CEO. The operation of a business is about managing relationships with others, and the development of trust and credibility with stakeholders is necessary. Transparency is more important, and keeping hidden agendas or covering up information is more difficult. Relationships with others require a commitment to teamwork and partnerships, and managers must have the ability to build and sustain relationships. Finally, it must be remembered that managers are members of society and their behaviour is likely to reflect the standards of morality existing in society.[7]

All three—owners, boards of directors, and managers—are more aware than ever of the ethics of business and the resulting implications. This awareness also includes monitoring society's attitudes toward business.

LO 1.9 Integration of Business and Society

An article by Porter and Kramer made a good case for business and society needing each other. Business needs a healthy society in which education and health-care systems exist. There should be equal opportunity in the workforce and safe products for consumers. Carefully developed government policies increase the efficiency of business. This creates demand for products and services, and corporations pursuing profits at the expense of society are naive.

On the other hand, society needs successful companies. Business is needed to create jobs, wealth, and innovations that improve the standard of living for society. If business is weakened by governments and non-governmental organizations jobs disappear, competitiveness is lost, wages stagnate, and wealth declines.

In the past, too much focus has been placed on friction between society and business with not enough attention given to the interaction and integration between the two. There must be a shared value in which business and society both benefit. Illustrations of the benefits are provided throughout the book, although some of the frictions are described also. The direction of the ethics and responsibilities of business is toward reducing the frictions and increasing the benefits.[8]

The concept of a **social contract** is one way to describe this relationship between business and society. It is defined as "a set of two-way understandings that characterizes the relationship between two major institutions."[9] In this book, the two major institutions are business and society, and the relationship between them has changed over the years. Recent changes have been due to the recognition of many stakeholders other than shareholders that influence the corporation and are influenced by the corporation. As a result, society has increased its expectations of business relating to social, ethical, and environmental responsibilities. Some of these expectations have been established by government via laws or regulations, but most are shared understandings between two institutions. These shared understandings reflect mutual expectations about each other's roles, ethics, and responsibilities. Much of the social contract between business and society is not written, changes over time, and can create confusion and misunderstandings.[10]

Whether viewed from the integration or social-contract perspective, the relationship between business and society is complex and constantly changing.

Your advice to Vanessa . . .

....

Every day, everyone has some contact with business. Usually, this contact takes place under normal circumstances and with little thought to the implications for business and society. Sometimes, however, issues arise from the interaction with business. Quite often, the nature of the issues is complex and not easy to resolve. This is the situation in which Vanessa finds herself. Some possible courses of action are suggested but none are easy. Today, most business students are interested in economic, social, and environmental sustainability. In a course focusing on business and society, an understanding of the ethics of business and the responsibilities involved prepares students to answer questions like those posed in the vignette.

Summary

- The relationship between business and society is complex. To understand the relationship it is necessary to be knowledgeable of the business system and of capitalism in particular. There should also be an appreciation of the efforts being made by business to be responsive to society's expectations of its social and its economic responsibilities. (LO 1.1)

- Business integrity is the appropriateness of a corporation's behaviour and its adherence to moral guidelines acceptable to society such as honesty, fairness, and justice. The concepts used to describe the integrity of business are ethics of business, corporate social responsibility, corporate sustainability, the triple bottom line, and corporate citizenship. The integrity of business is no different from that of individuals or other institutions in society. Students in business programs are also challenged by issues of integrity. In particular, the behaviour of students has ethical implications, and they are no different than other stakeholders. (LO 1.2)

- The three main approaches to ethical thinking are deontological, teleological, and virtue ethics. (LO 1.3)

- The Canadian business system is referred to by various terms, but usually as a form of capitalism. The business system does have some defects, but it is constantly changing to reflect society's demands upon it. (LO 1.4)

- Several forms of business enterprise exist, but the most common is the incorporated enterprise referred to as the corporation. At one time, it was a privilege to form a corporation; that is, the monarch or government granted the right to incorporate. Today the corporation is viewed more as a free association of individuals who can incorporate as long as they are engaged in a legal activity. Thus, the modern corporation is accountable not only to the government, but also to society in general. (LO 1.5)

- Society allows business to function as a system to provide goods and services. Two concepts that help to understand this consent are legitimacy and social licence. Society's trust of business is necessary. (LO 1.6)

- Society's attitudes toward business vary over time, and its views are influenced by several factors. Corporate wrongdoing receives a lot of attention and creates negative views of business. (LO 1.7)

- Owners, boards of directors, and managers are the three most important stakeholders in the actual operation of the corporation. Each has a distinct role, and all influence the integrity of the corporation. (LO 1.8)

- Business and society are integrated. Business needs society and society needs business. One concept discussing the relationship is the social contract. (LO 1.9)

Key Terms

Integrity	Virtue ethics
Ethics of business	Economic system
Stakeholder	Capitalism
Corporate social responsibility (CSR)	Free enterprise system
Corporate sustainability (CS)	Laissez-faire capitalism
Triple bottom line	Responsible enterprise system
Corporate citizenship	Legitimacy
Responsible corporation	Social licence
Deontological ethics	Social media
Teleological ethics	Social contract

Critical Thinking and Discussion Questions

1. Do most Canadians understand the workings of the Canadian business system or capitalism? Do you? Give reasons to support your answer.

2. Do you agree with the position that the frequency of wrongdoing by business is about the same as for individuals or any other institutions in society?

3. Why do people disagree on what is morally appropriate behaviour? Which approach to ethical thinking do you practise?

4. How would you describe the Canadian business system?

5. Which two factors influence the integrity of Canadian business the most?

6. Should corporations be formed only with the permission of society as represented by government, or should they be allowed to form freely without much government oversight?

7. What is the connection between the type of approach to incorporation and society's expectations of the corporation?

8. Why should the members of the board of directors have any interest in the relationship between business and society?

9. What most influences your attitude toward business?

10. Should businesspersons be concerned about how they and business are portrayed in the media?

11. What are the integrity or ethical challenges you confront as a student?

Cases

1.1 SEARS CANADA'S BANKRUPTCY AND PENSIONERS

Most Canadians expect employers to provide pensions as one benefit of the employment contract. The expectations include not only coverage but also adequate funds to maintain a desired retirement lifestyle and security for the longevity of the pension. Government officials and financial industry spokespersons are warning of a crisis in the pension system, especially pensions in the private or business sector. Some claim that the crisis in pensions will have a negative impact on overall economic efficiency.

The two most common types of pension plans are defined benefit and defined contribution. Defined benefit plans guarantee a retirement payment based on income level and years of service. The risk of return and longevity is assumed by the employer; that is, the employer is responsible for deficits in the plan. The defined benefit type is the most common, but this type is experiencing a major problem: there are insufficient assets to support the payment of pension obligations to retired employees. The deficits in the plans have resulted from lower interest rates reducing earnings, stricter standards imposed by government regulations, and higher costs or payouts.

In defined contribution plans, employees and employer make contributions in registered retirement savings plan (RRSP)–type accumulation accounts, with employees allocating the funds among investment alternatives. The risk of return and longevity is transferred to individuals, something with which Adam Smith would most likely agree. The difficulty is that individuals are less able to bear the risk of failures and they are less knowledgeable of investment opportunities and dangers. Also, there is a possibility they will pay financial advisers too much to guide them in the investment process.

Defined benefit plans are particularly problematic when a business goes bankrupt, as Sears Canada did in January 2018. The 18,000 pensioners learnt that their pension plan was underfunded by $270 million. This meant that their pension payments would be reduced by 20 percent. In August 2018, the payments were actually reduced to 30 percent.

The questions became about what Sears' pensioners could do. The pensioners argue that bankruptcy laws favour corporations and management. In most jurisdictions, creditors have priority over pension funds, so any remaining funds could not be accessed to fund the $270 million shortfall. For years, governments have discussed the possibility of changing laws to give pensions a priority over creditors, referred to as super priority ranking. The argument against this is that it would upset the delicate financial balance that protects bankers and other creditors. As a result, companies may have less credit available to survive and grow, as lenders would become more reluctant to lend. Another proposal is to have governments back the pensions in case of bankruptcy. The Ontario government has proposed that some minimum be paid to pensioners when a corporation declares bankruptcy. Other governments are considering it. It is argued that governments should not bail out irresponsible employers and it would not be fair to other taxpayers.

The Sears pensioners have formed Sears Canada Retiree Group (SCRG), "a not-for-profit volunteer organization committed to the protection of the company pensions and benefits of all Sears Canada retirees and their surviving beneficiaries." SCRG has pointed out that Sears Canada's board has received over $600,000 in pay and another $600,000 in professions fees. In addition, financial advisers and lawyers are being paid. Also, $3 billion in dividends was paid to investors between 2005 and 2013 while the company was experiencing problems. SCRG argues that such extraordinary dividends and any funds generated by asset stripping should be returned.

There appears to be no easy solutions and SCRG continues with various legal actions.

Questions

1. How is the integrity of business illustrated, or not illustrated, with Sears Canada and its pensioners?

2. Which approach to ethical thinking would aid decision making regarding this issue?

3. How do the difficulties and changes being experienced by pension plans influence society's attitudes toward business?

4. What responsibility do corporations have to provide pension plans?

5. What responsibility and capability do employees have to manage their own pension plans?

1.2 DETECTING PLAGIARISM AND ACADEMIC INTEGRITY

Students and faculty at colleges and universities are concerned about cheating in the academic environment. The reasons given for cheating include high expectations, pressures to succeed, students feeling they were unfairly treated in some way, and the belief that "everyone is doing it." There are many forms of cheating, but one that is receiving a lot of attention is plagiarism.

Studies indicate that about one in three students admit to plagiarizing at some time in their academic program. About 5 percent admit to purchasing an essay online and handing it in as their own. Business, engineering, journalism, and education students were found to be the most likely to plagiarize. There is no definitive reason why business students are the worst offenders, but there is speculation they have a "bottom-line" mentality toward getting things accomplished.

One approach to combat this problem is for educational institutions to use plagiarism detecting services such as Turnitin.com and Plagiarism.org. Essays are submitted directly by students or by faculty members. These services identify copied materials and issue a report to the instructor.

In some schools, the use of the detection systems has not been opposed by students or faculty. It is considered normal practice and is compared to the use of metal detectors at airports. The argument is made that it ensures the integrity of a degree and reduces the possibility of someone obtaining a degree by improper means. The point is made that detection also takes other forms, for example paid invigilators at examinations. Use of detection systems ensures everyone plays by the same rules and serves as a deterrent to improper behaviour. Faculty time is saved and the detection process is simplified, reducing the need for faculty to play police.

In other schools, the detection systems are criticized for several reasons. Students are often given no alternative but to submit their papers. Students resent the assumption of guilt and the impression that students are being hunted down for violations. Some argue that it is an infringement of their copyright, but legal experts refute this claim. The fact that private companies are making a profit at detection is considered inappropriate. The reliability of the systems is questioned, as they detect only about 50 percent of the actual plagiarism. Overall, an antagonistic atmosphere is created that does little to resolve the underlying causes of plagiarism.

Questions

1. Academic integrity involves students, faculty members, and post-secondary institutions. Who is served by the use of detection systems?

2. What responsibility should professors take to detect plagiarism?

3. When should disciplinary action be taken against a student?

4. What should be done about the problem of plagiarism other than using detection systems?

5. Is cheating in school through plagiarism a predictor of cheating in business careers?

6. Which approach to ethical thinking would increase understanding of behaviour regarding plagiarism?

Capitalism provides most of society's goods and services.
Used © Shutterstock/Adam Melnyk

CHAPTER 2

Ethics and Capitalism

LEARNING OUTCOMES

After studying this chapter, you will be able to:

LO 2.1	Enumerate and discuss the eight fundamentals of a capitalist business system.
LO 2.2	Define the right of private property and identify ethical implications associated with it.
LO 2.3	Explain individualism and economic freedom and the related ethical implications.
LO 2.4	Define equality of opportunity and elaborate upon the ethical implications for business.
LO 2.5	Describe the competition fundamental and link ethical implications to it.
LO 2.6	Understand profits and the associated ethical implications.
LO 2.7	Link the work ethic to ethical implications.
LO 2.8	Define consumer sovereignty and understand related ethical implications.
LO 2.9	Explain the role of government in a capitalist business system and what the ethical implications are in this system.
LO 2.10	Define Canadian capitalism and recognize that capitalism exists in different forms around the world.
LO 2.11	Recognize the challenges to presenting the case for the ethics of capitalism.

What would you do if...?

Stephen Jacovich was enrolled in a joint arts and business program. He majored in sociology with a minor in business, as he felt this gave him a varied and broader view of society and business. The business minor might even help him in his career.

In the course classes and interactions with fellow students, he was noticing an increasing criticism of capitalism—in particular, of the current business system and the corporation. He was not surprised that some of his sociology professors and course materials made criticisms but he was surprised when business professors were critical of some aspects of capitalism.

The criticisms were wide-ranging. Inequity was the issue most frequently mentioned. Not everyone had the same opportunities and incomes were not distributed fairly. The concentration of income and wealth in 1 percent of society was resented, particularly the high incomes of business executives. What were perceived as excessive corporate profits was a concern. It was alleged that competition among corporations was not as rigorous as it should be in a market system. In fact, it appeared that monopolies existed where there was only one corporation providing a good or service and there were oligopolies where only a few corporations provided goods and services.

Many business practices were criticized. The damage to the environment from the inefficient use of resources and pollution worried many. Other issues were the encouragement of excessive consumption, unsafe products, and the failure of corporations to address complaints promptly and fairly. Layoffs of employees and closures of plants even when the business was profitable concerned many. They argued that the capitalistic system resulted in economic instability and unpredictability of results.

Stephen realized that some criticisms were the result of disappointments and personal experiences in their relations with business corporations. Many students resented business' presence on campus through sponsorships and naming privileges when donations were made. Also, the anti-capitalist views were reinforced by rhetoric from politicians, religious leaders, and union officials in addition to the comments of professors. As he viewed some sites on the Internet, he sensed that there might be a growing anti-capitalism movement forming. Many students were actively critical of business but so were Millennials who felt they were not receiving the rewards they expected.

Stephen was puzzled by the extensiveness of the criticism given society's prosperity and improvements in the standard of living. Also, he did not understand why there was so much criticism but at the same time so few suggestions as to what to do about it. In particular, the critics did not identify what should replace capitalism. It was not evident to him how to respond to the anti-capitalism views. Maybe he should just ignore them.

What is your advice to Stephen?

The purpose of this chapter is to describe capitalism in Canada through the commonly accepted fundamentals of this economic system. This provides the context in which business operates and identifies the ethical implications of a capitalist system.

LO 2.1 Introduction to the Fundamentals of Capitalism

The assumption made is that the Canadian economic system has been, and still is, largely composed of business enterprises operating in a market system. The majority of goods and services wanted by Canadians are provided by the market system, which coordinates and organizes economic activity. Even most of the goods and services needed by students are provided by this system as illustrated in Everyday Ethics 2.1. Most Canadians accept that an economic responsibility of business is to make a profit in providing goods and services. It is argued that this private system is less cumbersome and less costly to run than a centralized, government-operated system, and that it is more responsive to society's needs because it allows individuals and business corporations to be more innovative.

EVERYDAY ETHICS 2.1

How Capitalism Works for You

Think about the following goods and services you encounter on a typical day as a student. The cereal, fruit, and milk you eat for breakfast. The vehicle you use to get to classes. The smart phone you listen to music on. The coffee you purchase. The textbook you use in a course. The laptop or tablet you carry all day. The pens, pencils, and paper you use. The pizza you have for lunch. The video game you play to relax. The social media sites in which you participate. The cell phone or smart phone you use constantly in addition to iPads and other tablets. The Aspirin you take for a headache. The newspaper, magazine, or comic book you read during break. The clothing you wear. The fried chicken you eat for dinner at home. The television programs or movies you watch in the evening. The bed you go to sleep in.

In a capitalist system, business enterprises are responsible for providing most of these goods and services. Most are provided without a problem, but sometimes there are issues about this responsibility that relate to the fundamentals of capitalism.

The theory of capitalism can be described by examining some of the fundamental elements of such a system. In reality, it is more difficult to explain how the business system works. The ideal operation of the system is not expected, and much of the theory of the classical capitalist system is based on the philosophical underpinnings of the American system and may never have been applicable in Canada. These fundamental elements exist in different forms in various countries, and they are important to examine as they provide a basis for explaining some of the ethics and responsibilities of business that exist today.

In this chapter, eight fundamentals are described and some ethical implications of each are identified. The fundamentals are: the right of private property; equality of opportunity; competition; individualism and economic freedom; profits; the work ethic; consumer sovereignty; and the role of government. Capitalism requires a strong system of ethical behaviour; without it, the government and the justice system will intervene. The business system's approach to addressing economic, social, and ethical challenges is influenced by the form of capitalism in practice. The issues confronting managers today are assessed in the context of these fundamentals.[1]

LO 2.2   The Right of Private Property

The Fundamental

The right to ownership of property by individuals and corporations is fundamental to the business system. The **right of private property** is the legal right to own and use economic goods, for example land and buildings. Property is not owned by the state, and individuals may own property and use it as they see fit. Individuals are allowed to accumulate property and other forms of capital and wealth without restriction. This accumulation of privately owned property allows individuals to control their own destiny and not have decisions affecting them made by others. Other rationales for the right to private property are that the pride taken in ownership results in better care of property; the ownership of private property gives a sense of security and a feeling of satisfaction from participation in society; and private ownership develops respect for the property of others.

Ethical Implications

Individuals and corporations have been allowed to accumulate capital wealth, but there is an uneven distribution of wealth among members of society. This has led to demands for a more equitable distribution, usually achieved by government actions or abridgements to the right of private property. The government has "eminent domain" over property and can expropriate after payment of a fair price. Governments have even nationalized corporations and whole industries in some countries.

Taxation is one method of redistributing wealth. Despite this taxation, business retains some advantages because corporations are allowed to consolidate financial statements, to average taxable income over several years, to depreciate fixed assets, and to receive tax concessions. The government controls property through zoning regulations and restrictions on foreign ownership of property in some provinces. Most of the natural resources of Canada are still owned by the federal or provincial governments. Also, in the modern knowledge economy, the protection of another type of property—intellectual—is becoming increasingly important. **Intellectual property** is an umbrella term for patents, copyrights, trademarks, industrial designs, integrated circuit topographies, and plant breeders' rights.

Want to learn more about **the right to intellectual property**?

In theory, property rights guarantee an individual's security and freedom. Today, membership rights, such as those offered by labour unions, cooperatives, trade associations, and professional societies, are for some a preferred basis for security and freedom. This leads to the discussion of the desirability of having property in private hands versus held by governments or some form of collective. An example of the issues involved with property rights in the Indigenous communities are described in Everyday Ethics 2.2 and it is felt that the lack of these rights is contributing to economic inequality.

 EVERYDAY ETHICS 2.2

Indigenous Peoples and Property Rights

Many Indigenous Peoples are denied individual property rights, one of the basic freedoms of individuals and a fundamental of business. However, granting property rights on Indigenous lands has been discussed as a way to encourage economic prosperity. Currently the lands are owned by the federal government in trust for Indigenous Peoples living on them. This is a collective arrangement leading to an absence of a sense of ownership and belonging fostering dependence on the federal and Indigenous governments (band councils). An example of the consequence of collective ownership is that some individuals neglect their homes, allowing them to become uninhabitable.

It is proposed that full property rights be granted to individuals to buy, sell, mortgage, lease, and develop property. A benefit of this approach is that it creates an ownership culture leading to more productive use of the land. Privately owned property provides collateral for mortgages and capital for business enterprises. Overall, this will create wealth on Indigenous lands, lead to increased economic activity, and improve living conditions. In other words, Indigenous Peoples would have control over their economic destiny.

There are difficulties with granting individual property rights. The concept of individual property rights is contrary to their traditional way of life and their attachment to land in general. There would be some difficulties in allocating property among present band members, and whether or not members who had left but previously resided on the Indigenous lands had a right to some property. There is fear that a class system based on property may emerge. Another issue is whether or not individuals could sell their acquired property to non-Indigenous people. Some chiefs oppose the individual property rights as it will limit their power over the bands.

Property rights in some form do exist on a few Indigenous Peoples' lands and various possibilities are being considered. A land tenure system has to reflect a nation's culture and traditions by maintaining a sense of community and collective interest. A new property rights regime is under development. The 1999 First *Nations Land Management Act* is the most recent attempt to update the property regime contained within the *Indian Act*. There is tension surrounding the development of an individual property rights regime for reserve lands and treaty lands as some fear that the land base may be further reduced through land sales of individuals. The Nisga'a Treaty creates one solution by creating a Nisga'a collective property right defined in the Treaty.

LO 2.3   Individualism and Economic Freedom

The Fundamental

Individualism is the view that the individual, and not society or a collective, is the paramount decision maker in society and assumes that the individual is inherently decent and rational. Individuals should have the privilege of determining their own course of action; that is, of behaving in their own self-interest with the minimum of authority being exercised over them. The privilege of determining for oneself what actions to take encourages individual initiative and self-interest.

Individualism is linked to freedom, and this has provided a connection between the business system in Canada and a democratic form of government. In general terms, freedoms are identified as the capability to have and control property, freedom of association, freedom of information, and freedom of movement. **Economic freedoms** exist when the business system operates with few restrictions on its activities. Examples of economic freedom include the freedom of individuals to enter business; to locate anywhere; to enter contracts; to choose among competing goods and services; to choose an occupation; to access consumer and output markets; and to develop their own economic ends, and the means to attain these ends by choosing and utilizing resources as they see fit. This approach encourages entrepreneurial talent and innovation.

Individualism and economic freedoms were based on the division of labour, or specialization. Individuals did things that naturally contributed to the production of the goods and services required by society. Likewise, each corporation performed some functions in the production system, but several corporations were involved in the realization of the final product. The production system was based on specialization and was fragmented, but the idea was that if attention were paid to the parts of the system, the whole would take care of itself. Responsibility for Ethics 2.1 gives another description of economic freedoms.

 RESPONSIBILITY FOR ETHICS 2.1

Economic Freedoms

Conservative-oriented research organizations have developed indices of economic freedoms. Two examples are The Heritage Foundation and The Fraser Institute (in conjunction with several other institutes). How individuals view these economic freedoms has an effect on their ethical behaviour.

The following is a list of some factors that are considered when identifying and measuring economic freedoms:

- Property rights—Rule of law that protects property rights.
- Taxation—All taxes are considered harmful to economic activity.
- Government intervention—Economic freedom improves with less government.
- Regulation—Regulations should be straight forward, efficient, and at a minimum.
- International exchange—No restrictions should be on the movement of goods, services, or money between nations.
- Foreign investment—Few, if any, limits should exist on the extent of foreign investment.
- Money and inflation—Government maintains a tight monetary policy where the supply of currency does not exceed the demand.
- Wage and price controls—A free economy allows corporations to set the prices on the goods and services they require and to establish the wages they pay workers.
- Corruption—Corruption in the economy, as represented by a black market, should not exist.

For each of these factors, grading scales have been developed. After scoring the factors, a total score is ascertained by country and countries ranked. In recent years, Canada has been one of the top 10 countries on these economic freedom indices. Detailed descriptions of these freedoms are available at: current Index to Economic Freedom, The Heritage Foundation website at http://www.heritage.org/index/, and the most recent Economic Freedom of the World Annual Report, The Fraser Institute website http://www.freetheworld.com/release.html. Different freedoms are used in each index.

Ethical Implications

Many in society consider the emphasis on individuals inappropriate and believe that communitarianism is more important in society as individuals seek to join and identify with some type of community organization. Status is achieved by working with others rather than by struggling alone. Unions and cooperatives are examples of such organizations, as are the recent developments in industrial democracy and social enterprise.

It is argued that a systematic societal approach is preferable to the atomistic thinking of individualism. The whole society is viewed, rather than its parts, and understanding the interrelationships among the parts is favoured over a highly specialized, subdivided view of society.

The issue arises as to the extent individuals are responsible for their economic well-being versus governments or some form of collective organization. Governments operate many social programs for various members of society, and individualism and economic freedom become less important than social well-being, distribution of income, health, and education. Although most of the economic freedoms mentioned in the previous section exist to some extent, there have been abridgements to these freedoms. All business corporations now require some form of licensing prior to commencing business, and if an enterprise wishes to incorporate, it must be registered with the government. Also, the freedoms of employees are restricted by the corporations that employ them (dress codes, required purchase of firm's products) and by membership in unions (compulsory membership, allocation of work).

Recently, economic freedoms have been defined by various research organizations and national economies have been evaluated according to the extent that the freedoms exist. Ethical implications are present as the issue arises about the desirability of individual versus collective action, and about the extent to which economic freedoms should exist.

LO 2.4 Equality of Opportunity

The Fundamental

Equality of opportunity is the assumption that all individuals or groups have an even chance at responding to some condition in society. Many of those involved in Canadian business in the nineteenth and twentieth centuries were attracted to Canada because there was less influence exerted by nobility, landed gentry, or a rigid class system in North America than in Europe. There was less established wealth, and the "frontier" environment allowed individuals the opportunity to create their own wealth no matter what their background. This type of environment was appropriate for business: everyone was more likely to start the economic challenge of establishing and operating a corporation on about the same terms, and to have about an equal chance of succeeding. The opportunity existed to make one's own way by establishing a new business with minimum government intervention, and it was possible to pull up stakes and move to another part of the frontier.

Ethical Implications

In reality, equality of opportunity is challenging to achieve in a capitalist system. It is a societal issue because lack of equality of opportunity leads to economic or income inequality, which often is blamed on business. Many examples stem from income distribution, for example wages that are stagnant while profits increase, the gap between the poor and the rich (among individuals within an organization or a country and among countries), and male versus female income disparity. Gender equality is discussed in Responsibility for Ethics 2.2 particularly as it relates to economic income.

 RESPONSIBILITY FOR ETHICS 2.2

Business' Responsibility for Gender Equality

Gender equality means that women and men have equal means and opportunities for realizing their full human rights and responsibilities. There are many bases for inequality including economic, racial, health, education, and political. In Canada, women enjoy the same health and educational levels as men, but economic participation is not optimal.

Thus, business corporations must be concerned about women having the means and opportunities to participate in corporate economic endeavours and decision making. Gender equality is an issue for business because the inequalities are quickly disclosed, for example, by social media.

According to Statistics Canada, women's income based on hourly wages is 88 percent of that of men. Other measures provide insight into the wage gap. Annual earnings of full-time working women are 72 percent of those of men, and women's annual earnings for both full-time and part-time workers are 69 percent of those of men. Women are concentrated in lower-level and lower-income occupations, and too many are in contingent jobs—that is, part-time or seasonal. The McKinsey Global Institute completed a study that identified the potential growth in the world's GDP if economic gender equality were achieved. It developed a Gender Parity Score to measure the distance each country has advanced toward gender parity (that is, 1.00). Canada's score was 0.75, behind Norway, Belgium, Sweden, New Zealand, and Denmark. Although Canada is in the top 10 countries, there is room for improvement.

A Canadian Centre for Policy Alternatives study found significant differences in pay between male and female corporate executives. Among top executives, women make $0.68 for every dollar their male colleagues make, amounting to $950,000 less in pay a year. The ratio is $0.83 among all full-time workers.

There is a strong business case for improving gender equality: economic and social conditions are improved and productivity and economic growth enhanced. Countries with higher gender equality maximize competitiveness and economic potential. Studies have shown that better corporate performance, governance, and profits occur with higher gender equality. The pool of prospective employee talent is increased for business. Moreover, as women dominate the consumer base, their improved economic well-being creates product demand. Advancing women's equality in Canada would result in a 0.6 percent incremental GDP growth annually and in 10 years is forecasted to add $150 billion to the economy.

There are several initiatives that business can undertake to foster gender equality. Human resources policies that would facilitate gender equality include: increase access to education and training; ensure hiring and recruitment practices are not discriminatory; provide affordable child care; develop policies relating to employment maternity and paternity leave; provide for the same opportunity for a job regardless of gender; and allow flexible work arrangements and job sharing. Corporations can provide mentorship with successful female managers serving as role models, and develop practices and policies to provide equal opportunities for rising to positions of leadership. To increase representation in decision-making positions on boards of directors and in senior management, voluntary targets or quotas, and disclosure requirements could be used. Assistance could be provided to women wishing to become entrepreneurs and support given to female-operated businesses in the corporation's supply chain.

The Government of Canada is about to pass a *Pay Equity Act* to reduce pay inequality issues in areas of federal jurisdiction. Some provinces have similar legislation.

In place of equality of opportunity has come the call for equality of results, such as the desire for an adequate income, quality health care, good education, and retirement security. In other words, a more egalitarian society and a move away from opportunity, individualism, and personal freedom toward social, economic, and cultural levelling has been sought. Equality was redefined to be an equality of result, with all persons in society having nearly equal incomes, status, and power. The new equality was to be achieved through government involvement. The result has been a conflict between the motivational incentive provided by a competitive system and a system advocating equal reward to all despite the extent of effort or contribution.

Inequality is inevitable with a capitalistic system and has ethical implications. As economic growth occurs, the wealth created is not distributed equally and a debate centres on the relationship between growth and equality. Does faster growth necessarily cause greater inequality? Or, does greater inequality cause faster growth? If growth results in everyone being better off, most people are satisfied. But if the rich get richer and the poor get poorer, a problem arises in that social instability might occur. Another outcome might be demands for an engineered egalitarian society attempted through government initiatives such as affirmative action in employment and education, hiring quotas, and pay equity.

Want to learn more about inequality and why it is an issue for business?

As it is not possible to achieve equality of opportunities or results, an alternative is to think in terms of increasing equity or fairness in the business system. This approach would have the corporation striving to achieve greater perceived fairness in the distribution of economic wealth and in its treatment of stakeholder interests. Equity would involve fairness in the opening up of economic opportunity, fairness in the way stakeholders are treated by the corporation, and fairness in the way the economic pie is divided. Examples of inequities would be sudden and drastic layoffs, large drops in living standards, excessively high executive salaries, and fortunes for some while the bargaining power of others is reduced. Although it is difficult to define what is fair, it is easier to achieve equity than equality.

LO 2.5 Competition

The Fundamental

Competition is the condition in a market system in which many rival sellers seek to provide goods and services to many buyers. It is believed that competition is natural and desirable: it ensures that corporations provide the goods and services desired by society. The survival of the corporation is at stake as it exists in rivalry with others to provide goods and services to consumers who usually have alternative sources of supply. No one corporation or seller can influence the market by its behaviour—a multitude of sellers ensures competition, thus preventing concentration of economic power. The advantages of competition are that it ensures goods and services are provided at lowest costs; reduces waste and inefficiency and holds profits to a minimum; widens the choice of goods and services available to consumers; and regulates prices. Competition is the invisible hand that is responsible for the orderly operation of the market. Society rewards the most competitive firms, and only the fittest survive.

Ethical Implications

The circumstances described in the previous paragraph represent perfect competition—which seldom exists today. The pricing system is sometimes controlled or influenced by business or government actions. An **oligopoly**, where the few sellers in an industry behave similarly, exists in many industries, and even monopolies exist in others. Some business corporations have become very large and have diversified into many industries. Government regulates prices in some industries such as utilities, and in oligopolies there is a tendency for price leadership by one of the larger corporations. Some industries, such as real estate and insurance, tend to charge identical commissions or establish premiums from rate books available to all corporations in the industry. The professions have suggested price ranges for their services. Governments control or influence prices through direct control over wages and profits (as during the Second World War, or the period from 1975 to 1978), taxation, direct regulation, provincial barriers to trade, and tariffs.

No longer is it possible for corporations to easily enter some industries, as barriers to entry exist in the form of the size of plant necessary to achieve economies of scale, the domination of the market by one or a few corporations through advertising, or the inability to obtain the necessary technology. The ideal situation of perfect competition no longer exists, if it ever did. The invisible hand of a free market is now sometimes replaced by the visible hand of government or a market dominated by corporate giants. *The Economist* magazine argued that to restore public faith in markets, initiatives must be undertaken to restore competition.[2]

The nature of competition in an industry influences behaviour between the corporation and various other stakeholders, including other corporations in the industry, consumers, and suppliers. There are ethical implications of competitive behaviour, and governments in developed economies have attempted to influence this behaviour to protect various stakeholder interests. Everyday Ethics 2.3 is an example anti-competitive behaviour in an industry.

 EVERYDAY ETHICS 2.3

Flair Airlines and Fair Competition

Flair Airlines was formed in 2005 as a low-cost airline headquartered in Edmonton, Alberta, flying to several destinations in Western Canada, to Hamilton in Ontario, and to the Southern United States. It always faced competition but that increased when WestJet started a low-cost offshoot, Swoop, in June 2018. Swoop flew to several Canadian cities, the Southern United States, Mexico, and the Caribbean.

Flair complained about Swoop's aggressive competitive practices to the federal government's Competition Bureau, an independent law-enforcement agency that ensures Canadian businesses and consumers are treated fairly in a competitive marketplace. Flair claimed that Swoop was competing unfairly in three routes: Edmonton to Abbotsford, Edmonton to Hamilton, and Edmonton to Winnipeg. Swoop's practices resulted in Flair dropping its Edmonton to Hamilton service. Flair claimed to have lost $10 million between June and October as a result of Swoop's competition.

The Competition Bureau decided to investigate Flair's complaint with particular regard to flights out of Saskatoon, Thunder Bay, and Kamloops. The Bureau said it had reason to believe there was anti-competitive behaviour including low-cost pricing and unfair scheduling tactics being done by Swoop.

The complaint was being investigated in early 2019.

LO 2.6 Profits

The Fundamental

Profits are the excess of revenues over expenses and are closely associated with competition. The pursuit of profits spurs people into action and provides the drive and desire to do things. Corporations compete for profits, yet competition ensures that if excessive profits are made, others will be attracted to the industry. Profits are not only a regulator of efficiency, but also a measure of effectiveness. They can be retained in the business as a source of funds, and provide both an incentive to develop new products and technology and a reward for risk taking.

Ethical Implications

Many in society view profits with disdain, and some even consider them immoral. Many consider earning a profit to be appropriate, but some consider attempting to maximize profits through reducing competition to be inappropriate. As corporations have become larger and fewer in number in some industries, and more prices are government- or self-regulated, the role of profits as envisioned in classical theory has altered. Profits do not act as a "regulator" for many reasons. The introduction of taxation, especially income taxation, and the rates of inflation redistribute profits. The barriers to entry existing in many industries and the need for increasing size to achieve efficiency may have led to profits higher than normal under perfect competition. Competition not only is reflected by the number of corporations operating in an industry, but also is impacted by the services offered, advertising, brand loyalty, and image or reputation. Profits are controversial, as illustrated in Everyday Ethics 2.4.

 EVERYDAY ETHICS 2.4

Banking Industry Profits—Reasonable or Excessive?

The year 2017 was a good one for corporations in the banking industry. The following list gives an indication of the industry's profitability, referred to as net income, in 2017:

- Royal Bank of Canada - $11.5 billion
- Toronto-Dominion Bank - $10.3 billion
- Bank of Nova Scotia - $8.2 billion
- Bank of Montreal - $5.3 billion
- Canadian Imperial Bank of Commerce - $4.7 billion

Note that the word *profits* was not used by the corporations in the presentation of these financial data. Are these profits reasonable at a time when consumers are paying high service fees? Should the excessive profits be taxed by the government? Should the pricing practices in the industry be investigated?

Democracy Watch, a national non-profit, non-partisan organization and Canadian advocacy citizen group, is conducting a "Bank Accountability Campaign" to make them more socially responsible. The organization believes that "Canada's Big 6 Banks reaped these record profits in 2017 in part by firing thousands of people, cutting services, and hiking fees and credit card interest rates."

Bank profitability raises issues with ethical implications for the banking corporations, consumers, and government.

LO 2.7   The Work Ethic

The Fundamental

The **work ethic** is a code of values, or a body of moral principles, claiming that work is desirable, it is a natural activity, and it is good in and of itself. It has been assumed that work is the purpose of one's life and that unemployment is only a temporary misfortune. Individuals in society are assumed to be willing to support themselves and the members of their family. Work in itself is worthy, admirable, and both personally and socially valuable. The Protestant ethic reinforced the work ethic by claiming that hard work, diligence, thrift, and "busyness" were desirable for religious reasons; that is, work served as an earthly expression of God's will.

Ethical Implications

It is argued that individuals' attitudes toward work have changed as a result of government programs and society's expectations. Government programs now support the less fortunate, and the effects of unemployment have been reduced by Employment Insurance payments. These programs may not have a socially desirable impact, as sometimes labour markets are distorted—actually causing unemployment. Individuals now expect that more will be done for them, usually by governments but also by business corporations by way of working conditions, fringe benefits, and salaries—as illustrated, for example, in Responsibility for Ethics 2.3. The tendency toward government handouts and a somewhat more paternal attitude by employers has resulted in less need to work hard—or, as some argue, to work at all. The traditional form of the work ethic encouraged thrift and saving. In modern society, the desire to consume is a driving force, and individuals work hard to acquire material possessions. The resulting consumption ethic relates to the next fundamental, consumer sovereignty.

 RESPONSIBILITY FOR ETHICS 2.3

Work Ethic of the Millennials

If you were born between 1981 and 2000, you are a "Millennial." Millennials, also known as Generation Y or the Net Generation, have entered, or are now entering, the workforce. Some describe them as spoiled, narcissistic lay-abouts who spend too much time with social networking and (often illegally) downloading audio and video materials, and who have a tendency to plagiarize. Common misconceptions about Millennials include the following: overly self-confident, disrespectful and indifferent of authority, treat work as a way to personal fulfillment, and lack loyalty to employers. Managers often view Millennials as difficult to manage, requiring precise direction and more feedback, particularly praise. Some believe them to have unrealistic career expectations, hopping from one job to another seeking advancement, and putting unreasonable demands on employers because they think work should be not only fulfilling but also fun, with flexible hours, good salaries, and ample vacations. It is sometimes assumed that because Millennials grew up in good times, they believe they are entitled to a particular lifestyle and workplace environment. This has resulted in a perception that many Millennials have a poor work ethic.

Not everyone holds this view of the Millennials' work ethic and instead see them as computer-literate multitaskers who are good at online collaboration, making them natural team players. Some say they are smarter, quicker, and more tolerant of diversity. They provide fresh perspectives and ideas, and have lots of energy. They care about society's problems, respect the environment, believe in justice, value innovation, and insist on integrity.

The workplace circumstances in which Millennials find themselves should also be considered. Finding full-time work paying benefits and promising pensions is difficult. Instead, they must cope with the gig economy, in which part-time jobs are common and salaries have stagnated. Many are carrying student debt they find difficult to pay off. Often, they are not employed in their field of education. This is a generation experiencing many workplace problems and many do not feel that they have been treated fairly.

LO 2.8   Consumer Sovereignty

The Fundamental

Consumer sovereignty is the assumption existing in an economy that consumers have and exercise power over producers through the decisions they make in purchasing the goods and services provided by corporations. It is assumed that consumption is the end purpose of production. Consumers, by "voting" for a product when they purchase it, dictate the types, styles, and quality of goods and services provided by business. It is the consumers' evaluation and acceptance or rejection that determines the success of a business. It is clear that the producer is servant to the consumer and is to obey the instruction of the consumer, who commands and directs. Consumer sovereignty is a fundamental part of any competitive system, and generally the more competitive the market the stronger the power of the consumer.

Ethical Implications

Consumers often face challenges in exercising their sovereignty. Sometimes consumers are not aware of all alternatives available to them and sometimes they are not capable of understanding the technical complexities of many goods and services. With some goods and services there is less choice, or no choice, available to the consumer. Giant corporations are said to mould consumers' tastes and preferences through persuasive advertising. It is argued that producers have the power to ignore some consumer wishes, something necessary for mass production. On the other hand, it is suggested that there are too many products, or brands, with too little difference. Trivial product differentiation and artificial product obsolescence have encouraged this proliferation of products.

Canadian governments have passed legislation relating to consumer matters that has imposed many regulations, standards, and approvals prior to the introduction of a product. Governments influence or regulate in the "public interest," which frequently is more in the "producer interest." Monopolistic institutions are tolerated or created by the government, such as agricultural marketing organizations or professional associations. Tariffs and quotas on imported goods create contrived scarcities, increasing the prices paid by consumers. It is doubtful that consumers have much influence on the market compared to the impact of organizations of large corporations, government agencies, organized labour, or minority producer groups such as farmers. Everyday Ethics 2.5 describes one tactic that consumers use to assert sovereignty even though its effectiveness is doubtful.

 EVERYDAY ETHICS 2.5

Consumer Boycotts and Sovereignty

The word *boycott* derives from Captain Charles Boycott, who was a land agent collecting rents in Ireland for an absentee landlord, Lord Erne. Most land in Ireland was owned by outsiders who did not live in the country. They rented the land out to tenant farmers who in the late nineteenth century started demanding fair rent, free sale, and fixity of tenure. The Irish tenants refused to pay their rents and organized against the unfair treatment.

A definition of **boycott** is an act to abstain from using, buying, or dealing with a person, organization, or country as an expression of protest, usually for moral, economic, social, political, or environmental reasons. A boycott can be a form of activism where consumers refuse to purchase a good or service. Today, boycotts are frequently organized to support a cause such as protection of forests or animals. The goal is to damage the reputation of or place economic pressure on the business, organization, or country. Boycotts are more likely to be successful if participants are passionate about the cause, the cost to participate is low, the issue is easy to understand, and mass media is used.

Some boycotts are successful, but few result in substantial changes. It is difficult to measure the impact as they rarely cripple sales. Their success is increasing awareness of the issue and of the target's reputation. Boycotting can be a coercive act and it can inflict harm. Consideration should be given to whether or not the boycott is warranted; for example, jobs may be lost when corporation sales decline or misleading claims are made.

Social media has made it easier for consumers to organize boycotts and speeds up the protests. It is more difficult for corporations to control as they are more likely to be taken by surprise than with offline protests. Researchers have found that online protests can do financial, reputational, and sales damage if consumers are mobilized successfully.

Examples of boycotts include the following: bluefin tuna, as it is an endangered species; the farmed salmon industry, as it poses a massive risk to the environment and native species; Hermès, which sells luxury bags and belts made of skin from reptiles; Kellogg's, over the company's use of genetically modified organisms (GMOs); and L'Oréal, due to its continued use of animal testing for cosmetics.

LO 2.9   The Role of Government

The Fundamental

Government's role is to be kept to a minimum and is frequently expressed as a laissez-faire approach: "leave us alone." Although minimum government involvement is advocated, government is to provide for such things as national security, internal law and order, and a system of currency and measures. Government also provides the mechanisms for individuals to associate with others for a common, lawful purpose by evolving a body of law relating to contracts between individuals, which provide a basis for individual behaviour and expectations with respect to contractual arrangements. Government intervention in the business system for other than these types of activities is considered to lessen efficiency as the movement of resources is restricted and market pricing is interfered with.

Ethical Implications

Instead of the modest intended role of government, the government now is an influential stakeholder in the business system. Government involvement in the economy has always been greater in Canada than in the United States. Government was involved in building or financing transportation facilities very early in Canadian history. The National Policy of the 1880s and through the twentieth century, involving the imposition of tariffs to protect domestic manufacturers, has been a major intervention in the economy. Governments are now extensively involved in the economy through subsidies, taxation, tariffs, regulations and legislation, loans and grants programs, and ownership. Government is not only a monitor of business activity, but also an active participant in the system.

Want to learn more about **business fundamentals and the story of The Little Red Hen**?

Governments restrict capital movements and natural resource sales, impose product standards, and in some cases even prevent businesses from shutting down plants when they want. Legislation governs how employees are treated and regulates the types of contracts that can be made with customers. Competition legislation makes some types of trade practices illegal and attempts to prevent monopolization. Governments also influence a corporation's approach to ethics and responsibilities, a topic examined in Chapter 10.

These eight fundamentals are not isolated from but rather linked to one another and become the basis for the capitalist market system. Private property is the basis of individualism and economic freedom; competition regulates profits; profits motivate individuals and reinforce the work ethic; the work ethic is rewarded by profits and the accumulation of property; individualism is critical for competition and consistent with the work ethic; and consumer sovereignty is related to economic freedom, competition, and profits. The fundamentals are the basis of capitalism, but capitalism takes different forms around the world and at different times.

LO 2.10   Canadian and Other Forms of Capitalism

Capitalism is an economic system that allows for private ownership of the means of production (land, labour, and capital) and assumes that economic decision making is in the hands of individuals or corporations that make decisions expecting to earn a profit. Canadian capitalism satisfies this definition to some degree, but not all means of production are privately owned, not all economic decision making is in the hands of individuals, and many economic decisions are made where profit is not the motive.

Canada does not have a pure free-enterprise system, but instead a complex, "patched up" one. This patched system is the best that can be expected given human limitations; that is, no system can be perfect if it is to operate democratically. Moreover, the system is an integrated and complex one, making the separation of fundamental elements difficult. Government involvement has increased as the underlying assumptions of capitalism have become less valid in practice. Some would argue that laissez-faire capitalism was a myth in the first place and never really operational.

While capitalism takes one form in Canada, different forms or versions are in existence around the world. Also, the form of capitalism within a country can change. Canadian managers and entrepreneurs must recognize this phenomenon.

The following list outlines some of the more common forms of capitalism.[3]

Consumer capitalism—This form of capitalism is also referred to as *liberal market capitalism* and is practised in the United States, Britain, Canada, and Australia. Government involvement in the economic system is limited, there are open borders, and a profit mentality exists. Consumers have considerable influence over the market and producers respond to their wishes. Potential problems with this form are income inequity, low savings rate, and weak central governments.

Producer capitalism—This form emphasizes production, employment, and statist policies; that is, the concentration of economic controls and planning in the hands of a centralized government. As practised in Germany, it is referred to as a *social market economy* and is a regulated capitalist market with generous social welfare. Input is sought from other stakeholders, particularly employees or labour, a practice referred to as *co-determination*. Other forms of producer capitalism are practised in France, Japan, and Mexico. Potential problems with this form are that the social safety nets fray, innovation is slowed, and consumer dissatisfaction often occurs.

Family capitalism—Also referred to as *crony* and *Confucian capitalism*, this form is found in eastern Asian countries such as Taiwan, Malaysia, Thailand, and Indonesia. In some economies, extended clans dominate business activities and control capital flows. In many countries, the clans or families are created by Chinese descendants scattered throughout the region. In Japan, the form is based on the implicit belief in social balance and harmony or domestic peace. An emotional attachment is formed with groups, family, households, working teams, and nature, with an embracing of belongingness. This view differs from the Western beliefs in objectivity, equal treatment, and the "level playing field." Under this form, outsiders are not considered equal, modern corporate organizations are less likely to be formed, and money markets are restricted.

Frontier capitalism—Russia and China are examples of frontier capitalism, suggesting that capitalism is in its beginning stages. The fundamentals of business are being introduced as the government pursues for-profit business activities and an entrepreneurial class sprouts. The fundamentals are in various stages of being made operational. The role of government changes with the need to develop commercial law and regulation. The rule of law is not clearly established, and criminal activity often fills the void. Barriers to trade with other economies have to be removed. Mechanisms and institutions have to be developed that will facilitate a transition to consumer or producer capitalism.

State capitalism—A different type of capitalism being sought by some involves a greater role of government directly in the business system through the ownership of corporations. **State capitalism** is "an economic system in which governments manipulate market outcomes for political and social purposes." The financial crisis and economic downturn of 2009 shook the fundamentals of free markets, spurring countries to take control of property and financial resources within a country. The stimulus packages offered by governments included expenditures of goods and services and refinancing corporations, in particular in the banking and automobile industries, in which governments became a part owner. Many economists fear that government involvement in business for political or economic purposes will not result in the most efficient use of resources.[4]

Various forms of capitalism are advocated as a result of changes in society's view of business. The discussion of capitalist fundamentals and the differing forms of capitalism explains the lack of clarity surrounding the description given to the economic systems operating in particular countries. Students of business should appreciate that different forms of capitalism exist in different economies and that the form changes over time in the same economy. All this complicates the relationship between business and society.

LO 2.11   The Ethics of Capitalism

The ethics of capitalism are often questioned by members of society. As an economic system capitalism faces many challenges that lead to this doubt. On the other hand, many defend capitalism as a moral system.

The Challenges

Capitalism is a controversial economic system: many stakeholders advocate the benefits of the system, and many oppose or are critical of it. This has been the case with the financial crises, economic downturns, and occurrences of corporate crime. The following discussion examines some of the challenges.

Greed—Humans act in their own self-interest to some extent; that is, they desire to improve their situation. **Greed** is an excessive and selfish form of self-interest where individuals desire more of something than what is needed or fair. Of course, what is needed and fair is open to interpretation. Self-interest is harmful if channelled improperly through deceit, corruption, force, fraud, and theft; an example is given in Everyday Ethics 2.6. Some say capitalism is only about greed, but this is unfair as it is also about creativity, innovation, and entrepreneurship, which provide society with employment and goods and services.

 EVERYDAY ETHICS 2.6

Gordon Gekko's "Greed Is Good"

Michael Douglas played Gordon Gekko, a ruthless businessman who symbolized greed and corruption, in the 1987 movie *Wall Street*. In the movie, Gekko made an often-quoted reference to greed:

> *The point is, ladies and gentleman, that greed—for lack of a better word—is good. Greed is right. Greed works. Greed clarifies, cuts through, and captures the essence of the evolutionary spirit. Greed, in all of its forms—greed for life, for money, for love, knowledge—has marked the upward surge of mankind.*

In 2009, a sequel to the film came out with Michael Douglas again playing Gekko. In *Wall Street: Money Never Sleeps*, Gekko is back in business after being in jail for 20 years for insider trading—this time, though, he has a seemingly different view of morality.

Economic downturns—Economic cycles are a feature of capitalism. Because capitalism is based on a market system, there will be swings between prosperous times and recessions or even depressions. An example is the 2008 collapse of financial institutions in the United States and Europe. Several investment banks failed, followed by many banks in other parts of the world, resulting in a credit squeeze and fall in value of financial assets. This was attributed to the lack of government regulation and oversight plus business practices such as the focus on share value and incentive-based executive compensation. But markets are dynamic and correct themselves eventually.

Business failures—Another aspect of capitalism is failure that disposes of weak corporations and shifts resources to new or stronger ones. Thus, bankruptcy laws need to work well to transfer resources efficiently from less-productive to more-productive uses. Governments could become involved and bail out or prop up these corporations. This involvement is expensive, and the selection of which corporations to support is complicated. Nevertheless, those who have lost jobs and investments do pay a price for failure.

Income and wealth inequity—Critics of capitalism claim that a system based on a market system leads to inequities. Supporters of the system say that inequities are inevitable and necessary in a dynamic economy to provide incentive and prevent the regimentation of equality. A problem arises when particular groups in society are discriminated against economically to an extent that cannot be tolerated. Income and wealth is discussed further in Everyday Ethics 2.7.

 EVERYDAY ETHICS 2.7

Income and Wealth Inequalities

Income and wealth inequalities represent a major challenge to capitalism and the existing business system. There are numerous definitions but most identify income inequity as how evenly or unevenly household or individual income is distributed in society. Such income would come from wages, salaries, and return on investments or wealth that generates income from dividends, interest, and capital gains. Quite often, the focus is on the gap between the rich (1 percent or 5 percent of the population) and everyone else. Some researchers claim income inequality has been growing rapidly for 30 years according to any major statistical measure used.

The business community has an interest in the issue as indicated by publications from the Conference Board of Canada, the Fraser Institute, and Chartered Professional Accountants Canada (CPA Canada). There is a consensus among business organizations that capitalism is the best economic system at creating opportunity and a higher standard of living. There is also the view that if the issue is not addressed, social unrest could occur and/or oppressive taxes could be imposed by governments to solve the problem. Economic growth is diminished as poor people purchase less and business is not fully using the skills and capacities of workers. Inequality raises the questions of fairness and social justice; it is unfair to punish those who have bad luck and some simply do not have opportunities. More equality would lower poverty and could be achieved by providing good jobs, child benefits, affordable housing, and child care.

Government policies do address the issue. Spending on social programs transfers benefits to those with lower incomes and investments are made to increase accessibility to education and training opportunities. Minimum wages alleviate the problems, and changes to the taxation system would help, particularly taxing the rich. As business has the most to gain, it could also invest in employees by paying a fair wage and investing in their operations to improve productivity and increase innovation.

Not everyone considers income and wealth inequality to be an issue. The interpretation of the inequality data varies and there are points of view that the inequality is not as serious as claimed. It is not necessarily a bad consequence of the capitalist system as it is a driver of prosperity. Inequality is an incentive for people to seek out income-improving opportunities. In a capitalist system, inequality is simply part of economic progress, and despite the inequality there have been extraordinary increases in living standards.

Whether or not capitalism should be blamed for all the income and wealth inequality in society, business corporations are aware of the issue and assuming some of the responsibility for alleviating it.

Corporate crime and wrongdoing—Crime and wrongdoing exists in all societal institutions. As mentioned in Chapter 1, corporate crime and wrongdoing come in many forms and often receive considerable publicity and damages the reputations of businesses.

There are other challenges including the stagnant incomes of many Canadians at a time of higher and higher CEO salaries. Various forms of inequality exist particularly of income. It is claimed that capitalism lacks a caring view of weaker members of society. Damage to the environment is a challenge that business will have to address more urgently in the future. Lastly, a fundamental of capitalism is the reliance on a market system that seldom works perfectly.

Capitalism as an Ethical System

Given these challenges, many in society wonder whether capitalism operates with *any* ethics, while others argue that capitalism does not prevent the pursuit of what is good for society. Advocates of capitalism argue that it is a system that produces wealth, promotes prosperity, and provides greater human well-being than any other economic system. Capitalism allows creative and productive forces to operate that, in turn, create value in the form of superior goods and services resulting in a better quality of life. In a capitalist system, business must plan to be successful, which involves an empathy towards others or stakeholders. Cooperation is encouraged despite the existence of a market system based on competition.

For those arguing that capitalism is moral or ethical system, some features are significant. Capitalism respects freedoms including the right of individuals to set their own objectives and to pursue happiness as they perceive it to be. In other words, capitalism allows and encourages the virtues necessary for human life by safeguarding the freedom of an independent mind and the sanctity of the individual. Advocates believe that government would be less successful at respecting the freedoms of individuals.

The advocates of capitalism state that signs of an ethically minded business culture exist. Business has to respond to consumers demanding products consistent with their moral values and to society in general, for example, insisting on respect for the environment. Business is expected to address social issues and is increasingly accountable because of the Internet, in particular, social media. Business' efforts in responding to these demands is considered to be a virtue.[5]

At the level of the corporation, an assumption exists that moral individuals operate the business system and that they are in the majority. For capitalism to operate effectively, a strong system of moral behaviour and integrity is necessary. Aspects of this include the need to be honest and truthful, to operate by the rules of society and government, to keep one's word, to be responsible for actions, and to treat others as you would like them to treat you, including with compassion and forgiveness. Most corporations behave ethically because if they behave inconsistently with the values of society and its stakeholders their behaviour would be corrected in various ways. For example, employees would leave, customers would be lost, and governments would legislate appropriate behaviour. Integrity in business makes sense, and many contend that a more ethically minded business culture is emerging. Many demonstrations of this culture will be examined throughout this book.

The fundamentals of capitalism are to be viewed in light of ethically minded corporate developments such as social responsibility, business ethics, corporate citizenship, and stakeholder management. More importantly, how these fundamentals are interpreted in society influences the values held by businesspersons and managers. If capitalism is to be accepted as the economic system in society, businesspersons and managers must somehow take into account the ethical implications resulting from the workings of the fundamentals.

Other models or forms of capitalism are being proposed that take into account the ethics and responsibilities of business. But all incorporate the fundamentals in some way. Various stakeholders of the business system are impacted by how the fundamentals are interrupted or applied. It should be noted that many business organizations, businesspersons, and corporations are advocating greater responsibility and sensitivity to society and stakeholders. The following chapters will provide illustrations of these business initiatives, and Chapter 16 will describe new forms of capitalism that are being proposed.

The fundamentals were described as together they form the basis of Canadian capitalism. These elements give rise to many social or ethical issues that present challenges for Canadian businesspersons and managers. Therefore, the fundamentals discussed will provide a basis for an understanding of economic, social, or ethical responsibilities and of the relationships between business and its various stakeholders.

Your advice to Stephen ...

Of course, Stephen could attempt to explain the dynamics of a capitalist system based on the fundamentals described in LO 2.2 to LO 2.9. He can admit that capitalism is not without its problems—that is, that it is not perfect. He might challenge the critics to suggest alternatives to capitalism or to identify changes to capitalism's fundamentals that would improve it. He should not be silent when unsubstantiated claims are made. Lastly, he should appreciate that some in society are simply opposed to capitalism and there is no way to persuade them otherwise.

Summary

- Most goods and services needed by Canadians are supplied by business enterprises operating in a capitalist system. Many ethical implications arise as a result. Eight fundamental elements of Canadian capitalism were identified: the right of private property; equality of opportunity; competition; individualism and economic freedom; profits; the work ethic; consumer sovereignty; and the role of government. The elements represent values that must be held to some extent by a society in order for capitalism to operate effectively as an economic system. (LO 2.1)

- The right of private property facilitates the operation of business, but some in society resent a few acquiring large amounts. (LO 2.2)

- For capitalism to be acceptable to most Canadians, it must allow for equality of opportunity to share in economic well-being even though the results are not the same for everyone. (LO 2.3)

- To ensure that capitalism is regulated in the best interests of stakeholders, competitive rivalry must exist between sellers of goods and services to provide buyers with choice. The difficulty is that even in Canada's form of capitalism competitive markets do not exist. (LO 2.4)

- Individualism encourages people to participate in a capitalistic system, because they are free to make economic decisions in providing goods and services in a marketplace. Some Canadians resent the focus on individuals and believe the economy should be directed more by governments. (LO 2.5)

- In theory, when profits become too high in an industry, more businesses are attracted to that industry. Due to market imperfections, such as barriers of entry, this sometimes does not occur. (LO 2.6)

- How employees and employers view the work ethic influences the ethics and responsibilities of a corporation. (LO 2.7)

- The goods and services produced by capitalism should be determined by consumers as they make purchase decisions. Unfortunately, consumer choice is restricted by various business practices and some government regulations. (LO 2.8)

- Government has a role in a capitalistic system, but its involvement should be only to protect the interests of stakeholders unable to defend themselves and to provide the infrastructure for the market system to operate effectively. (LO 2.9)

- Capitalism exists in several forms around the world. The functioning of capitalism faces changes, but does operate most of the time with moral standards. New forms of capitalism are always being proposed to make business more responsive to society's needs. (LO 2.10)
- The ethics of capitalism involve several challenges, but an argument can be made that it is a moral system. (LO 2.11)

Key Terms

Right of private property	Profits
Intellectual property	Work ethic
Individualism	Consumer sovereignty
Economic freedoms	Boycott
Equality of opportunity	State capitalism
Competition	Greed
Oligopoly	

Critical Thinking and Discussion Questions

1. Identify the intellectual property you use in your studies. Have you always respected the rights of the owners of this type of private property?
2. Should equality of opportunity equal equality of results? What are the implications for business because of the inequalities that result from capitalism?
3. Why doesn't competition exist in some industries, and what are the ethical implications?
4. Assess the amount of economic freedom that exists in Canada today. How does this freedom, or lack thereof, influence Canadian businesses?
5. What is the connection between competition and profits?
6. Do you believe that employees no longer possess a genuine work ethic?
7. Does the Canadian consumer exert any sovereignty in the marketplace?
8. Is government's role in the Canadian business system increasing or decreasing?
9. What individual and societal values are involved with each of the fundamentals? Values are defined as core beliefs or desires that guide or motivate attitudes and actions.
10. Does capitalism or the free market system erode moral character?
11. Is ethical capitalism possible?

Cases

2.1 COPYRIGHT FAIRNESS

The *Canadian Copyright* Act protects the creators—that is, authors—of works published on paper or in digital form. The Act allows the use of these works without permission as long as certain conditions are met. Clause 29, Fair Dealing, allows use for the purpose of research, private study, or parody or satire.

The Canadian Copyright Licensing Agency (CANCOPY), known as Access Copyright, was established in 1988 by a collective of creators and publishers that provided educational and other institutions access to protected work.

It was a central organization to provide photocopy licensing of published works while ensuring rights holders would be fairly compensated for that copying. Access Copyright's role in protecting the rights of creators and publishers increased over the years.

The interpretation of fair dealing has been problematic. A court case decision in 2004 ruled that fair dealing was a "user's right." Another decision in 2012 determined that an educator could make copies for all students in a class. A revision of the Act in 2012 added "education" to the list of permitted purposes.

In 2011, York University opted out of Access Copyright. York and other universities in their association, Universities Canada, seized the opportunity provided by this decision and developed the "Fair Dealing Guidelines" that permitted extensive copying. Universities Canada said that these guidelines were a balanced approach to copyright fair dealing. Students would benefit, as there would be increased accessibility to materials, which would impact the quality of post-secondary education. The guidelines allowed for the use of short excerpts from works that were identified as up to 10 percent of a copyright-protected work, one chapter from a book, and a single article from a periodical. Costs to students would be reduced as a result.

Access Copyright was committed to upholding the rights of creators and publishers and was mandated to ensure they were fairly compensated when their works were used. As a result, it sued York University, claiming improper reproducing of protected works. Critics of the university pointed out that it was harming many of its own employees, who generated the works being denied royalties. Publishers pointed out that there were fewer Canadian works being written and that some publishers were experiencing financial difficulties and others had gone out of business.

In July 2017, the court ruled that York University didn't have the right to opt out of paying royalties and stated that the guidelines were not fair. The court concluded that the guidelines did not meet the test for fair dealing established by the Supreme Court of Canada. The judge stated that the guidelines were arbitrary and unfairly designed to get works without paying. York University is appealing the decision. Meanwhile, the government is reviewing the Act.

Questions

1. Is the protection of intellectual property important to business and society?
2. Should written works be protected?
3. Who are the stakeholders involved?
4. What is fair from the perspectives of the various stakeholders?

2.2 EXCLUSIVELY COKE

Corporations are making agreements with university and college administrations to become the sole provider of particular products or services on campuses. These exclusivity agreements have occurred in several areas, including banking services, travel agency services, fast food, soft drinks, and retail. In return for obtaining the exclusive right to provide a good or service, the university or college receives a payment, sometimes in the millions of dollars. School boards in some provinces have entered into similar agreements.

A common exclusivity agreement is for soft drinks for which Coca-Cola and PepsiCo compete. An example is the University of Calgary's announcement that Coca-Cola would receive the cold beverage provider contract. The university justified the decision by stating that Coca-Cola was "a trusted household name and a company with extensive history and experience in the beverage industry" and that the company is "dedicated to offering safe, quality drinks to consumers across the globe, and provides beverages to various industries including health care, universities, stadiums and other businesses around the world." A committee had selected Coca-Cola after a rigorous and fair process in which several criteria were considered, including quality, technology, student experience, retail, catering, and finances.

The University of Calgary's approach was not unusual. University administrators point out that the agreements are necessary as governments are not financing universities at the level needed. Thus, the universities are forced to obtain funds from other sources. Students have objected, pointing out that they loose the right to choose a brand, prices may be inflated, and monopolies are created. In addition, there is the morality of the practice. They, and others, are concerned with corporate control of campus life, and the attempt to snare young students who become lifelong consumers of the brand. Other students simply don't care. The companies view the agreements as good corporate citizenship where everyone wins. Student programs such as athletics are supported. The deals may include provisions whereby the winning bottler would refrain from other advertising on campus and keep price increases below the rate of inflation. On the other hand, the contracts usually contain minimum sales quotas; if not met, the contracts are extended until they are.

Questions

1. What fundamental or fundamentals of capitalism are involved in this practice?
2. Should educational institutions be involved with exclusivity agreements?
3. Which stakeholders are harmed and which benefit from these agreements?

A variety of stakeholders influence business and/or are influenced by business.
Used © monkeybusinessimages/Getty Images

CHAPTER 3

Identifying Stakeholders and Issues

LEARNING OUTCOMES

After studying this chapter, you will be able to:

LO 3.1 Recognize business as one institution in society and understand that its activities are influenced by other institutions and individuals referred to as stakeholders.

LO 3.2 Identify the corporation's stakeholders generally and the stakeholders relating to particular issues confronting the corporation.

LO 3.3 Understand the dynamic nature of stakeholder influence and that stakeholders have different goals and influence.

LO 3.4 Recognize the role of managers in relation to stakeholders.

LO 3.5 Formulate arguments supporting and opposing the stakeholder concept.

LO 3.6 Define an issue, describe issues management, and understand issue life cycles.

LO 3.7 Learn the importance of managing issues that become crises.

What would you do if...?

Tom Carroll operated a small construction business building new homes and renovating older ones. He had been in business for 20 years and had a good reputation for quality work completed on time. His company employed six workers year-round, but the number increased to about 20 between May and October when outside construction was viable. He operated his business "by the book" and attempted to be fair in dealings with employees and customers. In addition, he made a point of dealing with the Canada Revenue Agency fairly and did not avoid or evade taxes. He believed that this was not the case with many of his competitors.

Tom felt that some of his competitors were simply greedy. In chatting with them about evading taxes, they said that they were unlikely to get caught and customers did not care. Furthermore, they felt that it was necessary sometimes to survive and that entrepreneurs deserved the extra compensation for working hard and long hours. Although they believed that evading large amounts in taxes was a crime, evading small amounts was okay. There was a common feeling that small business pays too much tax, the government wastes money, and large businesses get more tax breaks than small businesses.

The two main areas where the contractors evaded paying taxes were paying workers off the books and hiding income. The downsides of paying off the books were the always-present chance of being caught, the inability to declare the labour costs as an expense, the liability in the event of worker injury, and the risk of worker disclosure. Income was more likely to be hidden when the business was struggling financially, the owner had close control of operations, the business's objectives were short-term, and workers were paid off the books. Hiding income was facilitated by customers paying cash, sometimes in exchange for a lower price.

Hearing all this got Tom to thinking. There were certainly opportunities to evade taxes with slight chances of being caught. It was clear that his competitors were benefiting from the evasion practices while he paid all his taxes. He raised the issue with his spouse, who said he should not follow the same practice. Despite this, he started considering the possibility.

What is your advice to Tom?

This chapter introduces three topics that enable managers to assess the overall business environment—that is, to understand the economic, ethical, and environmental circumstances in which a corporation finds itself. The first topic describes the stakeholder concept, lists the corporation's stakeholders, and examines the pros and cons of the concept. The second topic is the identification of the issues confronting the corporation. A related topic will be the managing of crises. The three topics are closely related, as issues always involve stakeholders, and issues sometimes become crises. The identification of the corporation's relevant and salient stakeholders along with the issues is one approach to scanning the environment and will assist in understanding the corporation's circumstances.

LO 3.1   The Stakeholder Concept and Business

The business system impacts the lives of all citizens. In Canada, and in other democracies with private economic systems, business operates in a pluralistic social system where a variety of groups and institutions use power or influence to represent the interests of particular groups of citizens. The business corporation is one of many institutions in a pluralistic society, but its influence is widespread.

A **pluralistic society** is one where influence or power is decentralized by dispersing it among a variety of institutions. No one institution is completely independent of others, but each institution does possess some autonomy to pursue its own interests. With power diffused in this way, society is somewhat protected from the dominance of one group or one institution. Business is subject to the influence of other institutions in society and must respond to the various participants in society. In this book, these participants are referred to as stakeholders.

A stakeholder is an individual, or group, who can influence and/or is influenced by the achievement of an organization's purpose.[1] Stakeholders may also be referred to as claimants, influencers, publics, or constituencies. Although all these terms have their merits, the term "stakeholder" is preferable as it provides the most general identification of the parties to which business is responsible or accountable.

It is important for managers to identify the complete array of stakeholders for two reasons: (1) to obtain resources, business has to recognize the groups that control scarce resources; and (2) to maintain the legitimacy of business as an institution in society, the support of other groups is required. Freeman argues that the use of the word "stakeholder" and the stakeholder concept is important for the following reason:

> By using "stakeholder," managers and theorists alike will come to see these groups as having a "stake." "Stakeholder" connotes "legitimacy," and while managers may not think that certain groups are "legitimate" in the sense that their demands on the firm are inappropriate, they had better give "legitimacy" to these groups in terms of their ability to affect the direction of the firm. Hence, "legitimacy" can be understood in a managerial sense implying that it is "legitimate to spend time and resources" on stakeholders, regardless of the appropriateness of their demand.[2]

Freeman points out that managers must seek out stakeholders and argues that if "you want to manage effectively, then you must take your stakeholders into account in a systematic fashion."[3] Furthermore, the corporation should undertake on its own to identify and to satisfy key stakeholders before a solution is imposed, often by government or the courts. It is important that corporations develop managers with the expertise to deal with stakeholders.

All stakeholders have expectations, such as reasonably priced and good-quality products, adequate wage levels, good working conditions, and a clean, safe environment. Business must understand the preferences and expectations of the various stakeholder groups. Managers cannot look only inward to the needs of owners; in order to be successful, managers must behave in a manner compatible with the beliefs and values of their stakeholders.

The complexity of business is often due to changing relationships between a corporation and its stakeholders. It should be remembered that the relationships are two-way. Corporations must understand how their activities influence stakeholders and also how stakeholders can influence their activities. Another approach to viewing these relationships is in terms of ethics and responsibilities. The corporation must consider the ethical implications of its behaviour toward stakeholders as must stakeholders toward the corporation. Corporations have responsibilities to stakeholders, depending on the situation and issue. Likewise, stakeholders must consider their responsibilities to the corporation depending on the circumstances of the relationship.

LO 3.2 | Identifying Stakeholders

The first step for business is to identify the stakeholders that influence the corporation and/or that are influenced by the corporation. The following is a generic listing (that is, a list that applies to most corporations) of a corporation's stakeholders. This list is not intended to be in any particular order of importance.

Owners

Owners of the corporation, usually referred to as shareholders, are those individuals or groups who have invested in the form of equity, or shares. Shareholders can number in the hundreds of thousands for large corporations, or be a single individual in the case of an unincorporated business. Large institutions, such as mutual or pension funds, may hold shares in corporations, as may a government. A corporation may be a shareholder in one or several other corporations. The influence shareholders have on business varies. One generalization is based on the number of shareholders: where there are thousands of investors, each holding a small number of shares, the individual shareholder's influence is usually minimal. But, where ownership is concentrated in the hands of a few shareholders, they usually exert significant influence over the corporation. In recent years mutual and pension funds, which in the past did not exercise their influence despite substantial holdings, have become more active in influencing major corporate decisions. Owners are stakeholders fundamental to the corporation and will be discussed in detail in Chapter 11.

Directors

Directors are elected by shareholders to represent their interests. They vary in number but are usually fewer than 20, and comprise a board that meets to decide on issues confronting the corporation. Directors can be from inside or from outside the corporation, in which case they are usually executives, managers, or owners of other corporations. The purpose of a board of directors is to determine the corporation's strategic direction, monitor and review the corporation's performance, and hire and fire the top executives. In theory, the ultimate responsibility for the corporation rests with the directors, but in reality, their influence varies. If the board comprises mainly insiders—that is, management—its influence on the corporation is substantial.

Often boards comprising outsiders are mainly token bodies that rubber-stamp management's decisions. However, the board of directors has the potential to be a very powerful body. The influence of directors will be examined in Chapter 11.

It should be noted that small, unincorporated business enterprises do not have directors. In these enterprises the owners are also the operators and/or managers, and no board of directors exists. However, even small enterprises can be incorporated, and the owner/manager often is the principal shareholder and serves on the small board of directors, which operates on an informal basis.

Employees

Employees are individuals who work for the corporation and are categorized in several different ways. Managers are employees involved in supervising tasks at low, middle, and top levels in the corporation. Workers may be thought of as blue- versus white-collar. Blue-collar workers are involved in manufacturing, production, or servicing tasks, while white-collar workers are office employees. A corporation employs several professional groups, such as engineers, lawyers, and accountants. Employees may be hired on a part-time or full-time basis, with part-time employment becoming more prevalent recently. Labour unions often represent some employees, especially blue-collar workers. One issue relating to unions is dealing with the corporate trend to seek wage and benefit concessions from employees during a period of economic downturn.

Retired employees, either managers or workers, have a stake in the corporation where company pension plans exist. Recently, more attention has been focused on the employment of disadvantaged groups, including women, minority ethnic groups, and persons with disabilities. Employees are considered among the most obvious and, perhaps, most important stakeholders. They have considerable influence for the simple reason that they are critical for the operation of the corporation. The ethics and responsibilities relating to employees will be discussed in Chapter 12.

Customers or Consumers

A corporation's customers may be members of the public, usually referred to as consumers; other corporations, referred to as industrial (or business-to-business) customers; or governments or government agencies. Customers are the source of revenue for the corporation and should be treated carefully. However, where a corporation is a monopoly, or where there is a lack of competition in the market, customers can be taken for granted. It is argued that the needs of individual consumers are ignored by large corporations that, through persuasive promotional practices, manipulate consumers. Instead of consumers influencing production decisions, producers influence or determine what consumers will purchase. Today, consumers are participating in various forms of ethical purchasing practices and influencing the ethics of corporations, as described in Responsibility for Ethics 3.1. The ethics and responsibilities relating to consumers will be discussed in Chapter 12.

 RESPONSIBILITY FOR ETHICS 3.1

Ethical Consumer Influences

Consumers are influencing corporations to offer goods and services that they consider to be "ethical" or "socially responsible." Also, many businesses have taken the initiative and are responding to these ethical consumers. This influence is reflected in the following:

- *Natural and organic food supermarkets*—Whole Foods Market is an example. This Austin, Texas, company claims to be the world's leading natural and organic food supermarket. All supermarkets now stock more natural and organic foods.

- *Fair trade products*—This involves the identification of products such as coffee, cocoa, sugar, and flowers that have been produced under conditions where human rights, good working conditions, and the environment are respected.

- *Product Red brand*—Corporations are allowed to license this brand, with a percentage of the profits going to The Global Fund to provide sustainable funding for programs to fight AIDS, tuberculosis, and malaria in developing countries.

- *Boycotts*—Organized boycotts of products or particular corporations are increasing in number as described in Chapter 2. These efforts have been made easier and more successful because of the Internet.

- *Local sourcing*—Farm and community markets offer goods produced in areas close to consumers, who consider them to be more ethical.

- *Vegans and vegetarians*—Consumers preferring this type of food have increased and stores are increasingly making this type of food available.

- *Websites*—There are sites that assist consumers in identifying ethical goods and services, an example being Ethical Consumer at https://www.ethicalconsumer.org/.

Lenders and Creditors

Different types of individuals or groups lend corporations money. Some lend for long terms by purchasing bonds or debentures, while others advance funds for short periods, as with trade creditors. The lenders may be individuals or other corporations, usually financial intermediaries that exist to lend money. This stakeholder has substantial influence: if the lender is not paid as agreed upon in the contract, the corporation's assets can often be seized. Mortgagees, lenders, and creditors have a prior claim on the assets of a corporation if it ceases operations or goes bankrupt.

Suppliers

Suppliers are usually other corporations that provide raw materials, component parts, or finished materials used in the manufacture or provision of the corporation's goods and services. The influence of suppliers varies. If a supplier is the only source of a particular material or component, then more of the corporation's attention must be devoted to this supplier. If the material component is available from several suppliers, the corporation has alternative sources and is not dependent upon a sole source. Sometimes, a corporation may, for a variety of reasons, own its supplier. The ethics and responsibilities relating to suppliers and supply chains will be discussed in Chapter 12.

Service Professionals

Service professionals are individuals who are not employees of the corporation but provide services on a fee-for-service basis. Included in this type of stakeholder are lawyers, accountants, engineers, and management consultants. Their influence is in the form of the advice they provide the corporation. It is in their own interest to see that the advice is reliable, as they are then more likely to be rehired. Corporations rely on service professionals as it is often too expensive to employ such expertise on a permanent basis.

A key professional in business is the accountant. Corporations must present financial and non-financial information according to certain standards to that stakeholders, in particular owners and lenders, can have confidence in the data. Chartered Professional Accountants Canada ensures that this is done and the organization is described in Responsibility for Ethics 3.2.

 RESPONSIBILITY FOR ETHICS 3.2

Chartered Professional Accountants Canada

Chartered Professional Accountants Canada (CPA Canada) is the national organization representing 210,000 accounting professionals with provincial branches. CPA Canada ensures that highly qualified professionals will demonstrate a commitment to providing the highest standards of accounting, ethics, and best business practices. It funds the development of Canadian accounting and assurance standards and the work of the independent standard-setting boards and oversight councils. This is important to ensure the financial and non-financial information in the private and public sectors is reliable, comparable, transparent, and credible.

CPA Canada follows the Chartered Professional Accountants of British Columbia (CPABC) Code of Professional Conduct. This Code is 177 pages in length and is based on five fundamental principles of ethics:

Professional behaviour—CPAs must conduct themselves in a manner that will maintain the reputation of the profession and serve the public interest.

Integrity and due care—CPAs will perform professional services with integrity and due care.

Objectivity—CPAs will not allow their judgment to be compromised by bias, conflict of interest, and undue influence of others.

Professional competence—CPAs will maintain their professional skills and competence by keeping informed of, and complying with, developments in their area of professional service.

Confidentiality—CPAs protect the confidentiality of information obtained as a result of professional employment.

Dealers, Distributors, and Franchisees

In some types of business, many other corporations distribute a firm's product to customers along a distribution or supply chain. A good example is the automobile industry, where hundreds of dealers form a distribution system. Wholesalers are also this type of stakeholder. Some corporations allow others to sell their product or service through a franchising system. The arrangement under which distributors or franchisees operate varies, but can be complex, especially in the case of franchising. The extent and complexity of these arrangements determine the influence a corporation has over the distributors or franchisees. But this influence is not one-sided, as the corporation depends on these types of businesses to get its products to the customers. If the corporation in question is a dealer, distributor, or franchise, the operations of the business will be impacted substantially by the agreement under which it operates.

Business Organizations

Corporations join together to form hundreds of organizations to represent their interests. An example of such an organization representing large business corporations is the Business Council of Canada, a group comprising the executives of Canada's largest 150 corporations. Chambers of Commerce or Boards of Trade exist in thousands of communities, and a national coordinating organization operates as the Canadian Chamber of Commerce. There are organizations representing small businesses, including the Canadian Federation of Independent Business and the Association of Chinese Canadian Entrepreneurs. Trade associations represent corporations operating within particular industries, for example the Forest Products Association of Canada or the Canadian Manufacturers & Exporters. Business also forms self-regulating agencies such as the Advertising Standards Council, which monitors advertising practices. In some areas, or industries, corporations are represented by employer associations usually dealing with industrial relations matters.

The impact of these types of organizations varies, but by uniting to speak as one they are bound to have more influence than by acting individually. Often it is difficult to obtain consensus within these groups, as not all businesspersons think the same way. The effectiveness of voluntary, self-regulating agencies has been questioned.

Competitors

Competitors are those firms that sell the same products. However, competitors should be viewed more broadly. Corporations producing substitute products should be identified and monitored. Not only should existing competitors be considered, but potential future competitors should be identified. With rapid technological advances, new products and services are constantly being researched and developed. Competitors should not be restricted to those from the domestic environment: those from foreign countries should also be considered. The ethics and responsibilities relating to competitors will be discussed in Chapter 12.

Joint-Venture Participants

Joint-venture participants are partners cooperating in a particular enterprise or project. Usually, written agreements outline the relationships between the corporation and its partners. Several other terms are also used to describe this cooperation, including alliances, consortia, networks, and partnerships. The word "strategic" is often used in conjunction with these terms, for example strategic alliances, cooperative strategies, and strategic partnerships.

Non-Governmental Organizations (NGOs)

A **non-governmental organization (NGO)** is any group outside of the public and private sectors that holds shared values or attitudes about an issue confronting society. Such organizations, previously known as interest groups, operate on a non-profit basis with volunteer members or networks, with many having paid employees. They are numerous, but their impact on the corporation varies. Examples of groups currently having considerable impact on the corporation are environmental, women's, and neighbourhood (community) groups. Chapter 13 will examine this stakeholder in detail.

Society at Large

This stakeholder represents the general public; that is, the views of society. The views of this stakeholder can be difficult to determine, making it difficult to ascertain this stakeholder's influence. In opinion surveys, members of society will express concern for energy conservation but continue to purchase high-gasoline-consumption vehicles or choose to live long distances from where they work. Communities in which businesses are located fall into this category, but their views are often made explicit to the corporation. A significant group in society at large are Canada's Indigenous Peoples.

Educational Institutions

Schools, colleges, and universities educate not only employees but also the general public. Business relies on these institutions to provide it with educated and skilled employees. These institutions also educate the public about economic systems and the role of business in society. Universities, in particular, are relied upon to perform basic research that is often applied to industrial situations. Educational institutions, although mainly government funded, are now seeking financial and other support from business, giving rise to the issue of commercialization involving corporate advertising on campus, research funding, and naming buildings after major donors. The student is also a stakeholder of the corporation in several ways including as a consumer of goods, as employees with part-time jobs while in school, and as potential employees in the future. The topic of educational institutions as stakeholders is discussed in Chapter 13.

Religious Groups

Churches often speak out on issues related to business. Religious leaders occasionally speak of concerns with capitalism and the dangers of the free market and profits.[4] Businesspersons are individually influenced by the values and beliefs upheld by religious groups. The influence of this stakeholder will be described in Chapter 13. There is even a patron saint of business, described in Responsibility for Ethics 3.3, who was an early practitioner of corporate social responsibility.

 RESPONSIBILITY FOR ETHICS 3.3

The Patron Saint of Business

The patron saint most closely related to business is Homobonus, who was a successful merchant and tailor, and is acknowledged for his good works in the community. Saint Homobonus (meaning "good man") is listed as the patron to merchants, cloth workers, tailors, and shoemakers. In addition, he is also recognized as the patron saint of businesspeople, the only saint recognized as such.

Homobonus Tucingo was born sometime during the first half of the twelfth century in Cremona, Italy, the son of a wealthy tailor and merchant. He never attended school but his father taught him the trade and how to conduct business diligently and honestly. He successfully operated the business after his father's death, and viewed it as an employment given him by God and as a means of serving both his family and the wider society of which he was a member.

He is described as an industrious and thrifty businessman, yet exhibiting boundless charity. His business prospered in spite of his generous charity to the poor. There is a claim that the more he gave away, the more prosperous he became. He died on November 13, 1197, and was canonized in 1199. It was unusual to canonize a layman, especially one in business, and to do it within two years after his death. An invocation or prayer to Saint Homobonus is:

St. Homobonus, you merited the favour of both God and man by being a doer of the Word, and not just a hearer. You have shown us that it is possible to live a Christian life in the world, for you, yourself were a prosperous businessman—yet you loved God with all your heart, and you loved your neighbour as yourself. We bring to you our petition [specifically mention here] and ask you to intercede before the Father on our behalf.

Source: Robert W. Sexty, "Recognizing Saintly Business: Lessons from Saint Homobonus," *New Academy Review,* Autumn 2003, Vol. 2, No. 3, 55–56.

Want to learn more about Saint Homobonus?

Charities

Charitable organizations receive some of their funding from corporations, and in return the business donors expect careful stewardship of the funding. In addition, some corporations have a direct involvement in charitable activities. Charities are a part of the non-profit sector and included in the civil society stakeholders discussed in Chapter 13. Some charities operate commercial enterprises.

Service, Fraternal, Cultural, and Ethnic Associations

Employees of business corporations join numerous service, fraternal, cultural, and ethnic associations, such as Rotary and Lions Clubs, Parents for French, and the Ukrainian Business Association. These memberships often involve volunteerism through the donation of employee time and efforts, and association with such organizations is often viewed as a source of business contacts. Responsibility for Ethics 3.4 is an example of a service organization attempting to influence the behaviour of its members.

 RESPONSIBILITY FOR ETHICS 3.4

Guiding Principles

Business networks and social organizations are involved in activities for the betterment of the communities in which they exist. Pledges, codes, and principles of these organizations impact the behaviour of members, most of whom are businesspersons. The Four-Way Test is an example:

The Four-Way Test

The test, which has been translated into more than 100 languages, asks the following questions:
Of the things we think, say or do

1. Is it the TRUTH?
2. Is it FAIR to all concerned?
3. Will it build GOODWILL and BETTER FRIENDSHIPS?
4. Will it be BENEFICIAL to all concerned?

The Media

The media cover events associated with business. Managers are interviewed and quoted on a corporation's plans or business issues. Media publicity about the practices of a particular corporation or the quality of its products or services can have a substantial positive or negative impact on a corporation's sales. On some occasions, the corporation attempts to influence media coverage through media releases and public relations initiatives. Recently, social media has been influencing business and is used by business to influence other stakeholders, as discussed in Chapter 13.

Government

It is important to recognize that government is not a monolith. Instead, government has several dimensions. In Canada, there are three levels of government: local, provincial/-territorial, and federal. Governments are formed by politicians and staffed by civil servants. Business must consider the impact of both of these groups within each level. Governments are organized by departments, and the influence of these departments on business varies by industry and by corporation. Governments have agencies that impact business operations, including regulatory bodies such as the Canadian Transport Commission, the Canadian Radio-television and Telecommunications Commission, and provincial public utility boards. Governments own many business enterprises, wholly or in part, and many government-owned financial institutions lend money to business corporations. Even foreign governments may have an impact by influencing sales in other countries.

Two other institutions are associated with governments: political parties and the legal system. Political parties play a role in business, and business supports these parties financially. The legal system is established and maintained by governments, and court decisions impact business corporations. Government is an influential stakeholder in the business system including its role in promoting corporate social responsibility as discussed in Chapter 10.

Other Possible Stakeholders

There is some controversy about whether or not the environment and animals should be identified as stakeholders. Some stakeholder theorists argue that the environment should be a stakeholder. Their main point is that this would give the natural environment prominence—or make it a priority—with management and stakeholders. Others disagree, saying that stakeholders must have a voice; that is, the capability to speak for themselves. The natural environment is unable to do this, but its well-being is certainly the concern of others. Furthermore, the environment does not meet the definition of a stakeholder upon which the theory is based. In this book, the natural environment is considered and taken into account and is described in Chapter 14, but not as a stakeholder.

In society, the treatment of animals varies: one view is that they have rights and a moral status in themselves and views continue to the opposite thought that there is no need to give them any status. Animals are not commonly portrayed as stakeholders of the corporation. There is an academic field that studies animal ethics, but there have been limited connections made to the ethics of business. Animals as stakeholders is described in Everyday Ethics 3.1.

 EVERYDAY ETHICS 3.1

Animals as Stakeholders

Animals have a prominent presence in society and can be categorized into several groups, each with issues relating to the treatment or welfare of animals. The most obvious group is the use of animals as pets or companions. The pet industry is huge and ranges from the provision of the medical care to marketers of pet food supplies. Exotic animals such as snakes and monkeys are illegally traded in the world. Animal shelters exist in every community to care for abandoned and abused pets.

Business and governments use animals in the development and testing of life-saving pharmaceuticals and other drugs. Consumers are concerned about the treatment of these animals and NGOs have been formed to protect them. Animals are admired in the wild through tourism and they also provide entertainment in zoos and circuses. The exploitation of wild animals is a concern, for example, killing them for ivory, for hides for clothing, or just for sport.

The harvesting of animals for human food raises issues. Wild animal species may be become extinct or seriously reduced in numbers. The raising of animals in farms for food is opposed by many consumers and NGOs. In many economies, animals still perform work related tasks such transportation and hauling or a source of power in agricultural cultivation.

There are different views towards the moral status of animals. One view is that animals should be treated so that the maximum welfare is achieved for the animal. Another view is that animals have the right to be treated respectfully and should not be harmed. A virtue view proposes that animals be treated with compassion and kindness.

Now that the stakeholders of the corporation have been identified, the following sections discuss other aspects of the relationships between corporations and stakeholders.

Want to learn more about **assessing information about stakeholders?**

LO 3.3 The Dynamics of Stakeholder Influence

Traditionally, the principal stakeholders or power groups were identified as owners, government, and labour (employees). This list is too simplistic: many others have a stake, and the enlarged view illustrated in the previous section is becoming more widely accepted. In effect, these stakeholders act as a system of checks and balances and business cannot act alone without considering the possible actions, and impacts, of groups other than government and labour.

All of these groups, or stakeholders, influence business decision making in a pluralistic society. However, this list is not exhaustive or definitive. It is not possible to list all stakeholders, and they vary by industry and corporation. A corporation's stakeholders may be defined differently for several reasons.

Each of the above stakeholder categories can be broken down further in a manner appropriate to a particular corporation. There are differing perceptions of stakeholders, and their power—or stake—varies depending upon one's point of view. One corporation may consider the influence of stakeholder groups not considered "legitimate" by another corporation, as the two have vastly different values—for example terrorist groups, which some corporations must take into account. The perceived relevance of stakeholders also varies with level of management and functional area. Middle managers conceptualize a different set of stakeholders as being more influential than do chief executives.

When identifying stakeholders it is important to know the corporation's relevant stakeholders, in particular those that have a moral claim. Some stakeholders have a limited or non-evident moral claim on the corporation. This varies with industries and corporations and over time. These factors add to the dynamics of stakeholder influence. An example of the stakeholders identified by one corporation is given in Everday Ethics 3.2.

EVERYDAY ETHICS 3.2

Catalyst Paper's Stakeholders

Corporations often identify their stakeholders in CSR or Sustainability reports in different ways and an illustration is provided by Catalyst Paper Corporation. Catalyst Paper manufactures a broad range of high-quality paper products and is one of the largest producers of mechanical printing paper. It is recognized for its sustainable business practices.

In its 2016 Sustainability Report, *Enduring Values: Constant Change,* Catalyst identified the following key stakeholder groups:

- Employees, retirees, communities
- Investors
- Non-governmental organizations
- Suppliers and business partners
- Indigenous Peoples
- Governments
- Customers

Source: "Catalyst in Context," Catalyst Sustainability Report 2016, page 18, Catalyst Paper Corporation, https://www.catalystpaper.com/sites/default/files/catalyst_csr_2016.pdf?utm_source=website&utm_medium=report&utm_term=web&utm_content=pdf&utm_campaign=Sustainability%20report. Used with permission.

Categorizing Stakeholders

No attempt has been made here to categorize the stakeholders as other writers do. Frederick, Davis, and Post[5] categorize the corporation's interactions with society as primary or secondary. Primary interactions are with employees (unions), shareholders, creditors, suppliers, customers, competitors, and wholesalers or retailers, while secondary interactions are with local communities, governments, social activist groups, media, business support groups, and the general public. The difficulty with such a categorization is that stakeholders' involvement and influence shift over time and vary among corporations. It is difficult to ascertain who should be on each list; for example, government is listed as secondary, whereas in Canada it is primary in regulated or protected industries.

Stakeholders are sometimes categorized as being external versus internal to the corporation. Mintzberg's external influencers are owners, associates, employee associations, the public, and directors, while internal influencers are the chief executive officers, line managers, operators, analysts of the technostructure, support staff, and ideology. This categorization serves Mintzberg well for conceptualizing power in and around organizations, but is not sufficiently detailed to identify all stakeholder groups in society. Problems also occur in identifying influencers as internal or external. Mintzberg considers owners to be external, but it might be argued that they are internal; directors might be considered to fit in between the two categories.[6]

Phillips identifies two types of stakeholders, making a useful distinction. Normative stakeholders are those to whom the organization has an obligation and stakeholders from whom the corporation has voluntarily accepted benefits. Examples are financiers, employees, consumers, suppliers, and the local community. In contrast, derivative stakeholders are those from whom the corporation has not accepted benefits, but they hold power over the corporation and may exert either a beneficial or harmful influence. Two examples are NGOs and competitors.[7]

Differing Goals and Power

Conflict may exist among stakeholders. The goals of the various groups differ and may or may not be compatible with those of the corporation. This is natural, as all are in effect sharing from one pot and benefits to one most likely represent losses to another. Corporation managers must be aware of this fact and, if necessary, negotiate an accommodation. The interaction between the corporation and stakeholders is very much a balancing act. If priority is given to profits for shareholders at the expense of benefits to employees or consumers, then these stakeholders will react. They may reduce the quantity or quality of their contribution (effort or purchases) until they receive what they perceive as a return commensurate with their contribution. Ultimately, such action can jeopardize returns on capital to shareholders.

It should be recognized that some stakeholders have more power or influence than others. There may be a shifting of power among the groups at various times, or coalitions may form to counterbalance a powerful group exerting too much influence. Business management may even attempt to co-opt an interest group's or regulatory agency's influence. When some stakeholders become too influential, other stakeholders may somehow counterbalance the power. An example is provided by a corporation's actions to exert control over its suppliers or purchasers: government may impose competition legislation or other laws to counter such restrictive trade practices. It is also argued that there is a managerial elite, comprising managers of larger businesses plus politicians and senior civil servants, that controls business within a nation, resulting in most important business decisions being made by a few. Hopefully, if such elite control is the case, other stakeholders will point this out (media) or initiate action (non-governmental organizations).

Just because a stakeholder is out of the limelight does not mean it is not exerting influence on business. Some stakeholders are just more evident than others; for example, the demands of unions, employees, and shareholders are usually known, while the demands of others are emerging. Also, the influence of stakeholders varies over time. Consumer interest groups were influential in the 1960s and 1970s but declined in the 1980s as government and public support was reduced. The reverse was the case with environmental interest groups. It is the task of managers to identify the most influential stakeholders; that is, those groups that make a difference to the well-being of the corporation.

LO 3.4 The Manager: A Special Stakeholder

The managers of Canadian business corporations are also stakeholders, of course: they can be employees, and may be shareholders as well. The uniqueness of managers is that they are in charge of corporations; that is, they are very influential in dealing with other stakeholders. Managers, and chief executive officers (CEOs) in particular, determine the corporation's social responsibility initiatives where the stakeholders supported are recognized as influencing the corporation.

Managers are responsible for carefully identifying and analyzing the stakeholders influencing the corporation and the stakeholders influenced by the corporation. They are also responsible for responding to stakeholders. This managerial responsibility might be outlined as follows:

- Identify stakeholders influenced by, or having an influence on, the corporation.

- Understand how the corporation currently views the stakeholders.

- Examine how each stakeholder will or might influence the corporation.

- Assess opportunities or threats, and the magnitude of their influence on the stakeholder.

- Rank stakeholders by influence.

- Prepare programs or policies detailing how to deal or cope with stakeholders.

A controversial issue is the level of compensation managers, in particular CEOs, should receive for their efforts. Everyday Ethics 3.3 lists the compensation of Canada's highest paid CEOs. High CEO compensation raises several ethical implications:

- Some executive compensation packages are so large they can affect the returns of shareholders, including employee pension plans.

- CEO compensation is increasing at a rate faster than that of workers, whose pay has been stagnant.

- Compensation often increases when the performance of the corporation declines.

- Employees feel unfairly treated when layoffs occur while the CEO's salary increases.

- Often the compensation packages are not disclosed or properly accounted for.

- Stock options are exercised before performance is achieved, and sometimes at share prices beyond the market price.

- Pension plans for executives are much more generous than for other employees, some of whom may not even have a pension plan.

- The highly paid executives are able to hire the best expert tax accountants to avoid paying taxes.

EVERYDAY ETHICS 3.3

Executive Compensation and Ethical Implications

A report by the Canadian Centre for Policy Alternatives (CCPA) found that the five highest-paid Canadian chief executives in 2017 were:

- Richard Baker, Hudson's Bay Co., $54.8 million
- Donald Walker, Magna International Inc., $26.4 million
- Keith E. Creel, Canadian Pacific Railway Ltd., $20.1 million
- James C. Smith, Thomson Reuters Corp., $18.7 million
- Linda Hasenfratz, Linamar Co., $16.5 million

These figures represent total compensation including salary, bonus, shares, and options.

It is argued that chief executive officers (CEOs) of Canadian corporations are earning a disproportionate share of the wealth. According to a study by the CCPA, the average compensation of the 100 best-paid CEOs was $10 million in 2017, while the average wage and salary earnings of Canadians was $50,759. CEOs made 197 times more than the average Canadian worker. The study found that the 100 highest-paid corporate executives earn an average Canadian's annual salary by 11:33 a.m. on January 2.

Several initiatives are proposed to counter the trend toward high compensation packages, including placing restrictions on the exercising of options, limiting severance benefits, delaying payment of bonuses until performance is clear, requiring shareholder approval of preferential pensions, and implementing the complete disclosure of all costs associated with compensation. Some governments, including those in the United States and United Kingdom, are regulating executive compensation in industries to which they have provided financial support. A simple approach would be to tax the compensation of highly paid executives at a higher rate.

Changing Executive Compensation

"Pay for performance" compensation schemes result in executives receiving not only large cash salaries but also stock and equity-linked incentives. The result of this approach is that executives think more about shareholders than other stakeholders such as labour and the talent on which the corporation depends. Boards of directors are complicit in this approach, as their pay is based on similar incentives. This results in a focus on the top of the corporation and shareholders, and contributes to income inequity.

In most cases when setting executive compensation, comparison is made to what executives are paid in similar corporations—that is, to a "peer group" of other CEOs. Thus, compensation is established on an external perspective, and some researchers argue that internal inequity would be more beneficial to the well-being of the corporation. It is argued that there should be an internal focus in setting executive pay. Other measures and metrics should be considered, such as employee engagement and retention, measures of productivity and customer service, and key risk factors in the supply chain. It is unlikely that this approach will be adapted any time soon.[8]

Another approach is the practice of tying executive compensation to environmental, social, and governance performance targets, known as *sustainable pay*. Few Canadian corporations have implemented this practice and the ones that have use past performance instead of pre-determined performance goals. Sustainable pay should be implemented as it protects and creates long-term shareholder value. Where sustainable performance measures are used, they are primarily directed at compliance, risk mitigation, and value protection rather than value creation.[9]

The next chapter will outline various ways managers can analyze relationships with stakeholders and their influence on the corporation and vice versa.

LO 3.5   Arguing the Stakeholder Concept

The Argument Against the Stakeholder Concept

Although the stakeholder concept has been widely accepted, some opposition does exist. The case against the concept can be summarized by four main points: problems of categorization, challenges in meeting expectations, dilution of top management focus, and the impracticality of shared governance.

Opponents argue that the list of stakeholders is extensive and diverse and the stakeholders often have contrary objectives. Furthermore, there is no agreement on the priority or importance of the stakeholders. In fact, it has been pointed out that there is not even agreement on the number of stakeholders.

Meeting the expectations of all stakeholders maybe an impossible challenge. There is no clear statement of stakeholder expectations except for shareholders. Determining the "share" each stakeholder should claim (or be entitled to claim) is difficult. There are complex trade-offs among the stakeholders, making it impossible to operate for the benefit of all.

To meet the objectives of the corporation, managers need a clear, unequivocal corporate purpose. The "social market" as represented by the communist and socialist economic systems has failed for the most part. The social goals of many stakeholders divert management attention from the measurable results necessary to judge corporate performance.

The corporation's governance structure does not accommodate multiple stakeholders, and efforts to do so have failed. It is challenging to have competing and conflicting interests attempting to govern the corporation. The corporation as it functions today is designed to confer advantages to one set of stakeholders, the shareholders.[10]

The Argument For the Stakeholder Concept

Advocates of the stakeholder concept argue that the opponents do not understand the basis for the concept. They argue that an appreciation for stakeholders is fundamental to understanding how to make money. Recognition of stakeholder interests does not promote equity, and certainly not equality. Responding to stakeholders is simply good business, as they are often capable of adversely impacting the performance of the corporation.

It is necessary not only to recognize the interests of all stakeholders but also to promote the loyalty of other individuals and groups. Shareholders are a principal stakeholder, but ignoring others—for example, employees, customers, and lenders—can have substantial economic consequences. Even interest groups or NGOs can prevent the corporation from accomplishing its goals. Stakeholder thinking identifies the full range of individuals and groups from whom loyalty is needed (or, in some cases, is not needed).

The purpose of the corporation in today's society is a complex combination of desires and expectations. The stakeholder concept is a systematic approach to recognizing these expectations and deciding whether to respond. Through an assessment of each stakeholder, the value of each to the corporation can be ascertained to suit the stakeholder and to suit the corporation's purpose.[11]

A topic related to the stakeholder concept is the process of issues management, which involves the identification of issues that confront business or the corporation as well as the development of appropriate responses. The following section describes issues and their management.

Want to learn more about **identifying and engaging stakeholders**?

LO 3.6 Issues Relating to Ethics, Responsibilities, and Sustainability

Issues arise from the relationships between business corporations and their stakeholders. In the context of business and society, an **issue** is a point in question or a matter that is in dispute where different views are held of what is or what ought to be corporate performance–based management or stakeholder expectations.

Wartick and Mahon expanded the definition of a corporate issue by identifying the following:

a. a controversial inconsistency based on one or more expectation gaps,

b. involving management perceptions of changing legitimacy and other stakeholder perceptions of changing cost/benefit positions,

c. that occur with or between views of what is and/or what ought to be corporate performance or stakeholder perceptions of corporate performance, and

d. imply an actual or anticipated resolution that creates significant, identifiable present or future impact on the organization.[12]

These definitions will assist in identifying economic, ethical, social, and environmental issues important to the study of business's relationship to society. They are the first step in establishing an issues management process.

Issues Management

Issues management is a systematic process by which the corporation can identify, evaluate, and respond to those economic, social, and environmental issues that may impact significantly upon it.[13] The definition suggests that corporations can manage the issues confronting them. The term "issues management" is considered a misnomer, as no corporation can manage or influence events to attain a desired outcome on a particular issue in all situations at all times. Issues management does not mean the corporation can create social change, or can control or manipulate society. Instead, the term refers to the process by which the corporation responds to economic, social, and environmental issues.

One purpose of issues management is to minimize surprises relating to events or trends in society by serving as an early warning system. Also, it prompts managers to be more systematic in coping with issues and stakeholder concerns by using foresight to anticipate change, and by participating in the resolution of existing issues. Issues management attempts to fill a void by providing a framework for assessing matters confronting the corporation that otherwise may be overlooked. It also provides the mechanism for coordinating and integrating management of issues that might confront several departments or units throughout the corporation.

There are several benefits to practising issues management: corporations are more likely to maintain a competitive advantage over rivals; corporate behaviour is more likely to be consistent with societal expectations; and the corporation is less likely to make a serious social or ethical mistake. Issues management enables the corporation to detect issues earlier and develop appropriate responses much sooner, sometimes even when the issues are emerging. The corporation's vulnerability is reduced and its credibility enhanced.

Like any other management methodology or technique, issues management does not just happen and appropriate conditions must exist for success. Top management must support it and be involved. There must be broad participation at the operating and staff levels. The approach must adapt to the culture and the management dynamics of the corporation. The issues management approach should be implemented gradually, making sure that it is supported by operating units. It is important to stress output (position papers, ideas, and interpretation of data) over process (the techniques and mechanisms used for issues identification, issues evaluation, and response development). Decisions must be made, and analysis cannot go on forever.[14]

Issue Life Cycles

One aspect of issues management is monitoring for issue life cycles. Issues can be viewed in two dimensions: over time and by degree of awareness. In Figure 3.1, the degrees of awareness at various stages of the cycle are identified as none or little, increasing, prominent, peak, and declining. Issues are often present that receive little or no attention (T1). It is also possible for an issue to be not evident at all. Managers should be aware of these possibilities, particularly when facing the early stages of a new issue or the re-emergence of an old issue. The public and media may not be aware of the issue and the government is most likely inactive. But NGOs and those stakeholders directly impacted may be aware of the issue.

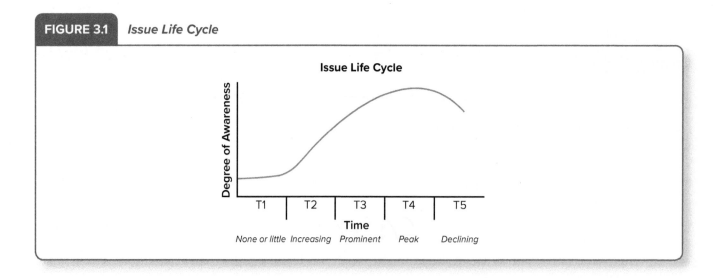

FIGURE 3.1 *Issue Life Cycle*

According to Coates, Coates, Jarratt, and Heinz,[15] early identification, in period T1, of an emerging issue having *any* of six characteristics is important. These characteristics are as follows:

1. The terms of the debate cannot yet be clearly defined.

2. One of the actors (stakeholders) will define the emerging issue and make it a current issue.

3. It deals with matters of conflicting values and interest.

4. It is not a problem that expert knowledge will automatically be able to resolve.

5. It is stated in value-laden terms.

6. Trade-offs are possible.

This list indicates that an emerging issue may not be easy to resolve in the short term.

In period T2, the awareness of the issue increases—for example, as the issue receives some media attention. It is unlikely that all corporations have formulated a response by this time. NGOs and other stakeholders will have become more active in exposing the issue and will attempt to draw more attention to it. Government is most likely reactive at this stage. The urgency of the issues is unlikely to be clear at this point.

In period T3, the issue is very prominent and cannot be ignored. Responses or solutions are widely discussed, and most corporations have taken a stance. The government becomes active and all stakeholders who are influenced recognize the importance and implications of the issue.

The issue peaks at T4 and corporations will be defensive. The issue may become a crisis at the time. NGOs would be seeking settlements or other solutions. Government would be proactive and may be proposing legislation to address the issue. The decline or maybe dormant stage (T5) should not necessarily be viewed with relief because issue awareness may not decline, as indicated in Figure 3.1 but instead turn upwards as a result of some event or change in actions by stakeholders. The issue may re-emerge and awareness increase, or awareness may remain constant. The challenge for managers is to be sensitive to the degree of issue awareness of society or a significant number of stakeholders.

LO 3.7 Crisis Management

Sometimes an issue will become a crisis for management. Crises could arise from issues such as industrial accidents, product failure or tampering, product recalls, product safety, technology failure, hostile takeovers, malicious rumours or media leaks, natural disasters, environmental problems, labour disputes, acts of terrorism, fraud or embezzlement, and violations of government regulations. These crises involve many stakeholders depending upon the incident. Issues that become crises can be addressed through approaches to crisis management.

Many discussions of crisis management make reference to Fink's "anatomy of a crisis."[16] A **crisis** is defined as a turning point, a crucial time, and a situation that has reached a critical point. Fink states that a crisis is an unstable time but the outcome may not necessarily be bad, and that there can be positive outcomes. He defines **crisis management** as an approach involving planning and removing much of the risk and uncertainty, allowing the corporation to achieve more control over events.[17]

Fink proposed that there were four stages to any crisis: prodromal, acute, chronic, and resolution, which are shown diagrammatically in Figure 3.2. The prodromal, or pre-crisis, stage is one where the corporation receives some warning or some symptoms appear, even if subtle. This stage represents a turning point that, if recognized, should not be ignored because an anticipated crisis is much easier to manage at this stage. Situations exist where management, even if aware of a crisis, may not be able to do anything in advance.

FIGURE 3.2 *Fink's Anatomy of a Crisis*

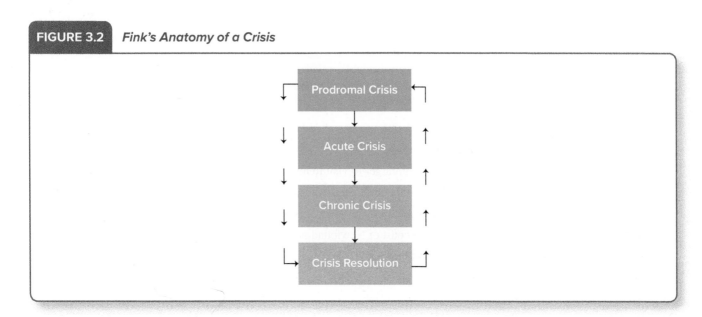

The acute crisis stage is the point at which the crisis has occurred and the damage has resulted. At this stage it is easier to control the response if the corporation is prepared; but there are often rapid developments that may be hard to control. The cleanup or post-mortem phase is referred to as the chronic crisis stage. This is a stage for recovery, investigations, audits, and self-analysis, as well as for further development of crisis management approaches. It is a stage that can linger for some time. The final stage is crisis resolution, when the corporation has recovered from the damage of a crisis.

Fink points out that all four stages may not be present, they may overlap, and their duration and intensity varies. Ideally, he says, the prodromal stage should be followed immediately by resolution, as shown by the arrows on the left side of the figure. The arrows on the right side indicate a learning process is possible so that previous stages of future crises can be dealt with more effectively.[18]

Fink's four stage framework is representative of the many models of crisis that exist. For example, Pearson and Mitroff's model had five stages: signal of detection, preparation/prevention, containment/damage limitation, recovery, and learning.[19] Augustine extended his framework to six stages including a final one "profiting from the crisis."[20]

Most corporations will experience crises to some degree and it is important to be prepared and, if possible, proactively invest in approaches to deal with a crisis. Managers should identify aspects of the corporation's operations where a crisis is mostly likely to occur. For example, a food manufacturer should anticipate a crisis involving food contamination, and a railway can plan for derailments that will inevitably occur. Managers and employees must organize responses and practice the procedures to follow. Crisis incidents should be monitored and analyzed and lessons learnt from them.

Crisis management always includes a discussion on communications. All the relevant or key stakeholders must be identified and contacted including the media, social media, and those stakeholders affected including governments. Internal stakeholders such as employees should be fully informed of the situation. Transparency is stressed, where the corporation tells everything it knows, what it does not know, and what it would like to know. There should be answers to all questions and the media should be provided with accurate and timely information. It is important to be honest, disclose all facts, and demonstrate concern.

A key ingredient is honesty. Telling the truth is viewed as the only policy as it is the ethical and practical thing to do. Incomplete information to guard against possible legal actions should be avoided. The correct facts should be stated clearly without media spin. Above all, there should be empathy for those stakeholders harmed. The spokesperson should be carefully selected and possess effective communication skills. Arm's length advisers should be engaged to objectively assess the corporation's communications approach.[21]

Most likely an apology is necessary. The apology should be timely, most likely soon after the incident, and not limited by possible legal consequences. An apology will contribute to rebuilding trust in and the reputation of the corporation. An apology must be sincere, include assuming responsibility, and not placing blame on others. Most corporations recover from a crisis if the response is properly managed.[22]

Everyday Ethics 3.4 lists examples of apologies made for corporate mistakes.

 EVERYDAY ETHICS 3.4

Apologies for Corporate Mistakes

There is a need for a prompt apology for the harm inflicted on stakeholders after a crisis or corporate mistake. The immediate response is needed as smart phones and social media communicate harms very quickly. An apology is sometimes needed even before management has all the facts or management has had time to assess the situation. Some corporations have "apology teams" in communications/public-relations departments that are able to respond quickly.

The following are examples of apologies that have received attention:

- Loblaw: alleged price-fixing of bread
- Facebook: violation of privacy
- United Airlines: forcible removal of passenger
- McDonald's: advertising that compared hamburger to visit to museum (hamburger better)
- Tim Hortons: sale of doughnuts in the colours of the Humboldt Broncos
- WestJet: misinformation about not being able to fly in when airports were operating
- Husky Energy Inc.: largest oil spill off the coast of Newfoundland and Labrador
- Boeing: executives apologize for 737 Max crashes

The use of the stakeholder concept and issue and crisis management provide good frameworks for examining the economic, ethical, and environmental responsibilities of the corporation. The following chapter will discuss the approaches to influencing or engaging stakeholders, and the approaches or tactics that stakeholders use to influence the corporation. Issues are associated with stakeholders and approaches to analyzing issues will be described.

Your advice to Tom . . .

What Tom is facing is a common dilemma that involves numerous rationalizations: taxes are too high and he pays too much, it is necessary to survive in a competitive business, and everyone is doing it. Several stakeholders influence Tom. Many of his competitors are doing it, so the government collects less tax revenue, which in turn places a larger burden on those who do pay taxes. Some customers are attracted by a lower price and will not care even though they may be liable for accidents on their property—and employees who are not covered by workers' compensation schemes have little recourse if injured. Tom would be wise to consult another person!

Summary

- This chapter defines and identifies the stakeholders in the business system and describes the management of issues that arise in the system. A stakeholder is an individual, or group, that has some share, interest, or "stake" in the business system and the activities of corporations. (LO 3.1)

- Nineteen types of stakeholders are listed and described, but several things should be remembered about the list:

  - The list is not necessarily complete but it includes the most commonly acknowledged stakeholders and comprises generic or general labels. The stakeholder names or participants have to be customized for each corporation. (LO 3.2)

  - Although some stakeholders—for example, employees, shareholders, and customers—are important to all corporations, the dynamic nature of the relationships between business and stakeholders means that the importance of other stakeholders will vary by corporation and over time. Because of this variability, the list is not categorized in any way so the reader is less likely to predetermine the influence of particular stakeholders. (LO 3.3)

  - Each stakeholder has different goals and expectations of the corporation. Sometimes conflict exists among stakeholders and/or the interests of stakeholders. Overseeing the various stakeholder interests is an important aspect of the modern manager's job. Stakeholders, and their influence, are referred to constantly throughout this book, as is the influence managers have over stakeholders. (LO 3.3)

- Managers perform a key role in the relationship between the corporation and stakeholders. Manager or CEO compensation is an issue and it proposed that executive compensation should be tied to ethical, social, and environment criteria. (LO 3.4)

- Despite the widespread use of the stakeholder concept in business organizations, it is not universally accepted as legitimate. However, today most managers believe that the stakeholder concept is a systematic approach to understanding and responding to various influences in the corporation's environment. (LO 3.5)

- The identification and management of economic, ethical, and environmental issues that may confront the corporation is described. Issues always involve stakeholders, and their appropriate identification and management is important. Issue life cycles should be identified. (LO 3.6)

- Some issues lead to crises and the response must be timely and comprehensive. Crises in business have been described and crisis management frameworks developed that enable the corporation to take appropriate actions in such situations. (LO 3.7)

Key Terms

Pluralistic society	**Issues management**
Owners	**Crisis**
Non-governmental organization (NGO)	**Crisis management**
Issue	

Critical Thinking and Discussion Questions

1. List the stakeholders that have influence and/or are influenced in the opening vignette of this chapter. What are the economic, social, and ethical issues involved?
2. How can all stakeholders be satisfied? Should a corporation be accountable to stakeholders, or take into account stakeholders?
3. Why can different stakeholders have more influence at one time and less at another time?
4. Access the websites of three large corporations and list the members of the board of directors by occupation. What are your conclusions about the type of people who serve on boards?
5. Discuss the influence that business corporations and businesspersons have on your educational institution.
6. Monitor the media's coverage of Canadian business in newspapers or on radio and television. Identify whether the coverage is positive or negative.
7. Why do some businesspeople still oppose the stakeholder concept despite its widespread adoption?
8. Identify the three main issues confronting business in Canada today.
9. Where in their life cycle are the following business and society issues?
   - Consumption of bottled water
   - Climate change
   - Obesity
   - Excessive executive compensation
   - Global outsourcing
   - Privatization of health care

Cases

3.1 "BOONDOCKING" AT WALMART

Ted McAfee owns the Blue Spruce RV Park on the outskirts of Prince George, B.C.—and he has a problem. Business has declined substantially in recent years as recreational vehicle (RV) owners are parking (or camping) in Walmart store parking lots for free.

The RV owners are allowed by the stores to park for free, but no facilities are provided such as electricity, fresh water, or waste water disposal. In RV slang this practice is known as "boondocking." The practice is also made possible as many of the RVs are self-contained with their own electrical systems and with water supplies for several days.

Parking in the Walmart lots has become more appealing to owners as the prices at RV parks have risen and the cost of gasoline increased. The lots provide a safe location as they are lighted all night and monitored by security cameras. Also, the stores are a convenient source for supplies and services such as pharmacies.

The Walmart stores have an RV-friendly policy although it is not an official one. A Rand McNally atlas sold at Walmart gives directions to every store, and RV owners can purchase a store locator from the RV website rvtravel.com.

In Prince George and many other communities, the practice of staying overnight in a store parking lot is not allowed by local city regulations. Prince George city authorities had Walmart put up signs informing RV owners of the regulations. But it is difficult to enforce the regulations, especially as Walmart does not care about the practice. In addition, there is a threat from RV owners who are organized, and in the U.S. communities that enforced the local regulations were boycotted.

Meanwhile, Ted McAfee and other park owners are losing business and may close down.

Questions

1. List the stakeholders involved and their influence. Identify any fundamentals of business or capitalism involved.
2. What are the issues for Walmart and stakeholders?
3. What can or should RV park operators like Ted McAfee do?

3.2 ALBERTA'S ORPHAN WELLS

Alberta's petroleum industry has been a main component of the province's prosperous economy for decades. One challenging outcome of the industry is the large number of inactive, and in some cases abandoned, oil and gas wells now existing in the province. The companies that drilled the wells are still responsible for them. Regulations require reclamation of these non-productive oil and gas wells, including a complete site assessment and restoration to its original condition.

It is estimated that there are 90,000 inactive wells in the province, many considered to be abandoned. The problem is that many of these wells were owned by companies that have failed and no longer exist. These wells are referred to as being *orphans* and it is not possible to cover the costs of reclamation. The Alberta Energy Regulator collects an annual levy from active oil and gas producers and remits the funds to the Orphan Well Association (OWA). The OWA is a non-profit organization whose mandate is to manage the abandoned oil and gas orphan wells and the remediation and reclamation of the sites. In 2018, the OWA had an inventory of about 1,900 wells and 4,121 pipeline sites. It had about $235 million to clean up about 700 wells.

The abandoned wells were problematic for farmers. They cannot refuse companies drilling on their property and have little say in their operation. Inactive wells may not be properly sealed and leak methane, contaminate soil and water, and pose a threat to livestock. Some farmers with abandoned wells have been refused mortgages and incurred legal costs in dealing with the companies. Abandonment regulations in the United States are stricter, but the Alberta government has been reluctant to tighten rules.

The estimated cost for reclamation of abandoned wells ranges from $27 billion to $47 billion. The OWA does not have sufficient funds and even operating companies will be challenged to finance the reclamation of thousands of wells, especially with the downturn in the industry. The existence of abandoned wells is being referred to as an economic and environmental disaster. The costly reclamation will take decades to complete and will be a burden for future generations.

Questions

1. What are the issues involved with oil and gas well abandonment?
2. Who are the stakeholders involved in the issues and what is the nature of their influence?
3. How can the problem of abandoned and orphan wells be resolved?

Even small businesses have stakeholders.
Used © Ariel Skelley/ Blend images LLC

CHAPTER 4

Stakeholder and Issue Analysis

LEARNING OUTCOMES

After studying this chapter, you will be able to:

LO 4.1 Explain stakeholder analysis in an organization.

LO 4.2 Describe stakeholder management capability.

LO 4.3 Understand stakeholder matrix mapping.

LO 4.4 Discuss the diagnostic typology of organizational stakeholders.

LO 4.5 Apply the stakeholder identification and salience typology.

LO 4.6 Explain the application of stakeholder influence strategies.

LO 4.7 Identify the use of stakeholder collaboration approaches.

LO 4.8 Learn about approaches to issue analysis.

What would you do if...?

Carol Duggan had recently been promoted to manager of The Coffeepot, one of several coffee shops owned by her boss, who had delegated responsibility for day-to-day management of the shop to her. It was a new shop and in addition to serving coffee and other beverages offered a light food menu including sandwiches and desserts.

Carol was interested in the shop doing well, because in addition to her salary she was to receive bonuses based on the shop's financial performance. Things were going quite well but she was always on the lookout for ways to increase business. Since she had become manager, she observed that some customers occupied tables and lounges for extended periods of time. She felt that many customers viewed the shop as a way to get out of the house or as a place to get away from other distractions.

Internet connections were provided free through a Wi-Fi service, and many customers sat for hours surfing the net. The shop also offered students a discount on purchases to encourage their patronage. Post-secondary students would purchase a coffee and then do their studying or assignments with books and computers spread out at the tables.

At the same time, she noticed that other customers could not find a table or a place to sit. Some students did give up their tables, but others did not. Several customers complained to Carol about the monopolization of tables by students. As a result, she decided to monitor the offenders and began to maintain a record of their behaviour. She found that some were staying three to four hours three or four nights a week despite the signs posted at the counter and on the walls requesting that table occupancy be limited to one hour.

The next step was to decide what to do. Carol faced a dilemma involving balancing profitability with a social service to the community. She was reluctant to address the offending individuals verbally, as this might lead to a confrontation or embarrassment. Instead, she slipped a small orange-coloured note to offending customers that stated "Your time is up. Please make this table available for other customers. Thanks." This action was taken only when the shop was busy and customers were seeking tables.

The reaction was immediate. Customers went online (some from within the shop!) on Facebook and Twitter to share their thoughts about this new practice with hundreds of contacts. Within 24 hours, various student leaders were proposing a boycott of The Coffeepot. A writing group announced that it would no longer meet there. Some students claimed that they paid for their food and drinks and were entitled to stay as long as they wanted. Others stated that they realized that the shop was a business and had to make profits. The incident became a feature story in the local media. Responses to Carol and the shop owner were split about 50/50 between negative and supportive.

What is your advice to Carol?

This chapter reviews the analysis of stakeholders and issues. The approaches to stakeholder analysis range from the basic listing and mapping to more complicated concepts such as stakeholder collaboration and social capital. The phrase *stakeholder management* is used for some approaches because this represents how managers perceive stakeholders; that is, as individuals or groups that could be "managed," suggesting that stakeholders could be controlled or even manipulated. Recently, stakeholder-theory academics and researchers have developed other approaches to understanding stakeholders, particularly those with a moral claim. Today, many enlightened corporations are using these approaches to enhance their understanding of stakeholder relations, referred to as **stakeholder engagement**—any efforts by a corporation to understand and involve relevant individuals, groups, or organizations by considering their moral concerns in strategic and operational initiatives.

Issue analysis is a logical accompanying process to stakeholder analysis. Two approaches to issues analysis will be described in the last section.

LO 4.1 Basic Stakeholder Analysis

All corporations should involve themselves in stakeholder management, even at a preliminary level. If nothing else, corporations should identify and attempt to understand the stakeholders that influence and are influenced by the corporation. At the least, the corporation should prepare a stakeholder map of its stakeholders.

The corporation can increase its understanding of these stakeholders by answering the following questions, which will capture the essential information needed for effective stakeholder management:

1. Who are our stakeholders?

2. What are their stakes?

3. What opportunities and challenges are presented to our firm?

4. What responsibilities (economic, legal, ethical, and philanthropic) does our firm have to all its stakeholders?

5. What strategies or actions should our firm take to best deal with stakeholder challenges and opportunities?[1]

A similar approach is to complete a stakeholder analysis worksheet for each stakeholder, like the one in Table 4.1. Note that two parts exist in the lower portion of the worksheet, for stakeholders that influence the organization and for those that are influenced by the organization. Some stakeholders are one or the other, while others may be both.

TABLE 4.1	Stakeholder Analysis Worksheet

Definition
Stakeholder—An individual or group who can influence, or is influenced by, the operations (or activities) of an organization.

Stakeholder Identification
Stakeholder _____
Subcategories _____

Stakeholder Analysis
Influences the organization _____
How? _____
Organization's response_____
How satisfactory is the response? _____
Influenced by the organization _____
How? _____
Stakeholder's response _____
How successful is this influence? _____

Basic stakeholder analysis may include a map or diagram of the stakeholders arrayed around the corporation. Such diagrams are of value in appreciating the extent of stakeholders influencing the corporation and that are influenced. Lines connecting the stakeholders to the corporation can include arrows to indicate the direction of influence. The thickness or colour of the lines can also be indications of influence. The main value of such diagrams is to gain an appreciation for the number of stakeholders and an understanding of real and possible influences. This is the beginning of an analysis, as the nature of the influence—the direction and extent of the influence—would have to be ascertained.

LO 4.2   Freeman's Stakeholder Management Capability

According to Freeman,[2] the process an organization uses to manage relationships with its stakeholder groups involves three levels: (1) identifying the organization's stakeholders and their perceived stakes according to the rational perspective; (2) determining the organizational processes used to manage relationships with stakeholders and fitting these processes with the stakeholder map of the organization; and (3) understanding the set of transactions or bargains between the organization and its stakeholders and deciding whether these negotiations fit the map and the processes. Thus, Freeman defines **stakeholder management capability** as the ability of managers to identify stakeholders and their influence, to develop the organizational practices to understand stakeholders, and to undertake direct contact with stakeholders.[3]

The rational level, the first level, involves preparing a stakeholder map that identifies specific stakeholders. For example, the stakeholder map should include the names of non-governmental organizations (NGOs) influencing the corporation, or the government agencies with which the corporation is involved. A problem arises in that membership among groups may overlap; for example, someone can be an employee but also a shareholder through stock purchase plans. There also may be networks or coalitions among stakeholders, and these should be indicated somehow. An attempt must be made to ascertain the "stake" of each group and the power it has, keeping in mind that different perceptions of stake and power exist.[4]

The second level, process, identifies the procedures used to assess stakeholders. Freeman mentions some possible procedures—including portfolio analysis, which he believes applies to some stakeholders but is too financially oriented, and strategic management, which applies if stakeholder questions are included in each component.[5] In some corporations, specific managers are responsible for stakeholder relations and examples are presented in Responsibility for Ethics 4.1.

 RESPONSIBILITY FOR ETHICS 4.1

Jobs in Stakeholder Relations

The following is a sample of stakeholder relations and engagement job opportunities. Such jobs may also be listed as *stakeholder management, communications, public relations*, and *community relations*. The posting of these jobs indicates the importance corporations are placing on stakeholders. Note that these listings are not the complete job descriptions.

- Ledor Group of Companies, Manager, Community and Stakeholder Relations, Vancouver: Involves the development and execution of a stakeholder and Indigenous engagement plan and building and maintaining relationships with key stakeholders within the communities.
- CAPREIT, Stakeholder Relations Manager, Toronto: Assists in the implementation of the Stakeholder Relations strategy, advises senior management of issues and/or risks to stakeholder relationships, and networks key stakeholders to gather intelligence on their concerns, attitudes, current work, and upcoming projects.
- GHD, Senior Stakeholder Engagement and Communication Specialist, Waterloo: Involves building the company's stakeholder engagement and strategic communication business by providing services such as public consultation, outreach and education, risk communication, crises communication, and stakeholder engagement.
- Gibson Energy ULC, Communications & Community Engagement Analyst, Calgary: Assists in the development and execution of communications and external engagement initiatives, and with various stakeholder engagement and corporate social responsibility activities including tracking and reporting metrics.
- Coca-Cola Company, Sr. Manager, Sustainability and Community Relations, Toronto: The development and execution of a strategy that elevates the company's social licence to operate and to work with partnerships to maximize its position as a community and environmental leader in Canada.

Finally, the "transactional" level deals with the actual interaction with stakeholders. It is important to employ managers with the appropriate value set to deal with particular stakeholders if the relationship is to be an effective one. An obvious example is dealing with the media. Some executives are not comfortable dealing with the media, and such contact should be assigned to someone with skills in that area.[6]

Freeman's work is the basis upon which other approaches to understanding stakeholders were formulated.

Want to learn more about **the principles of stakeholder management?**

LO 4.3 Stakeholder Matrix Mapping

The identification of stakeholders is an important first step, but the interpretation of the relationships between the organization and the stakeholders is important. Stakeholder theory has progressed substantially in recent years, and several methodologies or models now exist that can be used to understand or interpret the influence stakeholders have on the organization and/or the influence the organization has on the stakeholders.

Matrix mapping is a technique of categorizing an organization's stakeholders by their influence according to two variables, and usually involves plotting them on a two-by-two matrix. Managers need such a methodology for assessing the importance or power of stakeholders to achieve their demands and whether they have the means or resources to influence. Through a mapping process, management can ascertain the likely impact of stakeholder demands on the corporation's strategies and identify appropriate courses of action to counter or influence these demands.

The matrix in Figure 4.1 illustrates one methodology in which stakeholders are categorized according to their position on a particular issue or proposal and their importance. On the vertical axis, the stakeholders are identified and assessed on whether they oppose the corporation on the issue or support it. A numerical value of 0 to −5 is assigned to those stakeholders opposing, and a value of 0 to +5 is assigned to those supporting. The importance of stakeholders is measured on a horizontal axis and varies from least, at a value of 0, to most, at a value of 10. After the two values are agreed upon, the location of the stakeholder is plotted on the matrix.

FIGURE 4.1   *The Position/Importance Stakeholder Matrix*

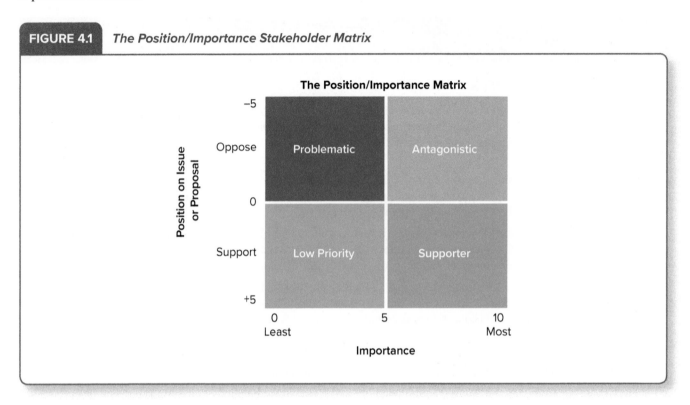

Four categories of stakeholders result from this analysis:

- *Problematic stakeholders*—those who would oppose the organization's course of action and are relatively unimportant to the organization.
- *Antagonistic stakeholders*—those who would oppose or be hostile to the organization's course of action and are very important to the organization.
- *Low priority stakeholders*—those who support the organization's course of action and are relatively unimportant to the organization.
- *Supporter stakeholders*—those who would support the organization's course of action and are important to the organization.[7]

An example of stakeholder categorization is given in Responsibility for Ethics 4.2 relating to the issue of a large retailer entering a small community.

 RESPONSIBILITY FOR ETHICS 4.2

Stakeholders and Large Retail Development

An ethical issue arises when large retailers such as Walmart or Canadian Tire enter smaller communities and compete against local, small businesses. From the perspective of the large retailer, the stakeholders involved with the issue are plotted on a position/importance matrix.

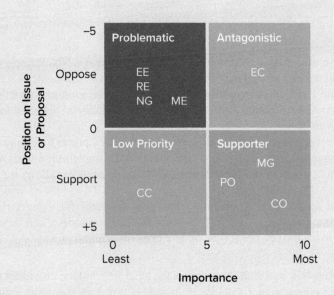

Stakeholders:

- Existing competitors (EC), including small businesses
- Municipal government (MG), mostly likely supporter; considers development desirable
- Consumers (CO), most likely supporter as prices lower and selection increases
- Chamber of Commerce (CC), supporter but some members may oppose
- Residents (RE) in area of the development
- NGOs (NG), especially environmental ones, would oppose
- Possible employees (PO) in development view as opportunity
- Employees (EE) of existing retailers
- Media (ME) would outline both positions

After all stakeholders are identified, the large retailer can develop strategies to influence some stakeholders and to counter the influence of other stakeholders.

After the categorization is completed, managers can develop tactics or strategies to most appropriately deal with each stakeholder. The following are examples:

- *Strategies for problematic stakeholders*—Target moderate stakeholders with educational programs, adjust corporate plans to accommodate stakeholders, and prepare defensive plans if coalitions of stakeholders form.
- *Strategies for antagonistic stakeholders*—Identify potential coalitions and take defensive action, prepare for under-mining of supporters, anticipate nature of objections and develop counter-arguments, engage selected stakeholders in bargaining, and determine plan changes to gain support.
- *Strategies for low priority stakeholders*—Provide educational programs and promote involvement with supporters.
- *Strategies for supporter stakeholders*—Provide information to reinforce position, and ask supporters to influence indifferent stakeholders.[8]

This stakeholder matrix mapping uses two variables relating to position and importance. Other matrices could use variables such as power/dynamism, or power/interest. Regardless of the variables used, the importance of the technique is a systematic analysis of stakeholders and their influence.

Want to learn more about **matrix mapping**?

LO 4.4   The Diagnostic Typology of Organizational Stakeholders

One methodology for assessing and managing stakeholders is outlined by Savage, Nix, Whitehead, and Blair[9] and appears to be based on Freeman's generic stakeholder strategies.[10] The authors claim that a stakeholder's significance or influence depends on the situation and the issues involved, and as a result managers must use the appropriate methods to deal with various stakeholders. Two assessments are considered critical: the assessments of stakeholders' potential to threaten the organization, and of their potential to cooperate with it.

Diagnosing the potential for threat involves ascertaining the stakeholder's power to disrupt the organization's accomplishment of its objectives. Diagnosing the potential for cooperation allows the organization to move beyond defensive and offensive strategies against a threat to a situation in which cooperation with stakeholders allows the organization to accomplish its objectives.

The stakeholder's potential for threat or cooperation becomes the basis for categorizing the types of stakeholders. Stakeholders can be classified into four types—supportive, marginal, non-supportive, and mixed blessing—and that different strategies exist for responding to each type. The following is a brief description of each stakeholder type and corresponding strategy.[11]

- *Type 1: Supportive stakeholder and strategy*—This is the ideal stakeholder, providing support by being a low threat and high on potential for cooperation. Examples are boards of directors, managers, employees, parent companies, and possibly suppliers and service providers. The strategy for managing this type of stakeholder is to encourage the cooperative potential and not ignore them or take them for granted.

- *Type 2: The marginal stakeholder and strategy*—These stakeholders are neither highly threatening nor especially cooperative. They potentially have a stake, but it varies by issue or is limited to particular issues. Examples are consumer groups, shareholders, and professional associations for employees. The strategy for managing stakeholders of this type is to monitor them closely while recognizing that their interests are narrow and issue-specific.

- *Type 3: The non-supportive stakeholder and strategy*—These stakeholders have a high threat potential, but low cooperation potential. Because of this, they are the most challenging to manage. Examples for a manufacturing firm are competing firms, employee unions, government, and perhaps the media. The strategy to follow with this type of stakeholder is defensive, attempting to reduce the organization's dependence on the stakeholder.

- *Type 4: The mixed blessing stakeholder and strategy*—These stakeholders play a major role in the organization as their threat and cooperation potential are high. Examples are employees who are in short supply, important clients, and organizations with complementary products or services. There are two possibilities for such stakeholders: to become supportive or non-supportive. The strategy to deal with this type of stakeholder is collaboration of some sort, for example joint ventures, alliances, or mergers.

Savage et al. outline a stakeholder management process based on these types of stakeholders. The first step is to identify the key organizational stakeholders by considering factors such as relative power, the specific context and history of the relationship, and specific issues that may be salient. Next, managers diagnose stakeholders according to critical dimensions of potential for threat or cooperation. Following this step, appropriate strategies are formulated to enhance or change current relationships with the key stakeholders. Finally, the strategies must be effectively implemented, including the possibility of transforming the stakeholder relationship from a less favourable to a more favourable one if appropriate. Strategies should attempt to satisfy the needs of marginal stakeholders minimally and to satisfy the needs of supportive and mixed blessing stakeholders maximally. Savage et al. recommend that managers develop objectives for the organization's relationship with current and possible stakeholders as part of an ongoing strategic management process.[12] Responsibility for Ethics 4.3 analyzes the issue of bank automated teller machine (ATM) fees and stakeholder types.

 RESPONSIBILITY FOR ETHICS 4.3

Bank ATM Fees, Stakeholders, and Strategies

The issue of fees charged by banks for ATM services has been contentious. Critics said the banks were not being responsible in that consumers were being charged high fees for withdrawing their money. The following is an analysis of this issue, the stakeholders involved, and possible strategies from the perspective of one Canadian bank.

Stakeholder Type 4—Mixed Blessing/Collaborate Strategy

- Government: non-interventionist, but could make election issue
- Minister of Finance: has power to regulate, but prefers not
- Competing banks: have same fee structure, but one may decide to go for lower or no fee
- Media: balanced reporting of issue, but do give voice to critics; also cover banks' views on issue

Stakeholder Type 1—Supportive/Involve Strategy

- Canadian Bankers Association: preparing case in support of existing fee structure
- University finance professors: view fees as "user pay"; research indicates fees reasonable
- Shareholders: keep informed and more concerned with dividends
- White-label ATM providers: may be concerned with future revenue and connections with banks

Stakeholder Type 2—Marginal/Monitor Strategy

- Consumers: 75 percent are not charged for service (i.e., use their own bank); no concern
- Consumer groups: given 75 percent of consumers do not view as issue, unlikely to do anything
- Credit unions: some do not charge customers fees; may decide to promote this feature

Stakeholder Type 3—Non-supportive/Defend Strategy

- New Democratic Party (NDP) raised the issue
- House of Commons Finance Committee: may force government to take action
- Consumers: 25 percent who are charged feel disadvantaged and overcharged
- Some media, for example *Toronto Star*, very critical of banks
- Society at large: general mistrust and dislike of banks due to high profits and poor service

LO 4.5 Stakeholder Identification and Salience

Despite the popularity of the stakeholder concept, little consensus exists on who (or what) the stakeholders of the corporation are and to whom (or what) managers pay attention. Mitchell, Agle, and Wood[13] developed a theory of stakeholder identification and salience based upon stakeholder possession of one or more of three attributes: power, legitimacy, and urgency. **Salience** is the degree to which managers give priority to competing stakeholder claims.

The authors provide an extensive review of stakeholder theory, develop a typology of stakeholders, formulate propositions concerning their salience to managers, and discuss research and management implications. Only the stakeholder attributes and the typology will be reviewed here.

Mitchell, Agle, and Wood define the three attributes as follows:

- **Power** is exercising a relationship among social actors in which one social actor, A, can get another social actor, B, to do something that B would not otherwise do. Power can be based upon force or threat, incentives, or symbolic influences.

- **Legitimacy** is a generalized perception or assumption that the actions of an entity are desirable, proper, or appropriate within some socially constructed system of norms, values, beliefs, and definition that is based on the individual, the organization, or society.

- **Urgency** is the degree to which the stakeholder's claim or relationship calls for immediate attention, and exists when a claim or relationship is of a time-sensitive nature and when that claim or relationship is important or critical to the stakeholder.[14]

Additional features make the stakeholder attributes dynamic: the attributes are variable—that is, they do not exist in a steady state; the attributes are socially constructed—not objective; and the consciousness and willful exercise of the attributes may or may not be present.

It is assumed that managers who wish to achieve a particular end will pay attention to the various classes of stakeholders, and that managers' perceptions dictate stakeholder salience. In addition, the various classes of stakeholders might be identified based upon the possession of one, two, or all three of the attributes power, legitimacy, and urgency. The authors group the stakeholders into the following classes: (a) those with one attribute are latent or warrant low salience, referred to as *dormant, discretionary,* or *demanding stakeholders*; (b) those with two attributes are expectant or moderately salient, referred to as *dominant, dangerous,* or *dependent stakeholders*; and (c) those with three attributes are definitive or highly salient, referred to as *definitive stakeholders*. Individuals or entities possessing none of the attributes are non- or potential stakeholders.[15]

The authors acknowledge that the typology they have developed may require refinement, further development, and testing. Its advantage not only is that stakeholders are identified, but also that their salience is assessed and the dynamic nature of stakeholder relationships emphasized. By acquiring a missing attribute or attributes, or by losing an existing attribute, the salience of the stakeholder changes. Managers must be aware of such changes and adjust their responses.

The typology presented incorporates the three attributes of power, legitimacy, and urgency that previously had been used in developing various stakeholder theories. It enables managers to perform a systematic categorization of stakeholder–management relationships, and allows them to deal with multiple stakeholder influences. The result is a more dynamic and comprehensive theory that will assist managers to more effectively deal with the corporation's stakeholders. The salience of one stakeholder is described in Responsibility for Ethics 4.4.

 RESPONSIBILITY FOR ETHICS 4.4

PETA's Milk Campaign and the Three Salience Attributes

Many businesses are confronted by the activities of People for the Ethical Treatment of Animals (PETA), an animal rights NGO. One of PETA's campaigns is to discourage the consumption of milk and, if possible, ban it. PETA's criticisms of milk include the following: it is produced on factory farms by inhumanely treated animals, it is an inefficient food source placing demand on the environment, and it is linked to various health problems such as allergies, constipation, obesity, heart disease, and cancer. PETA's ultimate goal is to convert people to vegetarianism.

This campaign concerns the dairy industry. The following is an example of how PETA, as a stakeholder in the dairy industry, can be evaluated according to the three salience attributes.

Stakeholder	Attribute		
	Power	Legitimacy	Urgency
PETA's "Milk Sucks" campaign	Through the media and the Internet there is some influence on consumers. To date, it appears that PETA lacks power to change the minds of many consumers. It uses celebrities to support its position.	PETA quotes medical studies and health researchers on the dangers of consuming milk. All this evidence can be countered by other scientists and health organizations.	The campaign should be monitored but other immediate action is not necessary. The industry would continue its advertising messages on the benefits of milk.
	Conclusion: Low	**Conclusion: Low**	**Conclusion: Medium**

Although the salience is relatively low when the attributes are considered together, the campaign cannot be ignored. Thus, there is some salience based on urgency, and PETA is therefore a "demanding" stakeholder.

LO 4.6   Stakeholder Influence Strategies

Frooman[16] takes another approach to understanding the relationship between the corporation and its stakeholders. He states that in developing responses to stakeholders, three general questions must be answered: who are they (that is, what are their attributes), what do they want, and how are they going to try to get it? He suggests that the first two questions have been addressed by researchers while the third has been neglected.

Frooman was interested in determining how stakeholders try to act to influence the organization's decision making and behaviour. In his research, he sought to answer two questions: What are the different types of influence strategies? and What are the determinants of the choice of influence strategy?

He chose resource dependence theory as a framework for answering these questions, as organizations are usually dependent on stakeholders for some of their resources. **Resource dependence** exists when a stakeholder is supplying a resource and can exert some form of control over it. For example, this control could be based on the amount of the resource controlled, the non-substitutability of the resource, or the essentiality of the resource.

Types of resource control and the types of influence pathways determine the influence strategies available to stakeholders. There are two general means of control over an organization: withholding strategies and usage strategies. **Withholding strategies** are those where the stakeholder discontinues providing a resource to an organization with the intention of changing a certain behaviour. **Usage strategies** are those in which the stakeholder continues to supply a resource but specifies how it will be used—that is, it attaches conditions to the use of the resource. Both strategies could be credible threats to an organization.[17]

A second source of power or influence involves the resource dependence that arises from relationships between stakeholders. An **influence pathway** occurs where withholding and usage strategies could be performed by an ally of the stakeholder with whom the organization has a resource dependence. Direct strategies are those in which the stakeholder itself manipulates the flow of resources by withholding or through usage conditions. Indirect strategies are those where the stakeholder works through an ally by having the ally manipulate the flow of resources by withholding or through usage conditions. Indirect strategies require substantial communication and cooperation between stakeholders and are difficult to sustain.[18]

The influence strategies available to stakeholders were summarized by Frooman in a typology of influence strategies based upon two questions: Is the stakeholder dependent on the corporation? and Is the corporation dependent on the stakeholder? In the four possible influence strategies created, the resource dependence is identified and the applicable influence strategies specified. The influence strategies chosen will be determined by who is dependent upon whom and by how much.

The four influence strategy possibilities are as follows:

1. Indirect/usage exists where the stakeholder is dependent on the corporation but the corporation is not dependent on the stakeholder, resulting in the corporation having power over the stakeholder.

2. Indirect/withholding exists where the stakeholder is not dependent on the corporation and the corporation is not dependent on the stakeholder, resulting in low interdependence.

3. Direct/withholding exists where the stakeholder is not dependent on the corporation but the corporation is dependent on the stakeholder, resulting in the stakeholder having power. This is illustrated by a consumer boycott; if successful, the stakeholder has the power.

4. Direct/usage exists where the stakeholder is dependent on the corporation and the corporation is dependent on the stakeholder, resulting in high interdependence. This is a more complicated result. An example is KFC restaurants directing suppliers to provide chickens that were produced under specified humane conditions. These types of influence strategies have become more common and are more challenging for managers.[19]

Managers can gain an understanding of stakeholders and their influence by being aware of these possibilities. If managers can forecast the influence strategies to be used, they can counter the influence strategy likely to occur. Instead of formulating their own strategies to influence stakeholders, it may be more appropriate for managers first to anticipate and understand the possible influence strategies available to stakeholders. Responsibility for Ethics 4.5 illustrates the use of influence strategies in the Canadian mining industry.

Want to learn more about influence strategies?

 RESPONSIBILITY FOR ETHICS 4.5

Stakeholders and Their Influence in the Canadian Mining Industry

This is a typology of influence strategy for corporations operating in the Canadian mining industry in general. Particular corporations and issues would result in a different allocation of stakeholders.

		Is the stakeholder dependent on the corporation?	
		No	**Yes**
Is the corporation dependent on the stakeholder?	**No**	*Low Interdependence Stakeholders:* • Environmental NGOs • Aboriginal groups • Religious organizations • Educational institutions ↓ *Indirect/Withholding Influence Strategy*	*Firm Power Stakeholders:* • Suppliers • Employees • Service professionals • Charities ↓ *Indirect/Usage Influence Strategy*
	Yes	*Stakeholder Power Stakeholders:* • Government regulators • Customers • Media • Local communities • Activist shareholders ↓ *Direct/Withholding Influence Strategy*	*High Interdependence Stakeholders:* • Owners/investors • Business organizations • Local communities • Suppliers • Competitors ↓ *Indirect/Usage Influence Strategy*

Note: The allocation of stakeholders could be challenged. It could be argued that environmental NGOs and Aboriginal groups currently have power over companies. Local communities are in two categories, as operations may depend on whether it was a single-industry community. The influence of suppliers and competitors would depend on the nature of the market.

LO 4.7 Stakeholder Collaboration

Recent research and consulting efforts focus on changing the relationship between the corporation and its stakeholders from "management" to "collaboration." Stakeholder management emphasized mechanisms of how an organization identified, monitored, and responded to its stakeholders. The mechanisms included issue analysis, consultation, strategic communication, and formal contacts. The impression was created that managers could direct and control the interactions with stakeholders, and that the main purpose was to buffer the organization from negative or challenging stakeholder activities. In the corporation, the responsibility for stakeholder management was assigned to functional departments rather than being a top-management task.

The recent approach focuses on building stakeholder relationships that are reciprocal, evolving, and mutually defined, and that are a source of opportunity and competitive advantage. **Collaboration** is a meta-capability to establish and maintain relationships that allows the organization to tap into a powerful source of creative energy, a large pool of innovative ideas, and a wider network.[20] The goal is to increase the organization's environmental stability and to enhance control over changing circumstances. The approach would be more integrated and company-wide, with responsibility for stakeholder collaboration assigned to a senior executive.[21] Stakeholder collaboration is also referred to as stakeholder engagement in the academic literature and in corporate reports. A summary of the approach is given in Table 4.2.

TABLE 4.2	Characteristics of Old and New Approaches to Corporate–Stakeholder Relations
Stakeholder Management	**Stakeholder Collaboration**
Fragmented among various departments	Integrated management approach
Focus on managing relationships	Focus on building relationships

Stakeholder Management	Stakeholder Collaboration
Emphasis on buffering the organization	Emphasis on creating opportunities and mutual benefits
Linked to short-term business goals	Linked to long-term business goals
Idiosyncratic implementation dependent on division interests and personal style of manager	Coherent approach driven by business goals, mission, values, and corporate strategies

Source: Reprinted with permission of the publisher. From *The Stakeholder Strategy*, copyrighted 1998 by Ann Svendsen, Berrett-Koehler Publishers, Inc., San Francisco, CA. All rights reserved. www.bkconnection.com

Svendsen provides a framework or guide for organizations that wish to develop collaborative stakeholder relationships. The framework, identified as FOSTERing stakeholder relationships, involves six steps:

- *Creating a foundation*—The beginning stage involves relationship building in a strategic mode by incorporating it into corporate missions, values, and ethics guidelines.
- *Organizational alignment*—The organization's internal systems and structures need to be aligned—that is, put in a state of readiness—to support the development of collaborative relationships including dialogue with stakeholders to obtain a clear understanding of their comments and perceptions.
- *Strategy development*—A strategy is necessary to forge new stakeholder relationships.
- *Trust building*—Trust is essential for stable social relationships as it promotes cooperation and understanding.
- *Evaluation*—The effectiveness of the relationship-building effort must be assessed and improvements identified.
- *Repeat the process*—The process is repeated to further improve social performance.[22]

Svendsen outlines the various tasks necessary at each stage, describes the tools and methodologies to be used, and identifies results to be expected. Stakeholder collaboration moves beyond the stakeholder management approach to a new level of stakeholder analysis and understanding. Many corporations consider stakeholder relations an important management function. Everyday Ethics 4.1 describes the approaches to stakeholder collaboration or engagement at one corporation.

 EVERYDAY ETHICS 4.1

Stakeholder Engagement at Celestica Inc.

Celestica Inc. provides technological solutions so that its customers can manage their supply chains more effectively. The solutions provided are in the areas of design and engineering, joint design and manufacturing, manufacturing services, precision machining, supply chain services, logistics and fulfillment, and after-market services.

Celestica has an extensive program of stakeholder engagement. The table below lists the stakeholders and the main engagement approaches.

Stakeholder	Engagement Approaches
Employees	Town hall meetings, internal communications, leadership meetings, employee surveys, sustainable workplace program, open-door policy, sustainability report, annual risk assessment
Customers	Teleconferences, voluntary reporting, surveys, audits, scorecards, collaboration projects
Academia	Working group meetings, surveys, research projects
Consortia (joint-venture participants or partners)	Meetings, working groups, seminars, webinars
Government	Local government regulations
Investors	Investor surveys
Non-governmental Organizations (NGOs)	Face-to-face meetings, teleconferences, on-site tours, collaboration projects
Suppliers	Emails, teleconferences, questionnaires, facility tours

More information on the company's stakeholder engagement is provided on pages 25–26 of its *2017 Sustainability Report*. In addition to listing stakeholders and engagement approaches it also identifies the topics dealt with for each stakeholder and the actions taken.

LO 4.8   Issue Analysis

The academic and practitioner literature has been giving more attention to issue analysis. This is a logical development as the stakeholder concept and analysis complement each other. This section presents two approaches to issue analysis: the issues management process and issue salience analysis.

The Issues Management Process

The following discussion is an outline of a typical issues management process, broken into six steps: identification, analysis, ranking, response formulation, implementation, and monitoring and evaluating. The description is a general one and is based on the steps outlined by Carroll and Bryson.[23] There may be variations in the overall process used, and different methodologies or techniques may be used in the steps. This description is meant to serve as a general description of the issues management process.

1. *Identification of issues*—This step involves the formulation of issues in many ways, including social forecasting, futures research, environmental scanning, and public issues scanning.

2. *Analysis of issues*—In this step issues are described and evaluated, usually in writing, so that a consensus is achieved among managers. All stakeholders who are influenced and/or can influence the issue should be identified. Everyday Ethics 4.2 identifies a major issue confronting the telecommunications industry and the relevant stakeholders.

3. *Ranking or prioritizing of issues*—The purpose of this step is to establish the importance of the issues identified, which should be possible after the description of each issue has been agreed to in Step 2.

4. *Formulating issue response*—The choices available to the corporation are identified and evaluated. It is important to identify all response alternatives that may be pursued to address the issue.

5. *Implementing issue response*—At this stage, specific plans are formulated to implement the response selected. A work plan is developed to ensure the implementation of the response.

6. *Monitoring and evaluating issue response*—The status of the issue and the response is reviewed on a regular basis.

 EVERYDAY ETHICS 4.2

Stakeholders and Cell Phone Towers

In order to provide cell phone service to larger geographic areas or to improve reception quality, a telecommunications corporation must erect towers. If the tower height is more than 15 metres, the corporation must consult with residents. However, if the tower is less than 15 metres, the corporation is allowed to erect the tower without consulting residents or even informing them. The industry is erecting towers 14.9 metres high in many cities without consultation.

The issue: How can telecommunications corporations erect needed cell phone towers in a socially responsible manner?

The stakeholders:

- Cell phone users: Consumers who have cell phones demand good service, and are unhappy when reception is not available or of poor quality. They put pressure on the corporations for better service.

- Community residents: People living near the cell phone towers are concerned about the effect they will have on property values and the health hazards associated with the radio frequency fields they give off.

- The federal government: Industry Canada regulates the erection of towers and has final say as to where they are placed.

- Local governments: Municipal governments receive complaints from residents, but have limited, if any, power to control the erection of the towers.

- Competitors: All telecommunications corporations are confronted by the issue.

- Health professionals: Health risks have been studied extensively and are believed to be low, although some European studies have found a risk. However, many persons living near the towers are not convinced that a risk does not exist.

- Churches: Towers are placed on church properties or structures as a source of revenue; neighbours often are annoyed.

- Shareholders: Most are concerned about profitability and dividends and thus want cell phone revenues to increase.

- Media: National and local media have given extensive coverage to the issue, making more people aware of it.

This process ensures that the most salient or critical issues are addressed. The remaining issues are not dropped, but are maintained in a list of issues that is reformulated on a regular basis.

Managers must identify and recognize all the relevant stakeholders for their corporation and also those that have influence on particular issues relating to the corporation's operations. From a managerial perspective, the next consideration is how to influence the stakeholders. Issues can be dealt with in a variety of ways, for example lobbying to influence the government, improving media relations, improving ethics programs, and consulting or engaging stakeholder groups such as NGOs. Some issues appear suddenly and require immediate and comprehensive responses; crisis management is required in these situations.

Issue Materiality

Issue materiality is a question or matter that is sufficiently important to warrant management's attention. It is also referred to as *sustainability materiality* and is described by the Global Reporting Initiative as an "aspect" that will

- reflect the organization's significant economic, environmental, and social impacts; or

- substantively influence the assessments and decisions of stakeholders.[24]

An aspect or issue that meets these criteria should be reported in a corporate social responsibility or sustainability report. Materiality has been used in financial reporting as a threshold to focus on particular economic decisions. Sustainability materiality is concerned with a wider range of stakeholder impacts, including those of an ethical, social, environmental, and financial nature.

Materiality can be assessed on a matrix in which the horizontal axis measures an issue's importance to the corporation and the vertical axis measures its importance to stakeholders. An example of a matrix is presented in Figure 4.2.

FIGURE 4.2 *Issue Materiality Matrix*

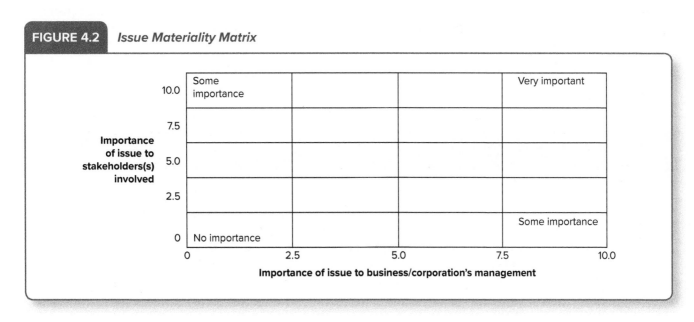

The results of this materiality analysis are plotted on the two-dimension matrix ranking the issues by importance to stakeholders and management. Issues are identified or captured through research of existing or emerging trends as appearing in industry publications, media, or public policy pre-announcements. Surveys and interviews of internal and external stakeholders can be used, as can roundtables and online forums. Monitoring or collaborating with stakeholders, especially NGOs, is another source of materiality information.

After the issues are plotted, they are ranked in decreasing order of importance. The priority issues for management would tend to be located in the upper right-hand corner. The next priority would be issues located in the upper left and lower right corners. Their influence on operations and the ease or difficulty of addressing the issues would be deciding factors for rating. Issues in the lower left corner are of little importance to stakeholders or management.

This approach was illustrated in Air Canada's 2016 Corporate Sustainability Report. The issues considered important to Air Canada's business were identified through internal interviews and workshops and those considered important to stakeholders were determined from surveys of customers, employees, and suppliers. The issues identified as being highly important to the corporation and stakeholders included safety, regulatory compliance, ethical business practices and policies, customer engagement, and fleet management. Issues considered less important included noise and air emissions, sustainable procurement practices, water management, and diversity. Air Canada's matrix was colour coded to indicate the stakeholders associated with each issue.[25]

Want to learn more about issue materiality with examples?

Various approaches to stakeholder and issue analysis have been presented leading to the most comprehensive and inclusive approaches. A corporation establishes many relationship networks with stakeholders through analysis, communications, consultation, participation, collaboration, and partnership. Stakeholder engagement is an integral aspect of corporate social responsibility or corporate sustainability. It involves creating value for all stakeholders and an honest, open, and respectful engagement of stakeholders vital to corporate strategy. Stakeholder salience analysis is increasingly being performed in conjunction with issue materiality analysis. This increases the understanding of stakeholders and related issues for the corporation and management.

Your advice to Carol . . .

Stakeholder relations or engagement exists in all types of business and not just in large corporations, as this vignette illustrates. Large corporations often have a manager or even a department devoted to stakeholder relations. In smaller business, stakeholder relations are looked after by operational managers already responsible for other business functions. Carol must be sensitive not only to who the coffee shop's stakeholders are, but also to the influence that these stakeholders have on her and the influence she might have on them. For example, Millennials may expect different amenities from a coffee shop than senior citizens would. It is important for Carol, like all managers, to think through the consequences of a decision for various stakeholders before acting.

Summary

- The appropriate identification of stakeholders is very important to business corporations as one approach to understanding the environment in which they operate. Identification should be only the first step, as managers must analyze the nature of the relationships between the corporation and its stakeholders. (LO 4.1)

- Freeman's stakeholder management capability provides a good starting point for understanding stakeholder relationships. Although he stresses the importance of proper identification of stakeholders, he also appreciates that appropriate organizational arrangements must be in place to understand the relationships and ultimately to interact with stakeholders. (LO 4.2)

- The various stakeholder matrix mapping methodologies give managers a practical approach to assessing the influence of stakeholders. Matrices can be based on a variety of dimensions and designed to suit the corporation's purpose in stakeholder understanding. The variables illustrated were position on an issue and importance of the issue to the stakeholder. (LO 4.3)

- The diagnostic typology of organizational stakeholders attempts to understand stakeholder influence by assessing the potential threat or potential for cooperation. (LO 4.4)

- The salience stakeholder typology increases the complexity of analysis by using three attributes to assess stakeholder importance: power, legitimacy, and urgency. (LO 4.5)

- Frooman's influence strategies provide another perspective on understanding stakeholders. He argues that managers should appreciate that stakeholders can influence one another and the corporation in direct and indirect ways and by withholding or specifying usage conditions. Understanding influence strategies further enhances managers' understanding of stakeholder actions. (LO 4.6)

- The most sophisticated approach to understanding stakeholders is through collaboration or engagement. Collaboration changes the approach from managing stakeholders to dialoguing with them. (LO 4.7)

- Issue materiality analysis has a logical connection to stakeholder analysis. Examining stakeholders and issues together increases management understanding of the environment in which the corporation operates. (LO 4.8)

Key Terms

Stakeholder engagement	Urgency
Issue analysis	Resource dependence
Stakeholder management capability	Withholding strategies
Matrix mapping	Usage strategies
Salience	Influence pathway
Power	Collaboration
Legitimacy	Issue materiality

Critical Thinking and Discussion Questions

1. Complete the stakeholder analysis worksheet for three stakeholders of a local business, or for your business program at a university or college.

2. How do corporations develop "stakeholder management capability"?

3. Write a job description for a "manager of stakeholder relations."

4. Why should corporations develop "stakeholder management capability"?

5. How does stakeholder matrix mapping help managers?

6. Can stakeholders be managed? If yes, why should they? If no, what can management do to influence stakeholders?

7. Some stakeholders are more important, or salient, than others. How do the concepts of power, legitimacy, and urgency assist managers in assessing stakeholder salience?

8. Explain how stakeholder influence strategies impact the corporation.

9. What are the benefits for management of performing both stakeholder and issue analyses?

10. Freeman identified three levels of "stakeholder management capability": identification, organization processes for understanding stakeholders, and establishing relations. Which of these levels are illustrated by the following:

   - Stakeholder analysis worksheet
   - A stakeholder manager position
   - Stakeholder matrix mapping

- The stakeholder typology based on salience
- Stakeholder influence strategies
- Stakeholder collaboration
- Issue materiality matrix

Cases

4.1 CSR AND THE CLOSURE OF A NEIGHBOURHOOD SUPERMARKET

On January 14, 2012, Loblaw Inc. closed its SaveEasy supermarket in the Churchill Square shopping centre in St. John's, NL. There had been a supermarket on the site for 55 years, originally operated by a local business but later acquired by Loblaw Inc. The Churchill Park residential area was developed after World War II and included a small-scale mixed retail square and open spaces.

The Square was located on the edge of the Memorial University of Newfoundland campus, which had about 20,000 students, faculty, and staff. By 2012, there was a predominance of retired persons living in apartment buildings and individual homes in and around the Square. The SaveEasy supermarket closure left a gap in the retail makeup of the Square. As one resident pointed out, the Square had a lot to offer including medical and dental offices, restaurants, clothing stores, and a pharmacy, post office, bank, hairdresser, coffee shop, pub, sports outfitter, and dry cleaner—but now no food store.

Most of the students did not own cars and many retirees either did not own cars or were unable to drive. As the nearest supermarkets were now a distance of about two kilometres away, both these groups were inconvenienced by the closure of the neighbourhood supermarket. The closure was consistent with the trend in food stores. The Churchill Square SaveEasy was a small-scale supermarket that, when built, replaced smaller local grocery stores. Recently, the model for supermarket stores used by Loblaw and other food retailers was to centralized, full-service stores as they followed the big-box store trend. Loblaw's centralization of its stores resulted in the closure of several other stores in St. John's.

Residents objected to the closure and contacted Loblaw. The information they received was that the store was not very profitable and the building was deteriorating, requiring expensive repairs. The Deputy Mayor expressed concern over the closure of SaveEasy grocery store in Churchill Square and asked that the Mayor write Loblaw expressing concern. In addition, the Deputy Mayor suggested that Council meet with Loblaw on the matter. A petition with hundreds of signatures was tabled at a City Council meeting, which read:

We the undersigned deplore the closure of SaveEasy in Churchill Square. We urge City Council not to approve any other kinds of uses of the location. A food store is absolutely essential to the neighbourhood, particularly for seniors and students.

A copy of the petition was forwarded to Loblaw. These initiatives had no impact.

Many residents and students felt that Loblaw was not being a good corporate citizen and referred to a quotation from the corporation's 2014 Corporate Responsibility Report: "We strive to be an exemplary corporate citizen..." The report described Loblaw's CSR commitment that included respecting the environment, sourcing with integrity, making a difference in communities, reflecting the nation's diversity, and being a good place to work. In 2015, Loblaw was one of *Maclean's* magazine's Top 50 Socially Responsible Corporations. Those opposing the closure felt that Loblaw was focusing more on its bottom line than on good corporate citizenship.

As the months passed, another issue arose relating to the closure: Loblaw would not allow another grocery store to rent or purchase the building, in effect keeping competition out. Considerable discussion took place in the local media about Loblaw's unwillingness to give up the space, creating what was referred to as "economic black holes." Some people argued that City Council should have a vacant building policy requiring the owners to allow the structure to be occupied if some business were willing to rent or acquire the space. It was pointed out that Loblaw was not breaking any laws and was paying the taxes on the building. Others pointed out that Loblaw could not be expected to help its competitors. Meanwhile, the vacant store was a constant reminder of the inconvenience imposed on several stakeholders.

Questions

1. Who were the stakeholders and what was their influence?

2. Is it socially responsible to prevent the former store from being rented or sold to another business?

3. Should City Council take any action in this situation?

4. Was Loblaw being socially responsible? Does it have a moral obligation to keep the store open?

4.2 THE ECONOMICS AND ETHICS OF TEXTBOOK PRICING

Several students were gathered around the section of the College Bookstore where business textbooks were shelved. Martin Tremayne heard comments about the outrageous and unethical prices being charged for the required books and that the cruel publishers were profiteering at the mercy of students. Martin decided to delay the purchase the Business Ethics book he had come to get.

Later over a coffee, Martin reflected about the incident. He had enough money with him to purchase the book but didn't want do so in front of his angry colleagues. Martin was having a good time at college. He was in a co-operative program and the work terms that paid most of his expenses. He lived at home, but had car payments and maintenance expenses. He had taken a couple of trips to the Caribbean while at college and attended several concerts in Toronto and New York. Overall, he has enjoyed his time at college.

Martin decided to find out about the textbook publishing industry and what caused the high prices. The industry was unusual in that textbooks were selected by professors who did not have to purchase them, that is, students were captive consumers in that they are required to purchase the book. The publishers market to professors and most selected the best textbook to meet the requirements for the course and seldom considered the price. According to studies, the cost of textbooks had increased about four times faster than the Consumer Price Index resulting in many universities and colleges becoming concerned about possible overpricing. On average, students spent between $500 and $1,000 per semester on textbooks and other course materials.

The publishers claimed that textbook publishing was competitive and that they were not profiteering. To ensure quality, textbooks were subject to an extensive reviewing process often involving 30 reviews. Textbooks were published on high quality paper, unlike trade publications, and involved sophisticated design with colour, graphs, indices, and photos. Publishers developed a large selection of books, not all of which were successful and some lose money. In addition, publishers had to provide instructor's manuals, lecture slides, test banks, and online platforms for each book. The publishers received 80 per cent of the retail price with the bookstores receiving the remainder.

Universities had responded in several ways. They suggested that professors change textbooks and editions only when absolutely necessary so that there was a second-hand market for the books. Some encouraged professors to assign books from the Open Textbook Library or Project Gutenberg where books were available for free online. The books were written by academics and were adequate for some courses. The use of other Internet materials was encouraged but quality control was a problem. Other universities started renting textbooks, most book stores purchased textbooks for resale, and sometimes several copies were put on reserve in the library. Some textbooks were published as digital copies which somewhat cost less, but these editions had expiration dates, cannot be copied and printing is limited. Students may have e-readers, but some still preferred the paper edition.

Students complained that new editions were published forcing them to buy new books despite minor changes, and often professors sometimes only used a small portion of the book. With increasing tuition fees and living expenses, students were accumulating increasing amounts of debt. The more money spent on textbooks meant less for food, transport, health, and leisure.

Martin wondered whether to go back and purchase the textbook or investigate other ways to obtain it.

Questions

1. What fundamentals of capitalism are relevant to this case?

2. Who are the stakeholders and what are the issues along the supply chain for textbooks?

3. Are textbooks too expensive? Is money spent on textbooks a legitimate expense in the educational system?

Applying for a job involves ethical issues.
Used © Shutterstock/ Rawpixel.com

PART III *Ethical and Social Responsibilities*

CHAPTER 5

Ethics of Business: The Theoretical Basis

LEARNING OUTCOMES

After studying this chapter, you will be able to:

LO 5.1 Define the ethics of business.

LO 5.2 Understand the different approaches managers and businesspersons take to assessing the ethical implications of their decisions.

LO 5.3 Identify the influences on ethical behaviour and define ethical relativism.

LO 5.4 Describe the seven common theoretical bases for ethical conduct.

LO 5.5 Outline a sequence of moral reasoning.

LO 5.6 Appreciate the challenges of ethics in business.

What would you do if...?

Jonathan Devereaux graduated with his Bachelor of Commerce but could not find the type of job he wanted and that matched his qualifications. He was competing for jobs not only with other recent graduates, but also with people who had been recently laid off because of the economic downturn. He had school loans that had to be repaid—and, because he no longer lived at home, he had living expenses to cover. After two months of rejections, Jonathan was getting desperate and somehow had to earn a living. He decided to apply for jobs for which he was overqualified in order to improve his financial situation until he could get his desired job. He applied for several positions, but was turned down because he was considered too qualified. Jonathan decided to overcome this hurdle by customizing—or "stripping"—his résumé. When applying for some jobs, he omitted his degree. When applying for others, he deleted information about academic awards received in high school and university. He altered his résumé to reflect the skills he thought were relevant to each specific job. He found this ironic as he had been enhancing his résumé in an attempt to impress potential employers. His conscience bothered him and it presented him with a dilemma, but he felt that he had no other alternative. One job he applied for was to work as a cook in a fast food outlet.

Rosemary Lynch was the manager of the fast-food outlet to which Jonathan had applied. She found him to be very personable and enthusiastic. She glanced over his résumé quickly and did not notice anything unusual. Few skills were necessary to be a cook in the fast-food outlet and she thought he could be trained very quickly. She was about to call to offer him the job when one of the staff approached and asked to have a word with her. The staff member said that she had seen Jonathan around the university and thought that he had graduated last year. This information presented Rosemary with a dilemma and caused her to rethink the job offer.

What is your advice to Jonathan and Rosemary?

Business ethics: Isn't that an oxymoron? Many stakeholders in society believe that business simply has no ethics. This position is unfair, and most likely reflects a lack of understanding of business—and of ethics. Ethics are involved in all aspects of human interaction and ethical implications exist in religious institutions, government, policing organizations, family life, and union organizations. As illustrated above, students are also confronted by ethical issues. It is no different for business, and so it is appropriate to use the phrase "ethics of business" instead of "business ethics."

This chapter presents materials that will enable you to better understand the ethical implications of business so that you will be better able to respond to this "oxymoron" argument. The phrase *ethics of business* is defined, and the influence on moral behaviour is identified. The most common ethical principles are described, and moral reasoning is explained.

LO 5.1 Introducing the Ethics of Business

Ethics has always been a concern for society and its various institutions. Business corporations and their managers are no different, despite the view held by many that businesspersons are somehow less ethical than others. To some extent this has been the result of the traditional view of the capitalist system, alleging that profits are the only motivating force for business, business activity requires and rewards deception, business evades the law, businesspersons and managers manipulate others, and business activity leads to materialism.

At times, business ethics became a focus for discussion in society and among managers, as in the latter half of the 1980s and the first years of the twenty-first century. The ethics of business is constantly in the media, especially after the financial crisis and economic downturn since 2008.

Many definitions of business ethics exist. The definitions include terms such as moral principles, morality of human actions, standards of conduct, rights and wrongs, truth, honesty and fairness, values, customs, the Golden Rule, and philosophy.

One researcher, Philip Lewis, developed a definition that synthesizes what he found to be the four most mentioned concepts in existing definitions: "**Business ethics** is the rules, standards, codes or principles which provide guidelines for morally right behaviour and truthfulness in specific situations."[1] Lewis and others argue that business ethics is difficult to define as it apparently means different things to different managers.

In this book, the preference is to use the term "ethics of business," which in Chapter 1 was defined as the rules, standards, codes, or principles that provide guidance for morally appropriate behaviour in managerial decision making relating to the operation of the corporation and business's relationship with society.

LO 5.2   Assessment of Ethical Implications in Business Decisions

Figure 5.1 illustrates how managers consider the ethical implications of business decisions or actions. Three levels of assessing ethical implications are identified: awareness, assessment based upon influences, and assessment based upon ethical principles.

FIGURE 5.1   *Levels of Ethical Assessment*

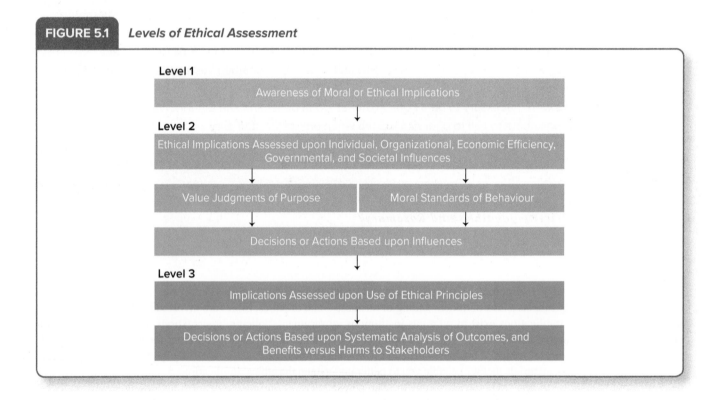

Level 1

Awareness of Moral or Ethical Implications

Level 2

Ethical Implications Assessed upon Individual, Organizational, Economic Efficiency, Governmental, and Societal Influences

Value Judgments of Purpose

Moral Standards of Behaviour

Decisions or Actions Based upon Influences

Level 3

Implications Assessed upon Use of Ethical Principles

Decisions or Actions Based upon Systematic Analysis of Outcomes, and Benefits versus Harms to Stakeholders

Level 1 assumes an awareness of moral or ethical implications of business decisions or actions. This may not be the case, as some managers behave in an amoral manner. Managers with an amoral approach to ethics disregard all moral responsibilities when making decisions. In order to assess ethical implications there must be an awareness of ethics.

The ethical implications of business decisions or actions can be assessed by individual and/or societal influences that are described as value judgments of purpose and moral standards of behaviour. **Value judgments** are subjective evaluations of what is considered important and are based on how managers intuitively feel about the goodness or rightness of various goals.[2] **Moral standards** are defined as the means by which individuals judge their actions and the actions of others based upon accepted behaviour in society.[3] Both types of influences can vary by culture, country, and time. Level 2 is the one most commonly used by managers, and most individuals.

Level 3 represents a more systematic analysis or assessment of ethical implications. The assessment is based on the use of fundamental ethical principles to evaluate the outcomes from decisions or corporate actions. A conscious effort is made to identify and analyze the distribution of benefits and harms to all stakeholders affected.

Levels 2 and 3 are described in the following sections.

LO 5.3 Influences on Ethical Behaviour

No definitive factor can explain ethical behaviour, but many influences can provide an understanding of behaviour. These influences become the bases for an individual's value judgments and moral standards that determine behaviour. For many individuals, value judgments and moral standards are used in making a Level 2 ethical-related decision. The action resulting is certainly better than a Level 1 assessment, and may not be inappropriate or even wrong. Furthermore, the assessment is not as comprehensive as it might have been if a Level 3 assessment were used.

The influences on ethical behaviour are summarized in five categories: influences of individuals, corporate or organizational influences, economic efficiency influences, government and the legal system influences, and societal influences.

Influences of Individuals

Managers often make ethical decisions based on the morals they acquire while growing up. The family or home environment is a major influence, making the personal convictions of individual managers a source of ethical standards. For some managers, religious upbringing and contact with religious organizations as an adult provide a basis for assessing and analyzing ethical decisions. The moral standards set by other businesspersons may become the basis on which an individual manager considers ethical issues. The educational process that a manager is exposed to may become a reference point. Ethical matters in general are examined in schools, and some managers may be influenced by university-level education in ethics or philosophy.

Corporate or Organizational Influences

The culture of a corporation or organization influences how a manager behaves. In other words, the behaviour of superiors and colleagues sets the tone or standard by which ethical decisions are made. Many corporations develop mission, vision, and values statements that identify the values that are held by the organization and reflected in the corporate culture. As described in Chapter 8, many corporations and organizations have codes of conduct and ethics. Corporate social responsibility objectives emphasize values or moral considerations to be considered when operating in society.

Many business or industry organizations encourage members to act ethically. One of the most widely known is the Better Business Bureau (BBB), described in Responsibility for Ethics 5.1. Business employs professionals such as lawyers, architects, engineers, and doctors. Ethical codes or guidelines have been developed by their respective professional associations and must be adhered to by their members. In some associations the codes are rigorously enforced, and expulsion from the profession is possible.

 RESPONSIBILITY FOR ETHICS 5.1

The Better Business Bureau's (BBB) Ethical Marketplace

Vision: An ethical marketplace where buyers and sellers can trust each other.

Mission: BBB's mission is to be the leader in advancing marketplace trust. BBB accomplishes this mission by:

- Creating a community of trustworthy businesses
- Setting standards for marketplace trust
- Encouraging and supporting best practices
- Celebrating marketplace role models, and
- Denouncing substandard marketplace behaviour

One BBB value is integrity by being honest and ethical in all business activities. Another is trust, and its standards for trust include the following: advertise honestly, tell the truth, be transparent, honour promises, be responsive, safeguard privacy, and embody integrity.

Economic Efficiency Influences

The capitalist economic system was discussed in Chapter 2 and the implications for the ethics of business were identified.

Some managers assess the moral implications of a decision by its economic consequences, and a moral justification is based on the workings of a market system. They believe it is necessary to maximize output as it is in society's interests to provide the essentials of food, clothing, and shelter. Adam Smith's *Wealth of Nations*[4] is held up as the foundation for this focus on economic efficiency whereby managers and corporations may appear to take selfish actions and be motivated by personal gains in business dealings. Self-interested actions in the marketplace are justified as they contribute to the efficient operation of the economy, which in turn results in prosperity and the optimum use of society's resources. Profits are maximized but are subject to market and legal constraints, and the role of the state is minimized.

The corporation's success is measured by its economic efficiency and competitive effectiveness, which leads to social betterment. Society benefits, or the public good is increased, when there is an improved use of scarce resources. This does not mean cutting corners and producing poor-quality products or providing unsafe working conditions for employees. But it does involve the substitution of capital for labour and making use of the economies of scale, scope, and experience. Abuses will be avoided if effective markets exist, and economic efficiency differs from self-interest in that business must operate within market constraints.

There are some difficulties with economic efficiency influences. Often non-competitive markets exist resulting in market domination and excessive profits. Economic efficiency leads to some stakeholders not participating fully, and inequalities will result. Those who oppose capitalism and those who advocate for alleviation of the perceived abuses of business frequently criticize this influence.

Government and the Legal System Influences

In order to maintain fair competition, fair treatment of stakeholders, and a set of laws governing business transactions, there has to be a central authority that has the power to enforce basic rules of conduct. In a democratic society, this authority is the government that enacts legislation and regulations; that is, a code of laws. Government legislation does influence business decisions. The *Competition Act* makes some questionable market practices illegal and thus discourages some managers from becoming involved in such practices. Government regulations require the disclosure of information to protect the interests of stakeholders—for example, when selling shares to the public, a corporation must clearly state certain information about its finances and operations.

The legal system makes certain behaviour illegal, and most managers are sensitive to behaving within the law. Many laws at one time were moral standards and became laws because practice showed it was necessary to control some behaviours. Businesspersons often argue that it is better to self-regulate or to self-police than to encourage legislation or regulations. This is one of the main arguments for corporations to practise social responsibility.

The minimal moral standard for some managers and corporations is to take actions that do not violate the law—that is, "It's legal so it's okay." This approach to ascertain what is right has some drawbacks. Morality is more than just what is legal versus illegal, and laws cannot cover everything. Laws or government regulations can be arbitrary and designed to further the interests of particular individuals or organizations in society. Nevertheless, for many in business the law does represent the minimal moral standards. Chapter 10 examines the ethics implications of government's regulation of the business system.

Societal Influences

Members of society form social relationships with those of similar interests, customs, beliefs, or values. These relationships can be based on the views of a particular community—for example, a town's reaction to a plant closure. Views of appropriate ethical behaviour may be influenced by a dominant culture, political views, and economic status. Some stakeholders of business represent societal views including volunteer, charitable, religious, service, fraternal, cultural, and ethnic organizations. The cultural traditions of a country or an ethnic group influence how managers view society and business practices especially for Canadian managers operating in a foreign country.

One test of ethical behaviour is whether the manager can defend the decision if it becomes known through the media. The numerous activist or advocacy groups in society known as NGOs (non-governmental organizations) can have an impact on business decisions. An example is the pressure NGOs applied to Talisman Energy for its alleged role in Sudanese genocide, eventually causing the company to divest its petroleum interests in that country.

Together these influences on ethical behaviour affect the decisions of managers and how they view moral issues. But, by themselves, these influences do not ensure any type of standardized or uniform behaviour. These influences result in individual value judgments and moral standards that affect the assessment of ethical implications by managers.

The reliance on a variety of influences illustrates **ethical relativism**, the belief that ethical answers depend on the situation and no universal standards or rules exist to guide or evaluate morality. In other words, ethics is relative and people set their own standards for judging their behaviour. One example of ethical relativism occurs when consideration is given only to one's self-interest and values with the assumption that different people have different beliefs. Another example is cultural relativism, where various societies have different customs and belief systems. What is considered morally appropriate in one society may not be so in another, and outsiders should be careful about condemning behaviours within a society. There are problems with ethical relativism. It is considered a lazy way to approach ethics as it lacks a rigorous analysis of the circumstances and consequences. Also, it contradicts everyday behaviour where individuals seek differing views and opinions. On the other hand, it is dangerous when individuals become moral absolutists, believing that they alone know what is acceptable in society.

Most of these influences are not based on any theoretical basis of ethical assessment. As a result, the degree of assessment of ethical implications is most likely not complete or thorough. Proper and acceptable decisions may be made, but to perform a more systematic assessment of business decisions or actions, managers should consider a Level 3 analysis, as described in the following section.

Table 5.1 distinguishes among value judgments and moral standards as discussed in this section, and ethical principles as described in the next section. The principles described offer some guidance for managers when confronted with decisions that have ethical implications. These principles by no means describe the only approaches to making such decisions.

TABLE 5.1	Distinguishing among Values, Morals, and Ethics	
Value Judgments	**Moral Standards**	**Ethical Principles**
Managers use value judgments when they must decide what is right or wrong	Managers turn to moral standards of behaviour in decision making	Managers can examine standards of behaviour and choice of goals by using the fundamental logic of ethical principles of analysis
Subjective evaluations of what managers think is important; based upon a manager's own values	Represent the expectations of society and the means by which managers judge their actions	Ethics is the study of what is good or right in human beings
The way managers intuitively feel about right or wrong	Vary with individuals and by culture, country, organization, and time	Ethics is a way of thinking about morality in a logical and systematic manner
Can be thought of as priorities or preferences and are variable	Are subjective gauges of conduct, and are the way managers bring intuitive feelings about right or good into decision making	Do not differ between people and remain the same
Used along with moral standards when confronted with a complex managerial dilemma	Are not objective, consistent, or timeless, as are ethical principles	Are the foundation of moral philosophy
		Are the fundamental rules by which moral standards and value judgments can be examined

LO 5.4   The Theoretical Basis for Ethical Conduct

Businesspersons do incorporate morality into decision making, but it is commonly based on value judgments and moral standards. Formal ethics principles exist, but they are often described in very theoretical, abstract, and complex language. The same principle is sometimes broken down into several categories that can be confusing for individuals without ethics education. Many businesspersons simply do not know how to apply ethics principles to business circumstances.

Hosmer claims that it is no longer necessary to recognize all the distinctions in ethical theories for them to be useful.[5] Moral problems should be defined as resulting in harms to some and benefits to others. This introduces more realism in the business context—for example, it takes into account the effects of competition. Some management actions have to be taken despite the harms to some stakeholders in order to maintain or enlarge the benefits to other stakeholders.

To enable businesspersons to apply ethical principles, the seven most cited principles of ethical analysis are described in more detail: self-interest, personal virtues, caring, utilitarian benefits, universal rules, individual rights, and justice. These ethical principles are applied the same way in any context. Ethical principles are not subjective measures that vary with cultural, social, and economic conditions. Instead, they are objective statements that transcend countries, religions, cultures, and times.

Self-Interest Ethic (Ethical Egoism)

The **self-interest ethic** means that individuals or corporations set their own standards for judging the ethical implications of their actions; that is, only the individual's values and standards are the basis for actions. Most individuals are influenced by their own interests and have a tendency to do what is right for them. Self-interest is always present and cannot be ignored, even though many moralists have a low opinion of it as a basis of behaviour. Self-interest is extended to organizations, and in particular to corporations, that are criticized for profit maximization.

There are problems associated with the self-interest ethic. Carried to the extreme, self-interest is not desirable as an ethic. It is considered an easy way out and implies laziness because the person is relying on their own beliefs without a more complicated analysis. In the short term self-interest is viewed as selfish behaviour even though the long-term results of a self-interested action may be beneficial. Individuals relying on this ethic may become absolutists who consider only what they think is right and fail to take into consideration the interests of others. Few in society practise extreme self-interest or egoism.

Yet, many observers fail to recognize that some degree of self-interest can be reconciled with morality and does include the consideration of others. Maitland claims that many people confuse self-interest with selfishness, self-absorption, disregard for the rights and interests of others, money-making, greed, materialism, hedonism, and profit maximization.[6] He argues that many people do not distinguish between morally acceptable and unacceptable expressions of self-interest.

Kaler admits that the line between self-interest and concern for others is blurred, but has attempted to make the distinction through the gradations of self-interest (egoism: totally self-interested) and morality (ultra-moral: self-sacrificial altruism). Egoism, or extreme self-interest, is excessive interest in oneself, ignoring completely the interests of others. The goals of altruists are to account for and be sensitive to the interests of others to the point where their own interests are sacrificed or neglected (ultra-moral).[7]

Many people find no fault with reasonable, measured, and proportionate self-interest, and it is acceptable for an individual to be appropriately self-concerned as long as the interests of others are considered. Maitland argues that it is in an individual's interests to not be too self-concerned. An appropriate gradation of self-interest draws the egoist into relations with others who are required to assist or enable the accomplishment of his or her self-interest. Thus, the enlightened egoist will be attentive to the needs of others, and self-interest provides an incentive to restrain one's self-interest. Maitland counters the various attacks on self-interest and argues that it is not the same as money-making, greed, and hedonism. Maximization of profits is acceptable in society as long as the interests of all relevant stakeholders have been considered and the corporation stays within the rules of operation provided in society through government.[8] An advocate of self-interest was Ayn Rand, who provides an explanation of the relationship between self-interest and ethics in Responsibility for Ethics 5.2.

 RESPONSIBILITY FOR ETHICS 5.2

Ayn Rand's Views on Ethics and Self-Interest

Ayn Rand (1902–82) was a philosopher whose writings have influenced many including the advocates of capitalism; she still has a substantial following. Rand developed a theory of objectivism that involved the concepts of reality of nature, reason, self-interest, and capitalism. She described her philosophy in the best-selling novels and films *The Fountainhead* (1943) and *Atlas Shrugged* (1957), in plays and short stories, and also in nonfiction writings.

She believed that rationality was an individual's basic virtue and rested on three fundamental values: reason, purpose, and self-esteem. For individuals, reason was the judge of values and the only guide to action, and the proper standard for ethics was humankind's survival.

Self-interest was to be discovered and achieved in individuals through a rational process instead of by a random means. The individual was an end in themselves but was not the means to the ends of others. Individuals were to behave in their own rational self-interest, not sacrificing themselves to others—this did not mean a right to sacrifice others in the pursuit of their self-interest. An individual's pursuit of rational self-interest and happiness was the highest moral purpose in life.

Want to learn more about **Ayn Rand**?

The self-interest ethic has been described in some detail because it is so pervasive in society (despite denials), it is often cited by critics of business as the only ethic businesspersons use, and it is widely misunderstood.

Personal Virtues Ethic

The application of self-interest, especially in the short term, may not result in the fair and courteous treatment of others. The lack of forceful interference is not enough even if the long-term result is good. The **personal virtues ethic** means that an individual's or corporation's behaviour is based upon being a good person or corporate citizen with attitudes and character traits such as courage, honesty, wisdom, temperance, courage, fidelity, integrity, and generosity. People should act in ways to convey a sense of honour, pride, and self-worth. Virtues are acquired or developed through learning and practise, and will become habits.

The moral decisions made are not necessarily based on being kind and compassionate, and are not necessarily concerned about rights or benefits. Instead, the decision maker is concerned about the virtuous basis for his or her own actions. An individual should ask, "Does this action represent the kind of person I am or want to be, or present the desired corporate image or reputation?" An illustration of undesirable virtues is given in Everyday Ethics 5.1. In this example, questionable virtue traits can harm a person's reputation and be expensive.

 EVERYDAY ETHICS 5.1

Business and Lance Armstrong's Virtues

Lance Armstrong's virtues have been a point of discussion for years. He was considered an outstanding athlete and had won the Tour de France cycling race seven times before retiring in 2011. He was a high-profile athlete and had sponsorships from sports shoe and apparel company Nike, brewer Anheuser-Busch, and bicycle manufacturer Trek. In 1996 he was diagnosed with testicular cancer and was admired for his fight to overcome it. The Lance Armstrong Foundation was established in 1997 to support cancer research, and Livestrong formed in 2003 to provide services and other support to cancer patients. There were various accusations during Armstrong's career that he used illegal performance-enhancing drugs, known as doping. He denied the accusations and was very critical of his accusers. Investigations were started but did not find evidence to support the accusations.

The release of a United States Anti-Doping Agency (USADA) report in October 2012 changed things. The comprehensive report was hundreds of pages long and contained eyewitness testimony from teammates, email correspondence, financial records, and laboratory analyses. The report accused Armstrong of running "the most sophisticated, professionalized and successful doping program that sport has ever seen." The doping included administration of testosterone, cortisone, human growth hormone, and blood booster erythropoietin (EPO). Armstrong was accused of having deep character flaws that included lying, bullying, cheating, and attacking people. As a result of the report, he was stripped of his seven Tour de France titles and barred for life from participating in Olympic sports. He later resigned from the board of Livestrong.

In January 2013, Armstrong confessed that he used drugs in interviews on the Oprah Winfrey Network. A common reaction to the interviews was that Armstrong did little to redeem himself, failed to convey a genuine sense of remorse, and lacked credibility. In a later media interview, he claimed that he was the fall guy for the cycling doping culture where cheating was common. Moreover, he claimed that doping existed in other endurance sports. It was felt that he did little to repair his tarnished reputation.

Armstrong's virtues continue to receive attention in the media. A negative story appeared in *USA Today* claiming that Armstrong suffers from a blind ego and arrogance. The story reminded readers how he treated those who threatened to expose him, and how he bullied, discredited, and defamed so many. On the positive side, a story in *The Guardian* raised the possibility that Armstrong might rebrand himself if his contrition felt less self-absorbed.

Another account of Armstrong's downfall is available at https://ethicsunwrapped.utexas.edu/video/armstrongs-doping-downfall.

Managers and corporations must be honest, open, and truthful, and should be proud of their actions. Standards of behaviour toward others reflect fair and courteous treatment of one another—or, in the case of business, the treatment of its stakeholders. Managers should ask themselves how they would feel if the bases and details of a moral action became known. Managers should ask, "Would I feel comfortable explaining to a national television audience why a particular decision was made?" The disclosure audience can be colleagues, friends, partners, family, or the public. The application of this principle in this manner is referred to as the "TV test" or "light of day test" by some ethicists (e.g., Pagano[9]). The personal virtues of managers and businesspersons do provide a basis for deciding what is the right thing to do in business.

Ethic of Caring

Managers should consider what is truly good for society. Honesty, truthfulness, and temperance are not enough, and there has to be some degree of caring, compassion, and kindness toward others. The **ethic of caring** gives attention to specific individuals or stakeholders harmed or disadvantaged and their particular circumstances. There should be some sense of responsibility for reducing the harm or suffering of others, and solutions are designed to respond to the needs of particular individuals or stakeholders. Decision makers will be concerned with equity, or what is appropriate in the circumstances. Exceptions to universal application are fine when they will relieve suffering and harm. Stated another way, this ethic assumes there should be a sense of responsibility to reduce actual harm to or suffering of particular stakeholders.

Managers and corporations should act toward others in a way they would expect others to act toward them. The moral decision should be examined from the perspective of other parties or stakeholders involved or affected to try to determine what response the other stakeholders see as the most ethical. This principle is referred to as the Golden Rule: "Do unto others as you would have them do unto you." Managers would take actions that would be caring and work toward building a sense of community. In the corporation, this would include developing people, recognizing effort, considering family responsibilities, responding to a community problem, and accommodating disadvantaged groups.

The advantage of this ethic is that it is responsive to immediate suffering or harm. It allows for flexibility, enabling the manager to respond quickly to changing circumstances, and precedents are not a concern. There are downsides to the use of this ethic in decision making. The consideration of individual stakeholder problems might result in losing sight of the bigger picture and thus unintentionally harming some other stakeholder. Quite often the caring actions rely on subjective criteria or gut responses that limit the understanding of all the factors involved. If used to the extreme, this ethic can result in decisions that appear subjective and arbitrary.

In business organizations, the ethic of caring is exemplified by developing employees, responding to family or community problems, and participating in affirmative programs for disadvantaged groups—an example of which is given in Everyday Ethics 5.2.

 EVERYDAY ETHICS 5.2

Raymond James Ltd.'s Approach to Caring for Communities

Raymond James Ltd., a North American independent full-service investment dealer, operates in Canada and the United States. It was established in 1962 on the principle of always putting the needs of clients first. But it is also concerned about the needs of others with its desire to give back to the communities in which it operates.

Through the Raymond James Canada Foundation, several giving programs are supported, but one in particular focuses on caring. In 2013, the RJ Cares Month was created and designed to emphasize employee volunteering and teamwork. During the month of May, employees focus their energy on team volunteer activities, donation drives, and charitable engagement initiatives at a local level.

In May 2018, 500 employees from 30 branches from across Canada participated. This involved 2,800 hours of volunteer time and benefited over 100 charities and non-profit organizations. One thousand pounds of food and 1,600 personal-care items were collected for those in need, 80 units of blood were donated, and 105 pounds of garbage were removed from shorelines.

The RJ Cares Month initiative was one of the reasons why Raymond James Ltd. was selected as one of B.C.'s Top Employers in 2018.

Utilitarian Ethic

The **utilitarian ethic** focuses on the distribution of benefits and harms to all stakeholders with the view to maximizing benefits. One approach to this ethic is that managers and corporations should make moral decisions that do "the greatest good for the greatest number." When managers make decisions, they should consider whether the harm in an action is outweighed by the good—that is, a cost–benefit analysis is conducted. If the action maximizes benefits, then it is the optimum course to take among alternatives that provide fewer benefits. Ethicists have described many variations of the utilitarian ethic, but this description is the most appropriate for business. It is particularly appropriate when managers are attempting to understand the impact of an action on society and its various stakeholders. Some ethicists prefer the utilitarian ethic instead of relying on government legislation and policies as those associated with government, such as politicians and civil servants, also have their self-interests.

As with other ethical theories, there are difficulties. The utilitarian ethic does not account for what is just. Also, there is a question of what is maximized to result in the community's happiness. There is no accepted means to accurately measure some costs and benefits, and even if there were, there is a risk of miscalculating them. Finally, there is no method for distributing the costs or benefits. Despite these difficulties, managers often make a moral decision based on what they perceive to be the greatest good for the greatest number.

Universal Rules Ethic

The determination of the net social benefit is good in theory, but it is difficult to apply, especially in business situations. It is challenging to distribute benefits and allocate harms fairly, as it is not possible to eliminate the self-interest of the person who decides. The **universal rules ethic** ensures that managers or corporations have the same moral obligations in morally similar situations. An example is the right to privacy, which most respect. Managers should behave in such a way that the action they take under the circumstances can be an appropriate decision or rule of behaviour for others in a similar situation. One way to express this principle is, "What individuals believe is right for themselves, they should believe is right for all others." Persons should be treated as an end in themselves, worthy of dignity and respect and never as a means to one's own ends. An advantage of the ethic is that it eliminates self-interest.

The ethic indicates there should be rules and morals in society that should be fair to everyone, that they should universally apply, and that they should apply over time. This principle is also referred to as *categorical imperative ethics*—that is, it is complete in itself without reference to any other ends. This means that a manager acts only if they were willing to have the decision become a universal law.

There are drawbacks to this approach to moral decision making. It can be difficult to determine whether or not someone is being used merely as a means to an end. Also, it is questionable whether it is possible to always work to universal rules, as exceptions usually exist. The ethic provides no scale between actions that are considered to be morally right or wrong.

Individual Rights Ethic

Given human nature, it is difficult—if not impossible—to eliminate self-interest. The **individual rights ethic** relies on a list of agreed-upon rights for everyone that will be upheld by everyone and that becomes the basis for deciding what is right, just, or fair. Examples of such rights are guarantees against arbitrary actions of government, the reinforcement of freedom of speech and religion, security against seizure of property, access to due process, and protection of privacy. Governments identify rights in constitutions, and the United Nations has published a *Universal Declaration of Human Rights*. The advantage of this ethic is that there is no need to determine the greatest good or to establish a universal duty.

Attention to rights is important in assessing behaviour. First of all, it is necessary is ask if the rights of all have been respected as a right is a justified claim on others. Rights depend on standards and their acceptance by individuals and society in general. Some rights are more concrete than others, for example, some rights are guaranteed by legislation. Responsibility for Ethics 5.3 identifies where the legal rights of Canadians are explicitly stated in law. Other rights are moral in nature and are standards that most in society acknowledge but they are not necessarily codified in law. Even legally guaranteed rights are disputed in court cases and moral rights result in different interpretations in society.

 RESPONSIBILITY FOR ETHICS 5.3

Rights and Responsibilities of Canadians

The legal rights of Canadians are based on the unwritten constitution of Great Britain, legislation by Canadian governments, English common law, the *Canadian Charter of Rights and Freedoms*, and the Constitution of Canada. These rights include the following:

- Freedom of conscience and religion
- Freedom of expression, including freedom of speech and of the press
- Freedom of peaceful assembly
- Freedom of association
- Mobility rights; that is, the choice of where to live within Canada and whether to enter and leave the country

- Aboriginal Peoples' rights
- Official language rights and minority language educational rights
- Multiculturalism as a fundamental characteristic of Canadian heritage and identity.

With rights come responsibilities, including the following:

- Obeying the law
- Respecting the rights and freedoms of others
- Taking responsibility for oneself and one's family
- Serving on a jury
- Participating in democracy, for example by voting in elections
- Helping others in the community
- Protecting and enjoying heritage and environment

Source: "Rights and Responsibilities of Citizenship," Citizenship and Immigration Canada accessed July 3, 2012, http://www.cic.gc.ca/english/resources /publications/discover/section-04.asp. Courtesy of Immigration, Refugees and Citizenship Canada (IRCC).

Problems exist in determining and agreeing upon the list of rights. Often rights are in conflict with one another, or there is a conflict between the holders of those rights, creating dilemmas that are not easily resolved. As a result, some rights might need to be limited. Rights should not be the sole determinant in ethical decision making. They are not absolute and overemphasis on one right may result in injustice. Moreover, there is not a universally recognized list of rights and the use of a particular right must be defended or justified. In business, stakeholders have various rights, some of which are supported by laws. Employees have a right to privacy, and shareholders to disclosure of information that will affect their investments.

Ethic of Justice

The **ethic of justice** considers that moral decisions are based on the primacy of a single value: justice which will result in an outcome that is fair. It is preferred by those who view ethical dilemmas as involving a conflict among rights that can be resolved by the impartial application of some general principle. Thus, the fairness of the process is important, but so is the equitable (but not necessarily equal) distribution of results. Each stakeholder has rights relating to the distribution of benefits or harms from an action or decision. In the equitable treatment of stakeholders, precedents should be avoided. There is a need to ensure that no stakeholders are left out, and an implicit social contract exists in society that the poor, uneducated, and unemployed should not be made worse off, in particular by any actions of business.

Ethicists have identified several forms of justice or fairness:

- *Procedural*—This involves the impartial application of rules or procedures.
- *Compensatory*—Stakeholders are compensated appropriately for wrongs or injustices that they have suffered, which can involve providing monetary payments.
- *Retributive*—This form is concerned with punishing an individual or corporation in a way that fits the offence but will be just and fair.
- *Distributive*—There is concern for how all stakeholders are treated. They are treated the same unless they differ in some relevant way. Criteria considered for similarity or difference include the stakeholders' contribution or productivity, merit or seniority, needs, and abilities. Benefits or harms are distributed in a way that is just and fair. This form of justice is often applicable in business situations.

The advantage to using this ethic is that it attempts to look at a dilemma logically and impartially. This ethic is appealing, as all are perceived to have an equal right to equitable treatment. Only when rights differ in some way relevant to the situation are there justifiable grounds for different treatment. Reasons of inequality might include: worked harder than others, accomplished more or performed better, contributed more to group or society, seniority, or a prior agreement about how the distribution should be made.

A disadvantage is that it is difficult to decide, outside of the law, who has the moral authority to reward or punish whom. Ensuring that benefits are distributed fairly to everyone is challenging, and there may be arbitrariness in deciding which rules to apply. Persons relying on this ethic may unintentionally ride roughshod over some stakeholders in favour of some abstract ideal. The immediate interests of particular stakeholders may be overlooked, and the ethic is perceived as being impersonal, inflexible, cold, and uncaring. Persons who prefer this ethic may tolerate harms to some stakeholders in the name of justice or some right. Discriminatory behaviour is acceptable as long as the relative inputs of those affected are considered.

With this ethic, managers should act to ensure a more equitable distribution of benefits so that all individuals get what they deserve and what is just and fair. But markets are unjust in the distribution of resources, resulting in poverty, some poorly educated citizens, and unemployment. Justice is reflected in the following business practices: the development of outstanding goods and services, employee skill and competency development, the use of teams, and fair and honest treatment of all stakeholders. Responsibility for Ethics 5.4 is an example of how one industry attempts to resolve customer grievances in a just manner.

 RESPONSIBILITY FOR ETHICS 5.4

CAMVAP: The Canadian Motor Vehicle Arbitration Plan

The Canadian automobile industry was concerned about the increasing number of customers who were frustrated by not having an accessible way to resolve disputes involving new-car warranties. In 1994, the industry created the Canadian Motor Vehicle Arbitration Plan (CAMVAP), which provides consumers with recourse to justice without going to court through a binding arbitration process.

CAMVAP is an arbitration program for resolving disputes with an automobile manufacturer. In a dispute, the consumer and the manufacturer agree to accept the decision of an impartial person, or arbitrator, who hears both sides of the case, considers the evidence, and makes a final decision binding on both parties. Fifteen manufacturers participate in the plan and CAMVAP claims several advantages including "fair, fast, free, friendly, and final."

The seven principles represent a wide range of ethical philosophy. The assessment of the appropriateness of behaviour would vary substantially among these principles. This is one reason why there is such a deviance of views regarding whether particular actions are correct. Managers and corporations can use these principles to become better informed of the consequences of their decisions. But decisions are not always easy to make and become complicated, resulting in an ethical dilemma.

Ethical Dilemmas

An **ethical dilemma** is a situation or problem where a person has to make a difficult choice between two alternatives, neither of which resolves an issue or problem in an ethically acceptable fashion. There are many types of dilemmas; some examples expressed in common terms are *the lessor of two evils, damned if you do and damned if you don't* (Catch-22), and *between a rock and a hard place*. The type of dilemma most applicable to business is the ethical dilemma involving a choice between moral imperatives or obligations. Often, a dilemma requires a choice between alternatives, both of which are considered wrong or undesirable.

Ethical dilemmas are the result of a variety of circumstances. They might arise because of pressure from management, complications with personal friendships, societal issues, or career and family life. In such situations, societal and personal ethical guidelines often provide no satisfactory outcome. In the workplace and in personal life, dilemmas are common.

One approach to handling them is to identify the ethical principles involved as discussed in the previous section. An issue or problem can be reviewed or analyzed using one or more of the ethic principles discussed above. Sometimes it is helpful to examine the issue or problem from an ethical perspective different from the one(s) used initially.

The following section describes moral reasoning, which will help in resolving dilemmas. Chapter 6 outlines aspects of leadership and approaches to management that will help in avoiding ethical dilemmas or at least assist in addressing them.

Ethical behaviour tends to be good for business and involves demonstrating respect for key moral principles that include honesty, fairness, equality, dignity, diversity, and individual rights.

Want to learn more about *ethical principles through videos*?

LO 5.5   Moral Reasoning

Moral reasoning is a systematic approach to thinking or reasoning through the implications of a moral problem or issue. In general terms, an approach to moral decision making includes the following steps, although variations to the sequence do exist:

- Define the moral issue or decision
- Gather all relevant information
- Identify the stakeholders involved
- Develop possible alternative solutions
- Consider the applicable value judgments, moral standards, and ethical principles
- Identify the distribution of harms and benefits to the stakeholders by each alternative with each ethical principle used
- Determine any practical constraints that might apply
- Decide on the action or decision to be taken that can be supported, explained, and defended if necessary

Hosmer argues that one or more of the ethical principles should be used to analyze a moral dilemma. For each principle the distribution of harms and benefits to the relevant stakeholders is identified. Because the principles represent a wide range of perspectives, and no one principle is necessarily consistent with the others, the conclusions reached through the use of each principle will vary. By using a range of perspectives, managers can increase their understanding of the various ethical implications of their decisions. It is unlikely that any single ethical principle can ensure a satisfactory analysis to every business decision or to a complex decision. The use of several principles provides a broad-based range of options to the manager, and identification of harms and benefits to stakeholders enables the manager to better understand the consequences of an ethical decision.

According to Hosmer, managers confuse ethics, morals, and values. Whereas ethics remain the same and do not differ among people, cultures, or countries, morals and values do. Decisions involving moral considerations are often based upon moral standards of society and value judgments held by individuals. It is important that managers use ethics principles as the basis of analysis and do not rely solely on morals and values. The moral standards and value judgments are partly determined by the influences mentioned above.[10]

Many managers rely solely on moral standards and value judgments, but this approach may not provide a sufficient analysis of the situation or result in the most satisfactory course of action. The ethical principles offer a form of analysis that systematically allocates the benefits and harms in a manner that recognizes the interests and rights of each stakeholder. This is more likely to result in an accommodation of stakeholders that will lead to more confidence and trust in the corporation.

Table 5.2 summarizes the approaches managers might take to consider the ethical implications of business decisions. Approach 1 is to ignore the ethical implications and not consider them, an approach increasingly considered unacceptable in today's society. Approach 2 represents Level 2 of ethical assessment, where value judgments and moral standards are considered. Depending upon the values and morals identified, this approach might be acceptable and result in a satisfactory

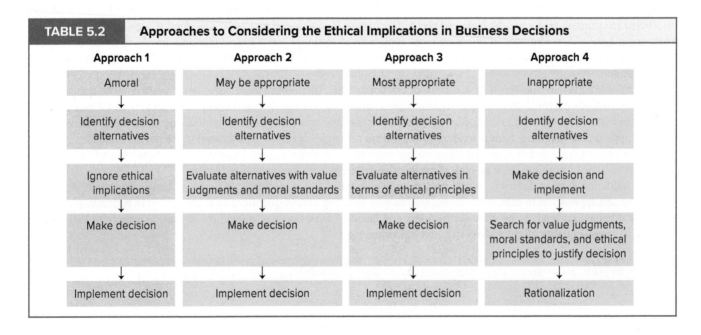

TABLE 5.2	Approaches to Considering the Ethical Implications in Business Decisions		
Approach 1	**Approach 2**	**Approach 3**	**Approach 4**
Amoral	May be appropriate	Most appropriate	Inappropriate
Identify decision alternatives	Identify decision alternatives	Identify decision alternatives	Identify decision alternatives
Ignore ethical implications	Evaluate alternatives with value judgments and moral standards	Evaluate alternatives in terms of ethical principles	Make decision and implement
Make decision	Make decision	Make decision	Search for value judgments, moral standards, and ethical principles to justify decision
Implement decision	Implement decision	Implement decision	Rationalization

consideration of ethical implications. Approach 3 involves the systematic evaluation of business decisions through the use of ethical principles. This approach would most likely result in a more satisfactory decision, because the distribution of harms and benefits among stakeholders is analyzed from different ethical perspectives and is viewed as being the most appropriate method.

In approaches 2 and 3, consideration of ethical implications is performed prior to making the decision. Approach 4 is thought to be inappropriate as the decision is made without any consideration of ethics but value judgments, moral standards, and ethical principles are searched for after the fact as justification of the decision. Such an approach would not be considered acceptable given today's sensitivity to social responsibility and ethics.

Kohlberg's Stages of Moral Development

How managers assess ethical issues and challenges varies greatly; one explanation is provided in this reading. Another commonly referred-to theory of moral reasoning was developed by Kohlberg and speculates that individuals have identifiable cognitive skill levels that they use in resolving moral dilemmas.[11] These skills are developed over time as a result of educational experience and the socialization processes in maturing from childhood to adulthood. Table 5.3 summarizes Kohlberg's six stages of moral development in three levels. He has also proposed a seventh stage, "Beyond morality and justice," which is not described.[12]

TABLE 5.3	Kohlberg's Stages of Moral Development
Pre-conventional Level	
At this level, individuals are focused on themselves and awareness of others is virtually non-existent. What is right is determined by self-interest.	
At this level, individuals are focused on themselves and awareness of others is virtually non-existent. What is right is determined by self-interest.	
Stage 1—Punishment and obedience orientation. There is obedience to rules and authority and concern for possible punishment if caught. Good or bad is decided in terms of the power to determine the rules. Authority is exercised and fear used as an influencer.	
Stage 2—Individual instrumental purpose and exchange orientation. The individual focuses on what they will get out of an exchange; that is, the reward involved or "what is in it for me." What is right is defined in terms of whether something serves one's own needs. The situation is evaluated on the basis of fairness to one's self or self-satisfaction.	
Conventional Level	
The individual is more aware of others at this level, and is group- or organization-focused. Individuals take into account the expectations and overall welfare of society and therefore are responding to notions of fairness and justice as outlined in laws, rules, and codes.	
Stage 3—Mutual interpersonal expectations, relationships, and conformity orientation. Individuals are concerned with being a good person. The well being of, and fairness to, others is considered. Group norms are followed and loyalty and belonging are important.	
Stage 4—Law and order orientation. Laws are viewed as promoting societal welfare and thus observed. What is right is determined by a sense of duty to society.	
Post-conventional Level	
Involves universal and humankind orientation. Concepts of rights and justice are considered when determining what is right. There is an increased capacity to consciously use principled judgment; that is, ethical principles. Rules and laws are questioned as the only basis for making moral decisions.	
Stage 5—Social contract orientation. Laws and morals may be in conflict, and another basis more appropriate for determining what is considered right is necessary. Societal standards apply that are established through consensus.	
Stage 6—Universal ethical principles orientation. Ethical principles are chosen as a basis for what is considered right regardless of society's views. Decisions are based upon one's conscience, and logical ethical principles are used.	

Kohlberg's work has been criticized on theoretical and methodological grounds but is often described in relation to the ethics of business. It is another approach to explaining how managers behave morally, and it is believed that most managers use stages 3 and 4. The stages of moral development suggest that managers learn through experience and training to consider the ethical implications of decisions differently over time and in different situations.

How can managers and businesspersons be moved toward Approach 3 identified in Table 5.2, and the Post-conventional Level in Table 5.3? Several things can be suggested in general terms. Managers should be encouraged to view situations from various points of view or from the perspectives of relevant stakeholders. They should be introduced to moral reasoning processes and engage in logical thinking or a reasoned argument. In addition, they should be exposed to moral controversy, through training or by example. Resource persons more experienced in moral reasoning should be available to advise managers and businesspeople.

LO 5.6 Ethics in Business: Some Challenges

Everyone is confronted by moral dilemmas and faced with difficult moral decisions, whether in one's personal life, the workplace, or management. Ethical breaches can never be eliminated, and it is idealistic or naive to think otherwise. But there should be some approach to keeping wrongs or harms to a minimum. Most individuals and organizations strive toward increasing the likelihood of "getting it right" through some systematic and thoughtful approach to resolve ethical dilemmas. Thus, there are challenges to ethics in business including simplistic approaches, myths, and lack of awareness.

Quite often the expression "just do the right thing" is proposed as a guide or standard for determining acceptable moral behaviour. This is not satisfactory because it is too open-ended and leads to many interpretations. What is "right" is in the eyes of the beholder and can have many meanings. Accountability is not achieved with this approach because no standard exists to measure or judge against. Instead, accountability is achieved by organizational processes and structures that will be examined in Chapter 6.

Treviño and Brown identified several myths pertaining to business ethics, three of which are applicable to this chapter. The first myth is *It's easy to be ethical*. Ethical decisions and theories are complex even when discussed in applied situations. They state that moral awareness—that is, ethical recognition and ethical sensitivity—is necessary as a first step in moral reasoning. Usually ethical decision making is a complex, multi-stage process, and the organizational context creates additional pressures and complexity.

Another myth is *Unethical behaviour in business is simply the result of "bad apples."* The first reaction is to look for a culprit who can be punished and removed. Most people are followers when it comes to ethics, and they engage in unethical conduct when directed by a boss. Ethics can be taught and the behaviour of adults influenced. Finally, it is a myth that *People are less ethical than they used to be*. Ethical behaviour today is not that different than in the past. The tendency is to remember recent unethical behaviour or events and forget those of the past.[13]

Another challenge relates to an individual's perception of his or her own morality. Most people believe that they behave ethically toward others, but self-perception often falls short. People are not objective in self-assessment; there are sources of unintended, unethical decision making that are an unconscious, implicit bias of which they are unaware. Banaji, Bazerman, and Chugh identified four biases: prejudice, favouritism, overclaiming credit, and conflict of interest.[14]

Implicit prejudice is a bias that emerges from unconscious beliefs such as stereotyping. Associations are made that may not always be valid. In-group favouritism is a bias that favours a group to which a person belongs or is associated. Such groups can be based on friendship, sharing a nationality, religion, social class, race, or educational affiliation. Extra credit is given for group membership leading to discrimination against from outside the group. Overclaiming credit is a bias that favours one's self. Many people hold positive views of themselves and believe that they are entitled to more than they deserve. Finally, conflict of interest is a bias that favours those who benefit the individual. Such conflicts lead honest, ethical persons to make decisions that are neither sound nor ethical.

Developments in society lead to new ethical challenges. Technological advances are demanding as new situations or circumstances occur, for example, the use of artificial intelligence in business and society has many implications for ethics. The ethical issues relating to robots, one aspect of artificial intelligence, is discussed in Everyday Ethics 5.3. Another responsibility for managers is to be knowledgeable of ethics and their application in new settings.

EVERYDAY ETHICS 5.3

The Ethics of Robots

A robot is defined as an engineered machine that senses, thinks and acts. More autonomous robots are being created and a challenge exists relating to how robots face ethical decisions, that is, how can they be designed to make moral judgments. Robots are presently used in manufacturing, the military, and automated aircraft, trains, and motor vehicles. From a consumer perspective, driverless cars and robo financial advisors are being designed. There will be increasing use of robots in the areas of research, entertainment, medicine and personal care.

Many issues relate to safety and errors. As an example, research is being undertaken to ascertain how a robot would make a decision between colliding with other cars and striking a pedestrian. Other issues involve the relationship between laws and robots. Laws must be designed that enable robots to be accountable for their actions and to insure their judgments will benefit the most. Ethicists, government, and engineers will need to cooperate in formulating appropriate laws. A third area of issues involves the social and economic impact of robots. In particular, economic disruption occurs as humans are replaced by robots leading to societal changes.

As robots acquire ability to act independently, society will have to decide whether or not robots should be allowed to make ethical and social responsibility decisions. To address this concern, roboethics is a new field of study and research that deals with the social, ethical, and legal implications of robotics technology. The field will attempt to create of an integrity framework that can be included in the design of robots. One issue is whether or not robots should be programmed to follow a code of ethics or conduct.

Want to learn more about **your ethics**?

This chapter identifies why business morality is complex and challenging. Managers can rely on intuitive approaches based on value judgments and moral standards to identify what they consider proper. This is not a reliable approach, as it may not consider the distribution of harms and benefits among all stakeholders. A more systematic approach is necessary, as frequently dilemmas exist and it is not possible to avoid harms. Ethics principles are relied upon to provide a more thorough approach.

Naturally, conflicts occur among the corporation's economic, legal, and social responsibilities. As discussed in Chapter 2, the market-based business system involves certain fundamentals, the application of which involves ethical implications. In addition, the corporation has legal responsibilities that must be obeyed, but the application of government requirements does not address all economic and ethical responsibilities. Chapters 7, 8, and 9 examine the ethical responsibilities—social and environmental—of business in its relationship to society. The next chapter describes how the ethics of business can be managed within the corporation.

Your advice to Jonathan and Rosemary ...

Several issues and stakeholders are involved in this situation. For Jonathan, it appears that self-interest is the primary motivator, but the personal virtues ethic also is evident. When considering other stakeholders, the utilitarian and universal rules ethics come into play. What about the consequences for other applicants who have the appropriate qualifications? What are the implications for employers? How do Jonathan's fellow employees feel about his being hired? If Jonathan thinks about the ethics of this situation at all, he is bound to be faced with a dilemma—but a different one from that facing Rosemary.

Summary

- The topic of business ethics has been "in" for the past decade and has been discussed extensively in the literature, the media, and the classroom as well as on the Internet. Ethical behaviour as it relates to a variety of contexts has been examined, for example as it relates to public administration and government, the environment, multinational corporations, banking, competitiveness, and industrial relations. An extensive examination of ethical behaviour has occurred not only as it relates to business and the corporation but also as it impacts the various interrelationships among business, society, and stakeholders. (LO 5.1)

- The operations of any business involve the potential that decisions will have ethical implications for managers and stakeholders. The preferred phrase *ethics of business* is defined as the rules, standards, codes, or principles that provide guidance for morally appropriate behaviour in managerial decision making relating to the operation of the corporation and business' relationship with society. (LO 5.1)

- The three levels of ethical assessment are (1) awareness of moral or ethical implications; (2) ethical implications assessed upon individual, organizational, economic efficiency, governmental, and societal influences, described as value judgments and moral standards; and (3) implications assessed upon use of ethical principles. (LO 5.2)

- The multitude of influences on ethical behaviour range from educational and religious backgrounds to professional organizations and governments. These influences lead to ethical relativism, the belief that ethical answers depend on the situation and that no universal standards or rules guide or evaluate morality. (LO 5.3)

- Seven theoretical bases, or ethics, for understanding ethical conduct are described: self-interest, personal virtues, caring, utilitarian, universal rules, individual rights, and justice. (LO 5.4)

- The process of moral reasoning is described. In particular, Kohlberg's theory of the stages of moral development is outlined in regard to its application to the ethics of business. The pre-conventional, conventional, and post-conventional levels and the six stages illustrate the attitude that managers may have toward assessing the implications of ethics in the business environment. (LO 5.5)

- The consideration of the ethical implications of the responsibilities of business is prevalent in what corporations do. The theoretical basis for ethics has been outlined and sets the stage for further examination of the ethics and responsibilities of business. But, there are several challenges to ethical behaviour in corporations. (LO 5.6)

Key Terms

Business ethics

Value judgments

Moral standards

Ethical relativism

Self-interest ethic

Personal virtues ethic

Ethic of caring

Utilitarian ethic

Universal rules ethic

Individual rights ethic

Ethic of justice

Ethical dilemma

Moral reasoning

Critical Thinking and Discussion Questions

1. Why should managers consider ethical relativism when doing business in a foreign country?

2. How is an ethical principle different from a moral standard?

3. Why can the self-interest ethic not be avoided when studying the ethics of business?

4. Which personal virtues are most important in the operation of a corporation?

5. Under what circumstances would a manager or a corporation use the ethic of caring in assessing the ethical implications of a decision?

6. What is attractive about the utilitarian ethic when analyzing business decisions?

7. How do corporate managers apply the universal rules ethic?

8. What are the rights of a corporation?

9. In what situations would it be appropriate to use the economic efficiency ethic in assessing ethical implications?

10. Is the ethic of justice applicable to capitalism?

11. Why is a system of moral reasoning important for managers?

Cases

5.1 WORKING OVERTIME

It was 9:05 p.m. and Tyler Simms was facing a dilemma. He was at the office working late, again, completing a report that his boss asked him to have ready for the next morning. She had received the draft report ten days earlier but waited until 4:33 p.m. that afternoon to return it for revision. Tyler felt that there was no excuse for the rushed revision because there had been plenty of time for his boss to give the feedback necessary to prepare the final draft. Tyler was becoming increasingly annoyed at having to work overtime under these circumstances. She had done this to him six times in the last month, and the practice was disrupting his family life. Other than for this annoyance, he liked his job, it paid well, and there were career opportunities. His dilemma was what he could do about this situation without risking his career.

The telephone rang. It was his spouse, who was experiencing a problem of her own. She had been helping their six-year-old daughter with a school project and was missing some supplies to complete it. It was getting late and she did not think she could get to any stores in time. Furthermore, she would have to get their one-year-old twin boys out of bed to go to the store with her. She said that she needed poster board, coloured markers, and tape. Given where his office was located, Tyler did not think he had time to get to a store stocking these supplies. He knew that the supplies were in the stationery cabinet in the outer office, to which he had access. He also knew that there was an explicit company policy not to use stationery for personal reasons. While on the phone, he wondered whether he should mention to his spouse the existence of the supplies in his office. He also pondered whether he should immediately leave and go to a store to buy supplies. If he did, there was a risk of not completing the report. Thus, a second dilemma emerged.

Questions

1. What are the issues involved with these dilemmas?

2. Who are the stakeholders?

3. What ethical principles could be applied to this situation?

4. What should Tyler do? Justify your choice using ethical reasoning.

5.2 PAYDAY LOAN INDUSTRY ETHICS

Payday loans are small (up to $1,500), unsecured, short-term loans with high fees and interest rates. The loan is made against the next paycheque, at which time it must be paid back. This type of lending began in the mid-1990s and today has about two million customers in Canada. There are more than 1,000 storefront locations in Canada and numerous online lenders. Some locations are open seven days a week, 24 hours a day. It is estimated that the industry does about $2 billion a year in business.

The operation of these stores and online lenders has become an informal banking system for a segment of the population. The loans are made and covered by postdated cheques cashed on the next payday. The average loan is about $300 and made for 10 days. The service offered is convenient, but expensive.

The Financial Consumer Agency of Canada compared the cost of a $300 loan for 14 days. Borrowing from a line of credit cost $5.81; an overdraft on a bank account, $7.19; a cash advance on a credit card, $7.42; and a payday loan, $63. It is even alleged by some consumer advocates that the payday loan business is illegal and a form of loansharking. The industry responds that their lending practices are better than the alternatives available to some in society who would have to resort to using pawnshops or unscrupulous lenders.

The payday-loan industry says that it is responding to a consumer need for short-term, unsecured loans. The chartered banks and credit unions are unwilling and/or unable to provide the service. In fact, it is argued that the banks have encouraged the industry by closing so many branches. The banks say they have overdraft and credit-card loans available. Some critics have determined that the payday-loan stores are increasingly being set up near banks.

Some consider the industry to be a scam against poor and financially illiterate consumers that traps many into a never-ending spiral of debt. Industry observers counter that there is a business case for the payday loans. First of all, there is a huge demand, suggesting a need. Flexibility is provided to consumers in managing their financial affairs, and other services are provided, such as cheque cashing and money transfer. The loans may be used to pay off other loans with even higher interest rates, such as those on some credit cards. The high interest rates and fees are justified as there is a high default rate, and there are high administrative costs involved with small loans.

The industry has been mostly unregulated, as there are jurisdictional complications, with the federal government being responsible for interest rates and the provinces for consumer protection. In recent years, several provincial governments have introduced legislation over various aspects of the business and municipalities have limited locations. An industry association, the Canadian Consumer Finance Association (CCFA), is attempting to clean up the industry's reputation and supports regulation by government. Its mandate is "to work with federal and provincial governments to achieve a regulatory framework that protects consumers while allowing for a viable industry to continue." CCFA represents 870 licensed stores and online businesses who must adhere to a "Code of Best Business Practices."

Questions

1. Analyze the ethics of the industry using utilitarian ethics. Which stakeholders benefit and which are harmed?
2. Do the benefits outweigh the harms or vice versa?
3. Is the payday-loan industry ethical?
4. Would you accept employment in the industry as a manager? Why or why not?

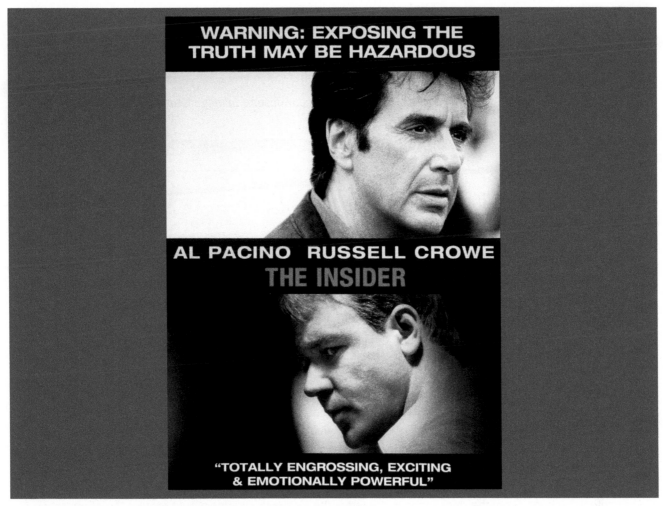

Some irresponsible corporate behaviour is disclosed by whistleblowers.
Used AF archive / Alamy Stock Photo

CHAPTER 6

Ethics of Business: Management and Leadership

LEARNING OUTCOMES

After studying this chapter, you will be able to:

LO 6.1 Recognize appropriate ethical leadership

LO 6.2 Define and describe the pros and cons of a statement of values.

LO 6.3 Make the distinction between codes of conduct and codes of ethics.

LO 6.4 Appreciate the purpose of ethics training in an organization.

LO 6.5 Define an ethics audit and explain the role of ethics officers and ethics committees

LO 6.6 Understand how ethics reporting systems work and define whistleblowing.

LO 6.7   Know who is responsible for managing the ethics of business.

LO 6.8   Identify the approaches to ethics programs.

LO 6.9   Evaluate ethics programs and list their benefits.

LO 6.10 Recognize that ethical misbehaviour may occur despite management efforts and the implementation of ethics programs.

What would you do if...?

Karl Langley, CEO of Reliable Auto Supplies Ltd., noticed the registered letter on his desk when he returned from a meeting. The envelope was marked "Highly Confidential" so the secretary had not opened it when preparing the mail. The letter was from one of the company's suppliers and accused Reliable's purchasing agents of demanding kickbacks on orders placed with them. The letter detailed the arrangements to facilitate the kickbacks that ranged from small gifts to about 2 percent of the order.

The supplier said that he had stopped most of the kickback scheme in which some of his employees had been involved and had even fired two. The supplier pointed out that after stopping the kickbacks, his company had received no orders from Reliable.

The letter was very upsetting. Karl did not know the supplier personally and the supplier had not identified any Reliable employees involved. Karl was aware that kickbacks had been a problem in the wholesale and retail industries in the past but believed that it was mostly under control. Besides, kickbacks were considered a corrupt payments offence in the *Criminal Code* of Canada. Karl had read in a newspaper that Costco had been fined $7 million for accepting illegal kickbacks.

Karl had several concerns. He considered that the supplier may be setting him up to cover up his own employees' actions. From the description in the letter, the kickback scheme would require the cooperation of several Reliable employees. He thought such a conspiracy was unlikely. He also wondered if his managers had been placing too much pressure on the purchasing agents, leading to this type of behaviour. Even more puzzling was the fact that Reliable had developed elaborate codes of conduct for all employees and strict guidelines for purchasing agents regarding the acceptance of gifts.

Karl wondered who he should contact and immediately thought of his lawyer. He was puzzled as to why Reliable's code of conduct and gift policy had not prevented this incident. He was not sure what to do next.

What is your advice to Karl?

Business has responded to the increased concern surrounding ethics and its social and environmental responsibilities. Various initiatives have been taken to institutionalize ethics; that is, to implement policies or programs that increase the awareness of ethics in the organization. Every organization has an ethics program, whether it knows it or not. In organizations there is a set of factors both implicit and explicit that communicate corporate values, define parameters of decision making, establish general rules for behaviour, and provide mechanisms for analysis. In order to implement policies or programs, the leadership of the corporation must support ethical behaviour by all corporate stakeholders including the CEO.

LO 6.1   Ethical Leadership Forms

Leadership styles have been extensively researched, but the styles applicable to ethics of business have not, according to Christensen et al. They reviewed research on leadership and identified possible styles or forms applicable to the ethics of business and corporate social responsibility. These forms are: ethical, responsible, and servant leadership.[1]

Leaders using an ethical form of leadership communicate ethical standards and encourage ethical conduct. They also provide a model of ethical behaviour and set an example for others in the corporation. Unethical behaviour is opposed and is dealt with promptly and appropriately. Decisions are made that consider the needs of different stakeholders, and encouragement is given to supporting worthy community activities including through volunteerism. The operations of the corporation reflect support for socially responsible activities, for example, designing safe products, treating employees fairly, and reducing pollution and other threats to the environment.

The concept of responsible leadership has two different orientations, a narrow one focused on financial performance and an extended one with a stakeholder view. The latter is consistent with corporate social responsibility where the corporation is not run to only make profits, but thinks of profits as an outcome likely to result from managing a purposeful and responsible business. Business is considered as a means, not an end, in addressing social problems and serving stakeholders in need. With this form of leadership, a manager might base actions on religious or spirituality beliefs.

A third form is servant leadership, which emphasizes concern for others, and combines the motivation to lead with the need to serve others. Characteristics of this form include: empowering and developing of people, acting authentically, showing of humility, and providing direction. Managers practising this form act as stewards who work for the good of the whole while creating value for relevant stakeholders. Focus is on all stakeholders and a wider set of goals than only profits. Social responsibility or sustainability is more likely included with the focus on disenfranchised stakeholders or maybe the environment. Most importantly the response of servant leadership is greater engagement with stakeholders, for example, including greater commitment, job satisfaction, and empowerment by employees. Survival of the corporation is important but so is responsibility to the community and meeting the needs of stakeholders.

The third form of leadership would include the design and implementation of some type of corporate ethics program and there are several components that managers or entrepreneurs can use. **Corporate ethics programs** comprise some combination of the following: a statement of values, code of conduct and/or ethics, ethics training, ethics audits and consulting services, ethics officers and committees, and ethics reporting systems.

Many initiatives can be taken, and several of these are described in this chapter. In the beginning sections, the explicit aspects of ethics programs are outlined. Toward the end of the chapter, the more implicit aspects of programs are described, including those responsible for providing leadership. The approaches of ethics programs are categorized and their evaluation discussed. Several components might comprise an ethics program, whether on a formal or informal basis. No model or standard program has emerged, and programs vary by business enterprise.

LO 6.2 Statement of Values

A **statement of values** contains a description of the beliefs, principles, and basic assumptions about what is desirable or worth striving for in an organization. Many corporations have articulated their values in such statements, also referred to as creeds and statements of philosophy. A statement of values also becomes the basis for a code of ethics. An example is provided in Everyday Ethics 6.1.

 EVERYDAY ETHICS 6.1

Values at Cameco Corporation

Cameco, one of the world's largest providers of uranium, has identified the following values that will guide its behaviour:

"Safety and Environment—The safety of people and protection of the environment are the foundations of our work. All of us share in the responsibility of continually improving the safety of our workplace and the quality of our environment.

People—We value the contribution of every employee and we treat people fairly by demonstrating our respect for individual dignity, creativity and cultural diversity. By being open and honest we achieve the strong relationships we seek.

Integrity—Through personal and professional integrity, we lead by example, earn trust, honour our commitments and conduct our business ethically.

Excellence—We pursue excellence in all that we do. Through leadership, collaboration and innovation, we strive to achieve our full potential and inspire others to reach theirs."

Source: Corporate Donations Cameco Corporation. Cameco Corporation, "Community," https://www.cameco.com/community accessed January 4th, 2016. Used with permission.

Most business corporations are concerned to some extent about ethical behaviour, integrity, employee health and safety, the environment, quality, and service. Such concerns are a part of corporate life today. A study of 15 Canadian multinational corporations found the top 10 corporate values to be integrity, honesty, justice, equality, objectivity (impartiality), loyalty, devotion, respect, prudence, and tolerance.[2]

There is no uniformity in content or format in these statements. Kooten found that a value statement may contain any combination of components, such as:

- the key interests to be satisfied and balanced; for example, the public or community interest, owners, employers, and suppliers;

- an emphasis on quality and/or excellence in relation to product and service, employees, and technology;

- efficiency as indicated by low cost, high productivity, and value for money or investment;

- the atmosphere or climate of enterprise; for example, a good place to work, an emphasis on teamwork, managers' support of staff, and development of employees;

- the observance of codes of conduct to enhance integrity and to ensure fairness in all dealings.[3]

By using a statement of values, managers are recognizing that individual and corporate actions are caused, in part, by the values that the individuals and the corporation have in common. Values need to be shared by everyone, at least to some degree, so that the values are reinforced and widely accepted. It is important that everyone in the corporation is able to identify the shared values and describe their rationale.

The values the organization wishes to operate with in the future are not necessarily the values implicit at the present. It is important to identify the organizational values desired, to compare them to individual values, and to ascertain how they can be reinforced. Value statements should be developed with the involvement, over time, of as many employees as possible. Although the production of a statement is the desired end result, the process used to accomplish that end is an important learning process.

What happens in practice is often quite different. The statements usually express the beliefs of the chief executive or top-level management and little, if any, effort is made to communicate or explain the values. In other cases, value statements, creeds, or philosophies are designed to improve the public image of the corporation and are only cited in advertisements, press releases, and newsletters. As a result, they are not taken seriously. A related problem is that no effort is made to instill the values throughout the corporation. In effect, the values are not shared and do not become a part of daily life—the ideals expressed are not reflected in reality, the meaning of the values is unclear, and employees and others do not understand the process.

Despite these problems, it is argued that management should be value-driven; that is, all plans, decisions, actions, and rewards are governed by a value focus. Thus, values have influence on organizational objectives, corporate plans, individual accountability, standards of performance, and reward systems.[4] This type of thinking is necessary if values are to influence corporate operations. Values must be identified, defined, prioritized, and then communicated throughout the enterprise, including corporate training programs and employee meetings. Whether the desired values are being practised should be measured within the organization and with customers or clients. In particular, current management practices must be monitored to ascertain the extent to which values are supported and incorporated into decision making, which may necessitate modifying leadership styles and management systems. Finally, values must be reinforced, including through a reward system.

Want to learn more about **giving voice to values**?

LO 6.3   Codes of Conduct and Codes of Ethics

A **code of conduct** explicitly states what appropriate behaviour is by identifying what is acceptable and unacceptable. A **code of ethics** is a statement of principles or values that guide behaviour by describing the general value system within which a corporation attempts to operate in a given environment. A distinction should be made between a code of ethics and a code of conduct even though academics and practitioners often do not do so; these differences are described in Table 6.1. As there is little consistency in the contents of the codes in practice, the following discussion refers to codes generally. Codes are referred to by a variety of titles, including "Standards of Practice," "Code of Behaviour," and "Standards of Professional Conduct," and can be 20 or more pages in length. Corporations often develop codes that are a mix of conduct behaviour and ethics guides.

TABLE 6.1	Distinction between Codes of Conduct and Codes of Ethics
Codes of Conduct	**Codes of Ethics**
Enforced by an external power and authority; convey rules that tell people what they must or must not do. Members of organizations must obey or face penalties for failing to do so.	Codes of ethics suggest guidelines to follow and empower individuals to act according to their consciences. Penalties are not imposed and writers emphasize the qualities they think members should have.
Key characteristics: • Imposed by others • What must be done or what must not be done • Rules	Key characteristics: • Self-imposed • Who we are • What we stand for • Guidelines or guiding principles

Codes have been developed at different levels in the business system, and they all contribute to the managing of ethics:

- *Corporate or business enterprise*—Individual corporations prepare codes for their own use (see Everyday Ethics 6.2).

- *Professional organizations*—Professions such as lawyers, accountants, and architects have been early users of codes and are influenced by them when employed by business enterprises.

- *Industry and sector*—Industry associations formulate codes that corporations in the industry or sector may voluntarily follow. Also referred to as *voluntary codes*, sometimes these codes are developed in conjunction with government agencies. Everyday Ethics 6.3 describes the "Codes of Ethics and Business Practices" outlining behaviour expected of corporations in the industry and in their relationship with consumers.

- *Single issue*—Non-governmental organizations (NGOs) or business associations develop codes applicable to a particular issue, for example sweatshop labour in developing countries.

- *Codes from national and international bodies*—International NGOs or agencies such as the United Nations or the Organisation for Economic Co-operation and Development (OECD) prepare codes.

 EVERYDAY ETHICS 6.2

Manulife Financial's Code of Business Conduct and Ethics

"The Manulife Financial Code of Business Conduct and Ethics (the "Code") reaffirms the Company's commitment to ethical conduct and its practice of complying with all applicable laws and avoiding potential or actual conflicts of interest. We should all be thoroughly familiar with its provisions and conduct ourselves according to both the letter and the spirit of the Code. With a long tradition of uncompromising dedication to the highest standards of business conduct, Manulife enjoys a reputation of unquestioned integrity and honesty. This reputation is among our most valuable assets and we must protect it."

The Code is organized into the following sections:

I. Why Ethics Matter—Outlines the purpose of the code and how it is applied.

II. Living Manulife's Values—Lists corporate values, which guide operations.

III. Ethics in the Workplace—Articulates workplace principles, fairness, professionalism, and safety.

IV. Ethics in Your Business Relationships—Includes fairness and honesty toward customers, compliance with laws, gifts to government officials, lobbying and campaign finance issues, and handling of media inquiries.

V. Conflicts of Interest—Identifies possible conflicts and indicates how to avoid them.

VI. Handling Information—Discusses appropriate information disclosure to ensure privacy of stakeholders, including that of employees, policyholders, and investors.

VII. Ethics and the Law—Stresses the need to be knowledgeable of appropriate laws and the duty to report inappropriate behaviour.

VIII. A Final Word—Reinforces the importance of employee conduct and good judgment as it impacts Manulife's reputation.

Each of the sections is described in more detail. An Ethics Hotline is available, enabling employees to ask questions about the Code of Business Conduct and Ethics or report suspected misconduct.

 EVERYDAY ETHICS 6.3

Ethics and Business Practices in the Direct Selling Industry

The Direct Selling Association (DSA) of Canada represents businesses that sell products or services directly to consumers away from fixed retail locations. Products sold this way include nutritionals, cosmetics, jewellery, gifts, and housewares. Well-known direct sellers are Avon, Amway, Mary Kay, Nu Skin, and Nygard Style Direct. The Association's mission is to "promote, serve and protect the interests of our member companies and independent direct sellers marketing their products, and ensure the highest level of business ethics and service to consumers."

In order to fulfil this mission, the Association has "Codes of Ethics and Business Practices" comprising three sections: ethical behaviour expected, business practices followed, and a code enforcement/complaints procedure. The Code of Ethics comprises 27 articles covering things such as pricing and terms, cooling-off periods, guarantees and warranties, after-sale service, refunds, complaints, and referral selling. The Code of Business Practices has 14 articles covering such things as recruiting, education, false or misleading statements, and disparaging remarks. The Code Enforcement and Handling Procedure comprises five sections. The codes are designed to cover behaviour among the direct sellers themselves and their relationships with consumers.

Source: "About the DSA," Direct Selling Association at https://www.dsa.ca/about-the-dsa/ and "Codes of Ethics and Business Practices," Direct Selling Association at https://www.dsa.ca/wp-content/uploads/2018/12/DSA-DSA-Codes-of-Ethics_ENG_2018.pdf accessed on January 20, 2019. Used with permission.

Codes are the most common approach to institutionalizing ethical behaviour, and aid in understanding relationships with stakeholders. They can improve customer confidence in the quality of a product or the level of service, and also help ensure ethical and fair treatment of customers. The reputation of the corporation or organization that develops codes is improved and attracts high-calibre employees and customers. Codes simplify the detection of unethical behaviour in competitors and employees by standardizing norms of behaviour. Lastly, codes provide for self-regulation, which is preferable to external control.

Overall, codes increase awareness, discourage ethical apathy, facilitate ethical decision making, and make it easier to refuse an unethical request.

Content

Today, the content of codes varies between corporations, but Table 6.2 identifies commonly found items.

TABLE 6.2	Content of Codes of Conduct and Codes of Ethics
A general statement of ethics, values, or philosophies	
Criteria for decision making and compliance with laws	
Responsibility toward employees, including items such as health and safety, diversity, a respectful workplace, and privacy	

Conflicts of interest, their identification, and how to handle them
Protection of corporate assets, including accurate accounting and record keeping, security or property, and insider information
Appropriate business practices, including honesty, fairness, obeying the law, and information disclosure
Appropriate conduct on behalf of the corporation; for example, relationships with customers, suppliers, competitors, creditors, and government
Responsibilities to society at large, including contribution to political parties, lobbying government, responses to media, treatment of communities, and concern for environmental protection
Implementation procedures, including familiarity with the code, reporting of violations, refusing unethical requests, and seeking help on ethical matters
Specification of enforcement/compliance procedures and the penalties for inappropriate or illegal behaviour.

Also, the content of codes has evolved over time and through five generations. The *first generation* focused on conflict of interest, involving the protection of company interests from employees, and was concerned with the shareholder interest and mostly excluded the public interest. Commercial conduct was emphasized in the *second generation,* including such things as bribery of foreign officials and arranging for kickbacks. It was argued that ethical practices protected the corporation's interest and reputation, as there was a relationship between ethical behaviour and profitability. The *third generation* focused on employee rights and the motivation of the workforce along with relationships with customers and suppliers. Ethical consumerism emerged with renewed mention of the importance of satisfying the customer. During this generation of codes, the exploitation of child labour also emerged. A wider responsibility was assumed in the *fourth generation* of codes, with attention to the protection of the environment and respect for communities in which corporations operated. Corporations wished to reduce legal liabilities as well as maintain their image. Finally, the *fifth generation* extended coverage to international concerns, for example countries whose governments ignored human rights, the rule of law, and labour conditions in developing countries.[5]

The development and implementation of codes has not been a static process. Corporations have been challenged by societal demands to address different social responsibilities. As a result, codes have become more challenging not only to develop but also to implement.

Criticisms

Some critics claim that codes of ethics or conduct are at best a minimal but unenforceable standard and at worst a hollow pretense. An implication of this claim is that most corporations and professions operate at an ethical level above that specified in the codes. It is for only the less scrupulous that the codes are intended, but the guidelines may not be very effective with this group. It is, therefore, difficult to enforce the codes and, even if they are enforced, the penalties may be insignificant. Those following a code may also be placed in a disadvantageous position because those who don't adhere to the code are not restricted in their actions. As a result, convincing everyone to comply is not easy. In corporations, codes are sometimes pointed to with pride but ignored in practice. Frequently, the codes are idealistic or written in meaningless generalities.

Sometimes, codes of ethics are developed merely to control competitive conduct among business corporations or individuals. They specify conduct that is considered unprofessional, such as pricing practices in some industries. In these cases the code of conduct is really designed to reduce competition, and this kind of self-regulation is sometimes a stop-gap measure of questionable intent designed merely to prevent government legislation and serve as a response to public criticism.

Nevertheless, the use of codes and their reasons for existing are no longer issues for many corporations. Codes are important devices for communicating and controlling employees' behaviour within the corporation, and the behaviour of corporations and industries in society. Codes can be made more effective through improving their content, increasing commitment to the codes, and creating mechanisms that encourage employees to embrace the codes and live by them on a daily basis.

LO 6.4   Ethics Training

Ethics training involves teaching employees about the values and policies on ethics they should follow in their decision making. The teaching sessions involve an orientation on values or ethics and related policies and deal with reputation and legal risks. A code of ethics or statement of values may be used in this teaching process, in addition to handbooks or policy statements. Such teaching can be done by managers or outside consultants and addressed to all levels of employees, but more emphasis has been placed on management levels.

Larger corporations have developed online exercises to increase awareness of ethical implications. Employees complete such exercises at their computers, with appropriate responses presented or a scoring of the employee's ethical awareness given. Such training programs are established not only to develop employee awareness of ethics in business but also to draw attention to the ethical issues to which an employee may be exposed.

Training involves giving participants practical checklists and tests to evaluate their actions. Training usually also includes a description of conflict of interest, something that inevitably arises in a discussion of ethics.

Checklists and Tests

Lists of questions, moral standards, and tests have been developed to assist managers in making ethical decisions. Writing in the *Harvard Business Review*, Nash argues that plainly worded questions, such as the following, should be used by managers when examining the ethics of a business decision:

1. Have you defined the problem accurately?
2. How would you define the problem if you stood on the other side of the fence?
3. How did this situation occur in the first place?
4. To whom and to what do you give your loyalty as a person and as a member of the corporation?
5. What is your intention in making this decision?
6. How does this intention compare with the probable results?
7. Whom could your decision or action injure?
8. Can you discuss the problem with the affected parties before you make your decision?
9. Are you confident that your position will be as valid over a long period of time as it seems now?
10. Could you disclose without qualm your decision or action to your boss, your CEO, the board of directors, your family, society as a whole?
11. What is the symbolic potential of your action if understood? If misunderstood?
12. Under what conditions would you allow exceptions to your stand?[6]

Nash refers to this approach as the "good puppy" theory, as it allows corporate morality to be defined and explored half-way between the rigorous moral analogy of the corporation being the "good person" and the purely amoral definition of good. According to Nash,

> *Moral capacity is perceived as present, but its potential is limited. A moral evaluation of the good puppy is possible but exists largely on concrete terms: we do not need to identify the puppy's intentions as utilitarian to understand and agree that its "ethical" fulfillment of the social contract consists of not soiling the carpet or biting the baby.*[7]

A second example is the Pagano model, which uses six clear questions that serve as several tests of the ethics of a particular action. Pagano identifies six tests that he feels provide useful insights into the ethics of a business' actions. The tests are as follows:

1. *Is it legal?*—This is a core starting point.
2. *The benefit–cost test*—This test employs the utilitarian perspective of the greatest good for the greatest number.
3. *The categorical imperative*—Do you want this action to be a universal standard? This test takes the view that if it's good for the goose, it's good for the gander.
4. *The light of day test*—What if your actions appeared on TV? Would you be proud?
5. *Do unto others*—This test uses the Golden Rule. Do you want the same to happen to you?
6. *The ventilation test*—Get a second opinion from a wise friend with no investment in the outcome.[8]

The author feels that this approach has the advantages of being compact and simple. Note that most of the questions represent the principles discussed in Chapter 5.

Understanding Conflicts of Interest

A conflict of interest occurs when there is a clash between the interests of an individual—that is, a manager or employee—and the organization that employs the individual. A **conflict of interest** is a situation in which an individual has a private or personal interest that is sufficient to appear to influence the objective exercise of that individual's duties.[9] The personal interest usually involves a financial gain or a promised future promotion or gift obtained by the individual or his or her immediate family. "Duties" refers to the responsibilities the individual was hired to perform in good faith and loyalty. Common conflicts are listed in Table 6.3.

TABLE 6.3	Common Conflicts of Interest
Self-dealing—Exists where a manager or employee takes an action in an official capacity that involves dealing with oneself in a private capacity and that confers a benefit to oneself. Today this extends to one's spouse, family members, and business partners.	
Accepting gifts or benefits—Involves the acceptance of some benefit.	
Influence peddling—The practice of soliciting some form of benefit; for example, asking for a kickback or gift from a supplier if a purchase is made.	
Using employer's property—The inappropriate use of an employer's property; for example, taking office supplies for home use.	
Using confidential information—The use for personal or private purposes of confidential information obtained from some other source, for example customers or suppliers, to gain some benefit.	
Outside employment or moonlighting—The work or activity in which an employee engages outside normal working hours for additional remuneration.	
Post-employment—Subsequent or future employment where information or contacts obtained during employment results in some benefit.	
Personal conduct—The situation where an employee's behaviour in private life may reflect adversely on the employer.	

Several complications exist in defining a manager's or employee's involvement in a conflict of interest. There are many variations of conflict of interest, from "influence peddling" to the improper use of company property. Interpretation of conflict of interest varies from one organization to another, from one department to another, and from one individual to another. Some conflicts of interest are defined in laws or regulations, but it is not possible to prohibit all possible business arrangements. Finally, it is difficult to distinguish among the types of conflict of interest.

The following are brief explanations of the three types of conflict:

- *Real*—A situation in which a manager or employee has knowledge of a private economic interest, or any kind of private or personal gain, that is sufficient to influence the exercise of their duties and responsibilities. Conflict occurs when there is an existence of a private interest, when it is known to the employee, and when there is a connection with the employer's duties or responsibilities that is sufficient to influence the exercise of those duties or responsibilities.

- *Apparent*—A situation where a conflict of interest can be deduced from appearances; exists when there is a reasonable apprehension that a well-informed person could make the connection.

- *Potential*—A situation that may develop into an actual conflict; exists when an employee can foresee that he or she has a private interest that may be sufficient to influence a duty or responsibility.[10]

Managers or employees must be aware of and concerned about all types and categories of conflict, and many corporations have statements describing potential conflicts. They must be familiar with any conflict of interest rules that exist, and also be able to recognize unidentified potential conflicts. Managers and employees must be continuously sensitive to conflicts of interest, as their reputation and the corporation's is at stake. Everyday Ethics 6.4 is an example of a corporation's conflict of interest policy.

Husky Energy Inc.'s Conflict of Interest Policy

Husky Energy Inc.'s Code of Conduct includes a substantial section on conflict of interest. In general it states that all employees and directors are to avoid all situations in which their personal interests conflict with their duties or the interests of the company. A potential conflict of interest arises when the employee or a related person engages in an activity that may result in receipt of a benefit at the expense of Husky or interfere with the employee's objectivity or effectiveness on the job.

A conflict of interest can arise when an employee accepts outside employment in areas similar to those in which Husky is involved, uses Husky's resources for outside work, participates in activities that reflect negatively on Husky's reputation, or holds a financial interest in a company doing business with Husky. Potential conflicts of interest must be immediately disclosed to the employee's supervisor. New employees must disclose any potential conflict of interest upon commencing work. If a violation of the policy is considered serious, disciplinary action will be taken, including possible termination of employment.

Source: Summarized from Husky Energy Inc. Code of Business Conduct, Conflict of Interest Section, pages 4–6 available at https://huskyenergy.com/downloads /abouthusky/coporategovernance/CodeofBusinessConductPolicy101.pdf © 2002-2013 Husky Energy Inc. Used with permission of Husky Energy Inc.

LO 6.5   Ethics Audits, Managers, and Committees

An **ethics audit** is a systematic effort to discover actual or potential unethical behaviour in an organization. It is designed not only to uncover unethical behaviour, but also to identify existing opportunities for unethical behaviour. There is a preventive as well as a remedial purpose. Audits are particularly useful when used in conjunction with a code of ethics, as the code can be the basis for comparison to establish how well or poorly the organization is doing. Regular audits foster ethical practice.

In recent years, several ethics audits or ethics accountability measures have been developed. These will be discussed in Chapter 9.

Consultants knowledgeable in the area of ethics advise management on how to put "integrity" into corporate culture. Ethics audits or surveys can be conducted by consultants to ascertain compliance to ethical standards, and consultants may be involved in training and code development. The consultants are usually persons external to the organization who have some education and experience in ethics management. The Ethics Practitioners' Association of Canada (described in Responsibility for Ethics 6.1) is attempting to improve the quality of ethics advice.

Ethics Practitioners' Association of Canada

The Ethics Practitioners' Association of Canada (EPAC) was formed in 1994 and "functions as a *community of interest* and a *community of practice* of individuals interested in ethics as applied in organizational life." Its members include ethics and values officers, compliance and CSR officers, consultants, educators, students, and others interested in applied ethics for any type of organization. Membership comes from all sectors: government, business, voluntary, and academic. EPAC has developed ethical standards for its members, a competency profile that describes functions a practitioner in the field of organizational ethics carries out, and a list of skills that such a practitioner should possess. Its activities are designed to encourage members to operate in an exemplary ethical and social manner locally and internationally.

Some corporations have gone beyond implementing codes, training, audits, and the use of consultants and established ethics officers, indicating that ethical issues are being treated seriously. An **ethics officer** is an independent manager, reporting to the board of directors or CEO, who reviews complaints or information from anyone in the organization or any stakeholder, studies the situation, and recommends action if necessary. Sometimes this role is performed by an ombudsperson or advocate, who also must be independent to ensure the trust of stakeholders. Such officers can alert the organization to ethical problems or issues before they become public knowledge, allowing time to prepare a defence or to take remedial actions. A similar position in some corporations is a **compliance officer** who is responsible for ensuring that all employees are familiar with the corporation's policies and codes, and with government regulations and laws. That person would also be responsible for ensuring that codes of conduct and ethics are being implemented. In Canada, the corporate secretary quite often performs this role.

An **ethics committee** is a group comprising directors, managers, or staff formed to monitor ethical standards and behaviour. The formation of such a committee, sometimes referred to as a business conduct committee, injects ethics at the highest level in the organization, and is a signal to all stakeholders of the company's commitment to ethical practice. This type of committee is involved in developing an ethics program and may monitor management and employee behaviour for ethical issues.

Ethics committees comprising management, employees, and outside stakeholders can also exist within the organization. Present practice appears to be that ethics committees are top-management focused. Such committees may also be called corporate ethics and responsibility committees, or advisory boards or councils, which usually comprise a variety of stakeholders.

LO 6.6 Ethics Reporting Systems and Whistleblowing

Corporations have established reporting systems so that they can become aware of issues and concerns relating to corporate ethical conduct or irregularities. The reporting systems are known by various names, the most common being "hotlines." Codes of ethics or conduct usually contain sections outlining the reporting system, and outside service providers are hired to process the reports. An example of one corporation's compliance and reporting system is outlined in Everyday Ethics 6.5. Corporations believe that such systems alert them to problems before they become public and allow time for remedial action. The system also reinforces the importance of the corporation's code of ethics or business conduct. The systems are a secure forum to report problems and enable individuals to be anonymous without fear of retaliation.

 EVERYDAY ETHICS 6.5

Compliance and Reporting at Barrick Gold Corporation

Corporate codes of ethics or conduct usually include a mechanism to identify issues arising from the codes, and to prevent and identify violations. This enables employees to seek guidance on these matters and allows the corporation to act prior to them becoming problems.

Barrick Gold has an extensive "Responsibilities to Comply with the Law and this Code, and Report Non-Compliance" section in its Code of Business Conduct and Ethics, which includes the following:

- All applicable laws, rules, and regulations must be respected wherever the company operates.
- There must be an annual acknowledgement of the Code.
- That employees and directors have a duty to report suspected code violations to the appropriate management level is clearly established.
- "Formal reporting channels" are identified.
- The matters that must be reported through the "formal reporting channels" are specified; for example alleged misstatement of financial statements, or known or suspected fraud.
- A compliance Hotline is available and is operated by an outside service provider.
- A statement is made about the confidentiality of any reports to the Hotline.

The practice of reporting alleged wrongdoing, code violations, and irregularities in corporate operations is commonly referred to as whistleblowing. **Whistleblowing** is an act of voluntary disclosure of inappropriate behaviour or decisions to persons in positions of authority in the organization. The term may have originated from the practice of English police officers blowing whistles to get someone's attention, or from the use of whistles by sports referees. The most frequent form of whistleblowing occurs in the workplace where employees, managers, or directors are concerned about some matter. Whistleblowers are also referred to as do-gooders, bell-ringers, lighthouse keepers, people's witnesses, snitches, rats, tattle-tales, and squealers.

Several issues relating to whistleblowing have ethical implications for whistleblowers and managers:

- The whistleblower is faced with the choices of silence, quitting, and disclosing when they become aware of the inappropriate behaviour. All these choices can be uncomfortable and involve risk.

- The range of concerns may go from clearly illegal, to maybe illegal, to an issue of morality, all of which may be difficult to define.

- The whistleblower is faced with several moral obligations to self and to professional, corporate, or industry codes. There most likely is an obligation to an employer due to a legal duty, loyalty, or confidentiality agreement. There may be an obligation to society at large.

- The whistleblower faces a credibility issue: Will they be believed? Will the disclosure be taken seriously? Is the matter important enough? Will the matter be addressed at all?

- Concern also exists about the perception of others toward the whistleblower: noble, honourable, ethical hero, or snitch, mole, traitor?

- When to tell and who to tell are often problems. The whistleblower must decide how far to let the concern continue before disclosure and then has the challenge of deciding whom to tell, particularly in organizations without reporting systems.

- The whistleblower must be concerned about their self-interest. There are costs and risks, consequences for personal and professional lives, and the possibility of retaliation to consider.

- Anonymity encourages reporting, but it might result in trivial claims that are a nuisance and unfounded.

- There is an issue of whether or not whistleblowers should be rewarded by government, regulatory organizations, or industry associations. Rewards encourage reporting but might result in perverse incentives such as reporting to government agencies instead of the corporation. Also, there is an issue of whether it should be necessary to pay whistleblowers to do the right thing when they should be doing it anyway.

Although this discussion has focused on workplace stakeholders—employees, managers, and directors—other stakeholders may be whistleblowers. Suppliers and consumers may disclose inappropriate corporate practices to the corporation's reporting system, the legal system, government regulators, or the general public. The media often are whistleblowers, as are non-governmental organizations (NGOs). The movie industry also has used whistleblowing in a business setting as a plot device (see Everyday Ethics 6.6).

 EVERYDAY ETHICS 6.6

Whistleblowing in the Movies

The ethics of business is the topic of many popular movies. The following is a list of some movies with a focus on whistleblowing in a business setting:

The Informant! (2009)—The story of a corporate executive who blows the whistle on price fixing in the large agri-business corporation where he works.

Michael Clayton (2007)—A ruthless corporate "fixer" faces a crisis of conscience when he is asked to work on behalf of a chemical company that knowingly contaminated an entire Wisconsin community and aims to cover it up.

Boiler Room (2000)—The story of a stockbroker operation using aggressive selling techniques to the disadvantage of clients. An employee discloses the abuses.

Erin Brockovich (2000)—A small law firm discovers that a chemical company is polluting and discloses the cover-up.

The Insider (1999)—Detailed account of an employee who discloses the misleading practices in the tobacco industry.

A Civil Action (1998)—Story of the disclosure of industrial pollution contaminating drinking water in New England.

The Rainmaker (1997)—Disclosure of the insurance industry's denial of health care payments to a dying client.

Silkwood (1983)—An employee tries to disclose that she and others have been exposed to radiation in the workplace. Based on a real story and widely considered the best movie on whistleblowing.

In addition to corporate disclosure or reporting policies, several government whistleblowing regulations impact on a corporation's reporting system. All are designed to facilitate regulation and enforcement in particular areas and may require employees to disclose corporate practices.

- *Canadian federal and provincial/territorial governments*—Whistleblowing provisions exist in many regulatory areas including environmental protection, health and safety, competition, and industrial relations. There is no comprehensive whistleblowing legislation except in New Brunswick. The federal government has passed regulations relating to whistleblowing within the public service including in the Competition Bureau.[11]

- *Canadian Securities Industry*—The Investment Industry Regulatory Organization of Canada and the Mutual Fund Dealers Association of Canada have whistleblower programs. In July 2016, the Ontario Securities Commission (OSC) adopted a whistleblower program that would reward informants up to $5 million when penalties for wrongdoing exceed $10 million. In February 2019, the OSC announced that it had awarded $7,499,000 to three whistleblowers on separate matters.[12]

- *United States government*—U.S. legislation impacts Canadian corporations with operations in that country. There is extensive legislation requiring disclosure and protecting whistleblowers, and the *Whistleblower Protection Act* applies to federal government employees. The *Sarbanes-Oxley Act* of 2002 contained several whistleblowing provisions, including prohibition against employment discrimination and the acceptance of social responsibility complaints.[13]

An ethics reporting system is challenging to administer and involves risks for the corporation and the discloser, but recently it has become an important component of a corporate ethics program.

LO 6.7 Ethics—Who Is Responsible?

A simple answer to the question "Who is responsible for ethics?" is "Everyone." But in a corporation it is argued that the responsibility for recognizing the importance of ethical behaviour in business and doing something about it has to start at the top—that is, with the board of directors.

Board of Directors Responsibility

Researcher Steven Bavaria claims that directors have been remiss in this area, especially the docile outside directors who have the independence to monitor ethical behaviour.[14] Gillies states that directors have two tasks in relation to ethics: to collectively identify values that determine acceptable behaviour in the firm, and to put in place a process that ensures values are reflected in action. Merely acting on the basis of one's own values is not sufficient, and it is necessary to deliberately consider the implications of unethical behaviour. Not all directors agree with this position, and the arguments for and against it reflect the general discussion of whether or not business has any social responsibility.[15]

The reasons given for the board's responsibility for ethical or moral behaviour include the point that it is simply good management to develop an appropriate culture that is sensitive to ethics issues. In addition, the board itself is involved in ethical questions such as conflicts of interest, compensation schemes, management buyouts, the rights of minority shareholders, and changes in management. Finally, it is easier to make decisions if the fundamental principles or values of the corporation are known and can serve as a reference point. In the past, and maybe the present, directors often were not aware that ethics were involved in a decision. They must be aware that values change over time and that their own values may not have altered. Because directors are the ultimate decision makers in corporations, they must demand that decisions made by management and all employees be based on ethical standards acceptable to society. Chapter 11 will also discuss the role of the board of directors in a corporation's social responsibility program.

Management Responsibility

The success of any ethics program depends on the commitment of top management. Managers must announce the program, champion its development and implementation, and always aspire to lead in an ethical manner. They must provide moral leadership as opposed to immoral or amoral leadership. Table 6.4 distinguishes the three models of moral management and leadership.

TABLE 6.4 **Management and Leadership Models**		
Immoral	Amoral	Moral
A posture or approach that is devoid of ethical principles and actively opposed to what is moral	A posture or approach that is without ethics, but not actively immoral	Conform to high standards of ethical behaviour or professional standards
Management's motives are selfish and it cares only about the individual's or the organization's gains	Two types: intentionally or unintentionally amoral	Aspire to succeed only within confines of ethical principles; for example fairness, justice, and due process
Management to some degree knows right from wrong and chooses to do wrong	Intentionally amoral leaders do not consider ethics, as they believe business activity lies outside of moral judgments; neither moral nor immoral, as different rules apply to business	Concerned with letter and spirit of the law
May be motivated by greed and profitability, and organizational (or personal) success is the goal to be achieved at any price	Unintentionally amoral leaders are morally careless, unaware of or inattentive to impact of their decisions on others	Prefer standards that are higher than the minimum set by the law
Do not care about claims or expectations of others	They lack ethical perception, sensitivity, or awareness	Assume leadership when ethical dilemmas arise
The law is regarded as a barrier to be overcome and will circumvent if it will achieve their ends	May be well-intentioned but unaware of harms from their actions	Make ethics a driving force of the organization
Do not make good corporate citizens	"Ethical gears in neutral"	
	Use letter of the law instead of spirit	
	Cannot make good corporate citizens	

Source: Adapted from and summarized from Perspectives on Corporate Citizenship, 1st Edition by Jörg, Andriof; Malcolm, McIntosh, published by Routledge 2002. Reproduced by arrangement with Taylor & Francis Books UK.

Carroll, in an article that summarized his views on moral leadership, identified seven attributes of a moral leader: having a passion to "do right," being morally proactive, considering stakeholder inclusiveness, having a strong ethical character, being obsessed with fairness, practising principled decision making, and integrating ethics wisdom with management wisdom.[16]

Inside the organization, managers are responsible for developing and supporting a variety of policies and procedures to ensure the ethical implications of decision making are considered. An ethics manual should be available, maybe even online. A values statement and codes would be included. Such a manual would include policies regarding such things as whistleblowing protection, guidelines for offering or accepting gifts, and the privacy of employee records. Codes of conduct or ethics would be supported through training, the appointment of an ethics ombudsperson, the establishment of an ethics hotline, and regular consultation with employees. Corporate publications or newsletters would feature articles on ethics, and consideration of ethics would be integrated into corporate planning, recruitment, and performance appraisals.

Managers not only must be supportive of ethics programs within the organization, but also must advocate for ethical approaches to management with external stakeholders. Executive speech making provides an example. Speeches should inform certain stakeholders that the business enterprise and its management are concerned about ethics and are responding to society's interest in the matter. It is not always clear to which stakeholders the speeches are directed, but they most likely address society at large, NGOs, business groups, students, and possibly even shareholders.

The next section outlines approaches to ethics programs.

LO 6.8 Ethics Programs: Approaches

From the materials presented, corporations can design a variety of programs to provide ethics leadership in an organization. The resulting programs are classified as formal, monological, and dialogical,[17] and as being compliance-based versus values-based.

Classification of Programs

A *formal approach* is based on organizational norms that are written as a code of conduct. This approach focuses on unacceptable practices or behaviour and emphasizes compliance and penalties. Usually the approach is top-down, as codes are imposed from top management. The advantages of such programs are that they provide clear guidance for decision making and that their fulfillment is measurable. The rights ethical principle is likely to be used in this approach. The disadvantages are that employees may resist the necessary coercion and indoctrination.[18]

The *monological approach* allows organizational members, for example managers and employees, to determine for themselves what is right or wrong. Codes of values, philosophies, and ethics would facilitate this approach. Organizational members are encouraged to reflect on the appropriateness of their behaviour by considering their own values, the circumstances of the incident or issue, and the alternative choices for resolution. This approach focuses on argument and reflection but leaves room to act upon specific circumstances. The justice ethic is the principle most likely to be used. On the other hand, performance is difficult to measure and the possibility exists that it will lead to differences in behaviour.[19]

The *dialogical approach* emphasizes communication before decisions are made and implemented. The stakeholders influenced or that can influence are consulted and an appeal is made for input. The approach is similar to that advocated in the collaborative view of stakeholder relations, and the values and opinions of all stakeholders involved are included. It seeks inclusive solutions and attention is given to the social dynamic side of ethical issues, usually based on the ethic of caring. The monitoring of these programs is more challenging, as it is based on the process and not on outcomes. There is a danger of ethical relativism, which may lead to differences in behaviour by the stakeholders involved.

The formal approach is the most commonly used and the dialogical approach the least common. Larger organizations most likely use a combination of approaches, especially formal and monological. Nijhof, Fisscher, and Looise state that it is challenging to combine the approaches, and suggest that it might be more appropriate to use different approaches in different circumstances.[20] Although conscientious programs have been discussed, it is possible that corporations will have informal, unwritten programs that are implemented implicitly instead of explicitly and without a structured, deliberate approach.

Compliance-based versus Values-based Programs

Increasingly in the literature and in practice a distinction is made between compliance-based versus values-based approaches to managing the ethics of business. Table 6.5 summarizes the differences between the two approaches.

TABLE 6.5	Compliance-based versus Values-based Approaches
Compliance-based	**Values-based**
Rules, laws, policies	Values, ethics, guiding principles
Conformity with externally imposed standards	Self-governance to chosen standards; self-imposed
Prevent criminal misconduct	Enable responsible conduct
Lawyer-driven	Management-driven
Educational approach: policies and rules, legalistic	Educational approach: policies and rules, but also guidelines and awareness through leadership
Employee discretion: limited	Employee discretion: increased
Control: auditing, penalties	Control: accountability, organizational systems, and decision processes

Code of Conduct:	Code of Ethics:
• Specific	• General
• Prescriptions/directives	• Values/principles
• Uniformity	• Judgment
• Enforceable statements of specific behaviour	• "Empowering" and "aspirational"

The compliance-based approach focuses on adherence to legal and regulatory requirements and to corporate policies. Clear rules guide ethics and the rules are clearly communicated, limiting an individual's discretion. These rules are enforced and sanctions are imposed for violating them. In contrast, the values-based approach is defined by organizational values and ethical standards, which are to be applied to decision making. This approach increases awareness of ethical issues through dialogue, training, and fostering an ethical corporate climate. It is the preferred approach, as many people do not like rules that cannot cover all the circumstances that are encountered.

The trend is to incorporate both approaches, because it is recognized that one alone cannot yield results. It is necessary to recognize compliance to rules or policies on the one hand, but also the positive effects of values on the other. A compliance-based approach has reduced misconduct, but a values-based approach is a more powerful influence on attitudes and behaviour. Combining the two approaches is referred to as **integrity management**. The codes of many corporations now follow this approach.[21]

Want to learn more about **a guide to practical ethics**?

LO 6.9 Ethics Programs: Evaluation and Benefits

The components of a corporate ethics program have been outlined. Just because a corporation is not involved in the components mentioned does not mean that it does not have an ethics program, according to Max Clarkson, the founding Director of the Centre for Corporate Social Performance and Ethics, University of Toronto. He argued that all corporations have programs, but that some of them were implicit. The implicit ethics programs were implemented through such things as the organization's culture, reward systems, valued behaviour, promotion policies, management example, general practice, and performance measures.[22]

Clarkson identified criteria for evaluating the effectiveness of an ethics program: visibility, ownership, fit, and balance. The components of an ethics program were clearly evident in statements such as codes, which should be widely distributed and communicated in a variety of formats. There was evidence of a commitment to the ethics program, as demonstrated by awareness and usage of the initiatives, and by their integration into the organizational culture. Initiatives should be appropriate to the circumstances of the corporation; that is, programs should be complementary with the type of business or industry. Lastly, there should be a balance in the programs among rules, redress, and principles, or a balance between "imposed control" and "self-control." Clarkson also identified criteria for evaluation of the program's implementation. Such criteria were the extent of resource commitment to the program, the CEO's involvement, the extent of communication about the program, and the training and education carried out.[23]

Business ethics is identified as an "in" topic, yet it has been discussed seriously for four decades. Much of the earlier material on ethics is still applicable. An article by Laczniak contains some ethical propositions that are still appropriate and can serve as criteria for justifying the formulation and implementation of ethics programs.

- Ethical conflicts and choices are inherent in business decision making.

- Proper ethical behaviour exists on a plane above the law. The law merely specifies the lowest common denominator of acceptable behaviour.

- There is no single satisfactory standard of ethical action agreeable to everyone that a manager can use to make specific operational decisions.

- Managers should be familiar with a wide variety of ethical standards.

- The discussion of business cases or of situations having ethical implications can make managers more ethically sensitive.

- There are diverse and sometimes conflicting determinants of ethical action. These stem primarily from the individual, the organization, professional norms, and the values of society.

- Individual values are the final standard, although not necessarily the determining reason for ethical behaviour.

- Consensus regarding what constitutes proper ethical behaviour in a decision-making situation diminishes as the level of analysis proceeds from abstract to specific.

- The moral tone of an organization is set by top management.

- The lower the organizational level of a manager, the greater the perceived pressure to act unethically.

- Individual managers perceive themselves as more ethical than their colleagues.

- Effective codes of ethics should contain meaningful and clearly stated provisions, along with enforced sanctions for noncompliance.

- Employees must have a non-punitive, fail-safe mechanism for reporting ethical abuses in the organization.

- Every organization should appoint a top-level manager or director to be responsible for acting as an ethical advocate in the organization.[24]

The propositions summarize many of the components described in this chapter. They also indicate that, within the corporation, directors and managers are all responsible for ethical behaviour, with top management assuming leadership. Despite being compiled more than two decades ago, these propositions provide practical guidance to the institutionalization of ethical behaviour in corporations.

It is not known how many corporations have formally organized programs, but there is no doubt that many are consciously attempting to increase awareness of ethical behaviour even though it may be done in an informal manner. Some benefits of programs to manage ethics are listed below.

- Many improvements in business practices and benefits to society have occurred as a result of attention paid to ethics in the past. Some practices are no longer considered acceptable, for example misleading advertising, child labour, and price fixing.

- Turbulent times have increased the awareness of ethics, and business leaders need a moral compass and to be sensitive to acting consistently.

- Ethics programs align corporate behaviour, especially that of managers and employees, with the principal ethical values preferred by the leaders of the business enterprise.

- Employees are prepared to face the reality of moral dilemmas; that is, to be sensitive to what might be considered good or bad.

- A focus on ethics sensitizes managers and employees to the legal requirements in a moral dilemma.

- Criminal acts are more likely to be avoided, as such behaviour is likely to be detected earlier and violations caught within the organization.

- Awareness of ethics helps managers to integrate values with quality management practices and strategic management.

- The implications or influence of management decisions on various stakeholders is more likely recognized.

- A more favourable public image is created for the business organization.[25]

The components of an ethics program can be evaluated by their focus. Some components are values-based, providing guidelines to influence behaviour with fewer specific rules or directions.

Another perspective involves executive ethical leadership. Treviño and Brown argued it is a myth that "ethics can be managed through formal ethics codes and programs." Compliance-based approaches including codes alone cannot address ethical behaviour and values-based approaches are also needed. It is necessary to reinforce an ethical culture every day. Another myth focuses on leadership: "Ethical leadership is mostly about leader integrity." Managers must lead others to behave ethically, not just be ethical themselves. Not all leaders are capable of this. Four types of executive ethical leadership were identified:

- hypocritical leader = strong moral manager and weak moral person

- unethical leader = weak moral manager and weak moral person

- ethical leader = strong moral manager and strong moral person

- ethically silent leader = weak moral manager and either a weak or strong moral person

Unfortunately, not all corporations are led by ethical leaders. The authors concluded their article by indicating what executives can do to provide ethical leadership. Their guidelines for effective ethics management are:

"First: Understand the Existing Ethical Culture

Second: Communicate the Importance of Ethical Standards

Third: Focus on the Reward System

Fourth: Promote Ethical Leadership Throughout the Firm."[26]

For ethics programs to be successful, the corporation must have an appropriate culture. **Corporate culture** is defined as a complex set of values, beliefs, assumptions, and symbols that define the way in which an organization conducts its business.[27] **Ethical corporate culture** can be defined as representing a "slice" or "subset" of the organization's broader culture and is maintained through an interplay and alignment of formal organizational systems, such as policies, leadership, authority structures, reward systems, training programs, and informal organizational systems such as peer behaviour and ethical norms.[28] Schwartz identified the three elements of ethical corporate culture as the existence of core ethical values, the establishment of formal ethics programs, and the presence of ethical leadership.[29] This chapter has outlined the organizational systems necessary to create an ethical corporate culture through management practices and leadership.

LO 6.10   Why Ethical Leadership and Programs Fail

There are frequent examples in the media of executives, managers, or corporations engaging in unethical behaviours such as accounting fraud, bribery, insider trading, price fixing, and Ponzi schemes. Sometimes these behaviours are portrayed as being a modern phenomenon, but in reality ethical mistakes have occurred throughout history, they are inevitable, and they come in waves or cycles. It is important to increase understanding of why unethical decisions are made by business managers and corporations even though the unethical behaviour occurs in other professions and institutions in society.

The issues of unethical leadership and failed ethics programs are not easy to explain. Conduct that is illegal, like the behaviours mentioned above, is relatively easy to condemn because laws or regulations are violated. Other conduct may be unethical or immoral but not illegal, in which case right versus wrong is often difficult to ascertain. Also, the literature on this topic presents contradictory findings and conclusions are often difficult.[30] The following discussion provides some explanations or answers from the literature.

Managers are morally imperfect—With well-designed systems and policies such as the organization's culture, governance system, and ethical programs plus the existence of government regulations to influence behaviour, it could be assumed that unethical behaviour is unlikely. But some individuals are morally imperfect and will take advantage when systems and regulations fail, and at the same time there is a good possibility of not being caught. Managers with moral commitment are less likely to be unethical. Note that personality screening for unethical predispositions is not an exact science and is unlikely to prevent bad behaviour.

Self-interest—Managers may do something wrong simply because they will benefit and they will get away with it. Self-interest also influences managers not to be unethical because of the possibility of being caught and the fear of punishment.

Rationalization and self-delusion—If managers observe others getting away with inappropriate behaviour, they are more likely to become involved in similar activities. When others are cheating and getting away with it, individuals feel that it is only fair that they should also. This is a form of rationalization and may even be self-delusion.

Threat of formal sanctions—When managers perceive that the threat of legal action and the imposition of sanctions are high, they may avoid unethical conduct. Unethical conduct is more likely when the sanctions are not imposed quickly, not highly likely to occur, and not punitive. Some research has found that the threat of formal sanctions or punishment does not deter unethical behaviour.

Threat of informal sanctions—An informal sanction such as social disapproval by colleagues, family, or society in general may be sufficient to discourage unethical behaviour.

Tolerance to risk-taking behaviour—Those managers who accept high risk taking are more likely to be involved in unethical behaviour.

Pressure in particular situations—Managers may be willing or forced to compromise their personal values when pressured to do so by superiors or a particular situation or requirement. Thus, bad behaviour may be exhibited by an otherwise good manager. An example of a situational pressure may be investor expectations to achieve returns, which may result in illegal activities such as price fixing, overcharging customers, or inappropriately polluting the environment.

Despite designing and implementing comprehensive ethics programs and an active role by management in emphasizing ethical behaviour, misbehaviour will still occur. When misbehaviour does occur, an issue arises relating to how much responsibility management, particularly top management, should assume for the misdeeds. The issue is complicated in large corporations when top management does not even know about the misbehaviour, and by the fact that they could not reasonably be expected to be aware of the circumstances.

Want to learn more about business ethics by joining a blog?

Your advice to Karl . . .

Managers often resort to legality as a basis for ethics. Karl's lawyer is unlikely to be of much help. He is better off verifying whether or not Reliable did business with the supplier and asking for an explanation of the transactions that have taken place in the last few years. Again, this is unlikely to help. However, he can review the purchasing policies with the managers and ascertain whether or not they were being followed. In particular, Karl can hold sessions with the purchasing managers reviewing various policies and ask for suggestions for improvements. All this is to be done without mentioning the kickbacks. The code of conduct should be reviewed with emphasis on acceptance of gifts or payment and the legal implications involved. A new policy should be instituted whereby the purchasing managers must read, review, and sign a copy of the code of conduct annually.

Summary

- As emphasized in Chapter 5, increasing sensitivity to the ethical implications of managerial actions in general is a start. In addition, corporations must take deliberate actions to reinforce the importance by considering ethical implications in decision making. Key to this is the appropriate form of ethical leadership. (LO 6.1)

- The components of a corporation's ethics program to accomplish this are described in the chapter. The initial stage should be a statement of values or the equivalent that states in general terms the behaviours expected. These values become the foundation for the corporation's ethics program. (LO 6.2)

- A code of ethics reflects the values of an organization. A distinction should be made from a code of conduct, which focuses on compliance to rules or regulations instead of values. The contents of codes are outlined and drawbacks are presented. (LO 6.3)

- Today, corporations are not leaving an understanding of morality to chance and are engaged in a variety of training for everyone in the organization. (LO 6.4)

- Ethics audits are becoming more common as an approach to assessing the ethical implications of a corporation's practices. Usually such audits are conducted by outside consultants, who can also provide a range of advice about ethics programs. In larger corporations, there is a trend toward an ethics officer of some type being responsible for all aspects of compliance and morality in the organization. Ethics committees in many corporations facilitate the implementation of ethics programs. (LO 6.5)

- Ethics reporting systems are being established. Closely associated with such systems is the practice of whistleblowing. Several complicated issues are associated with whistleblowing and whistleblowers. Managers must carefully monitor the practice to make sure its benefits outweigh the drawbacks. (LO 6.6)

- Someone must take responsibility for the development and implementation of ethics programs. The board of directors and top management must signal their commitment to any program if it is to be successful. A "moral" leadership model is necessary to achieve this. (LO 6.7)

- Approaches to ethics programs are described. The formal approach is most common; the dialogical the least. Most corporations have programs that are a combination of these approaches. Also, the components of programs can be identified as being compliance-based versus values-based. (LO 6.8)

- Ethics programs should be evaluated on a regular basis and the benefits clearly identified. The programs can be justified on several bases ranging from economics to doing the right thing. The components of an ethics program are either compliance-based, following rules and requiring conformance, or values-based, emphasizing values as a way to influence behaviour. In most corporations today, a combination of these approaches is used and referred to as integrity management. (LO 6.9)

- There are several explanations for why ethical leadership and programs fail despite the best efforts and intentions of the corporation and its managers. An ethical corporate culture is necessary for ethics programs to be successful. (LO 6.10)

Key Terms

Corporate ethics programs

Statement of values

Code of conduct

Code of ethics

Conflict of interest

Ethics audit

Ethics officer

Compliance officer

Ethics committee

Whistleblowing

Integrity management

Corporate culture

Ethical corporate culture

Critical Thinking and Discussion Questions

1. What values do you think corporations and their managers should observe in business? Which ones do you think they really follow?

2. How would the stakeholders of a corporation be influenced by codes of ethics or conduct?

3. What are the drawbacks to codes of ethics or conduct?

4. Is it possible or feasible to train managers in ethics?

5. Why is it becoming necessary to have one manager to coordinate corporate ethics programs?

6. What are the benefits of ethics reporting systems?

7. What are the positive aspects of whistleblowing? What are some downsides?

8. How are governments involved in whistleblowing?

9. Why should responsibility for ethics programs rest with top management?

10. Should ethics programs rely on compliance-based or integrity-based approaches?

11. What is the justification for corporate ethics programs?

12. In your experiences in the workplace or educational institution, have you been provided with appropriate ethical leadership?

Cases

6.1 THE PROBLEMATIC WHISTLEBLOWER

Paul O'Doherty is the ethics officer for a medium-sized petroleum company. The company has a comprehensive ethics program that is his responsibility. The program includes a code of business conduct that outlines the values that guide behaviour, identifies conflicts of interest, specifies appropriate and inappropriate practices, and provides an approach to reporting violations or suspected wrongdoing. One aspect of the reporting system is an employee Hotline; employees can contribute in written form, such as by email, or orally, by telephone or in person. Participants must identify themselves and all communications go directly to Paul. He reports directly to the corporate secretary and legal counsel; the identity of the employee is not disclosed and confidentiality is maintained except in rare cases where there is legal action.

Paul is a member of the Ethics Practitioners' Association of Canada (EPAC). According to EPAC, the skills of an ethics officer include "facilitating constructive dialogue on ethics-related issues, analyzing ethics issues and problems, and providing coherent, realistic solutions to ethical issues."[31] His job has been rewarding and he has enabled the company to keep abreast of developments in the ethics area. The company has received awards for its ethics program and is recognized as a leader in corporate ethics.

Recently, Paul has been experiencing a problem with the Hotline component of the ethics program. An employee is making numerous complaints to the Hotline, almost weekly. The complaints cover many aspects of the employee's department: unfair treatment by a supervisor, stealing of office supplies by coworkers, management favouritism in assigning holidays, reporting an employee who is moonlighting, and quality of service given to customers. All of the complaints have been investigated according to the procedures outlined in the corporation's reporting guidelines. The investigations have been costly, in terms of both money and time. None of the complaints has been determined to be justified and many lack credibility. Paul has reluctantly concluded that the employee is a whiner or trouble-maker, but he cannot state this to others. It appears that the employee's reporting practices have been damaging to department morale.

The challenge now is to decide whether something should be done about the situation.

Questions

1. What stakeholders are involved in this situation?

2. What actions should be taken to address this situation?

3. What are the ethical implications of each action?

4. What ethical principle or principles should be followed in resolving this situation?

6.2 HEIDI HEISE, SUB SAMARITAN

On June 3, 2010, a fire broke out in Heidi Heise's Dartmouth, N.S., apartment building. Several tenants had to find other accommodations, but fortunately Heidi's apartment was not damaged and she did not have to move out. Two of her neighbours were affected and, feeling sorry for them, Heidi offered them the use of her apartment while they looked for other accommodations.

Heidi had worked at three Subway fast-food restaurants during the previous three years, most recently including 10 months full time at one outlet. After the fire the neighbours to whom she had lent her apartment came to the restaurant to thank her. Because they were hungry and had no money, Heidi prepared two six-inch subs for them. As an employee working over her lunch period she was entitled to one free 12-inch sub, but decided to forgo it and gave it away. Store policy required that she record her consumption of the sub, but she forgot to do this.

A restaurant manager observed Heidi giving away the subs on a surveillance camera a few days later and fired her. Heidi was not impressed to have been fired for helping someone in need. She also believed that she had been a good employee: she had never receiving warnings or punishments related to her job. Several people intervened on Heidi's behalf, including her direct supervisor, but the general manager insisted on the firing. One of the neighbours and the apartment building manager also appealed to Subway in favour of Heidi.

A representative of Atlantic Subway Ltd. commented that the incident was unfortunate. Subway Restaurants Canada issued a statement saying that it was concerned, but personnel matters were the responsibility of the franchise owner. Calls by the media to Subway were not answered, but the incident received nationwide coverage. Reader comments to a Halifax *Chronicle Herald* story stated the following opinions:

- Subway had missed an opportunity to recognize an employee doing a good or right thing.

- The incident may have a negative impact on the morale of other employees.

- Subway should be boycotted.

About a week later, Heidi was offered a job by Subway competitor Quiznos, which also decided to donate $2 from the sale of subs to the victims of the fire.

Questions

1. What are the issues involved in this incident?

2. What ethical theories can be applied to analyze this incident?

3. Was Subway justified in firing Heidi?

4. As a manager, how would you have handled this incident? What aspects of an ethics program would have assisted you?

The automobile industry is aware of its ethics and responsibilities.
Used © mevans/Getty Images

CHAPTER 7

Corporate Social Responsibility: The Concept

LEARNING OUTCOMES

After studying this chapter, you will be able to:

LO 7.1 Describe corporate social responsibility (CSR).

LO 7.2 Debate the pros and cons of corporate social responsibility in Canadian business.

LO 7.3 Appreciate the various foundations of social responsibility theories.

LO 7.4 Explain Carroll's pyramid of corporate social responsibility.

LO 7.5 Define the four contemporary CSR concepts: corporate sustainability, reputation management, social impact management, and triple bottom line (TBL).

LO 7.6 Describe corporate and business citizenship.

LO 7.7 Explain the complexity of corporate social responsibility by understanding a unifying CSR framework.

What would you do if...?

George Lafontaine had always been an enthusiastic Volkswagen (VW) customer. As a young man, he drove a Beetle, then as he got older he purchased a Golf, then a Jetta, and most recently a Passat. It was time for George to purchase a new car, but he was hesitating at buying another Volkswagen. He had heard some disturbing news about VW's use of software manipulation devices to avoid regulated emissions standards. At first it was believed to be an isolated incident, the result of a few rogue employees. But, investigations by the media and others found that this was not the case. In fact, some believed that unethical behaviours were common in the auto industry.

George decided to research the Volkswagen website for information on ethics and social responsibility. He found a comprehensive code of ethics that included phrases like:

- we act responsibly, for the benefit of our customers, shareholders, and employees
- we consider compliance with . . . laws, and internal rules to be the basis for sustainable and successful economic activities
- we stand for respectable, honest actions. . .

In addition, he found detailed corporate social responsibility guidelines. Two of these guidelines related to the environment and product safety. The corporation claimed it was responsible to the environment by producing clean cars which would throughout their life cycle minimize their impact on the environment. Responsibility for their products would be designed to protect the health and safety of the customer.

Overall, the guidelines stated that VW viewed itself as a corporate citizen who took responsibility to society seriously. The VW corporation supported numerous CSR projects around the world related to the arts, sciences, education, health promotion, sports, and nature conservation as well as local infrastructure development. In Canada, for example, VW employees volunteered at Camp Oochigeas, a camp for children with cancer.

VW has placed advertisements in Canadian daily newspapers apologizing for their mistake and stating ". . .we won't rest until we earn back your trust and restore our integrity."

George was undecided about purchasing another VW product and disillusioned about CSR.

What advice would you give George?

This chapter defines social responsibility, reviews the case for business social involvement, reviews the arguments against involvement, and describes recent theories and approaches to corporate social responsibility including corporate citizenship.

LO 7.1 Describing Corporate Social Responsibility

Corporate social responsibility (CSR) has had many definitions to date; one is the way a corporation achieves a balance among its economic, social, and environmental responsibilities in its operations so as to address shareholder and other stakeholder expectations. CSR is known by many names, including corporate responsibility, corporate accountability, corporate ethics, corporate citizenship, corporate sustainability, stewardship, and the triple-E bottom line (economical, ethical, and environmental). CSR is a general management concern; that is, it is important to all aspects of business, and it is integrated into a corporation's operations through its values, culture, decision making, strategy, and reporting mechanisms.

A definition receiving some attention is the one developed by the International Organization for Standardization (ISO). This standards-setting organization already has formulated standards for risk, quality, environmental, and energy management. Its ISO 26000 standard defined social responsibility as the responsibility of an organization for the impacts of its decisions and activities on society and the environment, through transparent and ethical behaviour that:

- contributes to sustainable development, including health and the welfare of society;
- takes into account the expectations of stakeholders;
- is in compliance with applicable law and consistent with international norms of behaviour; and
- is integrated throughout the organization and practised in its relationships.[1]

The ISO views social responsibility as a holistic approach comprising seven core subjects: human rights, labour practices, the environment, fair operating practices, consumer issues, community involvement and development, and organizational governance. There are two fundamental practices: recognizing social responsibility and stakeholder identification and engagement.[2]

Rather than use a precise definition, researchers have identified the elements or topics that might be included. Buchholz identified five key elements found in most, if not all, definitions:

- Corporations have responsibilities that go beyond the production of goods and services at a profit.
- These responsibilities involve helping to solve important social problems, especially those they have helped create.
- Corporations have a broader constituency than shareholders alone.
- Corporations have impacts that go beyond simple marketplace transactions.
- Corporations serve a wider range of human values than can be captured by a sole focus on economic values.[3]

In another example of this approach, Dahlsrud examined 37 definitions through content analysis and found that five dimensions of CSR existed:

- Environmental: the natural environment
- Social: the relationship between business and society
- Economic: socio-economic and financial aspects
- Stakeholder: stakeholders and stakeholder groups
- Voluntariness: actions not prescribed by law

He concluded that existing definitions were largely congruent and that "the confusion is not so much about how CSR is defined, as about how CSR is socially constructed in a specific context."[4]

According to Wood, the "basic idea of corporate social responsibility is that business and society are interwoven rather than distinct entities" and that expectations are placed on business due to its three roles: as an institution in society, as a particular corporation or organization in society, and as individual managers who are moral actors within the corporation. These roles result in three levels of analysis—institutional, organizational, and individual—and can be expressed in terms of three principles of corporate social responsibility: legitimacy, public responsibility, and managerial discretion.[5]

The principle of *legitimacy* refers to society's granting of legitimacy and power to business, and business' appropriate use of that power and the possibility of losing that power. Corporate social responsibility defines the institutional relationship between business and society that is expected of any corporation. Society has the right to grant this power, to impose a balance of power among its institutions, and to define their legitimate functions. The focus is on business' obligations as a social institution, and society takes away power or imposes some sort of sanction on business if expectations are not met.

The principle of *public responsibility* means that business is responsible for outcomes related to its areas of involvement with society. The level of application is organizational—that is, the corporation—and confines business' responsibility to those problems related to a firm's activities and interests. This principle includes the view that corporations are responsible for solving the problems they create. The nature of social responsibility will vary from corporation to corporation as each corporation impacts society's resources in different ways or creates different problems. The principle involves emphasizing each corporation's relationship to its specific social, ethical, and political environment.

Last, the principle of *managerial discretion* refers to managers as moral actors who are obliged to exercise such discretion as is available to them to achieve socially responsible outcomes. Discretion is involved because the actions of managers are not totally prescribed by corporate procedures. The level of application is the individual who has the choices, opportunities, and personal responsibility to achieve the corporation's social responsibility.[6] Table 7.1 summarizes the three principles.

TABLE 7.1	Wood's Principles of Corporate Social Responsibility	
Principle of Legitimacy	**Principle of Public Responsibility**	**Principle of Managerial Discretion**
• External focus on expectations of society • Society grants the right to business to operate • Adherence to social norms of society • Pressures particularly strong on some corporations, e.g. large ones or consumer products	• Beyond general expectations of society, that is, at the corporation level • Determined by uniqueness for circumstances of the corporation • Resource dependence determines • Involves managing relationships with immediate environment	• Involves individual choice or managerial discretion • Individual decision makers or managers determine • Relates to latitude of action possible by management • Focuses on range of strategic options available to management

The many elements of corporate social responsibility have been introduced so that the concept's complexity is appreciated. A later section of this chapter will present a unified framework of corporate social responsibility as it relates to business and society.

The Importance of Corporate Social Responsibility

CSR is important because the business system is the mechanism selected by society to produce and distribute goods and services. Originally, people felt that a business corporation had fulfilled its social responsibility by surviving and realizing the maximum profit possible. The resources of society could be used by the corporation to make profits as long as the corporation complied with the few rules imposed by governments to check abusive practices. The market system provided the regulation necessary to police the system, and profits provided incentive and ensured efficiency. The work ethic and self-interest were the guiding principles of the system. By making a profit, corporations contributed to a growing, healthy economic system that provided employment and adequate incomes for all. In other words, corporate social responsibility was to operate profitably, and the corporation could not survive without profits, much less play a social role.

More recently, there has been a belief that business exists for more than profits (or economic goals), with the public expecting something else from business. As a result, the original concept of social responsibility involving the maximization of profits has been modified. Although profits are to be made, social goals are also to receive attention. Society depends on business to achieve social as well as economic goals—that is, social responsibilities are placed on business.

The issue of social responsibility cannot be easily resolved. To illustrate, consider the following questions: How should corporate performance in society be judged apart from traditional economic standards? Are there goals and measures that individuals inside and outside the corporation can use for guidance? Given the relationship between the corporation and its social environment, what is the scope of managerial responsibility? To what extent should the corporation involve itself in social concerns? How do corporations typically respond to social involvement issues? Is there a common process that will enhance the corporation's understanding of corporate social performance?

It must be appreciated that corporate social responsibility and a corporation's social performance are two of many factors in an extremely complex business environment in which the corporate manager is called upon to operate the business. Various stakeholders are constantly seeking a different role for business in society. Government continues to influence the business system and to change the forms and manner of this influence. Technological change is occurring at a very rapid pace. The media advise citizens quickly of events in the business world, allowing for quick public reaction.

The discussion of definitions and meanings of corporate social responsibility could be extensive, but the purpose here is to provide an introduction to and appreciation for social responsibility. Further understanding of the concept, its origins, and its interpretations is achieved by summarizing some of the debate surrounding social responsibility.

LO 7.2 The Corporate Social Responsibility Debate

The discussion of the appropriateness and meaning of social responsibility continues. This section outlines the cases for and against involvement in social responsibility, and includes a discussion of the ethical case for CSR or sustainability. Some confusion occurs because there are many theories used to represent the variety of views toward social responsibility. These theories are summarized in the next section.

The Case for Involvement

Many arguments support the involvement of business in society; that is, they support the social responsibility or social responsiveness of business.

Business must realize that society is a "system" of which corporations are a part, and that the system is interdependent. Therefore, if business institutions interact with others in society, the need for social involvement along with increasing interdependence brings the need to participate in the complex system that exists in society. There are many mutual involvements among individuals, groups, and organizations in society, or among subsectors of society. Business is vulnerable to the actions or events that occur in other subsectors. As a result, business should operate in such a way as to fulfill society's needs or expectations. It should do so for a very pragmatic reason: it is believed in some quarters that business functions by the consent of society and therefore must be sure to satisfy the needs of society. In other words, the existence of the business system depends on its acceptance by society. If business is to prevent criticisms or mutinous behaviour, it must be receptive to what is happening in society and respond in some way.

Corporations must be concerned with the public image and the goodwill generated by responsible social actions. A social responsibility role should be undertaken in order to prevent some public criticism and discourage further government involvement or regulation. This is a defensive approach designed to offset possible government action against those in the business system who use their power irresponsibly. Preventing is better than curing. It is better to take a proactive stance than a reactive one.

Social responsibility is in the shareholder's interest; that is, corporate virtue is good for profits, especially in the long term. A poor social responsibility role on the part of the corporation means poor management to some investors. They view failure to perform in society's interests in much the same way as they view the corporation's failure to perform in financial matters. Similarly, investors and consumers are showing increasing interest in and support for responsible business. Most top corporate managers consider social responsibility or corporate sustainability very important in their approach to management as illustrated in Everyday Ethics 7.1.

 EVERYDAY ETHICS 7.1

Managers' Views of Corporate Social Responsibility

These quotations were obtained from recent corporate social responsibility or sustainability reports. The terms *corporate social responsibility* and *corporate sustainability* are interchangeable. Note that a variety of industries are illustrated.

"Our goal in maintaining a CSR program is, as the title suggests, to earn the trust of our stakeholders by continuing to make ourselves accountable and by continually seeking ways to make a difference in the lives of the people we serve."

Brent Binions, President and CEO, Chartwell Retirement Residences, website at https://chartwell.com/en/about-us/corporate-social-responsibility.

"Sustainability is an integral part of Finning's purpose, vision and values, and is woven throughout our strategy and operations. We see sustainability in the same vein as operational excellence. They both capitalize on efficiencies, focus on doing the right things, and generate significant value for our company, our stakeholders, and the environment."

L. Scott Thomson, President and CEO, Finning International Inc., "2017 Sustainability Report," page 2, at https://www.finning.com/content/dam/finning/Global/Documents/sustainability/2017_Sustainability_Report.pdf.

"At Wheaton Precious Metals, we are committed to promoting responsible mining practices and giving back to the communities where we live and operate. The sustainability of our business and the industry is dependent on it. It is the right thing to do."

Randy Smallwood, President and CEO, Wheaton Precious Metals, website at https://www.wheatonpm.com/responsibility/approach/default.aspx

"Cenovus has long been recognized as one of Canada's most responsible oil and natural gas producers. When we launched in 2009, we made a strong commitment to operate in a safe, ethical, legal, environmentally and socially responsible manner, not just because it's the right thing to do, but because it makes good business sense."

Alex Pourbaix, President and CEO, Cenovus Energy Inc., "2017 Social Responsibility Report," page 3, at https://www.cenovus.com/reports/2017/2017-cr-report.pdf.

"Our business strategy is founded on corporate responsibility. The fundamental purpose of our actions is to ensure profitable growth for all: employees, shareholders, business partners and the communities we serve."

Eric R. La Flèche, President and CEO, Metro Inc., "Corporate Responsibility 2018," page 3, at https://corpo.metro.ca/userfiles/file/PDF/Responsabilite_entreprise/2018/2018_CSR_report.pdf.

Business must realize that social problems can become opportunities, or can lead to profits, lower costs, and reduced risks. Expenditures on pollution abatement may result in the retrieval of materials that were formerly disposed of as waste, or may allow for equipment to operate more efficiently, thereby generating more profits on future operations. Also with regard to social responsibility matters, business should take a long-run as opposed to a short-run view. Profits may increase in the long run as a result of actions taken at the present time. Judging the benefits of social responsibility becomes a simple matter of ascertaining whether it is in the corporation's longest-term self-interest to be conscious of social responsibility matters by reducing risk. Finally, some corporations have built their competitive advantage on social responsibility initiatives or strategies that set them apart from competitors.

Business should be given an opportunity to solve some social problems. The logic behind this argument is that business can solve problems as well as government can and that it certainly cannot do any worse than government has in the past. Business possesses the expertise, in its managers and executives, to develop plans to overcome social problems. As government is reducing its efforts to address some social problems, business needs to fill the gap. Businesspersons are also concerned citizens and humans; it is not appropriate for them to ignore social matters.

The Case Against Involvement

Although several arguments can be made for social involvement by business corporations, there also are many arguments *against* business social involvement.

Profit maximization is the primary purpose of business, and to have any other purpose is not socially responsible (as argued in Responsibility for Ethics 7.1). To have anything other than a profit-maximizing goal is to sabotage the market mechanism and distort the allocation of resources. Generally, then, it is contrary to the basic function of business to become involved in social matters. It should not be forgotten that business is an economic institution, not a social one, and its only responsibility is to manage efficiently within the law. The corporation would be irresponsible if it did not pursue profits and operate in the efficient market.

 RESPONSIBILITY FOR ETHICS 7.1

Milton Friedman

Milton Friedman, a Nobel Prize winner in economics, is often quoted as saying the only social responsibility of business is to make profits. Here is the quotation often used by proponents of a free economy:

> *The view has been gaining widespread acceptance that corporate officials and labor leaders have a "social responsibility" that goes beyond serving the interest of their stockholders or their members. This view shows a fundamental misconception of the character and nature of a free economy. In such an economy, there is one and only one social responsibility of business—to use its resources and engage in activities designed to increase its profits so long as it stays within the rules of the game, which is to say, engages in open and free competition, without deception or fraud. Similarly, the "social responsibility" of labor leaders is to serve the interests of the members of their unions.*

Source: Based on Milton Friedman, *Capitalism and Freedom: A Leading Economist's View of the Proper Role of Competitive Capitalism* (Chicago: The University of Chicago Press, 1962), 133.

Business corporations are responsible to the shareholders and, in effect, have no authority to operate in the social area. When a corporation becomes involved in social matters, there is a question of legitimacy. Even if corporations are sufficiently competent and powerful to bring about social changes in matters considered beyond the range of their immediate involvement, there is a real question as to whether such endeavours are appropriate. Managers should let shareholders decide whether or not they wish to become involved in social issues.

Social policy is the jurisdiction of governments, not business. Business lacks training in social issues, and lacks social skills necessary to carry out social programs. In other words, business is not competent to undertake social responsibility tasks. Furthermore, social responsibility is viewed by some as another excuse to let big business increase its power. The increase in power comes as a result of business becoming involved in social as well as economic matters. Imposing business values on social issues may lead to inappropriate domination: business already has sufficient power, and it would be inappropriate to extend that power to other matters.

Business involvement in social matters increases costs—not only costs to the organization, but also possibly even social costs—instead of decreasing them. This in turn may lead to business failures. There is no acknowledged source of reliable guidance or policy for business in social responsibility questions, and it is not easy to make the choice between responsible and selfish action in social issues. Social responsibility is an elusive concept for which few standards are available to evaluate and control the actions of corporations.

As institutions in society, business corporations cannot be held accountable for their actions in a way sufficient to satisfy demands for social involvement. Institutions involved in social matters should be accountable to society for that involvement. At the present time, few mechanisms are available to ensure that business corporations are accountable for their social actions.

It is particularly difficult to argue for CSR when events occur that are not clearly inappropriate or wrong even though the corporation has an elaborate and professional social responsibility or sustainability program. Recent examples are SNC-Lavalin, which was involved in bribery of foreign officials, and Volkswagen, when it deceived regulators about vehicle emissions. The reasons for these events is similar to why ethical managers fail as discussed in Chapter 6. Managers are not morally perfect and self-interest overtakes decision making. Pressure to perform may lead managers to take short cuts and violate clearly stated CSR policies. Another criticism is that some corporations may have CSR programs for appearances or because it has become the current trend when the culture of the organization and its managers are not committed to them.

Despite these points, there is increasing support in the business community for social involvement. The following describes one approach linking CSR and sustainability to ethical reasoning.

An Ethical Basis for CSR

Schaltegger and Burritt[7] related a corporation's business case to different ethical motivations as they influence corporate social responsibility (CSR) or corporate sustainability. They define a business case as "a rationale which guides management thinking and the justification of management decisions and activities."[8] Based on a review of the literature and their own research, the authors proposed four business cases based on management's view of the ethical basis for sustainability: reactionary, reputational, responsible, and collaborative.

The reactionary business case involves the protection of the conventional business functioning—that is, focusing on profit-seeking behaviour and minimizing the costs of doing business. CSR activities are added to the core business and not designed to strengthen the business. They are viewed as a cost that is necessary to preserve or protect the business through defensive actions. Philanthropy might be one such initiative. The focus is self-serving or determined by self-interest that is necessary to defend the conventional business approach. The approach would be comparable to Kohlberg's pre-conventional stage of moral development where self-interest is emphasized and the awareness of others—that is, society—is limited.[9]

A slightly enhanced business case of CSR is referred to as *reputational*—that is, how the business is portrayed in the media or in society. CSR activities would include impressions management, public relations, and communications to stakeholders with an emphasis on reputation, brand value, and maybe growth. Such activities might be viewed as greenwash and result in a decline in profitability. On the other hand, CSR activities can result in social and environmental benefits if the activities are linked to sustainability. The reputation business case of CSR is considered to be limited and may even be negative if not backed up by tangible initiatives favourably viewed by society. The authors claim that managers would think in terms of how sustainability initiatives would contribute to the corporation's financial success.[10]

The responsible business case for CSR involves striving for business performance excellence where the corporation's success is measured by economic, environmental, and social indicators. Performance excellence is achieved through efficiency gains, cost reductions, innovation, brand value, or sales. The business case is still focused on the corporation, its products, and direct relationships. Clean production and innovative product development are examples of initiatives that offer opportunities to improve operations and create new businesses. The business case is that sustainability initiatives will improve corporate operations.[11]

Dialogue-based management and engagement with a broad range of stakeholders leads to a collaborative business case for CSR. Business success is defined as more than maximizing profits and includes an understanding that initiatives will have social, environmental, and economic benefits. There is interaction or engagement with stakeholders that helps solve problems or vulnerabilities confronting stakeholders. Business is developed with stakeholder participation and collaboration leading to social, environmental, and economic benefits for the corporation and society. This is achieved by offering new solutions or improvements to products and services that are not environmentally sustainable, and by creating new participative structures in the market and with society.[12] Everyday Ethics 7.2 describes an initiative that would be a different approach to a social issue.

A main contribution of the research is the recognition that when responding to sustainability, managers may have different motivations resulting in different sustainability management initiatives leading to different kinds of business cases of or for sustainability.[13]

EVERYDAY ETHICS 7.2

A New Model for Corporate–Community Partnerships

In September 2018, the Bank of Montreal (BMO) committed $10 million over five years to address economic disparity or income inequity in Toronto communities. BMO CEO Darryl White stated that the old model of simply giving money was insufficient to address complicated social problems. Increasing inequality is creating "have" or "have not" neighbourhoods, which is not desirable.

Instead, BMO partnered with United Way Greater Toronto by providing the funding and launching an initiative to bring together business leaders to work with community stakeholders. Nineteen corporate leaders agreed to participate in a Local Economic Opportunity Leadership Table that would come up with breakthrough and creative approaches to increasing economic growth in all communities. The Table participants and community leaders were to look at economic disparity through a different lens and identify roles that the private sector would be able to play. Additional funds would be raised from others who also wished to address this major societal problem.

The arguments for and against CSR have been made. Various forms of CSR are widely practised and knowledge of the concept is essential for effective management in today's environment. The following section also addresses this debate but from a different perspective, summarizing the varying corporate social responsibility theories that exist. The existence of these theories helps explain why so many interpretations are associated with the concept.

LO 7.3 Social Responsibility Theories

Klonoski[14] sets out to address a fundamental question: "Does business and the corporation have a social nature, or not?" The answer given by any stakeholder can be associated with a theory of corporate social responsibility, and these theories fall into three categories: amoral, personal, and social.

The Amoral View

This category represents a traditional view of business and the role of the corporation; that is, the corporation is seen as a "highly individualized rights bearing economic entity designed for profit making and legitimatized by the laws governing incorporated businesses."[15] Free market defenders and legal recognition theorists are among those holding this view, including some who believe there is no such thing as corporate social responsibility. Over the years many theories have advocated this view of social responsibility; these are listed in Table 7.2. The amoral view is still held by some in the business community.

TABLE 7.2	Examples of Amoral-View Theories of Social Responsibility
Fundamentalism—The corporation has no or very little social responsibility.	
Legal recognition—The corporation is an autonomous entity and not the creation of society.	
Individual agreement—Corporations can be socially responsible, but only within the limits of a prior contractual agreement with shareholders.	
Traditional shareholders model—Beyond individual agreements, corporations are not ethically required to be socially responsible; they are responsible only to monies and to maximize profits (as so famously stated by Milton Friedman).	

Source: Summarized from Richard J. Klonoski, "Foundational Considerations in the Corporate Social Responsibility Debate," *Business Horizons* (July/August 1991): 9–18. With permission from Elsevier.

The "amoral" view should be carefully defined and not confused with an "immoral" view. Amoral refers to an activity without a moral quality; that is, something that is neither moral nor immoral: moral standards, restraints, or principles do not exist. This is quite different from immoral, which denotes activities that are not moral and do not conform to usually accepted or established patterns of conduct. Amoral means lacking in morals, good or bad, while immoral connotes evil or licentious behaviour. Although in some contexts being amoral is considered as reprehensible as being immoral, that is not the position taken by most advocates of the theories listed in this category.

The Personal View

This view discusses the nature of the corporation in ascertaining whether it can be held accountable. The question involved is whether corporations are "moral agents" or "full-fledged" moral persons. Corporations are viewed as collectives that act as individuals; they exist as legal persons and can be held responsible for their actions. This question has been extensively discussed in the literature.

Those arguing that corporations are persons claim that corporations are responsible for their actions in a way comparable to the actions taken by natural persons or individuals. Therefore, the corporation can be morally blamed in a way that is identical or very similar to natural persons. A strong counterargument in the literature claims that corporations are not persons. Supporters of this view argue that it is not possible to impose moral sanctions or punishments on corporations as corporations. It is possible to blame or punish the people who work for or manage the corporation, but not the corporation itself. Some punishments, such as fines, are in effect paid by shareholders or passed on as costs to consumers.

The debate over whether the corporation can be seen as a moral person does not provide an answer as to whether the corporation is a social institution. Those who claim the corporation is a person believe that it is socially responsible for its impact on society, and that it can be held morally accountable for its actions in the social sphere. Those who do not consider the corporation to be a person say that claims against the corporation by society need a different basis than that provided by the moral person or agency theory. The "personal" view represents a middle position between the amoral and social views.

The personal view leaves the debate unresolved. However, the arguments favouring the treatment of corporations as persons lead to the next theoretical view of corporate social responsibility: the social view.

The Social View

This view holds that the activities of corporations occur within an interpersonal and, most likely, social context. The corporation is considered a social institution in society, with social responsibilities. The social nature of business can rest in many different theories, some of which are listed in Table 7.3. The extent of corporate social responsibility depends on the theoretical foundation used to support the view.

TABLE 7.3	Examples of Social-View Theories of Social Responsibility

Social contract—An implicit social agreement exists between business and society that determines the social nature of the corporation, identifies its duties and rights, and is considered to be an evolving document.

Ideological/Historical—Society evolves and history gives rise to new social needs, societal demands, and changes in social values to which business is expected to contribute.

Stakeholder—There is a social responsibility function of the interrelationships developed by the corporation with groups that have a stake. This approach was also referred to as "constituency theory." This theory is one of the main underpinnings of this book.

Legal creator—The corporation is a creature of law, existing only in contemplation of law, and is thus made by society for the common good of society.

Social permission—Society can legitimately demand the corporation do certain kinds of activities and, if the corporation is harming the public good, can restrict or eliminate its activities.

Corporate citizenship—With the charter, the corporation becomes a legal entity with standing as a citizen similar to that of the individual and has duties as well as rights and privileges.

Social impact—Business has the power to change society and must consider social responsibilities.

Social interpenetration—Business is so intertwined with society that it cannot avoid social responsibilities.

Moral gratitude/reciprocity—As business operates within a social system, it should be socially responsible out of "gratitude" or have a moral responsibility to "reciprocate." Corporations benefit from and thus owe society.

Utilitarian—It is to the benefit of society or for the greatest good for the greatest number of people that corporations are socially responsible; social responsibility is in business' best interest.

Virtue-based—This view focuses on the development of good or morally virtuous people instead of principles or contracts. A morally responsible business is one in which good people make decisions based on generally developed moral character, self-discipline, moderation, hard work, courage, creativity, good humour, and intelligence.

Source: Summarized from Richard J. Klonoski, "Foundational Considerations in the Corporate Social Responsibility Debate," *Business Horizons* (July/August 1991): 9–18. With permission from Elsevier.

It is argued that the corporation should be considered a social institution, as it exists because individuals come together to achieve some objective related to the provision of goods and services. Today, corporations exist because society implicitly sanctions them to operate in that form. Many in society believe that corporations now operate within the "social" view of corporate social responsibility despite the continuing claims of those who argue the "amoral" view, with its incomplete vision of the corporation operating as a private institution with a solely economic purpose.

Many theories and frameworks have been presented to describe corporate social responsibility. Some of them overlap and some parallel the arguments for and against corporate social involvement. The existence of numerous theories supporting corporate social responsibility makes it difficult to find a comprehensive and precise definition, as mentioned in the previous section about describing social responsibility.

Despite the numerous views of corporate social responsibility, many business-supported organizations advocate it; some of these are listed in Responsibility for Ethics 7.2. The literature contains numerous models of social responsibility, and one has been selected for presentation. Carroll's pyramid of corporate social responsibility is a practical framework for managers that incorporates economic, legal, social, and ethical responsibilities.

 RESPONSIBILITY FOR ETHICS 7.2

Business-supported Organizations Working on CSR

Several organizations are promoting CSR with support from Canadian businesses:

Network for Business Sustainability (NBS)—The non-profit NBS network of international academic experts and business leaders was established in 2005 with its main office located at the Ivey Business School (Western University) in London, Ontario. It produces resources on important sustainability issues with the goal of shaping management practice and research. It connects with thousands of researchers and professionals worldwide who are interested in corporate social responsibility (CSR) and who believe in the value of research-based practice and practice-based research. NBS uses its academic and industry funding to commission research on the business community's top sustainability challenges.

Canadian Business for Social Responsibility—Founded in 1995, CBSR is a business-led, non-profit CSR consultancy and peer-to-peer learning organization that provides its members with candid counsel and customized advisory services as they formulate powerful business decisions that improve performance and contribute to a better world.

Conference Board of Canada—The Conference Board of Canada is an independent source of insights for business leaders. CSR is considered relevant to business, a key determinant of a corporation's relationship to the world. It conducts and publishes research, and disseminates knowledge to its members by conducting and publishing research and sponsoring conferences and seminars.

Corporate Knights—Founded in 2002, Corporate Knights Inc. is an independent, Canadian-based media company that publishes the world's largest-circulation magazine with an explicit focus on corporate responsibility.

Canadian Centre for Ethics and Corporate Policy (EthicsCentre.ca)—EthicsCentre.ca is a registered charity and independent ethics centre committed to promoting and maintaining an ethical orientation and culture in Canadian organizations. Its mission is to champion the application of ethical values in the decision-making process of business and other organizations.

Canadian Centre for Ethics in Public Affairs—CCEPA facilitates critical thinking, public discussion, and research into current ethical challenges in society. It promotes the public good through research into and dissemination of knowledge of ethical issues, which helps generate new insights, provide greater awareness, and heal misunderstandings.

Imagine Canada—Imagine Canada is a non-profit organization that helps charities and non-profit organizations fulfill their missions, champions corporate citizenship, and helps businesses partner in the community. It accomplishes this through research, developing public policy, promoting public awareness, and encouraging businesses to become better corporate citizens.

LO 7.4   The Pyramid of Corporate Social Responsibility

One way to view corporate social responsibility is through Carroll's[16] pyramid, which he claims presents the concept such that social responsibility will be accepted by a conscientious businessperson. There are four kinds of social responsibility—economic, legal, ethical, and philanthropic—which can be depicted in a pyramid, with economic responsibilities at the bottom, followed by legal, ethical, and philanthropic higher up. Carroll contends that all of these responsibilities have always existed to some degree, but ethical and philanthropic responsibilities have become significant only in recent years.[17]

Economic responsibilities relate to business' provision of goods and services of value to society. Profits result from this activity and are necessary for any other responsibilities to be carried out. It is assumed that corporations will be profitable, maintain a strong competitive position, and maintain a high level of operating efficiency. These are responsibilities that the corporation "must do" and the key stakeholders are shareholders, creditors, and consumers.

Society expects business to conform to laws and regulations formulated by governments that act as the ground rules under which business must operate. Corporations are expected to pursue profits within the framework of the law, which establishes what are considered fair operations. Society expects that all goods and services and relationships with stakeholders will meet at least minimal legal requirements.

Ethical responsibilities include those activities that are not expected or prohibited by society as economic or legal responsibilities. Standards, norms, or expectations that reflect concern for select stakeholder input are fair, just, or in keeping with their moral rights. Ethics or values may be reflected in laws or regulations, but ethical responsibilities are seen as embracing the emerging values and norms that society expects of business even if not currently required by law. These responsibilities can be thought of as things the corporation "should do." These responsibilities are more difficult for business to deal with as they are often ill-defined or under continual public debate. Ethical responsibilities also involve the fundamental ethical principles of moral philosophy, such as justice, human rights, and utilitarianism. The changing or emerging ethical responsibilities are constantly pushing legal responsibilities to broaden or expand, while at the same time expecting business' ethical behaviour to go beyond mere compliance with laws and regulations.

Philanthropic responsibilities involve being a good corporate citizen and include active participation in acts or programs to promote human welfare or goodwill. Examples are contributions to the arts, charities, and education. Such responsibilities are not expected in an ethical or moral sense, making philanthropy more discretionary or voluntary on the part of business even though society may have such expectations of business. Few in society expect corporations to have these responsibilities, and they can be thought of as things corporations "might do."

Carroll views the pyramid as a basic building-block structure, with economic performance as the foundation. At the same time, business is expected to obey the law, behave ethically, and be a good corporate citizen. Although the responsibilities are portrayed as separate elements, in practice they are not mutually exclusive; however, the separation aids managers to appreciate the different obligations that are in a constant but dynamic tension with one another. For example, there are particular tensions between economic and ethical responsibilities. In summary, Carroll views the total social responsibility of business as involving the simultaneous fulfillment of the four responsibilities—which, stated in pragmatic terms, means that the corporation should strive to make a profit, obey the law, be ethical, and be a good corporate citizen.[18]

Carroll's pyramid represents one of the earliest attempts to integrate the economic and social responsibilities of the corporation. Evidence is accumulating that supports consideration of economic (tangible) and social (intangible) responsibilities:

- Economic (profits) and social responsibilities (ethics) are not mutually exclusive.
- Research shows that economic and social responsibilities are often inseparable.
- Corporations that consider social responsibilities seriously tend to outperform solely profit-seeking corporations.

Resistance to this convergence of economic and social responsibilities does occur. Managers who incorporate social responsibilities into decision making are sometimes labelled as "do-gooders" who are ignoring profits. There are segments of society that suggest there is nothing good about business and that it cannot be ethical or concerned about social issues. It is argued that business should stay out of social responsibilities, as it is often difficult to judge what is right or wrong and managers are not prepared to make such decisions.

An outcome of this shift toward integrating economic, social, and environmental responsibilities has been the emergence of new concepts, several of which are discussed in the following section.

LO 7.5 Contemporary CSR Concepts

Corporate social responsibility is the terminology still widely used to represent business' social responsibilities. However, other terms have appeared that incorporate the consideration of economic responsibilities as well, including corporate sustainability, reputation management, social impact management, triple bottom line (TBL), and corporate citizenship. The first four terms will be briefly described here; corporate citizenship is a more prominent term and will be discussed in detail in the following section.

Corporate Sustainability

As with the definition of CSR, academics, consultants, and practitioners have formulated many definitions of corporate sustainability, some of which are similar to those for CSR. Corporate sustainability (CS) refers to corporate activities demonstrating the inclusion of social and environmental as well as economic responsibilities in business operations as they impact all stakeholders presently and in the future. Marrewijk identified five levels of CS that are similar to how CSR could be viewed:

- *Compliance-driven CS*—Involves following government regulations and responding to charity and stewardship considerations considered appropriate by society.
- *Profit-driven CS*—Consideration is given to the social, ethical, and environmental aspects of business operations provided they contribute to the financial bottom line.
- *Caring CS*—Initiatives go beyond legal compliance and profit considerations where economic, social, and environmental concerns are balanced, as it is the right thing to do.
- *Synergistic CS*—Well-balanced and functional solutions are sought that create value in the economic, social, and environmental areas, as it is a winning approach for all stakeholders.
- *Holistic CS*—Corporate sustainability is fully integrated and embedded in every aspect of the corporation's activities, as this is important to the quality and continuation of life on this planet.[19]

Corporate sustainability has been recognized by the financial markets because it creates long-term shareholder value by embracing opportunities and managing risks as the result of economic, social, and environmental developments.

> Want to learn more about **sustainability**?

Reputation Management

Reputation management is any effort to enhance the corporation's image and good name. In the past, the focus of these efforts was on media and public relations and, to some extent, crisis management. Today, reputation management is being extended to relations with all stakeholders. Many managers believe that reputation management enhances financial performance, improves competitive positions, and increases public approval of corporate activities, and studies support this view.[20]

A successful process to implement reputation management involves several stages: the identification of a desired perception of the corporation, the recognition of the significance of image with all stakeholders, an awareness of the influence of interactions with stakeholders on the corporation's reputation, and continuous efforts at maintaining relationships with stakeholders.

Reputations take a long time to establish and can be destroyed quickly. As a result, a reputation can be an asset but at times a liability. Managers must understand all the factors that encompass a reputation and be aware of the measures used to differentiate a good reputation from a bad one. Examples are provided by surveys appearing in the media, including "Canada's Best Managed Companies" in *Canadian Business* magazine; "Canada's Top 50 Socially Responsible Corporations" in *Maclean's*; and the "Best 50 Corporate Citizens in Canada" in *Corporate Knights: The Magazine for Clean Capitalism*. The purpose in describing these surveys is to establish that public measures assessing a corporation's reputation are available. It also establishes the importance of reputation and the need for managers to consciously monitor it.

> Want to learn more about *Corporate Knights*?

Social Impact Management

One of the main advocates of social impact management is the Aspen Institute. The Institute defines **social impact management** as "the field of inquiry at the intersection of business needs and wider societal concerns that reflects and respects the complex interdependency between the two."[21] This is very much a "business and society" approach, stressing the need for contemporary business to recognize and understand this interdependency if business and the society in which it operates wish to thrive. The Institute argues that this understanding is becoming increasingly important as corporations take on a bigger role and society increases pressure for corporations to address more essential social and environmental concerns.

The approach stresses the intersection of traditional business concerns (i.e., for financial or economic matters) and society's concerns for the consequences of the impact of the corporation (i.e., the social impact of business). Thus, social impact management is two-directional: society's influence on corporations, and the corporations' influence on the social and environmental concerns of society.

The Institute believes that "social impact management, as a way of thinking about business activities, explicitly considers and evaluates three aspects of a business:

1. Purpose: What is the purpose—in both societal and business terms—of a business or business activity?

2. Social Context: Are the legitimate rights and responsibilities of multiple stakeholders considered? Is a proposed strategy evaluated not only in terms of predicted business outcomes, but also in terms of its broader impacts—for example, on quality of life, the wider economy of a region, and security and safety?

3. Metrics: How is performance and profitability measured? What is being counted and what is not being counted? Are impacts and results measured across both short- and long-term time frames?"[22]

Triple Bottom Line (TBL)

The **triple-E (economic, ethical, and environmental) bottom line** evaluates a corporation's performance according to a summary of the economic, social, and environmental value the corporation adds or destroys. A variation of the term is the triple-P bottom line: people, planet, profit. The narrowest meaning of the term is a framework for measuring and reporting corporate performance against economic, social, and environmental indicators. Recently, a broader meaning has been attributed to the term in that the concept is used to capture a whole set of values, issues, and processes that corporations must address in order to minimize any harm resulting from their value-adding or destroying activities. This includes clarifying the corporation's purpose and taking into consideration all stakeholders. The triple bottom line approach is often the basis for corporate reporting of economic, ethical, and environmental responsibilities. Everyday Ethics 7.3 is an example of TBL at Novex Couriers.

EVERYDAY ETHICS 7.3

Triple Bottom Line at Novex Delivery Solutions

Novex Couriers, a B.C.-owned and -operated company, is one of the largest local same-day couriers in the Lower Mainland and has operated for over 30 years. Novex has a strategic plan to become a truly sustainable organization based on a triple bottom line approach. This plan focuses environment leadership, social and community leadership, and ethical business practices.

Novex understands that the nature of its business contributes to the growing environmental problem and accepts its responsibility by "going green." It uses a variety of emission-reducing vehicles including hybrids, electric, and ULEVs, all choices that minimize the company's carbon footprint. Waste-reduction and paper-conservation programs, energy-reduction initiatives, and environmental-awareness campaigns have been implemented. It is the first Carbon Neutral courier service in North America.

Novex engages with internal and external stakeholders. It is engaging its employees by supporting a diversity program, rewarding employees for their personal and organizational performance, and offering a training benefits program. In the community, the company and its employees support and assist in fundraising for a variety of social causes and community events including Kids Up Front, United Way, Juvenile Diabetes, and Boys and Girls Clubs of Vancouver.

As a result of its triple bottom line approach, Novex qualifies as a certified B Corporation (B Corp), a designation requiring the highest standards of verified social and environmental performance, public transparency, and legal accountability to balance profit and purpose.

Source: Novex Couriers, "About Us" at https://www.novex.ca/about-novex/ and "Sustainability," at http:www.novex.ca/sustainability accessed on January 31, 2019. Used with permission of Novex Couriers.

The triple bottom line approach has been criticized as being of limited value and even misleading. Norman and MacDonald argue that conceptually and practically the approach is not helping the discussion of CSR. According to these scholars, the claims made are difficult to assess and amount to misleading rhetoric. The authors claim that the use of the triple bottom line may be providing a smokescreen behind which corporations can avoid ethical and environmental responsibilities and reporting.[23]

LO 7.6 Views on Corporate and Business Citizenship

Corporate citizenship has recently become a commonly used term to describe the role of business in society. The term appears in the academic literature and business media and is used by corporations to describe their activities. Consulting firms promote their version of corporate citizenship and sell services to assist corporations in establishing and describing their citizenship activities. University research centres have been established on the topic, numerous books describe the concept, and there is a *Journal of Corporate Citizenship*.

Despite the common usage of the term, definitions vary. Corporate citizenship occurs when a corporation demonstrates that it takes into account its complete impact on society and the environment as well as its economic influence. It concerns the economic, ethical or social, and environmental responsibilities to all stakeholders involved, with consideration given to inputs from various stakeholders and the practices of corporations to develop relationships with stakeholders.

Many justifications for corporate citizenship exist, with one of the most frequently referenced being the "Business Case for Corporate Citizenship" that was posted on the World Economic Forum website.[24] According to this report, good corporate citizenship can provide business benefits in eight areas:

- *Reputation management*—A corporate reputation is built and maintained by fulfilling the expectations of multiple stakeholders.

- *Risk profile and risk management*—Risk is reduced when corporations understand stakeholder concerns.

- *Employee recruitment, motivation, and retention*—Obtaining and keeping employees is made easier for companies known as good corporate citizens.

- *Investor relations and access to capital*—Many investors are interested in non-financial as well as financial performance, and there is a proven link between good corporate citizenship and good financial performance.

- *Learning and innovation*—Corporate citizenship objectives can encourage creativity and innovation.

- *Competitiveness and market positioning*—Increasingly, consumers are inquiring about the corporate citizenship performance of companies and tend to be loyal to those with a good record.

- *Operational efficiency*—A focus on corporate citizenship can lead to direct improvements to the bottom line.

- *Licence to operate*—Companies with a good record of corporate citizenship are given greater leeway when problems occur and are less subject to unfair criticism.

This list illustrates the broad scope of activities and stakeholders that are impacted by corporate citizenship practices, including on a global scale. The report concluded that increasing corporate citizenship was an integral part of good business management. Everyday Ethics 7.4 is an example of how one corporation defines citizenship.

 EVERYDAY ETHICS 7.4

Corporate Citizenship at Imperial Oil

Some corporations are utilizing the concept of corporate citizenship to outline their relationship with society. Imperial Oil's "Corporate Citizenship Highlights 2016" report contains information such as:

- a commitment to health and safety with an Operations Integrity Management System to ensure the safety of employees and communities.

- a commitment to operating in an environmentally responsible manner through initiatives in climate change, air emissions, land use and biodiversity, land reclamation, tailings management, spill prevention, and water management. A balance would be sought between social and economic needs of communities.

- a summary of the economic contribution of the company through 5,700 employees, $5.2 billion paid in taxes, and $225 million invested in Indigenous suppliers.

- a shared commitment to an improved quality of life by investing in community-driven organizations and initiatives.

The quantity and diversity of the literature on corporate citizenship makes it difficult to concisely review. The following discussion attempts to organize the views that are held regarding corporate citizenship (inappropriate; limited, equivalent, extended; and business). The final section argues that a more appropriate term is *business citizenship*.

Approaches to Corporate Citizenship

Many have posed the questions, "Can the corporation be a citizen?" and "Is a corporate citizen the same as an individual citizen?" The nature of citizenship has its roots in political theory, philosophy, law, sociology, and psychology and is a complex phenomenon that has been discussed and debated for centuries. Individual citizenship involves the relationship of the person to the state, the rights and duties of citizens, and the national and cultural identity involved.[25]

Any attempt to extend the individual's role as a citizen to that of a corporation is thought by many to be completely inappropriate. A corporation is not an individual citizen, as it does not possess the attributes or characteristics of a person. Any attempt to project the qualities of a person to the corporation is false and meaningless. Given the prominence of corporate citizenship in the academic and practitioner spheres, this view is not widely held, although it does have its advocates. The following describe two approaches that researchers have developed to explain corporate citizenship.

The Limited, Equivalent, and Extended Views

Matten and Crane[26] described three views of corporate citizenship: limited, equivalent, and extended. These views will form the categories of how corporate citizenship is considered. A following section provides an explanation of why "corporate" citizenship would be more appropriately viewed as "business" citizenship.

A limited view of corporate citizenship involves giving back to society and is considered to be enlightened self-interest. The equivalent view is concerned with what society expects are the responsibilities of business. The extended view defines citizenship as a set of individual, social, civil, and political rights.[27]

Building on the "extended" view that citizenship is based on the shared understanding of basic social, civil, and political rights, a different way of considering corporate citizenship emerges. However, it is questionable whether social and political rights can be regarded as rights of the corporation. Instead, the corporations could be viewed as powerful actors that have a responsibility to respect individual rights.

Globalization has shifted responsibility for protecting citizenship rights away from governments, as seen by the activism of non-governmental organizations (NGOs). Instead of seeking from governments a solution to corporate misdeeds, NGOs pressure corporations directly or indirectly through stakeholders such as consumers and the media. The result is that many social changes are taking place beyond the power and influence of the nation-state. The absence of government initiatives has caused a gap in providing these rights, and corporations are increasingly filling this gap as they are principal actors in society and drivers of globalization.

Matten and Crane[28] cited some examples of change that have resulted as governments ceased to be the only guarantor of citizenship. There are areas where governments cease to administer citizenship rights, and corporations may step in or their role may become more pronounced, as illustrated in privatization and welfare reform. Another occurs where governments have not yet administered citizenship, for example in the regulation of sweatshop working conditions. Lastly, there are areas where the administration of citizenship rights may be beyond the nation-state or government, for example the creation of transnational institutions and global codes of conduct.

In this context, corporate citizenship is described as the role the corporation plays in administering citizenship rights for individuals, moving away from considering the corporation a citizen toward a view where the corporation administers some rights. Corporations would take on this role for altruistic, enlightened self-interest and pure self-interest motivations. This extended role of the corporation is represented in the following diagram:

Social role of the corporation in administering citizenship rights

↓

Social rights: The corporation as a *provider*

+

Civil rights: The corporation as an *enabler*

+

Political rights: The corporation as a *channel*[29]

This view describes the role of the corporation as being involved with administering citizenship rights for individuals rather than as a "citizen" as such. Matten and Crane's summary argument is that:

> *We have identified citizenship as an arena where two parties are involved: (1) the state (originally) as the party administering rights of citizenship and (2) the private citizen as the receiver of those rights. We have then argued that corporations have become major actors in this arena. Our extended conceptualization locates CC [corporate citizenship] in the administration of citizenship rights, which, in the liberal view, is clearly an aspect of citizenship. Of course, this does not mean that corporations "are" citizens or that they "have" citizenship, but they are certainly active in citizenship behaviors.*[30]

Corporate citizenship is considered at a different level; that is, not at the same level as for a private citizen. This view of corporate citizenship implies that corporations have replaced some of the functions of government as they administer citizenship. Corporations enter this different level on a discretionary or voluntary basis and accountability becomes an issue. The adequacy of such accountability will be discussed later.

The Business View

Wood and Logsdon[31] argue that the term "business citizenship" may better incorporate the broader perspective on business rights and duties, stakeholder relationships, and responses to the opportunities and challenges that accompany the global socio-economy of the twenty-first century. **Business citizenship** includes the responsibilities of corporate citizenship on a local and national basis and extends it to a global or universal scope.

The authors explain the status of citizenship for individuals and then compare this reasoning to the business organization or the corporation. Thus, the individual as citizen is local, community, and national in scope and the relationship of the individual is with the state and involves rights and duties. Today, the individual as citizen is global or universal in scope and concerned with common humanity, interdependence, and universalism, which are less grounded on fixed rules or laws.

Further, the corporation as citizen can be considered as either a "corporate" citizen or a "business" citizen. As a corporate citizen, corporations are a responsible player in local environments, involved with volunteerism, charity, and rights and duties in and for the community. Today, thinking in terms of being a corporate citizen associated with corporate–community relations may be too narrow to represent the depth and variety of business–society relationships. Thus, a "business citizen" would be responsible not only for local actions—that is, concerned with organizations' rights and societies within and across national and/or cultural borders—but also for global or universal actions. Wood and Logsdon provide the rationale for moving from individual citizenship to corporate citizenship by outlining the similarities and differences, and then moving the corporate citizen on a local, community, and national scope to the global or universal scope.[32]

The following quotation summarizes Wood and Logsdon's argument for using "business" instead of "corporate" citizenship:

"Business citizenship," . . . , provides an overarching rationale for corporate social performance, for the study of ethics in business, for stakeholder theory and issues management, for business-government relations and for concerns over major social, political and human issues such as labour rights and environmental protection. Business citizenship can be one of the conceptual balance beams of the long-standing paradox of self-interest and other interest, of individual versus collective outcomes.[33]

This presentation has provided background on the views of corporate and business citizenship in the literature and in practice. Currently, the more widely accepted term is *corporate citizenship*, but the use of business citizenship is considered more appropriate as it avoids the problematic discussion of whether or not the corporation is a citizen. It is also more inclusive as it incorporates the complete business system, including the global nature of business.

LO 7.7 The VBA Model: An Integration of CSR Concepts

Schwartz and Carroll developed a model of the business and society field that integrated and unified five frameworks in common usage by academics and managers: corporate social responsibility (CSR), business ethics (BE), stakeholder management (SM), sustainability (SUS), and corporate citizenship (CC). They named their framework the VBA model and believed that it would reduce the confusion resulting from the existence of the various frameworks. Three core concepts were identified as being common, to some degree, in all frameworks: value, balance, and accountability.[34]

The generation of value to business and society was found to be a fundamental element of all the frameworks. Value results "when business meets society's needs by producing goods and services in an efficient manner while avoiding unnecessary negative externalities."[35] A degree of balance occurs when some effort is made in "addressing and appropriately responding to potentially conflicting stakeholder interests and/or moral standards."[36] Other similar concepts are respect, weigh, trade-off, and satisfy. Accountability is present in all frameworks, meaning that while attempting to fulfill its economic, legal, and ethical responsibilities, business "must acknowledge responsibility for [its] actions and decisions and take steps to rectify failure and prevent them from happening again in the future."[37] The authors note that the three core concepts receive different emphasis in the frameworks, but they are present to some degree.

The VBA model integrating the frameworks is represented by the equation:

$$\text{Value} + \text{Balance} + \text{Accountability} = \text{Proper Role of Business in Society}$$

Schwartz and Carroll set forth the following normative proposition relating to their VBA model:

All organizations and individuals operating within a business context have a responsibility (CSR) as good corporate citizens (CC) to (a) contribute to sustainable societal value (SUS), and (b) appropriately balance stakeholder interests (SM), including shareholders or owners and/or moral standards (BE), while (c) demonstrating sufficient accountability.[38]

The integration of the five frameworks (CSR, BE, SM, SUS, and CC) and three core concepts (Value + Balance + Accountability) in the VBA results in the model's three key elements: creating sustainable value; demonstrating sufficient accountability; and achieving appropriate balance. The authors argue that by focusing on three core elements of the five frameworks, the VBA model integrates the shareholder theory and emphasizes the importance of others in managerial decision making while maintaining relevance for managers and ensuring a long-term global prospective.[39]

The VBA model clarifies the relationships among the various frameworks of corporate social responsibility presented in this chapter. In doing so, the confusion over the terminology should be reduced. The theoretical basis for social responsibility has been outlined, and the following chapters will discuss approaches used by corporations to implement or apply it and the methodologies used to evaluate it.

Want to learn more about CSR jobs?

Your advice to George. . .

George likely feels that he has been let down by the corporation and he likely has doubts about CSR. The issue is whether or not VW's reputation has been damaged so severely that he may not trust the corporation. He has not been personally harmed financially, but the environment is suffering because of VW's deliberate unethical behaviour. The challenge for George is how he can assess and believe the CSR claims of VW and for that matter, the claims of any automobile corporation. Unfortunately, some corporations become so focused on a goal, in this case to become the world's largest car manufacturer, that they are willing to ignore their own CSR policies.

Summary

- Rather than provide one definition of social responsibility, the chapter identifies the elements found in the majority of definitions. Corporate social responsibility is a reflection of the fact that business and society are interwoven and can be expressed in terms of three principles: legitimacy, public responsibility, and managerial discretion. The principle of legitimacy refers to society's granting of legitimacy and authority to business, along with business' appropriate use of that power; the principle of public responsibility means business is responsible for outcomes related to its areas of involvement with society; and the principle of managerial discretion refers to managers as moral actors who are obligated to exercise such discretion as is available to them to achieve socially responsible outcomes. (LO 7.1)

- The debate as to whether social responsibility is an appropriate concept is summarized in arguments for and against corporate social involvement. Arguments for and against corporate social involvement are provided and an ethical basis for CSR described. (LO 7.2)

- These arguments are reflected in Klonoski's summary of social responsibility theories, categorized according to three alternative views of the corporation as amoral, personal, and social. The arguments and theories are presented not to provide a definitive answer to the question of corporate social responsibility but to review the background to the debate. In fact, the debate has not been resolved to date, as evidenced by the critique of CSR in a leading business magazine. (LO 7.3)

- A pyramid of corporate social responsibilities is presented, based on economic, legal, ethical, and philanthropic responsibilities. A hierarchy of responsibilities exists; economic and legal obligations are primary and basic. In recent years, the ethical and philanthropic responsibilities have received more attention. (LO 7.4)

- Social responsibility has evolved and today other terminology is being used to describe the concept, including *corporate sustainability, reputation management, social impact management, triple bottom line,* and *corporate citizenship.* Definitions are provided so that a distinction can be made among the terms. (LO 7.5)

- Corporate citizenship is another term used interchangeably with CSR. It is an inclusive term to capture the economic, social, and environmental responsibilities of the corporation and relies on stakeholder theory. As with CSR various interpretations are given to the term, and it is argued that the term *business citizenship* would be even more inclusive as it is global or universal in scope. (LO 7.6)

- The VBA model is an attempt at unifying and integrating the various frameworks within CSR around three core concepts: value, balance, and accountability. This model reduces the confusion resulting from the various terminology used in the business and society and CSR field. (LO 7.7)

Key Terms

Reputation management

Social impact management

Triple-E (economic, ethical, and environmental) bottom line

Business citizenship

Critical Thinking and Discussion Questions

1. Why should corporations and their management be concerned with corporate social responsibility?

2. Distinguish among Wood's three principles of corporate responsibility: legitimacy, public responsibility, and managerial discretion.

3. Why do some corporations and their management oppose corporate social responsibility?

4. Can CSR be justified on an ethical basis?

5. Social responsibility is interpreted in many ways. State your understanding of corporate social responsibility.

6. List the 10 stakeholders you think have the greatest influence on a corporation's social responsibility.

7. Can the corporation have a conscience?

8. Do you agree that "economic responsibilities" are a component of corporate social responsibility?

9. What does a corporation have to do to have a "good" reputation?

10. Is the corporation a "citizen" of society?

Cases

7.1 WOULD YOU LIKE TO DONATE . . .?

Suzanne Valentine had been noticing an increasing number of businesses asking their customers to donate to charities when they make a purchase, a practice known as checkout charity or point of sale fundraising. One example was the Shoppers Drug Mart "SHOPPERS LOVE. YOU" campaign, which encourages customers to purchase a leaf for $1, a butterfly for $5, an apple for $10 or a bird for $100. All proceeds go directly to the women's health organizations chosen by each Associate-owner, best reflecting local community needs. Over the past five years, $57 million has been contributed to local, regional and national women's health initiatives.

Many other corporations have similar programs including Indigo, Loblaw, Walmart, and McDonald's. Even former Governor General David Johnston's "My Giving Moment" encourages participating in such programs.

Suzanne was directly affected by this type of corporate social responsibility fundraising. She worked part-time as a cashier at her neighbourhood grocery store where the owner established a donation scheme, "Pennies for Pets." The owner was a strong supporter of animal causes and the donations were to support the local animal shelter. All cashiers were instructed to ask customers if they wanted to donate $1 or $2 to the shelter.

Suzanne followed instructions but she had several reservations about the scheme. She felt awkward asking customers for the donation, particularly those who looked like they could not afford it. Some customers might be intimidated by the request and she did not believe that they should be put on the spot to say yes or no. Some customers may not wish to support this particular charity. As well, she was not convinced that the particular shelter deserved funding, as there had been some articles in the media about its poor management and treatment of animals. Lastly, she was not sure how much of the money collected was forwarded to the charity, and whether or not the owner matched the customer donations.

Questions

1. What are the ethical implications in this example of corporate social responsibility?

2. What information should the company provide to Suzanne and its customers?

3. Carroll has identified four corporate social responsibilities: economic, legal, ethical, and philanthropic. Which responsibilities are involved in "Pennies for Pets" or similar fundraising schemes?

4. How should Suzanne resolve her personal ethical dilemma?

7.2 THE TD GRADE ONE BOOK GIVEAWAY

The TD Bank Group (TD) supports several initiatives to encourage literacy and reading in Canada. TD believes that literacy is a key skill for the future. In 2000, TD established the Grade One Book Giveaway program after consulting ministries of education, school boards, and library organizations. The program is organized by the Canadian Children's Book Centre (CCBC), a not-for-profit organization dedicated "to the encouraging, promoting and supporting reading, writing and illustrating of Canadian books for young readers." CCBC focuses on books published in Canada and it is committed "to raising awareness and the quality and variety of Canadian books for young readers."

The program is the largest free-book program to school aged children in Canada. About 550,000 Grade 1 English and French students receive the book compliments of TD. They can keep the book and take it home to read with their parents and caregivers. The book distribution is supported by an author/illustrator reading tour across Canada. The books' printing and distribution costs are paid for by the bank and their logo appears on the front cover. Inside there is short letter from TD's CEO.

There has been some opposition to the program. In 2013, some school boards claimed that the books are corporate advertising and should not be distributed in the classroom. The boards claimed that it forces students to be exposed to advertising. As a result, the free book was not distributed in the classrooms that year but was made available at local public libraries in the area.

Defenders of the program state that the book has nothing to do with banking. Many Grade 1 students do not even know the letters T and D and the logo means nothing. The defenders suggest that the school boards have lost sight of their mission, that is, literacy. They state that there are all kinds of issues in the educational system and this is not one worthy of discussion.

Questions

1. Will the program promote a love of reading and a passion for books?

2. In whose best interests are the books being distributed?

3. Is TD being purely altruistic?

4. Are there other corporate programs where this issue exists?

Employee volunteers contribute to a corporation's social responsibility.
Used © Blend/ Image Source

CHAPTER 8

Corporate Social Responsibility: In Practice

LEARNING OUTCOMES

After studying this chapter, you will be able to:

LO 8.1 Identify the different responses to corporate social responsibility.

LO 8.2 Define corporate philanthropy and describe the forms it takes.

LO 8.3 Define corporate voluntarism and describe the implications for employees, employers, and the community.

LO 8.4 Define corporate sponsorship and identify trends in this approach to CSR.

LO 8.5 Understand the community investment approach to CSR including its use in Indigenous communities.

LO 8.6 Appreciate the challenges confronting small businesses in practising CSR.

What would you do if...?

Walter Zuberek once read a quote from Warren Buffett: "Giving money away is easy. Giving money away well is fiendishly difficult." He was learning just what Buffett meant.

Walter has just stepped down as CEO of York and Smith Limited after being associated with the company for 50 years. Walter came to Canada from Europe in the 1950s and went to work as an engineer for a small construction company known as York Construction. Over the years, the company expanded and acquired a building materials company from the Smith family, which led to the name change to York and Smith. Walter started as a site foreman, but steadily rose in the company as the owners recognized his managerial abilities. In the mid-1960s, the owners decided to sell the business and Walter was able to purchase it with financial assistance from a venture capitalist.

York and Smith grew into a $200 million a year business that manufactured and distributed building products for North American construction markets. The company served four construction market sectors: residential (both new construction and renovations), non-residential, agricultural and industrial storage, and infrastructure. The company believed in operating in a socially and ethically responsible manner and in providing the broadest possible opportunity for personal and professional development for its employees. The company also believed in giving back to the community and supported hospital and university capital fund campaigns, literacy programs, sports programs for persons who have a disability, and school lunch programs.

Walter's two sons now run the business, but Walter provides some oversight as chair of the board of directors. Because he is not as closely associated with the day-to-day operations, Walter has time to pay more attention to things that are of interest to him. He considers himself fortunate to have worked for York and Smith and to have been able to acquire the business. He is grateful for the opportunities provided in Canada, and appreciates the support he has received from various stakeholders over the years.

York and Smith Limited is experiencing good financial returns, with some discretionary funds available for social responsibility endeavours. Walter himself has accumulated a small fortune and wonders what to do with the money beyond leaving some to family members. He thought maybe it was appropriate to give something back to society.

Now that Walter is retired, a reassessment of the company's social contributions would be a good job for him, and at the same time he could investigate what he could do with his fortune. He wants to make sure the company's—and his—contributions to society are used in the most effective and efficient manner. This is a challenge, as Charity Intelligence Canada points out. There are issues about which charities to select, how the charities will spend the donation, and what the charities will achieve. Alternatively, Walter could set up a new charity for a cause that he and his family support.

···

What is your advice to Walter?

This chapter describes the various forms or approaches to practising or implementing corporate social responsibility (CSR) or corporate sustainability (CS) in corporations. Corporate social responsibility and the related concepts described in Chapter 7 have resulted in a range of activities. Corporate websites often contain details of all CSR activities. Professional associations provide advice to corporations, as do various newsletters. In addition, numerous consultant services are available to assist with CSR activities.

Corporations have moved from expressing CSR through corporate philanthropy in the form of donations to other approaches involving some form of direct community involvement or investment. Corporate giving, or donations, is the most traditional approach and is still practised. Many corporations now view writing a cheque to be insufficient or inappropriate to demonstrate their commitment to the community.

Corporations are now involved in voluntarism programs, corporate sponsorship, and community investment in addition to donations. Today, many corporations are involved in more than one of these approaches to CSR, with corporate philanthropy being the most common. In addition, the final section of this chapter will discuss CSR in small business as a separate topic. It should be noted that the corporation's CSR toward the environment is not dealt with in this chapter but is the focus in Chapter 14.

LO 8.1   Responses to Corporate Social Responsibility

Despite the widespread acceptance and practise of CSR, business corporations are responding to it in different ways. Table 8.1 identifies business responses to CSR, beginning with high acceptance and declining to little or none.

TABLE 8.1	Responses to CSR	
Response	**Explanation**	**Acceptance of CSR**
Social enterprise—social return	Organizations that operate with a social mission without the intention of operating to make profits with all earnings committed to social causes or projects. Example: Habitat for Humanity, Goodwill	High
Social enterprise—mixed return	Organizations that operate with a social mission but with the intention of making a profit. "Doing well by doing good" (social paradigm). A portion of profits are committed to social causes or projects with the remainder reinvested or returned to owners. Examples: Whole Foods Market Inc. and Value Village	High
CSR recognition or embracers	CSR and sustainability placed high on corporate agenda. Often are larger corporations and traded on stock exchanges. Corporate giving and citizenship are involved. Publish "social reports" of their initiatives. "Doing good by doing well" (economic paradigm).	Above average
Cautious CSR adaptors	Recognize CSR and sustainability but focus on savings from environmental projects, energy cost reductions, material efficiency, and risk reduction.	Some recognition
Tokenism or greenwashing	Corporations are not serious about CSR, but believe they should respond. Might be forced into initiatives by non-governmental organizations (NGOs), the media, or competitors. NGOs allege many multinational corporations are responding this way.	Low commitment
Amoral	Corporations, and their managers, simply ignore CSR, intentionally or unintentionally. Difficult to identify and measure numbers.	Very little, by chance, or legal requirement
Anti-CSR	As CSR is widely accepted and practised, it is unlikely that these corporations will identify themselves as being anti-CSR. Difficult to identify numbers.	Very little, most likely as required by law
Unknown	Businesses about which not much is known regarding CSR initiatives, including small businesses and privately held corporations. There is a modest literature on CSR in these types of enterprises.	Low, but not documented

The businesses most committed to CSR are social enterprises. Such businesses practise the *social paradigm*, which can be described as "Doing well by doing good." This means that the corporation will undertake socially desirable activities that will result in its doing well economically. There appear to be an increasing number of businesses responding to CSR in this manner. This approach is the highest level of CSR acceptance.

Many businesses are recognizing CSR as an essential aspect of management. Usually, these businesses audit their activities and report them to relevant stakeholders. This response is based on the *economic paradigm*, which can be described as "Doing good by doing well." This means that the corporation will do well economically and then undertake to do good socially. This view is illustrated by the CSR recognition and cautious adaptors responses.

The tokenism response is the one alleged by some non-governmental organizations (NGOs) when they evaluate CSR programs. The effectiveness of CSR efforts, particularly those made by multinational companies, is challenged. It claims to have revealed the true face of CSR—a false image and public relations. This response is often referred to as **greenwashing**, a form of advertising or public relations that deceptively provides the perception that a corporation's policies or practices are socially responsible.

An amoral response is illustrated by several views of CSR. Managers believe that a corporation has no or very little social responsibility, or that the corporation is an autonomous entity and not the creation of society. Others believe that the corporation is socially responsible only within the limits of a prior contractual agreement with shareholders. Finally, the traditional shareholder model argues that corporations are not ethically required to be socially responsible and their only responsibility is to maximize profits. This view is closely related to the fourth response, anti-CSR. Since CSR is a widely accepted conventional wisdom, those opposing it are unlikely to be vocal.

Lastly, the CSR response "unknown" has not been widely studied. Two examples are privately held corporations and small businesses. Small business and CSR will be discussed later in the chapter.

Not responding to society's demands for CSR can be risky. Several of these risks are listed in Table 8.2, emphasizing the need for corporations to plan their CSR initiatives.

TABLE 8.2	Risks of Not Practising CSR
The risks associated with not practising CSR include:	

Damaged reputation
- Negative media coverage
- Consumer boycotts
- Lost sales and revenues
- Labour disruptions
- Blockages, attacks against assets
- Decrease in share value
- More onerous financing or insurance terms

Increased spending to remedy past damage for core activities
- Increased shareholder activism
- Failure to attract and retain quality employees
- Civil lawsuits, including class-action initiatives
- Criminal and regulatory prosecution

Suspended operating permits
- Liability for the conduct of subsidiaries and arm's-length affiliates, for example suppliers
- Increased and onerous government regulation

Planning and Managing CSR Programs

When corporations are involved with CSR, there is a need to establish a planning process if the effort is to be most effective. To start with, there must be commitment from top management, including the board of directors. Without this commitment, any CSR efforts are unlikely to be as successful as they might be. Small as well as large businesses can plan for CSR although there is more media coverage of large corporation activities. CSR also involves many stakeholders both internal and external to the corporation that should be involved in the process.

The approach to CSR will involve one or more of the following most common activities: philanthropy or corporate giving, voluntarism, sponsorship, and community investment described in the following sections. Whatever the corporation decides to undertake, the outcome will be a CSR program, plan, or strategy.

The planning and managing of CSR programs is implemented in different ways. Large corporations have CSR or equivalent departments, with staff trained in the area that oversees the implementation of CSR initiatives. Other corporations rely on management consulting services to assist with CSR. Professional business associations provide advice to corporations, as do various newsletters.

Some corporations have committees that coordinate CSR efforts. A member of management, sometimes quite a senior member, is often given the responsibility for CSR. Others have more elaborate structural arrangements as illustrated in Responsibility for Ethics 8.1. METRO refers to CSR as corporate responsibility and its implementation is the responsibility of the Senior Director of Corporate Affairs.

 RESPONSIBILITY FOR ETHICS 8.1

CR Management at METRO

At METRO, corporate responsibility (CR) governance is part of the corporation's management structure and involves key individuals at each decision-making and implementation stage.

Governance Structure

Board of Directors: Approves policies and reviews the CR plans and reports.

President and CEO: Approves the CR strategy and ensures that the priorities are in line with METRO's business strategy.

Senior Director: Corporate Affairs: Defines the strategic CR directions and reports on progress to the management committee.

Senior Advisor, Corporate Responsibility: Oversees the implementation of the CR plan; coordinates the work of in-house teams and extended stakeholder relations.

In-House Teams: Ensure the advancement of the projects as part of the four pillars based on the set objectives and targets.

The following sections describe the various components that will make up a CSR program, plan, or strategy.

Want to learn more about **the most socially responsible corporations in Canada**?

LO 8.2   Corporate Philanthropy

Corporate philanthropy is the effort of business to contribute to society socially and is manifested by donations of money or goods and services in kind. Also referred to as corporate giving, philanthropy takes many forms.

Donations

Canadian business corporations donate to a variety of causes and organizations, including health and welfare agencies, educational institutions, community services, service clubs, civic projects, arts and culture groups, athletic organizations, and environmental groups. Some corporations spread contributions across a variety of causes, while others are more focused in their giving. In addition to the donation of money, corporate giving or philanthropy can involve the donation of goods and services. According to Statistics Canada, Canadians donate about $9 billion to charities, but it is not clear what portion is from corporations.[1]

Most Canadians believe corporations have a responsibility to provide support to charities and non-profit organizations, as illustrated in Everyday Ethics 8.1. This section provides arguments for and against corporate giving, examines how the decision to donate is made, and indicates trends in corporate giving.

 EVERYDAY ETHICS 8.1

Corporate Philanthropy Examples

Through philanthropy, Canadian corporations support many causes in society. The examples below illustrate the various approaches to philanthropy taken by corporations.

18 Asset Management (18 AM)—The company believes in giving back to the community and the charities and community organizations involved include United Way, London Community Foundation, Brain Tumour Foundation of Canada, Jesse's Journey, Greater London International Airport, Women's Community House, and the Ivey Business School.

BlueShore Financial—The company has a philanthropic donation program, which gives financial support to non-profit organizations and charities that provide services and programs to the communities served and that support their wellness philosophy.

GlaxoSmithKline Inc.—In 2017, the company donated $610,000 to Université du Québec à Montréal, Canadian Hospice Palliative Care Association, Save the Children Canada, Canadian Red Cross, United Way of Peel Region, and Centraide.

Smith's Funeral Homes—Smith's Funeral Homes operates from three locations in Ontario: Burlington, Stoney Creek, and Grimsby. The company supports dozens of organizations at each location.

Woodbine Entertainment Group—In 2017—18, Woodbine donated $898,036 to the following causes: building healthy communities, children and youth, the environment, and horse welfare and industry. Woodbine claims that "Every dollar donated to the local community returns a social value of $7.30."

Arguments For and Against Corporate Giving

The arguments for and against corporate giving are similar to those for social responsibility. Corporate giving is a widely used and acceptable approach to express social responsibility to the community and to show that business is not just concerned with society as a market for its goods and services. The act of corporate giving promotes an image of good citizenship and creates goodwill. This is important for the acceptance of business by society either in terms of legitimacy or a social licence to operate. Most businesspersons recognize that the volunteer sector provides some services very efficiently, and that even business corporations benefit from such services—as, for example, when employees belong to Alcoholics Anonymous.

Corporations receive significant benefits from a corporate community investment program in terms of employee commitment, corporate reputation, marketing visibility, and relationships with customers, suppliers, neighbours, and governments. It is argued that a corporation's success is tightly linked with economic health and social conditions in the community in which it operates, and thus a corporation should invest in the organizations that underpin community vitality.

Not everyone accepts the argument that business should be involved with corporate giving. It is argued that the funds given actually belong to shareholders, and it is presumptuous first for management to make the decision to give the funds, and then to choose particular recipients. Some claim that business corporations should not become involved with social welfare because that is the job of governments. Support for social causes could give business even more power in society at a time when many feel that it already has too much. By supporting any cause or charitable organization the corporation might become accountable for the actions taken by the charity, or adverse publicity could damage the corporation's image or reputation. Usually there are no guidelines, no standards to measure against, and no evaluation process for making decisions and monitoring corporate giving. The benefits of corporate giving are seldom measurable or directly related to the corporation.

Despite the arguments against corporate giving, most businesses, including small ones, are involved with corporate giving in some way.

Making Corporate Giving Decisions

In earlier times, corporate giving decisions were made by individual executives who often were members of the family at the helm of a corporation—the Eatons, Woodwards, Burtons, Molsons, and Labatts. This is still the case today as many wealthy individuals contribute large amounts to society.

On the other hand, many large corporations make donation decisions by committee consensus where the process is more complicated. In the most formalized processes, decisions relating to corporate giving are made in head offices by chief executives and boards of directors with assistance from a committee. The first decision relates to the donations budget. Budgets are set as a percentage of expected pre-tax profit, increased an arbitrary amount from the previous year, set in relation to industry norms or in comparison to peers, or set upon a formula based on number of employees. Assistance is available from several organizations, including the ones listed in Responsibility for Ethics 8.2. These organizations provide advice to individual executives and corporations including evaluations of a charity's efficiency and use of funds.

RESPONSIBILITY FOR ETHICS 8.2

Organizations Assisting in Corporate Philanthropy

Organizations outside the corporation that provide advice on corporate giving or donations include:

Imagine Canada (formerly the Canadian Centre for Philanthropy)—Established in 1980, the Centre's mission is to promote the generous application of charitable time and funds, and to strengthen the philanthropic community of Canada through research and training. The Centre initiated the IMAGINE program, a Canada-wide corporate and individual awareness program, to increase support for charitable non-profit organizations.

MoneySense—Each year this magazine and website evaluates the 100 largest charities in Canada on efficiency and where the money is spent.

Charity Intelligence Canada—This organization provides advice to donors and helps them identify which charities should receive money, how the donations are spent, and what the charities achieve.

Better Business Bureau (BBB) Canada—Corporations wishing to donate can check out charities to ascertain whether they comply with the BBB's Wise Giving Alliance *Charitable Accountability Standards*. Information provided about the charity includes how it is governed, how the money is spent, the truthfulness of their representatives, and their willingness to disclose information to the public.

Some corporations carefully establish the objectives for giving so that some guidelines are available to ascertain how much money is given and to whom. Criteria for evaluating requests are formulated and used by in-house staff or consultants in making decisions. Some givers perform cost–benefit analyses of the grant, while others require that social performance programs be proactive. Grants given in one year are evaluated prior to another grant being made. Some large corporate givers have managers to supervise the process. Despite the formalization suggested above, the single most important influence in the decision-making process is still often the chair of the board or the chief executive officer (CEO).

Either through formal or ad hoc processes, decisions are made to fund—or to reject—requests. A request is typically rejected when policy excludes a particular type of project or charity; there are not enough funds; a donation has already been made to an organization with parallel services; the organization is located outside the corporation's community; there is no Canada Revenue Agency registration number; there are inadequate financial statements; no new approaches are being accepted; the size of the request is too large; or the corporation receives too many requests.

Another form of rejection is the decision to cease giving to a particular organization. Such a decision may have serious consequences, including the failure of the organization. Many causes are rejected because they are somehow controversial. For example, many corporations are reluctant to support Planned Parenthood organizations because of possible backlash from pro-life groups. There is without doubt a tendency to seek out "safe" causes on the part of those who make the donating decision.

Trends and Concerns in Corporate Giving

A number of trends and concerns have occurred that have affected corporate giving. Large requests from institutions such as universities and hospitals have resulted in a higher portion of the donation budget being committed to five-year programs. This doesn't leave much opportunity to fund new causes or groups.

Business corporations in Canada are supporting a wide variety of charities, and this support has become much more important as government grants have declined. For those corporations that donate on a regular basis, philanthropy is a responsibility, a part of the cost of doing business. For other corporations, it is a frill. Some corporations support charities while they are experiencing good financial performance but in economic downturns or recessions reduce or stop corporate giving. It appears that some corporations are willing to give, but are becoming more selective and will have to be convinced to part with their money.

Some businesses or their owners choose to set up charitable foundations to handle corporate philanthropy. A **charitable foundation** is defined as a corporation or trust that is constituted and operated exclusively for charitable purposes. They are established by families of successful entrepreneurs, corporations, communities, special interest groups such as schools and hospitals, and governments. The foundations donate to a wide variety of causes including education, health, environment, community development, and arts and culture (see the examples provided in Everyday Ethics 8.2).

Philanthropy through Charitable Foundations

Philanthropic Foundations Canada (PFC) is a national membership organization for Canada's independent grant-making foundations and is a registered charity. There are about 10,800 public and private foundations in Canada that give away about $6.5 billion per year. Examples of foundations established by businesspersons are:

- The J.W. McConnell Family Foundation (various businesses including newspapers):

  The Foundation is a private family foundation funding programs to foster a more inclusive, sustainable, and resilient society The Foundation's purpose is to enhance Canada's ability to address complex social, environmental and economic challenges.

- The Birks Family Foundation (jewellery retailing):

  The mission of the Birks Family Foundation is to contribute to a higher standard of living and quality of life for all Canadians. It funds Canadian universities through capital campaigns and other special projects; hospitals, health services, long-term care institutions and specialized health organizations; social service agencies; and arts organizations that promote the development and understanding of Canadian culture.

- Donner Canadian Foundation (petroleum):

  The Donner Canadian Foundation funds public policy research and supports environmental, international development, and social service projects. Every year, the Donner Book Prize honours the best book on Canadian public policy.

Some of the strongest supporters of charitable organizations in Canada produce products that are not considered socially desirable by some—for example, tobacco, beer, and liquor. At issue is whether a group should be associated with the consumption of these products. Society might even find such support unacceptable. For example, in 1987 the federal government proposed legislation to prohibit the advertising and promotion of tobacco products. Yet corporations in the tobacco industry have been innovative and imaginative in their support of the arts. Groups that received support from the tobacco industry may find it difficult to obtain other sources of funding.

The trend to "marketing" and "business" orientations in supporting charities has raised concern. Marketing can be viewed as being "too commercial," as products or services are being directly promoted. Also, conditions can be placed on support, which is considered a threat to artistic or administrative freedom. Support may be given to activities and events where a marketing tie-in is possible, while other activities are neglected.

Some corporate giving is conditional on non-profit organizations becoming more efficient. The argument is that since corporations are tightening their belts, charitable organizations must also become more efficient. Included in this request for efficiency are demands that organizations share resources, avoid duplication, and reduce administrative costs. Charities must develop strategic plans, information and control systems, and generally improve their administrative systems.

Thus, pressure is on charities to produce returns, to be more accountable, and to ensure high visibility for their corporate supporters. Managers of charities argue that this restricts their activities and might prevent them from achieving their objectives. Corporations are also focusing their support on particular programs, projects, or events and are reluctant to provide support for basic operating expenses, placing even more pressure on the charitable organizations.

Another trend is toward **cause-related marketing**, where the purchase of a particular product results in a donation being made by the corporation to a non-profit organization's program. For example, the purchase of a particular brand of frozen vegetables results in a contribution to a food bank, or the purchase of a cake mix helps to fund a health cause. There are several criticisms of this approach, as it pushes philanthropy past even the marketing aspect of sponsorship.

Cause-related marketing is considered another way of making a profit, and there are fears that it will replace philanthropy by reducing the amount of no-strings corporate giving. The selection of causes is problematic. Safe, non-controversial causes are selected that will sell, and some companies base their selection of charities on opinion polls conducted to ascertain the most popular causes.

This approach to corporate giving is likely to continue as government funding declines, making commercial tie-ins inviting to managers of non-profit organizations. For business, it makes their product stand out, and if they can associate with the correct "hot" causes sales performance improves. Target audiences are chosen and promotional strategies are selected, making corporate giving "like selling soap suds," according to some critics. These critics question whether self-interested charitable investment or strategic giving is not becoming self-serving commercial activity.

Overall, these trends or concerns have given rise to strategic giving, an attempt to rationalize the shareholder interest with corporate philanthropy where the corporation benefits directly from the funds given. Some believe it is really shareholders' money that is being given away. To avoid complaints from shareholders, management should act in enlightened self-interest as a counterargument to the profit maximization position of shareholders. Thus, strategic giving is donating with an eye to the corporation's eventual best interests.[2]

Strategic giving leads corporations to make contributions within their own areas of interest. For example, funding of educational programs would be considered appropriate, as would support for a park facility that could be used by employees and their families. This enlightened self-interest, however, may not lead to support for women's shelters or housing for the poor, where the benefits to the corporation are not as evident. Although strategic giving is a way of justifying philanthropy consistent with shareholder interests, it would require managers to walk an ethical tightrope when rationalizing their proposals for support of particular charities.

Social Venture Philanthropy

A type of philanthropy being used more frequently is **social venture philanthropy**, the investment of human and financial resources by corporations in non-profit community development agencies to generate a social return instead of only a financial one. This approach is also known as *social venturing, the new philanthropy,* and *high-engagement philanthropy.*

Social venture philanthropy applies venture capital management practices to social responsibility. Investments are made, but a social return is expected rather than a financial one. There is a high engagement with the non-profit agency that provides leadership, bold ideas to address social problems, and strong teams with an active board involvement. Whereas venture capitalists plan an exit strategy, the social venture capitalist focuses on long-term funding and sustainability of the recipient.

Several examples of social venture philanthropy organizations exist in Canada, including Social Venture Partners (described in Everyday Ethics 8.3), B.C. Technology Social Venture Partners, Social Capital Partners, the Tides Foundation, and the Enterprising Non-Profits Program Vancouver.[3]

 EVERYDAY ETHICS 8.3

Social Venture Philanthropy and Social Venture Partners Calgary

Social Venture Partners Calgary's mission is to stimulate positive social change in Calgary. It is a partnership between needy not-for-profits and generous individuals, businesspersons, and others to create a new model of giving. Social Venture Partners Calgary combines the time, expertise, and financial and physical resources of its partners and turns them into a powerful tool of positive change for cash-strapped, advice-ready, and resource-constrained not-for-profits. These organizations get not only the commitment of money and resources over a number of years, but also the professional advice that leads to more successful outcomes. Examples of the investments made include the following:

Cornerstone Youth Centre—This is a charitable organization designed to teach life skills and "The 40 Developmental Assets" in order to best inspire and prepare youth for a successful life.

Connections Counselling and Consulting Foundation—This grant recipient empowers individuals by providing ongoing education, programs, and advocacy; ongoing family support to parents with an intellectual disability and their children; and counselling for persons with an intellectual disability.

Dare to Care—This non-profit organization addresses the pervasive and crippling issue of bullying, which continues to affect children, youth, and adults.

Although corporate giving or philanthropy is common in corporate social responsibility programs, other program components are volunteerism, sponsorship, and community investment, discussed in the following sections.

LO 8.3   Corporate Voluntarism

Corporate voluntarism is the time and talent employees commit to community organizations with support and/or consent from employers who recognize the value of such efforts to society. Corporations view voluntarism as giving something back to the community and society beyond monetary donations. In addition to employees, corporations now support the voluntary activities of retirees. Examples of volunteerism are given in Everyday Ethics 8.4.

EVERYDAY ETHICS 8.4

Corporate Volunteerism Examples

Canadian corporations encourage employee volunteerism in a variety of ways. Here are some examples:

The Home Depot Canada—Through their associate-led volunteer program "Team Depot," Home Depot associates are encouraged to become involved in voluntary activities. Annually, over 60,000 volunteer hours are contributed to more than 260 community projects across Canada.

PWC Canada—PWC's team volunteer programs focus on supporting young people through a variety of initiatives to address youth unemployment. During 2018, 3,271 employees participated in 365 firm-led team volunteer initiatives, contributing 24,250 total volunteer hours. Dollars for Doers grants are given in recognition of employees' efforts.

IGM Financial—IGM Financial companies encourage and empower their 3,500 employees, approximately 4,100 Investors Group advisors, and approximately 800 Investment Planning Counsel advisors to volunteer. Their commitment to community service involves facilitating volunteering with planned events and providing paid volunteer days across all of the IGM companies. Each year, several awards recognize outstanding volunteers.

WestJet—Referred to as "WestJetters," WestJet employees volunteer with their organization of choice. The volunteer hours contributed can be used to provide eligible non-profit/charitable organizations with the Gift of Flight to be used for fundraising purposes. Gifts are awarded for hours volunteered either individually or in groups.

Capital Power Corporation—Capital Power's EmPowering Communities program encourages employee volunteerism and recognizes the valuable gifts of time, skill, and knowledge that employees give to the community. In 2017, 136 employees were involved in the program, reporting 14,000 hours in volunteer time.

The principle of voluntarism is well established in society, and there is a continuing need to recruit and motivate members of society to support the many voluntary organizations. Employee voluntarism has become more important for two reasons: the decline of the professional volunteer of the past, the homemaker who did not work outside the home; and the increasing need for volunteers to serve. The former point results from more women working, and the latter refers to the increasing load on volunteers during cutbacks in government support and greater demand from an aging population.

There are benefits to employers, employees, and, of course, the non-profit organizations involved. But there also can be drawbacks, especially for employers and employees. Many of these benefits and drawbacks for the parties are summarized in Table 8.3.

TABLE 8.3	Employee Voluntarism: Advantages and Disadvantages

ADVANTAGES

- Benefits employee morale by enhancing professional skill development, providing a learning experience, and providing a personal experience
- Good for the community
- Good for the organizations supported
- Improves the corporation's local and national image or profile
- Good for the overall environment in which employees, customers, and the corporation must operate
- Can contribute to corporate team building, employee involvement initiatives, and employee retention
- Sets a good example
- Helps employees integrate with the community, provides a source of contacts or a network, and encourages a sense of community commitment

DISADVANTAGES

- Possible employee resentment at perceived coercion to participate
- Possible distractions from the job, corporate objectives
- Cost in dollars and time

DISADVANTAGES
• Implication of picking "winners" or "losers" from among community organizations; that is, deciding which to support
• Possibility of controversy over objectives of some voluntary organization reflecting adversely on the corporation
• Some employees may overcommit themselves, impacting upon job performance
• A controversy involving the efforts of an employee volunteer may reflect unfavourably on the corporation

The general benefits for employers include the creation of a better community environment, and opportunities for employee team building and corporate image building. For employees, general benefits are that the personal involvement improves the quality of life in the community; that contacts are made with community members, especially helpful to new employees in an area; and that an educational and broadening experience is received.

Corporate Support and Policies

A majority of corporations support voluntary activities and encourage employees to become involved in the community. Voluntary activities that are encouraged involve organizations such as the United Way, professional associations, business and trade associations, the Chamber of Commerce, service clubs, Junior Achievement, and community athletic groups. Several voluntary activities are usually excluded from employer support, for example working for trade unions (not in collective agreement), political parties, religious groups, and special interest advocacy groups.

The forms of support given to voluntary activities include providing facilities, allowing time off or schedule adjustments, assisting with personal expenses incurred while undertaking voluntary activities, extending special recognition to employees exhibiting outstanding performances, and issuing letters of thanks. Many corporations do not consider support and recognition for volunteer work to be an element in the regular performance review process. However, many corporate recruiters consider voluntary experience when assessing a candidate for employment.

Many corporations do not allow employee voluntarism to just exist without some policies formulated to serve as guidelines in the activity. Some corporate actions that would encourage involvement in the Volunteering section of their policies:

- Provide information for new employees on available volunteer organizations and opportunities.
- Provide recognition or awards to employees who volunteer in order to spur additional employee involvement.
- Encourage employees to volunteer via corporate-sponsored loaned executive and paid leave programs (a recent practice in this area is described in Everyday Ethics 8.5).
- Support programs for retirees.
- Establish formal programs and designating someone to give administrative support.

 EVERYDAY ETHICS 8.5

Corporate Service Corps

A recent form of voluntarism is "corporate service corps" set up by some corporations where employees donate their time to working on development projects in various countries. The IBM Corporate Service Corps was launched in 2008 as a corporate version of the Peace Corps and has involved 2,500 employees in projects. It is viewed as a form of training for global employees in addition to providing assistance in developing countries. IBM cooperates with various non-governmental organizations (NGOs) to place its volunteers, and placements are usually for only a few weeks. Other corporations with similar programs include Novartis Pharmaceuticals Corporation, Dow Corning Corporation, and FedEx.

A Canadian initiative is "Leave for Change" operated by the Uniterra Program, a joint effort of the Centre for International Studies and Cooperation (CECI) and the World University Service of Canada (WUSC) and financially supported by the Government of Canada. It is a corporate volunteering initiative that enables employees to spend a period on assignment in a developing country. Employers support the programs by investing in their human resources and because it demonstrates their social responsibility. Benefits are afforded to communities, employees, and the corporation. Communities receive pro bono help in solving problems confronting them economically, socially, and environmentally. Having the volunteers work in the communities increases international understanding. Benefits for the employee volunteers include gaining leadership training, experience in emerging countries, an opportunity to develop new knowledge and skills, and possibly increased job satisfaction. Corporations obtain insights into potential markets, and their employees obtain new skills and knowledge of developing countries.

It is questioned whether these volunteer placements of only a few weeks can accomplish much. Communities may be overwhelmed by enthusiastic volunteers promoting North American approaches to local problems. Projects may fail, creating ill will and not solving the problems of the communities.

Policies on voluntarism are of three types: encouraging, enabling, and promoting. Encouraging policy statements set the tone or position of the corporation relating to employee voluntarism, and are positive statements about the value of volunteer activities. Enabling policies provide guidelines to managers and employees regarding the implementation of the positive policy. They often set the boundaries and establish procedures relating to voluntarism; for example, the policy relating to a leave of absence to work for a voluntary organization. Overall, enabling policies facilitate the participation of employees in voluntary activity. The third policy category promotes participation in voluntary activity. These promoting policies recognize and reward employee achievement in voluntary activities. Taken together, these types of policies encourage employee voluntarism in Canada.

Employee voluntarism is most successful where top management, especially the chief executive officer, indicate it is a worthy and commendable activity. Top management support is vital for the corporate volunteer program to succeed. Employee voluntarism has endured even through the difficulties created by the economic downturns and will continue to be a significant way in which corporations contribute to the communities where they operate.

Want to learn more about **Canadian corporate volunteerism?**

LO 8.4 Corporate Sponsorship

Corporate sponsorship is defined as "a partnership, which has been established for mutual benefit between a business sponsor and an event or a non-profit."[4] A distinction should be made between corporate donations and sponsorship. A donation is a gift that goes one way, from a corporation to a charity, while a sponsorship, whether a single event or a series of events, confers benefits on both parties.

Sponsorship covers a wide range of sport, cultural, and educational events. There are also examples of extending corporate sponsorship programs to such social concerns as literacy, race relations, drug abuse, and environmental issues. Sponsorship provides a definite link between business and social issues.

Charity or Marketing?

Some acknowledge that corporate sponsorship has little to do with charity, donations, or philanthropy but instead is a business or marketing arrangement. Yet companies often mention sponsorships in "Involvement in or Contribution to the Community" sections of their annual or social reports. The trend toward sponsorships has been found to be attractive for a variety of reasons, including:

- favourable media exposure or publicity;
- opportunity to entertain clients;
- building a company/product presence;
- reaching select market segments; and
- business-to-business networking.[5]

Sponsorship is one way to increase corporate awareness, as broad exposure of a name or logo increases recognition and may result in a purchase decision. It is considered a positive and low-cost image-building approach and allows targeting; that is, the sponsorship can be directed at specific audiences or potential customers. Examples are given in Everyday Ethics 8.6 which illustrate the diversity of corporate sponsorship programs.

Corporate Sponsorship Examples

Canadian corporations sponsor a variety of events and causes.

Kent Building Supplies—The company's focus is on sponsoring non-profit events and registered charities that support growth, development, and wellness in the community. Examples of sponsorship are Ducks Unlimited Canada, the Kent Great Big Dig fundraising evening for the IWK Health Centre, Janeway Children's Hospital, the Leukemia & Lymphoma Society of Canada's Light the Night Walk, and the Canadian Red Cross.

Kruger Inc.—Kruger Inc. and its divisions have supported many causes including breast cancer, Ronald McDonald House Charities, women's curling, Earth Day Canada, Crohn's & Colitis Canada, and Log-A-Load for Kids Charity Hockey Tournament.

Sport Chek—The company sponsors several amateur sports organizations including Hockey Canada, Alpine Canada Alpin, Canada Snowboard, Canadian Olympic Committee, and Canadian Paralympic Committee. In addition, it supports several community sport programs.

Tim Hortons—The company sponsors and is the official coffee for several sports events including curling, hockey, football, soccer, and baseball.

SaskTel—Some of the events sponsored are SaskTel Saskatchewan Jazz Festival, bringing people together with music; SaskTel Indigenous Youth Awards, recognizing young Indigenous achievers; Saskatchewan Soccer Association, enriching lives through soccer; Robot Rumble, teaching about technology through fun and competition; and Ag in Motion, demonstrating the latest agricultural technology.

The corporate sponsor looks for a charitable situation that both satisfies the company's marketing ambitions and coincides with the needs of the charity group. There must be some common ground so that both parties benefit. To accomplish this, the sponsorship agreement should define clearly the role and needs of each partner. For the corporation, the sponsorship must fit into the marketing scheme, while the charity's integrity must not be threatened. A well-defined plan is necessary to avoid failure and disagreements. Many now consider corporate sponsorship to be a form of advertising.

Sponsorship is now so common that it has lost its novelty, and thus its capability to attract attention. The public may be cynical about cause-related sponsorships, or simply may not understand the linkage. Many question the appropriateness of the support given by alcohol companies to the arts and sports. The government might question whether some sponsorship violates advertising regulations.

Corporations may find it difficult to keep their hands off the event after the initial agreement is reached, and the relationship may turn sour. The return from a sponsorship is seldom precisely known, and it might be difficult to withdraw support without attracting attention. For example, the sponsorship of the Canadian equestrian team became awkward for some corporate sponsors when the sport experienced problems with drugs and dishonesty. But the withdrawal of support becomes a problem, as without corporate sponsorship many programs fail.

New approaches are being used by business to address social ills beyond giving money, social venture philanthropy, and social enterprises. Both assume that it is appropriate for business to solve social problems such as jobs in communities, training programs, and housing. The purpose of these approaches is to give the underprivileged the tools to create new opportunities by creating their own wealth instead of it being transferred to them.

LO 8.5   The Community Investment Approach

Community investment (CI) has become another approach to describing a corporation's CSR activities. It is defined as "the efforts of a corporation to help develop a community and create economic opportunities through a variety of means from donations to direct involvement in commercial undertakings." According to Business for Social Responsibility, "corporate community investment bridges traditional areas of philanthropy and volunteerism with commercial-community relationships in sourcing, workforce, financial investments, site selection, and the development and delivery of products and services."[6] The purpose of community investment is to develop CSR strategies in relation to corporate community–related issues and to link economic responsibilities with the social needs of the community. CI is more than philanthropic for some initiatives as it goes to the very heart of some organizations. One such organization is a **social enterprise**, a model business operation where some or all profits are deliberately used to further social aims. Social enterprises and social entrepreneurs will be described in Chapter 16.

In 2015 The Conference Board of Board conducted the first national survey of corporate community investment activity and produced a report on its findings, *Canadian Corporate Community Investment: Emerging Trends and Impact Measurement.*[7] The survey found that the most common elements of CI programs were: donations to organizations, sponsorship or marketing activities, contribution of in-kind resources, employee gift-matching/donations programs, and employee volunteer programs. The most commonly selected investment areas were: community, social, environmental, education and health. The choice of investment was most influenced by a fit with corporate values. Other influences were the ability to engage employees with project partners, the anticipated positive impact on corporate reputation, the ability to effect meaningful change, and the connection between the program and the corporation's products and services.

Senior leadership engagement was found to be very important to the success of any CI program. Several factors motivated senior leadership to support a CI program. The most important factor was the alignment with overall corporate strategy. Other factors included the enhancement of the corporation's reputation, the ability to engage employees, and a personal association with a program. Some corporations have CI professionals, that is, an employee informed on aspects of community investment. These professionals will be increasing demand and require various skills, including advocacy and public policy, social finance and impact investing, social innovation, product design, research, and supplier engagement and collaboration. Knowledge of the metrics in measuring and reporting community investment will also be necessary skills.[8]

CSR and Indigenous Peoples

Community investment is illustrated by corporations in resource industries that operate on or near Indigenous communities. These corporations are involved in wide-ranging initiatives relating to employment and skills training, education, engagement, youth development, economic participation and development, affordable housing, environmental projects, health and wellness, and cultural activities. The initiatives vary by corporation, as they focus on that which is most relevant to their operations. Committees or other engagement approaches are used to consult and engage the communities. Examples of the programs of several corporations are described in Everyday Ethics 8.7.

 EVERYDAY ETHICS 8.7

Examples of Corporate Indigenous Community Investment

Canadian corporations have undertaken several initiatives to invest in Indigenous communities. The following are some examples but they do not cover all the initiatives undertaken by the particular corporation.

AltaGas Ltd.—It has been a policy of AltaGas, an oil and gas producer, to build long-term collaborative relationships with Indigenous communities according to a set of guiding principles. Key action areas include a cultural awareness program, a First Nations Development Fund, and formal negotiated agreements covering such matters as training, education, and environmental protection.

Canfor Corporation—This integrated forest products company is partnering with Indigenous Peoples to provide economic opportunities through joint ventures, cooperative agreements, and collaborative initiatives. It has taken a proactive approach to community engagement through public advisory groups and extensive communication efforts.

HudBay Minerals Inc.—HudBay, a Canadian mining corporation, recognizes the lack of employment opportunities for Indigenous Peoples in Northern Manitoba. It stimulates business start-ups and small businesses near its operations that will develop job skills within Indigenous communities. As a result of this and other programs, 15 percent of its Manitoba employees are Indigenous.

Hydro-Québec—The company publishes a 12-page booklet outlining its relationships with Indigenous Peoples. Topics covered include the numerous partnerships and agreements developed over 40 years; initiatives to minimize the impacts of its projects and facilities on the environment and the communities concerned; and the positive benefits achieved for the company and Indigenous communities.

Pembina Pipeline Corporation—Pembina Pipeline recognizes that Indigenous Peoples have special and unique interests in the land on which it operates. Its Aboriginal Relations team is focused on four key undertakings: Aboriginal awareness training for employees and contractors, increasing Aboriginal employment, community relations and support for Aboriginal communities, and ensuring open and honest consultation.

Support for business ventures is often involved, for example assistance in establishing Indigenous enterprises that become suppliers to the resource corporation. Some Indigenous communities across Canada are establishing trusts to hold and manage the funds obtained from business activities and claims settlements (land claims, treaty land entitlement, hydro claims). Income from those funds helps Indigenous communities meet their immediate needs, but communities would align their short term needs with long term development aspirations and objectives using their values as a guide to decision making.[9]

Corporations should take a mutual benefit approach in their relationships with Indigenous communities and recognize the inherent rights of communities to determine their own futures. Words without appropriate actions may lead corporations to be accused of **redwashing**. This is "a term to describe the deception of the general public by government and industry in trying to cover up their theft of indigenous peoples lands, natural resources and cultural riches by pretending that they are acting in the best interests of the native peoples." Redwashing "occurs when time and money are spent on public relations gimmicks that make a pretence of acting ethically towards the indigenous nations of the Indigenous Nations of North America, when in fact the opposite is done."[10] Corporations present themselves as being benevolent, good neighbours through corporate giving and sponsorship in an attempt to cover up corporate initiatives that may have an adverse impact on the community.

Possible Reduced Commitment to Community Investment/CSR Initiatives

Despite all the evidence of community investment/CSR initiatives, there is concern that they will receive less attention during an economic downturn. There is a possibility that community investment and CSR generally might be less of a priority with corporations as turbulent economic conditions refocus attention to the bottom line. The advocates of sustainability or CSR fear that it may not receive as much attention by management and boards of directors, and that it would not be viewed seriously. Corporations may not mention CSR in their annual strategy statements to the financial market, or fail to produce comprehensive CSR or sustainability reports. Evidence to the contrary comes from consultants who claim that CSR has been temporarily derailed before and re-emerged in a revised form. It is pointed out that commitment to CSR in times of economic downturn is even more important for corporations as it differentiates them from competitors. Furthermore, CSR has moved into the mainstream because of climate change, financial scandals, and alleged human rights and environmental abuses. Corporations will continue commitment to CSR as they want to avoid government regulation being demanded by NGOs, while others argue that regulation is necessary—a voluntary approach does not work. Even with the doubts, the approaches discussed in this chapter illustrate an increasing belief that business should be investing in CSR or sustainability with the goal of a social return, and that business-type practices will be used in its implementation.

On a positive note, a multitude of awards and recognitions are designated for effective CSR or corporate sustainability programs. Examples of such awards are the *Corporate Knights* Best 50 Corporate Citizens in Canada, the *Maclean's* Top 50 Socially Responsible Corporations in Canada, and the Global 100 Most Sustainable Corporations in the World. Such awards are displayed on the corporation's website and in CSR or sustainability reports, and are mentioned in this book. Imagine Canada recognizes the best CSR programs with its Caring Company Program, described in Responsibility for Ethics 8.3.

 RESPONSIBILITY FOR ETHICS 8.3

Imagine Canada's Caring Company Program

Imagine Canada describes a Caring Company as one that is a good corporate citizen, drives social innovation, and invests money, ideas, and time in communities. It considers the Caring Company Program to be Canada's leading corporate citizenship initiative, and about 90 businesses are members. Membership assures stakeholders that the company is committed to investing in the community. Commitments necessary for membership include

- donating 1 percent of pre-tax profits to the community;
- championing and sustaining at least one community investment project; and
- publicly reporting their community investment activities.

Large or small corporations can become members once they agree to the principles of corporate citizenship and the benchmarks for community investment established by Imagine Canada.

In this chapter's last section, it is important to identify the role of CSR in small- and medium-sized businesses as they too contribute to business and society.

LO 8.6 Small Business and CSR

Many small business enterprises are involved with CSR but it has a lower profile. A survey of 500 small Canadian businesses found that over 90 percent felt it was their duty to give back to the community. About 75 percent found that CSR attracted like-minded employees, that customers expected CSR initiatives, and that the environment should be considered in decision making. Over 85 percent believed that the ability to contribute to the community is one of the rewards of business ownership.[11] Everyday Ethics 8.1, 8.4, and 8.5 include examples of CSR initiatives in small- and medium-sized businesses.

There are challenges to implementing CSR in small businesses. Entrepreneurs do not have time to devote to it as they are confronting the daily demands of their business. The expenses associated with obtaining the resources necessary, including consultants and employee time, may be beyond the means of a small business.[12] There is likely a lack of knowledge of CSR planning and monitoring methodologies, as resources relevant to small businesses are not readily available.[13]

The understanding of CSR that does exist is strongly influenced by the personal values of the entrepreneur. Small businesses must confront most of the social and ethical issues experienced by large business. But some issues are associated more with small business: entrepreneurs are more likely to participate in the underground economy, misleading advertising and financial reporting, improper gift giving and receiving, and tax evasion. In addition, human resource abuses are more common as entrepreneurs ignore or are unaware of workplace regulations. Entrepreneurs are sometimes accused of nepotism in the hiring and promotion of family members instead of employees.[14] Research has found differences between CSR practice in large versus small businesses; the findings are summarized in Table 8.4.[15]

TABLE 8.4	Differences in CSR in Large Corporations versus Small Businesses
Large Corporations	**Small Businesses**
• Accountable to a large number of stakeholders	• Accountable to fewer stakeholders
• Responsible to society at large	• Responsible to local communities
• Concerned with brand image and reputation	• Concerned about retaining business
• Shareholder pressure; ethical investing	• Pressure from lenders
• Based on corporate values	• Based on owner values
• Formal planning for CSR	• Unlikely to be formal planning
• Emphasis on standards and indices	• Emphasis on intuition and ad hoc processes
• Involvement of CSR professionals	• No dedicated personnel
• Prominent campaign; for example, cause-related marketing	• Small scale activities; for example, sponsoring local sports teams
• Awareness through CSR reporting, publicity	• Often unrecognized as CSR activities

The Network for Business Sustainability has developed a guide for small business involvement with local communities. A community comprises individuals or groups by issues, interactions, geography, or a sense of identity, and includes residents, community associations, sports leagues, online networks, parent–teacher associations, environmental activists, and religious groups. Examples of typical community concerns could be the hiring or laying off of local people, problems created such as pollution, and the construction of facilities. Working with community groups improves management decision making, creates legitimacy or social licence, and makes recruitment easier.[16] Table 8.5 outlines the three strategies for working with communities. Small business owners must carefully identify the relevant community groups, prioritize them, and then pick the best engagement strategy.

TABLE 8.5	Three Strategies for Working with Communities		
	Investment	**Involvement**	**Integration**
Company perspective	"Giving Back"	"Building Bridges"	"Changing Society"
Description	The company provides information or resources to the community	The company uses community input to shape its actions	The company and the community jointly manage projects

	Investment	Involvement	Integration
Communication	One-way	Two-way	Two-way
Number of partners	Many	Many	Few
Interaction	Occasional	Repeated	Frequent
Information/ knowledge	Goes from company to community	Goes from community to company	Is jointly generated
Control over process	Company	Company	Company and community
Tools and techniques	Advertisements; information kiosks; press releases; newsletters; door-to-door visits; information sessions; charitable donations; employee volunteering	Surveys; studies; interviews; consultative committees; interactive websites; public hearings; neutral forums	Strategic local or regional partnerships; sector discussion groups; joint brainstorming; conflict resolution; work groups

Source: Network for Business Sustainability, *Working with Community Groups: A Guide for Small Business*, November 5, 2012. Available at http://nbs.net/wp-content/uploads/SME-Resource-Community-Engagement.pdf. Used with the permission of Network for Business Sustainability.

Want to learn more about CSR and small business?

Although this guide is based on 200 studies of small business involvement in communities, it can be used by larger corporations at a local level, for example when building a plant in a community. Other assistance with CSR is available for entrepreneurs from industry associations, for example accessing the Canadian Federation of Independent Business, completing self-assessment checklists available on the Internet, cooperating with local non-profit organizations, and referring to the limited literature.[17]

Another Network for Business Sustainability study identified five strategies by which small- and medium-sized businesses could develop expertise in sustainability:

- Listen to stakeholders and be open to their suggestions and opinions.
- Start with small, easy, and inexpensive initiatives and learn from experience.
- Question operational methods through a continuous improvement approach.
- Call on external resources such as government agencies, organizations that provide consultation and coaching, and existing CSR standards and measures.
- Designate someone, usually the organization's senior management, responsible for CSR.

The study pointed out that there is not one set approach or strategy to follow; instead, small- and medium-sized businesses should explore and experiment to find something that fits their situation.[18]

Although not receiving the attention for their CSR practices that large corporations do, most small businesses and their owners do contribute to local communities. Small business entrepreneurs make donations to local charities, sponsor area sports teams and cultural activities, and volunteer in community organizations. An example of a small business practising CSR as a basis for operating is given in Everyday Ethics 8.8.

 EVERYDAY ETHICS 8.8

Citigrow Inc. and Urban Food

David Gingera, founder and president of Citigrow Inc., wanted to create a socially responsible business that would solve food problems through growing food in cities. He started Citigrow in Winnipeg in 2014 and connects property owners, gardeners, and food buyers, especially restaurants. The result is urban farms or urban agriculture, the process of growing food within the cities where it will be consumed. The approach produces fresh vegetables locally.

Property owners agree to utilize their available space to grow vegetables on small lots or "micro-farms." Citigrow coordinates the production, markets the vegetables, and pays the property owner a royalty. Customers can purchase the vegetables by a produce box system or at retailers and enjoy them at local restaurants. Gingera believes urban agriculture is the best way to grow better food, at lower costs and in a way that is better for the environment.

He and Citigrow have received several awards including Top 30 Under 30: Corporate Leaders in Sustainability and Canadian Social Responsibility Business of the Year.

Chapter 8 has provided an overview to corporate social responsibility as practised in Canada. Chapter 9 describes how CSR, sustainability, and community investment are measured, reported, and communicated to the corporation's stakeholders.

Summary

- A spectrum of corporate social responsibility and corporate sustainability approaches are described: corporate giving or donations, voluntarism, sponsorship, and community investment. Most corporations practise one or more of these approaches as they seek the most effective way to practise CSR. It is important for corporations to manage and plan their CSR efforts. (LO 8.1)

- There are arguments for and against corporate donations; in particular, the issue of whether such activity is in the best interests of the corporation and its shareholders has not been resolved. Once the corporation decides to become involved in corporate giving, another challenge emerges—how to manage the process. A decision-making process involving committees or foundations should be established if the corporation wants to be consistent and perceived to be treating all requests fairly. Although something positive can be gained from donations, there is the possibility of negative outcomes when requests are rejected. Rejections must be handled as professionally as successful requests. Philanthropic decision making is even more challenging given the increasing demands for corporate support and the limited amount of funds available. In addition, there is a trend toward tying giving to economic gains, an issue that re-emerges throughout the chapter. (LO 8.2)

- Voluntarism is receiving more attention as an approach to corporate philanthropy. Employees and retirees of corporations make contributions to charitable organizations, often with the encouragement of managers. Many corporations have well-defined policies relating to employee volunteer activities to avoid conflicts with work obligations or to protect the reputation of the corporation. Although voluntarism is usually encouraged, it is not without challenges for management. (LO 8.3)

- Sponsorship has grown as a form of philanthropy. Discussion continues as to whether such an activity is in support of a charity or an aspect of marketing. Corporations are pressured for greater return on donation funds, and tying support to sponsorship of projects or events appears to result. The discussion of sponsorship is a logical lead-in to the examination of the trend toward corporations seeking to satisfy economic as well as social objectives with corporate philanthropic initiatives. Corporate management is demanding more efficiency and accountability from non-profit charities, and receivers of support from corporations in "sin industries" are being challenged for accepting it. (LO 8.4)

- Some corporations prefer to implement CSR using the community investment concept. This concept is a comprehensive approach to CSR in the corporation's local, national, or international areas of operation. A good example is the efforts of resource industry corporations involved with social investments in Indigenous communities. Society should realize that corporations may reduce their CSR efforts. (LO 8.5)

- Small businesses are involved in CSR but receive less recognition than large corporations. CSR decisions are driven by the entrepreneur and focus on local community social issues. (LO 8.6)

Key Terms

Greenwashing

Corporate philanthropy

Charitable foundation

Cause-related marketing

Strategic giving

Social venture philanthropy

Corporate voluntarism

Corporate sponsorship

Community investment

Social enterprise

Redwashing

Critical Thinking and Discussion Questions

1. What is the strongest argument for business participating in corporate giving? What is the strongest argument for business not participating in corporate giving?

2. Why should corporations develop formal plans for implementing CSR?

3. How is the position that all corporate profits belong to the shareholders countered?

4. List guidelines that corporations might follow in developing and implementing a corporate giving program.

5. Why do some argue that corporate giving is now nothing more than corporate marketing or advertising?

6. Should business be involved in social venture philanthropy? Is business better than government at addressing social ills?

7. Should a charity accept donations from tobacco, alcohol, or beer companies?

8. What are the drawbacks to corporate voluntarism?

9. What criteria should be used in selecting a charity for a corporate voluntary program?

10. What are the positive features of sponsorship programs? What are the drawbacks?

11. Should corporations be thinking of CSR as an investment?

12. What are the implications if corporations reduce their support of CSR?

13. Why should small businesses become involved with CSR?

Cases

8.1 RESPONSIBLE ALCOHOL CONSUMPTION

Twelve producers of beer, wine and spirits have formed an industry association, Producers' Commitments, dedicated to the reduction of harmful drinking. The five key areas to be addressed are: reducing underage drinking; strengthening and expanding marketing codes of practice; providing consumer information and responsible product innovation; reducing drinking and driving; and enlisting the support of retailers to reduce harmful drinking. They also support the World Health Organization's (WHO) *Global Strategy to Reduce Harmful Use of Alcohol*. Two members of the association are Diageo plc and Molson Coors.

Diageo is the producer of beer and spirits including such brands as Smirnoff, Johnnie Walker, Captain Morgan, Barleys, Tanqueray, and Guinness. There are six main priorities to Diageo's Sustainability & Responsibility Strategy with the first one being "Alcohol in society." The company states that it wants to contribute to the World Health Organization's goal of reducing alcohol-related harm. It plans to do this by communicating about alcohol responsibly and tackling misuse through effective programs and policies. It will work with industry to promote responsible marketing, to provide appropriate consumer information, and to implement programs to address alcohol misuse.

Molson Coors Brewing Company states that one measure of success is to have their products consumed in the right way. Their brands include Carling, Coors, Black Horse, Black Ice, Becks, and Corona. The company is concerned about excessive consumption and in particular underage drinking. They have several programs targeting alcohol abuse including: Responsible Entertaining and Serving; Binge Drinking; Drinking and Driving; Underage Drinking; Drinking and Risky Activities; Drinking and Health; Drinking and Pregnancy; and Responsible Consumption.

Questions

1. Are beer, wine, and spirits producers good corporate citizens?

2. Is excessive consumption of alcohol a serious societal problem? Who are the stakeholders and what are the issues involved?

3. Are the CSR initiatives of Diageo and Molson Coors motivated only by economic self-interest?

4. What else the industry do about this social issue?

8.2 HAVING TO GIVE AT THE OFFICE

Roxanne Kampf was an accounts payable clerk for a large corporation. She enjoyed the job and was generally happy with her workplace. Her employer had an extensive corporate giving program and supported employee voluntarism, in which she participated. For example, Roxanne volunteered to participate in the cleanup of a park near the office. It was an enjoyable activity and involved social interaction with many colleagues. Overall, she was pleased to be working for a corporation that was socially responsible.

Roxanne had reservations about the corporate giving program—in particular, about the annual United Way campaign. Firstly, she did not agree with the purposes of some of the charities covered by United Way. Secondly, she preferred to contribute directly to the charities she supported and whose aims she endorsed. Lastly, she felt pressure from supervisors and peers to contribute. This last reservation caused Roxanne some anxiety.

She had been reading in the newspaper about workplace charity drives. A poll of readers of *The Globe and Mail* found that 51 percent liked to support charity drives, 36 percent preferred to make their donations privately, and 13 percent felt pressured to contribute. Obviously Roxanne was not alone in her concern.

Roxanne felt very uneasy about her direct supervisor heading up the campaign in her department. Although the actual canvassing was done by peers, she still felt pressure and anxiety. She was not sure how to say no or what excuse to make. She wondered if anyone would believe a statement that she had already used up her "charitable budget." Also, she was not sure how others would feel when she stated that she should be able to give to the charities she preferred and in private. Even more troublesome was her concern about how saying no would impact her career.

The campaign made her very uncomfortable and she was even feeling guilty. Fun campaign activities were organized in the office and it was obvious to all when she did not attend. Also, the office had a goal to raise $5,000 and she was not contributing as expected of team members. Roxanne faced a dilemma and did not know what to do.

Questions

1. What are the pros and cons of workplace charity drives? What are the issues involved?

2. Does Roxanne have an ethical dilemma? State what it is.

3. What ethical principles (from Chapter 5) might she use to analyze the dilemma?

4. What should Roxanne do?

Business is accountable for its social performance to society.
Used with the permission of Corporate Knights and Kaley McKean (artist).

CHAPTER 9

Measuring, Reporting, and Communicating CSR

LEARNING OUTCOMES

After studying this chapter, you will be able to:

LO 9.1 Understand the background to measuring and reporting CSR performance.

LO 9.2 Define corporate reputation and understand its relationship to corporate social responsibility.

LO 9.3 Identify the stakeholders who influence CSR reporting.

LO 9.4 Describe the relationship between CSR and corporate profitability.

LO 9.5 Enumerate and discuss the types of criteria used in social auditing.

LO 9.6 Recognize the criteria used to evaluate Canadian CSR reporting.

LO 9.7 Outline how CSR and sustainability results are communicated to stakeholders.

LO 9.8 Explain the role of business schools in CSR reporting.

LO 9.9 Discuss the future of CSR and CSR reporting.

What would you do if...?

Clare O'Neill was confused. She had been introduced to the ethics of business and corporate social responsibility (CSR) in a university business course. She had become very interested in business and in particular how corporations were responding to social and environmental issues. Her instructor had used various corporate websites and had reviewed several corporate responsibility or sustainability reports in class, and also had recommended that students who were interested in the topic should subscribe to *Corporate Knights*—described as "the magazine for clean capitalism."

Clare's confusion began when she received the 2019 results for "The Best 50 Corporate Citizens in Canada."[1] The list contained some prominent corporations that she recognized as socially and environmentally responsible, such as Mountain Equipment Co-op, Vancouver City Savings Credit Union, and The Co-operators. But also on the list were several industries that Clare did not feel were the most responsible, and she did not understand why they were represented. Popular media coverage was not always positive, and a series of documentaries she viewed at the college had been particularly critical.

The industries and corporations that Clare found doubtful included the following:

- *Petroleum*—Enbridge Inc. and Suncor Energy Inc. Clare viewed the petroleum industry as being irresponsible toward the environment, especially the operations in the Alberta oil sands. Recent reports had confirmed a significant increase in pollution in Alberta due to the oil sands developments.
- *Mining*—Iamgold Corp. and Teck Resources Ltd. Claire believed many mine properties were polluters and harmed the environment and local communities, especially when operating in developing countries.
- *Forestry*—Canfor Pulp Products Inc. and Cascades Inc. In Clare's view, forestry corporations were not doing enough reforestation nor making sufficient efforts to prevent harm to the environment. They also had closed many plants and laid off thousands of workers, many of whom had inadequate pensions.

Clare looked up the CSR reports for the corporations mentioned, and found that indeed they were involved with many significant socially responsible programs. She still viewed the industries as problematic in their responsibility to society. Also, she wondered if the corporations were reporting only good news and overlooking less favourable situations.

Clare wondered if she should cancel her subscription to the magazine. She also thought about writing a letter to the editor. She considered the possibility that she had misunderstood the CSR and corporate citizenship concepts. She was disappointed and confused.

What is your advice to Clare?

This chapter reviews how CSR and sustainability performance is measured, reported, and communicated in Canada by:

- Establishing the existence of this reporting and examining why it is taking place.
- Evaluating the quality of the reporting in terms of the reliability of the information.
- Reviewing the verification or assurance mechanisms used to enhance the credibility of the reporting.
- Identifying the efforts made by corporations to communicate the reports to stakeholders.[2]

Two other sections examine related topics: CSR education in business courses, and the future of corporate social responsibility and CSR reporting.

The terms CSR and sustainability are used interchangeably in this chapter.

LO 9.1   Auditing CSR

The first step in the measurement of CSR or sustainability performance involves some type of auditing. **Social auditing** is a systematic assessment that identifies, measures, evaluates, reports, and monitors the effects an enterprise has on society that are not covered in the traditional financial reports. The purpose of social auditing is to provide information to management and to various stakeholders about the impact of the enterprise on society, and to provide a basis of accountability for the social consequences of corporate activities. Such audits can be used to assess existing performance, to evaluate the performance of managers in relation to social objectives, to provide an information base for planning, and to serve as a measure for assessing future performance.

There are many social auditing approaches. The main ones are:

- *Inventory*—a listing of social activities without any evaluation.

- *Program management*—a statement describing particular programs or initiatives, including an indication of the resources committed.

- *Process*—a more elaborate approach incorporating the inventory and program management approaches. It includes an assessment of how each social program came into being, a statement of each program's objectives and the rationales behind each activity, and a description of what has been accomplished.

- *Cost or outlay*—a social–economic operating statement that tabulates the expenditures an enterprise makes on social objectives less the negative costs for social objectives not addressed. The approach is to measure the total social impact, positive and negative.

- *Social responsibility accounting*—a system of accounting that tabulates social costs and benefits with the objective of the best social return for the social investment made.

- *Social indicators*—an audit of the community is conducted using social indicators to provide data on the most pressing needs. Corporate social performances are compared or related to community or social indicators.

Corporations have moved beyond the social auditing approaches listed above. The following is a representation of the trend to the more sophisticated social auditing necessary for sustainability reporting:

- *Social objective setting*—In addition to economic objectives, corporations are establishing social and environmental objectives and reporting on their accomplishments in corporate annual reports.

- *Triple bottom line reporting*—Corporations prepare and publicize reports outlining economic, social, and environmental criteria and the extent to which they have been satisfied. Examples of such bottom lines are economic, ethical, and environmental, and people, planet, and prosperity.

- *Social reports*—Quite often the objectives and triple bottom line criteria are presented in comprehensive social reports prepared by the corporations themselves.

- *Sustainable guidelines*—Comprehensive sets of economic, social, and environmental criteria and performance indicators are being developed by organizations independent of corporations such as business research institutes, consultants, and non-governmental organizations (NGOs). These criteria and indicators are also referred to as guidelines or benchmarks and are being used in the preparation of social reports.

- *Externally verified social reports*—The corporations are using outside, independent organizations not only to develop the guidelines, but also to verify the corporation's performance relating to the guidelines. This independent verification is a major turning point in social reporting, or sustainability reporting. Although this practice is not widespread, it is gaining acceptance.

- *Consultation with stakeholders*—Some corporations are consulting stakeholders on the preparation of CSR or sustainability reports. Such consultation obtains the views of relevant stakeholders and is another approach to evaluating the corporation's CSR program.

The results of this auditing process become the basis for social reporting. **Corporate social responsibility (CSR) reporting** is a management function that documents the corporation's economic, ethical/social, and environmental responsibilities and initiatives, and communicates this information to relevant stakeholders. It is also known as *corporate sustainability reporting*.

Trends in Measuring Social Responsibility

Managers and businesspersons must now be familiar with the practices of measuring social responsibility and its implications. Traditionally they worried about financial audits, but now many corporations are performing audits or developing reporting mechanisms that measure how well the corporation is achieving its social responsibilities as well as its economic responsibilities. The formats and organization of these reports differ among corporations, with some being innovative and creative.

The approach to social responsibility measurement is shifting as trends emerge in Canada and elsewhere. Mandatory reporting requirements may be imposed by stock exchanges or governments; an example is the disclosure of greenhouse gas (GHG) emissions. Larger corporations tend to disclose more as they are subject to greater stakeholder scrutiny. Many corporations are opting for external assurance or confirmation of the information in their reports, a practice more common among larger corporations. Increasing numbers of corporations are reporting on their climate-related impacts and gender diversity is also receiving more attention. The measurement of social responsibility is constantly changing and Canadian managers must keep up with developments in the area.[3]

Three reasons why reporting is becoming increasingly necessary are to help maintain the corporation's reputation, to meet the demands of stakeholders, and to sustain corporate profitability.

LO 9.2   Corporate Reputation and CSR

Corporate reputation is "a perceptual representation of a corporation's past actions and future prospects that describes the corporation's overall appeal to all of its key constituents [stakeholders] when compared with other leading rivals."[4] It is often associated with corporate image, especially as promoted through public relations. The problem is that a corporate image has a temporary effect and is not an enduring solution to the relationship between business and society. Today corporate reputation is related more to the "character" of the corporation and involves corporate credibility, trust, and responsibility.

A distinction should be made between CSR and corporate reputation. CSR involves the way in which a corporation interacts with its stakeholders (as discussed in Chapters 4 and 8), whereas corporate reputation focuses on the perceptions that stakeholders have about the corporation as a result of the interactions. Thus, stakeholders' impressions are most often formed by a corporation's CSR performance. The drivers of corporate reputation include customer service, ethical conduct, community involvement, employee relations, quality of products and services, innovativeness, and environmental stewardship.[5]

The Conference Board of Canada report found that the three greatest reputational risks were product and service quality and safety; environmental impact; and mishandling of an incident or crisis. Canadian corporations had a greater interest in reputation because of the growing importance of intangible assets (for example, brand or intellectual property), the increasing complexity of supply chains, the growth and influence of social media, and higher stakeholder expectations. Corporations are managing reputation by preparing for crises, engaging stakeholders, and managing issues. Employees played a key role in reputation management and corporate reputation was influenced by the reputation of the industry, competitors, and suppliers.[6]

A connection exists not only between corporate reputation and stakeholders but also to issues management and strategy.[7] Stakeholders determine the issues that affect reputation, and managers must address stakeholders and the issues that concern them. Because reputation is good for business, it is the responsibility of all managers, starting with the chief executive officer (CEO). A corporate reputation builds trust with stakeholders, might enable the corporation to command higher prices, attracts qualified people, and minimizes the risk of damage from a crisis. Corporate reputation rather than image has become a key to a successful corporate strategy.

Researchers have found a relationship between corporate reputation and social responsibility, particularly when the corporation experiences a crisis or event that damages its image or reputation. A study by Minor and Morgan found that corporations with higher CSR ratings are more successful at overcoming setbacks.[8] Another study found that CSR created a layer of protection, and corporations known for social responsibility experienced less decline in stock prices when a crisis occurred.[9] Other researchers examined the influence that socially responsible images or reputations have on consumers. A commitment to ethics statements such as a values statement or code of ethics creates a reputation of responsibility that legitimizes a corporation in the eyes of consumers. They also found that consumers expect financially successful corporations to contribute to society. A corporation's reputation decreases consumer perception of purchase risk and increases consumer loyalty.[10]

Corporate reputation is an asset, though an intangible one, and thus is difficult to measure. In general terms, reputation is measured by being able to do the right thing, and through CSR reporting, corporations hope to convince stakeholders that they are indeed behaving this way. Everyday Ethics 9.1 describes the experience of one corporation whose reputation was threatened by a crisis and how their reputation was restored.

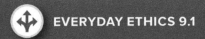

EVERYDAY ETHICS 9.1

Restoring the Reputation of Maple Leaf Foods

In the summer of 2008, Canada experienced a serious outbreak of listeriosis, which resulted in 57 persons becoming seriously ill and caused the deaths of 22 individuals. Listeriosis is one of about 250 food-borne illnesses that include salmonella, E. coli, and the Norwalk virus. It results from consuming food contaminated with a bacterium called *Listeria monocytogenes* and any form of disease or invasive infection that results is given the name *listeriosis*. The outbreak was traced to a Maple Leaf Foods plant.

There were several recalls of products and on August 23, 2008, Maple Leaf Foods decided that Michael McCain, the CEO, should make a national statement about the crisis. He apologized, admitted the problem, and took full responsibility for the crisis. This statement was considered to be the appropriate response, but sales of the company's products were impacted.

Over the next decade, McCain undertook a transformation of the company. Its purpose and vision were expressed as "To Be the Most Sustainable Protein Company on Earth." The company's sustainability strategy was based on "Better Food. Better Care. Better Communities. Better Planet." In May 2018 the company announced that its entire line of processed meats would be all-natural. As a result of its reaction to the crisis, the company's reputation was restored and Maple Leaf Foods is a member of Canada's Most Admired Corporate Cultures™ Winners Hall of Fame.

LO 9.3 Stakeholders Expect CSR Accountability

Several stakeholders are expecting—or even demanding—corporations to be accountable for their economic, social, and environmental responsibilities. The following is a list of the most influential stakeholders.

- *Shareholders and financial institutions*—Institutional investors and individual shareholders interested in ethical or social investing require additional information on CSR. Financial indexes have been formulated to guide investors, for example the Jantzi Social Index[11] in Canada and the Dow Jones Sustainability Index[12] in the United States. Responsibility for Ethics 9.1 describes the Jantzi Social Index.

RESPONSIBILITY FOR ETHICS 9.1

The Jantzi Social Index

The Jantzi Social Index (JSI) is a socially screened, common stock index modelled on the S&P/TSX 60 of 50 corporations that have passed a set of broadly based environmental, social, and governance rating criteria. Criteria have been developed to evaluate issue areas such as Indigenous relations, community involvement, corporate governance, employee and customer relations, environment, and human rights. Some indicators may exclude corporations with significant involvement in the production of nuclear power; the manufacture of tobacco products; and weapons-related contracting.

The index measures how a market for the selected corporations has changed over time. A benchmark is also established against which the success of the process is measured. Thus, the JSI provides a process against which institutional investors—for example, pension and mutual funds—can measure the performance of their socially screened stock portfolios. Also, the Jantzi–Sustainalytics Canadian Social Investment Database provides a comprehensive analysis of approximately 300 companies and income trusts, including all constituents of the S&P/TSX Composite Index.

- *Employees*—Informing employees of the corporation's CSR initiatives results in intangible benefits such as increasing employee satisfaction and reducing turnover. In a recent survey, about 80 percent of employees agreed with the statement that the more socially responsible their employer was the more motivated and loyal the employees became.[13]

- *Consumers*—Consumers are concerned about aspects of the goods and services they purchase including, for example, such things as the conditions under which they were produced, genetic modifications, environmental harm, and treatment of employees.

- *Society at large*—Local communities are interested in social and environmental issues confronting them. Corporate reporting is now addressing this by presenting materials by facility and community. Even students are seeking more information on corporate reporting, either for personal use or for use in classroom discussions or assignments.

- *Service professionals*—The professional accounting associations are recommending more elaborate CSR and sustainability reporting. An example is the Chartered Professional Accountants of Canada's (CPA Canada) efforts encouraging corporations to enhance sustainability along with financial reporting. Other professions also encourage increased disclosure.

- *Non-governmental organizations*—NGOs are constantly seeking information on corporations. In many cases, it is questionable how they use the information. For this reason, CSR reporting should be scrutinized and verified prior to release. This stakeholder will be discussed more in Chapter 13.

- *Charities*—CSR reporting informs the public of the corporation's philanthropic efforts. In addition, many social reports identify the corporation's giving policies, including areas of interest, and provide application information.

- *Media*—Journalists are constantly seeking story ideas or information to complete a story. The availability of CSR reports, especially online, is one quick source for them.

- *Government*—Numerous government acts and regulations require disclosure. On the other hand, governments are also interested in corporate self-disclosure because it avoids the need for legislation. Chapter 10 examines the association between ethics and government's role in society and its involvement with business.

Although this is not a complete list, it does indicate that many stakeholders are demanding or expecting increasing amounts of CSR or sustainability disclosure—one good reason why corporations should be serious about considering this type of disclosure, and the extent of transparency involved. Corporate transparency is important as it indicates to stakeholders how the data was obtained.

According to a paper from Globescan and SC Johnson, transparency is more than merely disclosing, as it involves two-way communication; that is, it not only involves telling stakeholders what the corporation is doing, but also seeking feedback and responding to it. It was found that transparency was one of the most important ways to build trust with and among stakeholders and create more shared value that will benefit society. Stakeholder scrutiny through increased transparency drives corporations to become more accountable. But it often requires a change in corporate culture, where secrecy is the norm.[14]

Social responsibility reporting will also increase stakeholders' understanding of the need for corporations to make profits.

LO 9.4 CSR and Profitability

It is generally accepted that the blind pursuit of maximum profits would be socially irresponsible. It is also believed that most corporations have multiple objectives, some of which are social in nature. If these statements are accurate, it is interesting to speculate about the relationship between the extent of socially responsible actions of a corporation and its level of profitability.

The relationship between profitability and CSR has been extensively studied, with mixed conclusions that can be summarized as follows:

- Expenditures on social responsibility initiatives do not contribute to profits.

- Expenditures on social responsibility initiatives do contribute to profits.

- Expenditures on social responsibility initiatives might contribute to profits.

A study by Laffer, Coors, and Winegarden found that CSR is not positively correlated with business profitability. Furthermore, the authors found some evidence that CSR activities lead to decreased profitability.[15] Another study found that up to some point, increased expenditures in social responsibility are associated with higher profits but further increases are associated with lower profit levels.[16]

An example of a study supporting the position that a positive relationship exists between CSR and profitability was a mega-analysis of 52 previous studies on the impact of CSR on profits by Orlitzky et al. Their findings confirmed that social responsibility and, to a lesser extent, environmental responsibility do have a measurable positive impact on profits. They concluded that their analysis established a greater degree of certainty with respect to the corporate social responsibility and corporate financial performance relationship than was assumed to exist by many business academics.[17]

On the other hand, a study by Margolis and Walsh expressed doubt about research methodologies used in examining the relationship. They examined the 30-year quest for an empirical relationship between a corporation's social initiatives and its financial performance—127 studies were analyzed, almost half of which pointed to a positive relationship between CSR and financial results. The other half reported a negative relationship, a non-significant relationship, or a mixed relationship. The authors argue that a definite link between CSR and profits may be more illusory than the research results suggest. Serious questions are raised about methodological difficulties, including problems with the sample used, concerns about reliability and validity of the measures used, and influence of moderating conditions.[18]

The research and debate on the relationship will continue, most likely without a definitive conclusion, for some time. However, the Network for Business Sustainability (NBS) has taken another view of the CSR and profitability relationship. It points out that 63 percent of the studies on CSR and profitability have found a positive relationship, 15 percent a negative one, and 22 percent a mixed or neutral one. NBS suggests calculating the return of investment of CSR by thinking in terms of creating value. Corporations have financial management systems and financial metrics or measures, but few metrics relating to CSR or sustainability. Initiatives can result in positive impacts, and the social and environmental benefits fall into one of three categories:

- *Firm processes*—The value created can be identified by readily available measures. The costs and savings of an energy conservation program can be measured, most likely with savings exceeding costs.

- *Firm outcomes*—The value created is less obvious and as a result may not be measured—but it should be. An example is provided by a conservation program that may improve employee satisfaction and increase productivity.

- *External outcomes*—The value created is in the more positive perceptions of external stakeholders, such as consumers who may view the corporation more favourably and increase their loyalty, thus increasing sales of the corporation's products.

Some of this value may have been overlooked in the past. NBS has identified three categories of metrics that business should use to capture this value. Financial metrics are the easiest to measure; for example, stock price or return on investment. Valuing CSR at this stage is relatively easy. The second metric is operational, which measures the direct bottom-line impacts of CSR activities and represents the direct costs and revenues associated with an activity. Lastly, strategic metrics are those that result in the corporation improving its strategic position. The metrics are less tangible but are value created from improved employee motivation, the creation of a culture of innovation, and greater brand loyalty.[19]

The economic performance, or profitability, is included in corporate social reporting as it is necessary if the corporation is also to be responsible for social and environmental contributions to society.

Now that reasons have been given for CSR reporting, the criteria used in evaluating such reports are discussed.

LO 9.5   Corporate Social Reporting Guidelines

The contents of corporate social reports reflect the guidelines used in social audits. Several guidelines provide illustrations of the criteria used to assess the ethics of business and identify socially responsible initiatives. Responsibility for Ethics 9.2 lists the most common guidelines used in corporate reporting.

 RESPONSIBILITY FOR ETHICS 9.2

Corporate Reporting Guidelines

There are several comprehensive guidelines; what follows are the most common:

- *Global Reporting Initiative (GRI) Standards*— The GRI Standards are the most widely used global standards for sustainability reporting. They feature a modular, interrelated structure, and represent the global best practice for reporting on a range of economic, environmental, and social impacts. Available at https://www.globalreporting.org/standards/.

- *The International Integrated Reporting Council (IIRC)*—A global coalition of regulators, investors, companies, standard setters, the accounting profession, and NGOs working to integrate financial and sustainability reporting. Available at http://integratedreporting.org/the-iirc-2/.

- *The Sustainability Accounting Standards Board (SASB)*—Has a mandate to create reporting standards for recognizing and disclosing material environmental, social, and governance impacts. Available at https://www .sasb.org/governance/.

- *OECD Guidelines for Multinational Enterprises*—Recommendations to multinational corporations operating in or from an adhering country. Available at http://mneguidelines.oecd.org/guidelines/.

- *United Nations Global Compact*—An initiative to bring together UN agencies, labour, and civil society to support universal environmental and social principles. Available at https://www.unglobalcompact.org/what-is-gc.

- *ISO 26000 CSR Standard*—The International Organization for Standardization (ISO) has developed a guidance standard for corporate social responsibility that relates to CSR reporting. The 14,000 standards apply to the environment. Available at https://www.iso.org/iso-26000-social-responsibility.html and https://www.iso.org /iso-14001-environmental-management.htm.

Other resources on CSR are available to Canadian businesspersons and managers. The Conference Board of Canada has a "National Corporate Social Responsibility Report: Managing Risks, Leveraging Opportunities" to help members better understand how to effectively manage and integrate CSR.[20] The Canadian Centre for Ethics and Corporate Policy operates EthicsCentre.ca, an independent ethics centre promoting an ethical orientation to Canadian organizations. It operates as a registered charity governed by volunteers and supported by corporations and individuals; it sponsors speaker events for members and publishes a newsletter, *Management Ethics*.[21] The Government of Canada has a very comprehensive guide, "Corporate Social Responsibility (CSR): An Implementation Guide for Canadian Business."[22]

Global Reporting Initiative (GRI)

As the **Global Reporting Initiative (GRI)** is the most comprehensive and widely used guideline, it is described in detail. GRI is an independent international undertaking to establish reporting criteria to help businesses and governments to understand and communicate their impact on sustainability issues. Its vision is to be "a thriving global community that lifts humanity and enhances the resources on which all life depends." Its mission is "to empower decisions that create social, environmental, and economic benefits for everyone."[23]

GRI's main activity is to develop Sustainability Reporting Standards that are made available as a free public good. They have been continuously developed over 20 years and represent global best practice for reporting on economic, environmental, and social issues. The use of the Sustainability Reporting Standards by corporations encourages accountability, enhances corporate reputation, and builds trust. Corporations are assisted in protecting the environment and improving society while at the same time thriving economically by improving governance and stakeholder relations.[24]

Table 9.1 summarizes the standards but only provides an overview to the extensive requirements of the standards. The standards are continuously reviewed and revisions are often announced and vary by industry.

TABLE 9.1	Global Reporting Initiative (GRI) Standards

Universal Standards

GRI 101 Foundation–Background on sustainability reporting and reporting principles.

GRI 102 General Disclosure–Report contextual information about the organization including its strategy, ethics and integrity, governance, stakeholder engagement, and reporting practice.

GRI 103 Management Approach–Management's approach to each topic and explanation to material topic and its boundary.

Economic Standards

GRI 200 Series—Topics covered in economic performance, market presence, indirect market impacts, procurement practices, anti-corruption, and anti- competition.

Environment Standards

GRI 300 Series—Environmental standards, materials, energy, water and effluents, biodiversity, emissions, effluents and waste, environmental compliance, supplier environmental assessment.

Social Standards

GRI 400 Series—Employment, labour/management relations, occupational health and safety, training and education, diversity and equal opportunity, non-discrimination, freedom of association and collective bargaining, child labour, forced or compulsory labour, security practices, rights of Indigenous Peoples, human rights assessment, local communities, public policy, customer health and safety, marketing and labelling, customer privacy, and socioeconomic compliance.

Source: GRI Standards Download Center, Global Reporting Initiative website at https://www.globalreporting.org/standards/gri -standards-download-center/. Used with permission.

GRI is an independent international organization that has pioneered sustainability reporting since 1997. GRI helps businesses and governments worldwide understand and communicate their impact on critical sustainability issues such as climate change, human rights, governance, and social well-being. This enables real action to create social, environmental, and economic benefits for everyone. The GRI Sustainability Reporting Standards are developed with true multi-stakeholder contributions and rooted in the public interest.

The GRI standards can be used for three purposes, among others: (1) benchmarking and assessing sustainability performance with respect to laws, norms, codes, performance standards, and voluntary initiatives; (2) understanding how the organization influences and is influenced by expectations about sustainable development; and (3) comparing performance within an organization and between different organizations over time.

Want to learn more about **the Global Reporting Initiative (GRI) with examples?**

LO 9.6   Evaluating Canadian CSR Reporting

CSR and sustainability reports cover the corporation's economic, social, and environmental responsibility initiatives as identified in the auditing process. At this time in Canada, CSR reporting is voluntary.

Dozens of codes and standards rank or evaluate corporations on every aspect of CSR. Corporations are confronted with lengthy forms and are required to meet various compliance practices. An issue that exists involves whether or not the standards and codes are valid measures of the numerous aspects of CSR. The information supplied by management may be manipulated to the corporation's advantage. Some corporations ignore all requests as there are too many, and too much work is needed to complete the surveys.[25]

Chatterji and Levine make several recommendations for improving the process:

- The codes or standards should be more transparent.

- The measures should be better explained and the source of weightings justified.

- Efforts should be made to reduce compliance costs by better designed forms and measures.

- The data used should be improved, with less reliance on information being supplied by management and more being sought from stakeholders.

- Financial performance measurement uses sophisticated methodology which should be incorporated into the measurement of social indicators.[26]

CSR reports are analyzed by several stakeholders. The analysis has identified best practices that corporations should consider when preparing a CSR report. These include:

- Identify the stakeholders to the target audience.

- Describe trends, risks, challenges, and opportunities facing the industry and the corporation. Give an outlook for the future.

- Identify issues, indicating which are priorities so the report has a focus.

- Identify major stakeholders and the approaches used to engage them. Report negative feedback as well as positive.

- Describe the reporting guidelines or standards used; for example, the Global Reporting Initiative. Consider having an external auditor verify the measures.

- Include objectives for the future and report on objective accomplishments from previous years.

- Use visuals such as photographs, illustrations, and graphs to effectively enhance appearance and readability.
- Identify the managers responsible for CSR in the corporation.[27]

Corporate social reports reflect the criteria used in social audits, which in turn determine the topics in corporate CSR reports. An example of a comprehensive report is in Everyday Ethics 9.2. The contents of reports will vary among corporations and in different years. For other examples of CSR reports, refer to "Want to learn more about the most socially responsible corporations in Canada?" in Chapter 8.

 EVERYDAY ETHICS 9.2

Corporate Responsibility Reporting at Scotiabank

Scotiabank's Corporate Social Responsibility Report is a comprehensive review and explanation of CSR at the bank. The 2017 Report included the following components:

- Comments for the President and Chief Executive Officer, and Chairman of the Board of Directors supporting CSR initiatives
- An explanation of the bank's CSR strategy
- Identification of economic, social, and environmental global mega-trends
- A description of the economic, social, and environmental value created for stakeholders
- Identification of Key Performance Indicators (KPIs) and the progress toward meeting major CSR priorities and measuring impacts
- An outline of stakeholder engagement and materiality
- A listing of priorities to create value for both society and the bank
- A description of CSR governance—that is, the organizational structure involved
- An outline of corporate governance and efforts to maintain trust
- A discussion of customers' access to finance and financial knowledge
- A discussion of employee diversity and inclusion
- An outline of community investment, in particular investing in young people
- Efforts in the area of the environment, including responsible finance and climate change
- A listing of the bank's GRI Standards Index 2017

Another aspect of CSR reporting is understanding how the report should be communicated to stakeholders.

Want to learn more about **evaluating sustainability reports?**

LO 9.7 Communicating CSR and Sustainability Results

The reports themselves are a form of communication that will enhance reputation, but the production of a report in itself is not sufficient. Efforts must be made to communicate it to stakeholders.

Within the corporation, various communications activities will inform employees: articles in newsletters, information on the employee intranet, agenda items at regular meetings, and corporate reputation committees. The integration of reporting with any performance measures is key so that employees are reminded constantly of CSR reporting.[28]

Communication with other stakeholders can be with the complete CSR report, or with brochures or mini-reports that mention only the highlights. These summaries can be inserted in customer invoices or billings, or other correspondence. Corporate websites should include electronic versions of the report that are easily accessed. Reporting is being segmented by audience to match messages with stakeholders, for example reports by facility site or community. Also, reporting should be communicated to those who are ready for it, or who are demanding it.

Managers should be aware that newspaper and magazine articles and television news programs are important sources of information for many stakeholders. Corporations must "manage the message," being honest in all communications and informing stakeholders how the corporation has promptly responded to issues or crises. Word of mouth should not be forgotten, as it is a form of communication among some stakeholders. Stakeholders who are influencers or opinion leaders should be identified and communications designed specially to reach them. Finally, communicating CSR and sustainability information is a continuous process, as is the practice of CSR.

A Network for Business Sustainability report found that four key attributes make sustainability information more useful for corporations and stakeholders:

- *Credibility*—information that is believable
- *Balance*—presenting an unbiased picture of organizational performance
- *Integration with strategy*—clearly tying sustainability goals with business goals
- *Comparability*—enabling comparisons to previous reports of the same firm and to information from the reports of other corporations[29]

The conclusion is that the preparation of CSR or sustainability reports requires design skills and must be carefully planned. In a corporation, one manager, department, or sustainability professional should be made responsible for the reporting process. Throughout this book, numerous Responsibility for Ethics and Everyday Ethics inserts have been obtained from corporate sustainability or social responsibility reports. An emphasis on CSR auditing, reporting, and communication will be part of the education received by future entrepreneurs and managers. Business programs are initiating changes to incorporate the ethics and responsibilities of business topics into their programs.

Want to learn more about **CSR in Canadian business**?

LO 9.8   Business Schools and Sustainability Reporting

Business schools are facing demands from society and the business community to better prepare their graduates to identify and address ethical implications in business. Ethics and social responsibility have received attention in business schools only recently, as the emphasis has been on functional areas—many of which have focused on financial rather than social responsibilities. Corporate corruption practices have increased awareness of ethical practice in business, and graduates who will be managers and businesspersons need a moral compass and sensitivity to acting consistently. In other words, graduates must be prepared to face the reality of moral dilemmas.

Corporations are increasingly using accountability audits to develop social responsibility reports for various stakeholders. Although very few business schools publish CSR reports on themselves, they are being held accountable for the integration of ethics of business and social responsibility topics into courses and programs.

The Association to Advance Collegiate Schools of Business (AACSB) is a global, nonprofit membership organization of educational institutions, businesses, and other entities devoted to the advancement of management education. AACSB assists business schools with the continuous improvement of their business programs and schools, including in the area of business ethics and social responsibility. Meeting AACSB's standards and other requirements is the business school is to receive accreditation.

AACSB does not require stand-alone courses in the ethics of business, assuming that the treatment of ethics is infused into other courses. Some controversy in the business and society academic community exists regarding this standard, with many arguing for stand-alone courses in addition to infusion. AACSB requirements relating to ethics and social responsibility of business schools include the identification of core values and how they are implemented.[30]

The sustainability of business schools and universities in general is now being ranked; two examples are *Corporate Knights* magazine and the *Times Higher University Education Social Impact Rankings*.

The performance of business schools is ranked according to their record in business sustainability. *Corporate Knights* magazine annually prepares the "Better World MBA Results." The schools are assessed on five indicators: institutes and centres, curriculum, faculty research, female diversity, and racial diversity.

Corporate Knights researched 141 MBA programs and 40 were ranked as leaders. Canadian schools included were Schulich School of Business, York University; Sobey School of Business, Saint Mary's University; College of Business and Economics, University of Guelph; Desautels Faculty of Management, McGill University; Gustavson School of Business, University of Victoria; Beedie School of Business, Simon Fraser University; Sauder School of Business, University of British Columbia; Haskayne School of Business, University of Calgary; John Molson School of Business, Concordia University; Rotman School of Management, University of Toronto; and Telfer School of Management, University of Ottawa.[31]

A new ranking of universities, *Times Higher University Education Social Impact Rankings,* was introduced in 2019. It assesses "universities against the United Nations' Sustainable Development Goals (SDGs)" (discussed in Chapter 15, LO 15.6). Eleven of the SDGs most relevant to higher education are used: SDG 3, Good health and well-being; SDG 4, Quality education; SDG 5, Gender equality; SDG 8, Decent work and economic growth; SDG 9, Industry, innovation, and infrastructure; SDG 10, Reduced inequalities; SDG 11, Sustainable cities and communities; SDG 12, Responsible consumption and production; SDG 13, Climate action; SDG 16, Peace, justice, and strong institutions; and SDG 17, Partnerships for the goals. The *Times* developed "indicators to provide comprehensive and balanced comparisons across three broad areas: research, outreach, and stewardship." More than 450 universities from 76 countries were reviewed and three Canadian universities were in the top 10: McMaster University (2), University of British Columbia (3), and Université de Montréal (7).[32]

Finally, a comprehensive business and society program for a business school will create a more favourable public image within universities, the business community, and society. An ethics program will enable business schools to contribute to university sustainability efforts and align their behaviour more closely with that demanded by society. Given the trends in society and in the field of business and management education, business schools need to prepare themselves for possible demands relating to the ethics of business and the implications of ethics on business programs and schools as well.

One approach to achieving a comprehensive business and society program is through participation in Principles for Responsible Management Education (PRME), "a United Nations–supported initiative founded in 2007 as a platform to raise the profile of sustainability in schools around the world, and to equip today's business students with the understanding and ability to deliver change tomorrow."[33] The Principles are Purpose, Values, Method, Research, Partnership, and Dialogue and are described in Chapter 16, LO 16.5. Involvement in PRME requires that participating business schools submit a Sharing Information on Progress (SIP) report that describes the school's progress toward sustainability.[34] Twenty Canadian business and management schools are PRME signatories and have submitted SIP reports. The PRME initiative enables business schools to report on their sustainability efforts, which they have not done sufficiently in the past, despite the advances in reporting of corporate sustainability.[35]

LO 9.9 The Future of CSR and Social Reporting

To understand the form CSR reporting will take, it is necessary to speculate on the future of CSR itself. The following are two views of what might happen with CSR.

In a report for VanCity Credit Union, Strandberg interviewed 47 CSR thought leaders about the future and a variety of views emerged. It is agreed that CSR is an aspect of the paradigm shift from industrial to sustainability capitalism. The progress on CSR has been slow, but it appears to be moving into the mainstream of business.[36]

Some of the interviewees felt corporations will lose interest in CSR and it will not move beyond a token baseline. Others thought CSR would develop quickly, especially if driven by high-profile wrongdoing. Continuous improvement would occur in CSR but it would be inconsistent across industry sectors. It was felt by some that CSR was part of a search for a new social contract between business and society. Despite the differences in views of the social impact and degree of corporate commitment, the majority agreed that in five to 10 years,

CSR will nonetheless become increasingly mainstream within business, even if not with the public consciousness. CSR tools, resources, language—all will become more aligned with business norms and systems. CSR standards—to greater or lesser effect—will be part of business basics and not an add-on.[37]

Strandberg identified a continuum of CSR possibilities, from "CSR Lite" to "Deep CSR"; these are presented in Table 9.2.

TABLE 9.2	Continuum of Future Commitment to CSR
Possible Future CSR	**Corporate Commitment**
CSR Lite	Superficial and marginal, may be required by law
	Concerned mainly about responsiveness to complaints
	May use indicators such as GRI and think they are in compliance
CSR Compliant	Voluntarily take on environmental and social obligations to maintain licence to operate
	Keep abreast of emerging standards and norms of CSR

CSR Strategic	Become compliant with standards and then create niches in areas more strategic to the corporation
	May use CSR as key to survival by providing goods and services acceptable to society
CSR Integrated	Believe the need to take social and environmental impacts and opportunities into account.
	Comprehensive CSR policies and operationalizing CSR principles through rigorous standards and objectives
Deep CSR	Business model where mission is to improve social or environmental conditions
	Move to addressing trade-offs between different elements of triple bottom line

Some other main findings by Strandberg are that:

- The role of stakeholders will become more important and consultation will become a core competency for managers. The relationship with NGOs will become more challenging and CSR will extend along the corporation's supply chain. Ethical consumers will be more powerful, and employees and investors will place more demands on the corporation.

- The top CSR issues will be the environment, reduction of poverty, governance, and accountability.

- There will be a new focus on CSR measurement and reporting with increased standardization.

- Governments may impose mandatory reporting.

- Corporations will be expected to play a greater role in social change.[38]

Overall, most participants in the study agreed that "CSR progress will be slow over the next ten years, but will become increasingly mainstreamed by business."[39] This observation is for the most part still applicable and the only finding that has not occurred is the imposition of mandatory reporting.

In another study, White developed three scenarios of the future of CSR: fade, integrate, or transform. Each of these is described briefly.

- *Fad-and-fade scenario*—Awareness and practise of CSR will decline significantly. This is the result of external trends or events beyond the control of the corporation. Government regulation emerges, replacing the self-regulatory purpose of CSR. The failure to address social, ethical, and governance challenges is also blamed.

- *Embed-and-integrate scenario*—CSR is accepted and the case for it no longer has to be made. Continuous enhancement of CSR approaches and practices occurs, and managers demonstrate a strong sense of moral and ethical commitment.

- *Transition-and-transformation*—Incremental changes to CSR are insufficient and stakeholders demand a redesign of the corporation. This will alter the nature and purpose of the corporation and broaden its social function. There is a challenge to the prevailing wisdom relating to the rights and obligations of the corporation. This became necessary as the public lost confidence in the corporation.[40]

Implications for reporting and communication exist depending what the future holds for CSR. Assuming that CSR becomes "CSR integrated" or "deep CSR," as argued by Strandberg, or that it follows the "embed-and-integrate" or "transition-and-transformation" scenarios proposed by White, the following are considerations:

1. A multiplicity of standards or guidelines exist, but it appears that the Global Reporting Initiative standards are the most commonly used.

2. The willingness of corporations to make the extensive disclosures necessary and the reliability of information provided are issues.

3. The process of independent verification has not become routine or formalized.

These points are still relevant and management must continue to consciously reinforce the CSR measuring, reporting, and communicating process within corporations. Acceptance of CSR reporting has been relatively slow, with only a small number of publicly listed corporations—usually in consumer products and resource industries—making the effort. It is clear that CSR initiatives must be sincere and benefit society, and this is not achieved by merely reporting token actions or approaching it as a public relations tactic.

Your advice to Clare . . .

This chapter identified some of the difficulties with CSR reports that would help explain Clare's confusion. You advise her to check out the methodology used when she is looking at any of the rankings or lists of the "best" corporations; the criteria that were considered in selecting the corporations will be identified and should explain how a particular corporation made the list. A best-in-sector lens is sometimes used; that is, the most socially responsible corporation in an industry is selected. Also, some criteria or measures are better than others. Clare also should keep in mind that corporations often "self-report," which may not be reliable. Furthermore, with any set of criteria, a corporation's good attributes may outweigh its (real or alleged) bad attributes. After reviewing the results, Clare also realized that corporations in the energy, mining, and forestry industries were more socially responsible than she thought.

Summary

- Corporate reporting of social responsibility and sustainability has become a management function in many organizations. Social auditing is performed and the results become the basis for social reporting. Today, economic, ethical, and environmental standards or measures are being developed and used by corporations. The ultimate in social reporting is to evaluate the corporation's performance on these standards and to have the results externally verified. (LO 9.1)

- An important reason for social reporting is to sustain the corporation's reputation; that is, the stakeholders' perceived views of the corporation. There are connections among reputation, the corporation's stakeholders, the management of the issues they raise, and the approach to strategic management. Today, corporate reputation rather than image has become important to a successful corporate strategy. (LO 9.2)

- Today, CSR reporting is expected, and even demanded, by several stakeholders, in particular shareholders, employees, consumers, society at large, service professionals, NGOs, charities, the media, and government. So many stakeholders are interested in the corporation's social and environmental initiatives that reporting cannot be ignored by management. (LO 9.3)

- The relationship between CSR and profitability has been extensively studied. A majority of studies have found a positive relationship, but the research approaches and techniques used are being questioned. (LO 9.4)

- Several organizations are establishing standards to be used in social auditing, which in turn determine the contents of CSR reports. Organizations assisting managers in this area include the Conference Board of Canada, the Accountability Project, and the Global Reporting Initiative. The latter is the most prominent, and its standards are utilized by many corporations in their CSR reports. (LO 9.5)

- The CSR reports produced by Canadian corporations are evaluated by newspapers, magazines, consulting firms, and professional organizations. This evaluation provides best-practice examples for corporations beginning to develop CSR reports. (LO 9.6)

- The act of producing the CSR report is a good learning exercise for the corporation, but it is necessary to communicate the results to stakeholders in various formats and delivery modes. (LO 9.7)

- Few business schools produce a CSR report on themselves. But they are being evaluated in terms of how they are integrating corporate social responsibility and the ethics of business into programs, courses, faculty activities, and student initiatives. (LO 9.8)

- The future of CSR and reporting is undergoing change. It is thought that it will become a required management function with a minimum baseline standard being established. What happens to CSR will determine the changes in social measuring, reporting, and communicating approaches. (LO 9.9)

Key Terms

Social auditing

Corporate social responsibility (CSR) reporting
(sustainability reporting)

Corporate reputation

Global Reporting Initiative (GRI)

Critical Thinking and Discussion Questions

1. Why should CSR measuring or auditing be externally verified?

2. What are the interrelationships among stakeholders, issues management, social responsibility, and corporate reputation?

3. Why are shareholders interested in social auditing and CSR reporting?

4. Why will the debate about the relationship between CSR and profitability not be resolved soon?

5. Why is transparency important in CSR reporting?

6. Why would a corporation use GRI's *Sustainability Reporting Guidelines* in its CSR reporting?

7. What kind of influence do the surveys of Canadian business' social responsibility and sustainability have on management?

8. What advice would you give to a manager responsible for preparing and communicating a CSR report?

9. What influence will business schools have on social auditing and reporting?

10. What is the future of CSR and corporate social reporting?

Cases

9.1 PHARMA INDUSTRY PAYMENTS TO DOCTORS

The Canadian pharmaceutical industry pays doctors and health-care organizations tens of millions of dollars a year for a variety of services. Doctors are paid for giving speeches, acting as consultants, spearheading treatment clinical trials, and teaching medical-education courses, and are reimbursed for travel expenses. Health-care organizations such as hospitals and university medical faculties also receive funding.

There has been considerable concern expressed about this practice, even from within the medical profession, as conflicts of interest are possible. Some studies have found a link between the payments and prescriptions. In response, Innovative Medicines Canada has attempted to self-regulate by implementing a voluntary framework on disclosure of payments. Innovative Medicines Canada represents the 45 firms who discover, develop, and deliver innovative medicines and vaccines, also referred to as *brand name pharmaceutical firms*.

Only 10 of the firms have endorsed the disclosure initiative. The information disclosed is not easily accessible as it is on the websites of the individual firms and not easily found. Dollar amounts of the payments are disclosed but no names or reasons for the payments are given. Several prominent physicians and researchers have established Open Pharma to advocate for greater disclosure in the health-care system. Its mission is "Transparency to Protect Trust and Enhance Science." The Canadian Medical Association (CMA) has endorsed the need for greater transparency.

Canadian governments are reluctant to become involved. The federal government states that the issue is a provincial matter. Only two provinces are considering legislation to require disclosure: Ontario and British Columbia. In the United States all payments over $10 must be disclosed with names, similar to requirements in other developed countries. Critics claim that the Innovative Medicines Canada initiative is a public-relations effort to stave off legislation, and not to improve transparency. The CMA says that it is continuing to improve transparency.

Questions

1. Who are the stakeholders influenced by the issue and/or who can influence the issue?

2. Is greater transparency needed in the pharmaceutical industry?

3. How does this issue affect the industry's reputation?

4. Is the industry socially responsible?

5. What is the best approach to achieving greater transparency?

9.2 DISCLOSING GMOS IN HENRY'S RESTAURANT

Henry Kline owns and operates a successful family restaurant that tries to respond to the wishes of his customers. Over the years, many suggestions have improved the restaurant's appearance and menu. Responding to some of the suggestions for menu changes has been challenging.

Suggestions for the addition of particular dishes were carefully considered and made if financially and nutritionally feasible. The identification of ingredients had become more difficult over the years. Customers were more concerned about the impact of some ingredients on their health and about various related social and environmental issues. As a result, the menu identified organic, vegan, and gluten-free dishes.

Recently, some customers requested that the menu indicate whether dishes contain any genetically modified organisms (GMOs)—that is. plant or animal content whose structure has been changed by scientists so that it can be produced more efficiently. Henry had not thought about GMOs much and had to do some research. The literature was overwhelming from those who opposed and those who supported GMO foods.

The debate about genetic modification started years ago and is ongoing. Proponents of GMO foods state that engineering genes gives plants useful traits: more resistant to disease and pesticides, better able to withstand colder temperatures or drought, and higher yields. The products may have better shelf life and taste, and better nutritional profiles. The government has approved 120 plants, including soybeans, canola, corn, and sugar beets, containing GMOs. It has not approved any animal products, but the United States has approved GMO salmon.

Those opposing GMO foods claim there is a risk to health, such as an increase in allergies and antibiotic resistance. Regulatory agencies in several countries, including Canada, have concluded that there is no risk to consuming genetically modified foods.

Henry would not be able to guarantee that dishes were GMO-free as there is no required labelling for the ingredients he uses. Even if there were sufficient labelling, it would be difficult to maintain separate inventories or prevent the accidental mixing of GMO-free ingredients with supplies containing GMO ingredients. Given the information he obtained, it would be difficult to label his dishes GMO-free with any assurance.

Questions

1. Is the issue significant to the operation and success of the restaurant?

2. Is Henry being socially responsible?

3. What should Henry tell his customers?

4. What should Henry do?

Business is regulated in several ways including by government.
Used © Lopolo | Dreamstime.com

CHAPTER 10

Regulating Business' Ethics and Responsibilities

LEARNING OUTCOMES

After studying this chapter, you will be able to:

LO 10.1 Understand the different types of regulation to enhance corporate ethics and responsibilities.

LO 10.2 Describe government initiatives to encourage corporate social responsibility and accountability.

LO 10.3 Learn about government's concern for business corruption and its attempt to prevent it.

LO 10.4 Identify the ethics and responsibilities associated with taxation.

LO 10.5 Acknowledge the involvement of business in politics and identify the related ethics and responsibilities.

LO 10.6 Define lobbying and understand its influence.

LO 10.7 Explain the role of corporate public affairs departments, and define corporate agenda and corporate welfare.

What would you do if...?

Luke Boychuk was in the kitchen reading the newspaper as his mother prepared dinner. He had graduated from a business program at the local college but was still living at home as he attempted to pay off his student loans. He said to his mother, "Here's another story about the federal government assistance to business. I really resent those big companies not paying back all their loans when I have no choice but to pay back my student loans with interest. They are nothing but corporate welfare bums."

Luke's annoyance was prompted by media stories he had recently seen. One article was about the $13.7 billion in assistance given to the Canadian auto industry in 2009, some of which has not been repaid. An article written by the Fraser Institute, "Bombardier and Canada's corporate welfare trap," claims that the company had received $3.7 billion in subsidies, some of which were loans not totally repaid. Even worse, a story claimed that business had received $6 billion in grants with no repayment required. And these figures only represented the corporate welfare dispersed by one federal government department and did not include assistance received from provincial and municipal governments. It is estimated that the federal government spends about $14 billion a year on business subsidies and the provinces spend even more.

Defenders of the government programs to business argued that employment has been created, although exact figures were not known. Also, these programs redirect or stimulate economic growth and development not otherwise likely to occur. Some starting businesses needed help to obtain financing as private lenders were not willing to provide. This was particularly the case in high technology industries. On the other hand, the Canada Student Loans Program requires students to start paying interest immediately upon graduation, and to start repaying their loans six months after graduation.

Luke's mother, a chartered public accountant, turned to him. "But aren't you some kind of a welfare bum? The government paid the interest on your loans while you were in school. Besides, while you were a student, you were eligible for the GST/HST tax credit, could deduct tuition and education expenses, and, when you moved, you could also deduct those expenses. Now you can deduct the interest paid on your loans. I don't recall you paying any income tax while you were in college. Today, students get an even better deal as they receive tax credits for transit passes and textbooks, and don't pay income tax on any scholarship, fellowship, or bursary income."

This information took Luke by surprise as he realized that individuals as well as corporations receive subsidies from the government. He thought he should reconsider the appropriateness of government programs to assist business.

What is your advice to Luke?

There are a variety of ways that the corporation's behaviour is regulated so that it is aware of ethical issues and recognizes and fulfills its responsibilities to stakeholders. This is accomplished through a range of regulation from government imposed to that provided by market forces.

Governments are involved in influencing corporate social responsibility in various ways. Furthermore, governments play major roles in controlling corruption and the administration of a fair taxation system. On the other hand, corporations attempt to influence governments through lobbying and the operation of public affairs departments.

LO 10.1   Types of Regulation

When considering the regulation of business, most think immediately of government regulation. This section also discusses types of regulation that influence corporations based on self-regulation, private regulation, and market forces. These types of regulation range from the most intrusive (government regulation) to the least intrusive (market regulation).

Government Regulation of Business

Government in developed economies like Canada will regulate parts of the economy that it believes to be the most critical to society's well-being. Standards are developed, applied, and enforced by government or its agents, and the standards apply to everyone. Government provides a countervailing power to business by reflecting society's concerns. On the other hand, government regulation is criticized for being oppressive, ineffectual, confused, conflictual, costly, rigid, weakly enforced, and amenable to capture by those it is regulating.

In Canada, government with few exceptions regulates the distribution and sale of alcohol beverages. The labour collective bargaining process is almost totally regulated directly by government with few aspects delegated to other types of regulation. Governments also are the principal regulators in competition policy, bankruptcy laws, and intellectual property. Governments are always introducing new regulations. In recent years they have regulated online transactions, tattoo artists, organic foods, ingredients in pet food, and the rights of airline passengers.

The influence and involvement of government in the business system is substantial and there are implications of ethics and responsibilities of business. The following list illustrates the scope of government in society:

- Government is the architect of economic growth, which is accomplished by expenditures, taxation, and policies.
- Government is a major purchaser of goods and services provided by business.
- Government is a major promoter and subsidizer of business.
- Government is a provider of financial capital through loans and grants.
- Government is a rescuer of failed business corporations.
- Government is the owner of business enterprises.

In addition to the above, there are four other areas where the government has a major influence on business' ethics and responsibilities: by prescribing legal rules of conduct, by protecting the interests of business, by protecting the interests of various stakeholders, and by using regulation to manage large areas of business activity.

The government provides the framework legislation enabling businesses to operate. This legislation includes laws relating to competition policy, anti-dumping, bankruptcy, incorporation, intellectual and industrial property, contractual agreements, and property rights. These laws provide the "rules of the game"—that is, the conditions under which business will operate.

Government is the protector of business interest, for example, the imposing of tariff and non-tariff barriers that exist to shield Canadian industry from foreign competition. Since 1879, Canadian manufacturing has been protected by tariffs and other barriers such as quotas and regulations. Industries receiving substantial protection in the past have included textiles and shoes, furniture, and appliances. It is argued that this has caused some Canadian industries to be less efficient than they might have been. Freer trade is reducing the influence of these protective measures. Protective measures also exist between provinces, and many businesspersons believe that these barriers are a greater impediment to free trade within Canada than between Canada and other countries.

Government is the protector of various interests in society against business exploitation and redistributes resources to meet social ends. Governments have legislated to protect the interests of those with low incomes (for example, rent control), minority groups facing discrimination, and the environment. Consumers have been protected by extensive legislation as they are often unable to represent themselves or make their voice heard. Corporations are involved in collecting taxes for governments, such as retail sales tax and payroll deductions of personal income tax. They also pay taxes on profits, but the total amount they contribute is substantially less than that raised by personal income taxation.

Government directly manages, through regulation, large areas of private business activity. In theory, the regulation of the economy and the business enterprise system should be done by the forces or influences of the marketplace. But in practice this is not the way it works, and a mechanism is required to control monopoly and oligopoly powers, to control the transfer of income from consumers to producers, and to increase efficiency in production. Regulatory organizations do a variety of things, including establishing prices and levels of service, mediating between corporations, advising governments on policy, controlling expenditures, administering acts or regulations (such as licensing), and operating as quasi-judicial bodies. A good example of the complications in regulations is provided in the discussion of the taxi industry in Responsibility for Ethics 10.1.

RESPONSIBILITY FOR ETHICS 10.1

Regulating the Taxi Industry

The taxi industry is one of the most regulated in Canada. Municipal governments impose numerous requirements on the industry, including driver qualifications, vehicle conditions, driver and passenger insurance, and conditions on where they can operate. Licences or permits are restricted and in some cities can cost tens of thousands of dollars. All the rules limit competition, reduce the supply of taxis, and force up prices, creating what could be viewed as a cartel. Much of this is not in the best interests of consumers.

The industry's regulations were challenged with the entry of ride-sharing apps by Uber and others. The ride-sharing taxis proved popular, providing better service at lower prices. The regulated taxis objected to the ride-sharing companies as they were taking business and did not have to adhere to the expensive regulations. Municipal governments are struggling to develop regulations that will allow the ride-sharing taxis to operate. Even Uber agrees that it should be subject to some regulation relating to safety and insurance.

In the meantime, some stakeholders are benefiting from the changes technology has enabled in the taxi industry while others are harmed.

Various governments regulate the operation of business enterprises through commissions, tribunals, agencies, and boards. The following are examples of industries regulated by government-sponsored regulatory agencies: petroleum; insurance; pipelines; some agricultural products, including dairy and poultry; utilities (electric, telephone); transportation (trucking, rail, airline, bus, taxi); communications (radio, television); and securities. Government, in one form or another, directly regulates about one-third of the economy through more than 600 organizations. Examples of such regulatory organizations are the Canadian Radio-television and Telecommunications Commission, the Canadian Transportation Commission, the National Energy Board, and the public utilities boards in most provinces.

Government regulation of some sort impacts every business enterprise, and every Canadian, but there are two trends reducing regulation by government: deregulation and privatization. These trends shift regulation from government laws and policies to private or civil regulation, market regulation, and self-regulation approaches.

Deregulation is the reduction of government influence or impact on the economy, allowing for a freer and more efficient marketplace. The reason given for deregulation is that fewer and simpler regulations will lead to a more competitive business environment, resulting in higher productivity, more efficiency, and lower prices. Those opposing deregulation argue that it results in reduced environmental quality standards; greater financial uncertainty, as occurred in 2008; and market control by monopolies.

Privatization, one manifestation of lessened government involvement, is discussed, as it has substantial implications for business corporations and society. **Privatization** is the "strengthening of the market at the expense of the state."[1] After reviewing several definitions of privatization, Goodrich concluded that they had four things in common: privatization is defined as the provision of public service by the private sector; there are degrees of privatization, complete or partial; there are many techniques or forms of privatization (for example, divestiture, contracting out); and different terms are used that have overlapping meanings (for example, *contract public agencies* and *contracting out service delivery*).[2]

The privatization trend provides numerous opportunities for business. Private-sector businesses can provide services formerly delivered by government in several ways, namely participation in conventional markets where buyers and sellers compete for projects or contracts to perform work; monopoly franchises where the private company provides services at specified standards; management contracts; and acquiring ownership of the corporation. The challenge for entrepreneurs and managers is to make sure they are aware of the possibilities by monitoring government initiatives.

Want to learn more about **your view of government regulation?**

Self-regulation

Self-regulation is regulation imposed by the corporation or industry, not directly by the government or market forces. Businesspersons advocating this type of regulation claim that it is faster, cheaper, and more efficient and effective than government regulation. It is more likely to be accepted because it is voluntarily developed and adapted. It improves the relationship between business and consumers, and allows government to focus on other priorities. An example of industry self-regulation is the Chemistry Industry Association of Canada's Responsible Care® Ethic described in Responsibility for Ethics 10.2.

Self-regulation is criticized because it impairs business competition and innovation due to self-serving restraint by industry participants. It may result in lower standards than those imposed by government, and it is ineffective whenever competition and other laws forbid compulsory membership necessary to ensure the worst offenders are involved. Its administration presents challenges, including the lack of adequate penalties for those who violate the regulations; insufficient financing, publicity, and promotion; and lack of public or consumer representation.

 RESPONSIBILITY FOR ETHICS 10.2

The Chemistry Industry's Responsible Care® Ethic and Principles for Sustainability

Launched in 1985 by the Chemistry Industry Association of Canada (CIAC), Responsible Care® is a UN-recognized sustainability initiative that has been adopted in nearly 70 countries around the world.

Commitment to Responsible Care inspires CIAC member-companies to continuously improve their health, safety, and environmental performance while delivering products essential to everyday life.

The Responsible Care® Ethic and Principles for Sustainability

We are committed to doing the right thing, and being seen to do the right thing.

We dedicate ourselves, our technology and our business practices to sustainability—the betterment of society, the environment and the economy. The principles of Responsible Care® are key to our business success, and compel us to:

- work for the improvement of people's lives and the environment, while striving to do no harm;
- be accountable and responsive to the public, especially our local communities, who have the right to understand the risks and benefits of what we do;
- take preventative action to protect health and the environment;
- innovate for safer products and processes that conserve resources and provide enhanced value;
- engage with our business partners to ensure the stewardship and security of our products, services and raw materials throughout their life cycles
- understand and meet expectations for social responsibility
- work with all stakeholders for public policy and standards that enhance sustainability, act to advance legal requirements and meet or exceed their letter and spirit
- promote awareness of Responsible Care®, and inspire others to commit to these principles

Source: Reprinted with permission from the Chemistry Industry Association of Canada, http://www.canadianchemistry.ca/responsible_care/index.php/en/our-commitment. Used with permission.

Industry or trade associations often facilitate this type of regulation, and initiatives are undertaken to address industry issues that, if not addressed, may lead to government regulation. Members of an industry can attempt to influence corporate behaviour and even enforce standards. The Advertising Standards Canada is an industry organization committed to the integrity of advertising through industry self-regulation with the Canadian Code of Advertising Standards. The Retail Council of Canada attempts to influence its members' behaviour in various ways, one of which is the Scanner Price Accuracy Voluntary Code. Another example is given in Responsibility for Ethics 10.3.

 RESPONSIBILITY FOR ETHICS 10.3

The REALTOR® Code

The Canadian Real Estate Association (CREA) promotes professionalism in the industry by its REALTOR® Code. The Code includes a Standard of Conduct statement to protect the rights and interests of consumers. The Code may establish obligations above those required by law.

The Code is outlined in a 27-page document and includes a Code of Ethics that was developed in 1959. The Code of Ethics states that REALTORS® are committed to

- professional, competent service;
- absolute honesty and integrity in business dealing;
- utmost civility; and
- cooperation with and fairness to all.

Personal accountability of REALTORS® is achieved through compliance with CREA's Standards of Business Practice.

To meet their obligations, REALTORS® pledge to observe the spirit of the Code in all of their activities and conduct their business, whether personally or through employees, associates, or others, in accordance with the Standards of Business Practice and the Golden Rule:

"Do unto others as you would have them do unto you."

The power to prevent abuses is usually limited, as the potential for anti-competitive behaviour or conflicts of interest limits the effectiveness of this type of regulation. In most industries, participation is voluntary, and even when a member violates the standards, enforcement and remedial action is limited.

Government prefers to have some industries and professions regulate themselves and grants this in legislation. An example is **self-regulatory organizations (SROs)**, industry or professional groups that are delegated or designated a regulatory function including the development, use, and enforcement of standards. An industry example is provided by the securities industry in Canada. The provincial securities commissions have delegated some aspects of securities regulation to the Toronto Stock Exchange (TSX) and various financial industry organizations such as the Investment Industry Regulatory Organization of Canada (IIROC) and the Mutual Fund Dealers Association of Canada (MFDA). Professionals such as accountants and lawyers are also regulated by SROs.

Private Regulation

In recent years, there has been a rise in **private or civil regulation**, defined as a non-profit, independent organization that sets standards for responsible business practices. *Private* refers to the non-involvement of the public, or government, sector. *Civil* refers to an organization from the civil society—that is, the voluntary, community, and social organizations or institutions that contribute to the functioning of society but are usually not related to or supported by government. The most common stakeholders involved in regulation are non-governmental organizations. A main approach of private regulation is the certification of products or services by third parties not linked to business or government. The penalties are social or market based rather than legal sanctions.

Third-party certification is an approval or endorsement by an organization independent of government and business after reviewing the production or provision of a good or service to ascertain whether or not the product complies with specific standards relating to such things as safety, quality, performance, or environmental responsibility. This review typically includes comprehensive formulation/material reviews, testing, and facility inspections. In effect, there is an audit that "certifies" compliance with standard requirements. Most certified products bear the certifier's mark or label on their packaging to help consumers and other buyers make informed purchasing decisions. Corporate websites often include a listing of these certification labels. This communicates unobservable product attributes to stakeholders, consumers in particular. Such certification allows stakeholders to credibly distinguish "good" and best performers. It is argued that both business and stakeholders benefit. It is assumed that certified corporations should gain some financial reward relative to non-certified ones, although there is little research to prove this occurs. Private third-party certification should not be confused with certification available from some self-regulatory organizations sponsored by a group of corporations or industry association. Examples of third-party certifications are given in Responsibility for Ethics 10.4.

RESPONSIBILITY FOR ETHICS 10.4

Examples of Third-Party Certifications

Dozens of products have third-party certifications and only a few are listed in these examples.

Marine Stewardship Council (MSC)—MSC sets standards, in consultation with stakeholders, for sustainable fisheries and traceable seafood supply chains. The MSC operates a third-party certification program carried out by teams of auditors who are experts in fisheries science and management and are independent of the fishery and the MSC. Additional information available at https://www.msc.org/about-us/standards/third-party-certification.

Forestry Stewardship Council (FSC)—The FSC offers a forest-management certification that is awarded to forest owners and managers whose operations and processes meet FSC standards, and a chain-of-custody certification that applies to businesses that manufacture or sell forest products. Additional information available at https://ic.fsc.org /en/for-business/types-of-certification.

Rainforest Alliance—The Alliance's little green frog is a symbol of environmental, social, and economic sustainability on farm and forest products around the world. Rainforest Alliance Certified™ products include coffee, tea, chocolate, soaps, and beef. Additional information at https://www.rainforest-alliance.org/find-certified.

Fairtrade Canada—Fairtrade Canada audits producers, traders, and companies to ensure compliance with the internationally agreed Fairtrade Standards. The certification provides assurance that the relevant economic, social, and environmental standards are met and that producers receive the Fairtrade Minimum Price and Premium. Certified products include coffee, tea, sugar, flowers, nuts, cotton, and herbs and spices. Additional information at http://fairtrade.ca/.

There are several reasons for the rise of this type of regulation and business' acceptance. In some instances, there is a lack of government willingness or capability to regulate. The legitimacy, governance, and implementation of this regulation is not based in public authority—that is, government—and is a form of private law rather than legally enforceable standards. Business may prefer this type of regulation to that provided by government. Private regulation is sometimes encouraged or facilitated by governments as they lack the capability to regulate them.

As civil society and citizen campaigns that name and shame corporations become more common, corporations are forced to accept CSR practices in response to this public criticism. Similarly, if a consumer brand is impacted, corporations are more likely to seek private certification. The adoption of a certification may avoid negative media. Lastly, a corporation may have to follow others in the industry who have adopted certification.

NGOs have become involved for a variety of reasons. Certification is a source of leverage used on corporations to change procurement practices. Lobbying of corporations, industry associations, and governments has not been as successful as hoped, prompting NGOs to use other influence tactics. The creation of alliances with corporations/industry is an example. This has led to the emergence of private regulations, legitimacy, and increased effectiveness such as the Marine Stewardship Council's label identifying sustainable fish.

Private regulation is common in forestry, fisheries, chemicals, marine transportation, computers and electronic equipment, electronic commerce, apparel, rugs, coffee, cocoa, palm oil, diamonds, gold, toys, minerals and mining, energy, tourism, and financial services (for example, bond ratings). It is commonly used as a global regulatory system as many countries no longer have exclusive authority to govern multinational firms and global supply networks. Most fair-trade and organic labels are examples of private regulation.

There are some downsides to private regulation. Many certification labels exist that confuse consumers, especially in the environmental area. Likewise, corporations may be faced with competing certification organizations, as exist, for example, in the palm-oil industry. It is possible that stakeholders may give undue credence to certification, believing that the standards are reliable. Others suggest that certification is little more than a marketing strategy. Enforcement of standards is challenging and penalties for violations are difficult to apply. Some host countries are unwilling to enforce violations by certified corporations for fear of losing jobs. Some certification organizations may not be as independent as portrayed, with undisclosed support from business. In the forestry industry, some considered the Sustainable Forestry Initiate a form of industry self-regulation, versus the Forestry Stewardship Council, which is more independent.

An example of the complications of private regulation involving certification is described in Everyday Ethics 10.1.

Earls Kitchen + Bar and Certified Beef

Earls Kitchen + Bar was started in 1982 by Leroy Earl Fuller and his son Stanley Earl Fuller in Edmonton, Alberta, and by 2016 had 67 restaurants across Canada and the United States with 7,000 employees. Over the years, Earls has made an effort to respond to the tastes of its customers. There was a growing demand for ethical beef—that is, meat from animals that were raised in comfortable conditions, were antibiotic and steroid free, and contained no added hormones. This demand arose to combat the negative social connotations of consuming beef. Earls started studying "conscious sourcing" in response to these consumer concerns.

After extensive study, Earls started sourcing beef that was certified by Humane Farm Animal Care (HFAC), an American non-profit certification organization dedicated to improving the lives of farm animals in food production from birth through slaughter. The HFAC grants a Certified Humane Raised and Handled® label for food products that meet its standards after inspections of farms or ranches and slaughter plants.

Earls started sourcing the HFAC-certified beef in 2014 but by 2016 was unable to find sufficient Canadian supply to meet the demand in all its restaurants. As a result, it decided to obtain its beef from a single HFAC-certified supplier in the United States.

This move resulted in an immediate uproar from Canadian beef producers, customers, and politicians. Social-media activity suggested that Earls should be boycotted. Canadian producers claimed that they produced beef that met HFAC-certification standards from other certification bodies. The B.C. SPCA's certified label was referred to as an example. A few days after announcing the decision to purchase American beef, the company backed down and said that it would make every effort to obtain its beef from Canadian suppliers. Eventually, Earls stated that it had made a mistake and admitted that it had failed to consult all stakeholders by neglecting farmers and ranchers.

Earls' experience illustrates some of the complications in private regulation. The commitment to one certification may limit supply especially when the single-supplier policy is adopted. Some grief could have been avoided by making sure all stakeholders were consulted. The existence of several certification bodies without a uniform system complicates certification for corporations and consumers. Some beef producers advocated for an increased role for government, which would provide a uniform system.

Market Regulation

If a rigorous and competitive market exists, there is less need for government-imposed laws or regulations, as the corporation is influenced or regulated by the dynamic forces of a free market. This could also be referred to as a laissez-faire approach, where government does not interfere with business. The market disciplines would include competitive rivalry among firms with entry to the market possible and substitutes available. Various stakeholders are involved in influencing the corporation and, in effect, regulate its behaviours. An example is consumers who can take action to force the corporation to behave in particular ways by refusing to purchase goods or services, or through organized action such as a boycott or applying pressure through social media. Abuses are possible, but are corrected by the market or stakeholder pressures. No economies rely on market forces exclusively.

Corporate self-discipline is a form of regulation where norms or standards are developed, used, and enforced by the corporation itself. This is accomplished through mission and values statements, codes of conduct or ethics, ethics programs, or adherence to social and environmental reporting guidelines. The acceptance and practice of corporate social responsibility (CSR) is the most general form of self-regulation (refer to Chapters 7, 8, and 9). Even though it has received substantial attention recently, CSR is still criticized. It has failed to live up to its promise, and some corporations have been accused of participating only for appearances or on a token basis. The desire for profit maximization still exists, and the corporation's behaviour is a function of market imperatives rather than management's values or corporate structures. There is no assurance that all corporations will participate, and enforcement is a problem. On the other hand, measures of CSR are being increasingly used and pressures are being applied by various stakeholders advocating socially responsible behaviour.

As a result of these four types of regulation, the outcome in society and the economic system is a balance between private (business and civil society) and public (government), two extremes on the spectrum. The private sector provides for innovation, investment, and risk taking that promotes growth and employment. On the other hand, government provides the institutions, rules, safety nets, education, research, and infrastructure to empower the private sector. There are two possibilities in the relationship: where business directly controls more of the economy than the private sector and where the government controls the economy through a variety of methods. The balance shifts back and forth with different consequences for business and society stakeholders.

In most forms of capitalism operating in democracies, a mixture of regulation provides a balance among government regulation, self-regulation, private regulation, and market regulation. The types of regulation discussed will confirm that regulation is not solely a government initiative. Also, regulation varies substantially among industries and even within industries.

The following sections will describe a variety of topics relating to regulation and the last section describes government involvement in facilitating corporate responsibility.

LO 10.2 Government Involvement in Corporate Social Responsibility

Governments have become involved in CSR through legislation, regulations, or simply by encouraging CSR or sustainability practices.

Demands to legislate CSR and accountability have occurred at various times. Some morality has been legislated through the legal system. For example, there are laws against dishonest business practices, laws to prevent monopolistic behaviour, laws relating to the health and safety of employees, and laws that prohibit conducting business with corrupt foreign regimes. This type of legislation has provided safeguards to various stakeholders, including investors, consumers, and employees. The demands increase after a corporate scandal. For example, American corporations were held more accountable after the Enron failure, the BP oil disaster in the Gulf of Mexico led to demands for greater regulation in the petroleum industry, and recent Ponzi schemes have prompted calls for more protection of individual investors.

Since 1993, the Federal Government has been involved in several initiatives that have influenced the corporate social responsibility of Canadian corporations in the extractive or mining industry. The mining industry, nationally and internationally, has a reputation for violating human rights and causing damage to the environment. As Canadian corporations have a major presence in the industry around the world, their business conduct impacts national reputation. The Whitehorse Mining Initiative was initiated by the Mining Association of Canada and brought together business, government, environmental NGOs, and Aboriginal groups to ensure social and environmental goals were considered in mining development.[3] In 2000, the Canadian government was involved in the Kimberley Process where diamonds are labelled to prevent the sale of those used to finance conflicts or produced by slave or child labour.[4]

In 2007, Canada joined the Extractive Industries Transparency Initiative to address corruption in resource-dependent countries.[5] This eventually led to "Building the Canadian Advantage: A Corporate Social Responsibility Strategy for the Canadian International Extractive Sector" which included a CSR Counsellor and CSR Centre of Excellence.[6] This was revised as the "Doing Business the Canadian Way: A Strategy to Advance CSR in Canada's Extractive Sector Abroad" in 2014.[7] The Government also committed Canada to the "Voluntary Principles on Security and Human Rights" in 2009. These principles provide a broad framework that helps companies operate in ways that provide security to their facilities while respecting human rights and fundamental freedoms.[8] These initiatives by the Federal Government were an attempt to influence the social, ethical and environmental conduct of Canadian corporations in the extractive industry.

Several federal government departments have extensive websites dealing with CSR, including Innovation, Science and Economic Development Canada; Global Affairs Canada; and Natural Resources Canada. Innovation, Science and Economic Development Canada has a website "Supporting Corporate Social Responsibility initiatives" that identifies various guidelines for multinational corporations.[9]

In 2018, Global Affairs Canada announced a revised program described in "Responsible Business Conduct Abroad" on its website. The program defined corporate social responsibility (CSR) "as the voluntary activities undertaken by a company, over and above legal requirements, to operate in an economically, socially and environmentally sustainable manner." It also described Responsible Business Conduct (RBC) as being "about Canadian companies doing business abroad responsibly in an economic, social and environmentally sustainable manner. It is also about conduct that demonstrates respect for human rights and is consistent with applicable laws and internationally recognized standards." Two new elements of responsible business conduct abroad were announced. An independent Canadian Ombudsperson for Responsible Enterprise (CORE) position was created and mandated to investigate allegations of human-rights abuses linked to Canadian corporate activity abroad. The second element was the creation of a multi-stakeholder Advisory Body to advise the government and the CORE on responsible business conduct abroad.[10]

The Natural Resources Canada website, under "Social Responsibility," defines CSR as "the voluntary activities of companies, over and above regulation, that serve to integrate social, environmental and economic concerns into their activities." The site contains links to several related social responsibility and sustainability sites.[11] This is only a sample of social responsibility information available as the government attempts to influence the conduct of Canadian corporations within Canada and around the world. Many provincial governments would also provide information on social responsibility.

There are hundreds of corporations owned by the federal, provincial, and municipal governments. Many of these operate with economic objectives but must also be socially aware of society's needs. They operate in every province and territory and in a variety of industries. Many are involved in supporting communities through donations, sponsorships, and employee voluntary efforts, but they are seldom involved in community investment projects. Everyday Ethics 10.2 gives examples of the social responsibility activities of government-owned corporations. Some of these corporations even have comprehensive social-responsibility reports.

 EVERYDAY ETHICS 10.2

Examples of Social Responsibility in Government-Owned Corporations

Export Development Corporation—The areas covered by the Corporation's report include environment and people, business integrity, their workplace, and community involvement. The Corporation has a Corporate Sustainability and Responsibility Advisory Council to advise on and guide its CSR practices.

Toronto Hydro—Toronto Hydro, owned by the City of Toronto, prepares a comprehensive corporate social responsibility report that highlights its sustainability progress in several key areas, including business operations, workforce, environmental footprint, and community outreach.

Liquor Control Board of Ontario—The social responsibility report discusses responsible product use, product quality and safety, sustainability, and community initiatives.

Canada Post—The Social Responsibility Report assesses key social and environmental performance measures. The Global Reporting Initiative (GRI) standards are used.

Gond, Kang, and Moon distinguished several modes of coordination between corporations and government over the content and process of CSR initiatives, some of which are applicable to Canada. The "CSR as self-government" mode operates alongside government and conforms to the philanthropic view of CSR where business makes discretionary contributions to society independent of government requirements. A second mode, "CSR as facilitated by government," involves government encouraging corporate responsibility through rhetoric and by providing incentives, one example being tax incentives for charitable giving. The "CSR as partnership with government" mode involves government, business, and sometimes civil society organizations combining their resources to deliver social benefits. The Canadian government had a public–private partnership to deliver aid projects in Burkina Faso but the program has been discontinued. From the discussion in this section, it is evident that various government roles are used in promoting CSR.[12]

There are two societal issues—corruption and taxation—that are of concern to governments. Corruption is monitored and punished, and efforts are undertaken to ensure that the taxation system is fair and equitable to business and society. These issues and the influence of government are discussed in the following two sections.

LO 10.3 Government Attempts at Dealing with Corruption

The approach to dealing with corporations and executives who had engaged in wrongdoing or corruption was not easy for government. Corporate crimes were difficult to detect and prosecute. There is disincentive for a corporation to report corruption or co-operate with authorities. The government can take the corporation to court or negotiate a guilty plea if charged with wrongdoing. A guilty conviction or plea would preclude the corporation from doing business with government customers. An alternative was for the government to not address the issue although they may want to discourage corrupt behaviour. This alternative may not be possible once the corruption is public knowledge and pressure could come from organizations such as Transparency International, media coverage, and social media discussions.

Corruption of Canadian public officials was covered by the *Criminal Code of Canada* and it was not until 1999 the *Corruption of Foreign Public Officials Act* (CFPOA) was passed covering foreign officials.[13] These laws were to discourage Canadian corporations from engaging in corrupt acts at home or abroad. The CFPOA covered bribery of public officials, the possession of proceeds derived from bribery of public officials, and money laundering. CFPOA investigations were often not disclosed by the government or the corporations. The first prison sentence for charges under the Act was in 2014.

Government's Integrity Framework

In 2012, the Government of Canada introduced its Integrity Framework to deal with the lack of action on this issue. The Framework "was established to protect the integrity of procurement and real property transactions managed by the department by ensuring that these transactions are carried out free from the influence of corruption, collusion and fraud and that the Government of Canada does not inadvertently support suppliers involved in such illegal activities." Its purpose was to safeguard public funds, to promote conduction of business in a fair, open, transparent, accountable, and cost-efficient manner, and to encourage businesses to engage in ethical conduct. The offences covered include: fraud under Federal Government legislation; money laundering; involvement with criminal organizations; tax evasion; bribery; secret commissions; forgery; and falsification of books or documents.[14]

Corporations wishing to do business with the Government must certify that they and any affiliates have not been charged with any of the offences anywhere in the world in the past ten years. If they have been charged, they are debarred from doing business with the Government for 10 years. Exceptions will be made if no other corporation is able to supply the goods, an emergency exists, or national security is involved.

Even with these exceptions, the Canadian framework is stricter than requirements in the United States, the European Union, and many other countries and was considered an overreaction to the corruption issue. In the United States and other countries, corporations may be prosecuted but legal action can be deferred or suspended. This is done where corporations agree to undertake remedial actions.

Business claimed that this pragmatic approach is not available in Canada and that the consequences are serious. Debarment might be considered a restraint of trade and lawsuits may result under the World Trade Organization and NAFTA. Debarment of a corporation may result in a loss of Canadian jobs, reduced foreign investment, and higher prices from reduced competition. It is argued that the Canadian Government's rule-based integrity framework should be more flexible and take into consideration that the corporation is taking remedial actions.

The Government was lobbied to revise the Framework by the industry associations including Canadian Manufacturers and Exporters, Canadian Council of Chief Executives, Information Technology Association, and the Canadian Chamber of Commerce. These initiatives resulted in the revision of the Framework announced in July 2015 with a name change to the Integrity Regime. The ten year ineligibility can be reduced to five years if the corporation cooperated with legal authorities or addressed the causes of the misconduct. The actions of affiliates would no longer automatically result in ten year ineligibility. The Government would have the ability to suspend a supplier for up to 18 months if the supplier is charged or admitted guilt to a listed offence. The Government also announced that would continue to consult anti-corruption experts and industry. Administrative agreements would be allowed which were agreements between the supplier and Government that reduced the risks of contracting with a particular supplier. It was not specified how these agreements would work.[15]

Canadian business leaders were still unhappy with the policy and critics claimed that the Government had caved in to business interests. The Integrity Regime was still harsh compared to legislation in Europe and the United States under the *Foreign Corrupt Practices Act* enacted in 1977. Also, there was no presumption of innocence until proven guilty and the five year debarment was still too long. The revised Framework still did not have provision for a type of negotiated settlement,

Remediation Agreements

Remediation agreements, also referred to as *deferred prosecution agreements* (DPA), were made possible by an amendment to the *Criminal Code* that came into effect in September 2018. This is a voluntary agreement between a government prosecutor and a corporation accused of committing an offence. The corporation agrees to remedial undertakings instead of being prosecuted. The agreement must be in the public interest and the terms fair, reasonable, and proportionate to the alleged crime. Such agreements might include the corporation acknowledging wrongdoing, dismissing employees involved, paying of penalties, implementation of compliance measures, declarations that the corporation will avoid wrongdoing the future, and undertaking anti-corruption policies. This type of agreement saves the corporation and employees from more negative consequences, but still addresses the issue. Charges are stayed, that is, no action is taken, and the corporation can be recharged in the future if it does not comply with the agreement and if it did, the charges are dropped.

Industry associations pointed out that a deferred prosecution agreement alternative would act as an incentive for corporations to disclose ethics breaches and co-operate with authorities. Deferred prosecution agreements would allow the corporation to take corrective actions, for example, firing employees guilty of misconduct and the implementation policies and ethics programs that would help prevent corruption in the future. The agreements would still hold the corporation accountable for unethical behaviour even if criminal charges were not laid.[16] Everyday Ethics 10.3 describes the impact of the Integrity Regime on one corporation.

SNC-Lavalin and the Integrity Regime

SNC-Lavalin one of the leading engineering and construction groups in the world operating in over 50 countries. Founded in 1911, it is headquartered in Montreal, PQ, has 40,000 employees, and revenues of about $7 billion with about two-thirds from Canadian projects.

Since 2012, SNC-Lavalin has faced corruption scandals including fraud, bribery and money laundering in Algeria, Bangladesh, Libya, and Montreal. Former managers face criminal charges relating to corruption of Libyan officials. The perpetrators and SNC-Lavalin's CEO were fired as a result.

In February 2015, criminal fraud and bribery charges were laid against the company under the *Corruption of Foreign Public Officials Act*. If convicted, the company would not be able to bid on Canadian government projects for five years. SNC-Lavalin executives say this is too harsh and warned that the company might be broken-up or cease to exist. If convicted and disbarred, innocent employees and investors would be harmed. Needless to say the company's reputation has been severely damaged.

SNC-Lavalin argues that charges should be laid against individuals, not the company. Moreover, since 2012 the company has gone through a rehabilitation process including: establishing an ethics hotline, forming an Ethics and Compliance Committee, making key leadership and structural changes, appointing a new Chief Compliance Officer, holding Ethics and Compliance Awareness Sessions, and updating the Code of Ethics and Business Conduct.

In September 2018, the government proceeded with criminal corruption charges. The Public Prosecution Service of Canada decided not to enter into a negotiated remediation or deferred-prosecution agreement.

SNC-Lavalin is facing a very uncertain future and the well-being of many stakeholders will be impacted.

This description illustrates how difficult it has been for the Canadian government to address corporate corruption. Taxation is another area of concern to governments, which must ensure that corporations and individuals pay appropriate and fair shares.

LO 10.4   Ethics and Responsibilities of Taxation

There are several ethical issues and responsibilities relating to the Canadian taxation of corporations and individuals. Society, as represented by government, has to decide what portion of taxation revenue is to be raised from business, both large and small, and individuals. Many Canadians believe that large corporations and high-income individuals do not pay enough taxes. The ethics of avoiding taxes is questioned by many Canadians, as they believe that corporations and high-income earners have a responsibility to pay their share. In any taxation system, issues occur in how the harms—that is, the highest rates—and benefits—that is, the lowest rates or no taxes—are distributed.

Corporate Taxation

The corporate tax rate for corporations has been lowered and is now perceived to be lower than the rate paid by individuals. The percentage of federal government revenue coming from corporate income tax has been declining while the percentage acquired from individuals has been increasing. In addition to lower rates, there are other factors that are reducing the taxes paid by corporations. Corporations have more possibilities for reducing taxes through legal tax loopholes, various tax credits, and tax loss carry-forwards. Several corporations pay almost no taxes and are able to do so legally.

Also, Canadian corporations are using **tax havens**, defined by the Canada Revenue Agency as a jurisdiction with one or more of the following characteristics: no tax, or very low rates of taxation; strict bank-secrecy provisions; a lack of transparency in the operation of its tax system; and a lack of effective exchange of information with other countries.[17] A Canadians for Tax Fairness report on the top 60 public corporations found they had over 1,000 subsidiaries in tax havens. Only four of the 60 had no subsidiaries in known tax havens. It was estimated that there was $284 billion in direct Canadian corporate investments in these tax havens, which meant $10 billion to $15 billion in lost tax revenue. The report stated that this practice was not illegal, but also recommended several actions to curb the use of tax havens.[18]

Another controversial issue is the transferring of profits on taxes to jurisdictions with lower taxation, particularly taxation havens, or, as they are now referred to, taxation efficient jurisdictions. The issue is where Canadian multinational corporations should pay income taxes on profits made on operations in other countries where taxation is lower. This is done through **transfer pricing**, the price set for goods and services sold between legal entities of the corporation. This practice is described in Everyday Ethics 10.4 involving Cameco Corp.

EVERYDAY ETHICS 10.4

Cameco Ltd. and Its Taxes

Cameco Ltd., with headquarters in Saskatoon, Saskatchewan, is one of the world's largest uranium producers with mines in Canada, the United States, and Kazakhstan. In 1999, it set up a subsidiary company, Cameco Europe Ltd., in Zug, Switzerland, a low-tax haven. This subsidiary purchases uranium produced by Cameco at US$10/lb and sells it to customers around the world. Over the years, the price has been as high as US$140 and is now about US$40. Cameco generates less profit in Canada, thus paying less tax. By locating the subsidiary in a tax haven, it has avoided paying tax on billions of income, saving about $1.5 billion in federal and provincial income tax.

Cameco states that having the marketing subsidiary in Europe is logical as it is closer to most customers. Cameco Europe has its own board of directors and one employee, the CEO, and operates out of an office rented from its law firm. Some paperwork is done in Zug but all other functions are done by Cameco employees in Canada. Uranium never goes to Zug as it is shipped directly from Canada to customers.

The Canada Revenue Agency (CRA) is disputing the corporate structure, saying it was only set up to avoid taxes. Also, CRA questions the transfer pricing arrangement. The U.S. Internal Revenue Service has also taken action against Cameco to recover avoided taxes. CRA won its court case against the company but the decision has been appealed by Cameco. It is estimated that Cameco might have to pay over $800 million in back taxes and penalties if it loses in court. Cameco claims that it is acting within the law.

In September 2018, the Federal Court of Appeal ruled in favour of Cameco, but CRA has appealed the decision.

A federal government policy has facilitated tax avoidance through its signing of tax information exchange agreements (TIERs), which enable countries to exchange information about taxpayers. According to the government, these agreements will combat international tax evasion and ensure tax fairness by implementing standards developed by the Organisation for Economic Co-operation and Development (OECD). These agreements allow Canadian multinational corporations to pay the lower taxes in other countries and bring back profits and pay no taxes in Canada. Taxation experts claim that Canada has little choice but to sign those agreements as other developing countries are participating and are granting their multinational corporations tax breaks and exemptions. In 2019, TIERs existed with 24 countries and six more being negotiated.[19]

There are some arguments for lower corporate taxation. It is argued that corporate taxation in Canada must be comparable to that in other countries. If not, Canadian operations will be transferred to other countries. Also, it is claimed that lower corporate taxation enables corporations to boost investments in their Canadian operations, creating jobs. A counter-argument is that corporate taxation should be low as ultimately it is a cost included in the price of goods and services purchased by consumers. Some corporations are unable to take advantage of the lower taxation opportunities, as they lack the resources to arrange them or their operations are not sufficiently mobile to allow the transfer of operations.

Small Business Taxation

A special case is made for lower taxation on small business enterprises. Governments believe that small businesses are a major creator of jobs in the economy and should receive a preferential tax rate. Studies have not proven this conventional wisdom and it has been pointed out that while many small businesses are created, few grow. The preferential rate applies to small businesses with less than $15 million in taxable capital and the first $500,000 per year of qualifying active business income. Almost 700,000 small businesses benefit annually from this lower rate.[20] Other arguments supporting a preferential tax are that small businesses should be compensated for their limited access to capital, the high costs of compliance to various laws and regulations, and cash flow concerns facing smaller businesses.

A study at the University of Calgary contradicted the view that small business tax concessions encouraged growth. They could result in corporations being broken into smaller, less efficient units merely to take advantage of the tax concession. Some individuals might create small businesses in order to reduce their personal tax liabilities rather than grow corporations. Lastly, a threshold effect might exist that holds back small businesses from growth beyond the size limits to qualify for the concession.[21] Another study by the C.D. Howe Institute also found that the tax rate concession had only a minor impact on investment by small businesses and came with a social cost. This cost is that the government must recoup the foregone tax revenue by cutting spending or imposing higher taxes on other business corporations or individuals. Furthermore, encouraging the expansion of small businesses at the expense of larger ones may not result in the most productive businesses, reducing the overall economic performance of the country.[22]

Individual Taxation

The federal government's tax system is increasing the proportion of total income tax revenue that is received from individuals. This increases the tax burden on individuals. As with corporate taxation, the issue of fairness arises, as many Canadians believe that wealthy individuals are able to avoid paying taxes. Legal schemes or loopholes are used by lawyers and tax experts to reduce the amount of taxes paid.

The Canadians for Tax Fairness is "a not-for-profit, non-partisan organization advocating for fair and progressive tax policies aimed at building a strong and sustainable economy, reducing inequalities and funding quality services."[23] It receives most of its financial support from Canada's labour union organizations and is criticized by many economists for its misleading presentations. The organization advocates for the closing of tax loopholes that are unfair and result in an ineffective tax system enabling some to avoid paying taxes. It wants a Financial Transaction Tax (also known as the Robin Hood Tax) imposed on international financial transactions, as is being done in some countries. The money collected under this system would help address global poverty and climate change, and be used to deal with the debt and deficit crisis. Also, the organization wants the Canada Revenue Agency (CRA) to clamp down on tax havens. A CRA study estimated that Canadians were hiding up to $240 billion abroad, avoiding taxes of $3 billion a year. Canadian businesses and individuals who are paying income tax question the fairness of a system that allows some to legally avoid paying taxes.[24]

Increasing the taxation of the rich is advocated by many Canadians. It is claimed that the rich do not spend all their income. Reducing taxes on lower income earners, who do spend all their income, sparks economic growth. An argument opposing this view is that rich Canadians deserve their good fortune as they are providing goods and services that consumers want. They have played by the rules and should be encouraged and not penalized for their success. Higher taxation of the rich has not been successful in other countries as it does not raise more revenue. Instead, it increases the legal avoidance of taxes by accountants and lawyers searching for ways to avoid taxes through tax shelter arrangements. Nevertheless, many perceive that taxing the rich is a matter of fairness.

The taxation system is complex and the issues not easy to resolve. Moreover, this discussion only dealt with income taxes at the federal government level. Taxes are also imposed by provincial and municipal governments and there are many different types of taxes levied. Canadians believe that corporations should behave ethically and accept their responsibilities by contributing to the financing of public services.

The next sections describe two approaches that business corporations use to influence government. Corporations monitor government policies and regulations and will present their views through lobbying. Also, corporations established public affairs departments whose role is to influence government.

Want to learn more about **Canadian taxation policies**?

LO 10.5 The Ethics of Business and Involvement in Politics

Many issues are associated with the involvement of business in politics either as corporations or businesspersons, and there are pros and cons to such involvement. It is a pluralistic right for business to be involved, as corporations are an institution in society and thus have a moral responsibility to take part in the political system. Business influences society and, in addition, corporations pay taxes. Businesspersons are very knowledgeable of economics and finances, and have the information and skills to make a contribution to the political process. Participation by business is necessary to counterbalance the anti-business activity of other groups, for example of unions.

On the other hand, some downsides to business involvement exist. It is argued that politics should be left to politicians, and business should be publicly neutral. Politicians have to address issues across a wide spectrum, and businesspersons are not necessarily qualified to deal with many of the social issues the government must address. Business is already accused of exerting too much power in society, and the involvement of businesspersons in politics could upset the pluralistic balance in society. Business involvement might also be interpreted as being biased, thus having an adverse effect on customers or shareholders, or conflicts of interest might exist. There is a risk of alienating a particular government that could result in legislation or regulation not desirable to business. It is difficult to find a satisfactory position on many of the emotional and highly political issues such as abortion, gun control, and human rights.

Nevertheless, business is involved in politics in several ways. The following is a discussion of this involvement.

- The financing of political parties—Corporations are a source of funds, but recent election laws limit the amounts. Corporations can also contribute "in kind"; for example, providing a party with free office space, or providing legal and other services to politicians during an election campaign. Also, corporations contribute to political leadership campaigns, where the money involved can be as great as for an election campaign.

- Publicly expressed support for a candidate or party—Support for a candidate or party can be expressed in several ways; for example, inviting campaigning politicians to address employees on company property, allowing the circulation of political materials to employees, endorsing a candidate in a newspaper advertisement with his/her affiliation mentioned, or allowing time off work to a particular candidate.

- Publicly expressed views on political issues—Business expresses views on political issues by purchasing advertisements, usually via contributions to industry or trade associations that support or oppose some political issues.

- Executives running for public office—Executives have management skills to bring to government, presumably as much as the occupational groups that are most common in elected positions now: lawyers, teachers, university professors, journalists, and engineers.

- Management's position on employee participation—Management must formulate policies relating to employee participation in the political process; for example, leave policy.

It is argued that Canadian business is very involved and influential in politics and is portrayed as having powerful influences on public policy without much accountability. Businesspersons must concern themselves with how they are perceived as influencing government policy and whether their positions are in the best interests of not only the corporation but also other stakeholders, including owners and society at large. Everyday Ethics 10.5 gives two illustrations of how corporations address the issue of business and politics.

 EVERYDAY ETHICS 10.5

Addressing Political Involvement

Canadian corporations address the issue of involvement in politics in their codes of conduct or ethics. The following are two examples of company policies:

Political Activity

As a Bombardier employee, you may, subject to applicable laws, engage in legitimate political activity, as long as it is carried out on your own time and without using Bombardier property. You may seek election or other political office, but you must notify your supervisor or the Compliance Officer to discuss the impact your involvement may have on your duties at Bombardier. You may express your views on public or community issues of importance but it must be clear at all times that the views expressed are not those of Bombardier. Bombardier and its employees abide by all laws and regulations governing political contributions in every jurisdiction where the Corporation does business.

Political Activities and Contributions

Repsol does not make any political contributions, including any "financial or in-kind support given directly or indirectly to political parties, their elected representatives or persons seeking political office." The company recognizes "the right of personnel to exercise freedom of expression, and to participate in political activities, provided these activities do not interfere with job-related performance."

The types of involvement in politics by business and businesspersons are one way to influence politics, and thus public policy. An even more direct approach to influencing government is through lobbying activities, which also involve ethical and responsibility issues.

LO 10.6   The Ethics of Business Lobbying

Lobbying is defined as all attempts to influence directly or indirectly any government activity, and includes any attempt to influence legislators, their staff members, public administrators, and members of regulatory agencies. Specifically, the practice of lobbying government can be defined as including attempts to influence:

- the making or amending of legislation and regulations;
- the making or changing of government policies or programs;
- government decisions in the awarding of grants, contracts, contributions, or any similar benefits; and
- government appointments to boards, commissions, and any other public office.[25]

There are several types of business lobbyists. The first is business corporations that attempt to influence government through lobbying performed by business interest groups or associations. Examples of business interest groups that act as lobbies include the Business Council of Canada (an organization comprising the chief executives of the largest corporations); the Canadian Federation of Independent Business; the Canadian Bankers' Association; the Electrical Association; and the Automobile Parts Manufacturers Association of Canada. It is estimated that there are hundreds of such associations that regularly lobby government by distributing literature and information; appearing before parliamentary committees, royal commissions, inquiries, and other bodies; and interviewing politicians and civil servants.

The second type of lobbyist is the consultant who specializes in government–business relations and is paid by a corporation, a group of corporations, or a business association to make contact with government, or to tell business how to influence government. Government relations consultants monitor government activities for clients, and help them develop strategies and actively lobby for their clients. Independent consultants are often former politicians, civil servants, and political staff, sometimes with industry experience, who operate as individuals or in small partnerships.

A third type of business lobbyist exists where corporations develop lobbying capability "in-house," often referred to as government relations or public affairs staff. Such departments usually report to top management and constantly monitor the political environment for developments that will impact the corporation and industry. They prepare positions for management and may be involved directly in lobbying, or in making presentations to government departments or agencies and civil servants. These departments are discussed in a following section.

There are pros and cons to business lobbying. It is argued that business must lobby to offset the influence of other groups. It should be pointed out that business groups are not the only lobbyists. Consumers, farmers, labour organizations, environmentalists, and religious groups, to name a few, all lobby governments. In fact, such interest group lobbying is part of a capitalist system in a democratic society. It is believed that with each group presenting its point of view, government is better prepared to formulate public policies satisfactory to Canadians. Business argues that its opinion or perspective must be made known to governments if informed decisions are to be made about public policies affecting business.

Lobbying is criticized for several reasons. In the past, some of the practices of lobbying groups were unethical, as seen, for example, by the use of bribes, the offering of gifts, the making of improper political contributions, and even blackmail. As a result, many view lobbying as a distasteful, undesirable activity. It is also argued that the business lobby is far too powerful and presents a view that is too one-sided. Other groups in society claim there is unequal access to government and that business is over represented while other stakeholders are underrepresented. The cost of business lobbying can be passed on to consumers through the prices paid for goods and services, while other groups, such as consumers and environmentalists, do not have the financial and human resources to lobby effectively.

Business lobbying activities have grown and there is continuing involvement of government in the business system. This has necessitated greater lobbying to ensure that business interests are protected. Also, once one corporation or group starts to lobby, others follow out of necessity. It should be remembered that business groups often lobby against one another in an attempt to influence a government decision. For example, Canadian bicycle manufacturers might lobby for increased tariff protection, but retailers that import bicycles might lobby for lower tariffs. This point illustrates that business lobbying is not just business against other groups in society.

Nevertheless, increasing concern was being expressed about business lobbying, and in 1988 the federal government passed an act respecting the registration of lobbyists. In this act, the definition of lobbyist referred to "paid lobbyists" and included those who lobby on behalf of clients and employees of enterprises and organizations that function as lobbyists. According to the government, the purpose of the legislation is not to regulate lobbying, but to make the lobbying process better understood by identifying who is doing it and on what issues. Responsibility of Ethics 10.5 describes some aspects of this legislation.

RESPONSIBILITY FOR ETHICS 10.5

The Lobbying Act

The *Lobbying Act* and its related Regulations came into force simultaneously on July 2, 2008. See below for key events in the history of the Canadian lobbyists registration regime.

The *Lobbying Act* is based on four key principles.

- Free and open access to government is an important matter of public interest.

- Lobbying public office holders is a legitimate activity.

- It is desirable that public office holders and the general public be able to know who is engaged in lobbying activities.

- The system of registration of paid lobbyists should not impede free and open access to government.

The Act applies to individuals who are paid to lobby. People who lobby on a voluntary basis are not required to register.

The Office has developed a Lobbyists' Code of Conduct available at https://ocl-cal.gc.ca/eic/site/012.nsf /eng/h_00014.html and lobbying activity can be searched at Lobbyists' Code of Conduct.

The government is a major stakeholder in the business system influencing business operations, and as discussed in this section business influences government policies, legislation, and regulation through involvement in politics and lobbying.

Want to learn more about lobbying government?

LO 10.7   Corporate Public Affairs Departments

Corporate public affairs is the management function responsible for monitoring and interpreting the governmental environment of the corporation or industry, and for managing the responses necessary to protect the interests of the corporation or industry. Public affairs or government relations departments have been established in many large corporations and managers of such departments should have knowledge of governmental decision-making processes and have credibility with relevant government officials or departments.

Although public affairs initially focused on the relationship between business and government, its role in some corporations has been expanded to include community relations, media relations, environmental monitoring, issues management, lobbying, and public relations. As a result, the corporate public affairs function is found in corporations under a variety of names. Also, corporate public affairs departments have expanded in response to the growing impact of government involvement in the business system, for example in the areas of diversity, environmental protection, occupational health and safety, and consumer protection. It has also been necessary to counteract the lobbying of other stakeholders in society promoting their interests, for example NGOs.

Corporate public affairs has evolved into an occupational profession represented by the Public Affairs Association of Canada (PAAC), a national, not-for-profit organization founded in 1984. Its principal objective is to help public affairs professionals succeed in their work by providing them with forums for professional development, the exchange of new ideas, and networking.[26] The PAAC has an extensive Statement of Ethical Principles, a portion of which is reproduced in Responsibility for Ethics 10.6.

RESPONSIBILITY FOR ETHICS 10.6

PAAC Statement of Principles

The Public Affairs Association of Canada (PAAC) is a gathering place for the interchange of ideas and ideologies, professional development, and practical networking. As the established national organization of public affairs professionals, the PAAC helps define appropriate conduct.

Public affairs professionals work with corporate, charitable, and political clients to engage various audiences. The public affairs profession is recognized increasingly for its high standard of practice and expertise, as well as the impact practitioners have on the development and debate of issues. It is acknowledged for the value and diversity of its contributions to Canadian society.

Public affairs practitioners will:

1. Avoid acting in such a way as to bring harm or disrepute to the profession, colleague, employer, or client.

2. Respect regulatory statutes and meet in full their obligations for disclosure in particular the Charter of Rights, the federal and provincial Lobbyist Registration Acts, Privacy Legislation, and municipal codes as they apply to the jurisdiction of practice.

3. Provide advice, guidance, and an informed opinion as to the nature of the business, policy, or legislative issue in a manner that is forthright and credibly reasoned.

4. Avoid personal and professional conflicts of interest and inform clients and employers as soon as the potential for conflict arises.

5. Ensure that any new engagement is subject to full disclosure with respect to regulatory requirements, the firm, and the client.

6. Be transparent in the management of financial accounts, contractual matters, obligations, and client/organizational interest.

7. Respect interpersonal confidences and confidential information.

Source: Based on "Statement of Principles," Public Affairs Association of Canada, http://www.publicaffairs.ca/who-we-are/ethical-principles/. Used with permission of PAAC.

Public affairs or government relations units continue to play a role when the corporation is attempting to influence government and in interpreting government's influence upon the corporation. Through the three approaches of involvement in politics, lobbying, and public affairs departments, business does influence government policy-making and regulation. These approaches raise the issues of corporate agenda and corporate welfare.

Those individuals and groups in society who question the increasing role of business frequently use the phrase **corporate agenda**, the real or imagined domination of public policy or government programs by corporations or business organizations in their own best interests. The concern is that corporations have too much influence over governments and the lives of individuals. Social activists and union leaders are prominent in their criticism of the alleged corporate agenda.

There is some consensus on the components of such an agenda. The corporate agenda usually includes some or all of the following:

• The reduction of government involvement in the economy through privatization, downsizing, and outsourcing.

• The deregulation of business and industry.

• Reduced corporate taxation and personal income taxation of higher-income earners along with an overall shifting of tax burdens to working individuals.

• Advocacy of deficit and debt reduction.

• Reduction in government expenditures on social services to low- and middle-income individuals.

• The enactment of free trade agreements and support for globalization.

• The weakening of unions and workers' right to organize.

• Increasing lobbying and involvement in the political process by business including the formation of partnerships between business and government.

Despite this alleged corporate agenda, corporations and industries appear increasingly willing to advocate for and accept government assistance referred to as **corporate welfare**—any action by municipal, provincial, or federal governments that gives a specific corporation or an entire industry a benefit not offered to others. It is a pejorative term attributed to Ralph Nader, who first used the term in 1956 to describe the special treatment received by business. The term "corporate welfare bums" was used by NDP leader David Lewis in the 1972 federal election campaign to emphasize the preferential treatment received by business.[27] The term contrasts with social welfare and suggests receiving a benefit without doing anything. All forms of government assistance are included, for example grants, loans, loan guarantees, tax breaks, trade barriers, and legislated monopolies. The practice is criticized as it is considered unfair to other corporations and to taxpayers and consumers. The term constantly appears in media stories relating to the subsidies received by business.

The hypocrisy of business lobbying for and accepting government assistance is not lost on many stakeholders. The corporate agenda advocates less government regulation and a reduction in social programs—that is, social welfare—while advocating for benefits to business.

Regulating business ethics and responsibilities involves several approaches to influencing the conduct of corporations. Regulation by government is the main approach used in the Canadian business system, but it is not the sole source of influence. On the other hand, corporations attempt to influence through lobbying and the operation of public affairs departments.

Your advice to Luke . . .

You advise Luke that you understand he may be somewhat quick in criticizing corporations for receiving government assistance; however, most citizens receive benefits from governments, including students. Hopefully, if loans are involved, they are repaid—unlike the practice with government assistance to business. Everyone should be cautious in accusing others of being social or corporate "welfare bums."

Summary

- Business is regulated by government, self-regulation by business itself, private or civil regulation, and market forces. Many in society believe that only government regulates business. Most economies rely on a combination of the four forms. (LO 10.1)

- The federal government has recognized the importance of corporate social responsibility and has been involved with several initiatives to ensure Canadian corporations behave in ways that are socially and environmentally responsible. (LO 10.2)

- The Canadian government is attempting to discourage corruption of corporations and their managers in Canada and abroad. As a result, the government is involved in anti-corruption initiatives. (LO 10.3)

- Government's taxation of corporate and personal income raises issues relating to the fairness of the taxation system and how some corporations and individuals can legally avoid paying taxes. This is accomplished by shifting operations to low-tax havens or finding loopholes in the system. (LO 10.4)

- Business is involved in Canadian politics through financing political parties, supporting particular candidates, expressing views on public issues, allowing employees to participate in the political process, and through businesspersons seeking public office. (LO 10.5)

- Lobbying is any attempt to influence directly or indirectly any government activity, and includes any attempt to influence legislators, their staff, public administrators, and members of regulatory agencies. Corporations or industry organizations can have their own employees as lobbyists or can hire consultants to perform the function. Lobbying is controversial and is being increasingly regulated. Even though business devotes considerable resources to lobbying, its efforts are not always successful. (LO 10.6)

- Corporate public affairs departments perform the management function responsible for monitoring and interpreting the governmental environment of the corporation or industry and for managing the responses necessary to protect the interests of the corporation or industry. Some claim that business' capability to influence government has resulted in a corporate agenda where it dominates government actions. While business advocates the reduction of government involvement in the economy, it also seeks government assistance and protection—a practice known as corporate welfare. (LO 10.7)

Key Terms

Deregulation

Privatization

Self-regulation

Self-regulatory organizations (SROs)

Private or civil regulation

Third-party certification

Remediation agreements

Tax haven

Transfer pricing

Lobbying

Corporate public affairs

Corporate agenda

Corporate welfare

Critical Thinking and Discussion Questions

1. Why do most Canadians believe that only the government regulates business?

2. What are the dangers of or downsides to business self-regulation?

3. What issues are involved in third-party certification?

4. Why should government be encouraging corporations to be socially and environmentally responsible?

5. What are the controversies associated with the government dealing with corporate corruption?

6. Why do corporations and individuals attempt to avoid responsibility for paying the taxes they owe? What should be done about it?

7. Should corporations and businesspersons be involved in the political process at all?

8. How can business lobbying of government be justified?

9. What are some of the dangers of business lobbying?

10. Why is it necessary for corporations to have a corporate public affairs department?

11. What evidence is there that governments operate with a corporate agenda?

12. Should corporate welfare be stopped?

Cases

10.1 YUKON ALCOHOL STUDY AND LOBBYING

The consumption of alcohol in Canada results in an economic cost of about $14 billion per year from lost productivity, direct health costs, and enforcement. Research has found that alcohol consumption increases the risk of breast and colon cancer, causes cirrhosis of the liver, and leads to impaired driving resulting in automobile and other accidents. A World Health Organization body, the International Agency for Research on Cancer, has established that alcohol consumption causes some cancers.

The Yukon government and the Yukon Liquor Corporation were concerned about the territory's higher heavy drinking rates. They felt that it was their social responsibility to inform consumers about the consequences of alcohol. They agreed to participate in a study to test the impact of alcohol warning labels using alcohol sales data and surveys in Whitehorse, Yukon, where products would be labelled, and Yellowknife, Northwest Territories, where they would not. Known as the Northern Territories Alcohol Study, it was to assess local attitudes, opinions, and behaviours related to alcohol, and the effect of warning labels. In May 2017, it was agreed that researchers from Public Health Ontario and the Canadian Institute for Substance Abuse, University of Victoria, would partner with the government and corporation to conduct this study. It was funded by Health Canada.

On November 22, 2017, warning labels were placed on alcohol products at the Whitehorse store. The labels advised consumers to drink in moderation and about the risks of alcohol, in particular the link between alcohol and cancer. There had been labels since 1991 warning that drinking alcohol during pregnancy can cause birth defects, but this was stopped with the new labels. Dozens of countries have mandatory health labelling on alcohol.

The national alcohol, beer, and wine trade associations expressed concerns about the labelling. They questioned the legislative authority to label the containers; moreover, labels were fixed without their consent and blocked out other information. There was also the possibility of the infringement of trademarks and possible defamation. The industries were also concerned about other jurisdictions starting similar labelling. The associations lobbied the Yukon government and contacted the research organizations, stating that the researchers were biased, the labels false and alarmist, and the study was fatally flawed. In particular, they questioned the link between alcohol and cancer.

On December 19, 2017, the study was halted when the government caved in to avoid legal action for defamation and trademark infringement. After discussions among the parties, the study resumed on February 15, 2018, using two labels to educate consumers: one that shows a standard drink size, and a second that provides low-risk drinking guidelines. The health-warning label about cancer would no longer be part of the study. Results of the study are expected in 2019.

Questions

1. What is the social responsibility of liquor commissions or the government?
2. Was the labelling appropriate and in the best interests of consumers?
3. Were the lobbying efforts of the national brand manufacturers appropriate?
4. What should the Government of Yukon and the Yukon Liquor Commission do if (1) the study proves that the labelling reduces alcohol consumption or misuse, and (2) the study proves that the labelling does not reduce alcohol consumption or misuse?

10.2 ZAPPING SALES AND TAXES

Julia Hoben had graduated from a college business program with a major in accounting. She designed her program so that it enabled her to obtain a Chartered Professional Accountant (CPA) designation within two years. She was employed as an accountant with a regional school board and she was enjoying the work.

Recently, her uncle asked if she was interested in doing some accounting for his restaurant. Julia first thought about this as moonlighting, which her employer might not approve of. She checked her employer's policy handbook and did not find any mention of moonlighting.

Julia had learned in a Human Resources course about moonlighting and the issues involved. Moonlighting, or outside employment, is defined as paid work in which an employee engages outside of the normal working hours of their primary job. The most common reason for engaging in such activity is to earn extra money to pay expenses, reduce debt, or save. Individuals also do it to gain experience, improve their skills, start small businesses, or simply because they enjoy it.

Employers are concerned about the possible interference with job performance and conflicts of interest. Moonlighting may result in employees being stressed or fatigued, reducing productivity. It could involve the inappropriate use of company resources, such as communications, computers, and copying facilities. Conflicts of interest can arise, especially if the work being performed is the same and in the same industry. Conflicts also occur when personal interests resulting from moonlighting clash with the interests of the employer who expects employee loyalty. As a result, employers often require that employees disclose outside employment. From a societal perspective, moonlighting is perceived as taking jobs that could be filled by unemployed persons, and governments are concerned about tax evasion.

Her uncle assured her that he needed Julia's services for a maximum of three hours a week and would pay her an hourly rate. Julia would not be performing bookkeeping tasks, because her aunt looked after that aspect. Her uncle wanted Julia to look after the various tax filings for the provincial government and the Canadian Revenue Agency (CRA) as the filings would be considered more reliable if prepared by someone with a professional accounting designation. Julia concluded that there was no conflict between working for a school board and in the restaurant industry, and agreed to the offer. She did not feel it necessary to inform her employer.

During the first months, Julia experienced several complications in this part-time employment. Her first concern was prompted when her uncle paid her in cash for the first two weeks of work. At first, Julia did not think much about this, but upon further reflection she acknowledged that cash payments to employees or suppliers in the restaurant industry were a possible approach to avoiding taxes.

Things got more complicated in the following weeks. The restaurant used a point of sale (POS) computerized system to record sales according to whether they were credit card or cash, and summarized sales by menu items and waiter. Julia reviewed the reports from this system in preparing taxation returns. She noticed that daily cash versus credit sales fluctuated greatly—more than would be expected. Also, she found two POS reports for the same day with differing totals.

Julia had read newspaper articles about tax avoidance in the restaurant industry. In fact, CRA had conducted an extensive investigation into tax fraud in the industry. One practice involved the use of "zapper" computer software to delete specific data, such as cash sales or employee hours. This practice was difficult to detect because a stand-alone software application was used that was contained on a CD or memory stick.

This situation placed Julia in a difficult position. First of all, family was involved and it would harm family relationships if she reported the practice to the taxation agencies, or if she even mentioned it to her uncle. Besides the personal dilemma, there was also a professional one. As a member of Chartered Professional Accountants she had to follow its ethical principles and rules of conduct. She was not allowed to provide services that could be unlawful, to present financial information that was misleading, or to be associated with any reports or statements she knows are false.

These principles and rules seemed very clear to Julia. Her conscience would not allow her to sign a taxation return when she suspected fraud. Julia felt very alone as she was not sure with whom she could discuss this matter, or, more importantly, what she should do.

Questions

1. What ethical issues are involved?
2. What fundamentals of capitalism are involved?
3. Why should individuals and businesses pay taxes?
4. What should Julia do?

Canadians can own responsible business corporations.
Used © Shutterstock/Jirapong Manustrong

CHAPTER 11

Responsible Ownership and Governance

LEARNING OUTCOMES

After studying this chapter, you will be able to:

LO 11.1 Identify the owners of Canadian business.

LO 11.2 List and explain the ethical and responsibility issues of ownership.

LO 11.3 Define and understand the challenges of responsible investing.

LO 11.4 Describe approaches to protecting owners and investors.

LO 11.5 Define corporate governance and discuss the issues relating to corporate governance.

LO 11.6 Explain the relationships among ownership, corporate governance, and social responsibility and ethical conduct.

What would you do if...?

Felicia Desterro was in the third year of a business program and recently had become interested in the role of responsible investing. Throughout her college years, she had also become interested in the environment including topics such as climate change, greenhouse gas, and CO_2 emissions. She regularly attended meetings of environmental groups held on campus and presentations by faculty or others on the damage occurring to the environment from our consumption of fossil fuels.

At one of the meetings, she was approached to become more active, and in particular, to organize a campaign to obtain a commitment from the College's Board of Governors to sell investments in fossil fuel corporations. College had an endowment fund of $275 million which provided student scholarships and an employee pension fund of $190 million. Over 40 colleges and universities in Canada, and hundreds around the world, had started such campaigns. In addition, municipal and religious institutions had become involved. Felicia decided to do some research into these campaigns.

The divestment of the stocks held by colleges and universities is not a new initiative, for example, there was a divesting of tobacco stocks in the 1990s. The Canadian Youth Climate Coalition (CYCC) has been heading up the student environmental movement nationally. In January 2013 CCYC launched its Fossil Free Canada campaign calling for individuals and institutions to divest from fossil fuels. It is requesting that institutions immediately stop purchasing any new investments in fossil fuel corporations and to divest all investments within five years.

Felicia would receive assistance from this group to prepare a campaign on campus. CCYC provided advice on how to launch a petition, build a team to assist, plan for the campaign, build support, press decision makers, and escalate the campaign with demonstrations. It provided posters, leaflets, buttons, toolkits, guides, and background materials. She learnt that most divestment campaigns were initiated by students, but faculty also participated in many cases. Any campaign would involve students, faculty, and the Board of Governors and would make a statement of the college's commitment to the environment.

During her research, Felicia came across some counter arguments to divestment. First of all, it is a complicated process as investments are often in pooled funds (such as hedge, mutual, and venture funds) as opposed to individual stocks, and that there were few funds completely free of non-renewable energy corporations. Educational institutions had legal and financial obligations relating to the endowment funds that had to be respected. There are likely to be economic costs, that is, lower returns on investments. Resources for scholarships may be reduced or in the case of pension funds, payments had to be made to retirees.

Furthermore, energy corporations were major contributors to college campaigns for buildings and programs in addition to hiring many graduates. The fact that many energy corporations were involved with renewable energy sources was ignored. The divestment campaigns were criticized for being anti-business and were mainly symbolic rather than substantive. Some critics claimed that divestment campaigns had little economic effect on the targeted corporations. The campaigns had little impact on the consumption of fossil fuels as society, including students, relied on the products and services of these corporations every day. The alternatives suggested were to invest in researching cleaner energy technology, and to work with corporations to change their behaviour towards energy consumption. It was also pointed out that colleges could establish low-carbon endowment funds to which students and faculty could donate.

What is your advice to Felicia?

Owners, also referred to as investors or shareholders, are key stakeholders in a capitalist system as they provide a major portion of the capital to finance corporations. Although many stakeholders influence the corporation, a corporation is for the shareholders; they own it, and should ultimately control it. The ownership patterns of Canadian business are changing, and owners have varying degrees of influence on corporate social responsibility and the moral behaviour of the corporation. Ownership will be the focus of the first four sections of this chapter.

The fifth and sixth sections will examine how the corporation is governed and discuss the main stakeholder involved, the members of the Board of Directors. A governing system includes the processes, structures, and relationships through which decisions are made. Corporate governance is defined and some aspects examined. The relationship between governance and performance is discussed along with the relationship to corporate social responsibility and the ethics of business.

LO 11.1   The Ownership of Canadian Business

Who owns Canadian business? A quick response would be "shareholders," but the answer is not as straightforward as this. Table 11.1 lists the main types of owners of Canadian businesses. Some owners personally own equity in the corporation either as investors, entrepreneurs, employees or managers, customers or consumers, or producers.

TABLE 11.1	Owners of Canadian Business

Investors—Investors are individuals who personally hold equity interests for investment purposes and who are not involved in the corporation as entrepreneurs or managers. Those individuals who have purchased shares in corporations listed on a stock exchange are an example of this type of owner.

Entrepreneurs—Ownership of business by individuals—that is, entrepreneurs—is a common form of ownership and has become increasingly so in recent years. Small businesses with fewer than 100 employees, are an important force in Canada, accounting for nearly 98 percent of all enterprises.

Employees and managers—Employees including managers may own all or parts of corporations. Employee ownership can take several forms, including participation in an employee stock purchase plan or employee share ownership plan (ESOP); cooperation with an entrepreneur to refinance a corporation and operate it as a going concern; and establishment of a worker cooperative.

Customers or consumers—The most common type of business organization owned by customers is the co-operative, and the most widely recognized among these are retail consumer co-operatives and financial institutions such as credit unions or caisses populaires. Co-operatives have been leaders in institutionalizing ethics and responsibilities.

Producers—Producer ownership is through co-operatives of various types. There are more than 150 agricultural marketing co-operatives in dairy, grain, poultry, and other endeavours. In addition there are farm supply, fisheries, and production co-operatives.

Ownership through mutual funds—A **mutual fund** is a pool of money from many individual investors that is invested on their behalf, usually in a specific kind of investment. Money contributed to equity mutual funds is invested by fund managers in a portfolio of shares in corporations. Ownership via mutual funds appeals to some investors as it allows them to participate in the stock market without having to make separate decisions about each purchase or sale of stocks.

Ownership interest through pension funds—A substantial portion of pension fund assets are invested in corporate stock. Thus, many Canadians are most likely unaware that they are investing in Canadian business.

Corporate ownership—Corporations often own shares in other enterprises. This inter-corporate ownership is widespread and is monitored by the government. The purpose of the monitoring is to ascertain whether monopoly behaviour occurs and to identify foreign ownership.

Private equity firms—**Private equity firms** manage large pools of money acquired from wealthy individuals or families and big institutions such as pension and mutual funds. The firms are private in the sense that they are not listed and traded on a stock exchange.

Venture capital companies—A **venture capital company** is a type of private equity firm that usually acquires part ownership of business enterprises for which they provide financial and management assistance.

Not-for-profit organization ownership—Examples of not-for-profit organizations are churches, non-governmental organizations (NGOs), foundations, and universities, and all are likely to be concerned with the integrity of business. Investment or endowment funds in these organizations sometimes own stock in corporations.

Government ownership—Canadian federal, provincial, and municipal governments all operate a large number of business enterprises, sometimes referred to as Crown corporations. Government-owned corporations have been used extensively as instruments of public policy implementation, and are considered by some to be part of the Canadian economic culture.

Challenges arise from any type of ownership but the issues facing investors are the most examined. In the situation when the ownership of the corporation is widely dispersed among thousands of shareholders, it is argued that management actually controls the corporation. Individual investors lack the means, and maybe the will, to unite and challenge management's decisions. At the other extreme, investors who are shareholders in corporations dominated by one or a few shareholders who have controlling interests are virtually powerless also. Their few votes make no difference, as sufficient votes are controlled by the dominating shareholder. Corporations with a dominant shareholder must be sensitive to treating minority shareholders with respect and fairness.

Traditionally, the ownership of one share meant one vote and, at least in principle, the owners of shares directed the affairs of the corporation by evaluating management's performance and deciding upon the acquisition and disposal of assets. In other words, shareholders had certain rights based upon their voting privileges. However, many corporations operate with **dual-class stock**, where more than one type of share or stock with different voting rights and dividend payments is issued by a single corporation. Also, **non-voting shares** or **restricted shares** (sometimes referred to as *uncommon shares*) are allowed on the Toronto Stock Exchange. Non-voting shares are common shares without voting privileges, while restricted shares involve some limit on voting, for example only one vote for every 10 or 100 shares owned. The creation of these types of shares allows management or majority owners to control the corporation by concentrating voting power in the hands of a few friendly shareholders. The result is ownership (or stake) without control (or influence), and the fundamental tenet that ownership entails control is contradicted. Such a circumstance is believed to represent a threat to economic democracy and might lead to a decay of a central feature of the free market system. Issues of fairness and rights of other shareholders arise when some shareholders have control through the use of non-voting shares. Often shareholders have no other recourse than to sell their shares if they disagree with the control exercised by the voting shares.

Investors or shareholders can be categorized as passive or active. **Passive shareholders** are those who do not attempt to influence the affairs of the corporation even though they have a legal right to do so. Many small shareholders simply cast their votes with management without considering alternatives. There may be a feeling of hopelessness, but nevertheless they have some responsibility for at least being informed about the corporation and exercising their voting privileges. **Active shareholders** are those who participate in the governance to the full extent allowed by the law. This can be an individual shareholder but also the individuals who manage pension and mutual funds. In the past, these shareholders were "passive"; that is, they did not exercise voting rights or otherwise attempt to influence the affairs of the corporation despite owning substantial numbers of shares. Active shareholders may take an interest in social responsibility issues as will be discussed later.

It is claimed that employee ownership increases morale and company loyalty, motivating employees to greater effort. Productivity rises, and higher profitability results. **Worker capitalism** is a term used to describe employee ownership as workers are turned into capitalists through stock ownership. If widespread, employee ownership could lead to a de-concentration of wealth. Employee ownership has been shown to be an important variable in reviving the fortunes of corporations that were not profitable enough to satisfy existing owners. Although not bankrupt, these corporations, or branch plants, were often abandoned by their owners and rescued by management, entrepreneurs, and employees. In this manner, jobs were saved.

Employee ownership is not without difficulties. Employees who invest in the corporation for which they work are in effect increasing their stake in the corporation. Their jobs, and often savings and pensions, depend now upon the fate of one corporation. Seldom do employees have majority ownership and control of the corporation. Management may still run the corporation as it wishes, not relinquishing control to employees. By not disclosing financial and operating results, employees are often kept unaware of how well the corporation is doing, and in some cases may be manipulated by management as needed information is not available. If employees own shares their participation in decision making may lead to nothing getting done, with the endless meetings, discussions, and votes being very time consuming. In some cases, only token democracy is practised in the workplace despite the employee involvement in ownership, and the prospects for job security are not enhanced.

Some issues directly related to ownership have been identified and the next section describes some issues related to corporate social responsibility.

LO 11.2 Ethical and Responsibility Issues of Ownership

There are ethical issues relating to how some owners are treated by others, and how owners treat other stakeholders. The actions of other stakeholders—for example governments, other corporations, and self-regulatory organizations—influence the owner stakeholder. Knowledge of how owners are influenced and/or influence is important to understanding the implications for corporate citizenship. The following are illustrations of the ethical issues relating to ownership and how they are acted upon.

Investor owners have limited influence in making the corporation more socially responsible, but some do attempt it through presenting shareholder resolutions to annual meetings. Examples are provided in Responsibility for Ethics 11.1. Few of these resolutions are successful, but they alert management to social concerns and so do have an influence. These resolutions are proposed by a variety of stakeholders, including individual investors, mutual and pension funds, financial institutions such as credit unions, and non-governmental organizations. The resolution topics tend to vary over time with some relating to a variety of social responsibility issues.

 RESPONSIBILITY FOR ETHICS 11.1

Social Responsibility Shareholder Resolutions

The *Canada Business Corporations Act* requires that shareholder proposals or resolutions be circulated to shareholders and voted upon at the corporation's annual meeting. Investor or shareholder resolutions are presented on a variety of topics, including those related to ethical, social, and environmental responsibility, but they are seldom passed and sometimes withdrawn after discussions with corporate management. What follows are examples of social responsibility–related proposals and corporations targeted during 2017–19:

- Prepare a report outlining how the company respects internationally recognized standards for Indigenous Peoples' rights in its business operations. (TransCanada Corporation)

- Publish a brief report every year in order to enable shareholders to assess its exposure to climate risk and its contribution to the transition to a low-carbon-emission economy. (Royal Bank of Canada)

- Assuring sound commercial practices regarding the sale of financial products and services by requiring executives to sign a statement confirming they will comply with principles of loyalty, integrity, and honesty in their customer relations, with disciplinary measures for failure to comply. (CIBC)

- Requiring the board undertake a review and report to shareholders on the feasibility, cost, and benefits of implementing a Living Wage policy covering employees, suppliers, and contractors. (Loblaw Companies Ltd.)

- Disclosure of company operations in Bermuda and other "low tax rate territories." (Manulife Group)

Want to learn more about what shareholders are demanding of corporations?

Mutual funds can be purchased that invest in corporations considered to have a social, ethical and environmental focus or objective. Some pension plans have also revised their investment strategy to acquire the stock of socially responsible corporations. Some pension fund managers have endorsed the purchase of ethically and environmentally responsible investments of corporations with a good record of corporate social responsibility. Even the Canada Pension Plan (CPP) fund now invests in equities and has a responsible investing policy. This policy may satisfy Canadian citizens concerned about social responsibility and alerts managers to criteria used by the CPP when investing in corporations.

The investment or endowment funds of not-for-profit organizations sometimes own stock in corporations. The extent of this ownership is not great, and any one organization seldom owns a large portion of a particular enterprise. However, the influence of these owners may be greater than their small holdings indicate. In particular, church groups or NGOs have achieved a high profile by questioning aspects of a corporation's operations at annual meetings and other public forums. Some of these NGOs, for example Oxfam, may operate commercially oriented social enterprises. The portfolios of universities are carefully scrutinized by students and faculty for investments in corporations involved in unethical activities or irresponsible behaviour. This scrutiny has led to many universities divesting investments in some corporations as advocated by the Coalition of Universities for Responsible Investing. Its mission is to increase awareness of integrating social, environmental, and governance issues into investment decisions.

Employee, consumer, and producer owners have formed co-operatives through which to achieve ownership. Ownership in all co-operatives is based on the principle that one member has one vote, and each member contributes the same amount of equity. Profits are not the purpose of co-operatives, but some do distribute surplus funds equally to members. Employees, customers, and producers most likely become involved in business ownership for social purposes; that is, to preserve jobs, to provide particular goods or services that are socially acceptable, and to establish socially appropriate distribution systems. Co-operatives have been leaders in institutionalizing ethics and responsibilities, as the examples in Everyday Ethics 11.1 illustrate.

Social Responsibility at Co-operatives and Credit Unions

Mountain Equipment Co-op (MEC) is Canada's largest retailer of quality outdoor equipment and has more than 5 million members, or owners, around the world. One MEC value is to operate ethically and with integrity. It fulfills this value by committing to the ethical sourcing of merchandise, constructing and operating "green" buildings, pursuing energy conservation and waste reduction, and supporting community conservation and outdoor recreation groups. In 2018, MEC had 22 stores with total sales of $445 million.

Vancouver City Savings Credit Union (Vancity) is a credit union providing banking, borrowing, lending, and insurance services. In 2018, it had over 525,000 customers, or owners, in British Columbia and total assets of $26.4 billion. It has received many awards for its social responsibility. It focuses on the environment by addressing climate change, practising green banking, indicating ways to grow the social economy, outlining socially responsible investing, and listing community initiatives. A "Greenhouse Gas Handbook Inventory Report" is published annually, outlining the procedures and methodologies Vancity uses to assess and estimate the emissions of greenhouse gasses associated with its business and business operations.

The accountability for economic, social, and environmental responsibilities has become common among publicly traded corporations. Other corporations are less, if at all, accountable, for example privately owned corporations and private equity firms. These corporations avoid much of the government regulation imposed on publicly traded corporations and can often ignore societal pressure. These companies do not have to disclose top management compensation and are not subject to the stock exchange disclosure requirements. This may change in the future as these corporations use capital provided by pension and mutual funds, which are more publicly accountable, often insisting on corporate social responsibility auditing and reporting.

The accountability, or control, of the corporations owned by the government has been a major public administration issue referred to as an "accountability dilemma." The trend to making Crown corporations operate in a more commercial manner has resulted in several accountability problems, including (1) the newly defined, commercially oriented objectives of many government-owned corporations that may be in conflict with social objectives in the national interest; (2) the consequences of evaluating performance based on commercial criteria (that is, profits); (3) the degree of autonomy that should be granted the corporations and their managements; and (4) the techniques for controlling and evaluating the commercial corporations. Just because government owns a corporation does not ensure it will practise appropriate corporate social and environmental responsibility.

Owners have an economic responsibility if they wish their corporation to survive while at the same time being concerned about the responsibility for the ethical or social impact of the business. Owners have varying influences over the operation of their businesses, including how the corporation responds to its social or ethical environment. Today, many owners are focusing on responsible investing, which is having an impact on how the corporation behaves.

LO 11.3 Responsible Investing

Responsible investment (RI) "is an approach to investing that aims to incorporate environmental, social and governance (ESG) factors into investment decisions, to better manage risk and generate sustainable, long-term returns."[1] These investments are usually stocks of publicly traded corporations, but some funds comprise bonds and other investments that are "balanced" between equity and debt. RI is also referred to as socially responsible investing, ethical investing, sustainable investing, community investing, mission-based investing, impact investing, or social conscience investment, and, in the context of the environment, green investing or environmentally friendly investing.

Two organizations promoting responsible investing are the Principles for Responsible Investment on an international level and the Responsible Investment Association in Canada. Both are described in Responsibility for Ethics 11.2.

RESPONSIBILITY FOR ETHICS 11.2

Organizations Promoting Responsible Investment

Principles for Responsible Investment (PRI)

The Principles were formulated in partnership with the UNEP Finance Initiative and the UN Global Compact by investors, for investors, with the objective of contributing to the development of a more sustainable global financial system. The initiative was prompted as environmental, social, and governance (ESG) issues can affect the performance of investment portfolios. The signatories to the principles represent a majority of the world's professionally managed investments and adoption is voluntary. The Principles are as follows:

Principle 1: "We will incorporate ESG issues into investment analysis and decision-making processes."

Principle 2: "We will be active owners and incorporate ESG issues into our ownership policies and practices."

Principle 3: "We will seek appropriate disclosure on ESG issues by the entities in which we invest."

Principle 4: "We will promote acceptance and implementation of the Principles within the investment industry."

Principle 5: "We will work together to enhance our effectiveness in implementing the Principles."

Principle 6: "We will each report on our activities and progress towards implementing the Principles."

Responsible Investment Association (RIA) in Canada

RIA comprises 100 organizational members, such as asset managers, asset owners, and service providers, and 250 individual members, such as advisors, consultants, and other professionals. Originally focusing on socially responsible investing, RIA has evolved with the industry and encompasses the broader scope of responsible investing, which incorporates environmental, social, and governance (ESG) issues in the selection and management of investments. Over $2 billion of investments were made using some form of responsible investing strategies.

RIA has five strategic priorities for encouraging responsible investment:

- **Market Education**—Driving awareness and demand for responsible investments
- **Integration**—Developing RI (responsible investment) capacity in investment professionals
- **Advocacy**—Shifting public policy and regulation to support RI
- **Brand and Reputation**—Strengthening the RIA's reputation as the leading voice for RI in Canada
- **Capacity Building**—Building the RIA's financial and human capital resources

Source: "About the PRI," Principles for Responsible Investment (PRI) at https://www.unpri.org/about-the-pri and "About," Responsible Investment Association, https://riacanada.ca/about/. Used with permission.

Awareness is growing surrounding the possibilities of achieving acceptable rates of return and social objectives at the same time. Individual investors have an appreciation of this, but the awareness has most likely been fuelled by the investment decisions of churches and other religious organizations, trade unions, women's organizations, co-operative systems, the environmental movement, universities and colleges, and pensions funds. The Canadian financial community has quickly responded to the growing awareness of and demand for socially responsive investments. An RIA comparison of market performance shows responsible investment exceeding that of the Toronto Stock Exchange's S&P Composite and S&P 60 indices.[2]

Decisions on responsible investment usually use three possible approaches: positive screening, negative screening, or best-of-sector. Positive screening leads to investing in corporations with good social and environmental records and enlightened industrial and stakeholder relations. Negative screening identifies objectionable corporations; those, for example, involved in alcohol, tobacco, weapons, and nuclear power. Examples of investment criteria included in the screens are listed in Table 11.2. Not all funds apply all these criteria.

TABLE 11.2	Responsible Investment Criteria

The criteria or screens used in making responsible investments vary by fund and provide a method by which a prospective investment is judged to be socially acceptable. Activities that might be considered socially irresponsible or unethical include:

- poor employee/labour relations
- failure to promote racial and sexual equality and affirmative action programs
- the manufacture of controversial weapons
- involvement in the nuclear industry
- use of fossil fuels, especially coal
- the manufacture of "sin" products such as alcohol or tobacco
- the conducting of business in repressive regimes
- the violation of human rights
- failure to involve Indigenous Peoples
- environmentally damaging operations, for example, those that pollute
- unsafe goods and services, questionable marketing practices, and exploitive marketing in developing countries
- use of animals in product testing
- involvement in gambling and pornography
- factory farm production of animals
- genetically modified product
- child or forced labour

The best-of-sector approach compares and ranks corporations within an industry. As few corporations have perfect social responsibility records or performance, this approach identifies corporations best in an industry. It is believed that it preferable to invest in these corporations and attempt to influence them in improving their social responsibility. An acceptable target period or date should be established by which the corporations will improve. Not investing in a corporation with less than a perfect record does not give the investor a voice to influence corporation behaviour. This engagement with the corporation sends a signal from investors that social responsibility is important to investment decisions. Boycotting, or not buying a stock, seldom works in that the corporation is not influenced. Through ranking within an industry, the investor is trying to have some influence.

The motives of the financial community raise compelling thoughts. Does it really believe in socially responsible investing or is this simply a response to a market demand? Are the funds merely shrewd marketing? The motives of investors can also be questioned. For how long would they continue to invest in a socially responsible corporation or fund that lost money? There are several stock indices of corporate social responsibility performance listed in Responsibility for Ethics 11.3 for persons interested in making responsible investments.

 RESPONSIBILITY FOR ETHICS 11.3

Responsible Investment Stock Market Indices

Here are examples of responsible investment stock indices:

Sustainalytics/Jantzi Social Index (JSI) (Canada)—A stock index of socially screened investments developed to create a benchmark against which investors can measure the performance of their responsible investments.

S&P/TSX Renewable Energy and Clean Technology Index (Canada)—This index measures performance of companies listed on the TSX whose core business is the development of green technologies and sustainable infrastructure solutions.

Dow Jones Sustainability Indices (U.S.)—The indices cover the top 10 percent of the biggest 2,500 companies in the Dow Jones World Index in terms of economic, environmental, and social criteria and the Dow Jones STOXX Sustainability Index, which covers the leading 20 percent in terms of sustainability of the companies in the Dow Jones STOXX SM 600 Index.

FTSE4Good Index Series (U.K.)—These indices are designed to measure the performance of companies demonstrating strong environmental, social, and governance (ESG) practices.

Another dynamic of responsible investing is the role of mutual and pension funds. It is possible that the managers of such funds will come under pressure from fund contributors to invest in such a way that reflects their social values. The managers, in turn, might make an investment decision on social criteria that pressures corporation managers to behave in socially responsible ways. Also, some fund managers purchase shares in some corporations in the hopes of changing the corporation's behaviour. The influence of such pressure is not clear at this time. Even so, individuals making investments through funds may be prompting decisions that influence managers to improve their corporation's social performance.

There have been responsible investing developments relating to Indigenous Peoples. The Responsible Investment Association (Canada) states that investors should learn about the cultures and histories of Indigenous Peoples. This awareness would help investors understand how corporate projects would affect Indigenous rights resulting in better relations with Indigenous organizations.[3] The Canadian Council for Aboriginal Business has a certification program, Progressive Aboriginal Relations (PAR), that allows for self-assessment of corporate performance in Aboriginal relations. The CCAB offers a certification to corporations recognized as good business partners, great places to work, and committed to prosperity in Aboriginal communities. There are several dozen PAR corporations.[4] The National Aboriginal Trust Officers Association (NATOA) has a Responsible Investment Committee that formulates the direction the association will take in providing information to the membership in the area of responsible investment, which includes socially responsible investing (SRI) initiatives, and ethical, sustainable, and governance (ESG) activities.[5] NATOA and the Shareholders Association for Research and Education (SHARE) has published a report, *Advancing Reconciliation in Canada: A Guide for Investors*. This report will provide information that investors can use in making reconciliation a part of decision making when doing business with Indigenous peoples.[6]

There are challenges to ascertaining what a socially responsible investment is. In particular, one researcher claimed that social investing was a myth. His critique made the following points:

- The data relied upon are sketchy and the research is highly selective.

- The ratings are not completely objective and misrepresent the complexity of the modern corporation.

- The screenings are tainted by anachronistic, contradictory, idiosyncratic, and ideologically constructed notions of social responsibility.

- Claims of the growing financial impact are questionable.

- No coherent case has been made for why the criteria used for social responsibility are better at effecting social change.

- The researcher concludes that the general approach of social investment advocates is one of vindication of the true believer, not investigation.[7]

It is not always easy to be socially responsible, but corporations are making the efforts. Furthermore, the concept of responsible investing is being taught in universities and colleges and centres to study it are being established. Investors or shareholders own the corporation and many efforts are made to ensure they are responsible stakeholders. Their influence includes the corporation's approach to corporate social responsibility, and the most direct way to accomplish this is through responsible investing, a trend that is increasing. Whether investors are concerned about responsible investing or not, there is still a need to protect their interests.

LO 11.4 Protecting Owners and Investors

Protection of owners or investors is a primary issue and several stakeholders are involved, including directors, governments, self-regulatory agencies, financial industry institutions and associations, shareholder activists, and managers. A term used to describe the responsibilities towards owners is **shareholder democracy**, the exercise of power of owners to ensure that they are treated fairly and enjoy equally the privileges and duties of ownership. There is general agreement that shareholders have some of the same rights as owners, namely voting power on major decisions, the transfer to ownership when desired, the entitlement to dividends, and accessibility to accurate and timely financial information. These rights vary with the type of share owned.

Want to learn more about **shareholder democracy**?

Several stakeholders attempt to ensure these rights; many of them are identified in Responsibility for Ethics 11.4. Given the numerous financial scandals, inappropriate market activity, and losses suffered by investors, governments and the financial industry are currently re-examining the adequacy of investor protection. Despite the numerous government initiatives, self-regulatory organizations, and industry associations, investors are still suffering losses due to illegal or unethical behaviour on the part of financial industry managers. Reliance on the government regulation does not appear sufficient to protect shareholders, and it is suggested that no one is guarding the guards—that is, the regulators, whether government or self-regulators.

⚖️ **RESPONSIBILITY FOR ETHICS 11.4**

Stakeholders Protecting the Rights of Owners

Governments

- Incorporation and securities laws, for example the *Canada Business Corporations Act*, protect shareholder rights. Such laws exist at the provincial level also.

- The *Sarbanes-Oxley Act* of 2002, which is U.S. legislation passed to protect investors by improving the accuracy and reliability of corporate disclosures. Canadian corporations are affected if they obtain capital on U.S. markets; this Act established practices later included in Canadian legislation and regulations.

- The RCMP's Integrated Market Enforcement Teams, which are groups of highly specialized investigators dedicated to ensuring that those who commit serious capital market fraud offences will be detected, charged, and prosecuted.

Self-Regulatory Agencies and Organizations

- Stock exchanges—in particular the Toronto Stock Exchange, the largest in Canada—which provide markets for trading equity capital, and develop and enforce their own rules and regulations relating to corporate listings and the protection of investors.

- Securities Exchange Commissions in each province and territory, of which the Ontario Securities Commission is the most influential. The 13 securities commissions have formed the Canadian Securities Administrators organization to coordinate and harmonize regulation of the Canadian capital markets.

- Investment Industry Regulatory Organization of Canada (IIROC) is the national self-regulatory organization that oversees all investment dealers and trading activity on debt and equity marketplaces in Canada.

- The Canadian Investor Protection Fund is a not-for-profit organization that provides investor protection for investment dealer bankruptcy.

- The Mutual Fund Dealers Association of Canada, which oversees the sale of mutual funds. It regulates the activities of members and ensures they adhere to the rules, bylaws, and policies of the MFDA, as well as applicable securities legislation.

Organizations Representing Shareholders

- The Small Investor Protection Association, a volunteer member organization committed to fair practice in the investment industry.

- The Shareholder Association for Research and Education (SHARE), a non-profit organization created by the Canadian labour movement to improve institutional investment practices to protect investors.

- The Canadian Foundation for Advancement of Investor Rights (FAIR) is an independent national non-profit organization advocating for Canadian investors by providing information and education to the public, governments and regulators about investors' rights and protections.

Want to learn more about investment scams and frauds?

Although government and other stakeholders are attempting to ensure that owners are treated fairly, the role of boards of directors and managers should not be ignored. Many corporations have investor relations departments. The managers of these departments strive to maintain the confidence of investors and are active in communicating information about the corporation to existing and potential investors.

There are challenges associated with the ownership and control of Canadian business corporations. But, the situation should not be viewed as one of hopelessness. The composition of ownership is always changing, and at the same time there is a shifting influence, or control, by various owners. Given the dynamic nature of the Canadian business system, there will always be owners and other stakeholders who care enough to challenge the existing centres of influence.

The governance of the corporation is a topic related to ownership and the trend to responsible investing. The following section defines corporate governance and the major stakeholder involved, the board of directors. A final section will link governance to corporate responsibility.

LO 11.5   Corporate Governance and the Board of Directors

How corporations are governed became an issue in the 1990s, when many corporations failed and it appeared that boards of directors were not performing their function well; that is, they were not protecting the interests of shareholders. In the 2000s, major scandals and bankruptcies reinforced the interest in governance. The board of directors has been the object of many suggestions for reform. The result has been the reform, or reorganization, of the board as the principal body involved with the processes, structures, and relationships through which decisions are made. Owners or shareholders have also been pressuring for change through the use of resolutions examples of which are given in Responsibility for Ethics 11.5.

RESPONSIBILITY FOR ETHICS 11.5

Governance Shareholder Resolutions

The *Canada Business Corporations Act* requires that shareholder proposals or resolutions be circulated to shareholders and voted upon at the corporation's annual meeting. Many investor or shareholder resolutions are related to governance, but they are seldom passed. Below are examples of governance proposals, including issue and corporation targeted, during 2017–19:

- Disclosing of direct and indirect lobbying activities so that investors can assess whether the company's lobbying is consistent with the company's expressed goals and in the best interests of shareholders. (SNC-Lavalin)

- Proposing the adoption of a bylaw authorizing the nomination by the public of two directors, who shall be elected by the shareholders, each serving for a term of one year or until a successor is elected or appointed. (CIBC)

- Requesting a formal, written board diversity policy to increase gender diversity on the board of directors and amongst senior management. (Canfor Corporation)

- Adopting a policy to require the chair of the board to be an independent director. (Loblaw Companies Ltd.)

- Disclosing the use of the equity ratio in the CEO compensation-setting process. (Manulife Group)

- The board of directors adopting a policy to give shareholders a "say on pay" for executive compensation. (Power Corporation of Canada)

The definition of corporate governance has evolved over time. One definition of **corporate governance** is the processes, structures, and relationships through which the shareholders, as represented by a board of directors, oversee the activities of the corporation. A second frequently used definition is from the literature: Governance is concerned with the intrinsic nature, purpose, integrity, and identity of the institution, with a primary focus on the entity's relevance, continuity, and fiduciary aspects. Governance involves monitoring and overseeing strategic direction, socioeconomic and cultural context, resources, externalities, and constituencies of the institution.[8]

In the first definition the owner and director stakeholders were mentioned, representing a more traditional view. In the second definition, the scope is much greater and the word *constituencies* is used in recognition of the numerous stakeholders that influence the governance of the corporation. A third definition is a more practical or applied one: "Corporate governance" means the process and structure used to direct and manage the business and affairs of the corporation with the objective of enhancing long-term value for shareholders and the financial viability of the business. The process and structure define the division of power and accountability among shareholders, the board of directors, and management, and can have an impact on other stakeholders such as employees, customers, suppliers, and communities.[9] Again the influence of stakeholders is identified. The definitions illustrate how corporate governance has changed. The changes have involved many issues, some of which will be examined.

At an international level, the inclusion of stakeholders in the definition of corporate governance was an important step and has been endorsed by the OECD. The OECD Principles of Corporate Governance included a section on the role of stakeholders. This role includes the following points:

- The rights of stakeholders are respected when established by law or mutual agreements.

- Effective redress should be available to stakeholders when their legally established rights are violated.

- If stakeholders participate in the governance process, they should have access to all the information necessary to carry out their role.

- Stakeholders should be allowed to freely communicate concerns about illegal or unethical practices to the board without fear of retaliation.[10]

Members of a corporation's board of directors are the stakeholders directly involved with governance. A **board of directors** is a group of individuals elected by shareholders to govern or oversee the corporation's affairs. The role of the board is to monitor and evaluate the corporation's activities and performance. The board has the power to select, evaluate, and terminate the chief executive officer and top management. The directors are required to provide shareholders with financial statements and an auditor's statement, and other financial and operational information required by the articles, by-laws, or a shareholder agreement. This information is usually presented as an annual report. The board should be planning for the longer term by participating in a strategic planning process, and ensuring continuity and succession in the management team. Usually major transactions and ventures are evaluated and approved. The role described includes what are referred to as **fiduciary duties**, obligations owed by directors to shareholders that are prescribed by laws or regulations.

The board of directors selects chief executive officers, monitors their behaviour, evaluates their performance, and, if necessary, dismisses them. Some CEOs have not been sufficiently accountable to the board, and thus to the owners of the corporation. It is suggested that there has been an imbalance of power as some managers behaved like absolute monarchs or military dictators. Corporate governance reform has restored power to the board and taken it away from the all-powerful CEO. The board is now more independent; in particular, its audit committee is a much more independent body.

Corporate governance practices have changed substantially in the past few years. In the past, directors may have questioned management's decisions but rarely countermanded them even though they had ultimate authority over key policy decisions. They are now playing a bigger role in determining and assessing strategy, acquisition decisions, succession planning, crisis responses, financial reporting practices, relations with stakeholders, and ethical responsibilities. Boards are meeting more often; seeking more qualified directors, often with particular competencies; meeting without management present; and hiring their own experts on various matters including executive compensation, accounting policies, and legal issues.

Large institutional investors believe that good governance leads to better performance. Many of these investors have formed the Canadian Coalition for Good Governance (described in Responsibility for Ethics 11.6) to develop investor interest and promote changes in governance.

 RESPONSIBILITY FOR ETHICS 11.6

Canadian Coalition for Good Governance (CCGG)

Institutional investors such as pension funds, mutual funds, and third-party money managers have formed CCGG to represent their interests. This is accomplished by encouraging best corporate governance practices in the corporations in which they own shares, mostly corporations that are members of the S&P/TSX Composite Index. CCGG members manage about $3 trillion in assets on behalf of Canadian investors.

CCGG researches and publishes information on governance issues such as executive compensation, majority voting, director compensation, board shareholder engagement, and disclosure of financial and governance information. By making submissions on governance-related matters to stock exchanges, securities commissions, and governments, it attempts to influence the regulation of the securities industry.

Each year, it prepares a Best Practices for Proxy Circular Disclosure report to assist managers and board members. Also, it annually awards Governance Gavel Awards such as the "Best Disclosure of Corporate Governance and Executive Compensation Practices" won by Emera Incorporated in 2018.

CCGG members believe that good governance practices result in a greater return to investors who are participating in the financial market through indirect pension and mutual funds ownership.

Five major issues relating to governance and boards of directors are the structure and members of the board, board diversity, executive compensation, disclosure and transparency, and board evaluation.

Board Structure and Membership

Most boards comprise 10 to 15 members who also serve on various committees. The number of committees varies, as does the type. Common committees include audit, finance, human resources, pension, compensation, nominating, governance, and strategic planning. Often these areas are combined, usually resulting in three to six committees. A recent development has been the formation of social responsibility or environment committees.

The separation of the board chair and CEO positions has been controversial. Corporate governance experts and regulatory bodies recommend that different persons occupy the positions and that an independent director act as chair. The independence of the board is at issue and many boards have adopted the separation of the positions.

Becoming a board member was once a closed process with corporate executives dominating membership, acquaintances of executives appointed, and the existence of interlocking directorships; that is, directors serving on one another's boards. Corporate governance reform has altered this process in most publicly listed corporations. Director positions have job descriptions outlining what is expected. New members are sought through a nomination process, given an orientation to the corporation, and provided with a continuing education program. The qualifications of a director are varied. Financial acumen and the capability of identifying risk are essential. Operating experience is an asset, and knowledge of governance processes is expected.

A major issue on board memberships has been their independence from the operations and management of the corporation. A definition of an **independent (or unrelated) director** is "a director who is free from any interest and any business or other relationship which could, or could reasonably be perceived to, materially interfere with the director's ability to act in the best interests of the corporation."[11] Family members, current executives, recently departed members of management, and professional advisers such as lawyers are not considered independent. There must be a majority of independent board members or an appropriate explanation provided. Prospective directors must be interested in the quality and reputation of the existing board, the quality of governance processes, the board's independence, and the corporation's approach for integrity and social responsibility.

Board Diversity

The recruitment of women and, to a lesser extent, minorities is receiving attention. About 24 percent of the directors of Canada's largest corporations are women depending upon the corporations surveyed. Modest progress has been made in increasing the number of women. Many corporations say they want women directors, but few heed the advice and elect them. It is argued that the pool of qualified applicants is small and that women lack experience as chief financial officers and CEOs. A "critical mass" of three or more female directors is required before they influence the board. Responsibility for Ethics 11.7 describes organizations involved in enhancing the board membership diversity. Mandatory quotas have been suggested, but they are opposed by most advocates who want to of increase board diversity.

 RESPONSIBILITY FOR ETHICS 11.7

Organizations Promoting Board Diversity

Several organizations are promoting diversity of membership on boards of directors. The Canadian Board Diversity Council is promotes a range of unrepresented communities while the 30% Club and Catalyst are concerned mainly with gender representation. DiverseCity OnBoard focuses on volunteer boards.

Canadian Board Diversity Council (CBDC)—The Council was set up to promote diversity on Canadian boards of directors by increasing the representation of women, visible minorities, Aboriginal Peoples, persons with disabilities and the LGBTQ community. CBDC conducts research on the progress of the diversity and publishes an annual report card. It has an education program in governance to create a greater number of highly skilled diverse board candidates and maintains a database of qualified people from across Canada who have the competences to serve on boards.

30% Club Canada—This organization exists in many countries and is committed to increasing gender balance on board and in senior management to at least 30 percent. In 2019, about 24 percent of board members were female. It cooperates with Catalyst Canada.

Catalyst Canada—This is another international non-profit research and advocacy organization dedicated to creating opportunities for women and business in Canada. The Catalyst Canada Honours annually recognizes individual champions of women in business. The Catalyst Accord is a call to action for the largest corporations to increase the representation of women on their boards.

OnBoard Canada—This program connects qualified, pre-screened candidates from underrepresented communities to volunteer board positions. It provides training in governance through an online learning campus supplemented by in-person discussions and events.

In December 2014, Canadian Securities Administrators (CSA) issued the NI58-58-101 Disclosure of Corporate Governance Practices rule, which required corporations to disclose corporate governance practices including the number women on boards of directors and in executive officer positions, the policies relating to the identification and nomination of women directors, and targets for women on boards and in executive officer positions. This rule became known as "comply or explain."

Surveys and reports have found that there has been little progress in increasing gender diversity on boards. The Canadian Board Diversity Council (CBDC) prepares an Annual Report Card on the representation of women, minority groups, Indigenous Peoples, persons with disabilities, and LGBTQ on the FP500 boards. In the past 15 years, CBDC has found little change in diversity, including the finding in its "Annual Report Card 2017: Advancing Diverse Leadership on Canada's Corporate Boards" of a 1 percent change since 2016.[12]

The Canadian Securities Administrators (CSA) reviews corporate disclosures relating to the number of women on boards since its Disclosure of Corporate Governance Practices rule. Here are the key findings of the 2018 review:

- The total percentage of board seats held by women increased to 15 percent in 2018, from 11 percent in 2015 (on companies CSA reviewed).

- When board seats became available and were filled, nearly three in 10 were filled by women.

- The number of issuers with at least one woman on their board increased to 66 percent in 2018, from 49 percent in 2015.

- 42 percent of issuers had adopted a policy on identifying and nominating women directors in 2018, representing an almost threefold increase since 2015.

- Issuers that adopted targets for the representation of women on their boards increased to 16 percent in 2018, from 7 percent in 2015.

- The number of issuers with at least one woman in executive officer positions increased to 66 percent in 2018, from 60 percent in 2015.[13]

Institutional investors and organizations advocating for gender representation on boards of directors have set a 30 percent goal by 2022. Some progress has been made, but board diversity is still a significant issue for Canadian corporate governance and initiatives are underway to continue addressing it.

Executive and Director Compensation

A controversial item involving disclosure and transparency is the compensation of executives and directors. Securities regulation requires disclosure of executive compensation in publicly traded corporations, and many have detailed statements of compensation. The compensation received by executives has several components including salary, bonuses, incentive plans, share grants, and options in addition to various perks such as health and pension plans. Issues exist for all forms of payment and include the criteria used to determine salary, the magnitude of the compensation, the basis for bonus and incentive plans, the inverse relationship that sometimes exists between salary and corporate performance, the amount and pricing of options, and excessive severance and pension payments. Two recent developments had increased attention to the appropriateness of compensation.

Say-on-pay is the ability of shareholders to vote on the remuneration of executives. It is an annual shareholder advisory vote on the board's approach that provides shareholders with an opportunity to express their satisfaction with the board's approach to executive compensation. Many public corporations in Canada have adopted this policy, but it has been criticized as being ineffective. Most shareholder votes on compensation have been supportive, but there are exceptions where over 50 percent opposed the proposed compensation. There are instances when a majority or even a minority of shareholders opposed the compensation scheme, changes were made. Some shareholder democracy are advocating for mandatory requirement for say-on-pay as it increases the accountability of boards to shareholders.[14]

Another board accountability initiative is the disclosure of a **CEO pay ratio** that has been implemented by the U.S. Securities and Exchange Commission in August 2015. This is the ratio of the compensation of the corporation's chief executive officer (CEO) to the median compensation of the corporation's employees. It is an indication of income inequality in society and will provide shareholders more information when voting on "say on pay." This initiative has not been adopted in Canada but is being discussed.[15]

Director compensation has also become an issue recently as it has increased to reflect the demands being placed on directors. Directors can receive an annual retainer, board meeting fee, annual committee retainer, and committee meeting fee. Some directors receive options, considered appropriate because some boards require directors to own shares in the corporation to enhance their stake. A director's compensation for a Canadian corporation can now amount to hundreds of thousands of dollars.

The compensation of executives and boards is an issue that has received a lot of attention recently.

Disclosure and Transparency

Corporate governance reform has focused on disclosure and transparency of the corporation's operations, in particular financial reporting and disclosure, and how the board functions. This became an issue with the failure of many American and Canadian corporations in the 1990s and early 2000s, quite often due to inappropriate behaviour on the part of executives and directors.

In Canada, the regulations of the Canadian Securities Administrators, the stock exchange regulations, and the self-regulatory organizations have had some impact, but not nearly as extensive as in the United States. An example of the influence the securities administrators are attempting to gain is outlined in Responsibility for Ethics 11.8 where they argue for the improvement in the disclosure of governance practices. In order to more effectively regulate, it is proposed that a national securities regulator be formed instead of relying on the provincial ones now operating.

 RESPONSIBILITY FOR ETHICS 11.8

Disclosure of Corporate Governance Practices

The Canadian Securities Administrators require that corporations listed on Canadian stock exchanges provide to shareholders information regarding their governance practices. Examples of the information required are:

- Board of directors—Identification of independent directors, other directorships held, and independence status of chair.

- Board mandate—Provide the text of the board's mandate.

- Position descriptions—For the board and committee chairs, CEO.

- Orientation and continuing education—Lists measures to familiarize board members with role of the board, its committees, and its directors, and the nature and operation of the corporation's business.

- Ethical business conduct—Disclose whether the board has adopted a written code of its directors, officers, and employees.

- Nomination of directors—Describe the process used to identify new candidates for board positions.

- Compensation—Describe how the compensation for the corporation's directors and officers is determined.

- Other board committees—List and describe functions of committees.

- Assessments—Indicate whether the board, its committees, and individual directors are regularly evaluated.

The document used to communicate with shareholders is the **management information circular** (also referred to as the management proxy circular or proxy circular disclosure report). The document is sent out to shareholders prior to the corporation's annual meeting and outlines the important matters to be discussed. It includes the information listed in Responsibility for Ethics 11.8. The Canadian Coalition for Good Governance recommends that the following matters also be included: board composition and succession planning, director continuing education, director attendance, director compensation and share ownership, strategic planning oversight, risk management oversight, shareholder engagement, and a Chair's Letter to Shareholders.[16] It also solicits proxy votes from shareholders who are not able to attend the annual meeting. The shareholder will vote to approve the slate of nominations for board of directors or have their vote withheld. There will also be voting for the selection of the auditor, any major decisions, shareholder resolutions, and sometimes other items such as say-on-pay.

In addition to these disclosure requirements, more responsibilities are being demanded of boards and their members. Corporations listed on Canadian stock exchanges are required to disclose the text of a board's written mandate. Such a mandate would include not only items mentioned above but also the following:

- The board's satisfaction with the integrity of the CEO and other executive members, and that they are creating a culture of integrity throughout the corporation.

- The board's approach to developing governance principles and guidelines specific to the corporation.

- Identification of measures for receiving feedback from stakeholders, including the possibility of them contacting independent directors directly.

- Listing expectations and responsibilities of directors to fulfill their duties, for example by attending meetings and reviewing materials prior to meetings.[17]

The OECD promotes good corporate governance practices by issuing the OECD Principles of Corporate Governance, which includes some responsibilities in addition to those mentioned in the National Instrument:

- Treating all shareholders fairly where board decisions affect different shareholder groups differently.
- Applying high ethical standards and taking into account the interests of stakeholders.
- Monitoring and managing potential conflicts of interest among management, board members, and shareholders.
- Ensuring the integrity of the corporation's accounting and financial reporting systems.
- Overseeing the process of disclosure and communications.[18]

An important contributor to disclosure and transparency is the board's **audit committee**. An audit committee comprises members of the board of directors and oversees the internal and external accounting auditing function to ensure that financial statements accurately and appropriately represent the condition of the corporation and that regulated disclosures are made. The committee makes sure that the corporation is in compliance with all regulations and often oversees the corporation's codes of conduct and/or ethics. Today, corporations are expected to prepare a "charter" for the audit committee that discloses the names of committee members, indicates whether they are independent, and describes the experience and education of each member.

Evaluation

The evaluation of board performance is one of the most challenging governance reforms to implement. The evaluation of board and director performance has not been common in the past despite the performance appraisal process being widely used in other levels of the corporation. There has been reluctance by many directors who do not believe evaluation is necessary, that the process may expose weaknesses in the governance process and be embarrassing, and that the collegial relationship among board members may be disrupted. Someone must initiate and champion the process, usually the chair or the board's governance committee. The criteria for assessing the board's performance must be established, but are usually based on regulatory requirements. Also, a process must be put in place to deal with the weaknesses uncovered in the evaluation.

Directors must represent shareholder interests, give advice on how to increase shareholder value, challenge management of goals and results. In order to do this, they review the legal, financial, business and governance functions of the corporation. Today directors are expected to evaluate the social responsibility of the corporation. Included in this aspect of evaluation would be the monitoring of the external environment for social trends and stakeholder influences, overseeing ethics programs and the corporate social responsibility initiatives.

Various organizations recognize the best practices of boards or board members; an example is the Canadian Coalition for Corporate Governance's "Governance Gavel Awards" mentioned in Responsibility for Ethics 11.6. *The Globe and Mail* annually publishes "Board Games: Annual Corporate Governance Rankings" and the Clarkson Centre for Business Ethics and Board Effectiveness prepares a "Board Shareholder Confidence Index," both of which are described in Responsibility for Ethics 11.9.

 RESPONSIBILITY FOR ETHICS 11.9

Best Corporate Governance Practices

The Globe and Mail Board Games: Annual Corporate Governance Rankings

Each year, *The Globe and Mail* identifies the corporations with the best governance practices in Canada. About 235 companies and trusts in the S&P/TSX Composite Index are examined. Extensive criteria are used in assessing the boards of directors' performance, including board composition, independence of directors and management, board evaluation, board diversity, committee structure, compensation of the CEO and directors, board output, director assessment, and shareholder engagement.

In 2018, the five corporations with the best governance practices were Manulife Financial Corp., Intact Financial Corp., Emera Inc., Canadian National Railways, and Royal Bank of Canada.

Clarkson Centre for Business Ethics and Board Effectiveness Confidence Index

The Clarkson Centre for Business Ethics and Board Effectiveness, University of Toronto, measures and monitors shareholder confidence with a "Board Shareholder Confidence Index," published annually. Companies on the S&P/TSX Composite Index are assigned a score out of 150. The Centre assists in the preparation of *The Globe and Mail's* annual "Board Games" corporate governance rankings.

Corporate governance has been reformed extensively and the new responsibilities for ethics and social responsibility have been added or enhanced.

LO 11.6 Ownership, Governance, and CSR

National Instrument 58-101 contains a clause relating to ethical business conduct that the Canadian Securities Administrators recommends is implemented. This clause is given in Responsibility for Ethics 11.10. Many corporate boards now have a code of ethical business conduct that applies to all, including directors.

 RESPONSIBILITY FOR ETHICS 11.10

Disclosure of "Ethical Business Conduct"

National Instrument 58-101, Clause 5, requires that corporations disclose the following in relation to ethical business conduct:

(a) "Disclose whether or not the board has adopted a written code for the directors, officers and employees. If the board has adopted a written code:

    (i) disclose how a person or company may obtain a copy of the code;

    (ii) describe how the board monitors compliance with its code, or if the board does not monitor compliance, explain whether and how the board satisfies itself regarding compliance with its code;

    (iii) provide a cross-reference to any material change report filed since the beginning of the issuer's most recently completed financial year that pertains to any conduct of a director or executive officer that constitutes a departure from the code.

(b) Describe any steps the board takes to ensure directors exercise independent judgment in considering transactions and agreements in respect of which a director or executive officer has a material interest.

(c) Describe any other steps the board takes to encourage and promote a culture of ethical business conduct."

Owners are taking more responsibility for the social, ethical, and environmental impacts their corporations have on society. Corporate governance practices have come under increasing scrutiny and owners pressure the corporation's main governing body, the board of directors, to address corporate responsibility and sustainability challenges. Some owners are becoming more active, pressuring the board to implement governance improvements and to account for the corporation's social and environmental performance. In particular, institutional investors—that is, mutual and pension funds—have become more demanding of boards, directors, and management. The trend to responsible investing has also applied pressure to the board and management, but criticism continues.

Directors are the protectors of shareholders' interests and the overseers of strategy and financial responsibility. Recently, directors have also become overseers of CSR and ethical conduct—this is because they are ultimately responsible for everything that happens in the corporation. Pay systems, incentive plans, and performance goals can lead to misconduct on the part of executives and employees. Being responsible for ethical management practices is now another concern in looking after shareholders' interests. Colero recommends that directors ask the following five questions about the corporation's ethics management:

- What is our company's strategy to manage ethics?
- Who is responsible for ethics in our company?
- Are people in our firm equipped to recognize and resolve moral dilemmas?
- Are people in our organization provided with a safe opportunity to discuss ethical issues of concern?
- Do we reward or punish ethical integrity and moral courage if it has a negative impact on the bottom line?[19]

Another perspective on corporate governance, CSR, and ethical conduct relates to an appropriate response to external environment factors, trends, or events. Schacter argues that four factors have to come together requiring boards to pay attention to CSR: globalization, loss of trust, civil society activism, and investor interest in CSR.

Globalization has made it necessary for corporations to consider the economic, social, and environmental impacts on society, including those in developing countries. Corporations are also facing increasing demand to do something about these impacts. Several corporate scandals, excessive executive compensation, outsourcing of jobs, environmental disasters, and stock market declines have resulted in a loss of trust in business and the corporation.

Civil society organizations, including NGOs, are more active and effective in pointing out the mistakes and misdeeds of corporations. Finally, many investors, including mutual and pension funds, have become more interested in responsible investing. Added to this list is the growing pressure for improved corporate governance, more management accountability for the corporation's economic, social, and environmental issues, and increasing regulation.[20]

Since Schacter's research, other issues have emerged that require the attention of boards, even though his list is still relevant. The issues are climate change; Indigenous Peoples' rights and interests; diversity of all types; vulnerability of employees due to technology and declining pension coverage; maintenance of an appropriate corporate culture; shareholder democracy; impacts of artificial intelligence; protection of data in particular consumer information; and the appropriate level of social responsibility or sustainability disclosure.

Directors are still responsible for the creation of wealth for shareholders, but there is a reputation risk involved in not responding to CSR and ensuring appropriate ethical conduct. Shareholder wealth may be adversely affected by boards of directors ignoring CSR and ethics management. The long-term interests of owners and stakeholders are interlinked, and through good governance practices boards must set an example for all the corporation's stakeholders and show that they are concerned about CSR and ethics management.

Your advice to Felicia . . .

....

Felicia's dilemma is not unusual. Just as it is often challenging to ascertain ethical versus unethical behaviour, responsible investing is often difficult to identify. Not everyone agrees on what is irresponsible corporate economic activity. Also, corporations that can appear responsible may lapse for some reason, sometimes beyond their control. The decision is further complicated by the expected dividends, or return, that the shareholder seeks. Which investment—or investments—to make is a judgment call involving pros and cons. Felicia should obtain all the information she can about a particular investment to make an informed decision.

Summary

- Although other stakeholders have an influence on the corporation, it is owned by shareholders or investors. There are several types of owners including investors, entrepreneurs, managers, employees, producers, and mutual, pension, and investment funds. Issues arising from ownership include the appropriateness of widely held versus concentrated ownership, the treatment of minority shareholders, non-voting shares, dual-class shares, the pros and cons of employee ownership, the accountability of private corporations, and the accountability of government-owned corporations. (LO 11.1)

- Several issues relate to ownership with one in particular being of interest, the influence of owners on the corporation's social responsibility. One approach used by investors is to sponsor shareholder resolutions advocating that the board of directors and corporate executives take action on a particular economic, social, environmental, or governance issue. Cooperatives by definition are more socially sensitive and NGOs can use small share holdings to make corporations aware of social issues. (LO 11.2)

- Responsible investing is the screening of investments by corporations or mutual and pension funds for their response to social or ethical responsibilities as well as their financial or economic actions. This process is also referred to as ethical, green, environmental, and social conscience investing. Investments are examined by a screen comprising negative or positive criteria, and best-of-sector. Several stock market indices identify corporations that qualify for responsible investing. (LO 11.3)

- It is necessary to protect the rights of owners through government legislation, self-regulatory agencies, industry association, and institutional activists. Corporations are mindful of owners and often have investor relations departments to maintain good relations. (LO 11.4)

- The definition of corporate governance has changed over the years to reflect developments in the area. Traditionally, the definition referred only to shareholders, but stakeholders are now included. The board of directors is elected by the shareholders and is mandated to represent shareholder interests. The board oversees all the affairs of the corporation and today this includes the ethical conduct and social responsibility of the corporation. Many corporations now have charters specifying the board's mandate. Several issues are related to corporate governance, including the board structure and membership, board diversity, executive and director compensation, disclosure and transparency, and evaluation. (LO 11.5)

- A connection exists between ownership, corporate governance, and ethical conduct and CSR. In fact, governance is now considered one influence on corporations to conduct their affairs appropriately in the interests of shareholders and other stakeholders, and as a part of the corporation's overall corporate social responsibility. (LO 11.6)

Key Terms

Mutual fund

Private equity firms

Venture capital company

Dual-class stock

Non-voting shares

Restricted shares

Passive shareholders

Active shareholders

Worker capitalism

Responsible investment (RI)

Shareholder democracy

Corporate governance

Board of directors

Fiduciary duties

Independent (or unrelated) director

Say-on-pay

CEO pay ratio

Management information circular

Audit committee

Critical Thinking and Discussion Questions

1. Why are owners an important stakeholder of the corporation? How does the corporation influence them, and how do owners influence the corporation?

2. Do owners always control the corporation?

3. How can owners influence the corporate social responsibility of the corporation?

4. How can an investor identify a responsible investment?

5. What can be done to protect the interests of owners or shareholders?

6. What are the responsibilities of the board of directors?

7. Why is diversity of the board of director's membership important?

8. Do the "say-on-pay" and "CEO ratio" initiatives make any difference to shareholders?

9. Why is disclosure and transparency important to shareholders and stakeholders?

10. What is the connection between corporate governance and the corporation's ethical conduct and social responsibility?

Cases

11.1 AUNT MABEL'S EXPERIENCE WITH OWNERSHIP

Karl Stillings' Aunt Mabel called him on a Saturday morning and wondered if he could drop in to visit her that afternoon. Aunt Mabel was a widow; Uncle Richard had passed away about 18 months ago. She was quite concerned about her investments and would appreciate Karl's advice since he had recently graduated from a business program.

During his visit Karl was not surprised to learn that his aunt had no investment experience—his uncle had looked after all financial matters. She had become a widow at 62 and found she had cash assets of about $200,000 from an insurance policy and savings. She approached a financial institution and was assigned an adviser. The adviser had Aunt Mabel sign an account agreement, which she admitted to Karl she did not read in detail as it was several pages and in small print. Besides, she trusted the financial institution and the young and very personable adviser.

The adviser initially invested the money in low-risk money market funds. A few months later he moved the money into higher risk equity or stock funds with higher fees and commissions. He then arranged a $100,000 loan secured against her existing equity, which he invested in very high-risk equity. Aunt Mabel questioned this, but was told it was allowed in the agreement she'd signed. While visiting the adviser recently, Aunt Mabel was told, after she had insisted, that she had lost $40,000 on her investments. She told the adviser she wanted out, but the adviser said there would be expensive redemption fees. Also, he advised waiting a while as markets turn around, and there was a possibility for making a lot of money. Aunt Mabel became very upset and did not know what to do. She decided to seek someone else's advice and that is why she contacted her nephew.

Over a cup of tea and biscuits, Aunt Mabel asked Karl what she should do now.

Questions

1. What type of ownership was involved? What can be assumed about this type of ownership? Was it appropriate for Aunt Mabel?

2. What stakeholders are involved?

3. What are the ethical issues or implications involved?

4. What ethical responsibilities do the adviser and the financial institution have toward any type of investor, and in particular toward an inexperienced and naïve one?

5. What advice should Karl give?

11.2 STOCK MARKET TEMPTATION

Jing Chen is 48 years old, married with two teenage children. Recently, he has been thinking more about plans for his family's income when he and his spouse retire. He has been considering investing in the stock market as one component of the retirement plan.

Inter Pipeline Ltd. came to his attention. The Calgary-based company is in the business of petroleum transportation and storage and natural gas liquids processing. It also operates 23 petroleum and petrochemical storage terminals in Europe and is involved in a major project to convert propane into polypropylene plastic used in packaging, textiles, and other products. It is listed on the Toronto Stock Exchange with the symbol LPL. The current price was $21.10 with a dividend of $1.71 for a yield of 8.10 percent. This return was higher than most other investment possibilities and the income would be eligible for a tax credit.

Jing was concerned that the high yield may be too good, as high-yielding stocks often experience cash-flow problems and reduce or drop the dividend. It was recommended as a "Buy" by several financial analysts. He analyzed the corporation's financial data and found that total revenue was over $2.2 billion, net income $527 million, total assets $10.4 billion, and total equity $3.5 billion. The financial statements presented a very positive picture.

His spouse pointed out that Inter Pipeline was in the oil and gas business, which was causing climate change, and the production of plastic products leads to environmental pollution. His spouse stated that investing in Inter Pipeline was hardly responsible.

Jing went to Inter Pipeline's website and found that it had extensive social responsibility and sustainability initiatives. In particular, its facilities removed 311,000 tons of CO_2 and recycled over 2.7 million m^3 of water. It had no fines, penalties, violations, or events of non-compliance with environmental laws and regulations. The corporation published an extensive Sustainability Report and summary statistics used the GRI standards.

Jing was now undecided about the investment.

Questions

1. What are the issues regarding investing in Inter Pipeline?
2. What are the pros and cons of investing in Inter Pipeline?
3. Can Jing justify claiming that Inter Pipeline is a responsible investment?

Employees are key stakeholders in corporate social responsibility programs.
Used © Hero Images/ image Source

CHAPTER 12

Ethics and Responsibilities in the Workplace and Marketplace

What would you do if...?

Phyllis Cramer enjoyed her job as an assistant manager at a large discount department store. It was a demanding job, but she liked the quick pace and the dynamic atmosphere. Among her duties was responsibility for implementing the store's loss prevention, or shoplifting, policy. The policy had recently changed, and Phyllis was concerned about the consequences.

Between 1.5 and 2.5 percent of retail sales are stolen or lost in some way depending on the type of merchandise. About 40 percent of the loss is due to shoplifting by customers, about 35 percent is due to employee theft, about 20 percent is due to administrative and paper errors, and the remaining loss is due to vendor mistakes or theft. Because preventing any loss contributes directly to the store's profitability, the reinforcement of a loss prevention policy is important to the store's financial success.

Of most concern to Phyllis is the loss experienced through customer shoplifting. The store had been very strict about shoplifting and prosecuted everyone regardless of the dollar amount stolen. She realized that this zero-tolerance policy was expensive to enforce. Lawyers' fees and court costs were substantial. Not only was her time involved, but employees had to testify in court on company time. In addition, sometimes the local police force expressed concern at the resources it had to devote to petty thefts.

The new policy would excuse first-time thieves when the value of shoplifted merchandise was less than $25. The store manager said this would allow Phyllis to focus on the professional shoplifters rather than teenagers, and to devote more time to preventing employee theft. The manager also indicated that the new policy would be less costly to implement.

Phyllis was concerned about the difference in treatment of shoplifters based upon dollar amounts. To her, stealing was stealing no matter how small the amount. She agreed with employees who felt the policy undermined their efforts and might even encourage more shoplifting. She believed the policy really avoided the problem rather than solving it.

Phyllis worried about the ethical implications of such a policy for the store, its employees, and customers who did not steal. Most importantly, she agonized in her own conscience about the policy, in particular letting some thieves get away without any punishment. She did have some sympathy with first-time teenage shoplifters and their parents, but to let them off scot-free was not appropriate either. Phyllis knew that implementing the new policy was not going to be easy.

What is your advice to Phyllis?

The purpose of this chapter is to examine the influence of four stakeholders on the corporation and how the corporation influences them. The four stakeholders to be discussed are employees, consumers, competitors, and suppliers. Employees are stakeholders internal to the corporation and their relationship gives rise to many ethical issues, one of which is illustrated above. Consumers are obviously important, because without them the corporation has no reason to exist. Competitors and suppliers are business-to-business stakeholders primarily involving economic or commercial relationships, but ethical issues also are evident. The analysis of supply chains is especially important in identifying a corporation's ethics and responsibilities and is therefore dealt with separately. For most corporations, all four are significant stakeholders in that numerous ethics and responsibilities are associated with them.

Issues relating to ethics and responsibilities will be identified for each stakeholder and will serve as the basis for discussing them. The purpose of this chapter is not to provide readers with a comprehensive examination of each issue, but instead to provide an appreciation of a wide range, multiplicity, and complexity of issues existing in this area.

LO 12.1 Employees in the Workplace

Employees are almost always identified by corporations as critical or key stakeholders. The relationship with this stakeholder group has always been a challenge, and given the downsizing, retrenchment, and technological changes of the recent past it will be even more so. There are many issues relating to ethics and responsibilities between employees and employers, including working conditions, workforce reduction, workplace privacy, fair compensation, employee loyalty and duties, diversity management, right to due process, and employee engagement. This list illustrates a range of issues in the relationship between the corporation and the employee stakeholder. Not all of the issues will be examined, but the following sections will focus on the work ethic, employee loyalty, and diversity and discrimination. Two movements related to diversity and discrimination will be discussed: LGBTQ and #MeToo along with the influence of feminist ethics. A concluding section will summarize the relationship between employees and CSR.

There are several competitions to identify the best employers in Canada through nomination or survey processes. Corporations that make the list publicize the achievement on letterhead, advertisements, and reports. The presence of these competitions promotes good employee relationships. Responsibility for Ethics 12.1 gives examples of the competitions and winners. These surveys provide insights into what makes a good employer or place to work.

 RESPONSIBILITY FOR ETHICS 12.1

Canada's Best Employers

Best Employers in Canada 2018—List prepared by Aon Hewitt Associates, a human resources firm, and published in *Maclean's*. Forty-nine employers were recognized as "organizations where people do great work—and love doing it."

Canada's Best Employers 2018: Small- and Medium-Sized Companies—There are two winning categories: Platinum companies are those in the top-scoring 25 percent of all companies; Gold companies are those in the 67 percent to 75 percent percentile of all companies. The listing is prepared by Aon Hewitt and published in *Canadian Business*.

Canada's Top 100 Employers 2019™—™—This is a competition to determine the best employers who offer exceptional workplaces for their employees. The competition is sponsored by Mediacorp Canada Inc. and the results are published in *The Globe and Mail*.

Many employees are seeking greater participation in decisions affecting the work environment. Moreover, many businesspeople are also committed to greater employee involvement as an approach to improving working conditions and performance. Many aspects of how employees are treated are legislated by governments, but the status of employees is influenced by voluntary actions of employers or advocated by employees seeking greater participation. The result might be viewed as employee claims to certain conditions in the workplace, or employee rights.

The concept of the work ethic has been used to establish the different positions employees and employers find themselves in today. Work has changed, and so has the approach to employees. Although employees may be still considered a critical resource, many issues confront human resource management.

The Work Ethic

The work ethic is a set of values that holds that work is important to members of society insofar as work influences the qualities or character of individuals; that work is a purposeful activity requiring an expenditure of energy with some sacrifice of leisure; that some gain, usually monetary, is involved; and that through work a person not only contributes to society but becomes a better individual. The work ethic as a concept had some origins in religion as labour was believed to be the worthy way to serve God, a calling through which one proved one's worthiness of redemption. Leisure or hedonistic activities were not considered appropriate.

Working hard and accumulating wealth were seen as outward signs of a person's morality. They also provided some assurance of a good life on Earth as well as a good afterlife. The basis for the work ethic is not clear, for while religion is involved so is economics. Although the work ethic was considered as divine dignity, the concept lost some of its piety because the accumulation of wealth countered the religious basis of the ethic, and consumption, much of it conspicuous and made possible by the earnings of work, was inconsistent with saving and investment, or frugality.

Today there are often calls for a return to the work ethic of the past. Arguments can be made for both positions. Many people consider work as only a part of life and instead want time to spend with family, satisfaction from what they do, and a sense of purpose from their job and life. This phenomenon is also described as "backing off the fast track" and focusing more on the quality of life. Work, by itself, is no longer as sufficiently fulfilling as it was in the past. This is manifested in several ways, for example:

- opting out of the labour force; for example, early retirement
- collecting employment insurance or welfare payments rather than accepting low-paying or unattractive jobs
- changing careers
- refusing to perform overtime work
- feeling alienation caused by pressure in the workplace
- questioning traditional authority.

One counterargument for this is that employees are working harder than ever and that more is expected of them in terms of productivity and improved quality, with comparisons made to Japanese workers. Evidence of the work ethic includes the long hours that management and professional persons spend at their jobs or places of business. Work has become an obsession to many, as people have to work harder to keep up with inflation or to make ends meet, and more work is expected from the same or fewer number of employees. Workers fear job loss, and fewer people are available for backup.

Canadians were surveyed about whether or not they still believe in the work ethic. Canadian attitudes toward work ethic include the following, suggesting that the work ethic still exists.

- Canadians are, in principle, committed to work.
- Canadians choose work over most leisure activities when they have to make that kind of choice.
- Canadians would rather work than collect employment insurance.

Other studies have found that Canadians are strongly motivated to work and that most express overall satisfaction with their jobs.

In the past decade an employment trend known as the *gig economy* has complicated the view toward the work ethic. The **gig economy** refers to persons whose participation in the labour force is via short-term, temporary jobs, contracts, and self-employment. These persons may have more than one job as they are often part-time and necessary to make a living. The growth in the gig economy is the result of many factors, including a decline in traditional manufacturing jobs, technology enabling the establishment of small businesses, and the rise of online shopping. The winners in the gig economy are high-skilled workers such as IT experts and computer programmers. The reasons for working in the gig economy are to have more autonomy and control, making extra money on the side, balancing career and family life, and earning while seeking another job. The losers are those whose jobs can be eliminated due to automation or outsourcing. The downsides include no medical, dental, or disability benefits; no sick pay; low wages, and the inability to meet living expenses.[1]

Table 12.1 lists some issues associated with the work ethic today. It is not known how all these issues affect the work ethic. There is evidence that employees are working longer and harder, yet employers are willing to lay off workers even when skills shortages exist in many occupations.

TABLE 12.1	Contemporary Implications on the Work Ethic

- Workplace stress has increased, according to recent studies. The stress is created by a variety of factors, including many of the items mentioned below.
- Increasing use of part-time or temporary workers has raised concerns about how they are treated.
- Moonlighting has increased.
- Challenges presented by the gig economy. It may result in a strong work ethic, as workers are totally dependent on their own efforts to earn a living. On the other hand, it may result in feelings of insecurity and disappointment.
- Fringe benefits are changing in response to employee demands and efforts by some employers to retain highly qualified workers; for example, elder care, working from home, job sharing, child care, discount programs, and recreational facilities. On the other hand, benefits received from health care and pension plans are declining as employers find them too costly.
- The makeup of compensation is changing, with greater emphasis on pay for performance through cash bonuses, stock purchase, and grant plans.

- Employees are more concerned about being able to balance work and personal life
- Job insecurity has increased as employers are willing to lay off employees on short notice and even when the corporation is profitable.
- There is a consensus that Canada is suffering a labour skills shortage and that the shortage will become worse.

Many issues exist with employees in the workplace. Only three will be discussed: loyalty of employers to employees and vice-versa, employee privacy, and diversity in the workplace.

Employee Loyalty

Loyalty creates that extra effort and extra drive in employees to perform. It encourages self-motivated behaviour, and reflects employees' confidence in management, their vision, and the corporation's purpose. Loyalty means commitment by employees to the organization they work for. In turn, employers are loyal to employees by providing career-long employment, good salaries, and other benefits. But has this relationship changed with the new employment environment?

Most managers probably believe that employees should be loyal. Signs of a lack of commitment are easy to detect (turnover, early retirements), but measuring loyalty is much more difficult. Low turnover is not necessarily a sign of loyalty, but instead may mean that employees are tied through benefit plans (particularly pensions), or that no other job opportunities exist. Managers should also be cautious of extreme loyalty; overzealous behaviour by an employee does not necessarily mean that the employee is performing in the best interests of the enterprise. But, given the pressures of change, it may not be possible for management to provide some of the things that in the past encouraged loyalty—for example, job security and good compensation packages.

Employees in today's society often want to be entities unto themselves and are seeking challenging opportunities. Some consider loyalty to self more important than to the corporation. Such employees might be seen to be loyal and dedicated to the job itself, rather than to the corporation they are employed by to do that job. On the other hand, many employees wonder why they should be loyal when corporations may lay them off. It is management's responsibility to provide the environment that engenders loyalty. Intelligent human resource management goes a long way toward doing this. Employees must first be trusted and managers must be loyal to employees. It is critical for managers to give trust and loyalty before expecting it. Managers often assume that they cannot expect loyalty, but loyalty and the commitment it involves can be generated by management initiatives.

In order to improve loyalty, managers must communicate a persuasive corporate image to employees. Employees who demonstrate loyalty must be appropriately rewarded—not only by monetary compensation. In pursuit of loyalty, management should bear in mind the following: loyalty must be a corporate priority and it must start at the top with the CEO; persons at all levels in the organization must be involved; the process takes a long time; and token, one-shot efforts must be avoided. Managers must be careful to distinguish between employee loyalty to individuals and to the corporation. Loyalty to individuals represents personal loyalty and is not as beneficial as loyalty to the organization, which is more enduring.

The blind loyalty of employees that may have existed in the past is unlikely today. On the other hand, managers are finding it more difficult to demonstrate that employees owe them loyalty. Corporate loyalty might need to be redefined in the context of the current situation, where jobs are less secure. It is unreasonable to expect dedicated efforts from employees whose future is insecure. But employees still basically want to think well of the company they work for, as it means thinking well about themselves. Employers will have to honestly explain the need for retrenchment, technological change, and heavier individual workloads. Another issue related to employee loyalty is whistleblowing, which was described in Chapter 6. Management may view it as an indication of disloyalty, and employees may be reluctant to engage in it for the same reason. Nevertheless, many corporations are establishing whistleblowing policies and procedures.

Workplace Privacy

Workplace privacy is a sensitive issue with many legal and ethical challenges, only some of which will be discussed. A fundamental component of privacy is use of an employee's personal information. Employees have the right to control access to personal information, but employers have some rights to obtain information. Privacy of personal information is regulated by the federal government's *Personal Information Protection and Electronic Documents Act* (PIPEDA) and other provincial legislation. PIPEDA requires that organizations hold personal information in a responsible manner, permit individuals to access and correct personal information, and allow individuals to have control over information about themselves. Responsibility for Ethics 12.2 summarizes the Act's "Fair Information Principles."

RESPONSIBILITY FOR ETHICS 12.2

Personal Information Protection and Electronic Documents Act (PIPEDA)

The Act requires that businesses and organizations manage personal information according to the following "Fair Information Principles":

- *Accountability*—put systems and people in place to manage information
- *Identifying purposes*—understand the uses to which the information will be put
- *Consent*—obtain permission to use personal information
- *Limiting collection*—collect only information that is appropriate and necessary
- *Limiting use, disclosure, and retention*—restrict the use of personal information
- *Accuracy*—minimize the collection of incorrect information
- *Safeguards*—make sure the information is stored and accessed appropriately
- *Openness*—must make information about its policies and practices relating to the management of personal information publicly and readily available
- *Individual access*—allow individuals to see their personal information
- *Provide recourse*—arrange for individuals to have a course of action if they have an issue with their personal information

Employers have a responsibility for workplace privacy, but they also have a right to some personal information. When hiring, employers need to know the applicant's qualifications and previous work experience. On the other hand, they have no right to personal information such as weight, age, medical records, race, blood type, fingerprints, or marital status. Employers are challenged to justify which aspects of an employee's personal life are relevant to the job—for example, whether that applicant has AIDS/HIV or uses illegal drugs. Testing for substance abuse is a controversial issue for both employees and employers, especially where a stakeholder's safety may be at risk.

Workplace privacy has been challenged by the emergence of electronic technology and social media. Employees have access to email systems, the Internet, wireless telephones, and other devices that may be used inappropriately. One issue is the appropriate use of electronic technology, particularly in relation to social media. Employees should be cautious when participating in social media such as Facebook. A related issue is the surveillance or monitoring of email and Internet usage; another is the use of cameras. Employers claim that such monitoring is necessary to avoid liability, to improve productivity and avoid excessive use, and to maintain network security. Employees claim that the employers are violating their personal privacy. As future employees, managers, or entrepreneurs, students will no doubt be exposed to the issues surrounding workplace privacy.

Want to learn more about privacy in the workplace?

Managing Employment Diversity

Despite the improvements in labour and human rights legislation, some individuals or groups in the workforce still claim that they are being treated unfairly by employers. **Discrimination** is the preferential (or less than preferential) treatment on bases not directly related to qualifications of the job or performance on the job. The discrimination occurring is often prejudice against certain persons that could be based on such grounds as race (including Indigenous), gender, nationality, age (young and old), disability, marital status, physical appearance, sexual orientation, and health (for example, HIV/AIDS). Sometimes discrimination is obvious, but it also can be based on habit, custom, and tradition and be barely noticeable.

Most discrimination is addressed by employment equity legislation and corporate policy. **Employment equity** is the fair and equal treatment of employees. Federal and provincial/territorial governments have legislation to implement employment equity. An example of federal government legislation is the *Employment Equity Act,* whose purpose is to:

achieve equality in the workplace so that no person shall be denied employment opportunities or benefits for reasons unrelated to ability and, in the fulfillment of that goal, to correct the conditions of disadvantage in employment experienced by women, aboriginal peoples, persons with disabilities and members of visible minorities by giving effect to the principle that employment equity means more than treating persons in the same way but also requires special measures and the accommodation of differences.[2]

Accompanying legislation is the *Canadian Human Rights Act* (R.S., 1985, c. H-6); its purpose is to:

extend the laws in Canada to give effect . . . to the principle that all individuals should have an opportunity equal with other individuals to make for themselves the lives that they are able and wish to have and to have their needs accommodated, consistent with their duties and obligations as members of society, without being hindered in or prevented from doing so by discriminatory practices based on race, national or ethnic origin, colour, religion, age, sex, sexual orientation, marital status, family status, disability or conviction for an offence for which a pardon has been granted.[3]

The Canadian Human Rights Commission administers the *Canadian Human Rights Act* and is responsible for ensuring compliance with the *Employment Equity Act.* Both laws ensure that the principles of equal opportunity and non-discrimination are followed in all areas of federal jurisdiction.

Provincial governments have passed anti-discrimination laws to ensure fair employment practices. Most provinces prohibit discrimination on the grounds of race, religion, national origin, colour, sex, age, and marital status, and in selected cases the prohibited grounds include political beliefs, ethnic origin, physical disability, creed, and sexual orientation.

Laws themselves do not prevent discrimination and enforcement is a problem. Some employees are still discriminated against and have little recourse through which to seek remedial action. To a large extent, the individual employer must be relied upon to treat employees and possible employees fairly. The corporation has a major role to play in reducing employment discrimination.

Most corporations comply with legislation and many are involved with **diversity management**, a voluntary initiative that goes beyond what is required by law to eliminate workplace discrimination. Many corporations now practise diversity management and are recognized by the Canada's Best Diversity Employers 2019 award.[4] Everyday Ethics 12.1 describes some aspects of diversity management at BCE Inc.

 EVERYDAY ETHICS 12.1

Diversity at BCE Inc.

BCE Inc. is one of Canada's Best Diversity Employers 2019, awarded for the company's extensive diversity management program overseen by its Diversity Leadership Council. Its Diversity and Inclusion programs cover several minority groups, including persons with disabilities, women, and Indigenous Peoples both in the workforce and senior management. Resource groups include Women at Bell and LGBT Network established in 2009.

Diversity and inclusion is extended to the board of directors and its supply chain. Women make up 30.1 percent of senior management and 31 percent of the non-executive directors on the board. In 2014, the company launched a supplier diversity program to increase involvement of businesses owned by women, Indigenous Peoples, LGBTQ+ persons, and other members of minority groups in its supply chain.

In addition to the Diversity Employers award, BCE Inc. has been recognized by the following employer awards: Canada's Top 100 Employers 2019, Canada's Top Employer for Young People 2019, and Montréal's Top Employers 2019.

Two related causes have received attention recently: the LGBTQ+ movement and the #MeToo movement. The following sections discuss these causes. Another related topic is feminist ethics, described after the #MeToo section.

LGBTQ+ and Business[5]

LGBTQ+ stands for lesbian, gay, bisexual, transgender, and queer or questioning. The plus sign indicates the need to be inclusive of all identities to ensure that none are left out. Sometimes a *2* is included to represent both masculine and feminine spirits and is used by some Indigenous people to describe their sexual, gender, and/or spiritual identity.

Business corporations are increasingly recognizing LGBTQ+ individuals. It is a challenge to develop policies relating to LGBTQ+, as they must be carefully worded not to offend and must not omit any persons who feel they are in this group.

LGBTQ+ inclusion is now considered necessary, as it improves access to talent and increases creativity, and it cannot be ignored as a market segment. However, corporations must be innovative in their inclusive approach to this segment of the population.

There must be commitment to inclusiveness at the top of the corporation. There is a need to identify how employees experience inclusiveness and to engage them to get ideas of what should be done. Some experimentation will likely be necessary. One organization that recognizes the importance of LGBTQ+ and can assist management is Pride at Work Canada, described in Responsibility for Ethics 12.3. Dozens of Canadian businesses have joined this organization, including Air Canada, Bell Canada, CIBC, Enbridge, Husky Energy, Loblaw, and McDonald's.

RESPONSIBILITY FOR ETHICS 12.3

Pride at Work Canada

Pride at Work Canada's national and regional partners collectively employ over 1 million Canadians and include leading employers from across the Canadian economy. Each of these employers recognizes LGBTQ2+ individuals as key to a productive, engaged workforce. Their membership brings them into a network of sharing good practice, and helps them establish best-in-class workplace initiatives. Educational programs are offered.

Pride at Work Canada's Mission is "Through dialogue, education and thought leadership, we empower employers to build workplaces that celebrate all employees regardless of gender expression, gender identity, and sexual orientation."

Pride at Work Canada's Vision is "A nation where every individual can achieve their full potential at work regardless of gender expression, gender identity, and sexual orientation."

Pride at Work Canada's Values are "Inclusion, Collaboration, Empowerment, Recognition, and Professionalism."

Source: Used with permission. Pride at Work Canada at https://prideatwork.ca/about-us/.

#MeToo and Business

The #MeToo movement has raised awareness of sexual harassment in society's institutions, from Hollywood to the everyday workplaces of women around the world. Statistics Canada has seen a rise in police-reported sexual assaults with the average daily number of reports increasing from 59 to 74.[6] While these numbers are likely still lower than reality, since only a small number of assaults are ever reported, one can see the movement has helped empower people to feel more confident in reporting.

The world of business is no exception to sexual harassment, which exists in all corporate levels, from lower level employees to management. Since #MeToo, there has been greater exposure of the issues involved, but the problem has always been present. The hashtag has increased management's awareness and resulted in the re-examination of corporate practices and policies.

There is no doubt that sexual harassment has existed in the workplace, but its prevalence is hard to establish as the systems to encourage people coming forward have not always existed. Surveys have found that both men and women have experienced sexual harassment, misconduct, or assault during their careers but have not always felt they could report the incidences to their company. Many people fear the consequences of reporting, even as victims, for fear of not being believed or even retaliation such as not being able to advance in their career or even losing their jobs. There have even been instances where the harassment has been reported but settled in house with non-disclosure agreements, thus silencing the victim and not allowing any kind of warning to current or future employees.

Some commentators question whether the #MeToo movement has gone too far. Others believe that the pendulum has not swung far enough. There is a fear of false accusations based on fabricated stories or of becoming a victim of a mob on social media. The anonymity of the accuser facilitates reporting, but may be unfair to the accused. An action may result in the accused's reputation being ruined, as well as their being financially ruined and psychologically harmed. On the other hand, there may be a backlash for the accuser at work.

Possible remedies can create their own problems. Investigations might result in the offender being suspended or reinstated and even fired. Policies need to therefore be in place to ensure that the accuser and the offender have the right to due process. In some cases, someone might assess whether the offender takes responsibility for what they have done versus merely feeling regretful because they were caught. A genuine apology, and a commitment to change behaviour could lead to redemption, and the possibility of restorative justice achieved with an honest effort to admit wrong. Surveys indicate that most offenders are not repeat offenders, but for some, the question is open as to whether or not offenders deserve to be forgiven for a sexual harassment incident.

Management and boards of directors must be proactive in addressing sexual harassment and the issues involved. Actions that need to be taken include putting in place procedures for reporting harassment, establishing independent helplines, increasing training programs and refreshing training materials, revising codes of conduct, and including more diverse voices in executive and board positions.

Many stakeholders, including customers, shareholders, employees, boards of directors, and NGOs, are asking for information on what protection from sexual harassment is being provided. Thus, it is essential that sexual harassment policies are in place. There are costs of ignoring such policies, including threats to a corporation's reputation, reduced productivity, increased turnover, and maybe declining sales. The #MeToo movement has shone a light on an issue that desperately needed more attention; the next steps will be to take that attention and turn it into action.

Influence of Feminist Ethics on Business Ethics and CSR

Feminist ethics is defined as "a diverse set of gender-focused approaches to ethical theory and practice."[7] The objective is to develop non-sexist ethical principles, policies, and practices in society. With regard to business organizations, women traditionally have not advanced as owners, managers, professionals, and members of boards of directors relative to men, creating a demand for gender equality and dignity for women. In addition, it is argued that feminist ethics can improve a corporation's overall approach to business ethics and CSR.

It was argued that traditional ethical theories did not consider or value the "traditional" women's moral experience. The theories were more concerned with traditional "men's issues," and ignored more traditionally prescribed traits of women, such as nurturing or caring. Traditionally "masculine" traits like independence, autonomy, hierarchy, and domination were overemphasized in comparison to "feminine" traits of interdependence, community, and collaboration. Moral reasoning favoured typically "male" ways of thinking based on rules, rights, justice, and universality, which was believed to lead to fair, objective, and consistent treatment or outcomes.

There were many gender-centred approaches to ethics, but they can be categorized as either care- or power-focused. Care-focused ethics highlight the differences between men and women and the perceived inferior status of women. It was believed that women were more likely to consider the views of others and assess situations differently than their male counterparts. Also, the perception was that women have a more nurturing and mentoring approach, and place more consideration on relationships through attachment, networks, and connections. The power- or status-focused approach emphasized issues related to domination and subordination of women. Power and how power was used to oppress women was described. Gender equality would be achieved through changes in systems, structures, institutions, and practices that differentiate between the roles and status of men and women in organizations.[8]

Borgerson discussed why feminist ethics should be harmonized with business ethics and CSR. Borgerson argued that feminist ethics placed emphasis on three concepts that provided better approaches to recognizing, evaluating, and addressing ethical concerns: relationships, responsibility, and experience. The focus of feminist ethics on these concepts would result in a superior appreciation of business ethics than that of the traditional theories discussed in Chapter 5.

Greater attention has been given to the role of interpersonal relationships in business. In traditional theories, individual or group autonomy when considering ethical action and decisions was viewed as appropriate. But more reflection on relationships advocated by feminist ethics increased the stakeholders considered or consulted. A distinction was made between taking and having responsibility. Active willingness was necessary when taking responsibility. There were implications for those not included or chosen in the responsibility taken, and this applied whether women and others were involved. Feminist ethics supported having responsibility, which was beyond the choice of deciding whether or not to take responsibility. Finally, experience involved taking an interest in understanding marginalized individuals or groups. Feminist ethics advocated listening to other voices, which resulted in a broader acknowledgement of human involvement or interaction. Thus, there was a sensitivity to the lives of others that encouraged a more critical reflection on a social or ethical issue or dilemma.[9]

The approaches of feminist ethics allow for deeper insight into decisions relating to business ethics and corporate social responsibility than do traditional ethical theories. Not only is the status of women in business considered, but the status of all stakeholders. The concepts of relationships, responsibility, and experience are critical in stakeholder relationships, assessing ethical issues, and formulating social responsibility programs.

Employees and CSR

Research has found that a connection exists between corporate social responsibility and sustainability and **employee engagement**, defined as the emotional and intellectual commitment of an individual or group to an organization that supports building and sustaining business performance.[10] A study by Hewitt Associates and CBSR (Canadian Business for Social Responsibility) found a strong correlation between employee engagement and employees' views of the employer's record on CSR. Corporations with a "high employee engagement have a higher degree of readiness to focus on CSR as a strategy to improve overall organizational performance and better meet the needs of employees and external stakeholders." The most frequent CSR activities were community investment, waste reduction, business travel reduction, and responsible purchasing.[11] A later Hewitt Associates study found that when employees had a positive view of their employer's CSR there was greater employee engagement, which corporate managers stated was important to long-term success.[12]

When employees believed that supervisors acted ethically, they also were likely to behave ethically. In other words, a direct correlation exists between the ethical behaviour of supervisors and that of employees.[13] Similarly, it was found that when employees believed their company was adhering to high ethical standards, the employees were more committed to the company.[14] Employers effectively communicating CSR within the corporation are more likely to attract and retain employees. Satisfied employees need to link work to personal life through CSR, feel connected to the corporation, and take opportunities for self-enhancement—all of which increase loyalty, productivity, and commitment.[15] Another study found that employees who gave money or time to social causes felt more committed to their employers. Through helping colleagues, employees considered themselves and their employers to be more caring.[16]

Related to this, research has found that students are searching for meaningful work as demonstrated by a prospective employer's involvement in social issues. Students want their work to align with social and environmental causes such as climate change, renewable energy, and innovative products and processes. In other words, employers are expected to incorporate sustainability and social responsibility into the design of jobs.[17] A Network for Business Sustainability study identified the sustainable practices that are being demanded by future employees. It was found that students wanted employers to promote environmental efficiency through reduced waste and to encourage carbon regulation. Independent evaluation that employers were meeting their social licence was expected along with increased CSR transparency. Students wanted increased involvement in business and increased community engagement by corporations.[18]

LO 12.2   Consumers and Consumption

While employees are internal workplace stakeholders, consumers are external marketplace stakeholders. Their role is critical to corporations: without their participation through purchases, corporations cannot succeed. Fundamental to understanding the consumer stakeholder in the marketplace is knowledge of the consumer sovereignty concept.

Defining Consumer Sovereignty

A review of the literature does not disclose a definitive definition of "consumer sovereignty," but several essential characteristics of a definition are included in the following:

- Consumers, not producers or governments, dictate the type, quality, and quantity of goods and services to be provided.
- Elements of democracy are present, including the idea of voting through purchase decisions, and that these decisions are made based upon the preferences of a majority.
- Consumers are free to make their own choices and are not unduly influenced by producers or governments.
- An economic system operates more efficiently when consumers determine production.[19]

The concept is imperfectly defined as its objective could be considered impossible and its realization in the market far from perfect. Yet consumer sovereignty is a fundamental of capitalism as described in Chapter 2. Government has become involved and is making many decisions that, in theory, should be made by consumers. Economists say consumers should be protected from those who are convinced they know better than consumers what is best.

The distinction between consumer and producer (any corporation, for example a manufacturer or farmer) is an important one to make. It is argued that consumers have relinquished their sovereignty to producers. Producers and consumers may have conflicting interests and the producers' notions of what satisfies consumers may be influenced by what satisfies them as producers. As a result, consumers become impotent as influencers in the economic system.

The principle of consumer sovereignty is unlikely to be observed unless consumers have freedom of choice and are actually allowed to register their preferences in a market. In this respect, consumer sovereignty is really a front for the individualistic ethic, which holds that freedom is valuable in itself. If this ethic is accepted, one must accept the freedom to offer choices as well as the freedom to choose. Businesspersons often argue the former, but forget the latter. It might be argued that governments forget that consumers should have the freedom to choose.

Consumers and the Marketplace

The conditions of consumer sovereignty are seldom fulfilled in the marketplace, as buyers face high information costs, offensive and often misleading advertising, and shoddy and unsafe goods. Consumers may be manipulated by persuasive, at times misleading, advertising. It is also argued that as a small number of large firms dominate the market for some goods and services, consumers are being forced to purchase what producers provide. Consumer preferences are manipulated by large corporations in which market power has become concentrated. Also, in product development, there may be a difference between what consumers think the alternatives are and what producers think they are, meaning that the actual market choices may not reveal what consumers really want.

On the other hand, consumers do have some influence on the corporation and the marketplace. The most obvious way is of course their decision whether or not to purchase a corporation's products or services, but there are other influences. Consumer sovereignty exerts influence through **consumerism**, a social movement seeking to protect and augment the rights and powers of buyers in relation to sellers. An objective of the consumer movement is to make consumers aware of their place or role in the marketplace. Consumerism is considered necessary because some goods and services supplied by corporations fail to meet acceptable standards relating to product safety, information, performance, and pricing. Consumers may experience poor after-purchase service and might be the victims of retail misbehaviour, such as high-pressure sales tactics and misleading advertisements.

Consumers have formed organizations to promote their interests. One example is the Consumers' Association of Canada, formed in 1947, which is a voluntary, non-profit organization committed to the improvement of the standard of living in Canadian homes. It studies consumer problems and issues and brings the views of consumers to corporations and governments. The most well-known consumer advocate is the American Ralph Nader. In Canada, Phil Edmonston formed the Nader-style Automobile Protection Association to represent car owners. In addition, dozens of small consumer organizations exist across Canada. Being informed also enhances the influence of consumers in the marketplace. Print and broadcast information informs consumers, as does access to the Internet. From consumerism, a set of consumer rights have emerged. These rights, with accompanying responsibilities, are presented in Responsibility for Ethics 12.4.

 RESPONSIBILITY FOR ETHICS 12.4

Consumer Rights and Responsibilities

Rights illustrate a source of influence for consumer stakeholders, but with rights come responsibilities. The first four rights were outlined in a speech in 1962 by U.S. President John Kennedy. U.S. President Gerald Ford added the fifth right in 1970, and over time other rights have been added by consensus.

Consumer Rights	Consumer Responsibilities
To safety	To follow instructions and take precautions
To choose	To make independent, informed consumption choices
To be heard	To make opinions known and to complain in a constructive manner
To be informed	To search out and use available information
To consumer education	To take advantage of education opportunities
To redress	To fight for the quality and service expected
To a healthy environment	To minimize environmental damage by careful choice and use of goods and services

---

The consumer influence may also be exerted by government. Governments have enacted legislation and regulations to protect the consumer, and one example is the federal government's *Competition Act.* The Act is intended to promote and maintain fair competition so that Canadian consumers can benefit from competitive prices, product choice, and quality services. Responsibility for Ethics 12.5 summarizes legislation to protect consumers in the area of advertising and deceptive market practices.

RESPONSIBILITY FOR ETHICS 12.5

Protecting the Consumer

The Competition Bureau promotes truth in advertising in the marketplace by discouraging deceptive business practices and by encouraging the provision of sufficient information to enable informed consumer choice. The *Competition Act* is a federal law governing most business conduct in Canada. It contains both criminal and civil provisions aimed at preventing anti-competitive practices in the marketplace.

False or misleading ordinary selling price representations—The ordinary selling price provisions of the *Competition Act* are designed to ensure that when products are promoted at sale prices, consumers are not misled by reference to inflated regular prices.

Performance representation not based on adequate and proper tests—Businesses should not make any performance claims unless they can back them up. The *Competition Act* prohibits any representation in the form of a statement, warranty, or guarantee of the performance, efficacy, or length of life of any given product that is not based on adequate and proper testing. The *Competition Act* prohibits:

- the sale or rent of a product at a price higher than its advertised price
- "bait-and-switch" selling, which occurs when a product is advertised at a bargain price but is not available for sale in reasonable quantities
- the supply of a product at a price that exceeds the lowest of two or more prices clearly expressed in respect to the product
- any promotional contest that does not disclose the number and approximate value of prizes and the odds of winning
- misleading warranties and guarantees
- the unauthorized use of tests and testimonials, or the distortion of authorized tests and testimonials

Pyramid selling—Pyramid selling is illegal in Canada. It is a multi-level marketing plan that includes either compensation for recruitment, required purchases as a condition of participation, inventory loading, or the lack of a buy-back guarantee on reasonable commercial terms.

Consumer sovereignty can lead to excessive consumption, resulting in an antagonism toward materialism, selfishness, greed, and the destruction of mankind's natural virtue. It is an expression of individualism as opposed to collectivism. There is no doubt that the concept concentrates on the individual instead of society as a whole, and largely ignores the higher purposes to which the narrow interest of individuals should be subservient. But this is true of any economic system based upon individualism and competitive markets. The assumption is that individual decision making is preferable to centralized, unitary decision making. If individualism and self-interest are acceptable as motivators in a business system, it seems logical that they should also be motivators for consumers. Everyday Ethics 12.2 discusses whether or not this means "the customer is always right."

EVERYDAY ETHICS 12.2

"The Customer Is Always Right"

The meaning of consumer sovereignty would suggest that the customer, or consumer, is always right. Although consumers have rights, they also have responsibilities and are expected to behave in an ethical manner.

Sometimes consumers are wrong. Consumers are sometimes ill-informed or overwhelmed by information and thus may not make a decision in their best interests. Some consumers behave badly, for example, requesting a refund for an item not sold by the retailer, making abusive remarks to employees or treating them badly, or returning failed products after misusing them.

There are situations when customer demands involve morals. There may be commercial reasons for accommodating consumers but moral reasons for not, for example, selling pornographic materials, consulting one service provider and then having another perform work, or demanding unjustified returns.

On the other hand, there may be moral reasons for accommodating consumers but stronger commercial reasons for not doing so, for example, overbooking aircraft or costly product recalls.

The cliché "The customer is always right" illustrates the challenges of attempting to accommodate all stakeholders. There are other stakeholders—for example, employees—and consumers have to be reasonable in their expectations.

Consumers and CSR

Consumers are demanding a wide range of ethically, socially, and environmentally responsible products—that is, goods and services. This is referred to as **ethical consumerism**, a form of activism where consumers buy products, goods, and services that are ethically produced and/or not harmful to the environment and society. Goods and services that fall into the ethical category include organic produce; fair trade goods; electricity from renewable energy; green products, such as those made from recycled paper and wood products; locally produced goods or services; and goods and services provided by non-profit or social enterprise enterprises.[20]

According to research, about 20 percent of consumers based purchase decisions on ethical or socially responsible considerations. Three factors motivate consumers to make these purchases: CSR information must be available; there must be a moral alignment of CSR practices with the consumer on moral values; and the products must be considered affordable.[21]

Business is responding and Table 12.2 lists the types of ethical products available in the marketplace. Many issues are associated with this list. Consumers are often conflicted; for example, they are critical of big-box stores (such as Walmart), but still patronize them. Corporations, in particular retailers, are able to charge higher prices for ethical products and increase profits. Retailers such as Whole Foods Market and The Body Shop have built profitable corporate strategies based upon ethical products. Government policies or non-governmental organization (NGO) pressures may restrict consumer choice, for example banning eggs from caged birds on university campuses.

TABLE 12.2	Examples of Ethical Products
Food: • Organic • Local • Fair trade **Housing:** • Energy efficient **Clothing:** • Eco-chic—fashionable clothes from organic cotton, hemp, bamboo, flax, soy • Slow fashion—eco-friendly design • Recycled (Value Village, etc) • Fair trade fashions (Fair Indigo, etc) • Organic sneakers **Cosmetics:** • Natural ingredients • No animal testing **Green weddings:** • Efforts made to use particular clothing, special catering requirements; not using expensive limousines	**Financial Products:** • Ethical and green mutual funds • Ethical and SR stock (sustainability) indices • Green mortgages **Travel:** • Eco-travel • Carbon offsets (e.g., Air Canada) • Eco-resorts **Jewellery:** • Gold and diamonds—certification of source **Energy:** • Fluorescent light bulbs • Energy-saving devices • Clean sources of energy • Biofuel (ethanol and bio-diesel) **Transportation:** • "Terror-Free Gas"—gasoline sourced in nations that do not support terrorism • Hybrid vehicles • Carbon offsets

Want to learn more about **ethical products and services**?

Corporations promoting socially and environmentally friendly products are accused of greenwashing—that is, making token efforts, or saying one thing and doing another. It is questionable that some products are actually ethical. The meaning of *organic* is not clearly established and the term is used inappropriately sometimes. Certification standards and systems have not been established in some areas, and labelling can be misleading.

In the case of food, the calculation of "food miles" is difficult and misleading. The calculation of benefits must take into account all factor costs in the food production life-cycle and not just transportation miles or costs. Furthermore, consumers in developed countries demand more than can be produced locally and must rely on imported items. Locally produced food is often more expensive and the benefits to the environment are not certain.

A major issue with ethical products is whether socially conscious consumers are willing to pay for these types of products. Two researchers undertook a study to review 30 years of literature to ascertain the following: "Are consumers willing to reward firms for their sustainability actions with price premiums or increased purchases?" Many influences, impediments, and enhancements affected three consumer behaviour intentions—willingness to change behaviour, willingness to pay a premium, and willingness to punish. The main finding of the study was that ". . .the average premium for socially conscious products and services is 10%. Some consumers will demand a discount for 'unsustainability', even greater than the premium for sustainability."[22]

Other research studied the trade-offs consumers are willing to make when paying more for products with ethical features. Socially conscious features are definitely more important to some consumers and social features will make a difference when functional and price features are satisfied. It was found that some social features were more important than others; for example, avoiding child labour was more important than working conditions and animal testing more important than the use of animal by-products.[23]

It has been found that consumers react differently to various types of ethical initiatives. Park studied consumers' reactions to five types of ethical possibilities: fair trade, sustainable or green products, locally produced products, buy one and get one free, and donations to charities. It was determined that consumers were most interested in fair trade products, followed by buy one and get one free and donations. The author concluded that there are different types of ethical consumers that must be considered when designing ethical initiatives.[24]

There are many issues relating to ethical or sustainable products and services. Some consumers are willing to pay a higher price for these products and corporations are responding, but the ethical claims must be legitimate.

LO 12.3 Competitors and Competition

Competition is necessary, even crucial, for an effective market economy. It encourages innovation, productivity, entrepreneurship, and efficiency. The principal beneficiary when competitive forces exist is the consumer, who is provided with quality products, choice, and the best possible price.

Competition, as one of the fundamentals of the business system, was discussed in Chapter 2. In the context of business, competition is a struggle or rivalry for supremacy, often expressed among corporations as *market share*. Two or more corporations offer the same or similar product or service in many ways—for example, by offering a better product, through use of advertising, or by superior distribution or service. Competition might result in the defeat or destruction of one of the corporations. Business failures do result from competition, and if only one corporate structure survives a monopoly situation exists. Although competition does result in the failure of some corporations, the usual result is that some survive and new businesses enter the industry. Thus, competitors are a stakeholder group that most managers must recognize and respond to in some way.

Competition: Ethics and Responsibilities

Implications for social responsibility are associated with the degree of competitive rivalry existing in a business system. One position is that increased competition and pressure to be competitive has resulted in an increase in unethical or questionable practices. Industrial spying, espionage, and sabotage are now of such concern that industrial or economic security has replaced national security as a major national issue. Practices range from eavesdropping and theft of research and development technology, to hiring the competitor's key employees. It is argued that the practices are much more widespread than reported and that many remain undisclosed either because companies are unaware of them or are too embarrassed to report them.

Several causes of this trend have been identified, including the cutthroat global economy, aggressive competitive tactics, and shorter product cycles necessitating faster responses to competitor initiatives. The copying or counterfeiting of products appears more common and increasingly difficult to control, as there appears to be little reluctance to steal ideas from others.

Society is concerned about the concentration of corporate power in a few corporations or a few groupings of interconnected corporations. There is a concern that a few large corporations may have too much influence over the economy and possibly too much influence over government. Concentration of corporate power can also be measured within a single industry by providing the percentage of sales controlled by the four or eight largest firms.

There are two concerns about industrial concentration—the possibilities for collaboration and higher profitability. In highly concentrated industries, corporations often behave in a similar fashion. For example, packaging changes are copied and prices matched. In less concentrated industries, it is much more difficult to keep track of all competitors and to predict their behaviour. Economists have been concerned that corporations in highly concentrated industries tend to be more profitable.

The high degree of market concentration in some industries plus the high degree of concentrated ownership constitutes a centre of power in society. When this concentration is combined with a capability to influence other stakeholders, especially governments, a controlling power structure is set in place. Many Canadians are fearful of this.

Government Influence to Encourage Competition

Competitive behaviour or the conduct of business in Canada is regulated by the *Competition Act* (R.S.C. 1985, c. C-34). This Act establishes the basic principles for the conduct of business in Canada so that competition is encouraged and maintained. The purpose of the Act is to promote the efficiency and adaptability of the Canadian economy; ensure that small and medium-sized corporations have an equitable opportunity to participate in the Canadian economy; and provide consumers with competitive prices and product choices. If it could be accomplished, this purpose would result in an ideal marketplace. Responsibility for Ethics 12.6 lists clauses in the *Competition Act* that apply to how competitors should behave.

 RESPONSIBILITY FOR ETHICS 12.6

Regulation of Competitors

The *Competition Act* governs business conduct among competitors. Some of the Act's features are as follows:

Conspiracy—This is any agreement, arrangements, or combination designed to lessen competition unduly in relation to supply, manufacture, or production of a product and includes fixing prices, or preventing competitors from entering the market.

Bid-Rigging—Any arrangement between two or more persons or corporations where one party will refrain from bidding in a call for tenders, or where there was collusion in the submission of bids.

Predatory Pricing—There are two types of predatory pricing: (i) selling products in one region of Canada at prices lower than in another region for the purpose of lessening competition; and (ii) selling products at unreasonably low prices where the intent is to lessen competition.

Review of Mergers—When a merger occurs, the Competition Bureau may decide to examine it and recommend whether or not actions should be taken to preserve competition.

Abuse of Dominant Position—The Competition Act provides for remedies where dominant corporations in a market engage in anti-competitive behaviours, such as acquisition of a customer who would otherwise be available to a competitor to impede a competitor's entry into the market; purchase of products to prevent the reduction of existing price levels; and selling articles at a price lower than the acquisition cost to discipline or eliminate a competitor.

Although the role of government in encouraging competition in the Canadian economy is important, it is only one of several factors determining competitive behaviour. The following is a selected list of such factors:

Entrepreneurship—It should be remembered that the business system involves a life-cycle process in which corporations are formed, grow, and dissolve. There is a constant supply (or birth) of new small businesses, many of which grow in stature and provide competition for large, well-established firms.

Deregulation and privatization—Government initiatives to deregulate some sectors of the economy have influenced the growth of businesses, and efforts to sell off the business corporations it owns have increased opportunities for entrepreneurs (discussed in Chapter 10).

Technology—A multitude of technological developments have encouraged competitive rivalry. New technology has led to new business corporations, for example in electronics and various computer-related industries, and has changed how other industries operate.

Decline of natural monopoly—Utility-type companies often operated as natural monopolies, for example in telephone and cable television. With deregulation and new technologies, neither of these industries can now be considered a natural monopoly. Competition exists in the telephone industry and cable television is under pressure from wireless and new providers.

Global trends in trade—The reduction of some barriers to trade is increasing competition in Canada. This is accomplished through trade agreements such as the World Trade Organization (WTO); the North American Free Trade Agreement (NAFTA), being renegotiated as the Canada–United States–Mexico Agreement (CUSMA); the Canada–European Union (EU) Comprehensive Economic and Trade Agreement (CETA); and the Trans-Pacific Partnership (TPP), an agreement among 11 Pacific Rim countries. Despite free trade agreements, many barriers to trade exist, especially non-tariff barriers.

Mergers/takeovers—Mergers or takeovers tend to occur in cycles, with the later 1970s and 1980s being two periods of high acquisition activity. Such acquisitions can reduce competition, especially if they are acquisitions in the same industry.

The following two sections will discuss the supplier stakeholder and the importance of the supply chain to sustainability.

LO 12.4   Suppliers as a Stakeholder

In **Business-to-business** commercial activity, one corporation (a supplier) sells goods or services to another corporation rather than to consumers. Traditionally, the relationship between suppliers and their customers was an adversarial one. Today the relationship is more likely to be one of mutual interdependence based on trust and collaboration. Everyday Ethics 12.3 is an example of a customer attempting to influence the behaviour of suppliers. Purchasers or buyers are recognizing suppliers who cooperate with them and are committed to considering social and environmental responsibilities.

 EVERYDAY ETHICS 12.3

Influencing Suppliers

An example of how a corporation influences its suppliers is the use of "supplier codes of business conduct." A good example is the *Canadian Tire Principles of Business Conduct,* which includes a section on "Expectations of Suppliers."

- Compliance with laws
- Employment standards
- Wages and benefits
- Working hours
- Child labour
- Forced or slave labour
- Discrimination/human rights
- Disciplinary practices
- Workplace environment
- Environmental protection
- Confidentiality and privacy
- Unlawful payments
- Dealing with the company's employees
- Sub-suppliers

Also included are descriptions of supplier certification, supplier assessment and monitoring, enforcement of the code, and reporting and addressing code violations. The reason for selecting this code is that it appears comprehensive. Other retailers and manufacturers have similar codes.

The relationship between customers and suppliers is governed informally by several rights. The supplier expects to have the right to supply goods and services to a customer. Preferential treatment is not expected from the customer or received by the supplier. A fair deal is expected, which is negotiated ethically without lies, deception, non-disclosure, or threats. Conflicts of interest are expected to be disclosed. Loyalty by both sides may exist, but not to imply automatic acceptance of terms or conditions offered.

The influence of suppliers varies. Where the customer has several sources of goods and services, the customer will exert more influence over the supplier. If the supplier is the sole source of particular goods or services, the supplier will have greater influence over the transaction.

The buyer's purchasing staff and the supplier's sales staff are sometimes confronted with ethical dilemmas when bribes, kickbacks, gifts, and hospitality are offered. Suppliers and their customers have formed professional associations, such as the Supply Chain Management Association (SCMA)™, to guide the behaviour of these employees. Responsibility for Ethics 12.7 provides an outline of the Code of Ethics formulated by SCMA.

 RESPONSIBILITY FOR ETHICS 12.7

Supply Chain Management Association (SCMA)™

Supply Chain Management Association (SCMA)™ is a professional association of supply management managers and provides training, education, and professional development. It offers a training program leading to a diploma/certificate in supply management. The association embraces all aspects of strategic supply chain management, including: purchasing/procurement, strategic sourcing, contract management, materials/inventory management and logistics and transportation.

A condition of membership is adherence to its Code of Ethics. Components of the code include:

- Standards of conduct: Avoidance of conflicts of interest; protection of confidential or sensitive information; maintenance of business relationships; acceptance of gifts, gratuities, and hospitality; and promotion of environmental and social responsibilities.

- Professional principles: Professional competency; professionalism; honesty and integrity, responsible management, serving the public good; and compliance with legal obligations.

Enforcement procedures outlined are compliant process, conduct of investigations, and nature of sanctions.

Government legislation governs the relationship between buyers and suppliers. Responsibility for Ethics 12.8 lists clauses in the *Competition Act* that apply to this relationship. As discussed in this section and the one that follows, suppliers are now regulated more by other stakeholders, such as consumers, their business customers, and NGOs.

 RESPONSIBILITY FOR ETHICS 12.8

Regulation of Suppliers

The *Competition Act* contains the following provisions to ensure suppliers do not take advantage of their customers:

Exclusive dealing, tied selling, and market restrictions—These practices generally occur when a supplier places conditions on the supply of a product that constrain the customer in terms of, for example, what else the customer must buy to obtain supply, where the customer may subsequently market the product, or what other product lines the customer may or may not carry. Although not illegal in themselves, they will be investigated if they are found to have caused, or to be likely to cause, a substantial lessening of competition in a market.

Price discrimination—This exists when a supplier charges different prices to competitors who purchase similar volumes of an article.

Price maintenance—This involves attempts to influence upward or to discourage the reduction of price at which another corporation supplies or advertises a product, or refusing to supply anyone because of that corporation's low pricing policy.

Refusal to deal—Refusal to deal involves situations where a buyer cannot obtain supplies of an available product on usual trade terms and, as a result, is substantially affected in their ability to conduct business, resulting in an adverse effect on competition.

Two issues relating to supply management are discussed in the next sections: local supplier favouritism and supplier diversity.

Local Supplier Favouritism Issues

Localism is defined as "a social movement that supports economic practices oriented toward strengthening local economies and reducing reliance on nonlocal resources." It is often referred to as *buying local* and as *locavorism* when involving food. Advocates of this practice want consumers and businesses to purchase from local independent businesses and not from large national retail chains or foreign sources. Thus, buy local has been a rallying cry against big-box stores by independent business. It is argued that it is a person's civic duty to shop locally and that there are economic benefits for the community. From a business perspective, it has been found that business organizations with more community identity orientations will be more likely to source locally.[25]

Two business associations that support localism are the Business Alliance for Local Living Economies (BALLE), whose mission is "to create local economies that work for all,"[26] and the American Independent Business Alliance (AMIBA), a non-profit organization "dedicated to helping communities become more self-supporting and resilient through fostering a culture that values and supports independent business and local entrepreneurs."[27]

Buy-local policies are implemented by federal, provincial, and municipal governments with the best of intentions. However, there are downsides to these policies. They are a form of protectionism to shelter local providers. It is argued that these policies coddle the weak, do not stimulate innovation, and prevent local businesses from taking advantage of the global supply chain. Usually, the result is higher prices, meaning customers have less to spend elsewhere in the local economy. In some instances, retaliation results, with similar policies being enacted against those that were the first to impose such policies. The exclusion of outsiders may cause a "them" versus "us" mentality, limiting business opportunities. Buy-local policies raise economic, social, and ethical issues and create harm to stakeholders and economies.[28]

Supplier Diversity

Supplier diversity is defined as "reaching out to groups not traditionally included or underrepresented in the supply chain or within the purchasing process of major corporations or governments." In order to advance supplier diversity, Supplier Diversity Alliance Canada (SDAC) was established in 2016 by the Canadian Gay & Lesbian Chamber of Commerce (CGLCC), representing LGBTQ-owned businesses; the Women Business Enterprises Canada Council (WBE Canada), representing women-owned businesses; and the Canadian Aboriginal and Minority Supplier Council (CAMSC), representing Aboriginal and minority groups suppliers.[29] The CAMSC is described in Responsibility for Ethics 12.9.

 RESPONSIBILITY FOR ETHICS 12.9

Canadian Aboriginal and Minority Supplier Council (CAMSC)

CAMSC is an example of an organization promoting supplier diversity.

CAMSC's vision is to "be the nationally recognized, respected and trusted business partner, leading supplier diversity in all industry segments with proven results in wealth and job creation for Aboriginal and minority groups suppliers. Economic value is created by deepening business and diverse supplier relationships through the innovation, competitiveness and brand loyalty in the supply chain."

CAMSC's mission is to "champion business relationships and economic growth of the Canadian supply chain through the inclusion of Aboriginals and Minority suppliers."

CAMSC, in collaboration with corporate members, provides a range of programs and services to assist suppliers in better accessing business opportunities with major corporations. It is associated with several other diverse supplier organizations.

Source: "About CAMSC," Canadian Aboriginal and Minority Supplier Council website at https://www.camsc.ca/about_camsc accessed March 8, 2019. Used with permission.

The purpose of supplier diversity organizations is to provide corporations owned by Indigenous people and minority groups an equal opportunity to become suppliers to major corporations and governments. They provide support, guidance, and consultation in approaches to developing and applying effective inclusive procurement policies and practices. By purchasing from diverse suppliers, corporations and governments are creating jobs, generating tax revenue, and increasing economic empowerment and spending power in the diverse communities. In other words, supplier diversity provides market-access opportunities to those underrepresented in the supply chain.

The next section looks at the supply chain in more detail to reveal how complex the sustainability relationship is between a corporation and its suppliers.

LO 12.5 Supply Chains and Sustainability

A **supply chain**, or value chain, is the route that a product travels from the procurement of raw materials, the transformation into intermediate goods and then final products, and the delivery to consumers through a distribution system to its ultimate disposal by the consumer. Planning, scheduling, and controlling the supply chain appropriately means that the corporation has the right product, in the right place, at the right time, and in the right condition. Figure 12.1 is a basic supply chain applicable to most products.

FIGURE 12.1 *Stages in a Supply Chain*

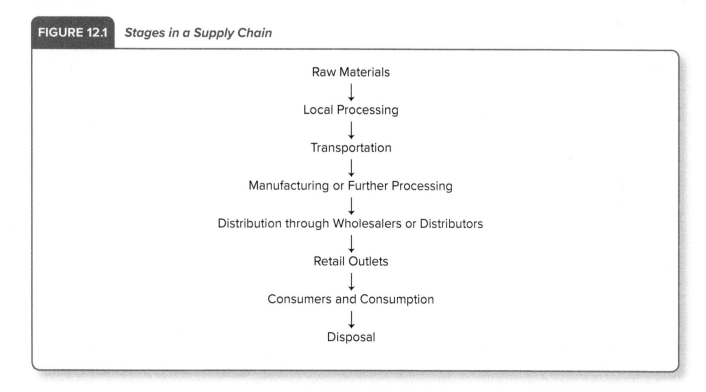

Today supply chain management includes paying attention to ethical, social, and environmental issues along with the accompanying responsibilities. When this is done, the supply chain is referred as being ethical or sustainable.

Raw materials may come from several sources and are often from developing countries. Materials such as wood, minerals, and petroleum have many associated environmental issues. Materials from developing countries frequently involve issues such as human rights, child labour, low wages, and dangerous working conditions. Sometimes the raw materials are shipped out of the country for processing, depriving local workers of employment.

Not all products follow the same chain; some may involve additional stages and some fewer. Retailers may purchase directly from manufacturers, bypassing wholesalers, or consumers may buy directly from manufacturers. Although a single chain is shown, branches may exist as by-products are produced, or the product at some stage may be sold to another corporation as ingredients for another product. Waste may be produced at different stages, which must be disposed of or sold to be used in other products. More attention has been focused on final product disposal and who is responsible. Profitability varies along the chain and with the type of product. Different issues impacting different stakeholders exist along the chain. NGOs often play major roles in improving conditions for workers in raw material production facilities. Governments tend to be more influential in downstream sections of the chain.

Global supply chains add another dimension for management and often these chains are more complicated. The Network for Business Sustainability published a study that provided guidance and listed best practices. The first step is to list all stakeholders that influence a corporation's approach to sustainable supply chains. The study found that the following stakeholders want sustainable supply chains: consumers, government, general public, activists (NGOs), media, industry peers, employees, and investors. The key sustainability issues in supply chains included working conditions, the environment, CSR, low wages, human rights, child labour, health and safety, forced labour, and sweatshops. According to the study's authors, there are three steps to developing a sustainable global supply chain:

- Identify Motivators: What is motivating change in the industry? What does the corporation stand to gain and lose? The key motivators were found to be customers, compliance, costs, competitive advantage, and conscience.

- Assess Levers: Seven key levers can facilitate or inhibit efforts to build a sustainable supply chain. Internal levers are purpose—that is, alignment of sustainability with organizational strategy; clear policy statements/codes of conduct; and people—that is, leadership/management support. External levers are industry collaboration; partnerships, including trust in supplier engagement; supportive government regulation; and power as represented by organizational size or influence over suppliers.

- Improve Practices: The four most prevalent practices were found to be a code of conduct that set expectations throughout the supply chain, certification as a screening device in selecting suppliers, rigorous selection process to reduce supply risks, and monitoring or auditing to ensure compliance with expectations.[30]

Global supply chains are now influenced by industry codes of conduct established by socially responsible corporations in collaboration with NGOs, trade unions, universities, and sometimes governments. The Fair Labour Association (FLA) is an example which has a Workplace Code of Conduct.[31] Another example is the toy industry's International Council of Toy Industries' code called ICTI Care (Caring, Awareness, Responsible, Ethical), a program to promote ethical manufacturing, in the form of fair labor treatment, as well as employee health and safety.[32]

These codes and others vary in their success as implementation depends on how rigorously compliance is enforced and what remedial action is imposed. The existence of reliable auditing processes is key especially when the audits are verified by a third party. In developing countries, the extent of corruption and the influence of governments are factors in determining how successful such codes are. In some cases, the codes are not delivering improvements. When adequate investments of time and money are made other codes have resulted in improvements.

The following section elaborates on approaches to sustainability in a supply chain, whether local or global.

Sustainable Supply Chains

The focus on ethics and responsibility in purchasing is described as *sustainability purchasing*, *extended producer responsibility* or *product stewardship*, and *life cycle thinking*. Other terms associated with this approach to purchasing are *responsible purchasing*, *ethical sourcing*, and *ethical trade*. Fair trade also involves sustainable supply chains and is discussed below.

Sustainability purchasing is defined as

…selecting goods and services which promote a healthier community and environment by considering the costs as well as the environmental and social impacts of products and services through all stages of their lifecycle: from product/service development and manufacturing through product/service use and ultimately to the disposal of whatever remains of the product/service at the end of its useful life. This process is achieved by incorporating key environmental and social factors with traditional price and performance considerations in purchasing decisions.[33]

This definition makes it clear that sustainability purchasing applies to the complete product chain, which could also be equated with the life cycle of the product. Sustainability purchasing is a form of regulation imposed on the corporation or industry by stakeholders other than government. Consumers, usually with the help of or prompting by NGOs, apply pressure to change purchasing practices. Retailers often prompt action after being influenced by consumers or NGOs.

Corporations recognize this influence and in turn respond through professional or trade associations (as illustrated by SCMA), or by participating in networks promoting sustainable purchasing, an example of which is given in Responsibility for Ethics 12.10. This type of network enables corporations to find suppliers who endorse sustainability practices.

RESPONSIBILITY FOR ETHICS 12.10

BuySmart Network

The BuySmart Network was established in 2005 in Vancouver as the Sustainability Purchasing Network. It is a non-profit organization supported by partners and sponsors interested in sustainability purchasing that will forge healthier, greener, and socially beneficial supply chains in Canada.

Some of the features of the Network as identified on their website are:

- The goals of the BuySmart Network are to: encourage the demand for and use of products and services that support positive social, economic and environmental impacts; and help organizations meet their strategic goals through sustainable procurement.

- Explaining the programs and services offered, including being a resource centre, a learning hub, and a place for advice.

- "Resource Centre" page includes lists of purchasing organizations, case studies, topics in sustainability purchasing, supplier directories, and tools and tips.

Other approaches to describing sustainable supply chains are extended producer responsibility and life cycle assessment.

Extended producer responsibility is "an environmental policy approach in which a producer's responsibility, physical and/or financial, for a product is extended to the post-consumer stage of a product's life cycle."[34] *Producer* in this definition refers to manufacturers or distributors. The responsibility for disposal is being shifted upstream to producers and away from consumers and local governments responsible for waste management. The policy is to provide incentives to producers to take environmental considerations into the design of the product. Extended producer responsibility is also referred to as *product stewardship*. This view of sustainability is being influenced by several stakeholders external to the corporation, including customers and consumers, non-governmental environmental organizations, voluntary standards organizations, institutional investors, and government authorities.[35]

Life cycle thinking (LCT) is "about going beyond the traditional focus on production site and manufacturing processes to include environmental, social and economic impacts of a product over its entire life cycle." The approach is also referred to as *life cycle assessment* and *social life cycle*. A typical product life cycle is as follows: natural resources; extraction of raw materials; design and production; packaging and distribution; use and maintenance; disposal, including incineration and land-filling. Inside the cycle are the possibilities for reuse and recycling of materials and components. In each life cycle there is the potential to reduce resource consumption and improve the performance of products. The UN's "Life Cycle Initiative" website contains extensive information on LCT.[36]

Want to learn more about sustainability in supply chains?

Fair Trade and Sustainability

Another influence on sustainability purchasing is the fair trade movement. **Fair trade** is commonly used to identify products that are involved with sustainability purchasing but usually focuses on the beginning of the product chain. The Fairtrade Foundation's definition is as follows:

Fairtrade is about better prices, decent working conditions, local sustainability, and fair terms of trade for farmers and workers in the developing world. By requiring companies to pay sustainable prices (which must never fall lower than the market price), Fairtrade addresses the injustices of conventional trade, which traditionally discriminates against the poorest, weakest producers. It enables them to improve their position and have more control over their lives.[37]

The fair trade movement is not anti-capitalist, but instead intends to use the market system to enhance the influence of the supplier stakeholder. The best known fair trade products are coffee, spices, tea, cocoa, and fruit, but today retailers carry many fair trade products including wine, flowers, and beauty products. In Canada, Fairtrade Canada is the coordinator of fair trade initiatives and performs three functions: (1) it is responsible for certifying that Canadian products bearing the Fairtrade certification marks meet international Fairtrade standards; (2) it licenses Canadian companies to use the Fairtrade certification marks and attempts to ensure that licensed companies abide by the standards required of the marks; and (3) it promotes the use of Fairtrade certification marks and certified products. It is a member of Fairtrade International, which is responsible for the international coordination of Fairtrade standards, organizing support for producers around the world, developing fair trade strategy, and promoting global trade justice.[38]

Controversy arose in early 2013 related to the certification of fair trade products in Canada. Competition in labelling has emerged between Fairtrade International and Fair Trade USA. Fairtrade Canada is a branch of Fairtrade International, which uses a circle symbol with the image of a producer against a blue and green roundel with a black background. Fair Trade USA uses a green/white/black label with a farmer holding a bowl. Fair Trade USA has started to certify products in Canada.

Fairtrade International/Fairtrade Canada allows only democratically organized groups of farmers in a cooperative to be certified and does not allow privately operated farms. It signs up farmers who must meet specified labour, environmental, and social standards and secures buyers in developed countries who pay more for the products. Farmers are guaranteed a minimum wage or return. Twenty percent of the product's ingredients must be fair trade to obtain the certification.

Fair Trade USA split from Fairtrade International because it felt that the latter's certification was too strict and not able to provide the volume of products needed in the market. It certifies non-cooperative farms that are privately owned estates or plantations. The certification label is applied to ingredients within a product; that is, the whole product does not have to contain a specified amount of fair trade ingredients. The existence of two fair trade labels in the Canadian market will likely cause some confusion for consumers. This is another illustration of buyer beware, depending upon which specifications a consumer believes are appropriate.[39]

The entrepreneurs promoting fair trade products claim that the local suppliers in developing countries are now receiving a higher price for their product. Initially fair trade was sponsored by NGOs such as Oxfam, Rainforest Alliance, and Traidcraft, but corporations are now developing their own sources in countries where the products are produced; this often occurs in partnership with NGOs. An example of an international organization promoting fair trade is given in Responsibility for Ethics 12.11.

 RESPONSIBILITY FOR ETHICS 12.11

The Ethical Trading Initiative (ETI)

The Ethical Trading Initiative (ETI) is an alliance of companies, trade unions, and voluntary organizations that work together to improve the lives of workers in developing countries that make or grow consumer goods. It is working toward a world where all workers are free from exploitation and discrimination, and work in conditions of freedom, security and equity. The alliance enables ETI to tackle many of the issues that cannot be addressed by individual corporations.

ETI's Base Code is founded on the conventions of the International Labour Organization (ILO) and covers the following:

- Freedom of employment
- Freedom of association and the right to collective bargaining
- Safe working conditions
- No child labour
- Living wages are paid
- Working hours are not excessive
- No discrimination is practised
- Regular employment
- No harsh or inhumane treatment

Corporations that are members include Gap Inc., The Body Shop International, H&M, Marshalls, and Next.

Fair trade has been criticized for several reasons, and some critics claim that the fair trade movement has failed. It is claimed that little of the extra paid by consumers for fair trade products actually reaches the producers or farmers, and a positive impact is difficult to prove.[40] Further, a criticism is that not only is the lot of poor farmers not improved, but fair trade also may actually help to impoverish them because problems exist with certification. The poorest farmers may not be able to afford the fees for certification. It is claimed that the certification process is lax and almost impossible to monitor, as farmers and middlemen can get around the system.[41]

Other criticism includes the claim that exploitation of labour still exists. Even with the focus on labour practices, the cocoa industry still has slavery, poor working conditions, and illegal farming on protected land. Some critics argue that the focus on labour practices has resulted in neglecting farming techniques and pesticide use. There are challenges for the users of fair trade commodities in developed countries. The proliferation of labels and organizations licensing and certifying commodities is confusing and unreliable. The use of fair trade ingredients by Canadian businesses is more expensive, supply is not always available, and quality can be inconsistent. Overall, critics claim that fair trade is more about easing the consciences of consumers in developed countries than reducing poverty in developing countries.[42]

Employees, consumers, competitors, and supplier stakeholders are among the most influential for any corporation. The economic, social, and environmental issues are numerous, and this chapter has provided an introduction to them. The following chapter examines other stakeholders that might be influential: non-governmental organizations (NGOs), the media, policy development institutions (think tanks), and religious and educational institutions.

Your advice to Phyllis . . .

You understand that Phyllis faces a dilemma with the contradictions that confront managers. As an employee, she is faced with the task of implementing a policy with which she may not totally agree. What is involved are different approaches to ethical reasoning. A caring ethic would suggest that exceptions should be made. A justice ethic would attempt to treat all so that equitable outcomes occur. A utilitarian ethic would attempt to identify stakeholders and the benefits and harms to each. It appears that Phyllis's concern is that not all shoplifters should be treated the same and maybe they have rights. Her dilemma is not an uncommon occurrence in the retail workplace.

Summary

- Canadian employers and employees face many challenges in their relationship. Most Canadians still believe in the work ethic; several factors affect the loyalty of the employee to the employer; and employment diversity is a matter that employers must manage in today's workplace. Diversity management now includes the LGBTQ groups and the #MeToo movement. (LO 12.1)

- According to consumer sovereignty, consumers should be determining what goods and services are available in the marketplace. In reality, this does not occur and consumers must also rely on rights and government legislation and regulation. Corporations are placing numerous products in the marketplace in response to ethical consumerism. (LO 12.2)

- It is desirable that competitive rivalry exists in the marketplace, but many ethical and responsibility issues arise. Government has enacted legislation to encourage honest, fair, and open competition in the marketplace. Several factors in the economy determine competitive behaviour. (LO 12.3)

- Pressure on suppliers and the supply chain to consider ethics and responsibilities in the marketplace has increased. In general, the relationship between suppliers and their customers has changed from an adversarial one to a co-operative one including the emergence of supplier diversity. (LO 12.4)

- The supply chain identifies the progress of a product from raw material sources through to the consumer and ultimately disposal. Sustainability purchasing takes into consideration ethical, social, and environmental factors in acquiring materials and products. Fair trade is a version of this type of purchasing that attempts to improve the economic well-being of people working in the upstream component of the supply chain. (LO 12.5)

Key Terms

Gig economy	Business-to-business
Discrimination	Localism
Employment equity	Supplier diversity
Diversity management	Supply (or value) chain
Feminist ethics	Sustainability purchasing
Employee engagement	Extended producer responsibility
Consumerism	Life cycle thinking
Ethical consumerism	Fair trade

Critical Thinking and Discussion Questions

1. Is the work ethic concept relevant in today's workplace?
2. Why should employees be loyal to the corporation? How does the corporation express its loyalty to employees?
3. What does the corporation gain from workplace diversity?
4. Should corporations respond to recent diversity movements such as LGBTQ and #MeToo?
5. To what extent does the consumer sovereignty concept apply in today's marketplace?
6. Are consumers adequately protected in the marketplace?
7. What are the pros and cons when competition results in the failure of a business?
8. Can the government encourage competition? If so, how does the government do it?
9. Which stakeholders are influencing the commercial activities along the supply chain?
10. Who should be responsible for the disposal of a product after it is used by the consumer?
11. What are the benefits of sustainability purchasing to corporations?
12. Why are fair trade products popular with consumers?

Cases

12.1 JUSTIFYING LOCAL PREFERENCE

In January each year, the City of Easton issues a tender call for horticultural supplies for the following summer season. Most of the supplies are trees, shrubs, and perennials, which are planted in the various parks and landscaped areas throughout the city. The City's Works Department takes pride in its gardening program and the City's efforts have been recognized by several awards despite the very limited budget.

This year, six bids were received: three from nurseries in another province and three from local firms. All three out-of-province bids were lower than any of the local nurseries. The successful bid was for $35,000 and the other bids ranged up to $49,000. The lowest local bid was $39,000.

At its meeting on March 16, City Council awarded the contract to the lowest out-of-province bid. One councillor inquired about the fact that the supplier was not local and suggested the City should support local business. The Deputy Mayor stated that she believed the lowest bid had to be accepted according to provincial legislation.

Callers to a local radio call-in program expressed dismay and outrage at this decision. Some referred to the councillors as idiots for not supporting local business. Others made the point that local nurseries should be awarded the contract because they provide employment in the city. Several pointed out that the difference of $4,000 was insignificant and that the City should be willing to pay this difference.

Mike Manston was the owner of the local nursery that submitted the lowest local bid. He was disappointed, as he considered himself to be a responsible corporate citizen. He employed six persons year-round and dozens more in the summer. He belonged to local service clubs, served on the boards of local charities, and sponsored cultural events and sports teams.

Mike was not sure what he should or could do about the situation.

Questions

1. What fundamentals of business (Chapter 2) are involved with this situation?
2. What stakeholders influence the decision and/or are influenced by the decision?
3. What are the pros and cons of a protectionist policy?
4. What should be done about the city's policy of not giving preferential treatment to local businesses?

12.2 DILEMMA OF EATING ETHICALLY

Ananya Banerjee is a single mother with two sons, aged eight and 10, living in Toronto. Since her spouse had passed away, the family was living on a modest income from Ananya's job and a small payment from her spouse's estate. She was managing to cope but she had to be very careful with money. She had avoided taking any social assistance and did not visit food banks.

Ananya was aware of many food issues, particularly the desirability of consuming locally produced organic food. But she was confronted with the reality that this type of food was more expensive and not easily accessible. The prices at the farmers' market were often higher than at the local supermarket. She appreciated that the food may be fresher and grown in a sustainable environment. The farmers' market where locally grown food could be purchased, especially in the summer, was a long distance away. Travelling to it would involve a bus trip, which would limit how much she could carry back home.

In her research about organic and locally grown food, she learnt some disturbing information. Besides locally grown food often being more expensive, there was no assurance that it was organic, as there was no reliable certification system. Although it was claimed that local and organic food was better for her family's health, the health benefits were questionable, according to some articles she had read. Some health professionals suggested that, nutritionally, it might be just as well to buy frozen vegetables.

This left Ananya with a dilemma. Despite the criticism, she felt the organic food was better for her family; on the other hand, she doubted that she could afford it. It appeared that ethical food was for the wealthy, who could afford it.

Questions

1. What are the ethical issues involved?
2. How could reasonably priced and local organic food be made available to lower income consumers?
3. How can Ananya resolve her dilemma?
4. What should the government or a community organization do to help persons in this situation?
5. Is organic and locally grown food actually better for consumers?

NGOs' role in the business and society relationship is increasing.
Used © FatCamera/ Getty Images

CHAPTER 13

Civil Society Stakeholders

LEARNING OUTCOMES

After studying this chapter, you will be able to:

LO 13.1   Define non-governmental organization (NGO) and describe NGO issues and tactics.

LO 13.2   Describe the media as a stakeholder of the corporation and explain the influence of the media on the corporation and the corporation on the media.

LO 13.3   Define policy development institutions (think tanks) and their influence.

LO 13.4   Describe the influence of religious organizations on business.

LO 13.5   Understand the relationship between education institutions, and business and society.

What would you do if...?

Debbie Belbin is crazy about animals! She and her boyfriend have two dogs and three cats all living together in a third floor one bedroom apartment. They spend much of their spare time caring for the pets including extensive walks and runs with the dogs.

Debbie has always loved animals and grew up in the household with various pets. She was aware of several organizations, or NGOs, that advocated for the fair treatment of animals. She supported the local branches of the Humane Society of Canada and the Society of the Prevention of Cruelty to Animals and volunteered at shelters for abused and abandoned animals. Over the years, she had made donations to NGOs dedicated to animal welfare and rights including: People for the Ethical Treatment of Animals (PETA), Vegetarians International Voice for Animals, the Sea Shepherd Conservation Society, and the Animal Alliance of Canada.

However, she was becoming increasingly concerned about the operations and tactics used by some of the NGOs. Her concerns included:

- The use of misleading advertisements, in particular billboards and fake news, by some groups.
- The inappropriate expenditure of funds raised, and the alleged large salaries and perks paid to some animal NGO management.
- The threats made against corporate executives, including the picketing of their homes and families.
- The destruction of property during protests.
- Blockages of access to properties for unreasonable periods of time and sometimes causing harm to employees.
- The illegal entry into business properties, for example, breaking into barns and releasing animals.
- Campaigns against the consumption of some food, in particular, PETA's campaign against children drinking milk.

Debbie acquired a business degree three years ago and now worked for a computer company. She did not believe that everything done by corporations was evil or unethical. She was concerned that some of the tactics used by these NGOs not only harmed business but other stakeholders as well. There appears to be moderate NGOs concerned about animal welfare, that is, how animals are treated, but extremist ones exist advocating animal rights, that is, animals should be treated as humans. She wondered how she could sort out the "good" from the "bad" animal protection NGOs to ascertain which she should support.

What is your advice for Debbie?

Civil society comprises the voluntary, community, and social organizations or institutions that contribute to the functioning of society but are usually not related to or supported by government. Civil society institutions are corporation stakeholders; examples include non-governmental organizations, the media, community-based organizations, civic clubs, trade unions, charities, social and sports clubs, cooperatives, environmental groups, professional associations, policy development institutions, educational institutions, and organized religion.

In this chapter, two civil institutions that have substantial influence on business will be discussed in detail: non-governmental organizations (NGOs) and the media. Corporations and their managers must develop a relationship with these institutions in which managers not only learn about these stakeholders but also recognize their role in society and develop mechanisms for interacting with them. This focus is not one-way but instead is a proactive relationship in which managers understand and respect the roles of these civil society stakeholders. In addition to NGOs and the media, other civil society stakeholders influence business and/or are influenced by business; three are described briefly: policy development institutions (think tanks), religious institutions, and educational organizations.

LO 13.1 The Non-Governmental Organization (NGO) Stakeholder

The definition of this stakeholder is problematic because different terminology can be used—for example, "public interest," "special interest," or just "interest" groups. Such groups are usually discussed in the context of their influence on public policy formulation, thus the *public interest group* terminology. *Special interest group* is used to describe an association that seeks the advancements of financial interests of its members, for example doctors or lawyers. Although both groups indirectly influence business, the focus of this section is on interest groups that interact with or influence business more directly. Current practice is to refer to these groups as non-governmental organizations (NGOs). A well-known example of such an organization is Mothers Against Drunk Driving (MADD); see Everyday Ethics 13.1.

EVERYDAY ETHICS 13.1

Mothers Against Drunk Driving (MADD)

Mothers Against Drunk Driving (MADD Canada) is a non-profit, grassroots organization that is committed to stopping impaired driving and supporting the victims of this violent crime. At the heart of MADD Canada are volunteers who include not only mothers, but also fathers, friends, business professionals, experts in the anti-impaired driving field, and concerned citizens who want to make a difference in the fight against impaired driving. There are 100 branches and 7,500 volunteers across Canada to deliver its programs.

MADD Canada's aim is to offer support services to victims, heighten awareness about the dangers of drinking and driving, and to save lives and prevent injuries on our roads. Driving while under the influence of alcohol or other drugs is a terrible crime that touches all of our lives and it is an irresponsible, dangerous, and intolerable act.

Source: Adapted from Mothers Against Drunk Driving (MADD Canada); "About Us," http://www.madd.ca. MADD Canada, used with permission.

A non-governmental organization (NGO) is any group that holds shared values or attitudes about an issue confronting society and advocates for changes relating to the issue. NGOs make claims or demands that business take actions that will be consistent with the group's attitudes or principles. It should be noted that these groups are part of the private sector, not part of government, and are usually but not always non-profit organizations supported by volunteer members and activists. The distinction from government is an important one to make as NGOs are able to do things that governments will not or cannot do. NGOs operating in developing countries are sometimes supported by governments, for example those involved with the distribution of foreign aid as contractors acting on behalf of governments unable or unwilling to perform the necessary functions.

NGOs are not new to society; they have existed for hundreds of years. For example, NGOs have opposed slavery in various parts of the world and foot binding in China, advocated for women's voting rights, demanded better working conditions for children, and supported minimum wage laws. In recent times their numbers have proliferated; they can be locally based in a community or operate around the world. There are many economic, ethical, and environmental issues that form the basis or belief for an NGO; some of the most common issues that influence business are listed in Table 13.1.

TABLE 13.1	Examples of NGO Societal Issues Relevant to Business

Numerous societal issues are addressed by NGOs, and this list identifies some of those relevant to business organizations. Some issues may overlap, and particular NGOs may be involved in more than one. The issues are at both the domestic and international or global levels.
Animal welfare versus rights—Some advocate for the entitlements of animals as humans. Others are concerned about animal welfare, that is, the care given animals. Extreme groups oppose consumption of any meat products and promote vegetarianism.
Technology—Opposed to biotechnology developments; for example, genetic modification of foods. Also concerned about reproduction of life forms.
Economic—Often oppose capitalism and advocate for forms of collectivist enterprise or government ownership. Concerned about concentration of ownership and domination of the economy by the "corporate agenda" or the corporate elite.
Social development—Concerned with the gap between the rich and poor in Canada but particularly in developing countries. Promote community development, cultural and social activities, and social services such as housing and health care.
Workers'/human rights—Identify the working conditions of labour especially in developing countries. Advocate for union organization and codes of practice. Also concerned with human rights.

Environment—One of the most common causes of NGO activity. Covers all aspects of the environment in Canada and around the world.

Religious activism—Form of activism that is more common recently, especially in the U.S. Local churches and alliances of evangelical churches pressure corporations on their support of social issues such as gay rights and abortion.

Managers must be aware of the variety of approaches or tactics used in an attempt to influence the corporation or its stakeholders. Understanding the possible tactics is important because of a shift in the focus of influence. At one time, NGOs concentrated their efforts on lobbying or otherwise influencing government policies or regulation toward business. Some NGOs attack or attempt to influence corporations by taking actions directly against them. There has been a shift in recent years to indirectly influencing corporations through other stakeholders, for example shareholders, consumers, or suppliers. Responsibility for Ethics 13.1 lists some commonly used tactics to influence corporations.

 RESPONSIBILITY FOR ETHICS 13.1

NGO Tactics

The following are examples of tactics used by NGOs to influence the ethical conduct of corporations:

- Putting pressure on governments and politicians to change policies or regulations
- Generating damaging publicity on the corporation in the media
- Disrupting annual meetings
- Developing shareholder social policy resolutions (after purchasing a few shares)
- Damaging physical property or sabotaging activities
- Occupying corporate premises
- Sponsoring demonstrations or picketing corporate locations
- Picketing managers' homes
- Sponsoring demonstrations or picketing corporate locations
- Organizing boycotts to prevent purchases
- Organizing buycotts (that is, campaigning to buy the products or services of a particular company or country) to recommend purchases from preferred sellers
- Launching letter-writing campaigns, including letters-to-the-editors of newspapers
- Participating in digital protest movements
- Holding public meetings
- Using social media to initiate campaigns on social or environmental issues
- Initiating legal proceedings
- Participating in hacktivism, the non-violent use of the Internet for activist protests
- Developing anti-business or anti-corporate websites and "Watch"–type sites—for example Walmart Watch
- Supporting the development of anti-business documentaries and facilitating their distribution
- Providing support for alternative sources of goods and services (e.g., fair trade products, credit unions, employee-owned enterprises)

Want to learn more about **digital protest movements**?

The Case For and Against NGOs

Corporations and their managers should not dismiss NGOs as a nuisance or useless stakeholder. Their members are very dedicated to their cause or issue and their existence in society supports structures that allow for a wider cross-section of society to influence events. NGOs facilitated the preparation of the agreements on global warming, and they made available lower-cost drugs in developing countries. They generate ideas, knowledge, and solutions; disseminate information on issues; and, of course, pressure for results. Some NGOs have developed product certification systems that corporations have used in their marketing. NGOs can be agents for change, and can confer legitimacy when governments cannot act alone.

Governments and business will listen to NGOs when they operate in a transparent manner, are accountable for their actions, and are accurate in their claims or information.[1] In a report prepared by Canadian Business for Social Responsibility (CBSR), the benefits from partnerships with NGOs include identifying opportunities and risks, influencing public opinion, developing possibilities for innovation, enhancing reputation and trust by the public, creating expertise with in-depth knowledge of specific issues, facilitating employee engagement, and building large networks with other stakeholders.[2]

NGOs may advocate diverse views about the same issue. An example is provided by free trade, to which some NGO groups are opposed, yet the Global Freedom to Trade campaign advocates for global trade freedom. Other NGOs, such as Oxfam Canada, support freer trade under certain conditions, and many forms of fair trade practices exist. Managers must not only identify the NGOs related to industry-relevant issues, but also must understand the positions held about these issues because some may be supportive.

Many NGOs do represent a threat to business. Many of the tactics listed in Responsibility for Ethics 13.1 can disrupt business operations. Many are clearly anti-business and anti–free trade or globalization, reducing the support for business in society. Their beliefs in redistribution of wealth and equality of results are inconsistent with business beliefs in economic markets and efficiency measures. Some NGOs are simply "anti" everything associated with business and constantly criticize while offering few if any alternatives.[3]

Strategies for Relationships with NGOs

NGOs pressure corporations directly and indirectly through other stakeholders. If an indirect approach is the case, Spar and LaMure state that there are three key turning points for the corporation: (1) the NGO must be able to threaten the corporation with significant harm; (2) the corporation must respond to the threat by changing business practice; and (3) the change must serve to advance the NGO's goals. They argue that the corporation becomes the conduit by which outside stakeholders—that is, NGOs—attempt to achieve non-market objectives.[4]

Corporations cannot ignore the influence of NGOs and should not underestimate their power or tenacity. Many corporations do take NGO activism seriously and respond in different ways depending on the corporation's particular position or the type of industry. Spar and LaMure propose that the corporation's response to NGO activism is influenced by three variables: transaction costs, brand impact, and competitive position. There are also three possibilities when corporations are faced with NGO tactics. Resistance is possible, but not recommended in most situations. Capitulation may be the most advantageous in some cases, and pre-emption in others.

Transaction costs relate to capital and sourcing, and if substantial expenses are involved to meet the NGO's demands, the corporation is more likely to resist the demands. This is usually the case in natural resource industries where capital investments are high, or in industries where no other source of supply exists. In consumer goods industries, capitulation to NGO demands is usually less expensive and alternate sources of supply are available.

The greater the value a corporation places on its brand, the more susceptible it is to pressure from the NGO. In this situation, capitulation to the demands is a more logical response. Brand-name footwear and apparel companies can easily switch their sourcing and few, if any, capital costs are involved. By doing so, the corporation is more likely to gain a reputation as a socially responsible citizen.

In very competitive industries, being the first to meet or capitulate to NGO demands might provide a competitive advantage. This is particularly the case where brand recognition is high. Such action would be a pre-emptive strategy to gain on competitors.[5] Table 13.2 summarizes the strategies and the responses.

TABLE 13.2	Strategies for Relationships with NGOs		
Three Variables Influencing Response	**Transaction costs**	**Brand impact**	**Competitive position**
	↓	↓	↓
Responses	Resistance (resource industries)	Capitulation (consumer goods)	Pre-emption (competitive industries)

Managers do not always reply based on resistance, capitulation, and pre-emption. They may have personal motives and beliefs that can also motivate their decisions. Managers have values and ethical beliefs as a result of their upbringing or education that provide guidance in moral issues. It should not be assumed that managers always make decisions relating to NGO demands based on cost–benefit analysis or competitive positioning.[6]

A more aggressive response toward NGOs is possible but not recommended. An effort could be made to discredit NGOs with negative attacks, or to launch legal action. Both responses could backfire and complicate the relationship. However, it may be feasible to demand more accountability from NGOs, just as they are demanding the accountability of corporations. Some NGOs do not account appropriately to donors, or they spend funds on questionable activities. It can be pointed out that unrepresentative activists undermine the effectiveness of credible NGOs, and the corporation can provide evidence of its serious efforts at dialogue with some NGOs.

Some of the anti-business tactics used by NGOs are difficult to tolerate, but at times corporations find that ignoring their extreme positions may be preferable to attempts at countering. Business organizations have countered NGO-sponsored websites with NGOWATCH.org, a site that compiles factual data about NGOs, including analysis of relevant issues, treaties, and international organizations where NGOs are active. Lastly, business can suggest that NGOs also need a code of ethics and/or conduct to guide their operations.

Want to learn more about **"watch" sites**?

Based upon Spar and LaMure's article and from the discussion of NGOs, some observations are possible about how corporations can view and build their relationship with NGOs:

- A preferable strategy is to proactively engage the NGOs and expect to interact with them.
- Do not underestimate the influence of NGOs on the corporation directly or indirectly through other stakeholders.
- Reversing a decision or withdrawing from a project should not be viewed as a defeat.
- Sometimes selective concessions are sufficient to address opposition from NGOs.
- Sometimes it is appropriate to establish a dialogue with "realist" NGOs and ignore the "radical" and "idealist" ones.
- A pre-emptive strategy may be feasible.

Questions that managers should pose to learn about an NGO's approach include the following: Who are they? What do they want? What will they do to achieve their objectives? What is the best way to deal with them?

Partnership Relationships with NGOs

A Canadian Business for Social Responsibility (CBSR) report presents another view being advocated regarding relationships with NGOs—one of partnership. The report explores a different type of partnership between business and NGOs: domestic partnerships that build business leadership through social, environmental, and economic success. It is pointed out that philanthropic partnerships have supported and empowered NGOs; for example, Microsoft Canada's partnership with the Royal Canadian Mounted Police and the Toronto Police Service to establish the Child Exploitation Tracking System. However, another form of partnership drives social success and innovation in business by involving all three sectors: business, government, and civil society.[7]

This type of partnership brings together business and NGO resources to address an issue including human, technical, financial, and knowledge interests. The process is not without risks to all involved; damage to reputations, high start-up costs, conflicts of interest, and alienation of stakeholders may be concerns. CBSR identifies four key ingredients to defining the success of a partnership:

- Corporate and NGO leaders must show leadership.
- The corporation must be open to change.
- There must be a commitment to being committed.
- Partners must have a shared goal.[8]

An article at Network for Business Sustainability identified the key lessons for collaboration with NGOs from a different perspective. It must be recognized that different perspectives exist; this can be challenging but also valuable as each partner's knowledge, expertise, and capabilities complement the others'. Secondly, it is important to assign a person responsible for the project and give that person authority and decision-making ability. This champion is necessary to overcome resistance and to indicate to the NGO that the corporation is taking the relationship seriously. Also, the NGO engagement must be part of the corporation's core business—that is, integrated into the operations of business units and not maintained as a separate, standalone operation. Lastly, the relationship must be allowed to evolve over time and accommodate changing circumstances as they arise. Corporate and NGO partnerships are challenging to management, but they can be beneficial to both partners.[9]

World Wildlife Fund (WWF) is extensively involved with corporate partnerships and has an elaborate description of why and how it works with business.[10] WWF's approach is described in Everyday Ethics 13.2.

World Wildlife Fund Canada Corporate Partnerships

WWF's approach to working with the private sector is constructive and solutions-oriented. It is both collaborative in its methods, rigorous in its standards, and challenging in its objectives.

"Our guiding principles for corporate engagement are:

- Measurable results that support our conservation objectives

- Transparency

- The right to public commentary

Our cooperation with partners is based on a common understanding of issues, shared ambitions or activities, and a willingness to speak out in public. In general, we distinguish four types of partnerships with companies:

1. Driving sustainable business practices;

2. Communications and awareness raising;

3. Philanthropic relationships; and

4. Employee engagement."

WWF Canada publishes an annual report describing the rationale for its involvement in partnerships. In its 2017 report, partnerships were described with Loblaw Companies Ltd., TELUS Corporation, The Coca-Cola Company, Royal & Sun Alliance Insurance Company of Canada, HSBC, HP Inc., Procter & Gamble Inc., Domtar, and Ontario Lottery and Gaming Corporation.

Sources: "Working with Business," World Wildlife Fund Canada website at http://www.wwf.ca/about_us/howwework/business/ and "Corporate Partnerships Report: Overview of WWF-Canada Corporate Partnerships Fiscal Year 2017," at http://assets.wwf.ca/downloads/f17_final_cp_report.pdf ?_ga=2.19673464.1517368719.1552221306-1290159524.1552221306 accessed March 11, 2019. Used with permission.

A more elaborate example was the completion of the Canadian Boreal Forest Agreement (CBFA). In May 2010, an agreement was reached among nine environmental non-governmental organizations (ENGOs) and 21 forestry corporations on the management of the Canadian boreal forest. It was considered a significant agreement illustrating cooperation between ENGOs and the forestry industry. It was considered a historic event and was a model of ENGO–business cooperation.

The agreement had been criticized on the grounds that NGOs have no right to determine public policy, especially through the use of intimidation and threats based on unproven claims. Some argue that the boreal forest was not under threat of destruction, and that the agreement would result in higher prices, fewer jobs, zero impact on climate, and reduced profits. The agreement was terminated in 2018 and illustrated the challenges of business and ENGO cooperation.

This section has described NGOs and some of the relationships that exist between NGOs and business. Although NGOs have been an increasingly influential stakeholder, another civil society stakeholder, the media, plays an important role in influencing the corporation.

LO 13.2   The Media Stakeholder

This section explores the relationship between business and the media—newspapers, periodicals, television, radio, and the Internet. The media is a stakeholder that can influence the views held by the public about business, and cannot be ignored. In turn, business has some influence over the media. Most media operations are owned by private-sector enterprises, and advertising is a main source of revenue for them. In recent years business has taken on improved respectability in the media and this has led to increased coverage, especially for international business and personal finance.

Business is a major institution in society, and as with any other major institution, people have an intrinsic curiosity about it. People have developed the belief that they have a right to know about things that affect them, and this belief has been reinforced by access-to-information law. Thus, over the years, veils of secrecy that sheltered many institutions and organizations have been removed, or at least lifted. People now want to take a closer look at business and are asking tougher, more pointed questions.

The media stakeholder is divided into two categories: traditional and social. The traditional media—mainly print and broadcast—will be discussed in the next sections, including its influence and the media–business relationship. Social media is discussed in the following sections with a concluding section on media and CSR.

The Influence of Traditional Media

Traditional media is composed of written and broadcast approaches including newspapers, periodicals, books, television, film documentaries, movies, and Internet websites that portray the operations of business and its relationship to society. Some of the portrayals are positive, but many are negative and receive a lot of attention. The extent to which the popular media influences the attitudes of various stakeholders toward business is not known for certain. However, one study found that corporations receiving extensive coverage of corporate social irresponsibility relating to environmental, social, and governance issues faced a higher financial or credit risk.[11]

Numerous newspapers and periodicals cater to business audiences, or those interested in the ethics of business and its responsibilities. Daily newspapers have some business coverage, even if it is simply an abbreviated stock market listing. Many Canadian corporate histories and business biographies have been written, along with general books about the business system. Popular television programs also have mixed views of business with business often portrayed unfavourably. Documentaries made for television and movie theatres have become popular. Although some crossover occurs between documentaries and movies, movies often focus on the ethics of business and corporate social responsibility. The Internet is a source of information that is critical about business. Many large companies are the subject of "watch" sites, such as Walmart Watch, and industries are subject to similar sites, for example, MiningWatch. Some websites are critical of business in general, for example CorporateWatch.

Coverage of business has changed from domination by print to domination by live television. Television and radio have extensive and immediate coverage of business topics. CBC-TV has a business-related program called *Marketplace*, and the cable television channel Report on Business devotes all programming to business and related topics. However, even newspapers respond to events quickly, with lengthy analyses of major business-related events. Their online editions are updated constantly. This trend to instant news has also resulted in the instant expert opinion. If a company produces an unsafe product or pollutes a waterway, experts are available to offer their analysis or comment, although sometimes biased or peripheral.

The nature of regulation is important to consider. Print media content is self-regulated by editors and by reviewers for book and article publications. The newspaper trade association News Media Canada receives consumer complaints about the content of advertising, articles, and editorials. A National Media News Council and local councils have been established to receive and adjudicate complaints from "individuals and organizations who are concerned about the ethical conduct of a newspaper in gathering and publishing editorial content."[12] A federal government administrative tribunal, the Canadian Radio-television and Telecommunications Commission (CRTC) regulates and supervises broadcasting and telecommunications in the public interest, including some aspects of the Internet.[13] The Canadian Association of Broadcasters (CAB) represents private broadcasters and regulates the industry through its Code of Ethics, and codes covering violence in television programming, equitable portrayal, and advertising to children.[14]

At any time, one or a combination of the above factors influences attitudes. Even though the factors can be listed, it is unlikely consensus will occur on which factors are the most influential. Nevertheless, society's attitudes toward business change through time and businesspersons must always be aware of these changes. Monitoring attitudes toward business is important as it operates as the consent or permission of society.

Want to learn more about **the efforts of OpenMedia.ca to keep the Internet affordable?**

Issues in the Business and Media Relationship

Businesspersons have complained about what they consider to be inappropriate coverage in the media. On the other hand, the media complains about attitudes held by most businesspersons about its reporting practices. Table 13.3 summarizes complaints from both perspectives.

TABLE 13.3	Business–Media Relations

Business Complaints about the Media
- Reporters are not sufficiently knowledgeable about business and economics and fail to do their homework.

- The media is interested only in "bad" news that can be sensationalized.
- The media is unable to place the information into the correct context.
- The media has an inherent bias against business and is dominated by leftist journalists who neither support nor understand a market economy.
- Business reporting is not only biased, but also oversimplified and lacking in insight.
- Reporters do not respect "off-the-record" comments.

Media Complaints about Business

- Businesspersons confuse issues by waffling on details, stonewalling, attempting to hide negative information, or by lying.
- Businesspersons use the excuse that they are accountable only to shareholders, not the media.
- Businesspersons overreact to the process of reporting events and covering issues.

Some managers have attempted to manage the relationship to suit their purposes; press releases are an example. The media is viewed as a tap that can be turned on or off depending on what managers think stakeholders should know. Some corporations fear the damage that can be done by a reporter to a manager's or corporation's image. But the consequence of not responding to requests from the media is also dangerous. If the media is rebuffed it will turn to more cooperative sources of information—which may not be sympathetic to the business view. For their part, businesspersons and managers have threatened to cancel subscriptions when (or if) negative stories are carried. Advertising has been withdrawn by some businesses as retaliation for an editorial view or certain news coverage.

Another phenomenon influencing media coverage, in particular the publication of books, is *libel chill*. **Libel chill** occurs when a business threatens legal action if a particular article or book is published. With this threat present, writers, editors, and publishers impose on themselves a form of self-censorship, holding back on potentially controversial stories. This situation has an impact on the freedom of speech and the public's right to know. Publishers often back down for fear of a long and expensive court case and the possibility that they might lose.

Another challenge in business coverage is *media spin*. Corporations have access to the services of public relations experts who are frequently able to put a particular "spin," or interpretation, on corporate events or information. This spin is incorporated into corporate press releases supplied to the media, often with supporting materials. Reporters, facing looming deadlines, have been accused of simply repackaging corporate press releases without further input. In turn, reporters may put their own spin on corporate news, particularly news that is not favourable to the corporation. The result is that some business news should be interpreted carefully.

The issue is one of balance. The media should not get away with irresponsible, inaccurate, or scandalous reporting, but neither should businesspersons be allowed to unduly influence reporters and publishers. This discussion of the relationship between business and the media leads to a discussion of unfairness and biased reporting.

It is difficult to prove whether media has a left-leaning, anti-business, big-government bias that tends to favour politically correct welfare-state solutions and downplay market realities, or a right-wing, corporate-agenda bias that tends to favour solutions that benefit the wealthy and powerful elite to the exclusion of marginalized and ordinary working people.

A question arising from this discussion of fairness and bias in the media is whether it makes a difference. Corporations certainly think so. Managers worry about the type and tone of information that appears in the media and the influence this has on a company. Research into the relationship between media exposure and change in corporate reputation has for the most part been inconclusive. A study on the relationship between intensive media exposure and changes in corporate reputation concluded that media is a pervasive element in society and appears to be an important influence on the performance of modern companies.[15] Despite some positive findings, the author concluded that much remains to be done before the relationship is fully understood.

Another dimension in the relationship between business and the media comes about because business enterprises own and operate media outlets. Ownership of broadcast, telecommunications, and print media is now concentrated in multimedia business corporations. Several issues emerge as a result of this ownership, including those surrounding (1) the newspaper monopolies held in some cities by large corporations; (2) the interlocking ownership between print and broadcasting media; (3) the licensing process in broadcasting where some corporations are allegedly favoured over others; and (4) the operation of newspaper chains that are concerned more with financial performance than professional journalism.

The power associated with media ownership is one issue. A related issue is the centralization of the media. This involves the concern that there may be too few voices in the media. Newspapers are suffering declining readership, especially with some age groups, and some have failed. But the availability of magazines has increased, as have alternatives available on television and radio. A problem with control arises when all media is concentrated with one or a few owners; this is not yet the case.

However, although the independence of the media is an aspect of free privilege, this is countered by the professionalism of journalists and managers in the media.

Business topics and issues appear to have gained a new respectability in the media in recent years. In particular, there is increased coverage of the ethics of business and corporate social responsibility (CSR) in the media. Business's ethical, social, and environmental responsibilities are of increasing interest to the public. This seems to have led to increasing coverage of business topics and issues by the media. Also, corporations that own the media have recognized their responsibility for CSR or sustainability. Responsibility for Ethics 13.2 describes the newspaper industry's awareness of its impact on the environment.

 RESPONSIBILITY FOR ETHICS 13.2

Newspapers and the Environment

News Media Canada is a trade association representing over 800 print and digital media organizations in Canada. Various industry stakeholders, including consumers, advertisers, and advertising agencies, are interested in whether or not the paper products used are supplied by producers who are sustainable and environmentally responsible. In order to inform these stakeholders and their members, News Media Canada prepared a report, "Newspapers and the Environment: What You Need to Know."

The report posed the question "Are newspapers environmentally friendly?" The sustainable fibre used in producing newspapers was harvested according to five principles: harvest legally, regenerate promptly, promote recycling and recovery, welcome independent scrutiny, and reduce greenhouse gases (GHGs). The industry supports recycling and Canada has some of the highest rates of waste diversion of old newspapers.

The industry supports Ontario's *Waste-Free Ontario Act* 2016, which requires new producer responsibility where producers are individually responsible and accountable for their products and packaging at end of life. The B.C. members of News Media Canada prepared a stewardship plan for residential newsprint which was submitted to the Ministry of Environment on September 29, 2017.

The Challenges of Social Media

Social media has a dynamic influence on the relationship between business and society. One definition of social media is the various forms of online interaction or communication enabled by technology-based tools, most of which are Internet based. These tools allow business and society stakeholders to share opinions, insights, experiences, and perspectives through networking platforms such as Facebook, Twitter, Instagram, YouTube, LinkedIn, Snapchat, and Pinterest; the use of webcasts, blogs, and Internet forums; and the existence of websites. These tools allow individuals and organizations to create, share, and exchange information in the form of written materials, pictures, and videos through virtual communication networks. Also, online news coverage about business and society can be viewed online instead of in printed newspapers and on network news programs.

Social media has several characteristics that enable it to influence business in ways that are different from other media. Exchanges of information are instant, often interactive, cover all topics, and require minimum knowledge of the technology involved. It allows wider access to receive and publish information, potentially globally. The costs to participants are low or even non-existent, allowing large numbers to publish and receive information. It is usually interactive, which is not the case with most traditional media. Stakeholders can comment on and edit published materials, making it difficult to control content. Participation in social media can be for personal use—that is, at home—or used in the workplace, blurring the boundaries between personal and work life.

Social media has created new connections between business and society, in particular with employees, customers, suppliers, and non-governmental organizations. Social media can build, or destroy, a corporation's reputation. Many issues have resulted that present challenges. Also, social media is less monopolistic and may not depend on advertising and the need to generate profits.

Social media has enabled society to hold business more accountable. Unethical practices are more likely disclosed, and sooner. Bloggers are free to make comments about the corporation that may or may not be accurate, placing the corporation in a difficult position to respond or counter untruths. Fake blogs might exist that portray corporations negatively. The Edelman Trust Barometer found that 71 percent of Canadians were still concerned about false information or fake news being used as a weapon.[16] Although commonly used in politics, the reputation of corporations could be threatened. Some social media experts state that corporations have lost control over how they communicate, while bloggers are free to say what they want. From a positive perspective, corporations can view participation on social media as a way to interact with stakeholders and as a source of feedback on their performance.

Several issues exist in the human resources area. A prominent issue is how much time employees should spend on social media during working hours. Contributing to a social media site is a time waster and the acceptable level of monitoring employees' use is not easy to determine, as their right to privacy should be respected. Another problem is what action should be taken when employees make negative comments about the corporation. Employers could, if they wanted, scan social media for employee involvement and comments, and the possibility for discipline or even termination exists. Also, employers could scan social media for information when evaluating potential employees for positions. Applicants might be disqualified based on inaccurate information that appeared on a social media site.

Marketing and advertising practices also give rise to some issues. Corporations may distort endorsements by misrepresenting credentials, affiliations, and expertise or by placing fake stories. Some marketers may inappropriately collect data on consumers or use social media as a source of email addresses for spamming purposes and profile creation. On the other hand, social media can be used to engage customers more directly, including providing them with more information. However, micro targeting advertising to consumers is resented by many.

The security of computer systems is an issue, especially when corporate websites are hacked and confidential employee, customer, or supplier information disclosed. Any activities involving harassment or cyberbullying by posting misleading or incorrect information about competitors are inappropriate.

It is recommended that corporations develop written policies that prevent or resolve the issues arising from social media. The corporation's expectations for social media should be clearly outlined. Employees must understand that they are responsible for what they contribute to social media both personally or on behalf of their employer. The legal and reputational consequences of their actions should be considered.

Social Media Issues and Ethics

Social media gives rise to many ethical issues for businesses and individuals. The use of social media by corporations is a matter of balancing harms versus benefits—that is, a utilitarian ethic perspective. The identification of the rights of various stakeholders is necessary, for example the rights of privacy for consumers and employees. Involvement in social media should be guided by virtues such as honesty, trust, openness, respect, and fairness.

Social networks create conditions by which false information and misinformation can be spread, including about business corporations. A challenge for social platform providers is ascertaining which information should be banned, for example, hate speech. This leads to the dilemma of freedom of speech versus censorship if social platforms remove too much. On the other hand, if the platforms allow too much harmful content, they risk losing users and advertisers. The platforms have been accused of wanting to increase revenues as a priority while controlling content is a secondary consideration.

The collection of data without paying, and its manipulation for profit without permission or consent, is questionable. This is especially the case when access is obtained to an individual's personal information and opinion. The analysis of an individual's use of the Internet is not appropriate.

Given the ethical issues, the need to regulate social media has arisen. At this time, social media platforms are mostly regulated by the industry. However, the sloppiness regarding privacy, failure to protect personal data, tolerance for inaccuracy, and reluctance to admit mistakes has increased demands for government intervention, especially if industry does not act. Government actions could include investigations by the Competition Bureau and the CRTC, the enactment of a consumer bill of rights, and legislation to control data collection and use.

There is an issue of whether or not social media platforms should be responsible, even liable, for misinformation such as fake news. The platforms have responded that they are increasing transparency in several ways. They are now employing fact checkers and artificial intelligence to review content to reduce the spread of false news and misleading content.

Society's trust in the media is important regardless of which source is used. When asked which media source should be trusted for general news and information, Canadians responded as follows: 71 percent trusted traditional media; 62 percent, search engines; 49 percent, online media; and 31 percent, social media. In response to the question about the most credible corporate spokesperson, 65 percent thought a corporation's technical expert was credible. The credibility of others was as follows: academic expert, 64 percent; successful entrepreneur, 51 percent; NGO representative, 46 percent; journalist, 43 percent; and CEO, 41 percent.[17]

Two civil society stakeholders—NGOs and the media—have been discussed in detail, but many other institutions can influence business or be influenced by business. The following discussion briefly describes three others: policy development institutions or think tanks, religious organizations, and educational institutions.

LO 13.3 Policy Development Institutions (Think Tanks)

A **policy development institution** or think tank is an organization that researches and analyzes various important social, economic, and political issues confronting business and society. Responsibility for Ethics 13.3 lists some examples the better known think tanks. They attempt to influence society's, in particular government's, position on various business and social issues. They try to bring fresh thinking to an issue and mould government public policy. Although they claim to be non-partisan and independent, the brief descriptions in Everyday Ethics 13.3 suggest that various ideological views are represented. Think tanks are not directly affiliated with political parties, but some do have a political agenda and are supportive of some ideological movements. Many think tanks have charity status for taxation purposes if no more than ten percent of their resources are devoted to political advocacy.

 RESPONSIBILITY FOR ETHICS 13.3

Policy Development Institutions or "Think Tanks"

Most of these institutions are non-profit, non-partisan, and charitable organizations claiming to be independent.

- *C.D. Howe Institute*—Aims to improve Canadians' standard of living by fostering sound economic and social policy through independent research and analysis.

- *Caledon Institute of Social Policy*—Does research and analysis; seeks to inform and influence public opinion and to foster public discussion on poverty and social policy; and develops and promotes concrete, practicable proposals for the reform of social programs.

- *Canadian Centre for Policy Alternatives*—Conducts research and analysis concerned with issues of social and economic justice, and develops workable solutions to the policy questions facing Canadians today.

- *Canadian Labour and Business Centre*—Acts as a centre for business–labour dialogue and consensus building to develop effective public policy in labour market and skills issues.

- *Conference Board of Canada*—Builds leadership capacity for a better Canada by creating and sharing insights on economic trends, public policy, and organizational performance.

- *Fraser Institute*—Has as its objective the redirection of public attention through economic and social research to the role of competitive markets in providing for the well-being of Canadians.

- *Institute for Research on Public Policy*—Conducts research that aims to enhance the quality of the debate on the issues that matter most to Canadians by focusing on the strategic choices they must make to promote economic performance, social progress, and sound democratic governance.

Lists of think tanks can be obtained from Canajun Guide, "Think Tanks and Policy Research," at http://canajun .com/canada/politics/think.htm and "Canadian Think Tanks," at https://www.mcgill.ca/caps/files/caps/guide _canadianthinktanks.pdf.

 EVERYDAY ETHICS 13.3

Think Tank Views on Business and Society Issues

The following are examples of recent reports or studies produced by various think tanks. Note the variety of topics. The think tanks are good sources of views on many business and society issues.

- Fraser Institute: "Carbon Pricing in Alberta" finds that the province's carbon tax is unlikely to meaningfully reduce global carbon emissions.

- Canadian Centre for Policy Alternatives: "Jobs vs the Environment? Mainstream and alternative media coverage of pipeline controversies" explores media coverage of pipeline controversies by focusing on pipeline projects that connect Alberta's oil sands to export markets.

- Conference Board of Canada: The "Working Together: Indigenous Recruitment and Retention in Remote Canada" report examines the current situation of Indigenous recruitment and retention for organizations and finds that the most important strategies for improving retention target education, training, collaboration, and cultural awareness.
- Public Policy Forum: "Food Innovation in Canada's North: The case for a social enterprise cluster: An Action Canada Task Force report" is a preliminary study of the feasibility of an Arctic Food Innovation Cluster in Canada. The intent of such a cluster is to advance increased access to affordable, culturally informed, healthy food across northern regions.

Usually think tanks are not connected to government, although government may provide funding. Most funding is provided by business corporations and trade unions. Wealthy individuals, foundations, member contributors, universities, and the sale of services (e.g., consulting, publications, etc.) finance others. Most Canadian think tanks were established in the 1970s and 1980s; they exist in most democracies, with some being international in scope.

Critics claim that think tanks lack transparency. Quite often who funds them is not identified on websites and if it is, the amount of their financial contribution is not. Foreign funding is allowed but is criticized. Some think tanks are merely public relations fronts and advocates for industry or labour sponsors. The research publications are often one sided and others are the result of research that is ideologically driven by member interests.

A question for business and managers is whether the think tanks have much influence. Some argue that they have little influence, while others claim they can change the language of public debate. At the least, the think tanks most relevant to a corporation's industry, or that examine an issue of importance to the industry, should be monitored.

LO 13.4   Religious Institutions

Four topics discuss the influence of religion in business: the impact on managerial decision making, the existence of businesses supplying religious goods and services, spirituality in the workplace, and corporate response to religious activism.

The influence of religion on managerial decision making has been discussed extensively. Many argue that religious beliefs or practices have an influence on a manager's perceptions of what is ethical versus unethical, and can play a role in management education. Romar advocates Confucianism as a compelling managerial ethic because it is compatible with accepted managerial practices, it requires individuals and organizations to make a positive contribution to society, it recognizes hierarchy as an important organizational principle and demands managerial moral leadership, and its virtues provide a moral basis for hierarchical and cooperative relationships.[18] The Metanexus Institute is involved in an interdisciplinary social scientific research initiative on the economic and social consequences of religion and spirituality, referred to as "spiritual capital."[19] The Roman Catholic Church has commented on the relationship between business and society over the years. Responsibility for Ethics 13.4 summarizes a recent church publication that addresses business leadership in society and proposes six practical principles for business.

 RESPONSIBILITY FOR ETHICS 13.4

The Church's Reflection on Business Leadership

The Roman Catholic Pontifical Council for Justice and Peace studied the role of business in society and concluded that the vocation of the businessperson was a genuine human and Christian calling. But, in dealing with the complex issues facing society and business, a need existed for businesspersons to base decisions on the foundational principles of human dignity and the common good. These principles should provide direction for business in organizing the labour and capital employed in a market system, and the processes of innovation.

The following summarizes a portion of the findings:

SIX PRACTICAL PRINCIPLES FOR BUSINESS

The principles of respect for human dignity and pursuit of the common good are the foundations of the Church's social teaching. Joined with the six practical principles of business, they can offer more specific guidance on the three broad business objectives.

Meeting the Needs of the World through the Creation and Development of Goods and Services

1. Businesses that produce goods which are truly good and services which truly serve *contribute to the common good.*

2. Businesses maintain *solidarity* with the poor by being alert for opportunities to serve deprived and underserved populations and people in need.

Organizing Good and Productive Work

3. Businesses make a contribution to the community by fostering the special *dignity of human work.*

4. Businesses provide, through *subsidiarity*, opportunities for employees to exercise appropriate authority as they contribute to the mission of the organization.

Creating Sustainable Wealth and Distributing It Justly

5. Businesses model *stewardship of the resources*—whether capital, human, or environmental—they have received.

6. Businesses are *just* in the allocation of resources to all stakeholders: employees, customers, investors, suppliers, and the community.

The study also recommended that the Reflection be discussed by faculty and students to: ". . . see the Challenges and opportunities in the world of work; judge them according to the social principles of the Church; and act as leaders who serve God." The study provided a checklist for following the six principles.

Religion is generating many commercial opportunities in the economy: a religion-based theme park called Holy Land Experience in Florida; Christian literature publishers; retailers, including Walmart, selling religious items, music, and video games; and faith-based mutual funds.[20] A *BusinessWeek* article described how organized religion is even learning to operate like a business. Huge churches are being constructed, seating thousands, with large orchestras and choirs and state-of-the-art electronic communications.[21]

Effort by some businesses to integrate religion into the workplace is also discussed extensively in the literature.[22] The types of activities carried out in the workplace include spiritual, faith-based, and Bible study sessions; devotional prayer services; and the hiring of corporate chaplains to counsel employees. The introduction of religion into the secular corporation makes some feel uneasy. Although most activities are voluntary, employees may still feel pressure from religious employers. Customers have been subjected to open evangelizing by Christian-dominated corporations. Such activities are not necessarily associated with organized religion. Instead, they are referred to as **spirituality**, an individual's sense of peace or purpose with themselves and the connection to others and even nature that provides meaning to life and a sense of one's self. Responsibility for Ethics 13.5 describes two initiatives relating to spirituality in the workplace. Even if discussed only briefly, it is possible to recognize that the relationship between business and religious institution stakeholders gives rise to many issues.

 RESPONSIBILITY FOR ETHICS 13.5

Spirituality in the Workplace

Two organizations that are promoting and facilitating spirituality in the workplace are described below.

Corporate Chaplains Canada (CCC)

CCC's main purposes are

- supporting business owners, management, and employees as they face life's reality at work and home; and

- fostering relational, emotional, and spiritual growth and health as these individuals serve their companies, families, and communities together.

CCC cares for employees at corporations in B.C., Alberta, and Ontario. The chaplains promote the overall relational health of employees, stress caring for extended family needs, and provide moral and spiritual support when requested. The intended result is a work environment that is a better, more profitable place for employees and employer alike.

Workplace Centre for Spiritual and Ethical Development

The mission of the Workplace Centre for Spiritual and Ethical Development is "to serve the business community by advancing spirituality and ethics in the workplace." It "promotes the benefits of individual spiritual well-being; supports the study and practice of business ethics; and organizes programs and events which advance the understanding of spiritual values and ethical standards at work." Its values are listed as spiritual wholeness, cultural diversity, ethical business practices, wisdom of all communities of faith, individual dignity, and environmental sensitivity. The Centre is located in Vancouver, B.C.

Business must be careful in responding to religious activism or it might get caught in crossfire, particularly with conservative groups. *BusinessWeek* referred to this possibility as "culture wars" and posed the question, "When should companies take public positions on social issues?" Some of the social issues of concern identified in the article included support for gay rights, advertising on unacceptable television programs, and the pursuit of embryonic stem-cell research. The article concluded that the only way for a company to respond is to return to its core values. Companies should consider themselves the ultimate judge of what is socially acceptable and not be driven by the dogma of particular religious activism.[23]

LO 13.5   Educational Institutions

The appropriateness of business involvement in the education system has been controversial. The issue has become more prominent recently as various educational institutions seek assistance from business after government support has declined. Business is now involved in education from the kindergarten to post-secondary levels. The extent of involvement can be illustrated at the university level, where the following are of concern: the establishment of private, for-profit colleges; funding for buildings or centres from private sources with some conditions attached; conflicts of interest in the funding of research; the commercialization of research; and exclusivity agreements to provide goods and services.[24]

There are two views regarding the issue. The modern, pragmatic view looks at education and corporate money, or involvement in any form, as a mutually beneficial partnership. An example occurs when a business donates money to a school's athletic program and is allowed to advertise on team uniforms. The other view is that educational institutions should be places of unencumbered thought and considered a custodian of rights of the liberated human spirit. This view is strongly held in universities by many students and faculty. There are many variations between these extreme views, and the circumstances vary depending on the type of institution.

Many businesspeople sincerely believe in the partnership and that it helps the economy. The demands of the global marketplace and information age require skills that are best provided in the educational system. Thus, business has a role in improving the quality of education, and it is in its own interest to become involved. Partnerships have appeal for educators, from kindergarten teachers to university presidents, as resources formerly provided by governments have been reduced. As educators are financially squeezed, they overlook the ethical implications that might accompany the acceptance of assistance from business.

Many students and faculty oppose partnerships as they fear "market-driven" learning, leading to students being taught only topics of interest to them, universities dropping areas that are not currently popular, job "relevance" being the main criterion for what is taught, and efficiency being emphasized at the expense of social concerns. It is believed that the results would be greater social and economic disparities and loss of competitiveness in technology. There would be negative effects from this narrow focus as it alters the way society invests in higher education as a fundamental social institution. The economic needs of business are met, while the broader and more basic social and cultural needs are ignored.

There is a fear of losing control over what is taught and that the traditional role of the university would be changed. The university was traditionally viewed as a community of free and independent scholars, as an open forum for ideas, and as an institution that could be critical in its assessment of other societal institutions. Many fear that this traditional, and desirable, role would be reduced and possibly eliminated.[25]

Although this discussion has focused on post-secondary institutions, corporations also have economic, social, and environmental responsibilities to primary and secondary schools. An example is the marketing of unhealthy food and beverages to these schools, as illustrated in Everyday Ethics 13.4. It appears that business practices are not consistent with what is considered best for the health of children.

◈ EVERYDAY ETHICS 13.4

Food Marketing in Schools

Due to the prevalence of obesity, there have been many calls to restrict food and beverage marketing to children under 16. One area of concern is food marketing in primary and secondary schools. This marketing is mostly self-regulated, although some provinces, in particular Québec, and some school boards have some regulations.

Canadian health opinion leaders, health professionals, and researchers developed several policy recommendations to address the issue, referred to as the Ottawa Principles. One of the principles is to restrict commercial marketing in settings such as schools, childcare and early childhood education facilities, and sports and recreation centres.

A group of researchers from the University of Ottawa studied the type of food marketing in Canadian schools. Their finding were as follows:

"Overall, 84% of schools reported at least one type of food marketing and the median number of distinct types of marketing per school was 1 (range 0–6). The most frequently reported forms of marketing were the sale of branded food, particularly chocolate, pizza, and other fast food, for fundraising (64% of schools); food advertisements on school property (26%), and participation in incentive programs (18%). Primary schools (n = 108) were more likely to report participating in incentive programs (25%) and selling branded food items (72%) compared to secondary schools (n = 46; 2 and 43% respectively). Conversely, secondary schools were more likely to report food advertising on school property (56%), exclusive marketing arrangements with food companies (43%), and food product displays (19%) than primary schools."

Their conclusion was that current efforts by food marketers were not sufficiently regulated to protect Canadian schoolchildren.

NGOS, the media, policy development institutions, religious organizations, and educational institution stakeholders all influence business, and business influences them in return. Today's managers require the skills and talents to engage all these stakeholders.

Your advice to Debbie . . .

As an animal lover, Debbie believes in supporting organizations taking care and protecting animals, but she will have to research these NGOs. Most publish reports including financial statements and from these she should be able to identify responsible NGOs. She may wish to distinguish between NGOs that advocate animal rights versus animal welfare. Animal rights supporters believe that animals should have the same rights as humane treatment and protection from exploitation and abuse accorded humans. Animal welfare groups are more concerned with the animal care and whether or not their mental and physical needs are being met. If any of the NGOs are registered charities, she can check and Canada Revenue Agency (CRA) website. CRA examines the purpose of the charity and how their funds are spent.

Summary

- Civil society stakeholders are voluntary, community, and social organizations that represent society's views on business and society issues. They can influence the behaviour of corporations through advocacy. A full description and example of an NGO is given, providing a full picture of issues around which they form, and a list of their tactics and strategies for influence is provided. (LO 13.1)

- The media stakeholder is one that can influence society's attitudes toward business and one that business can influence. There is increased coverage of the ethics of business and corporate social responsibility (CSR) in the media, leading to increased public interest in business. Media themselves have recognized the importance of their own CSR. (LO 13.2)

- Policy development institutions or think tanks are numerous and advocate various points of view on business and society issues. They influence government's—and society in general's—attitudes toward business. Many of these think tanks are supported by trade unions, universities, and corporations and views consistent with capitalism are promoted. (LO 13.3)

- Some businesspersons are influenced by organized religions or by spirituality. Corporate values can be determined by religious beliefs and reflected in business operations. Business must be careful when responding to religious activism. (LO 13.4)

- Considerable controversy surrounds the relationship between business and the educational institution stakeholder. Businesses are increasing their presence on campus by supporting research, financing buildings and programs, and operating services. Some students and faculty members believe that the presence of business has an adverse influence on the educational institution, in particular reducing its academic independence. (LO 13.5)

Key Terms

Civil society

Libel chill

Policy development institution (think tank)

Spirituality

Critical Thinking and Discussion Questions

1. What roles do NGO stakeholders play in business and society?
2. Are all the tactics used by NGOs appropriate—that is, ethical?
3. What strategies should corporations use in dealing with NGOs?
4. What are the benefits and dangers of forming partnerships with NGOs?
5. What influence does the media stakeholder have on business and what influence does business have on the media?
6. Does business manipulate the media?
7. What challenges do the new forms of participatory media present to business?
8. What roles do the policy development institutions (think tanks) play in business and society?
9. Should religion—organized or spiritual—be associated with business? How can you integrate your faith into your work?
10. What are the benefits and dangers of business' involvement with the educational institutions stakeholder?

Cases

13.1 PIPELINES, NGOS, AND FIRST NATIONS

The construction of petroleum pipelines is a controversial issue in Canada. Applications to build several have been denied, in particular the expansion of the Trans Mountain Pipeline by Kinder Morgan. The pipeline was opposed by the Government of British Columbia, and several environmental NGOs including Tides Canada, the David Suzuki Foundation, the West Coast Environmental Law Foundation, Living Oceans Society, and the Rainforest Conservation Foundation. Some Indigenous communities also opposed the pipeline.

The opponents claimed that pipeline accidents would damage the environment and are hard to clean up. There was particular concern about oil spills in the waters off the west coast, would be difficult to clean up. Also, it was alleged that there were significant dangers to killer whales from the increased number of tankers in the area. All opponents believed that the continuing and increasing use of fossil fuels was a danger to the environment because of increased greenhouse gases. NGOs and Indigenous communities received considerable attention from the various tactics used, including organized protests, launching of lawsuits, discrediting of regulators, and constant lobbying of governments.

The Tsleil-Waututh Nation took the Government of Canada to court to halt the construction of the pipeline. The Federal Court of Appeal decision on August 30, 2018, held that the National Energy Board's (NEB) decision to exclude the increased marine traffic associated with the project from the environmental assessment was unreasonable, and that the Government of Canada did not adequately consult and accommodate affected Indigenous Peoples. This halted work on the Trans Mountain Pipeline project.

Several First Nations had opposed the pipeline and the Union of B.C. Indian Chiefs stated that the project would worsen climate change, devastating forests and causing floods. Some First Nations felt that the NGOs were misleading them about their agenda and implied that all First Nations agreed with the NGOs campaigns. It was alleged that the NGOs created the view that more First Nations opposed the pipeline than did. Many First Nations had signed benefit agreements with Kinder Morgan and were to receive cash, jobs, and assistance with business ventures.

An Indian Resource Council represented First Nations oil and gas producers and advocated for responsible energy development. The Council was composed of "First Nations across Canada that have oil and gas production on their land including those that have the potential for production." The Council believed that "the management and development of our resources is important for the socio-economic development and well being of our people." Indigenous Peoples live on the lands through which pipelines pass, and in some cases, have Aboriginal title to lands. They express their concerns about the environment and the exploitation of their lands, and their exclusion from decision making. It is essential that they are consulted about projects. First Nations and Indigenous groups can speak on their own behalf and it is not necessary for NGOs to claim that they are working on behalf of Indigenous Peoples. The Council questions why NGOs want to deprive First Nations of economic prosperity and the possibility of gaining autonomy from the federal government that energy development on First Nations lands would make possible.

Questions

1. Who are the stakeholders and what is their influence? Describe the different Indigenous stakeholders.
2. Did the NGOs behave ethically?
3. What is your view of the Indian Resource Council's position?
4. Should pipelines—in particular, the Trans Mountain expansion—be constructed?

13.2 SLAPPING GREENPEACE CANADA

SLAPP is an acronym for Strategic Lawsuits Against Public Participation. "SLAPPs are legal actions (usually defamation actions such as libel and slander) launched for the primary purpose of shutting down criticism, and without a strong cause of action. The plaintiff's goal in a SLAPP is not to win the lawsuit, but is rather to silence a critic by instilling fear of large legal costs and the spectre of large damage awards." Despite their right to free speech, critics or defendants may be frightened into silence. They may be required to take down websites, remove comments made online, remove printed materials, withdraw statements, and issue apologies.

Resolute Forest Products was accused of using a SLAPP against Greenpeace in 2013. The company took legal action against Greenpeace claiming $5 million in damages plus $2 million for punitive damages. It claimed that Greenpeace was using threats, intimidation, false accusations and harassing Resolute's customers to disrupt operations at the company's pulp and paper mills. Greenpeace was accused of spreading defamatory malicious falsehoods and intentionally interfering with the company's business. The NGO circulated defamatory articles about Resolute's forestry and corporate practices, and threatened and intimidated customers. As a result, jobs were lost in Northern Ontario and the economic well-being of communities threatened.

In addition, Resolute launched a campaign against Greenpeace and ForestEthics to counter what it said were inaccurate allegations. The campaign included full page advertisements in national and regional publications, direct mail, digital advertising, and social media campaigns. Five hundred municipalities, unions, and many Indigenous Peoples in Ontario and Quebec have expressed concern about the NGO actions. In newspaper advertisements, Resolute urged readers to email the NGOs telling them to stop the campaign against the company which was harming the lives and livelihoods of many Canadians.

Resolute has received dozens of awards in recognition of its sustainability practices. Examples of 2018 awards are Business Intelligence Group Awards for Business (Green Company of the Year; Green Product of the Year); iNOVA Awards (for 2017 Annual and Sustainability Report winning gold); Canada's Top 100 Corporate R&D Spenders (for being one of Canada's 2018 innovation leaders); The American Forest & Paper Association (AF&PA) Sustainability Awards (for Leadership in Sustainability); and Excellence Awards (for 2018 North American Excellence Award for Corporate Responsibility).

In January 2019, an American court dismissed most of the lawsuit against the NGOs.

Questions

1. Should SLAPPs be used against NGOs or even individuals who criticize a corporation or industry?
2. What stakeholders are involved in this issue?
3. What are the ethical implications of the use of SLAPPs and media campaigns?
4. What the ethical implications of the NGOs actions?

Businesses' environmental policies are a key component of CSR.
Used © desighsource09©123RF.com

CHAPTER 14

The Environment and Business Responsibilities

LEARNING OUTCOMES

After studying this chapter, you will be able to:

LO 14.1   Understand the extensiveness of business' responsibilities toward the environment.

LO 14.2   Describe the influence of government in addressing environmental concerns.

LO 14.3   Define environmental non-governmental organizations (ENGOs) and appreciate their influence on corporations.

LO 14.4   Explain how market-driven environmentalism approaches work.

LO 14.5   Describe a corporation's responses to environmental concerns in the context of the main functions of business.

LO 14.6   List the sustainability measures and standards that exist and become aware of corporate and industry initiatives to report on their environmental responsibilities.

LO 14.7   Appreciate that there are dissenting views on the environment and consider how business should respond.

LO 14.8   Identify the opportunities and challenges for a corporation's response to environmental concerns.

What would you do if...?

Vivian Duveen was standing by the fish counter in her local supermarket. She planned to purchase salmon for her family's dinner but hesitated. Fresh salmon had become very popular; it was a healthy meal, and her family enjoyed it. Today she noted that she could choose between fresh wild or farmed salmon, which was a little less expensive.

Vivian had been researching salmon as a food and the pros and cons of wild versus farmed sources. She found that it was a complicated issue with contradictions in articles and lots of unsubstantiated claims on both sides. There were numerous issues including nutritional value, the operation of farms, and the impact on the environment.

Many sources claimed that wild salmon was nutritionally superior to farmed salmon. Wild salmon was firmer, 20 percent less fatty, and contained 20 percent more protein. Other sources disagreed with these figures. Because it was fattier, farmed salmon contained more omega-3 acids, a desirable characteristic. Dietitians recommended eating two servings of salmon a week whether it was wild or farmed as it was one of the healthiest foods.

Farmed salmon were confined to crowded pens where they were fed daily to saturation, resulting in their growing faster and producing an oilier product. The fish were fed pellets of concentrated nutrients that included plant-based proteins, fish meal, and antibiotics as necessary. It was alleged that the farms produced excessive waste from uneaten food and that some fish escaped to interbreed with wild stocks threatening to weaken the wild salmon's gene pool. Critics of farms claimed that toxins, including PCBs and pesticides, in the fish produced were up to ten times greater than in wild stocks. The farm operators denied these claims.

In contrast, wild salmon lived in natural surroundings, but were subject to many stressors as they did not feed regularly and had many predators. They were carriers of furunculosis, a devastating bacterial disease that farmed salmon were vaccinated against. Sea lice were a problem with salmon but an antibiotic could be included in the food for farms to eliminate them. Some toxins were found in wild salmon depending on their habitat.

In Canada, fish farming was regulated by government to prevent abusive practices. The harvesting of farmed salmon followed strict regulations. The fish were starved for seven days to clear the alimentary tract to ensure a quality product. Also, the process of harvesting farmed fish was monitored, while harvesting practices for wild fish were unclear. The farm economies of scale resulted in lower prices for consumers, but it was alleged that these lower prices threatened small wild fishing operations.

Fish farms supplied about 50 percent of the fish consumed worldwide. The existence of farms for popular fish such as salmon has taken the pressure off wild stocks and prevented their depletion. The industry has been talking with ENGOs about ways to improve their practices. The farm operators argued that farming was more sustainable and socially responsible than wild catches. The industry claimed that wild fish cannot supply the world's demand for fish.

Vivian reached into the refrigerated display case and picked up a package of salmon.

What is your advice to Vivian?

There is increasing concern for the natural environment in Canada and around the world. The need to preserve and protect the environment is now so compelling that there is no question of its relevance for business—the natural environment is an issue that must be addressed. In other words, business has responsibilities toward achieving a sustainable environment.

Concern for the environment has been intensified by disasters such as Chernobyl and Three Mile Island (nuclear plant meltdowns), the Love Canal (pollution in New York), the *Exxon Valdez* (oil spill in Alaska), the BP oil disaster in the Gulf of Mexico, and the tsunami in Japan (and resulting nuclear power plant disaster). In addition, the depletion of the ozone layer, the greenhouse effect, acid rain, deforestation, pollution, energy depletion, and waste management are steadfast reminders of how compelling an issue our natural environment is.

This chapter describes how environmental concerns affect corporations and the many issues that arise with stakeholders. All stakeholders have an obligation to the environment and the key stakeholders influencing it are identified. The various ways that business is responding to its obligation to the environment are identified, as are the challenges involved for management.

LO 14.1   Business, Its Stakeholders, and the Natural Environment

Environmental issues confront virtually all aspects of the corporation, from the input of resources to the manufacturing process, and from workplace conditions through to the way products are packaged and sold. Managers must cope with planning, organizing, leading, and controlling all the aspects of the environmental issue. The ethical and responsibility issues identified in Table 14.1 are diverse; thus, a comprehensive environmental management approach is necessary. The following sections identify how corporations deal with the environment.

TABLE 14.1	**Principal Stakeholders and Issues Involved in Business' Response to the Environment**
Stakeholder	**Ethical Issues and Responsibilities for Managers**
Shareholders	Investment decisions influenced by the handling of the environment Risk associated with environment problems or disasters Establishment of "green" investment criteria
Directors	Getting environment issues on the board agenda Liability for environmental contamination Challenge of motivating management to address the issue
Employees	Workplace exposures to environmental problems (e.g., indoor air pollution) Refusal to perform tasks causing environmental problems Whistleblowing on employer
Customers/Consumers	Inconsistencies between concerns expressed about the environment and the consumption of environmentally unfriendly products Unwillingness to pay higher prices for environmentally friendly products/services if necessary The viability of "green" products
Lenders/Creditors	Need to assess increased financial risk
Suppliers	Must respond to demands for more environmentally friendly products Reassessing most appropriate transportation and packaging of supplies
Service Professionals	Familiarity with laws and regulations Design of appropriate audits Identification of full environmental cost accounting methods
Competitors	Consequence of competitive edge being obtained by making products more environmentally friendly

Stakeholder	Ethical Issues and Responsibilities for Managers
NGOs	How to respond to groups based upon environmental concerns
Media	How to respond to media coverage of environmental problems
Government	Complying with laws and regulations Influencing public policy

Although most business and society scholars do not consider the natural environment to be a stakeholder of business, there is agreement that it is influenced by stakeholders and/or has an influence on stakeholders. As a result, the natural environment can be viewed as a **commons**, or a resource used as though it belongs to all. Business has been able to use shared resources such as the environment simply because it wanted or needed to. In the past, for example, pollution was put into the environment without thinking about the damage and little regulation existed to prevent it. Through uncontrolled use, many in society believed that the environment as a commons was being destroyed. Often this destruction was occurring even though it was not the intent of the user—that is, business—and ownership was not an issue.

The concept of the commons was popularized by an article published in 1968 by Garrett Hardin.[1] Hardin described what would happen to a commons as illustrated by an unregulated pasture where all sheep herders added more sheep at no cost to them but their actions might lead to the destruction of the pasture for everyone. This behaviour can be explained, in part, by the individualism and economic freedom fundamental of capitalism described in Chapter 2 and the self-interest ethic described in Chapter 5.

Want to learn more about the "tragedy of the commons"?

Fortunately, most corporations and their stakeholders have recognized the real and potentially damaging impact of their actions on the environment. The environmental ethic and sustainable development are two concepts that aid business and society in understanding the environmental challenges.

The Environmental Ethic and Sustainable Development

Business' responsibilities to the environment are exemplified by the environmental ethic corporations practise and by management's understanding of sustainable development.

An **environmental ethic** is the set of values or principles that govern a corporation's practices relating to the environment. Concern for the environment has existed for some time, and an environmental ethic is evolving from this focus on ecology. Society and many businesspersons now have some sense of obligation or moral responsibility to the environment, which is expressed in different ways. For a business corporation, the values or principles include the idea that new business development needs to take account of the environment from the design stage through to ultimate disposal; that environmental management should be the responsibility of staff at all levels as an integral part of their job; that environmental performance should be built into the reward structure of the organization; that product and process responsibility should occur from cradle to grave; and that agreed-upon values and beliefs should be used as the guiding principles for conducting all business.[2]

The environmental ethic can be related to the three main approaches to ethical thinking described in Chapter 1: deontological or rule-based, consequential or utilitarianism, and virtue ethics theories. These three approaches to ethical thinking present different views of how the environment is considered.[3] The deontological approach is based on rules and regulations that are universally applied. Thus, the corporation is acting socially responsible if it adheres to regulations that give it the right to take certain actions relating to the environment. This is an approach often used by corporations in their environmental reporting. Its application is limited as only rational beings are treated as ends and everything else is considered as a means to an end, thus the approach is not capable of moral consideration in the context of the environment.

The utilitarian approach balances the negative or positive outcomes of a corporation's influence on the environment. This approach is often used and decisions are based on the relative costs or harms and benefits of a particular action. It has limited usefulness as the approach only considers foreseen consequences and is unable to identify unanticipated results or intrinsic values. On the other hand, virtue ethics allow for subjective evaluation of ethical decisions as it encompasses not only concern for human well-being but also concern for the well-being of the natural environment. Personal values and motivations are included, allowing for a wider outlook and a subjective evaluation based on virtuous traits.

When preparing environmental reports corporations tend to use the rule-based and utilitarian approaches to describe environmental decisions. Stakeholders not closely related to the corporation tend to evaluate the decisions based on the virtue ethics approach.[4]

The concept of *sustainable development* has received attention from governments, international agencies, and some business quarters. **Sustainable development** is defined as development ensuring that the use of resources and the impact on the environment today does not damage prospects for the use of resources or the environment by future generations. This was a theme in the report of the United Nations World Commission on Environment and Development (1987), which concluded that continued economic growth not only is possible, but also is necessary to reduce poverty and to sustain future generations.[5] Sustainable development has been endorsed by many businesspersons as an approach that allows environmental and economic concerns to coincide and makes economic progress possible.

Business sustainable development means "adopting business strategies and activities that meet the needs of the enterprise and its stakeholders today while protecting, sustaining, and enhancing the human and natural resources that will be needed in the future."[6] This definition was developed by the International Institute for Sustainable Development (IISD), a non-profit, private corporation established and supported by the governments of Canada and Manitoba to promote sustainable development in government, business, and individual decision making. This definition captures the sense of the concept as presented in the World Commission's report, but focuses on areas of specific interest and concern to business. It recognizes that economic development must meet the needs of the corporation and its stakeholders. The definition also highlights the dependence of the corporation's economic activities on human and natural resources as well as on physical and financial capital.

Environmental Concerns in Business and Society

In order to illustrate the extensiveness of the environment issue in society and the challenges that confront business, the following list defines the major concerns. Some terms overlap or are interrelated, but all are frequently used and should be understood.

- *Acid rain*—**Acid rain** is a generic term used for precipitation that contains an abnormally high concentration of sulphuric and nitric acid. Industrial activities create general gas emissions that combine with water to form the acids.[7]

- *Air pollution*—Air quality is affected by various pollutants resulting from the burning of fuels, emissions from industrial sites, and emissions from transportation vehicles. Smog is one form of air pollution.

- *Ecosystems*—An **ecosystem** is a biological community of interacting organisms and their physical environment. It is recommended that industry take an ecosystem approach to the environment—that is, recognize the interrelationships among land, air, water, wildlife, and human activities.[8]

- *Energy production and consumption*—The generation of energy is usually damaging to the environment, as are the pollutants released when the energy fuel is used. Industry is responsible for many of the problems created, but so are consumers. Business has been emphasizing the efficient use of energy through the development of new technologies for itself and consumers.

- *Nature and wildlife*—There is concern for the harm caused to birds, mammals, fish, and plants by the operations of business. Endangered species are of particular concern.

- *Ozone*—**Ozone** is a naturally occurring gas, formed from normal oxygen, that protects Earth by filtering out ultraviolet (UV) radiation from the sun. The thinning of the ozone layer in the upper atmosphere has resulted in increased UV radiation.[9]

- *Pollution*—Pollution involves any form of contamination in the environment. Business is under pressure to reduce its polluting of the environment.

- *Waste management*—**Waste management** is "disposal, processing, controlling, recycling and reusing the solid, liquid, and gaseous wastes of plants, animals, humans and other organisms."[10] Wastes often are hazardous, making the process more challenging. Recycling is described by the four Rs: reduce, reuse, recycle, and recover.

- *Water quality*—Water quality is determined by the presence of contaminants affecting its chemical and bacterial composition. Supply of safe drinking water is a concern in Canada. Corporations take on different environmental projects, as illustrated by Royal Bank's decision to focus on fresh water as described in Everyday Ethics 14.1.

 EVERYDAY ETHICS 14.1

The RBC Blue Water Project

RBC's Blue Water Project is dedicated to protecting the world's most precious natural resource: fresh water. The main focus is a 10-year donations program supporting projects that help protect and preserve water. RBC has made a $50 million charitable commitment to support initiatives to protect water in towns and cities. The project also supports conferences, economic reports, and events that help increase awareness about the importance of water.

RBC's Environmental Blueprint commits to reducing the use of landscape irrigation, reducing consumption by incorporating water-efficient technologies, and using environmentally responsible cleaning products to help protect water quality.

A term that captures the effects of the concerns listed above and that is frequently used today is *climate change,* also referred to as *global warming.* **Climate change** is "the result of human activities altering the chemical composition of the atmosphere through the build-up of greenhouse gases that trap heat and reflect it back to the Earth's surface." This process has resulted in an increase in global temperatures and more frequent weather events. **Greenhouse gases (GHG)** "are gases that absorb and trap heat in the atmosphere and cause a warming effect on earth. Some occur naturally in the atmosphere, while others result from human activities. Greenhouse gases include carbon dioxide, water vapor, methane, nitrous oxide, ozone, chlorofluorocarbons, hydrofluorocarbons and perfluorocarbons."[11] Climate change is a major issue for society and cannot be ignored by business. Business corporations and individuals can learn about the amount of GHGs they contribute to the atmosphere by using carbon footprint calculators listed in the Want to Learn More link below.

Want to learn more about **calculating your carbon footprint?**

LO 14.2   Government's Influence

Extensive government involvement exists through public policy formulation and the regulation of all aspects of the natural environment. The federal and provincial governments have passed environmental legislation, and are considering further legislation. Governments have announced various programs to create cleaner air, land, and water; to encourage sustainable resources; to develop parks and wildlife areas; to protect the Arctic regions; and to reduce global warming, ozone depletion, and acid rain. This section does not examine government initiatives in detail, but instead discusses the coordination of public and corporate policies on environment and identifies a range of policies that will impact on business.

Corporations should engage in a dialogue with government agencies so that their interests are protected and to contribute to the resolution of environmental problems. Governments may directly regulate activities of the corporation or introduce policy changes through taxation rates, the elimination or establishment of subsidies, international agreements, or the creation of markets in tradeable pollution permits. Business enterprises must establish mechanisms so that they can "listen" to what government is considering, and mechanisms so that they can "talk" to government.

Government departments and agencies have been established not only to regulate the activities of corporations, but also to assist them in meeting environmental performance targets. Governments have passed legislation to protect the environment that places obligations and responsibilities on business. It is not uncommon for the legislation to require that an environmental audit be undertaken by corporations or governments involved in environmentally sensitive projects. Environment-related legislation is enacted by the federal, provincial, and territorial governments in Canada.

Government legislation often stipulates that an environmental assessment document, or report, be submitted to relevant departments of the environment for review and approval. Although legislation varies among the federal and provincial governments, the report usually has to contain a description of the project, a list of reasons for the project, alternatives to the project, an outline of how the project and its alternatives will affect the environment directly or indirectly, an identification of the actions necessary to prevent those effects, and an evaluation of the advantages and disadvantages of the project to the environment and alternative ways to carry it out. The report is submitted for evaluation to an environmental assessment agency and often is followed by public hearings. Most corporations are now familiar with the environmental process and incorporate it into their decision making. Corporations also conduct audits and assessments even when not required by governments. Such audits often are of the whole organization and not restricted to particular projects or plants, and are designed to provide a "total picture" of the environmental circumstances of the corporation.

An example of such legislation is that overseen by the Government of Canada's Environment and Climate Change department, which administers over a dozen Acts of Parliament and is responsible for meeting numerous obligations spelled out in legislation. Three Acts illustrate the legislation. The *Canadian Environmental Protection Act* is "aimed at preventing pollution and protecting the environment and human health."[12] The *Federal Sustainable Development Act*, through which "the Minister of the Environment is responsible for developing the Federal Sustainable Development Strategy, setting out goals and targets for all federal departments."[13]

The most recent federal legislation is Bill C-69, "An Act to enact the Impact Assessment Act and the Canadian Energy Regulator Act, to amend the Navigation Protection Act, and to make consequential amendments to other Acts" was given Royal Assent on June 21, 2019.[14] The government's news release stated that the legislation will strengthen environmental protection; provide assessments on both the positive and negative environmental, economic, social, and health impacts; clear expectations and shorten timelines for project reviews; and recognize Indigenous rights, culture, and interests in projects.[15] The Canadian Environmental Assessment Agency will become the Impact Assessment Agency of Canada.[16]

The Canadian government has been involved in international agreements to control climate change, most of which failed. Reports stated that expected reductions in emissions were nowhere near projected goals and forecasts indicate that the government's targets under various plans will not be met. The most recent attempt at influencing climate change is the UN Framework Convention on Climate Change (UNFCCC) described in Responsibility for Ethics 14.1.

 RESPONSIBILITY FOR ETHICS 14.1

UN Framework Convention on Climate Change (UNFCCC)

In December 2015, 195 nations met in Paris, France, to negotiate an agreement to combat climate change that will unleash actions and investment towards a low-carbon, resilient, and sustainable future. The main aspects of the agreement are:

- Limiting the raise in temperature to 1.5 degrees Celsius above pre-industrial levels in this century.
- Accounting for climate action through a transparency system and global stock-take. This requires for nations to submit action plans (nationally determined contributions) that detail their future objectives to address climate change.
- Strengthen the ability of countries to deal with climate impacts.
- Strengthen the ability to recover from climate impacts.
- Provide financial support for nations to build clean, resilient futures.

Climate finance will be increased to US$100 billion by 2020 and a further financing goal established by 2025. The increased financing will assist in accomplishing the last three aspects and in particular in developing countries.

In December 2018 The 24th Conference of the Parties to the United Nations Framework Convention on Climate Change (COP24) met and agreed on rules to implement the Paris Agreement, which will come into force in 2020. This is a rulebook on how governments will measure and report on their emissions-cutting efforts.

The agreement is available at http://unfccc.int/resource/docs/2015/cop21/eng/l09.pdf.

Source: "United Nations Framework Convention on Climate Change (UNFCCC) accessed March 20, 2019 and "COP24: Key outcomes agreed at the UN climate talks in Katowice," Carbon Brief, December 16, 2018, at https://www.carbonbrief.org/cop24-key-outcomes-agreed-at-the-un-climate-talks-in -katowice accessed March 20, 2019. Used with permission.

LO 14.3 Environmental NGO Influence

Environmental non-governmental organizations (ENGOs) are groups that hold shared values or attitudes about the challenges confronting the natural environment and advocate for changes to improve the condition of the environment. Dozens of these groups exist in Canada; some are described in Responsibility for Ethics 14.2. The activities, policies, and initiatives of these groups should be monitored to assess the potential impact on the corporation. This monitoring function may be performed by the environmental affairs department, by the managers responsible for environmental matters, or by consultants.

 RESPONSIBILITY FOR ETHICS 14.2

Examples of Environmental Non-Governmental Organizations (ENGOs)

- *Evergreen*—Evergreen is focused on "creating and sustaining healthy urban environments in our schools, our public spaces, in housing and transit systems, and communities themselves." Its mission is "to enable flourishing cities" and its vision is "We dream of flourishing cities."

- *Friends of the Earth Canada*—Friends of the Earth (FOE) Canada is a charitable, non-profit environmental organization. Its mission is to be "a voice for the environment, nationally and internationally, working with others to inspire the renewal of our communities and the earth, through research, education and advocacy." It takes action to confront polluters, holding governments to account for their promises and insisting they enforce laws.

- *Environmental Defence Canada*—Environmental Defence Canada's purpose is to "challenge and inspire change in government, business and people to ensure a greener, healthier and prosperous life for all." It adheres to the following principles: being politically non-partisan, sticking to the facts, getting results, working cooperatively, and following the law.

- *Canadian Parks and Wilderness Society (CPAWS)*—CPAWS is "Canada's only nationwide charity dedicated solely to the protection of our public land and water, and ensuring our parks are managed to protect the nature within them." Its vision is to "protect at least half of our public land and water so that future generations can experience Canada's irreplaceable wilderness."

- *David Suzuki Foundation*—This is a national, bilingual non-profit organization headquartered in Vancouver, with offices in Toronto and Montréal. The Foundation's activities are conducting evidence-based research, educational programs, and policy analysis for the purpose of conserving and protecting the national environment and helping to create a sustainable Canada.

The list in Responsibility for Ethics 14.2 illustrates the ENGOs' diversity of interests covering the concerns listed above. Environment groups are not always easy to deal with and use a variety of tactics. They can be involved in protests, blockades, boycotts, court cases, and sometimes make use of annual shareholders' meetings as platforms for protest. Canadian environmental groups are also often part of a global network of organizations. Protests about logging the Clayoquot Sound forests in British Columbia, as an example, are an alliance effort and have received impressive international attention.

A study identified the factors that lead ENGOs to target particular corporations. Hendry reviewed existing research on the environmental movement, stakeholder theory, and corporate social performance from which he formulated eight propositions that might explain how target corporations are selected. Five case studies of ENGOs were used to examine the validity of the propositions. Hendry found that the factors ranked as follows, from most influential to least:

- The greater the certainty among ENGOs that the firm is the source of an environmental impact, the more likely ENGOs are to target the firm.

- The more consequential the firm's actions are for the natural environment, the more likely ENGOs are to target the firm.

- The denser the relationships among the firm's ENGO stakeholders, the better able those ENGOs are to monitor the firm and share information about the firm, and the more likely those ENGOs are to target the firm collectively.

- The larger the firm, the more likely ENGOs will target the firm.

- To maximize the effects of mimetic isomorphism, ENGOs target corporations that are influential in their organizational fields and therefore likely to be imitated.

- The more previous interactions between the firm and a particular ENGO, the more likely the ENGO will target the firm.

- The closer the firm is to consumers in the supply chain, the more likely ENGOs will target the firm.

- The more well-known the firm's brands are, the more likely ENGOs will target the firm.[17]

Although this discussion has focused on ENGOs targeting corporations, an increasing amount of cooperation or partnership is occurring between business and ENGOs as discussed in Chapter 13. Many corporations recognize the contributions of individuals and organizations in their efforts to protect the environment, and examples have been used throughout the book. Nonetheless, some ENGOs are reluctant to cooperate with corporations as they do not trust them and view such cooperation as a "sell-out" to business.

LO 14.4   Influence of Market-Driven Environmentalism

In addition to environmental initiatives being driven by government or pressures from ENGOs, there is a market-driven response to the environment. **Standard environmentalism** occurs when government regulation is a necessary remedy for the market's failure to provide enough environmental amenities. On the other hand, **market environmentalism** exists where economic incentives created by the market are more effective at protecting the environment than is government intervention.[18] Not everyone agrees with the market approach and argues that regulation and new technologies are more effective.[19] Nevertheless, market approaches are being considered and to some extent implemented.

The market factors influencing environmentalism are economic growth, free trade, and property rights. The differences among these approaches are summarized in Table 14.2, and highlight why free-market environmentalism is a possible approach.

TABLE 14.2	Differences between Standard and Market Environmentalism	
Factors	Standard	Free-Market
Economic Growth	Viewed as destructive, because producing more creates more environmental harm	World is dynamic and two forces counteract harm: (1) increased income drives a demand for more environmental quality, and (2) stimulation of innovation that improves environmental quality
Free Trade	Considered part of the problem: prevents countries from following own higher levels of protection; and belief that rich countries exploit poor	Forces industries to be more competitive, accelerating adoption of newer, cleaner technologies; trade restrictions possible to protect environment under WTO; countries open to trade grow faster
Property Rights versus Regulation	Faith in government to solve problem for the public good	Powerful tool for protecting because ownership incentive creates stewardship incentive and gives individuals power to protect the environment.

Source: Summarized from Laura Jones, "A Different Kind of Environmentalist," *Fraser Forum*, April 2001, 4–6. Used with permission.

The debate on a market orientation to environmentalism is only beginning, and standard environmentalism dominates at this time. However, examples of market-driven environmentalism are **carbon pricing**, a financial instrument that businesses and governments are using to reduce carbon (GHG) emissions, which can be done in one of three ways:

- **Cap-and-trade** where governments cap total carbon emissions and then give or sell companies carbon permits that add up to the cap. Companies can then trade permits with each other, with those who can reduce emissions cheaply and easily selling permits to those who cannot. The price of the permits is variable depending on the market. But generally, the lower the cap, the higher the price. Also referred to as *emissions trading*.

- Carbon pricing: governments impose a fee on carbon; the more a company or individual emits, the more they pay. Also referred to as a *carbon tax*. The price determines how effective the policy will be at lowering emissions—the higher the price, the greater the reductions.[20]

- **Output-based price system**: instead of paying the charge on fuels that they purchase, industrial facilities in the system will face a carbon price on the portion of their emissions that are above a limit, which will be determined based on relevant output-based standards (emissions per unit of output).[21]

These approaches price carbon and create economic incentives to reduce emissions and increase green technology. They generate revenue and can reduce emissions more effectively than regulations. These approaches to carbon pricing are controversial; some political parties and governments oppose them as they are considered to be another tax and ineffective. On the other hand, many corporations and business associations support carbon pricing programs.

Another approach is to offset carbon emissions by promoting clean-energy projects—for example, wind generation, solar installations, geothermal plants, or biomass energy generation—that replace emissions from polluting sources. Another possibility is to finance carbon removal activities, for example reforestation. **Offsets** or **emissions-reduction credits**, are credits purchased from other corporations or organizations to mitigate greenhouse gases released into the environment. The funds generated are used to finance undertakings that will result in the reduction of emissions. Everyday Ethics 14.2 describes corporations involved in the provision of offsets.

EVERYDAY ETHICS 14.2

Offset Providers

There are many offset providers operating and examples are:

- *Tree Canada*—Tree Canada's vision is "improving the lives of Canadians by planting and nurturing trees while teaching about the value of trees." Its "Grow Clean Air program allows Canadians to offset their carbon emissions through the planting of native trees in Canada."

- *coolAction.com*—coolAction helps individuals and companies take action to reduce global warming by reducing their global emissions of greenhouse gases (GHGs). It is possible to become carbon neutral by purchasing GHG Emission Reductions. which helps finance and implement coolAction.com emission reduction projects.

- *Bullfrog Power*—By purchasing from wind and low-impact hydro generators, Bullfrog Power considers itself a completely green electricity retailer. These sources are viewed as producing clean, renewable electricity that is non-polluting and non–CO_2 emitting. Corporations or consumers access their electricity supply from Ontario's electricity grid but are actually purchasing it from Bullfrog.

Corporations are examining the possibility of storing their carbon emissions through **carbon capture and storage (CCS)**. With CCS, carbon dioxide emissions are captured and injected into underground formations. The practice is sometimes referred to as carbon sequestration or geosequestration. Downsides are that it is expensive, because the infrastructures do not exist, the underground storage may weaken, it requires a large amount of energy to implement, and it needs a 1,000-year monitoring program. Alberta's Energy Resources and Conservation Board has approved Shell Canada Limited's CCS carbon capture and storage project north of Edmonton, but imposed 23 conditions regarding additional data collection, analysis, and reporting.[22]

Recently, a policy development institution or think tank, has been established to promote market-driven environmentalism, Canada's Ecofiscal Commission. Its aim is to increase awareness of practical options on the protecting the environment. Responsibility for Ethics 14.3 describes the Commission. It is funded by corporations and foundations.

RESPONSIBILITY FOR ETHICS 14.3

Canada's Ecofiscal Commission

The Ecofiscal Commission was formed by economists from across the country who wanted to broaden the discussion of ecofiscal policy reform. An ecofiscal policy corrects market price signals to encourage the economic activities such as job creation, investment, and innovation while reducing greenhouse gas emissions and the pollution of land, air, and water.

Ecofiscal policies put a price on pollution. When this is done there are incentives for investment in innovative technologies. This enables society to benefit economically from the country's natural resources while also providing better protection to the environment. The revenue generated from ecofiscal policies can create further economic benefits; for example, by reducing income and payroll taxes or investing in new technologies or critical infrastructure.

The Ecofiscal Commission and its Commissioners are fully independent and aim to inform the public and policy-makers across the political spectrum, at all levels of government. It conducts research on environmental and economic policies and prepares reports on a variety of topics. The website contains case studies of how ecofiscal policies are implemented and gives reasons why Canada needs ecofiscal solutions.

Source: Adapted from "What is Ecofiscal," Canada's Ecofiscal Commission accessed March 21, 2019, http://ecofiscal.ca. Used with permission.

Preston Manning, member of the Ecofiscal Commission Advisory Board and former Leader of the Official Opposition, Canada, has proposed that there should be a greater balance between environmental and economic impacts when projects are being reviewed. He admits that in the past economic development took precedence resulting in damage to the environment. The result was environmental-impact assessment requirements being put in place by governments. He claims that now, in some cases, environmental protection takes precedence over economic development and little, if any, consideration is given to economic feasibility and benefits. Manning argues that those proposing projects requiring environmental protection measures should also be required to complete an economic-impact assessment to ensure a balanced assessment.[23]

Controversy surrounds market-driven environmentalism. Its effectiveness is questioned, that is, whether there is an actual reduction of emissions. It is viewed as image polishing with no real commitment to the environment. Corporations are able to continue damaging the environment by avoiding addressing their environmental problems. Effective trading systems are being developed, but to be successful there supported by business and government.

LO 14.5 Businesses Response to Environmental Issues

Whether corporations are forced by governments, pressured by environmental non-governmental organizations, or involved in market-environmentalism, managers must adapt the corporation by making changes to its organizational structure and by identifying its strategic approach.

Management positions and committees should be created to deal with the environment issue. Structural arrangements are put in place to ensure environmental matters are addressed starting at the top with the board of directors; some boards have environmental committees. It is key to have top management commitment so that there are practical principles to guide the corporation's environmental efforts, to integrate environmental affairs with operations, and to encourage environmental professionals to meet mounting environmental requirements.

Some business corporations are hiring senior managers and other staff to focus on environmental matters alone. Senior managers' positions carry titles such as vice-president, environment; environmental director; corporate manager of environmental affairs; and environmental coordinator. In addition to senior managers there are numerous titles for staff with various specialties in the environment, for example vegetation management biologist, hydrogeologist, and site remediation engineer. One of the challenges is to find individuals with the appropriate environmental expertise and knowledge and adequate managerial capabilities, as a combination of managerial and technical expertise is necessary.

From a strategic perspective, corporations can choose different approaches to environmental concerns. A token response focuses on damage control as problems arise and attempts are made to fix them. This is a reactive strategy still adopted by some corporations, but given the increased attention to the environment by many stakeholders, it is not recommended. The next level of approach is a concern that the corporation is in compliance with laws and regulations. There is concern about exposure to lawsuits and prosecution has motivated many directors and senior executives to adopt strategies of compliance.

In a comprehensive environmental management strategy, management seeks to gain a competitive advantage by taking an active stance on environmental issues. In these corporations, everyone becomes involved in environmental management and environmental issues are integrated into all aspects of corporate management. This strategy has been widely adopted within certain industries in some industrialized countries. A final strategy involves a commitment to sustainable development where corporations integrate the concepts of sustainable development into their business strategies and environmental policies. The strategy requires that management consider the effect of its activities on the environment and on the long-term interests and needs of shareholders and stakeholders. These corporations engage in a different type of dialogue and consultation with their stakeholders. Their business strategies and activities are designed to balance the need for financial returns with the needs of the environment and various stakeholder groups. Mechanisms such as advisory panels and committees are established to facilitate communication with stakeholders. Corporate reporting expands in relation to the needs of stakeholders. They may also engage independent auditors to attest to their report's accuracy and reliability.[24]

Corporations need comprehensive environmental policies and programs, referred to as *environmental management systems* (EMS). These plans ensure that environmental practices become an important component of the corporation's overall strategy. It also is important to plan strategically for the long term by establishing long-term goals, identifying opportunities to further reduce the impact on the environment, and taking advantage of these opportunities.[25]

No matter which approach or management system is used, corporations must understand and plan for the impact they are having on the environment. Research suggests that environmental practices and performance are key elements to corporate success, including achieving market leadership and keeping ahead of competitors. A study found that environmental activities enabled corporations to stay ahead of competition.[26] According to research by the Network for Business Sustainability, a corporation should consider environmental impacts and develop policies for reasons that include reducing costs, responding to investor demands, facilitating regulatory approaches and mitigating operational risk, hiring the best employees, and meeting consumer demand for "green" products and services.[27] These are convincing reasons for responding to environmental concerns.

The following sections outline some corporate initiatives relating to the environment in the main functions of business, financial management, marketing, human resources, and operations. Although this approach does not cover all areas of a corporation's activities, it does address the main ones.

Financial Management

Financial management now includes consideration of environmental factors and involves many aspects, for example:

- Accounting guidelines require companies to unequivocally state on their balance sheets the estimated liability for restoring capital assets to environmentally sound conditions.

- "Eco-insurance" products are now available in response to the liability associated with environmental problems.

- The banking industry has also been affected by the environmental issue. Environmental assessments are necessary to determine the influence on financial performance and liability.

- Investments are being screened for environmental performance. Individual investors usually seek out environmentally friendly mutual funds. To obtain information on this aspect of performance, institutional investors use sustainability indices such as the Dow Jones Sustainability Indices (DJSI) or from the Toronto Stock Exchange including the Carbon Efficient Index, Fossil Fuel Free Index, and Renewable Energy and Clean Technology Index. An example of how seriously institutional investors are viewing climate change is given in Everyday Ethics 14.3.

- Shareholders unhappy with a corporation's environmental policy may hurt its financial performance, maybe more than the actions of ENGOs. A concerned shareholder can submit a resolution at the annual meeting arguing that the corporation is increasing its environmental risk and thus the financial risk to shareholders. Investment analysts are more influenced by such resolutions than by the actions of ENGOs such as boycotts, protests, lawsuits, demonstrations, or sit-ins to raise awareness of a corporation's poor environmental record.[28]

 EVERYDAY ETHICS 14.3

The Carbon Disclosure Project (CDP)

Several Canadian financial institutions are among the 803 institutional investors who collaborate in the Carbon Disclosure Project (CDP), an independent not-for-profit organization holding the largest database of primary corporate climate change information in the world. Its goals are to tackle climate change through the reduction of greenhouse emissions, to promote sustainable water use by business and cities, and to mitigate environmental risk in corporate supply chains. The largest corporations in the world are sent questionnaires requesting disclosure of information on their greenhouse gas emissions. The investors view the information as critical in helping them decide how to allocate capital. The data are also made available to corporations, public-sector organizations, government bodies, academics, and the public.

Two hundred of Canada's largest corporations were surveyed each year and a separate report prepared, *The Carbon Disclosure Project Canada Report 2017*. Although emissions are growing in Canada, corporations have invested in carbon reduction projects that have reduced the growth rate of emissions. Canadian companies with ambitious carbon reduction targets include Bank of Montreal, Air Canada, Canadian Tire Corporation, Canadian National Railways, and TransAlta Corp.

Financial regulators also recommend greater disclosure of environmental information. In 2008, the Ontario Securities Commission (OSC) issued National Instrument 51–102, *Continuous Disclosure Obligations*, which requires public corporations to disclose information about environmental matters such as environmental liabilities, asset retirement obligations, financial and operational effects of environmental protection requirements, environmental policies fundamental to operations, and environmental risks. The OSC concluded that a meaningful discussion of material environmental matters is important to achieve fair presentation of the corporation's financial condition. The risks and liabilities associated with the environment must now receive more attention by boards of directors and audit committees. Critics point out that quantifying the risks will be difficult as there are no agreed-upon standards of measurement.[29]

In March 2017, the Canadian Securities Administrators (CSA) decided to review the disclosure risks and financial impacts requirements associated with climate change. This review resulted in CSA Staff Notice 51-354 *Report on Climate Change Related Disclosure Project*. Below are the key findings from this review:

- Materiality is the determining factor in considering whether information must be disclosed to investors and the review found a wide range of perspectives on the materiality of climate change–related risks and opportunities.

- There is a variation in current disclosure practices and there is room for improvement.

- All users were dissatisfied with the state of climate-change disclosures and believe that improvements are needed.

- There were concerns about mandatory disclosure requirements such as the regulatory burden and over emphasis on climate-related risks.

As a result of these findings, the CSA intends to undertake work in the following three areas: developing new guidance materials and educating users on the disclosure of risks, opportunities, and financial impacts related to climate change; considering new disclosure requirements on risk governance; and monitoring the ongoing development of climate-change-related disclosure practices.[30]

This section on financial management was from the perspective of the corporation and what was required by industry regulators. Chapter 11 discussed corporate finances from the perspective of investors or owners.

Marketing

Green seems to be the most popular colour with business today, since it expresses society's concern for the environment. **Green marketing** involves selling environmentally friendly goods and services to consumers. Providing such products is necessary for many corporations if they are to survive, and doing so can provide a new opportunity to make money.

Dozens of so-called "green" products are on the market: liquid soap products that offer plastic refill pouches to reduce packaging waste; coffee filters made without bleach; recyclable or degradable trash bags; dishwasher detergent that is phosphate-free; and foam plates and cups without chlorofluorocarbons. Packaging is an obvious area where the four Rs—reduce, reuse, recycle, and recover—can be practised, and is getting considerable attention.

Consumers have access to substantial information on the environmental friendliness of products. One way that consumers can increase their awareness of environment issues is by purchasing products displaying eco-labels. Some common eco-labels are listed in Responsibility for Ethics 14.4.

 RESPONSIBILITY FOR ETHICS 14.4

Common Environmental Labels in Canada

Common green labels and claims are:

- Eco-Logo™: The Canadian EcoLogo (also known as Environmental Choice) helps you identify products and services that have been independently certified to meet strict environmental standards that reflect their entire life cycle—from manufacturing to disposal.

- ENERGY STAR: The international ENERGY STAR symbol marks products that are among the most energy efficient on the market.

- EnerGuide: The Canadian EnerGuide label lists a product's estimated annual energy consumption and compares it to the energy performance of similar products.

- Marine Stewardship Council Certification Logo: Products bearing the Marine Stewardship Council (MSC) label come from fisheries certified to have met the MSC standard for sustainable fishing

- Fairtrade Canada Logo: Fair trade schemes, such as Fairtrade Canada, set standards to ensure that certified products are produced in a socially and economically fair, and environmentally responsible manner.

- Canada Organic Logo: Food products that meet the Canadian standard for organic production (at all stages, from growing to marketing) and contain at least 95 percent organic ingredients and no GMOs (genetically modified organisms) may display the Canada Organic label.

- Möbius loop: The recycling symbol (or Möbius loop) indicates that a product or packaging is recyclable, contains recycled content, or both.

Information on eco-labels is also available from these sources:

- Ecolabel Index at http://www.ecolabelindex.com/.

- Global Ecolabelling Network at https://www.globalecolabelling.net/.

- Consumer Reports: Greener Choices at http://greenerchoices.org/labels/.

Source: Adapted from *Common Environmental Labels and Claims in Canada*, Office of Consumer Affairs (OCA), Government of Canada at http://www.ic.gc.ca/eic/site/oca-bc.nsf/eng/ca02523.html accessed March 20, 2019.

Consumers are increasingly considering eco-labels when purchasing products. These labels are sponsored by government, ENGOs, and business associations, and there are about 113 in Canada.[31] There are issues about whether or not consumers actually act upon the eco-labels or trust them. Despite the multiplicity of the labels, only one in five consumers actually purchased eco-labelled products.

In order to increase the legibility and trust in eco-labels, third-party certification is occurring (discussed in Chapter 10). This is the practice of having an independent auditor, such as an NGO or professional consulting firm, confirm that the eco-label participant meets the label's requirements. This would include verifying that the eco-label participant accurately discloses its environmental impacts and efforts to protect the environment. As there is an economic objective for corporations, business sponsored eco-labels would be monitored to ensure that consumers were not being misinformed about environmental performance.

A study by Darnall *et al.* found that consumers appear to have greater confidence in eco-labels sponsored by governments and ENGOs than those sponsored by business associations. When there is trust in the label, consumers did not differentiate between certified versus uncertified eco-labels. The findings for business-association-sponsored eco-labels differed. There was distrust of private business to provide credible environmental information and this discouraged the use of eco-labels sponsored by business organizations. However, business-sponsored eco-labels could overcome the distrust if certified by independent third party auditors.[32]

Another issue remains as to whether consumers are willing to pay the increased prices often necessary for many green products. Research has found that the attributes of the sustainable products influence these purchase decisions. Attributes like "safe and gentle" were valued for products like baby shampoo; attributes like "strong and tough" were preferred when purchasing car shampoo. Also, consumers were more likely to use green products when being watched.[33] The latter point was found to also be the case in other studies. Although consumers expected corporations to address environmental issues, they liked to give the impression that they are environmentally conscious when this may not be so. Consumers responded more positively to advertisements informing them how they can save money than to those advertisements promoting the benefits to the environment.[34]

The consumer perspective of CSR, particularly relating to environmentalism, is also discussed in Chapter 12.

> Want to learn more about **an environmental folk song**?

Human Resources

Eco-friendly policies and practices are influencing the recruitment and retention of employees. Such policies are emphasized in recruitment when prospective employees ask recruiters about the employer's environmental practices.[35] Students in particular are searching for environmentally friendly workplaces.

A green workplace is even more important in retention of employees especially in tight employment markets. Employees satisfied with their employer's environment policies are proud of working for the company. Those employees not satisfied are likely to leave if they can find a green workplace.[36] Some of the practices that create an environmentally friendly workplace are listed in Table 14.3.

TABLE 14.3	Practices and Policies to Create the Green Workplace

- Offering a recycling program for office products, including donating and discounting used office furniture to employees or charities, and banning disposables such as plastic utensils and paper cups and plates.
- Conserving energy by using energy-efficient lighting systems and equipment, and installing automatic shutoffs of idle equipment.
- Reducing consumption of paper, packaging, and other office supplies, including not printing electronic documents.
- Encouraging employees to be more environmentally friendly by promoting walking, biking, and using public transport to work or car-pooling. Providing bike stands, showers, and fare subsidies.
- Creating a pesticide-free green landscape with trees, lawns, and gardens.
- Reducing emissions through less travel and climate control, and striving for carbon neutrality.
- Purchasing renewable energy credits.
- Conducting virtual meetings through video and teleconferencing thus reducing travel.
- Using natural lighting, with windows and skylights.

- Investing in community environmental initiatives.
- Requiring suppliers to be green.
- Publicly disclosing sustainability initiatives through reports that identify objectives and detail the progress made in achieving them.
- Convincing employees of program benefits and top management support.
- Providing incentives for environmentally friendly behaviour.
- Organizing employee committees to provide advice on practices.

The benefits to employers of a green workplace include improved employee morale, a stronger public image, increased consumer confidence, a positive bottom line, and healthier employees. Barriers to a green workplace are implementation and maintenance costs, lack of top management support, lack of employee commitment, and concern for lower employee productivity. One study found that one-half of corporations surveyed had environmentally friendly workplace policies and believed that they benefited from them.[37] Another study found that when employees believe their employer is committed to the environment, they are more likely to become involved in eco-initiatives such as recycling and saving energy. In order to encourage such initiatives, management should develop environmental policies and communicate them to employees.[38] There appears to be a trend toward green workplace policies and practices.

There is increasing coverage in the media about environmentally friendly employment and Aon-Hewitt, a human resources consulting firm, annually identifies "Canada's Greenest Employers."[39] Of interest to students is the high demand for individuals with skills and experience in the green or environmental sectors.[40] An indication of the interest in "green" jobs is a job site that specializes in environment-related employment.[41]

Chapter 12 also discussed the influence of CSR on employees.

Operations

Business is trying to implement environmentally friendly processes and technologies into all aspects of operations or the production function. Environmental issues have added complexity to supply chains, with pressure coming from consumers, competitors, employees, NGOs, and governments. Three areas of activity have been briefly mentioned: pollution reduction, waste management and recycling, and energy conservation. Everyday Ethics 14.4 describes one standard of certification for environmentally friendly practices in the construction industry.

 EVERYDAY ETHICS 14.4

"Green" Construction

The Canada Green Building Council's (CaGBC) mission is to lead and accelerate the transformation to high-performing, healthy green buildings, homes, and communities throughout Canada. It works to change industry standards, develop best design practices and guidelines, and advocate for green buildings.

CaGBC's mission is accomplished through the Leadership in Energy and Environmental Design (LEED) Green Building Rating System™. This system encourages and accelerates global adoption of sustainable green building and development practices through the creation and implementation of universally understood and accepted tools and performance criteria. A whole-building approach to sustainability is promoted in five key areas of human and environmental health: location and transportation, sustainable site development; water savings; energy efficiency; materials selection; and indoor environmental quality.

LEED is a third-party certification program and an internationally accepted benchmark for the design, construction, and operation of high-performance green buildings. It provides building owners and operators the tools they need to have an immediate and measurable impact on their building's performance.

All Canadians pollute the environment, and the volume of garbage is growing faster than the Canadian population. Pollution comes from many sources, including aerosols, hydrocarbons, automobile exhaust, untreated sewage, and pesticides. Even packaging is a form of pollution; for example, many convenience goods are packaged in throwaway containers. Often pollution is attributed to large business enterprises that dump wastes into the water, air, or landfills. But consumers also create pollution. Thus, corporations are concerned with reducing not only their own pollution activities but also those of consumers.

Waste management is the handling and disposal of unwanted materials left after industrial production or individual consumption. The traditional method of getting rid of our garbage has been to bury it in landfills. These are easy to operate and are relatively inexpensive. But the problem exists of finding locations for new landfill sites: no one wants to live near a dump. As a result, many governments and businesses are developing methods to reuse or manage waste. Research and development and design take the impact of particular materials on the environment into account. Waste from the manufacturing process can be recycled as an input in the production of another product. The reduction of waste is sought, but there is also emphasis on recycling, the retrieval and reuse of suitable waste material such as paper, glass, metal, and plastics. An example of effective use of material that might go to waste but instead saves trees in given in Everyday Ethics 14.5.

EVERYDAY ETHICS 14.5

Jeff Golfman + Woody Harrelson = Tree-Free Paper

Jeff Golfman is a Manitoba entrepreneur who has started and sold several businesses. For the last 15 years he has been interested in producing paper from non-wood fibre, and in particular, agricultural fibre such as wheat straw. He noticed that Prairie farmers had to dispose of straw after harvesting their fields. This straw was sometimes burnt which produced carbon and proposed a health risk. Producing paper from wheat straw was difficult as long fibres were necessary to give paper its strength and straw fibres were short.

Woody Harrelson, actor and environmental activist, was interested in green manufacturing and the production of tree-paper caught his attention. Harrelson became aware of Golfman's efforts, met with Jeff, and together they became the co-founders of Prairie Paper Inc. Harrelson has invested in the project, promoted the product, and attracted other investors. Prairie Paper manufactures Step Forward Paper™, a revolutionary copy paper made up of 80 percent wheat straw waste and 20 percent Wood-Fibre, which is FSC ® certified.

Prairie Paper started selling photocopier paper in 2012 and later professional grade paper at several retailers including Staples and Basics. The paper is produced in India as there was no paper mill in Canada capable of producing it. Plans to construct a mill in Canada are underway but there are financing and raw material supply challenges.

Once a good has been used by the consumer, it can be disposed of as waste in a landfill or it can become a recyclable product. As a recyclable product, two alternative means of disposal exist: incineration or reuse. Incineration can be used to generate energy, which in turn can be utilized by consumers or manufacturers, although the process discharges some pollution to the environment.

Reuse involves collecting and sorting items, and is often performed by corporations. New technology for processing recycled materials and the availability of markets for recycled materials are making recycling businesses more viable. But problems still exist. The public has been so enthusiastic about recycling materials that the capacity of recycling facilities has been overtaxed. Markets for recycled materials have not grown fast enough to keep pace with the collection of recyclable materials. Once processing of the materials has occurred, they are recycled as raw materials in the manufacturing process.

Canadians are great users and abusers of energy, and growth in energy consumption has been levelling off only recently. As consumption rises, additional sources of energy must be found, placing demands on the environment. Hydro sites and petroleum production areas must be established. Furthermore, preserving the environment adds costs to energy that consumers may not be aware of.

Business is taking many actions to conserve energy. Companies are reducing their consumption in producing and marketing goods and services as well as in the construction of energy-efficient buildings. Also, corporations are introducing products that will enable consumers to conserve energy.

LO 14.6 Measuring and Reporting on Environmental Sustainability

Business can use several measures of sustainability to audit, monitor, and evaluate its environmental performance. These measures have been developed by business organizations, non-governmental organizations, and government agencies; some of these are described in Responsibility for Ethics 14.5.

⚖️ **RESPONSIBILITY FOR ETHICS 14.5**

Environmental Sustainability Measures and Standards

- *Coalition for Environmentally Responsible Economies (Ceres)*—Ceres is a non-profit organization comprising investors and environmental organizations who work with corporations to address sustainability challenges such as climate change. (As a matter of interest, Ceres is the Roman goddess of fertility and agriculture.) Its network of investors, companies and public interest groups to accelerate and expand the adoption of sustainable business practices and solutions to build a healthy global economy.

- *International Organization for Standardization (ISO) Relating to the Environment*—ISO is an international non-governmental organization comprising standards institutions in 162 countries. It provides standards for environmental management with its ISO 14000 family of International Standards including ISO 14064 and ISO 14065 to help organizations to quantify their greenhouse gas emissions and communicate on them, and ISO 14001 and ISO 50001 promote good practice in environmental and energy management.

- *International Institute for Sustainable Development (IISD)*—IISD is a Canadian-based, not-for-profit organization promoting change toward sustainable development. It is working to develop, enhance, and apply measurement and assessment tools to assist business in better managing environmental issues.

The indicators used to evaluate environmental performance are extensive. Examples include the following:

- Type and amount of materials used to provide the good or service, and cooperation with suppliers
- Source of energy and efficiency of use
- Source and quality of water
- Impact on biodiversity; that is, impact on location of operations, land use, nature, and species
- Reduction of emissions, effluents, and waste including hazardous materials
- Design of products and services to minimize impact on the environment
- Compliance with environmental regulations
- Use of efficient transportation mode[42]

Chapter 9 discussed the approaches to measuring and reporting corporate social responsibility and sustainability. Most of the measures discussed there apply to environmental sustainability reporting. An example is the Network for Business Sustainability's guide for measuring environmental impacts. The guide comprises four steps: Step 1 defines success by identifying pressures and establishing goals for addressing them; Step 2 decides what to measure for materials, energy, water, biodiversity, emissions, products and services, compliance, and transport; and Step 3 determines how to measure impacts, for example through life cycle analysis or environmental footprint, and to value them through ecosystem service valuation, or environmental input–output modelling. Finally, Step 4 incorporates the environmental measures into management decision making.[43]

Many corporations have prepared environmental policy statements or codes. The purpose of environmental codes is much the same as it is for codes of ethics: to increase awareness of the issue throughout the organization and to signal to other stakeholders that the corporation is active in this area. Many corporations are assisted in practising environmental ethics and sustainability using standards or codes established by industry associations. Corporations are being recognized for their efforts at minimizing their impact on the environment.

The ethical approaches used to describe decisions in environmental reports were more likely to use the rule-based and utilitarian ethics approaches according to a study by Leanne Morrison et al. while stakeholders not as closely associated with the corporation viewed them using a virtue ethics approach. There appeared to be a difference in how external stakeholders viewed or understood the ethical decision. This led to a gap between how the environment is described in corporate reports and stakeholders perceptions of the corporation's environmental impacts. As a result, there is a question of whether or not environmental reports are written in a way to which stakeholders can relate. This gap reduces the possibility of meaningful and effective stakeholder engagement on environmental issues.[44]

LO 14.7 Dissenting Views on the Environment

Not everyone agrees that business should be playing a leading role in protecting the environment. Some business journalists are particularly critical of sustainability for a variety of reasons:

- The concept is difficult to define and understand.
- It means stopping, or constraining, economic development.
- It implies that capitalism is unsustainable and morally lacking.
- It lacks understanding of markets and the moralistic system of markets.
- Executives are being misled into responding to it as a social issue, and the interest many have is merely as a public relations exercise.[45]

Many researchers have challenged environmentalism and sustainability; a prominent critic's view is described in Responsibility for Ethics 14.6.

RESPONSIBILITY FOR ETHICS 14.6

Bjørn Lomborg and The Skeptical Environmentalist

Dissenting views on the state of the environment exist. A controversial one was presented by Bjørn Lomborg, a Danish statistician, in his book *The Skeptical Environmentalist: Measuring the Real State of the World.* He challenged widely held beliefs that the global climate was getting worse, and even claimed that it was actually improving. The main points of his argument were that green activists and the media are overstating the environmental problems, technology that can reduce the damage is improving, Western lifestyles are environmentally sustainable, and the Kyoto Protocol was bad policy and too costly. He used statistics to support his position and was accused of misleading research; these charges were later dismissed. In 2004, he and others organized the Copenhagen Consensus Center, a think tank that increases awareness of the best ways to spend development money on addressing the major challenges facing the planet. In 2012, these challenges were as follows: armed conflict, biodiversity, chronic disease, climate change, education, hunger and malnutrition, infectious diseases, natural disasters, population growth, and water and sanitation. A second book, *Cool It: The Skeptical Environmentalist's Guide to Global Warming,* is also a film documentary and makes the case that many of the expensive and elaborate solutions to climate change will have little impact on the environment. Lomborg believes most solutions are based on emotional rather than strictly scientific assumptions.

Adding to these dissenting views are the mixed reactions received from consumers. It is not easy to interpret public opinion, as illustrated by consumption patterns, concern for jobs, and the reluctance to pay for improvements.

- Despite polls that confirm the concern Canadians have for the environment, consumers still purchase environmentally unfriendly products. Canadians still lead the world in energy consumption and generate the most household garbage.
- Canadians express strong views about conserving forests, reducing pollution, and halting hydroelectric projects. But if job losses result, their concerns about the environment are reduced.
- As most actions to improve environmental quality cost money, the issue becomes one of who will pay—that is, government, business, or consumers. Ultimately, the consumer and/or taxpayer pays, and many are unwilling to assume the costs. Most direct charges to consumers are resented.

Public opinion may express concern for the environment, but this concern is not always reflected in consumption patterns, the desire for jobs at the expense of the environment, and the reluctance to pay. These dissenting views leave corporations and managers uncertain about the course of action to follow.

A poll of Canadian business leaders also indicated that they are not serious about the environment. Only 12 percent had a policy for auditing the impact of greenhouse gases from their operations. While 83 percent thought a corporation's responsibility was to earn a return for shareholders, 56 percent did indicate that corporations had an obligation to adopt low-emission environmental practices. Many of the respondents doubted the reliability of the science behind climate change, and some thought Kyoto was a scam.[46]

The contradictions are illustrated further by what appears to be a paradox. Everyday Ethics 14.6 gives some common inconsistencies in various initiatives that are promoted as being good for the environment but also have unintended consequences. Some researchers have argued that a greater environmental paradox exists. The Millennium Ecosystem Assessment concluded that the capacity of ecosystems to provide services is low, which should mean that human well-being is declining. The Human Development Index, which measures literacy, life expectancy, and income, is improving in both rich and poor countries. The researchers are questioning why this is the case and what the implications are for society.[47]

EVERYDAY ETHICS 14.6

Paradoxical Environmentalism

Various stakeholders, governments, NGOs, or consumers often advocate for initiatives they claim will reduce damage to the environment. Many of these initiatives have unintended consequences that do not lead to the results expected. In some, there are trade-offs that reduce the benefits alleged to be gained. These contradictions challenge the course of action for business. The following are some examples that may be labelled "showcase environmentalism" in that they do not result in the environmental benefits claimed:

- *Fluorescent (CF) versus incandescent light bulbs*—Incandescent bulbs may use less energy but they contain mercury and the disposal of these bulbs has not yet been resolved.
- *Electric versus gasoline cars*—Electric cars reduce petroleum emissions but require a lot of energy to make the necessary batteries, not to mention the copper and aluminum needed to build them.
- *Plastic versus other bags*—Single-use plastic bags are environmentally unfriendly. However, decomposable plastic is available. Reusable cloth bags can become contaminated with repeated use.
- *Organic versus regular milk*—Fewer hormones and antibiotics are used in organic milk production but the low yields results in more cows being needed, which requires more feed and produces more methane.
- *Local versus global food*—It is claimed that local food is safer and reduces transportation costs. However, consumer choice is reduced and prices are higher with less competition.

LO 14.8 The Environment: Corporate Opportunities and Challenges

Corporations face many challenges and opportunities as they attempt to develop an environmental ethic and practise sustainable development. These challenges are both opportunities and threats.

The reputations of corporations that make an effort to address the environmental issue are most likely enhanced, and they gain greater prominence in the marketplace. An example of being recognized is the *Corporate Knights'* Clean200 described in Everyday Ethics 14.7. Customers are attracted, as investors might be, after a positive investment screening for environmental matters. Costs are reduced through recycling of materials, better control of pollution, energy conservation, and lower insurance. More competent staff might be attracted, and the corporation becomes better integrated with the local community.

EVERYDAY ETHICS 14.7

***Corporate Knights'* Clean200**

Corporate Knights magazine prepares a list of the 200 cleanest corporations. It uses a "carbon-free definition that captures a larger portion of the economy beyond energy efficiency, green energy, and zero emission and hybrid vehicles." The list excludes "oil and gas companies and utilities that generate less than 50 percent of their power from green sources, the top 100 coal companies measured by reserves, the top 100 oil & gas companies as measured by reserves, as well as all fossil fuel companies, majority fossil-fired utilities, pipeline and oil field services companies, and other fossil fuel-related companies…" The 21 negative screens used also included farm animal welfare, weapons manufacturers, gambling, pornography, and child/forced labour.

The nine Canadian corporations included in the 2019 Clean200 were (ranking in parentheses): Bombardier Inc-B (20); Canadian National Railways Co. (22); Telus Corp. (31); Canadian Solar (64); Stantec (141); Cogeco Communications Inc. (155); Transcontinental Inc. (156); Resolute Forest Products Inc. (176); and WSP Global Inc. (189).

Corporate Knights stated that "the Clean200 companies [have] been experiencing higher growth than the Forbes 2000 list of the world's largest stocks." It also claimed that the trend was clear: "Fossil fuels are disappearing and carbon-free business lines have stepped out of the clean energy niche and now touch the entire economy."

Source: "Introducing the 2019 Clean200, Corporate Knights posted February 19, 2019, at https://www.corporateknights.com/channels/leadership/introducing-2019-clean-200-15505561/ and "2019 Clean200 results," Corporate Knights posted February 19, 2019, at https://www.corporateknights.com/channels/leadership/200-cleanest-corporations-2019-15505560/ both accessed on March 18, 2019. Used with permission.

Business opportunities emerge from the development of new technologies or expertise to address environmental concerns. More efficient ways of producing products are found and better products are marketed. There is increasing evidence that responding to environmental concerns need not be costly, and that profitability can even be improved. The environment itself is an opportunity for some who provide the technology or expertise to address the concerns. Environmental product manufacturers include those that provide equipment for water pollution control, air pollution control, solid waste management, measuring instruments, chemicals for pollution control, and noise control. Examples of environmental services include waste handling, consultation services, assessment and control functions, laboratory services, and environmental research.

Several challenges for corporations exist if the environment is ignored. The corporate image deteriorates, and revenues may suffer as customers prefer products and services less damaging to the environment. Investors become more difficult to attract as the corporations cannot meet the criteria for environmental and ethical screening. Material and production costs may increase faster than for corporations practising reduction and recycling. The financial penalties are becoming higher and directors and managers are being held legally responsible for pollution. Insurance premiums are high for corporations that do not reduce their pollution risk. Alienation may occur from the local community, and failure to act may provoke stricter legislation and regulation.

From a Linear to a Circular Economy

Corporations and societal stakeholders are changing the way they think about the challenges to the environment. One approach is to view the economy as circular instead of linear. The consumption of resources since the industrial revolution can be described as a *linear economy* approach. A linear economy is one where raw materials are used to produce goods or products that are used and not recycled or may be even non-recyclable. This single use of resources is unsustainable as the world is consuming resources 50 percent faster than they are being replaced. A change in approach is needed. Thus, in the past couple of decades, recycling initiatives have resulted in the *reuse economy,* where after use, some goods are recycled and reused in production but the remainder is still waste.

With the world's population and the consumption of goods growing, this reuse economy is not sufficient as resources become scarce and there are damaging impacts on the environment. As a result, environmental NGOs and some governments and corporations are advocating a change in approach referred to as the **circular economy.** A circular economy is restorative and regenerative by design so materials constantly flow around a *closed loop* system preserving value rather than being used once and then discarded.

There are many features of a circular economy. Manufacturers must make efficient utilization of resources, design goods to eliminate waste, and build goods to last. Goods produced must be not only reusable, but capable of being repaired, refurbished, and repurposed. Energy used in the provision of goods must come from renewable sources. Businesses should offer programs to take back, trade in, and buy back goods to remarket. These types of initiatives are also referred to as *extended producer responsibility* (EPR) and *life cycle thinking* (described in Chapter 12), which requires businesses to assume the financial and operational responsibility for the efficient use and recovery of resources. Governments must enact legislation that will move business and society toward a more circular economy.[48] One organization advocating for a circular economy is the Circular Economy Leadership Coalition (CELC) described in Responsibility for Ethics 14.7.

RESPONSIBILITY FOR ETHICS 14.7

Circular Economy Leadership Coalition (CELC)

CELC's vision is to "make Canada a world leader in building a sustainable, prosperous, zero-waste, low-carbon-emitting Circular Economy that benefits the lives of people at home and abroad." The circular economy generates economic activity; aligns environmental and economic priorities; enables governments to increase companies' competitiveness with better policy and regulatory tools; and is an engine of innovation and a solution to some of the world's most pressing environmental challenges.

One of its initiatives is identifying a plastics circular economy that recirculates materials, keeping plastics out of the environment and in the economy. The report outlines the barriers and benefits to a circular economy in Canada and lists solutions and recommendations for policy-makers.

Below are two examples of corporations implementing a circular economy approach:

- Unilever Canada: The company is reconsidering plastic packaging toward circular economy thinking. It recognizes plastic packaging as a growing problem and is transforming its use of plastic packaging by 2025.

- IKEA Canada is taking steps to become a circular, climate-positive business. Included in these plans are use of renewable energy, wood and cotton from sustainable sources, and the more efficient use of water.

The management of the natural environment is a challenge for managers. Business must take on some of the responsibility for the environment, and many have already. For others, it is a matter of what type of response is appropriate and when. As an ideal, corporations should be evolving an environmental ethic to enhance sustainable development in society.

Your advice to Vivian . . .

This vignette illustrated how an everyday purchase decision can involve several economic, social, and environmental issues. The decision also illustrates a dilemma, and is a paradox for a consumer facing complex and contradictory information. It is difficult for consumers to be aware of all the issues, much less to research them extensively; this is but one decision among many on any given trip to the grocery store. The ultimate decision is up to the consumer because there is no authority to provide a definitive answer.

Summary

- Concern for the natural environment is widespread in society and business has a responsibility to respond. Responding to this concern is challenging as many stakeholders and issues influence corporations. Corporations must develop an environmental ethic or set of values relating to their practices toward sustainable development in the economy. Each corporation must develop strategies and practices to meet its own and its stakeholders' needs today while ensuring that future resources will be available. Environmental concerns are summarized in the descriptions of several topics: acid rain, air pollution, ecosystems, energy production and consumption, nature and wildlife, ozone, pollution, waste management, and water quality. Together, these topics influence climate change or global warming. (LO 14.1)

- Governments have implemented environmental policies through legislation and regulations and the establishment of various agencies. Environmental assessments by businesses are now commonplace. However, the federal government is reducing its regulation of environmental impacts. (LO 14.2)

- Influence of a different type comes from environmental non-governmental organizations (ENGOs). Hundreds of such organizations exist and corporations are learning how to respond to or cooperate with them. (LO 14.3)

- Another possibility is to leave solutions to environmental concerns to market-driven initiatives. Instead of being required by governments to respond, it is argued that relying on market forces is more effective. Emissions trading and offsets are two examples. (LO 14.4)

- When corporations act on environmental concerns, the responses must be managed with appropriate organizational structures, environment management systems, and corporate strategies. As corporations attempt to respond to environmental concerns, there are implications for all the major functions of business: financial management, marketing, human resources, and operations/production. (LO 14.5)

- Many sustainability measures and standards have been developed by ENGOs, business organizations, and industry associations. Indicators that measure a corporation's environmental performance are used. Many corporations issue elaborate environmental reports. (LO 14.6)

- Dissenting views on the environment are held in the business community and by other stakeholders. Not all businesspersons believe that climate change is a problem. Even public attitudes are mixed in that surveys indicate consumers are concerned, but this concern is not always reflected in purchasing decisions. This inconsistency complicates business decision making. (LO 14.7)

- The environment presents corporations with opportunities and threats. But, many corporations are developing an environmental ethic that achieves sustainable development. (LO 14.8)

Key Terms

Commons

Environmental ethic

Sustainable development

Business sustainable development

Acid rain

Ecosystem

Ozone

Waste management

Climate change (global warming)

Greenhouse gases (GHG)

Environmental non-governmental organizations (ENGOs)

Standard environmentalism

Market environmentalism

Carbon pricing

Cap-and-trade

Output-based price system

Offsets (emissions-reduction credits)

Carbon capture and storage (CCS)

Green marketing

Circular economy

Critical Thinking and Discussion Questions

1. Is the concept of the commons applicable today? Give examples.
2. What is the relationship between an environmental ethic and the theories of ethics?
3. What should be government's role in influencing business' response to environmental concerns?
4. What should be the relationship between corporations and ENGOs?
5. How can market forces help achieve sustainable development?
6. Should carbon pricing be imposed by the government?
7. What strategic approach should a corporation implement regarding society's concerns about the environment?
8. When evaluating major projects, should there be a requirement for an economic assessment as well as an environmental assessment?

9. What purposes do sustainability measures and standards serve?

10. Why do dissenting views exist on the seriousness of the danger of business activities to the environment?

11. Do the opportunities presented by sustainable development outweigh the threats?

12. How close is society to a circular economy?

Cases

14.1 A DOG'S "ECO-PAWPRINT"

Geraldine Churchill had graduated from her business program and had accepted a job with an accounting firm. This meant she was leaving home and moving to another city where she would be living alone. For company and security, she planned to get a pet, most likely a dog adopted from an animal shelter.

She had given this move some thought and had done some research. Thirty-five percent of Canadian households had a dog as a pet. Articles on pets identified some benefits of dog ownership. They enhanced the owner's health by increasing physical activity, for example, dog owners walked farther than others. There were psychological benefits as a dog provided companionship and there was trend with young persons to have pets for this reason.

There were also challenges. There was a risk of the dog contracting an infection, so hand hygiene was important. The food would have to be carefully selected to insure the appropriate and adequate nutrition. Health care was critical and veterinary and drug expenses could run into thousands of dollars. Grooming was necessary and would have to be done by Geraldine or at a pet grooming shop. Dogs required some training and lessons would be necessary. It may be necessary to find a dog daycare, and if she travelled, it would be necessary to board the dog somewhere. It was estimated that owning a dog could cost $2,500 and more per year. Owning a dog meant assuming responsibilities and considerable expenses.

A big surprise for Geraldine was the "eco-pawprint" of a dog on the environment. First of all, there was the amount of food a dog eats. The environmental imprint for food was substantial including the land, fertilizers, pesticides, water, energy, production equipment, packaging and transportation. Much of the dog food sold contains more protein than necessary and can be as much as humans consume. This adds a burden to the environment and takes resources that could be used to feed under nourished persons in the world. Also, she read that dogs in Canada produced over 600,000 tonnes of solid waste per year most of which goes to landfills. One article claimed that owning a dog was more environmentally unfriendly than operating a vehicle.

Geraldine was rethinking her plans for a pet.

Questions

1. What are the issue(s) and stakeholders involved?

2. Are pets a burden on the environment?

3. What should Geraldine do?

14.2 IS DR. SEUSS MISLEADING CHILDREN?

For generations, books by Dr. Seuss have been read to and by children. His books were often commentaries on social and political issues; for example, *Yertle the Turtle* had a theme based on totalitarianism, *The Sneetches* dealt with discrimination, and *How The Grinch Stole Christmas* criticized the commercialization of holidays. *The Lorax* discusses the threat to the environment.

The principal character in *The Lorax* is the Once-ler, who represents business. He cuts down the beautiful Truffula Trees to make a Thneed, which could be used for many things including shirts, hats, or gloves. The Lorax, a small, "mossy" creature who spoke for the trees and animals in the forest, asked the Once-ler to stop cutting down the Truffula Trees. But the Once-ler recognized the market potential of the Thneed and he set up a factory to manufacture even more of them.

The business grew bigger and the Once-ler cut down more and more trees to meet the demand. Animals that depended on the Truffula Trees lost their source of food. Smog and water pollution were created by the factories. The Once-ler said he had rights and was going to continue his business expansion. Eventually the last Truffula Tree was down, ending the production of Thneeds. The Once-ler realized his mistake and asked the readers to take the last Truffula Tree seed and plant it, take care of it, and protect it from those who want to chop it down.

Dr. Seuss wanted to make several points: the planet faces environmental problems such as pollution and the depletion of resources; these problems have serious implications for society; and there is some urgency necessary to address them. The story delivers a message that business is rapidly destroying the environment and that things will not change until people start to care and do something to stop the destruction.

In March 2012 the animated movie *The Lorax* was released to theatres in 2-D and 3-D. Most reviewers felt that it followed the book's pro-environmentalism and anti-capitalism themes. The movie stressed the dangers of over-consumption and corporate greed, and the virtue of conservation. There was a consensus that the movie was very colourful, the musical numbers were mediocre, and the voices of the characters were excellent. Many reviewers felt that young audiences might be influenced by the warnings against rampant capitalism which led to deforestation. In 2017, *The Lorax* opened as a musical/play in Toronto and a reviewer stated that its message seemed more pertinent than ever.

The story both in print and on-screen is very pessimistic and treats the business system harshly, and may be giving children an overly negative view of business. The positive aspects of the business system are not discussed; for example, explaining how business is essential to ensuring a high standard of living, how it creates employment, and how it provides innovative products and services. The story does not suggest that the environment and business activity can coexist.

Questions

1. Is it appropriate that children's stories contain anti-business messages? What are the ethical implications of this practice?

2. Today, who performs the role of the Lorax?

3. How would Dr. Seuss view sustainable development?

4. What other media contain messages that are critical of business?

5. Will you read *The Lorax* to children (including your own)?

Today CSR extends around the world.
Used © Janrysavy/Getty Images

CHAPTER 15

Globalization and Business Responsibilities

LEARNING OUTCOMES

After studying this chapter, you will be able to:

LO 15.1 Define globalization, identify related issues, and list the pros and cons.

LO 15.2 Describe the role international non-governmental organizations play in influencing business.

LO 15.3 Name the main supranational institutions influencing globalization.

LO 15.4 Understand the connection between globalization and Canadian business and society.

LO 15.5 Become familiar with the international standards that are guiding and influencing the behaviour of multinational corporations.

LO 15.6 Appreciate the special challenges confronting business as a result of globalization.

LO 15.7 Link the reduction of poverty in developing countries to aspects of capitalism.

What would you do if...?

Claudia Merchant was viewing a website that offered for sale an Hermès Birkin handbag that was exactly what she had been looking for. She had always wanted a bag of this type and this one was being sold for a fraction of the price. Claudia began filling out the order form, and then paused.

Her Business Law professor had devoted a whole class lecture to discuss the counterfeiting and pirating of intellectual property, which was a major issue in the globalization of business. Claudia recalled her referring to an intellectual property crime statistics report by the RCMP. The main types of products involved were footwear, clothing and accessories, copyrighted works, consumer electronics, and pharmaceuticals. In one year, the RCMP had seized more than $38 million in counterfeit and pirated goods with China being the primary source.

The professor emphasized the seriousness of the problem, explaining why it even threatened Canada's economic integrity. Local merchants were unable to compete and sometimes failed as a result. Because the products were produced overseas, jobs in Canada were lost. These products were not produced to Canadian standards and often threatened the health and safety of consumers. Real dangers were associated with purchasing counterfeit medications, electrical and electronic devices, alcohol and food products, toys, cosmetics, condoms, and sporting equipment. In a report, the Canadian Anti-Counterfeiting Network stated there were some troubling ethics about the culture of piracy in Canada and that more had to be done to change the view that it was ethically acceptable to purchase these goods.

According to Claudia's professor, counterfeiting and piracy were big business globally and were very profitable for those involved. Another aspect of the problem, according to the RCMP report, was that organized crime, criminal gangs, and even terrorist organizations increasingly were involved. Consumers were often attracted to luxury products, such as the Hermès handbag Claudia was interested in, by prices that saved them a lot of money. Many of these street vendors and Internet sites appeared quite legitimate and induced consumers to make innocent purchases.

The picture of the handbag was very clear and there were close-ups of the stitching and finish. The handbag looked legitimate, but the price was very low. Claudia started wondering about the website, and realized she did not recognize the name of the corporation. She wondered whether or not she should go ahead and purchase. The handbag would really go well with several of her outfits.

What is your advice to Claudia?

Globalization is placing challenges on Canadian business, including new economic, ethical, and environmental responsibilities. Canadian corporations have no choice but to face the challenges presented by the more complex world economy that is evolving. Many believe that international business activities have the potential for distributing goods and services more equitably and for improving the standard of living for all people. Corporations subject to market forces and managed by private, rather than government, employees are believed to be more efficient at supplying the goods and services needed by the citizens of any country.

Globalization is not a new phenomenon. Historians have recorded trade in goods between regions since ancient times. Civilizations around the Mediterranean Sea traded among each other over land and by sea. Indigenous Peoples in the Americas traded with one another. As transportation and communications technologies improved, European traders ventured farther to the Far East and the Americas. At times freer trade flourished, but over the centuries there have been periods of protectionism when countries believed it was in their best interests to restrict international commerce. The most recent occurrence of this was in the twentieth century until about 1980; after two World Wars and the Great Depression of the 1930s, governments became very protectionist and began to perform more of the economic functions in society. Gradually, this view changed, and in the last two decades of the century attitudes toward trade and market systems evolved. Today, this new view toward trade and markets is referred to as *globalization.*

This chapter describes globalization, its impact on corporations, the challenges associated with it, the standards of conduct that are influencing it, and the emergence of capitalism as the predominant economic system in the world. Throughout the chapter, the increasing complexity of the corporation's economic, ethical, social, and environmental responsibilities in the global marketplace is identified.

LO 15.1 Defining Globalization and the Implications for Business

A general definition of **globalization** is a process of decreasing constraints on the interactions among the nations and peoples of the world. There are several dimensions to globalization; three important ones for business are economic, political, and social or cultural.

Economic globalization involves the integration of fragmented markets into a global economy. The markets for goods and services, information, capital, and labour become worldwide, leading to free trade among nations; although progress has been made, the world has a long way to go before this is fully implemented. Barriers still exist to free trade among nations even through developing nations are now the producers of many goods and services consumed in industrialized economies. This could eventually mean worldwide standards or practices for product quality, pricing, service, and design. This is the type of globalization that is most commonly being referred to when the term is used.[1]

Political globalization is the process by which world power relationships change and there is a loss of sovereignty by the state. The reduced role of the state is replaced by power being assumed by multinational corporations, religious organizations, non-governmental organizations, social movements, and transnational terrorism. New forms of governance emerge, for example United Nations organizations (such as the Global Compact described in Responsibility for Ethics 15.1), the Organisation for Economic Co-operation and Development (OECD), the European Union (EU), and the World Trade Organization (WTO). Thus, economic activity is less hindered by political boundaries.[2]

 RESPONSIBILITY FOR ETHICS 15.1

The United Nations Global Compact

The Global Compact asks corporations to embrace, support, and enact, within their sphere of influence, a set of core values in the areas of human rights, labour standards, the environment, and anti-corruption. More than 9,500 corporations from 160 countries have signed on to the Compact, but only 85 are Canadian. Below are the Ten Principles of the UN Global Compact:

Human Rights

- *Principle 1:* businesses should support and respect the protection of internationally proclaimed human rights; and
- *Principle 2:* make sure that they are not complicit in human rights abuses.

Labour Standards

- *Principle 3:* businesses should uphold the freedom of association and the effective recognition of the right to collective bargaining;
- *Principle 4:* the elimination of all forms of forced and compulsory labour;
- *Principle 5:* the effective abolition of child labour; and
- *Principle 6:* the elimination of discrimination in respect of employment and occupation.

Environment

- *Principle 7:* businesses should support a precautionary approach to environmental challenges;
- *Principle 8:* undertake initiatives to promote greater environmental responsibility; and
- *Principle 9:* encourage the development and diffusion of environmentally friendly technologies.

Anti-Corruption

- *Principle 10:* businesses should work against all forms of corruption, including extortion and bribery.

Source: "The Ten Principles," *The United Nations Global Compact* at https://www.unglobalcompact.org/what-is-gc/mission/principles © 2016 United Nations. Used with permission.

Social or cultural globalization is the emergence of a worldwide cultural system. This system emerges due to a variety of social and cultural activities, including common patterns of consumption, such as demand for American entertainment and brand-name clothing; worldwide sporting events, such as football competitions and the Olympic Games; increasing tourism travel; movements common around the world, such as environmentalism and the trend toward holding business accountable for social and environmental responsibilities; and health problems affecting most of the world, such as AIDS and flu pandemics. As a result, the world is thought of more as a single place.[3]

Globalization increases business' economic, social, and environmental responsibilities, including issues arising from the following:

- Damage to the environment occurring as a result of using natural resources, including pollution and depletion.
- Business' alleged support for oppressive governments.
- Criticism of the marketing practices of many industries and corporations, for example tobacco, pharmaceutical, and baby formula products.
- Businesses associated with the arms trade are blamed for facilitating violence and warfare in various parts of the world.
- The treatment of employees in developing countries, the existence of sweatshops in industrialized as well as developing countries, and the attempts to prevent union formation.
- In many parts of the world, including Canada, Indigenous Peoples are attempting to regain control over ancestral lands.
- Income and gender inequity in developed versus developing countries.
- Genetic modification of plants and animals has aroused concern, as has the patenting of life forms in the production of food.
- Corruption, bribery, and questionable payments are involved with doing business in some countries.

As a result of these issues and others, the desirability of globalization is open to debate.

Globalization has generated considerable controversy. The pros and cons of globalization have been discussed extensively and the main arguments on each side are summarized in Table 15.1. **Globalists**, individuals and organizations that support globalization, make the arguments for globalization; **anti-globalists** are individuals and organizations that oppose globalization or are critical of it.

TABLE 15.1	The Pros and Cons of Globalization
Globalists' Arguments	**Anti-globalists' Arguments**
• Trade is encouraged as it leads to the most efficient production of goods and services from which all gain. • Private corporations and open markets provide better goods and services to society. • Opportunities for employment and higher incomes are enhanced in developing countries. • The standard of living has increased in most developing countries. • The transfer of capital, technology, intellectual property, and even skilled labour occurs. • Several stakeholders benefit, including owners, consumers, suppliers, and employees. • Cost of living reduced in developed countries.	• The expansion of global corporations is undesirable as decisions are based on profit-making or greed. • Conspiracies exist between corporations and governments resulting in any benefits being received by a few. • Unemployment is created in developed economies. • Poverty and inequality increases in the developing economies. • Periodic financial crises are caused disrupting the economies of many countries. • There is destruction of local environments as standards are lowered to attract developments. • The cultures of societies are lost or changed. • Human rights are violated, in particular in relation to sweatshops. • Questionable payments are made to governments or their officials to facilitate business. • Intellectual property is not respected. • The sovereignty of nations is undermined. • Worldwide organizations such as the World Bank, the International Monetary Fund, and the World Trade Organization have too much influence.

Globalization and Freer Trade

One of the features of globalization is economic, as mentioned above. The world economy has increased in the past 50 years as a result of expanding global trade relationships. Various trade organizations have been formed, such as the World Trade Organization (WTO). The WTO is "the only global international organization dealing with the rules of trade between nations." WTO agreements are negotiated and signed by the world's trading nations with the goal of ensuring that trade flows as smoothly, predictably, and freely as possible.[4]

Canada has signed many trade agreements, but only three major ones are well known. The North American Free Trade Agreement (NAFTA) oversees trade among Canada, the United States, and Mexico. It was renegotiated and modernized in 2018 as the United States-Mexico-Canada Agreement (USMCA) but in 2019 had not been confirmed by the three countries. Canada has also signed the Comprehensive Economic and Trade Agreement (CETA) with the European Union and the Comprehensive and Progressive Agreement for Trans-Pacific Trade Partnership (CPTPP) with 11 countries bordering the Pacific Ocean. Ethic issues are involved in trade, whether it is freer or restricted.

The WTO and trade agreements encourage greater trade among countries, improving economic well-being. Although referred to as *free trade* agreements, in practical terms they enable "freer trade" as totally free trade in unlikely. Unfortunately, trade protectionism occurs when barriers, such as tariffs and quotas, are imposed, having a negative impact on economic well-being. In particular, protectionism makes consumers worse off and damages the economies of developing countries. Recently, two world events are threatening globalization. Great Britain's decision to leave the European Union makes trade more challenging, and the United States' decision to not participate in some trade agreements and to become more protectionist by imposing tariffs on some goods appears to counter globalization.

There are winners and losers with globalization but it is unlikely that it will be halted even if its pace is slowed, referred to as **slowbalisation**. Businesspersons, as well as governments, should devise approaches to overcoming some of the downsides of globalization so that even more stakeholders benefit from the process. The existence of international non-governmental organizations, many of which oppose globalization, must be recognized and appropriate responses formulated.

 LO 15.2 Globalization and International Non-governmental Organizations (INGOs)

Business is being made aware of its responsibilities arising from globalization. **International non-governmental organizations (INGOs)** are groups that hold shared values and attitudes about the issues relating to globalization and advocate for changes to improve the conditions in developing countries. Many issues arise in addition to those listed, and INGOs are putting pressure on corporations and governments. Many INGOs are opposed to globalization and attempt to counterbalance what they consider the excessive influence of multinational corporations. Some address all issues of globalization, while others focus on human rights or the environment. Sometimes INGOs are referred to as transnational non-government actors (TNGAs), or transnational social movement organizations (TSMOs). Responsibility for Ethics 15.2 gives examples of INGOs.

 RESPONSIBILITY FOR ETHICS 15.2

Examples of INGOs

- *Corporate Watch*—This is an INGO whose purpose is to hold corporations accountable for their actions. It investigates and exposes corporate violations of human rights, environmental crimes, and fraud and corruption around the world. It works to foster global justice, to promote independent media activism, and to gain democratic control over corporations.

- *Oxfam International*—"Oxfam International is a confederation of 19 organizations working together with partners and communities in more than 90 countries to find lasting solutions to poverty, suffering and injustice." Its vision is "a just world without poverty" by helping to create lasting solutions to the injustice of poverty.

- *Amnesty International*—Amnesty International (AI) is a worldwide organization with 7 million members, supporters, and subscribers in 150 countries and territories. It campaigns for internationally recognized human rights; one current campaign is "Corporate Accountability." In this campaign, AI maintains that globalization through the existence of multinational corporations has changed the world we live in and presents new and complex challenges for the protection of human rights.

- *Greenpeace International*—Greenpeace is an independent global organization focusing on worldwide threats to the planet's biodiversity and environment. Issues addressed include climate change, the well-being of forests and oceans, food, toxic chemicals, and nuclear energy.

Such organizations have received considerable attention, particularly with demonstrations at world economic gatherings. A coalition of civil society and environmental INGOs plus labour organizations has disrupted various WTO and World Bank meetings, and G8 and G20 Summits. In addition, their publications, media events, and websites are influential.

INGOs believe that they have a role to play in globalization by representing those with the little or no voice, including the poor, sick, and uneducated; the victims of civil wars; and Indigenous Peoples. This role is an important contribution in civil society and cannot be ignored by governments or corporations. Not all INGOs are alike or hold the same views, and not all are opposed to globalization. However, they do believe that poverty and inequality must be addressed. They are concerned that rich countries are becoming better off and that rich persons within countries are becoming richer at the expense of the poor. It is believed that corporate influence is dominating government decision making and that corporate ownership of the media prevents alternative views from being aired.

On the other hand there is increasing cooperation between corporations and INGOs, as described in Chapter 13 where the pros and cons of partnerships with NGOs are discussed. Everyday Ethics 15.1 describes a partnership between INGOs and a corporation in the forestry industry.

 EVERYDAY ETHICS 15.1

Domtar Corporation, Ecopaper, and INGOs

Domtar is a large Canadian manufacturer of fibre-based products including communication papers, specialty and packaging papers and absorbent hygiene products.

Domtar and INGOs Forest Stewardship Council® and Rainforest Alliance have collaborated to verify Domtar's EarthChoice® Office Paper as being environmentally friendly. The Forest Stewardship Council® (FSC®) certification "ensures that forests are well managed, habitats are protected and that the rights of local communities are respected." Domtar also has the Rainforest Alliance Certified™ seal (a green frog) along with the FSC® trademark on qualifying products.

Domtar must maintain forests according to FSC standards relating to biodiversity, protection of water sheds, and support the rights of those whose livelihoods depends on the forest. Rainforest Alliance certification assesses Domtar's operations through audits that include species inventories, forest inspections, management plan reviews, and with input from interested parties. EarthChoice® Office Paper is also endorsed by the World Wildlife Fund and displays an Ecolabel® and the recycling symbol.

LO 15.3   Institutions of Globalization

No one global governance institution exists as such, but several organizations have an influence on the global economy beyond that of a particular nation. This type of organization is known as a **supranational institution**, an international organization that transcends national boundaries where the member states share in decision making on particular issues pertaining to the members. They are usually viewed as economic agencies, but they can also have an impact on the ethical, social, and environmental responsibilities of the corporation. INGOs are often critical of such institutions as they promote globalization. Five supranational institutions are described: the World Bank, the International Monetary Fund, the International Labour Organization, the World Trade Organization, and the World Economic Forum.

The World Bank was established with the objective of providing financing to enhance the economic development of countries after the Second World War. Today it focuses its financial and technical assistance to developing countries in Africa, Asia,

Latin America, and the Middle East. The bank is owned by the 189 member countries and aims to reduce poverty and improve living conditions in developing countries. Low-interest loans, interest-free credit, and grants are given for education, health, infrastructure, communications, and other purposes.[5]

The International Monetary Fund (IMF) is "an organization of 189 countries, working to foster global monetary cooperation, secure financial stability, facilitate international trade, promote high employment and sustainable economic growth, and reduce poverty."[6] Although monetary and financial policies are a focus for the organization, it is also concerned with the social impacts of these policies.

The International Labour Organization (ILO) is the United Nations agency that "seeks the promotion of social justice and internationally recognized human and labour rights." It formulates standards of basic labour rights including the freedom of association, the right to organize, collective bargaining, abolition of forced labour, and equality of opportunity and treatment. This organization has been influential in the area of accountability for sweatshops in developing countries. It also established the World Commission on the Social Dimension of Globalization to assist people coping with changes brought about by globalization. The Commission is searching for innovative ways to combine economic, social, and environmental objectives.[7]

The World Trade Organization (WTO), which came into force on January 1, 1995, is an international body that oversees and coordinates agreements reducing trade barriers. There have been many NGO demonstrations at WTO meetings, mostly opposing the liberalization of trade. The issues identified include the unfairness to developing nations, the abuse of workers, the low prices received by producers, the arbitrary practices of multinational corporations, and the loss of jobs.

The World Economic Forum (WEF) is different than other supranational institutions. Under Swiss law, the role of the Forum is as an independent International Institution for Public-Private Cooperation, not created or sponsored by governments. It meets with leading political, business, and other leaders in society to influence global, regional, and industry agendas. It claims that its activities are influenced "by a unique institutional culture founded on the stakeholder theory, which asserts that an organization is accountable to all parts of society." WEF is studying significant global challenges and it states that its areas of impact are "building awareness and co-operation; shaping mindsets and agendas and driving collective action." It prepares reports on the broad range of global issues and a World Economic Forum Annual Meeting is held in Davos-Klosters, Switzerland, each January.[8]

> Want to learn more about **the World Economic Forum**?

These institutions are viewed as being focused on economic matters, but as outlined above they are also influential in social, ethical, and environmental issues confronting the countries they are attempting to assist.

LO 15.4 Globalization and Canadian Business and Society

Canadian business is influenced by globalization and must respond; there are several implications. With global markets emerging, Canadian business is under pressure to forge international links as there will be less distinction between domestic and foreign enterprises. Ownership and control of business will be less important than performance at supplying goods and services. Canada, and Canadian business, has no choice but to meet the challenges of global market restructuring as new trading agreements are completed by governments. Several developing nations are becoming major economies—for example India, Brazil, Russia, and China—and Canadian business must prepare for the opportunities and threats that are emerging.

Canada must attract more investment in plants that further process our natural resources. Such investment will lead to productivity growth, increased competitiveness, and greater employment opportunities. On the other hand, Canadian direct investment abroad is a critical element in globalization. Businesspeople must be willing to invest money in operations outside of Canada. Governments must "think globally" when developing programs and policies, and be aware of the trend to globalization and encourage business to react appropriately.

In this global economy, Canadian corporations must be competitive with those from other countries in order to also behave as responsible corporate citizens. One measure of this ability to compete is the "Competitiveness Scoreboard" published annually by the International Institute for Management Development, which surveys the competitiveness of most national economies. Four factors are measured: economic performance, government efficiency, business efficiency, and infrastructure. In 2018 Canada ranked 10th out of 63 and on the four factors its rankings were 13th, 9th, 7th, and 7th. Canada's ranking will face challenges in the future as its lowest scores were in international trade, employment, public finance, and productivity and efficiency.[9]

A second measure of competitiveness is provided by the "Global Competitiveness Report" published by the World Economic Forum, an independent international organization committed to improving the state of the world by engaging leaders in partnerships to shape global, regional, and industry agendas. A Global Competitiveness Index provides an overview of a country's productivity and competitiveness based on nine factors. In 2018 Canada ranked 10th but Canada's score is being dragged down by weakness in infrastructure, information and communications technology, product market, market size, and innovation capacity.[10]

How well Canadian business is able to compete in the global market influences how well Canadian corporations can respond to social, ethical, and environmental responsibilities associated with globalization. Many Canadian corporations with global operations willingly accept, or are being pressured to accept, these additional responsibilities.

Many Canadian corporations are attempting to behave as responsible corporate citizens in the countries where they operate. Some of these corporations are identified by the Global 100 Most Sustainable Corporations in the World ranking described in Everyday Ethics 15.2.

 EVERYDAY ETHICS 15.2

Corporate Knights' Global 100

Each year *Corporate Knights: The Magazine for Clean Capitalism* compiles a list of the Global 100 Most Sustainable Corporations in the World. The five priority metrics used in the selection are:
Universal Key Performance Indicators (apply to all corporations)

- Percentage Tax Paid
- Pension Fund Status
- Supplier Sustainability
- Women in Executive Management
- Women on Boards of Directors
- Sustainability Pay Link (executive pay tied to sustainability)
- Sanctions Deductions (fines, penalties, and settlements)
- Clean Revenue (from products considered "clean")

Other Key Performance Indicators (KPIs) are scored when considered "priority KPIs" for the industry. These are:

- Energy, GHG, water, waste, volatile organic compounds, nitrogen oxides, sulphur oxide, and particular matter productivity.
- Injuries, fatalities.

The six Canadian corporations in the 2019 rankings were: Bombardier Inc. (22nd); Teck Resources Limited (37th); Sun Life Financial Inc. (41st); Suncor Energy Inc. (44th); Canadian Tire Corporation (91st), and Celestica Inc. (94th).

Source: "2019 Global 100 results," *Corporate Knights* at https://www.corporateknights.com/reports/2019-global-100/2019-global-100-results-15481153/ accessed March 20, 2019, and "Overview of Corporate Knights Rating Methodology, *Corporate Knights* at ttps://www.corporateknights.com/reports/2019-global-100/2019-global-100-methodology-15353681/ accessed March 20, 2019. Used with permission.

The Canadian mining industry operates around the world and responsible corporate citizenship is particularly important. A specific example of this citizenship is provided by Agnico Eagle Mines Limited and described in Everyday Ethics 15.3.

 EVERYDAY ETHICS 15.3

Agnico Eagle Mines Limited as a Corporate Citizen in Mexico

Agnico Eagle is a Canadian gold-mining company producing precious metals, gold and silver, from eight mines located in Canada, Finland, and Mexico with exploration and development activities in each of these regions as well as in the United States and Sweden. The company is committed to responsible mining and a sustainable development policy that "reflects an emphasis on health and wellness, our commitment to the protection of Human Rights, and a commitment to minimizing impacts to environment and risks associated with the management of tailings and water."

A focus is respecting the communities in which Agnico Eagle operates and this is exemplified by its social investment program (SIP) in the Mexican mines. After consultations with local stakeholders, a program was designed to focus on four areas of need to improve the health and socioeconomic well-being of local communities:

- *Education*—rehabilitated and modernized community schools at the preschool, elementary, and high school levels

- *Infrastructure and environment*—purchased waste collection equipment and established new waste storage areas that helped to promote a cleaner environment

- *Social development*—built a sport centre and partnered with the government of Mexico to build a cultural centre

- *Community wellness initiatives*—partnered with a local Lions Club and the Center for Recycling and Distributing Lenses to provide new glasses to children with vision problems and recycled lenses to older adults

As Canada is the home for many resource industry corporations such as mining and petroleum, it is important for these corporations to have corporate responsibility and sustainability programs. One reason for this is the fact that there are several international standards of conduct ensuring accountability of these corporations.

LO 15.5 Standards of Conduct and Accountability for Global Business

Numerous codes, guidelines, or principles provide direction to corporations operating in the global economy. These measures are developed by various INGOs, some in cooperation with business, supranational institutions, business associations, or other civil society organizations. Corporations can use the standards to assess their response to social and environmental responsibilities relating to international business.

Standards of conduct apply to the worldwide operations of a multinational corporation (MNC) and are applicable to all, although compliance is voluntary. Responsibility for Ethics 15.3 lists some of the common standards, but many others exist.

 RESPONSIBILITY FOR ETHICS 15.3

Global Standards of Conduct Developed by International Organizations

- *Caux Round Table: Caux Principles*—The "Caux Principles of Business" were developed by a network of senior business leaders from both industrialized and developing nations. The principles cover responsibilities to all stakeholders, economic and social impact of business, business behaviour, respect for rules, support for multilateral trade, respect for the environment, and avoidance of illicit operations.

- *OECD "Guidelines for Multinational Enterprises"*—This is one of the oldest guidelines and has influenced corporate behaviour around the world. Clauses include disclosure, employment and industrial relations, environment, combating bribery, consumer interests, science and technology, competition, and taxation.

- *Principles for Global Corporate Responsibility: Benchmarks for Measuring Business Performance*—This is a comprehensive set of more than 100 principles, 129 criteria, and 118 benchmarks to measure business' social and environmental performance. It was developed by interfaith organizations from several countries including the Taskforce on the Churches and Corporate Responsibility of Canada (TCCR, now KAIROS-Canada).

- *The Equator Principles (EPs)*—The Equator Principles is system for determining, assessing, and managing environmental and social risk in projects; it is primarily intended to provide a minimum standard for due diligence to support responsible risk decision-making. The EPs have been adopted by 82 financial institutions in 36 countries.

- *The United Nations' Principles for Responsible Investment (PRI)*—The Principles were formulated in partnership with the UNEP Finance Initiative and the UN Global Compact and developed by an international group of institution investors. The initiative has prompted as environmental, social, and corporate governance (ESG) issues can affect the performance of investment portfolios.

- *United Nations Global Compact Network*—In 1999, the World Economic Forum developed a set of principles referred to as the Global Compact, covering human rights, labour, and environment.
- *Global Reporting Initiative (GRI)*—GRI guidelines cover all aspects of economic, social, and environmental reporting and apply to multinational corporations. Refer to Chapter 9 for a description.

The following topics are covered in standards of conduct, but vary from one standard to another:

- *Political factors*—MNCs must respect national sovereignty and observe domestic laws, regulations, and administrative procedures. Corporations must not interfere (illegally) in the internal affairs of the countries in which they operate and adhere to taxation policies.
- *Sociocultural objectives and values*—MNCs should respect the social and cultural objectives, values, and traditions of the countries in which they operate.
- *Disclosure of information*—Information about operations should be available, but not to the extent that business confidentiality is violated. MNCs will issue CSR and environmental reports.
- *Competition*—Activities should not be undertaken that adversely affect competition by abusing a dominant position of market power.
- *Financing*—Corporate financing should be arranged to consider the impact on national balances of payments and credit policies.
- *Employment and human resources*—MNCs should respect the right of their employees to join trade unions, observe standards of employment and industrial relations, train persons from the local labour force, and be sensitive to the impacts of layoffs and closures. MNCs should respect human rights, not be involved in child or forced labour, and provide safe and healthy workplaces.
- *Science and technology*—MNCs must cooperate with the scientific and technological policies of the countries in which they operate and grant licences for the use of industrial property rights under reasonable terms.
- *Corrupt practices*—MNCs shall refrain from offering, promising, or giving any payment, gift, or other advantage to the benefit of a public official or politician.
- *Environmental protection*—MNCs shall carry out their activities in accordance with national laws, regulations, administrative practices, and policies relating to the preservation of the environment of the countries in which they operate and with due regard to international standards of sustainability.
- *Stakeholder consideration*—MNCs shall consider the interests of all stakeholders. Consumers must be dealt with fairly, marketing and advertising practices must be honest, privacy must be respected, and products sold must be safe and of good quality. The views of INGOs should be taken into consideration. Local supplier capacity should be developed.
- *Corporate governance*—The MNC shall follow appropriate governance practices.

Most of the standards cover a range of economic, ethical, and environmental measures. Human rights are included in most, but corporate governance practices in only some. They are a valuable resource for corporations and can be modified by industry. They provide a basis for reporting and guidelines for establishing policies. If used, there is need for annual auditing of compliance, preferably by an independent body or consultant. If not used or followed, any benefits from the standards will be lost.

LO 15.6 Special Challenges of Global Business

Some special challenges confront Canadian business as it participates increasingly in the global economy: the presence of corruption, respect for human rights, the use of sweatshop production, and the reduction of poverty.

Corruption

When operating in a global economy, Canadian corporations must be aware of the legal and ethical circumstances existing in various countries. Transparency International (TI) has developed an index of corruption, the Corruption Perception Index (CPI), to assist corporations in coping with particular countries. TI defines **corruption** as "the abuse of entrusted power for private gain" and their "Corruption Perception Index" measures the perceived level of public sector corruption in countries and territories around the world."[11] Table 15.2 lists the CPI scores for the five least corrupt countries and the five most corrupt according to TI. In 2018, out of the 180 countries surveyed, Canada ranks 9th with a score of 81, and the United States 22nd with a score of 71.

TABLE 15.2	Corruption Perceptions Index Scores 2018 (score out of 100)		
Least Corrupt Countries	CPI Score	Most Corrupt Countries	CPI Score
Denmark	88	North Korea	14
New Zealand	87	Yemen	14
Finland	85	South Sudan	13
Singapore	85	Syria	13
Sweden	85	Somalia	10

Bribery is a type of corruption that is widespread and insidious in some parts of the world. When managers of Canadian corporations operating overseas are confronted with this practice, ethical dilemmas arise. **Bribery** involves making questionable payments, or bribes, to government officials to influence their decisions. Sometimes bribes are referred to as *facilitation payments,* and involve smaller payments to expedite something an official should be doing by encouraging them to do it faster and more efficiently. Such payments may be justified as necessary to do business in a particular country and often are rationalized since everyone does it; bribery is an accepted practice and considered akin to a commission, tax, or compensation.

On the other hand, there are numerous arguments against making such payments: it is viewed as being simply wrong, unacceptable, and illegal. The practice compromises a manager's ethical standards when honesty and fairness should be practised all the time. Some corporations simply refuse to deal with corrupt governments because, in the long term, limited benefits exist and, once started, the practice is unlikely to stop. Bribery illustrates *ethical relativism,* described in Chapter 5. In some cultures and national environments bribery is an acceptable practice, and it is argued that foreigners accept it. Thus, managers can justify acting according to the circumstances in which they find themselves.

Canadian corporations and managers must adhere to the *Corruption of Foreign Public Officials Act* when doing business globally. This Act features three offences: bribing of a foreign public official; laundering of property and proceeds; and possession of property and proceeds. In addition to this act, the federal government is participating in anti-corruption initiatives through organizations such as the Organisation for Economic Co-operation and Development (OECD), the Organization of American States, the Council of Europe, the Commonwealth of Nations, and the United Nations.[12]

Several organizations monitor and measure bribery practices. In particular, the Organisation for Economic Co-operation and Development (OECD) has a program on "Bribery and Competition" that covers not only international business but also public sector integrity, sports, tax and crime, education for integrity, whistleblower protection, and public procurement. In March 2011, the OECD released a report pointing out that Canada is doing a poor job at enforcing bribery practices. Canada has prosecuted and convicted only one case, in 2005, and has one ongoing prosecution and more than twenty cases under investigation. The report made the following recommendations to the Canadian government:

- Provide more resources to its lawyers to prosecute more cases.
- Clarify the Act to apply to all conduct, not just "for profit" business.
- Make sanctions more effective.
- Make sure to prosecute Canadian businesspersons for bribery.
- Eliminate factors such as national economic interests and relations with a foreign state from consideration in making a decision to prosecute.[13]

In early 2013, OECD's concern appeared to be confirmed when several Canadian corporations were highlighted in the media for their corrupt behaviour. Several allegations of corruption were facing SNC-Lavalin Inc., a Montreal engineering firm, including alleged ties with the deposed regime of Moammar Gadhafi in Libya, and alleged bribery involving a bridge project in Bangladesh. Griffiths Energy International Inc., a Calgary oil and gas company, was fined $10.5 million for bribing government officials in Chad. The federal government stated that it would be cracking down on the corrupt practices of Canadian corporations.[14] As recently as March 2019, the OECD Working Group on Bribery expressed concern about the allegations of interference in the prosecution of SNC-Lavalin.[15]

Corporations operating in the global economy are increasingly disclosing information or being transparent about their activities and behaviour in the countries where they do business. Responsibility for Ethics 15.4 describes one organization's efforts to increase disclosure in the petroleum and mining industries. As Canadian corporations in resource industries operate around the world, Canadian managers are aware of the efforts to avoid corruption. An indicator of an increased effort against corruption and bribery, TRACE International, a non-profit anti-bribery group, argues that anti-bribery enforcement maybe gaining ground.[16] More countries are enacting legislation and taking more enforcement actions.[17]

Want to learn more about **global corporate corruption**?

 RESPONSIBILITY FOR ETHICS 15.4

Extractive Industries Transparency Initiative (EITI)

The Extractive Industries Transparency Initiative (EITI) is a global standard that promotes the open and accountable management of oil, gas, and mineral resources. It accomplishes this by encouraging revenue transparency through monitoring and reconciling corporation payments and government revenues at the country level. It believes that in countries that are rich in oil, gas, and minerals, the revenues received from the extraction of these resources should be used to foster economic growth and reduce poverty. When the government systems are inadequate, the revenues may be lost through corruption or used to finance conflicts. EITI aims to strengthen governance by improving transparency and accountability in the extractives sector. The process is overseen by participants from the government, corporations, industry associations, INGOs, institutional investors, and supranational institutions. The Canadian government supports EITI financially. More than 90 of the world's largest oil, gas, and mining corporations support and actively participate in the EITI process including the Canadian corporations Barrick Gold, Goldcorp, Kinross, and Teck Resources.

An effort at disclosing bribery, Publish What You Pay, has been undertaken by a coalition of more than 680 NGOs and calls for the mandatory disclosure of all payments to governments made by companies in extractive industries such as oil, gas, and mining.[18] In Canada, the Canadian Centre of Excellence for Anti-Corruption (CCEAC) has been established at the University of Ottawa to serve as a national and international centre to address corruption-related issues. It collaborates with industry, public and private organizations, academic institutions, and several key anti-corruption organizations, subject-matter experts, and stakeholders. It is involved in training, mentorship, education, advocacy, research, and other activities to tackle corruption and bribery.[19]

Human Rights

Human rights are the fundamental rights and freedoms to which all individuals, groups, and societies are entitled. The list of rights involved is large and has been expanded over the years, but one reference point is the United Nations' *Universal Declaration of Human Rights*, adopted in 1948.[20] Canadian corporations operating on a global scale need proactive human rights policies and practices both globally and within Canada. Financing and human talent may be harder to obtain without attention being given to human rights. Respect for human rights is a key to establishing market footholds in developing countries—which is important as they are the largest untapped market, estimated at more than three billion.

From a Canadian business perspective, two human rights codes or principles are significant: the United Nations' "Guiding Principles on Business and Human Rights" and the "Voluntary Principles on Security and Human Rights." The UN's Guiding Principles were developed recognizing the existing obligations of countries to respect, protect, and fulfill fundamental freedoms. Business corporations were required to comply with all applicable laws and to respect human rights. Corporations were expected to respect human rights and the responsibilities of corporations were specified, including the responsibility to have human rights policies and processes in place.[21]

The Voluntary Principles are relevant to Canada as they apply specifically to extractive and energy industries. Three participants were involved in applying the Principles: governments, corporations, and NGOs. The Principles fall into three categories:

- *Risk assessment*—The corporations were required to accurately assess risks present in their operating environment that were critical to the security of personnel.

- *Interaction between corporations and public security*—Governments have the primary role of maintaining law and order, security, and respect for human rights, but corporations have an interest in ensuring that actions taken by governments are consistent with the protection and promotion of human rights.

- *Interactions between corporations and private security*—It may be necessary for corporations to engage private security providers as a complement to public security, particularly where governments are unable or unwilling to provide adequate security.

Participants were to respect human rights throughout the world and guide corporations in maintaining the safety and security of their operations so as to encourage respect of human rights. The participants agreed to a dialogue ensuring that the Principles continued to be relevant and efficient.[22]

Sweatshop Production

The sourcing of products from sweatshops in developing countries—and to a lesser extent within Canada—is an issue with most retailers. Goods are supplied at low costs, but the plants where they are produced violate many human rights through the abuse of workers. The abuses include child labour, low pay, poor working conditions, poor health and safety, and overall mistreatment of workers. Even with extensive audits of production facilities in developing countries, there is no assurance that abuses will not occur. This has become a major issue to which retailers have responded; one example is given in Everyday Ethics 15.4.

 EVERYDAY ETHICS 15.4

Reitmans (Canada) Limited's Code of Conduct for Suppliers

Most retailers relying upon global sources for merchandise now have supplier codes and require suppliers to follow them. Reitmans, a Canadian clothing retailer, provides an example of such a code. The components of their Code of Conduct for Suppliers include:

- *Child labour*—Workers must be at least 15 years of age. The only exceptions are where 14 years old is allowed by law in a country, or younger if the compulsory school requirement is completed.

- *Forced labour*—Not allowed.

- *Discrimination*—Workers must be hired on the basis of ability and not subjected to discrimination in any aspect of employment.

- *Freedom of Association/Collective Bargaining*—Suppliers will not restrict workers from joining organizations protecting their well-being.

- *Wages and benefits*—Suppliers will pay minimum wages plus benefits in compliance with local laws.

- *Working Hours*—These will be in compliance with all applicable laws and regulations

- *Environment*—Suppliers must comply with all applicable environmental laws and regulations in the country in which they are located.

- *Working conditions*—Workers are to be treated with respect and dignity, and must work in a safe and healthy environment. They must not be subject to corporal punishment or any form of harassment. The required working conditions are listed, as are standards for dormitories if applicable.

Reitmans specifies a monitoring program for all suppliers, and their representatives must be allowed to inspect plants. To enforce the Code, Reitmans has the right to terminate its contract with the supplier if the Code is violated.

In addition to corporations developing policies and codes, many industries also have done so. Many INGOs monitor production facilities, often on behalf of the corporations. Consultants have specialized in the area of verifying the conditions and practices of these plants. Despite all these efforts, some suppliers in developing countries are avoiding labour rules and inspections.[23] Others argue that sweatshops are a stage in the industrial development of a country; they provide employment where there would be little or none and the developing economy is better off, which eventually leads to further economic development.[24]

The production in sweatshops has been increasingly regulated by governments, INGOs, business organizations, and the corporations themselves. The regulation has covered wages, working conditions, and environmental impact. It is generally believed that sweatshop employment is preferable to alternatives in developing countries. Although sweatshop employment is considered desirable, there are some issues that arise from this regulation.

Increasing regulation does increase wages and improve working conditions for those employed. This improves the local economies and may increase non-sweatshop employment. However, it may result in less employment as manufacturers automate and even move production to other lower-cost countries. The price of the goods produced may increase reducing demand and employment. The profits of sweatshop owners may decrease resulting in the owners exiting the country, or discouraging other sweatshop manufacturers from entering the country. Sweatshop regulation reduces the economic freedom of owners and may decrease economic efficiency. The regulation of sweatshops may have unintended consequences that may harm local employment.[25]

Global Poverty

Global poverty is extensively discussed in the media and in the publications of NGOs and governments. In this section, only two sources are outlined: Oxfam's efforts and the development of the United Nations' Sustainable Development Goals (SDGs).

Oxfam International's purpose is to reduce world poverty; it produced a significant report in 2016 entitled "An Economy for the 1%," which is summarized in Everyday Ethics 15.5. Oxfam continues to report on a variety of topics relating to poverty; for example, a recent focus is on women's rights. It believes that "gender is the most persistent predictor of poverty and powerlessness in our world today."[26]

 EVERYDAY ETHICS 15.5

Poverty and Oxfam

Oxfam's vision is "a just world without poverty" and its mission is "to build lasting solutions to poverty and injustice with a focus on improving the lives and promoting the rights of women and girls."

In 2016, Oxfam International released a report on the world inequality crisis—that is, the gap between the rich and the poor—which found that it was getting worse. Oxfam concludes that this growing economic inequality is bad for society as it undermines growth and social cohesion. Among the findings of the report were the following:

- The richest individuals—the 1 percent—have more wealth than the rest of the world's population. Sixty-two individuals have the same wealth as the 3.6 billion poorest people in the world.

- The wealth of the richest has grown while the wealth of the bottom half of the world's population has fallen.

- A global network of tax havens enables the richest individuals to hide $7.6 trillion.

- The average annual income of the poorest 10 percent of the world's population has risen by less than $3 in the last 25 years.

The report proposed several policy actions that could be taken to address the issue, including paying workers a living wage, promoting women's economic equality, sharing the tax burden fairly, making medicines affordable, and ending the era of tax havens.

Human rights and sweatshop labour abuses are related to the reduction of global poverty. This issue has been receiving more attention in part because of the United Nations' Sustainable Development Goals (SDGs), which identify the needs of the world's poorest. Private corporations will have to be involved if the goals are to be met, and some Canadian corporations have initiated projects to address various goals. Although governments shoulder much of the responsibility for human development, it is in business' interests to participate. An opportunity exists to capture future markets, corporations benefit from the stability of enhanced human development, and the risks of doing business are reduced. Business brings inherent skills to meet the goals, including providing leadership through partnerships and cooperative undertakings.[27] The Sustainable Development Goals are listed in Responsibility for Ethics 15.5.

RESPONSIBILITY FOR ETHICS 15.5

United Nations' Sustainable Development Goals

The United Nations' Sustainable Development Goals (SDGs) were adapted in 2015 to replace the Millennium Development Goals (MDGs). The SDGs are as follows:

Goal 1: End poverty in all its forms everywhere.

Goal 2: End hunger, achieve food security and improved nutrition and promote sustainable agriculture.

Goal 3: Ensure healthy lives and promote well-being for all at all ages.

Goal 4: Ensure inclusive and equitable quality education and promote lifelong learning opportunities for all,

Goal 5: Achieve gender equality and empower all women and girls.

Goal 6: Ensure availability and sustainable management of water and sanitation for all.

Goal 7: Ensure access to affordable, reliable, sustainable and modern energy for all.

Goal 8: Promote sustained, inclusive and sustainable economic growth, full and productive employment and decent work for all.

Goal 9: Build resilient infrastructure, promote inclusive and sustainable industrialization and foster innovation.

Goal 10: Reduce inequality within and among countries.

Goal 11: Make cities and human settlements inclusive, safe, resilient and sustainable.

Goal 12: Ensure sustainable consumption and production patterns.

Goal 13: Take urgent action to combat climate change and its impacts.

Goal 14: Conserve and sustainably use the oceans, seas and marine resources for sustainable development.

Goal 15: Protect, restore and promote sustainable use of terrestrial ecosystems, sustainably manage forests, combat desertification, and halt and reverse land degradation and halt biodiversity loss.

Goal 16: Promote peaceful and inclusive societies for sustainable development, provide access to justice for all and build effective, accountable and inclusive institutions at all levels.

Goal 17: Strengthen the means of implementation and revitalize the global partnership for sustainable development.

Want to learn more about **the United Nations' Sustainable Development Goals**?

Globalization has increased the reliance on markets and corporations providing goods and services around the world. The accomplishment of the Sustainable Development Goals requires use of these features of a capitalist economic system.

LO 15.7 The Acceptance of Global Capitalism

The emergence of globalization has occurred with the increasing acceptance of capitalism around the world. The trend to greater reliance on market systems rather than government initiatives is illustrated by some recent initiatives: the "Bottom of the Pyramid" concept, fair trade, microfinance, and increasing entrepreneurship in developing countries.

Business corporations may appropriately play a greater role in alleviating poverty in the world by applying the concept of the Bottom of the Pyramid (BOP). This concept was popularized by an article by C.K. Prahalad and Stuart L. Hart in 2002,[28] and by a book Prahalad wrote on the concept in 2005.[29]

The concept is that corporations should not ignore—as potential customers—the segment of the world's population living in poverty. An estimated three to four billion persons are in this segment, living on less than $2 per day. Individually they do not have much purchasing power, but collectively they do. The market potential for these people is often overlooked as corporations focus on the few wealthy customers or the emerging middle-income people in a developing economy.

If corporations are innovative enough, they can profitably market goods and services to those living in poverty. If corporations succeed in this, they will experience growth and profits while at the same time improving the living conditions of those persons and aiding regional development. This approach empowers those at the bottom by providing new options for improving their state. It allows corporations to make money and at the same time be socially responsible. Thus, the concept appeals to businesses that are pressured by various stakeholders to be more socially responsible.

Prahalad and Hart outlined the commercial infrastructure necessary at the bottom of the pyramid:

- Creating Buying Power: Giving persons in poverty access to credit that can be used to establish economic activity to generate income.

- Shaping Aspirations: This can be accomplished through consumer education and sustainable development of developing countries' resources.

- Tailoring Local Solutions: The solutions include targeted product development appropriate to developing economies and bottom-up innovation.

- Improving Access: Developing distribution systems and communication links within countries to facilitate economic activity and trade.

For success at the bottom of the pyramid, all aspects of this infrastructure must be put together in an appropriate way to facilitate the commercial efforts.

In June 2007, the Aspen Institute's Business and Society Program issued a bulletin on the Bottom of the Pyramid concept. It identified how the concept is being incorporated into the curricula for business programs and the university centres interested in the concept. Teaching materials were also identified. The bulletin asked some interesting questions about the BOP concept:

- Is the concept merely an academic fad, or will the trends of increasing curricular exposure to the topic continue?

- Why is a discussion of the concept noticeably absent from most top academic journals?

- Will corporations address the felt needs of the poor when providing goods and services or rather exploit marketing tactics to promote any potentially profitable product?[30]

Another example of a business approach to addressing the globalization issue relating to the low prices received by producers in developing countries has been fair trade. The Fairtrade Foundation, Oxfam, and Traidcraft have agreed on the following common definition of fair trade: "an alternative approach to conventional international trade. It is a trading partnership which aims at sustainable development for excluded and disadvantaged producers. It seeks to do this by providing better trading conditions, by awareness raising and by campaigning."[31] The fair trade movement is not anti-capitalist, but instead intends to use the market system to enhance the influence of the supplier stakeholder. The best known fair trade product is coffee, and today most retailers carry a fair trade product. Other fair trade products are flowers, tea, spices, and cocoa. The entrepreneurs promoting fair trade products claim that the local suppliers in developing countries are now receiving a higher price for their product. Fair trade was also discussed in Chapter 12.

Microfinance is the provision of financial products, such as micro-credit, micro-insurance, and savings accounts, to persons living in areas of poverty without access to banking services. Organizations providing these services are often referred to as microfinancial institutions (MFIS). Micro-credit has received the most attention and involves making small loans to poor persons to start or expand small businesses. Women are often the entrepreneurs who borrow money. The practice started about 30 years ago; the pioneer in this approach was Muhammad Yunus and the Grameen Bank in Bangladesh (see Everyday Ethics 15.6). Today, as many as 10,000 other institutions are involved in the practice, including government, business foundations, and aid agencies as well as commercial banks.[32]

 EVERYDAY ETHICS 15.6

Muhammad Yunus and the Nobel Peace Prize

The 2006 Nobel Peace Prize was won by Muhammad Yunus and the Grameen Bank for initiating the microfinance approach with the poor in Bangladesh. Small loans are made mainly to women to start or expand businesses, with no collateral but with significant interest rates. The loans are for business activity, not for consumption purposes. Yunus formed the Grameen Bank, which is more than 90 percent owned co-operatively by its customers.

Although promoted as an approach to alleviating poverty, microfinancial institutions have been criticized. The primary criticism is the high rates of interest charged, which is at 20 to 30 percent. The rates are justified on the higher costs of administering, making, and collecting the loans and administering small savings accounts. Some MFIS have been accused of pursuing growth by ignoring the ability to pay and using coercive collection tactics. Overlending is another problem, where multiple loans are made to the same person. There has been consideration of regulating the MFIS, for example by limiting the interest rates, but this may discourage lenders and force borrowers to less scrupulous lenders. Other initiatives to improve the industry include the establishment of credit bureaus, requirement of more transparency, and stronger ethical and regulatory framework. These actions are similar to the regulation of the payday loan industry in Canada. Finally, an issue is the morality of profiting by providing services that are intended to alleviate poverty.

The role of small business in improving the circumstances in developing countries has increased. This is illustrated by the Grameen Bank, which is a commercial, profit-making operation. One view of reducing poverty is to rely more on business models and less on aid or charity, which have failed in many cases to reduce poverty. The assumption is that the poor are assisted more by unleashing their energy, creativity, and entrepreneurial spirit. Corporations must realize that doing business with the poor benefits the poor *and* themselves. It will be necessary for some governments to eliminate the barriers to private enterprise or capitalism. Challenges are involved, including poor infrastructure, illiteracy, religious/racial/tribal tensions, crime, corruption, and excessive government regulation.

The trends and drivers behind implementing this new thinking and creating a favourable environment to start engaging the poor include the following:

- Many corporations see a need to break out of mature market sectors.
- Framework conditions in many developing countries are improving.
- Communications are faster and cheaper, making the world a smaller place.
- Public expectations of corporations are changing.
- New and better partners are available.
- Aid and investment are beginning to reinforce one another.[33]

Thousands of examples exist where corporations are cooperating with governments and INGOs in programs to enhance entrepreneurial capability as an approach to reducing poverty. Society benefits from more employment and the corporation increases its business.

Globalization has resulted in a reduction of government involvement in most economies and an increase in the reliance on markets and capitalism to provide society's goods and services. This trend reinforces the definition of globalization stated at the beginning of the chapter. It involves more than economic activities and is interwoven with the social and environmental responsibilities of business. Some question exists as to whether globalization will be influenced by an economic downturn. It appears that the trend may be slowing, but it is doubtful that it is being reversed.

Your advice to Claudia . . .

Many Canadians do not realize that globalization is impacting them in many ways every day. The ethics involved with selling counterfeit and pirated products is one example. Persons purchasing these products will benefit by allowing self-interest to influence their purchase decision. But other stakeholders are harmed, for example Canadian business retailers and their employees. It could be argued that the workers in China benefit, but they are likely working for low wages and in poor working conditions. You advise Claudia that you know her personal ethics and responsibilities are being challenged in this situation and it is important that she is aware of the ethical issues. Globalization impacts everyone in society, often in unexpected ways.

Summary

- The globalization of business has brought numerous issues relating to business' economic, social, and environmental responsibilities. A general definition of globalization is a process of decreasing constraints on the interactions among the nations and peoples of the world. The three global dimensions important to business are economic, political, and social. Those in favour of globalization (globalists) and those opposed (anti-globalists) continue to debate the pros and cons. (LO 15.1)

- Many non-governmental organizations focus on globalization. They have exerted considerable influence on international corporations and in some cases are partnering with business on projects to reduce poverty in developing countries. (LO 15.2)

- Supranational institutions are influencing globalization economically, socially, and environmentally. Four prominent supranational institutions described are the World Bank, the International Monetary Fund, the International Labour Organization, and the World Trade Organization. (LO 15.3)

- Globalization affects Canadian business and society in several ways. Canadian business must remain competitive with corporations from other countries. Many Canadian corporations are setting an example for corporate citizenship in developing countries. (LO 15.4)

- Several international standards of conduct have been developed that provide guidelines for corporate activities in developing countries. These standards can also be used as frameworks for reporting of their global responsibilities. (LO 15.5)

- Along with globalization comes the trend to rely on market systems and corporations more than requesting government involvement. This trend presents some special challenges for business, including responding to corruption, accommodating human rights in all operations and in particular in sweatshops, and contributing to the accomplishment of the UN's Millennium Development Goals. (LO 15.6)

- Globalization has embraced capitalism. Today, corporations are more likely to be privatized than nationalized. Microfinance and fair trade are examples of initiatives based more on business models than government ones. Entrepreneurship is increasingly taking hold in developing countries. (LO 15.7)

Key Terms

Globalization

Economic globalization

Political globalization

Social or cultural globalization

Globalists

Anti-globalists

Slowbalisation

International non-governmental organizations (INGOs)

Supranational institution

Corruption

Bribery

Human rights

Microfinance

Critical Thinking and Discussion Questions

1. Why has globalization occurred at this time?

2. Do the benefits of globalization offset the drawbacks?

3. Do INGOs play a significant role in business' response to globalization?

4. How do supranational institutions influence globalization?

5. Why is the competitiveness of Canadian business important?

6. What function do the various standards of conduct have?

7. What happens when corporations do not adhere to the standards or guidelines of conduct?

8. Why is the Canadian government so interested in corruption in the extractive industries?

9. How do Canadians know whether or not they are purchasing products produced in sweatshops?

10. Why should business support the UN's Sustainable Development Goals (SDGs)?

11. What is the relationship between capitalism and globalization?

Cases

15.1 KINROSS GOLD AND A CHALLENGE IN BRAZIL

Kinross Gold Corporation is a Canadian gold-mining company with mines and projects in the United States, Brazil, Chile, Ghana, Mauritania, and Russia. Kinross employs approximately 9,000 people worldwide and is committed to responsible mining. Its mine in Brazil, the Morro do Ouro Mine near Paracatu, is operated by a subsidiary, Kinross Brasil Mineração, and has created substantial controversy.

INGOs Above Ground, Justiça Global, and Business & Human Resource Centre have been very active in criticizing the mine and Kinross Gold. Their focus is on ensuring that Canadian corporations or those supported by the Canadian government respect human rights wherever they operate. An Above Ground report provided details about several issues, including the expelling of local peoples from their lands; the conflict between artisanal miners and local residents attempting to extract remnants of gold from the mine's tailings; environmental and health concerns; and Canadian public support for the mine. This latter issue relates to the $850 million in financing Kinross Gold has received from Export Development Canada (EDC) and the investment of $60 million by the Canada Pension Fund. The report recommended that the Canadian and Brazilian governments have an obligation to protect human rights in this type of large-scale extractive project.

Kinross Gold responds that it is acting ethically and transparently, respects human rights, and engages with stakeholders. Brazilian courts have ruled that Kinross Gold's purchases of lands and their use are legal. Trespassers attempting to steal gold are putting themselves and employees in danger. The arsenic from the mine is not a public concern and levels are normal. The corporation maintains communications with residents and monitors that its operations continue to benefit the community.

The corporation points out the socioeconomic benefits to Brazil from this mine in 2017: 1,632 employees, $71 million paid in wages and benefits, $463.5 million spent on goods and services, $11.9 in payments to governments, and 96,600 beneficiaries of its community programs. Kinross Gold's "2017 Corporate Social Responsibility Summary Report" outlines efforts to be a responsible miner. Kinross has contributed $10 million to the community to support schools and adult literacy and cultural programs. Its environmental footprint is carefully monitored and regulations have been followed. Energy and water use, and GHG emissions, have been reduced. Tailings management has been strengthened and the cyanide code certification has been maintained. Occupational illness has been reduced and programs to prevent serious injuries started.

The corporation received several awards for its Paracatu mine. It received the Best Place to Work (one of the 150 best companies to work for) award by Você SA in 2016; was named the 2017 Company of the Year (Mining Sector) by *Brazil Mineral* magazine; received the 2017 Compliance Brazil for Excellence in Social Responsibility Management from GrupoVerde Ghaia; and received a Merit Award for Business from Casa do Empresário in 2017. Kinross Gold has linked business performance to the UN's Sustainable Development Goals and given priority to goals 3 (good health and well-being), 4 (quality education), 5 (gender equality), 6 (clean water sanitation), 8 (decent work and economic growth), 12 (responsible consumption and production), 15 (life on land), and 16 (peace, justice, and strong institutions).

Questions

1. Do the socioeconomic benefits from the mine justify its existence?
2. Should the Government of Canada support gold mining in Brazil?
3. How should Kinross Gold respond to the INGOs?
4. Is Kinross Gold being socially responsible?
5. Is there anything else Kinross Gold can or should do?

15.2 FOOD RETAILING IN INDIA: REVOLUTION OR EVOLUTION?

Modern retailing approaches are evolving in India, especially in the food sector. It is common practice to shop for groceries in *kirana* stores, small neighbourhood shops and produce markets operated by entrepreneurs. In these retail outlets, the fruits and vegetables often are not good quality or in good condition, and the shops are not attractive or comfortable for shoppers. The owners are known for being wasteful, buying in small quantities, selling at high prices, lacking storage capability, and having no expertise in inventory control. There are about 12 million of these small family-operated outlets. In addition, there are 200 million pushcart vendors and hawkers who depend on the highly fragmented retail market for their livelihood.

Large Indian corporations have entered the market, such as Reliance Retail Ltd., with 300 stores in 30 cities across India. Some are opening modern North American–style supermarkets and hypermarkets while others are operating chains of produce shops. These stores are air-conditioned, brightly lit and clean, with trained workers. A greater variety of higher quality fruits and vegetables are available. Goods are neatly packaged, accurately weighed, and refrigerated. Most importantly, prices are lower. Modern retailing supply chain practices are being introduced, including distribution efficiency, high technology farming, and waste reduction. Some suggest that the farmers will receive more for their products as middlemen will be eliminated from the supply chain.

Another dimension of this issue is the restriction on foreign retailers' entry into the Indian market. Foreign retailers cannot sell directly to consumers. To circumvent this regulation, foreign corporations are entering at the wholesale level or in joint ventures or partnerships with Indian corporations. For example, Walmart has a joint venture with Bharti Enterprises, an Indian conglomerate. Other foreign retailers are attempting to enter the Indian market, including the U.K.'s Tesco PLC, and France's Carrefour SA, but success has been limited.

The operators of the smaller stores have protested this trend and have called upon government to stop the large corporations from entering the market. They feel that they cannot compete with the new retailers and would become unemployed with no other form of work available to them. The Indian government is monitoring this retail revolution closely and is under political pressure from the small shopkeepers, opposition parties, and socialist groups. There is concern that the arrival of modern retailing reduces the opportunities for self-employment, especially among the poor.

Even online retailing is challenging in India as Amazon and Walmart are spending billions to attract customers. Online retailing faces the same government regulations. It is difficult to get around these laws that protect local shopkeepers or *kirana* stores. Their grocery business appears safe for the time being.

Questions

1. Who are the stakeholders involved and what are their positions?
2. What are the issues relating to business and society? What dilemmas arise for Indian business and society?
3. How are the harms and benefits of the retail trade liberalization distributed?
4. Should foreign corporations be allowed to operate freely in India?

Events in society cause reactions in business.
Used © Rainer Zapka | Dreamstime.com

CHAPTER 16

The Socialization of Capitalism

LEARNING OUTCOMES

After studying this chapter, you will be able to:

LO 16.1 Define and learn about the Fourth Sector of the economy.

LO 16.2 Recognize that the socialization of capitalism can be achieved through a corporate sustainability strategy.

LO 16.3 Identify new corporate structures involved with socialization.

LO 16.4 Become aware of concepts associated with socialization and how it is expressed in the economy.

LO 16.5 Link the socialization of capitalism to business school programs and activities.

LO 16.6 Understand that capitalism changes and appreciate that capitalism will change in the future.

What would you do if...?

Leah Bromberger started three businesses that were very successful and employing about 50 persons. The businesses were all computer and Internet related: one designed web pages; a second provided consulting services on social media for corporations, governments, and civil society organizations; and a third solved computer systems and software problems being encountered by consumers.

Leah read about a new program being launched by Canadian Business for Social Responsibility (CBSR): "Do Business Like a Canadian." First she decided to learn more about CBSR. It is a business-supported, non-profit, professional association whose purpose is to help Canadian business and governments to build and benefit from a sustainable future. Its mission is to accelerate and scale corporate social and environmental sustainability in Canada by bringing together stakeholders to collectively tackle key issues. Another aspect of its mission is to be the most relevant sustainability business network in Canada and to influence progressive public policy toward its vision. It believes that businesses do better—by every measure—when they operate in a socially and environmentally responsible way.

These are CBSR's values:

"Collaboration—Working with others to achieve shared goals and to produce results with sustainable value

Innovation—Introducing or adopting new ways of thinking and acting in order to achieve our purpose

Integrity—Being honest and always acting in accordance with our principles

Vision—Looking ahead to conceive and plan for a better future"

CBSR's activities include the following:

- The CBSR Education Foundation is focused on advancing corporate social responsibility and sustainability in Canada by disseminating thought leadership, case studies, research, tool kits, and resources to industry, governments, academia, not-for-profits, non-governmental organizations, and civil society.
- Helping organizations and people work toward the Sustainable Development Goals (SDGs)
- The "Transformational CSR Framework and Approach" that provides a road map for corporations to transform from their present business models toward sustainable ones.[1]

By sponsoring the "Do Business Like a Canadian" program, CBSR believes that doing business responsibly can be a competitive advantage for Canadian corporations. This advantage is possible because of the Canadian business values that it has identified: collaborative, eco-conscious, ethical, gender balanced, globally minded, inclusive, innovative, and purpose driven. These values form the foundation for "Do Business Like a Canadian." Each value is explained and several business stories are presented illustrating the values.[2]

CBSR has partnered with *The Globe and Mail*, Ramp Communications, Export Development Canada, Nutrien, Bayer, and Keurig Canada to present a national event series with an accompanying print and social media campaign to promote Canadian business values and the resulting business leadership in environmental stewardship, inclusivity, and innovation.[3]

Businesspersons such as Leah can sign a pledge supporting the initiative. By making this pledge, participants agree to have their name listed as a supporter of Canadian business values and receive updates from CBSR about the campaign.[4]

Leah wondered whether or not she should sign the pledge.

What is your advice to Leah?

The title of this chapter requires some explanation as the "Socialization of Capitalism" is not a commonly used term. The **socialization of capitalism** is the process through which the business system conforms to the expectations of society resulting in desired, socially responsible outcomes. The process recognizes society's consensus about the role of capitalism and establishes norms, customs, and values that will enable capitalism to adjust to the society's desires or expectations relating to social purpose.

There is increasing emphasis on the **social purpose** of the corporation in addition to its traditional financial focus. Throughout this text, there have been many examples of this emphasis:

- Chapters 1 and 2: The discussion of the fundamentals of capitalism and the various forms that exist.

- Chapters 3 and 4: The development whereby corporations now consider a greater variety of stakeholders when making decisions. This has led to the development of engagement practices and a greater effort at issue identification and analysis.

- Chapters 7, 8, and 9: All the forms of corporate social responsibility and the accountability of corporations for their ethical, social and environmental responsibilities in addition to financial ones.

- Chapter 10: Various types of regulation have been involved in encouraging corporations to be more socially responsible.

- Chapter 11: Ownership of corporations is now influenced by owners preferring responsible investing and initiatives in shareholder democracy.

- Chapter 12: Stakeholders in the marketplace, consumers, employees, competitors, and suppliers, influence the corporation in a matter that increases its social purpose.

- Chapter 13: Civil society stakeholders, NGOs, the media, think tanks, and religious and educational institutions, are also increasing corporate social awareness.

- Chapters 14 and 15: Today, business corporations can seldom ignore their social, environmental and economic responsibilities as they relate to the environment and globalization.

Thus, there is a movement toward making capitalism more aware of the impact of its actions on society. At the same time, social organizations such as charities are using economic or commercial methods to finance their social goals. This chapter will describe various approaches to socialization that is occurring in Canadian capitalism. The first section describes the concept of the Fourth Sector, that is, a sector of the economy in addition to the traditional private, social, and public sectors. The Fourth Sector illustrates the interrelations between these sectors for social purposes.

The socialization of capitalism is illustrated by a sustainability approach to strategic management that is occurring in many corporations. Several sections discuss aspects of socialization that are occurring in Canadian capitalism: new corporate structures, different approaches to social undertakings in society, and the approaches to social integration. Another section describes the impact of socialization on educational programs in business schools. The final section considers what capitalism will be like in the future.

LO 16.1 Socialization of Capitalism and the Fourth Sector[5]

One approach to illustrating the extent of socialization of capitalism is to look at the traditional sectors in the economy, private, social, and public. The **private sector** is that part of economy not controlled and operated by government. It is run by individuals and corporations whose intention is to make profits. It is sometimes referred to as the citizen or free market sector. The **social sector** includes charities and non-profit organizations and is also referred to as the non-profit or voluntary sector. Technically this sector operates privately but a distinction is made from the private sector as it operates for social purposes with no intention to make profits. The **public sector** is operated by government departments, agencies, and organizations usually not to operate businesses or make profits. Governments function to provide such things as a legal system, policing and prison services, defence organizations, transportation infrastructure, and educational and health institutions.

In the economy, organizations in the three sectors are changing because of pressures from society. With its entrepreneurial incentive and efficient organizational skills, capitalism has influenced the social and public sectors. In the social sector, non-profit or charitable organizations are using business approaches to commercialize some of their activities. Likewise, the public sector uses business approaches to commercialize some of its operations and has even privatized, or sold off, operating units to the private sector.

There are reasons for this in each sector. The private sector is under pressure from stakeholders to be socially and environmentally responsible. The social sector, with its limited access to resources, has resorted to using business practices to enable them to fulfil their missions. The public sector partners with the private sector or utilizes business practices to provide the goods and services for which it is responsible. An example is the **public–private partnership (PPP)** defined as a cooperative venture between the public and private sectors, built on the expertise of each partner, that best meets clearly defined public needs through the appropriate allocation of resources, risks, and rewards. These partnerships among the sectors increase the involvement of the private sector, for-profit, and non-profit in the provision of government infrastructure and services. All this is necessary as society's stakeholders are demanding that inequity, poverty, short-term thinking, and greed be addressed.

In order to address society's concerns, new ways of thinking leading to changes in the design of organizational structures. Existing forms of organizations in private, social, and public sectors are not sufficient to generate the economic, social, and environmental benefits being demanded. The result is a **fourth sector** of the economy where new organizational forms integrate business or private, social and public methods, sometimes referred to as *hybrid organizations*. The result is illustrated in Figure 16.1 in which examples of fourth sector organizations are given.

FIGURE 16.1 *Sectors of the Economy*

Private Sector	Social Sector	Public Sector
↓	↓	↓
Social Initiatives or Trends	Commercialization of Activities	Commercialization and Privatization of Activities
↓	↓	↓
Fourth Sector Examples		
Corporate Social Responsibility Social Auditing Sustainability Reporting Stakeholder Engagement Environmental Management Volunteerism Employee Ownership Philanthropy Community Investment Social Impact Management Corporate Sponsorship Green Marketing Social License Social Venture Philanthropy	Social Entrepreneurship Microfinance Co-operatives Faith-Based Enterprises Fair Trade For-benefit Corporations B-corporations	Government-Owned Corporations Sale of Corporations and Other Assets Public–Private Partnerships Privatizing Goods and Services

While the mission and method of many new organizations in the business (private), social, and government (public) sectors are becoming steadily more similar, something more than simple blurring of the boundaries is occurring. Pioneering organizations in the three sectors are in fact converging toward a blending of economic, social, and environmental aims using business approaches. Not everyone agrees that a fourth sector exists but rather that organizations in the three sectors are merely working together to address society's concerns.[6]

The following sections describe some of the initiatives that are in some way addressing the integration of economic, social, and environmental purposes in today's organizations.

LO 16.2 Socialization of Capitalism Through Corporate Sustainability Strategy

Social, ethical, and environmental responsibilities are increasingly being integrated into the strategic management process. This widely practised planning approach has traditionally focused on the economic responsibilities and the financial performance of the corporation, but this approach is changing. The result is a **sustainability strategy**, a plan that views economic, ethical, social, and environmental responsibilities more intensively and integrates corporate social responsibility (CSR) into all facets of the corporation's operations. A sustainability strategy is also referred to as a CSR strategy by some corporations.

There is no one approach to developing a sustainability or CSR strategy, and the strategies developed vary with management preferences, how well managers understand CSR, and industry environments. In order to understand the different variations of a sustainability strategy, a corporation's approach can be assessed using a four-stage continuum:

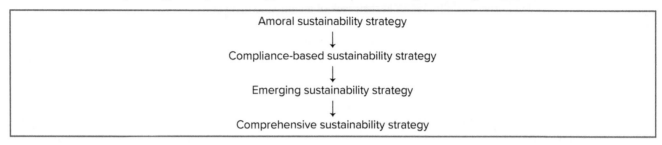

Amoral sustainability strategy
↓
Compliance-based sustainability strategy
↓
Emerging sustainability strategy
↓
Comprehensive sustainability strategy

The purpose of this continuum is to assess the extent of a corporation's sustainability strategy. It also provides guidance to the development of plans and to make improvements in an existing strategy. Although four stages are identified, it is unlikely corporations will fit perfectly in one stage. Table 16.1 identifies some of the characteristics of each strategy. This book provides illustrations of CSR being practised by Canadian corporations in many different ways.

TABLE 16.1	Main Characteristics of Sustainability Strategies			
	Amoral	**Compliance-based**	**Emerging**	**Comprehensive**
Awareness	Little or none; avoids sustainability practices	Motivated by legal requirements and public disapproval; some written policies	Beyond legal requirements; voluntarily accepts 3E responsibilities	Full acceptance and understanding; key element in economic strategy
Stakeholder focus	Owners	Most likely customers, lenders, employees, suppliers, and government	All identified and consciously considered	Stakeholder engagement
Management/ staff involvement	No training or rewards	Negative sanctions; some rewards Enforcement by HR and legal departments	Responsibility of senior manager or compliance officer Support resources provided Stronger focus on rewards and recognition	High-level management responsibility Integrated with compensation and performance appraisal systems
Board involvement	Unlikely	Restricted to that legally required and to maintain corporate reputation; no committee	Receive regular reports; possibility of CSR committee	Board committee oversees
Ethics program	None explicit Reflects management views	Rules-based Possible code of conduct	Codes of conduct and ethics Deliberate program	Complete, explicit program
CSR program	Ad hoc donations	Donations, sponsorships, voluntarism Public relations focus	More comprehensive, with community investment	Complete, explicit program
Reporting	None	Possible mention in annual reports	More extensive; possible separate report	Separate report with evaluation such as Global Reporting Initiative (GRI)

With an amoral sustainability strategy, the corporation ignores sustainability but cannot be viewed necessarily as deliberately doing so. It simply does not address economic, social, and environmental issues in a deliberate or explicit manner. Also, some corporations may consciously avoid or resist the consideration of sustainability practices. Corporations adopting this strategy are vulnerable to sustainability issues as their lack of attention to them reduces their preparedness if problems or issues arise.

Some consideration is given to sustainability in a compliance-based strategy, but it is motivated by legal requirements and the possibility of public backlash or disapproval of corporate behaviour. Thus, sustainability is accepted because of the possible economic consequences of doing nothing and the fear of negative publicity. The strategy is legalistic, focusing on what should not be done, what is within the law, and what is required by government.

Strategy extends beyond what is legally required and the corporation voluntarily considers its economic, ethical, and environmental responsibilities in an emerging sustainability strategy. Many more aspects of ethics and corporate social responsibility are taken into account.

The comprehensive sustainability strategy becomes a key component of the corporate strategy in corporations that fully understand and embrace their economic, social, and environmental responsibilities. Implementation requires integration with all aspects of the corporation's planning and operations. This process needs managers who understand sustainability, and corporations are establishing management positions to oversee sustainability or corporate social responsibility. The positions have a variety of names, and can be as high-level as a vice-president. The Network for Business Sustainability identified "10 Things New Sustainability Managers Need to Know":

1. Whether there is payback on investments in sustainability, for example in cost savings or customer loyalty.

2. How to make sustainability a part of corporate culture.

3. How to make the supply chain competitive and sustainable.

4. Whether customers will pay more for sustainable products or services.

5. How to best engage stakeholders.

6. How to identify the best measurements of a corporation's environmental impact.

7. Whether corporate sustainability attracts and retains employees.

8. How a corporation can mitigate and adapt to climate change.

9. The meaning of business sustainability.

10. How to identify resources, including research, about sustainability and related issues.[7]

In addition, corporations and managers must be aware of the challenges and opportunities presented by the trend towards thinking in sustainable terms. The Network for Business Sustainability prepares a list of the opportunities; past lists have included collaborating for sustainability, addressing climate change, building stakeholder trust, designing effective sustainability communications, turning sustainability into strategic priority, transitioning to green products and services, and respecting free, prior, informed consent (consultation and accommodation with impacted stakeholders).[8]

An approach to achieving a comprehensive sustainability strategy is through the use of **strategic management**, the process through which a corporation establishes its mission and objectives, analyzes the environment and resource capabilities in order to formulate strategy, creates the organizational systems and processes needed to implement the strategy, and devises mechanisms for evaluating performance. Managers are increasingly recognizing the potentially positive relationship between sustainability and financial return. Many corporations are consciously using the strategic management model to improve their performance economically, ethically, and environmentally. Another model of corporate sustainability strategy to accomplish the same is described in Responsibility for Ethics 16.1, The Transformational Company.

 RESPONSIBILITY FOR ETHICS 16.1

The Transformational Company

A guide that managers can use to achieve comprehensive corporate sustainability is "The Transformational Company Qualities." The guide provides a benchmark for managers who wish to improve their corporation's social and environmental impact. The benchmark was developed by the Canadian Business for Social Responsibility (CBSR), "a think tank and professional association for forward thinking business leaders across multiple sectors and regions in

Canada." CBSR researched a new approach to corporate social responsibility and identified 19 qualities of a transformational company that could be used as a guideline for corporations.

The list of the qualities is available at https://www.cbsr.ca/transformational-company; the CBSR is willing to share it so that corporations can improve their CSR and sustainability efforts in order to systematically address society risks, challenges, and opportunities.

To provide examples of the qualities, CBSR published case studies from across a variety of industry sectors and companies. CBSR believes that the "Transformational Company Qualities foster innovation, enhance a company's social license to grow, foster customer and supplier loyalty and help to attract, retain and engage employees."

Source: Adapted from "The Transformation Company," Canadian Business for Social Responsibility (CBSR) website at https://www.cbsr.ca/transformational-company. Used with permission.

Some managers are using sustainability concepts as rhetoric to maximize profits, or appear to be formulating and implementing a sustainability strategy when in reality it is superficial or done without commitment. However, many corporations today are taking sustainability seriously, viewing it as critical to their success or longevity.

LO 16.3 Socialization of Capitalism and New Corporate Structures

Some new forms of corporate structures have emerged that facilitate the integration of social and economic purposes.

Social Enterprise

A social enterprise is "a model of business operation where some or all profits are deliberately used to further social aims." There are several other definitions; one reason for this might be because there are several types, as outlined in Table 16.2. The type used is determined by the need for operational flexibility, financing and funding sources, preferential taxation treatment, and public perception. The use of social enterprises reduces reliance on donations from the public or corporations, foundations, or governments. In all cases, a feature of social enterprises is that they use business structures to accomplish a social purpose.[9] More information on social enterprise in Canada is available at the Social Enterprise Council of Canada (SECC), "an alliance of social enterprise leaders who leverage their networks, knowledge and experience in order to build a strong and enabling environment for social enterprise."[10] Examples of social enterprises are given in Everyday Ethics 16.1.

TABLE 16.2	Types of Social Enterprise
Type	Characteristic
Non-profit organization	Have charitable status. Organized only for charitable purposes. Must meet Canada Revenue rules. Can issue donation receipts.
Non-profit organization	Without charitable status. Exempt from taxation. Operated only for charitable purposes.
Co-operative	Member controlled and operates for their social benefit. If profits occur, returned to members.
Hybrid corporation	With caps on dividends and asset distribution. Examples: Community Contribution Company in B.C. and Community Interest Company in NS. No tax advantages.
For-profit corporation	Owned by non-profit organization and can operate as subsidiary earning profits. Could be B Corp.
For-profit corporation	Owned by investors. Can involve private returns to owners as well as committing a portion of profits to social purposes. Could be B Corp.

EVERYDAY ETHICS 16.1

Examples of Social Enterprises

St. John's Bakery, Toronto, ON—Operates a bakery "to provide our customers with outstanding artisan breads and sweets" and "to be and to build an inclusive community through the gifts and the needs that each of us brings."

Cleaning Solution, Vancouver, B.C.—Provides "meaningful employment for local residents who have experienced mental illness and best-of-market, environmentally-friendly cleaning services…"

Internet Café, St. John's, NL—Conceived as a "social enterprise operation where individuals struggling with barriers to enter or re-enter the workforce would have an opportunity for meaningful employment and work experience."

EthniCity, Calgary, AB—Provides Canadian work experience and training to immigrants in their transition to Canada.

Just Us! Coffee, Wolfville, NS—Canada's first fair trade coffee roaster, Just Us! is a worker cooperative exclusively roasting specialty grade, certified fair trade, and organic coffee.

Lists of other examples are available from Social Business Creation at https://socialbusinesscreation.hec.ca/social-business /social-enterprise-examples/and the Pond-Deshpande Centre at http://www.ponddeshpande.ca/sociale-enterprise-examples/.

Social enterprises are dynamic business operations capable of improving the well-being of citizens while making money, but are distinct from charities and from private-sector companies that practise social responsibility. Although the idea has received attention recently, it has existed for some time, for example in the cooperatives of the 1800s. Social enterprises take various forms, including community enterprises, credit unions, commercial operations of charities, employee-owned businesses, cooperatives, development trusts, housing associations, and companies operating under fair trade principles.

Although social enterprises take various forms, there are some common characteristics. They have an enterprise orientation; that is, they are involved in the production of goods or provision of services to a market, with the intention that revenues will exceed costs. They have social aims, such as providing employment, training, and investment funding. There is a commitment of local capacity building, and they are accountable to their members and community stakeholders. They are autonomous organizations with governance and ownership structures based on participation by stakeholder groups such as users and local community groups or shareholders. Profits are distributed to stakeholders or used for the benefit of the community.[11]

Social entrepreneurship involves the activities undertaken to enhance social wealth in some innovative way. A **social entrepreneur** is an innovative, visionary leader of a non-profit or for-profit business with real-world problem-solving creativity and a high awareness for ethical, social, and environmental considerations. Social entrepreneurs seek out innovative approaches to social issues in the community and use business skills to achieve social objectives. They also have the ability to meet community needs while being financially self-sufficient and paying attention to market forces. Successful social entrepreneurs do not believe that capitalism and profits are societal evils, but instead believe that business enterprises can be operated to enhance social aims. It is also possible to have **social intrapreneurship**, "the process of addressing social challenges from inside established organizations," and **social extrapreneurship**, "the process of inter-organizational action that facilitates alternative combinations of ideas, peoples, places, and resources to address social challenges."[12]

Several centres focus on social enterprises and entrepreneurship; these are usually associated with universities, and sometimes are in association with regular entrepreneurial studies. In Canada, colleges and universities offer programs or courses that focus on social entrepreneurship, and many business graduates are seeking employment in social enterprises where they apply their business and managerial skills. In order to gain experience in social entrepreneurship and social enterprises, university and college students can participate in Enactus groups or teams as described in Everyday Ethics 16.2.

EVERYDAY ETHICS 16.2

Enactus

Enactus, formerly Students in Free Enterprise (SIFE), is a student leadership organization whose purpose is to create community empowerment projects with the assistance of academics and business leaders. Each project can be considered a social enterprise that uses the power of entrepreneurial spirit and skill to transform lives and shape a better, more sustainable world. It is an international non-profit organization with groups around the world, including about 64 teams at Canadian universities and colleges, involving 2,734 students and 280 projects. Student participation in Enactus provides an opportunity for students to develop talents and skills necessary for leadership roles in business. The values encouraged are imagination, courage, determination, partnership, accountability, and curiosity.

Source: From Enactus website at http://enactus.org/ and https://enactus.org/country/canada/ accessed March 30, 2019. Used with permission of ENACTUS.

Social enterprises and social entrepreneurship are stimulating business innovation with integrity and passion. Closely related organizational structures doing the same are for-benefit and B Corporations, discussed next.

Want to learn more about Canadian social enterprises?

For-benefit and B Corporations

A social enterprise can operate as is a **for-benefit (or benefit) corporation** that aims to make profits but also has a strong commitment to addressing social and environmental problems. For-benefit corporations are expected to have a material impact on society and to consider how their actions affect stakeholders. Accountability and transparency are requirements, and they are expected to publicly report their social and environmental performance using recognized third-party standards.[13] In the United States, several states have passed legislation allowing for the incorporation of for-benefit corporations, giving them legal status. No for-benefit incorporation legislation has been passed in Canada as it is considered unnecessary.[14]

A variation on the for-benefit corporation is the **B Corporation (or B Corp)**. A B-Corp also operates to make profits but has a strong commitment to addressing social and environmental problems. A certification process is required in order to be eligible to receive the designation of B Corp. The requirements for certification are making amendments to corporate documents—for example, bylaws—to permit boards of directors to consider other stakeholders, and meeting rigorous and independent standards of social and environmental accountability and transparency.

In Canada the certification is performed by B Lab Canada. There are over 2,300 Certified B Corporations in 60 countries across 150 different industries. There are over 230 in Canada in nine provinces. B Corporations are a diverse community with a unifying goal to redefine success in business.[15] Everyday Ethics 16.3 lists examples of Canadian B Corporations.

 EVERYDAY ETHICS 16.3

Examples of Canadian B Corporations

Bullfrog Power, Toronto, ON—A green energy provider to homes and businesses through renewable energy solutions that reduce the impact on the environment.

Salt Spring Coffee, Richmond, B.C.—Coffee roasters that have formed farmer partnerships with a vision to be at the leading edge of coffee in quality, sustainability, pioneering, and origin.

PeaceWorks Technology Solutions, Waterloo, ON—Provides technology solutions that enable organizations to achieve their mission with increased ease and efficiency.

Enviro-Stewards, Elmira, ON—A company of engineers and scientists helping clients conserve their resources and effectively address their environmental liabilities.

Animikii Inc., Victoria, B.C.—An Indigenous-owned digital agency that works with Indigenous-focused organizations to drive positive change for Indigenous Peoples through technology.

Business Development Bank of Canada, Ottawa, ON—The only financial institution with a focus on small- and medium-sized enterprises and entrepreneurs through financing, advisory services, and capital. It is Canada's first B Corp bank.

One organization could operate as several types of organizations; for example, a new corporate form organization, a charitable organization, and a profit-making enterprise. The result is several organizational entities under one umbrella organization forming a portfolio. The following section describes an approach to managing this portfolio or organizations.

Social Enterprise/Non-profit Sustainability Matrix

Social enterprises and non-profit organizations must consider their sustainability in terms of how well they accomplish their social aims or objectives and how they are able to maintain themselves financially. As with for-profit corporations, they must think strategically to survive. One approach to assessing strategic sustainability is to evaluate the organization on two dimensions: its purpose, that is, the social impact on society intended in the organization's mission, and whether or not the organization is financially viable.[16]

The assessment of the social impact depends on the mission of the organization. Some general criteria could be: the contribution to the intended mission, for example, jobs created or clients serviced; how well the services were performed; evidence that an unmet need was addressed; contributions to the community; and cooperation with other organizations. Financial viability would be assessed against the level of expenses and availability of funding, the meeting of budgets, the success of revenue generating enterprises, and the diversity of funding sources. The matrix in Figure 16.2 illustrates the four strategic sustainability possibilities created by degree of social impact versus financial viability.

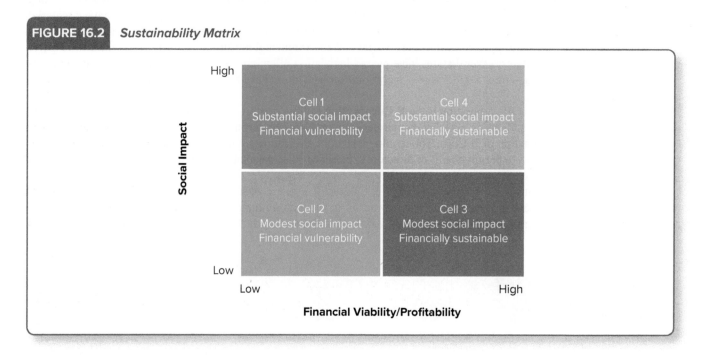

FIGURE 16.2 *Sustainability Matrix*

Cell 1 indicates that the organization is making a substantial social impact but may have inadequate funding to sustain this level of activity. Cell 2 is a *status quo* situation where a modest impact is being made but at the same time, finances are sufficient. In Cell 3 the situation is one where there is sufficient funding for the social impact being made, and the enterprise could reassess its social impact, or reallocate funding. The best situation is illustrated in Cell 4 there substantial funding is available for the social impact being made.

The Matrix can be used to assess the strategic sustainability on an organization in two situations. A social enterprise or non-profit organization could assess itself to ascertain where it is on the matrix and then take the appropriate action. For example, if the enterprise assesses themselves in Cell 1, it will seek more funding. The second situation is where a social enterprise or non-profit organization has several programs or operating units. The programs should be balanced against one another. For example, it may be appropriate that programs in cells 3 and 4 could support or subsidize programs in Cell 1.

Social enterprises and non-profit organizations should think and operate in strategic sustainable approaches the same manner as commercial enterprises.

LO 16.4 Socialization of Capitalism Concepts and Expressions

There are many concepts and expressions of the socialization of capitalism in the academic literature, the business media, and in practice. This section describes several of the most common ones.

Social Licence

In Chapter 1, social licence is defined as the privilege of operating in society with minimal formalized restrictions—that is, legislation, regulation, or market requirements—based on maintaining public trust by doing what is acceptable to stakeholders in the business and society relationship. Social licence is a term that is increasingly appearing in media stories.

In a general sense, social licence involves society's trust that the activities of business are legitimate and consistent with social expectations and the values of stakeholders. Social licence is based on ethics, values, expectations, and self-regulation and is considered preferable to social or government control, which is based on legal regulation, legislation, litigation, and compliance. In practice, a balance exists between social licence and control, where the former is a proactive approach and the latter reactive. The balance can be shifted with intervention in the marketplace by government or the actions or demands of stakeholders—for example, through consumer boycotts.

In recent years, social licence has been a concept applied to individual projects. This is significant in Canada as a major portion of the economy is based on the resource industries where development projects involve social and environmental issues or risks. As a result, the application of social licence has become a concept increasingly discussed. Today, most new projects require the approval of the local community and other stakeholders, in particular NGOs. A social licence is based upon the beliefs, perceptions, and opinions held by the stakeholders, and is in effect granted by those harmed or benefiting from the project. The life cycle of the project is involved, including a properly conducted environmental assessment, careful design of the project, effective operation practices, and a closure strategy.

Some business persons are questioning the need for such a licence. They claim that the harms of development projects should be balanced with the creation of jobs, generation of business activity, and encouragement of investment. The rules, procedures, and processes for obtaining a social licence are vague making it difficult to obtain. Besides, there is already in existence a regulatory system, such as exemplified by the National Energy Board and environmental assessment agencies, that have been set up by government to oversee most development projects. The social licence is in addition to these formal requirements meaning that not only government must be satisfied but also another stakeholder, that is, society. The requirements for obtaining the social licence are too open-ended, undefined, and biased with unaccountable tests. According to the critics, this should not be the basis for decision making and the stakeholders involved, in effect, have too much power. There is uncertainty concerning which stakeholders should be consulted, for example, NGOs, business, courts, and public opinion. Also, there is an issue relating to how the feedback should be measured and evaluated for its significance. Complete consensus is doubtful, especially for controversial projects. Thus, two licences are necessary, the first from the regulatory agency or government, and a second one from society. Some business persons wonder if the public interest has been ignored in this complicated process.

The existence of the social license is another indication of the need to integrate economic, social, and environment issues between business and society. Corporations and their managers must develop the skills and competences to deal with this development.

Social Innovation

In a general sense, social innovations are new ideas, products, services, institutions and relationships that offer a new way of addressing economic, social and environmental challenges. The problems that need be to addressed include climate change, poverty alleviation, income inequality, social conflicts, and environmental degradation. Social innovations occur at the edges of the private, social and public sectors of the economy and might be considered a part of the fourth sector. One definition of **social innovation** is "a novel solution to a social problem that is more effective, efficient, sustainable, or just than current solutions" where the "value created accrues primarily to society rather than to private individuals."[17]

Advocates of social innovation believe that society's most difficult and important problems cannot be understood and solved without involving the private, social, and public sectors of the economy. This involves an exchange of ideas and values, shifts in roles and values, and the integration of private capital with public and philanthropic support. Some social innovations permanently alter the perceptions, behaviours, and structures in society. An example of the changes in corporate structures is given in the previous section where social enterprise and for-benefits corporations were discussed. Social innovation is another expression of the socialization of capitalism and two examples of Canadian organizations involved with social innovation are described in Everyday Ethics 16.4.

 EVERYDAY ETHICS 16.4

Two Canadian Social Innovation Organizations

There are many organizations involved with social innovation and the following represent different approaches.

The Centre for Social Innovation (CSI)—This is a social enterprise with a mission to increase the presence of social innovation in Toronto and around the world. CSI believes that society is facing unprecedented economic, environmental, social, and cultural challenges, and that new innovations are the key to turning these challenges into opportunities to improve communities and the planet. Its members include 1,000 non-profits, charities, and social ventures employing over 2,500 people and generating annual revenues of $250 million.

The McConnell Foundation—The Foundation's purpose is to enhance Canada's ability to address complex social, environmental and economic challenges and one program is the Social Innovation Fund. The Fund is to support work that will result in breakthrough ideas and approaches, game changing strategies and collaborations, and continuous innovation. The Fund supports work on early stage innovations and established organizations already operating successful social innovations so that they scale up to meet growing demand.

Want to learn more about social innovation?

Social Impact Investing

Social impact investing is the financing of initiatives to address social and environmental challenges and that generates a financial return and measurable benefits to society. Social impact investing is also referred to as **social finance**, which has a similar definition: "investments intended to create a measurable social or environmental impact as well as to generate financial returns."[18]

The new forms of capital and investment vehicles used include microfinance, various types of bonds including social impact, green and community, venture philanthropy, social enterprises, B Corps, and socially focused mutual funds. These new forms act as a bridge between the private, social, and public sectors with regard to the financing of initiatives. The initiatives can relate to a wide range of investments including in clean technology, green construction, renewable energy, water, sustainable agriculture and food, and community economic development, for example, affordable housing, and health and educational facilities.

Impact investment is different from traditional investment in three ways: (1) Investors expect to receive a financial return with a defined societal impact. These investors include: high net worth individuals, foundations, community finance organizations (Indigenous financial institutions and community loan funds), financial institutions (credit unions and chartered banks), pension funds, and governments. (2) Investees' business models are constructed to seek both financial and social value. (3) Both investors and investees expect to be able to measure social impact. The financing tools used include social impact bonds, community bonds, and green bonds.

There are several impact measurement frameworks:

- Impact Reporting and Investment Standards (IRIS) and the Global Impact Investment Rating System (GIIRS). These frameworks allow investors to compare across sectors, regions, and organizational sizes.

- Social Return on Investment (SROI). This framework is used to assign monetary value to the social value created by the initiatives financed.

- Environmental, Social and Governance (ESG) metrics. These are commonly used in conventional financing.

- Demonstrating Value. This is a measurement tool that combines business performance monitoring with social impact evaluation.

Governments are also involved in building the capacity for impact investment. They provide the investment rules and requirements and sometimes co-invest. Taxes, subsidies, reporting requirements and intermediation are established by governments. They also enable the corporate structures such as the Community Contribution Company (CCC) in British Columbia and the Community Interest Company (CIC) in Nova Scotia.[19]

In 2017, the federal government formed the Social Innovation and Social Finance Strategy Co-Creation Steering Group. In 2018, the Group submitted its report, "Inclusive innovation: New ideas and new partnerships for stronger communities." It describes social innovation and social finance and contains the recommendations of the Group. One of its recommendations was that the "Government create a Social Finance Fund ('the Fund') to accelerate the development of social finance ecosystems across Canada."[20] In fall 2018, the government announced the establishment of a $755 million Social Finance Fund to support innovative solutions on a broad range of social challenges and attract new private sector investment to the social finance sector.[21]

Social finance differs from social responsible investing (SRI) in that the intent of social impact investing is made in organizations whose core mandate is to do social or environmental good. With SRI the economic, social, and governance risks are integrated into an analysis of all investments. SRI uses screens to avoid investing in corporations with poor economic, social, and governance practices. Negative screens use factors to disqualify investments, while positive screens use factors that identify corporations as the best or leading in their industry.[22]

The Sharing Economy

Some consumers are interested in the social purpose of business and one expression of this is referred to as the **sharing economy**, and sometimes as *peer-to-peer e-commerce* and defined as a sustainable social and economic system involving the sharing of human and physical resources. Examples of the trend include: swapping, exchanging, bartering, collective purchasing, shared ownership, renting or borrowing, and trading of used goods. Also associated with the trend are microfinancing, micro-entrepreneurship, social enterprises, and cooperatives. The trend is consistent with the philosophy of reducing, reusing, and recycling.

There is a greater desire in society to share rather than own as many believe that fewer resources should be used in the production and consumption of goods and services not only by individual consumers but also by business corporations. Technology, in particular the Internet, has enabled this trend to increase its presence in the economy. There are many areas where the sharing economy is appearing. Airbnb allows individual householders to rent accommodations in their homes without having to establish a bed and breakfast operation. By using Eatwith and Feastly, individuals with a talent for cooking can share their skills with others in their homes. In transportation, Uber and Lyft enable private operators to provide taxi services for others without belonging to a taxi company. CarShare, AutoShare, and Student Car Share enable individuals to rent vehicles on short terms. The borrowing or exchange of goods is made possible by eBay, and Swapsity facilitates bartering. Swap Working Holidays finds jobs for those interested in working abroad.

It is argued that the sharing economy has come about because of market failures or imperfections. The sharing economy is market- and exchange-based and offers opportunities to consumers and providers of services that were not being provided in the past. A downside is that the regulation of businesses in the sharing economy has been challenging. Most sharing economy businesses operate outside, or with little, government regulation, and it is difficult to apply traditional regulations. This leads to unfair competition in some industries and consumers may be unprotected. The livelihoods of some are destroyed and work security reduced. The gap between those fully employed and those working as casuals in the sharing economy may grow and cause dissatisfaction. Governments have not yet implemented regulations or policies that are applicable to how sharing economy businesses operate. Whatever regulation emerges, it should not impede growth, as a new economic sector has surfaced that is contributing to the economy.

Want to learn more about the sharing economy?

Philanthrocapitalism

The Economist referred to the new approaches such as social venture philanthropy and social enterprise as *philanthrocapitalism*. **Philanthrocapitalism** draws upon modern business practices, that is, the philosophy of capitalist style objectives and criteria with an entrepreneurial spirit to get more from non-profit or social organizations.[23] It is a new approach for the philanthropy of the world's wealthiest "one percent." These philanthropists, or philanthrocapitalists, want to bring new ideas to social initiatives and to be more involved with the operations. Their donations can be used where others have not been or to take advantage of opportunities others have missed. One initiative to encourage the world's wealthiest persons to share more of their wealth to address the needs of the world is the Giving Pledge described in Everyday Ethics 16.5.

EVERYDAY ETHICS 16.5

The Giving Pledge

Bill and Melinda Gates and Warren Buffett issued a "Giving Pledge" challenge to billionaires in June 2010, urging them to give away more than half of their fortunes. By 2019, 204 billionaires from 23 countries had pledged. The Giving Pledge website states:

The Giving Pledge is a movement of philanthropists that is aimed at encouraging a culture of generosity. One of the most important things about the Giving Pledge is that it's inspiring people to give more, establish their giving plans sooner, and give in smarter ways.

A list of current pledgers is available on Givingpledge.org. Canadians who have participated include Jeff Skoll (born in Montreal and the first president of eBay), Charles and Edgar Bronfman (whose family established Seagrams), Elon Musk (founder of Tesla and SpaceX), Garrett Camp (co-founder of Uber), and John and Marcy McCall MacBain (founder of Trader Classified Media).

Both domestic and international causes will receive funding. Each pledger decides how his or her money is to be allocated and there is no central agency to distribute the funds. The process will work on an honour system; that is, the pledge is non-binding and represents a moral commitment rather than a legal one. The Giving Pledge community has an annual meeting, in addition to smaller gatherings throughout the year. The purpose of the annual gathering is for the Giving Pledge community to learn and share knowledge in order to continue to improve the effectiveness of their philanthropic giving.

Source: Adapted from "The Giving Pledge" at http://givingpledge.org/ accessed March 28, 2019. © 2010–2013 Giving Pledge LLC and its licensors and suppliers, February 10, 2018, 10, 11. Used with the permission of The Giving Pledge.

This philanthropy by the world's elite has become a new charitable paradigm in international development. Its goals are to address social issues in the developing world including improving human well-being (health and education), reducing poverty, and promoting equality. Despite the generosity of the givers, there are criticisms.

Attention was drawn to philanthrocapitalism when Facebook's Mark Zuckerberg and his spouse, Priscilla Chan, announced that they were contributing 99 percent of their shares, valued at $45 million, to better the lives of millions. The legal structure that Zuckerberg used was questioned when he contributed the shares to a limited liability company (LLC) instead of a foundation. Using the LLC allowed the Zuckerbergs to retain of control of the corporation and influence its operations. Also, there were fewer restrictions on oversight than if a charitable foundation had been used. Zuckerberg can stay involved, gets a charitable deduction on this tax return, and does not pay capital gains on the shares.

Other criticisms are that they are undermining the work of NGOs and that the good causes pursued are dependent on the whims of a few. Avoiding taxation reduces the revenues that the government would have to address the same causes. Some critics say that the initiatives are undertaken merely to ease the social consciences of the donors and rarely tackle fundamental political and economic inequity. It is suggested that the individual initiatives lack collaboration and coordination with aid agencies, which may result in duplication of effort. One critic referred to the approach as philanthropic colonialism providing band aid solutions that fail to find and address the underlying causes of the complex problems being addressed.[24]

Social Capital

The concept of social capital is used by a growing number of sociologists, political scientists, economists, and organizational theorists to improve the understanding of social relationships among individuals, organizations, and within and between societies.[25] Stakeholder concept researchers are beginning to use social capital as another approach to understanding the relationships between the corporation and its stakeholders.

As social capital is a broad concept and can be used in understanding many different types of relationships, many definitions and perspectives of the concept exist. This discussion examines social capital as it applies to understanding corporate stakeholder relationships.

Social capital is any aspect of a corporation's organizational arrangements that creates value and facilitates the actions of stakeholders within and external to the corporation. Social capital is created when the relations between stakeholders and the corporation change in ways that facilitate increased understanding, cooperation, and coordination. In effect, the corporation's stakeholders are a network; that is, a pattern of ties linking the corporation with those it influences and those that can influence it.[26]

Another perspective views social capital as the trust or goodwill existing between the corporation and its stakeholders. This is a valuable resource to the corporation and its source is in the relationships established with stakeholders and the nature of these relationships. The more trust and goodwill the better off the corporation is because it works more efficiently with stakeholders. Corporations benefit from social capital because it facilitates cooperation and coordination that minimizes transaction costs, such as boycotts, legal actions, negotiations, and disruptions in production. More effective and efficient relations with stakeholders may provide a competitive edge over corporations that possess less social capital.

A research report prepared for the Canadian Institute of Chartered Accountants outlined how value is created through social capital obtained from stakeholder relationships.[27] The report identified three levels of organizational culture that explain how corporations orient themselves toward stakeholders. Level 1 is a compliance culture that preserves the value of stakeholder relationships as established by laws and norms and seeks to avoid unacceptable destruction of value. Level 2 is referred to as a relationship management culture where value is created but often is traded off, usually after the demands of the shareholders are satisfied. Maximum value is created at Level 3, a sustainable organizational culture. This culture maximizes the creation of value simultaneously in economic, ethical, and environmental terms.[28] The research focused on corporations at Levels 2 and 3.

From the research, a model of social capital and business value creation was developed; it is shown in Figure 16.3.

FIGURE 16.3 *Model of Social Capital and Business Value Creation*

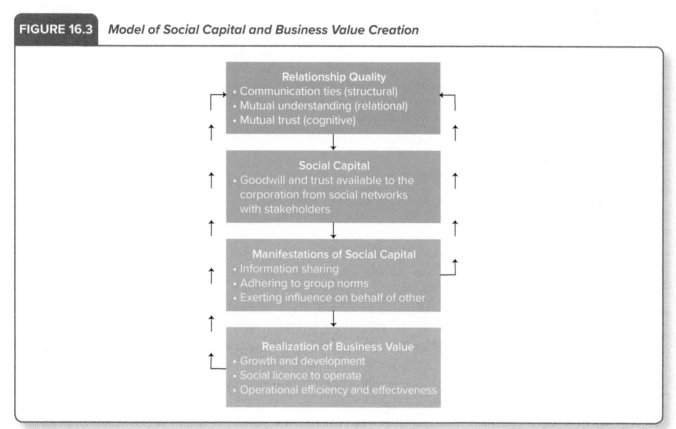

Source: Ann Svendsen, Robert G. Boutilier, and David Wheeler (2003). *Stakeholder Relationships, Social Capital, and Business Value Creation* (Toronto: The Canadian Institute of Chartered Accountants), 12. Reprinted with permission of Chartered Professional Accountants Canada, copyright 2003. Any changes to the original material are the sole responsibility of the author (and/or publisher) and have not been reviewed or endorsed by the Chartered Professional Accountants of Canada.

Svendsen, Boutilier, and Wheeler summarize the source of social capital as three dimensions or attributes: structural, represented by the networks in which the relationships are embedded; relational, referring to trust and reciprocity; and cognitive, involving mutual understanding. Three manifest benefits of social capital were identified:

- Willingness to share information.
- Willingness to exert one's influence or power to benefit the other where influence also means control and power.
- Solidarity/norm adherence referring to group cohesiveness.[29]

The researchers identified the potential business value created by the benefits of social capital. The following are some examples:

- Information allows employees to access new ideas from external networks.
- Information and norm adherence enables employees to share information and work collaboratively.
- Norm adherence establishes a strong emotional connection between the corporation and its customers.
- Influence can be obtained by making a valuable contribution to the community.
- Influence and norm adherence allows the corporation and union to have reciprocal debts to each other that merge their interests in each other's success.[30]

The concept of social capital is an additional approach to understanding stakeholder relationships and illustrates the sophistication possible in the analysis of stakeholder relationships. The argument that business value is created will most likely encourage other corporations to become involved with methodologies to increase their understanding of stakeholders.

Sustainable Capitalism

Al Gore, former U.S. vice-president, and David Blood, financial industry executive, have developed a document on an appropriate economy system for the future, *A Manifesto for Sustainable Capitalism: How businesses can embrace environmental, social and governance metrics.* They argue that it is time to move from short economic thinking to a longer-term version that they call **sustainable capitalism** which they define as an "economic system within which business and trade seek to maximise long-term value creation, accounting for all material ESG (environmental, social and governance) metrics."

Business must mobilize the financial resources to address challenges facing society such as climate change, water scarcity, poverty, disease, growing income inequality, urbanization, and massive economic volatility. This more responsible form of capitalism is a "framework that seeks to maximize long term economic value by reforming markets to address real needs while integrating environmental, social and governance (ESG) metrics throughout the decision-making process." Embracing sustainable capitalism will result in benefits for corporations:

- Sustainable products and services can increase a corporation's profits, enhance its brand, and improve its competitive positioning.
- Money will be saved by reducing waste and increasing energy efficiency in the supply chain, and by improving human-capital practices.
- Environmental, social, and governance metrics enable corporations to achieve higher compliance standards and better manage risk.
- Financial benefits such as lower cost of debt and lower capital constraints will result.

Investors should focus on the long-term value and potential of corporations when they make investment decisions. In order to respond to the urgency of the present threats, they recommend five key actions:

- Identify and incorporate risk from stranded assets, that is, those whose value would dramatically change, either positively or negatively, when large externalities are taken into account, for example, attributing a reasonable price to carbon or water.
- Mandate integrated financial and ESG performance reporting, which will enable corporations and investors to make better resource allocation decisions.
- End the practice of issuing quarterly earnings guidance which causes executives to manage and investors think in the short term instead of the longer term.
- Align compensation structures with long-term sustainable performance.
- Encourage long-term investing in securities that investors are loyal to in the long term.[31]

Sustainable capitalism has been discussed from an investor perspective. A corporation and management view was provided in LO 16.2.

Corporate Social Integration

Porter and Kramer argue that corporations have not analyzed CSR initiatives using the same frameworks that guide their core business choices. CSR should not be thought of as a cost, constraint, or charitable deed, but instead as an opportunity, innovation, and competitive advantage. The authors viewed most CSR initiatives as being reactive and many as being merely cosmetic; that is, public relations, media campaigns, and glossy reports. According to Porter and Kramer, reports seldom offer a coherent framework for CSR activities.

The authors identified the prevailing justifications for CSR and their limitations. The moral obligation for corporations to do the right thing does not always provide guidance. Sustainability that involves environmental and community stewardship is subject to self-interest and trade-offs. The license to operate means that outside stakeholders have control over the social agenda. The emphasis on reputation as a justification focuses on external stakeholders. All these prevailing justifications focus on tensions between business and society, and that to improve CSR there must be a better understanding of the interrelationship between the corporation and society.[32]

The authors proposed that the CSR model should become a corporate social integration model approach, which would integrate social perspective with business strategy. This would be accomplished by identifying the points of intersection between business and society, choosing which social issues to address, creating a corporate social agenda, and integrating inside-out and outside-in linkages.

The interdependence between business and society takes two forms: inside-out linkages, which represent the corporation's positive and negative influence on society through its operations, and outside-in linkages, which represent society's positive and negative influences on the corporation.[33]

Social issues must be prioritized into three types: generic, value chain, and social dimensions of competitive context. Generic social issues are those that do not significantly affect the corporation but are important to society. Value-chain social issues are significantly affected by the corporation as it carries out business. Lastly, social dimensions of competitive context are "factors in the external environment that significantly affect the underlying drivers of competitiveness in those places where the company operates."[34]

Porter and Kramer categorize a corporation's involvement in society into two approaches, responsive and strategic. Responsive CSR includes the generic social impacts and efforts to mitigate harm from value-chain activities. More importantly, strategic CSR includes transforming "value-chain activities to benefit society while reinforcing strategy," and "strategic philanthropy that leverages capabilities to improve salient areas of competitive context."[35]

Strategic CSR is beyond best practices and will identify a competitive position advantageous to the corporation. Inside-out and outside-in dimensions must work together to produce shared value opportunities. In this way the social dimension is enhanced while at the same time reducing the constraints on the corporation's value chain. Several examples are given, including Marriott's training program for hospitality industry employees; Nestlé's efforts to purchase from small producers in developing countries; and Whole Foods's value proposition of selling organic, natural, and healthy food products.[36]

Porter and Kramer conclude that CSR should be viewed more appropriately as corporate social integration. Instead of thinking in the short term, viewing CSR as correcting something business has done wrong or merely corporate giving, think of it as creating shared value for all stakeholders involved, in particular governments, NGOs, and corporations themselves.[37]

This section has identified and described several concepts along with some expressions of the socialization of capitalism. When considered together, these concepts and expressions are evidence of a trend in capitalism towards greater attention being given to integrating social purpose with a corporation's economic purpose.

The programs in Canada's business schools must incorporate sustainability concepts, frameworks, and theories into course work and research. The schools themselves might have sustainability reports, and students can be involved in sustainability initiatives.

LO 16.5   Socialization of Capitalism and Business School Programs

Business programs in colleges and universities are responding to the increasing awareness of the ethics and responsibilities of business. The response takes various forms and business education programs are feeling the impact. More important is the benefit for students. When they enter the workplace, they will be confronted by ethical dilemmas and a requirement to respond to social and environmental issues. When they become managers they will encounter various aspects of ethical business practice and be confronted by numerous business and society issues that will affect their corporations.

This section highlights some of initiatives to increase the awareness of the socialization of capitalism undertaken in business schools through the curriculum redesign and other activities.

Teaching Sustainability in Business Schools

This chapter has been describing various initiatives to transforming the approach to business through the socialization capitalism. However, it is important to educate and train future leaders on the integration of economic and social factors. Business schools are ideal places to provide new ways of thinking about business and society and to challenge the established precepts.

Corporations have ethics or social responsibilities programs and there is increasing discussion of similar programs at business schools. Such programs might have several components:

- There could be a statement of values or philosophy.
- The curriculum could include core and elective courses on ethics and related areas such as social enterprise and sustainability. Degree programs could be offered that focus on ethics and corporate responsibilities.

- The faculty could follow codes of ethics or conduct relating to teaching and research. Teaching materials, such as cases, could be developed in addition to publications in academic journals.

- Students could have their own code of ethics or conduct, and form and support organizations related to social responsibility. Students could be involved in volunteer activities and take pledges or oaths committing themselves to ethical and socially responsible behaviour.

The Association to Advance Collegiate Schools of Business (AACSB) has joined the Aspen Institute's Business and Society Program, the European Foundation for Management Development (EFMD), and several other leading associations as co-conveners of the United Nations Global Compact to craft the first iteration of a global set of principles that acknowledge business schools' critical role in advancing socially responsible business leadership. These principles are known as the six Principles of Responsibility Management Education (PRME) and are listed in Responsibility for Ethics 16.2. Business schools take pride in being identified with these principles of responsible management education as corporations do with the various awards that exist for practicing sustainability. Involvement in PRME requires that participating business schools submit a Sharing Information on Progress (SIP) report that describes the school's progress toward sustainability.

 RESPONSIBILITY FOR ETHICS 16.2

The Six Principles of Responsible Management Education

Principle 1

Purpose: We will develop the capabilities of students to be future generators of sustainable value for business and society at large and to work for an inclusive and sustainable global economy.

Principle 2

Values: We will incorporate into our academic activities and curricula the values of global social responsibility as portrayed in international initiatives such as the United Nations Global Compact.

Principle 3

Method: We will create educational frameworks, materials, processes and environments that enable effective learning experiences for responsible leadership.

Principle 4

Research: We will engage in conceptual and empirical research that advances our understanding about the role, dynamics, and impact of corporations in the creation of sustainable social, environmental and economic value.

Principle 5

Partnership: We will interact with managers of business corporations to extend our knowledge of their challenges in meeting social and environmental responsibilities and to explore jointly effective approaches to meeting these challenges.

Principle 6

Dialogue: We will facilitate and support dialogue and debate among educators, business, government, consumers, media, civil society organizations and other interested groups and stakeholders on critical issues related to global social responsibility and sustainability.

We understand that our own organizational practices should serve as examples of the values and attitudes we convey to our students.

Many business schools are going a step further and establishing sustainability centres to help create a more sustainable business model that integrates economic and social purposes. This is done by enhancing research and teaching programs as well as working with industry to make social and environmental change. Some examples of sustainability centres at Canadian colleges and universities are listed in Everyday Ethics 16.6. The Network for Business Sustainability maintains a directory of more than 150 sustainability centres from around the world.[38]

EVERYDAY ETHICS 16.6

Business School Sustainability Centres

Each year *Corporate Knights* magazine ranks MBA programs on sustainability. The ranking criteria includes institutes and centres, curriculum, faculty research, female diversity, and racial diversity. Eleven Canadian schools were included in the 2018 Better World MBA Ranking of 40 schools from around the world. The criterion for selection of the institutes and centres is the focus of sustainability initiatives. Examples at Canadian business schools are:

- *Haskayne School of Business, University of Calgary*—The Centre for Corporate Sustainability disseminates knowledge and seeks to find a balance in environmental, social, and economic approaches in energy (https://haskayne.ucalgary.ca/ccs).

- *Peter B. Gustavson School of Business, University of Victoria*—The Center of Social and Sustainable Innovation helps the school, its students, and the greater community become change agents and role models for a sustainable and responsible approach to business (https://www.uvic.ca/gustavson/research/research/centres/index.php).

- *College of Business and Economics, University of Guelph*—The John F. Wood Centre for Business and Student Enterprise looks for innovative and sustainable solutions to economic, social, and environmental problems (https://www.uoguelph.ca/johnfwoodcentre/about).

- *John Molson School of Business, Concordia University*—The David O'Brien Centre for Sustainable Enterprise (DOCSE) develops sustainable practices through academic research, programs, and outreach within the community (http://www.concordia.ca/jmsb/research/centres/david-obrien.html).

Other Canadian university business schools included in the top 40 are York, Saint Mary's, McGill, Simon Fraser, British Columbia, Toronto, and Ottawa.

Source: "Making the grade," *Corporate Knights*, Fall 2018 Issue, November 9, 2018 accessed at https://www.corporateknights.com/magazines/2018-better-world-mba-issue/making-the-grade-15417432/ on January 2, 2019. Used with permission.

It is believed that the initiatives of business to expose students to the concepts and expressions of the socialization of capitalism will change the ways students think about the relationships between business and society. For example, Wiek *et al.* identified the competences that students acquire when exposed to business programs that focus on sustainability. These competences were: systems thinking necessary to understand the complex economic, social and environmental issues; capability to consider long- and short-term implications of actions; consideration of the moral implications of actions; strategic thinking relating to stakeholder engagement and issues; and the importance of collaboration. The authors also identified the approaches used to develop these diverse competences in students: embedding sustainability into existing business programs; creating new courses and programs; and insuring that students were exposed to real-world problems.[39]

Another view of how students should be prepared to address sustainability challenges in their careers was described by Hoffman in an article titled "Management as a Calling." He described several ways to make a "whole manager," including requiring reflection about future careers, requiring a critical review of future capitalism, teaching about responsible lobbying, requiring more critical examination of the "purpose" of the corporation, and adding natural environment science to the curriculum.[40]

The various exposures to sustainability in business schools through courses and programs, providing sustainability-focused exchange and service learning opportunities, empowering students to make real-world impact through supervised projects, and engaging students to co-organize educational events will hopefully result in the development of future responsible managers. Some sustainability related initiatives by students are described in the following section.

Students and Sustainability

Stakeholders in society expect business to adopt and practise sustainability. It must be remembered that sustainability is the responsibility of all stakeholders, including students.

Students should check out their college or university's sustainability policy or strategy, as some have comprehensive policies. At some colleges, the Student Union will also have a sustainability program. Many universities have investments in endowment funds used to support scholarships or research. Students can lobby officials to follow socially responsible investing as described in Chapter 11. Some universities already belong to the Coalition of Universities for Responsible Investing (CURI), a forum for dialogue, collaborative action, and education on socially and environmentally responsible investing among Canadian universities.[41]

Students can also become directly involved in sustainability initiatives. Volunteering for campus or community projects and in support of social causes is possible, or local issues could be studied. Community-Based Research Canada (CBRC) is a network of people and organizations engaged in research to meet the needs of people and communities. Several Canadian universities are involved with CBRC.[42]

International volunteer service in a developing country is another possibility. This could involve travel with the purpose of studying an issue or aspect of life in a particular country. There is the possibility of living in a country for some time by seeking out a semester internship or a volunteer position. Some well-known organizations involved in this type of learning are Engineers Without Borders, Students Without Borders (Uniterra), CUSO International, and Projects Abroad.

Students participating in these programs are involved in a form of **service-learning**, a method of teaching combining classroom learning with service to the community either locally or in developing countries. It can be done for credit and involves a service activity to fulfill a community need and provides a way to gain further understanding of course content. More can be learned about service-learning at the Canadian Alliance for Community Service-Learning (CSL) website.[43]

Pledges or oaths to engage in ethical behaviour have been formulated. The *Graduation Pledge of Social and Environmental Responsibility* is taken upon graduation to emphasize consideration of the social and environmental consequences of the jobs students may accept and widely used in the United States.[44] Another example is the MBA Oath, a volunteer pledge for MBAs to create value responsibly and ethically.[45] Considerable controversy surrounds these pledges and oaths, with critics pointing out that they are window dressing or greenwashing and that they cannot be enforced. But they increase student awareness of ethical, social, and environmental issues.

LO 16.6 Capitalism in the Future

In Chapter 2, LO 2.10, descriptions of various forms of capitalism were defined: consumer, producer, family, frontier, and state capitalism. These can be considered descriptive of traditional capitalism. In the past two decades, various individuals and organizations have proposed other descriptive terminology that reflects what they think capitalism should be. Examples of these new terms for capitalism are summarized in Table 16.3 and reflect some aspect of the socialization of capitalism.

TABLE 16.3	Contemporary Terms for Capitalism
References are provided for more information or when the term can be attributed to a particular individual or organization.	
Responsible enterprise system—An economic system operating as a free enterprise system but incorporating the element of accountability. This definition implies that business enterprises are responsible to society for their actions and are answerable or accountable for being the cause, agent, or source of something. This term emerged in the debate following the 2008 financial crisis. The term recognized the need for a new economic system to restore trust in business, to create a different balance between finance and other sectors, and to encourage corporations to take a long-term view.	
Stakeholder capitalism—An economic system in which corporations accept broader obligations beyond financial ones for shareholders. Corporations are expected to balance the interests of shareholders with those of other stakeholders in the business system, for example employees, suppliers, customers, and the community at large. In stakeholder capitalism, corporations are expected to behave with greater social responsibility and be sensitive to the ethical consequences of their actions.	

Clean capitalism—*Corporate Knights* (CK) magazine uses this term to associate capitalism with social responsibility. The magazine defines clean capitalism as "an economic system that incorporates the social, economic and ecological benefits and costs, and actors know the full impacts of their actions." CK is the first print business magazine and research firm in the world to be a certified B Corp.

Conscious capitalism—Conscious capitalism builds on the foundations of capitalism, voluntary exchange, entrepreneurship, competition, freedom to trade and the rule of law. These are essential but conscious capitalism has other elements—trust, compassion, collaboration, and value creation—and is based on four pillars: higher purpose, stakeholder orientation, conscious leadership, and conscious culture.

Creative capitalism—This is a new form of capitalism that places the resolution of social needs as a primary goal of economic activity, rather than as a secondary consequence of economic activity and performance. It was described initially by Bill Gates of Microsoft, who was concerned by the inequities between the world's rich and poor peoples. He asserts that non-creative capitalism does not have to concern itself directly with the well-being of people. It took for granted its benefits to all, through its mechanisms of social Darwinism, competition, and evolutionary success of the fittest.

Moral capitalism—Moral capitalism is advocated by the Caux Round Table for Moral Capitalism (CRT), which "is an international network of principled business leaders working to promote a moral capitalism." It has formulated "Principles for Business" through which "principled capitalism can flourish and sustainable and socially responsible prosperity can become the foundation for a fair, free and transparent global society."

Inclusive capitalism—Inclusive capitalism is an approach that would address "the growing inequality in the distribution of income and wealth; to unemployment especially among the young; to falling social mobility; to the 1% vs the 99%; to poverty more generally and how capitalism can help to alleviate it." The approach is advocated by the Coalition for Inclusive Capitalism, a non-profit organization that "engages leaders across business, government, and civil society in their efforts to make capitalism more dynamic, sustainable, and inclusive."

Progressive capitalism—Joseph E. Stiglitz, a Nobel laureate in economics, recently published a book in which he describes this new form of capitalism, *People, Power, and Profits: Progressive Capitalism for an Age of Discontent*. He is concerned with inequality and the low levels of opportunity in society in an exploitative business system. There is a need to recognize the role of government in making the market system serve society. This involves the regulation of business to ensure competition, realigning the relationship between corporations and employees, and a new social contract that allows business and society to work together. Read Stiglitz's article "Progressive Capitalism Is Not an Oxymoron," *New York Times*, April 19, 2019, at https://www.nytimes.com/2019/04/19/opinion/sunday/progressive-capitalism.html.

Sustainable capitalism—Sustainable capitalism would be included, but it is discussed in LO 16.4.

Despite all these new forms of capitalism being proposed, there is still dissatisfaction with capitalism as an economic system. There have been surveys in the United States indicating that students and young adults are becoming less respectful of capitalism and are losing faith in the system. They feel that capitalism is unfair and they are being left out of the benefits. Capitalism should be more inclusive and the benefits shared more broadly. There is concern about the attacks on organized labour, the concentration of corporate power, excessive executive pay, and the downsides of trade policies that cause Americans to lose jobs. Overall, the sentiments centre around equality and opportunity, but those who are dissatisfied do not have suggestions on how capitalism might be changed in response to their complaints.[46]

In academic literature and business media there is extensive discussion of how capitalism should change. The headings of this discussion include *reimagining capitalism*, *redefining capitalism*, *renewing capitalism*, *rebooting capitalism*, or *reinventing capitalism*. All approaches outlined propose a more responsible capitalism. The contemporary terminology in Table 16.3 represents some possibilities for renewal of capitalism. Whether or not these ideas will satisfy those who are dissatisfied is not clear.

Concluding Comment

The Canadian capitalism system is becoming more aware of society's changing needs as reflected in corporate CSR and sustainability programs. This chapter has outlined the paradigm shift that has occurred in the relationship between business and society during recent decades, referred to as the *socialization of capitalism*. The business system is constantly changing along with the relationship between business and society.

The characteristics of the business system or capitalism are influenced by the fundamentals described in Chapter 2. The fundamentals are the same, but vary in influence over time. In turn, this impacts the ethics in Canadian business and society. Stakeholder influence changes over time, as do the issues that have an impact on the corporation. This leads to changes in the ethics of business and how corporate social responsibility or corporate sustainability is defined, practised, and reported.

Some stakeholders are more influential than others, and/or are influenced more by the corporation. The regulation of business is always present, but it varies, as illustrated by the increase in self-regulatory and private mechanisms including CSR. Recently, the role of owners has changed and corporate governance has been reformed. Civil society stakeholders, in particular non-governmental organizations, are increasing their influence, but corporations are also making efforts to influence them. Two areas of focus today are the natural environment and globalization. Managers cannot ignore these areas and must attempt to understand the consequences for their corporations.

Lastly, ethics of business, corporate social responsibility, or corporate sustainability now represents a strategic competence of management. This trend is unlikely to change in the near future.

Your advice to Leah . . .

If Leah believes that these are particular values associated with Canadian business practice the pledge should be signed. Before signing, the businesses must be reviewed to ascertain their consistency with contemporary corporate social responsibility and sustainability practices. In particular, there should be clarity on what the values mean in the context of the businesses. It is doubtful that signing the pledge will increase the revenue of her businesses, but signage about the membership may be of interest to customers and enhance their views of how the business operates. The only downside is that the businesses will have to live up to the values; if they don't, someone may draw it to their attention and expect accountability.

Summary

- The fourth sector is an illustration of the socialization of capitalism, or our business system today. The blurring of the boundaries among the private, social, and public sectors of the economy has created another sector where new organizational forms integrate private, social, and public approaches to providing goods and services in society. (LO 16.1)

- Corporate sustainability is a more comprehensive form of corporate social responsibility (CSR) that integrates social/ethical, environmental, and governance issues into the corporation's planning through strategic management. Corporations are at different stages on the sustainability continuum: amoral, compliance-based, emerging, and sustainability. There is no definitive description of a sustainable corporation, but the socialization of capitalism is occurring through corporate sustainability (LO 16.2)

- The socialization of capitalism has been facilitated by the creation of new organizational forms, in particular, social enterprises, for-benefit corporations, and b-corporations. (LO 16.3)

- There are numerous expressions of the socialization of capitalism and the concepts associated with it. These are: social licence, social innovation, social impact investing, the shared economy, philanthrocapitalism, social capital, sustainable capitalism, and corporate social integration. (LO 16.4)

- Business school programs are emphasizing the ethics of business and sustainability. Students are being prepared for confronting ethical dilemmas in the workplace and for understanding corporate responsibilities to society. Students can contribute to sustainability while attending colleges or universities. (LO 16.5)

- Capitalism is changing and becoming more sensitive to society's concerns about corporate ethical behaviour, social responsibility, and sustainability practices. It is not clear what capitalism will look like in the future but business management must be prepared so that corporations will be successful. (LO 16.6)

Key Terms

Socialization of capitalism

Social purpose

Private sector

Social sector

Public sector

Public–private partnership

Fourth sector

Sustainability strategy

Strategic management

Social entrepreneurship

Social entrepreneur

Social intrapreneurship

Social extrapreneurship

For-benefit (or benefit) corporation

B Corporation (or B Corp)

Social innovation

Social impact investing

Social finance

Sharing economy

Philanthrocapitalism

Social capital

Sustainable capitalism

Service-learning

Stakeholder capitalism

Clean capitalism

Conscious capitalism

Creative capitalism

Moral capitalism

Inclusive capitalism

Progressive capitalism

Critical Thinking and Discussion Questions

1. Why has the fourth sector of the economy emerged in recent years?

2. Why are there different stages of sustainability strategies?

3. What is the relationship between strategic management and sustainability strategy?

4. What should be included in a job description for a "sustainability manager"?

5. What role do profits have in the social enterprise type of corporate form?

6. Should a social licence be required? Is the need for a social license for projects preventing the economic development of the country?

7. What is the difference between social impact investing and socially responsible investing (also discussed in Chapter 11)?

8. Are the giving initiatives of the "one percent" (philantrocapitalists) improving social well-being in the world?

9. Is "sustainable capitalism" practical or feasible?

10. What approach should business programs take toward the socialization of capitalism?

11. How can students participate in the socialization of capitalism?

12. What should capitalism be like in the future?

Cases

16.1 STADIUMS, TAXPAYERS, AND SPORTS MILLIONAIRES

Calgary Mayor Naheed Nemshi and City Council were considering a proposal by the owner of the Calgary Flames to build a new arena and recreation complex. Calgary Sports and Recreation Corporation, which includes the NHL's Calgary Flames and the Canadian Football League's Calgary Stampeders, proposed a $890 million arena plus a combination stadium/field house for the downtown area. The complex would be financed with the corporation putting in $200 million, the City of Calgary $200 million, $250 million raised by a ticket tax, and $240 million by a community development levy where the taxpayers would be repaid by increased economic activity. In effect, Calgary taxpayers would be providing $440 million plus the land.

Similar schemes have been proposed by the owners of professional sports teams in other Canadian and American cities. Most involve wealthy franchise owners expecting taxpayers to subsidize the construction of new facilities. Sometimes pressure is applied by suggesting that the team will relocate to another city unless the new subsidized venue is not forthcoming. Often the new facilities are promoted as a stimulant to renewal of downtown areas and creating economic spinoffs thus having a multiplier effect. The schemes are usually complex and not easy for the public to understand.

Critics argue that the cities are victims and saying that taxpayers are giving money to the owners and well-paid players. The cities should be using the money for essential services such as affordable housing or improved social services. Numerous studies, including those by academics, have found that subsidizing new stadiums does not generate new full-time jobs, growth, or tax revenue. The wealthy owners of the sports franchises get a new facility and new revenue streams thereby increasing their profits. The subsidization is referred to as another form of corporate welfare. These critics state that if the new facility is not economically viable, then it should not be built.

Yet many cities do get involved in the schemes. Some believe that economic benefits are generated. Others simply get involved for emotional reasons: civic pride, the thrill of the game, and cheering for the "home" team.

Negotiations came to a standstill, and Mr. Nemshi was re-elected as mayor despite the efforts of the Flames' ownership to defeat him. The City Council has set up a committee to work on reopening the talks to replace the arena.

Questions

1. Who are the stakeholders involved in the construction of new sports facilities?

2. What are the issues involved? How do these issues relate to the Fourth Sector approach to economic activity?

3. Can the building of these sports facilities be justified, and if so, on what rationale?

4. Should cities become involved in this type of private–public partnership?

16.2 ADONIS CHRISTOPOULOS AND PLACES TO STAY

Adonis Christopoulos and three friends are planning a trip between semesters to the Southern United States. The purpose is to visit as many auto racing events as possible. They had researched the events and plotted out a route to attend 16 races over one month. Adonis was assigned the task of finding places to stay.

Adonis considered hotels, hostels, and maybe camping. The hotels were fairly expensive and many would not allow four adult males to occupy one room. Hostels were not available at many locations and some looked somewhat seedy. Camping was a possibility, but they did not have the equipment, which would take some effort to assemble and was costly, even second-hand. In discussing the accommodations with his friends, one of them mentioned Airbnb. Part of the sharing economy, this was an online marketplace and hospitality service accessed via its easy to use website and mobile app.

There was lots of information on the Internet about Airbnb. There was a wide selection of accommodations at all the locations. Full houses were even available that could accommodate all four friends. Adonis had communicated with some of the hosts, who were very personable and offered all kinds of help relating to the local area. Overall, Airbnb seemed to offer value for money and would be more affordable than hotels.

In his searching, Adonis also noticed some downsides. Some users felt they had been misled in that the accommodations did not live up to appearances and descriptions. Some hosts added fees not clearly specified in the listing and required minimum stays of two or more days. One problem mentioned by users was the right of the hosts to cancel reservations on short notice, leaving them without accommodations. Most sites did not have the pools, spas, or gyms that interested the guys.

In addition, there were some societal controversies. The hotel industry alleged that Airbnbs were unfair competition as they operated under no or few regulations. Local residents, including apartment dwellers and condo owners, opposed the presence of Airbnbs, and some municipalities had altered bylaws to restrict them in some areas. Social agencies claimed that the presence of Airbnbs reduced the availability of affordable housing.

Adonis found an abundance of positive and negative Airbnb experiences posted on various social media sites. Now he had to decide whether or not to go ahead and make reservations.

Questions

1. What are the issues associated with Airbnbs?
2. Who were the stakeholders influenced and/or who influenced each issue?
3. Should sharing economy businesses exist with fewer regulations?
4. Overall, are there more benefits than harms resulting from sharing economy businesses?

Ethics, Responsibilities, and Sustainability Cases

Energy Drinks at Prairie Pharmacy[1]

Victor Lukasik has just taken over the operation of the family drug store, Prairie Pharmacy. The pharmacy was started by his grandfather and carried on by his father, who now is semi-retired working as a relief or part-time pharmacist. The pharmacy was located in a Western Canada community of about 5,200 that was also served by a large retail drugstore chain. Despite the competition, Prairie Pharmacy continued to prosper because the loyalty of long-time customers and its personalized service. The pharmacy had started as a prescription filling outlet and sold a few over the counter medications. Over the years, the pharmacy had grown and now sold a large variety of over-the-counter medications, snack food, candies and soft drinks, cosmetics, greeting cards, magazines, and personal care products. It had a Canada Post franchise outlet.

Victor completed a pharmacy degree and then went to work as a sales representative for a pharmaceutical company for five years. During that time, he completed an MBA part time and through distance education courses. Victor now felt that he had sufficient education and experience to take on the management of the family pharmacy. Besides, it was good to return to his hometown.

Victor had several ideas about operating the pharmacy and about how it would compete against the larger chain store. One area that particularly interested Victor was the social responsibility of the retail pharmacy industry. An issue of concern to him was the unhealthy products that were sold in the store. One such product was energy drinks, and he had done some primarily research.

What is an Energy Drink?

An energy drink is a beverage that is supposed to make a person more alert and give more energy. Common brands are Full Throttle, Monster, Tab Energy, Rockstar, Red Rain, Go Fast!, Rip It, and Red Bull. Most of these drinks contain caffeine, sugar, taurine, vitamins and herbs. Caffeine is a main ingredient and can be found in coffee, tea, chocolate, cola and certain medications. The range of caffeine in energy drinks ranges from 50 mg per can to above 200 mg per can, above the recommended daily intake for most children and teens. Too much caffeine can cause irritability, nausea, heart palpitations, feelings of hyper-energy, nervousness and loss of sleep, and is not recommended for children or young teenagers.[2]

Many energy drinks sold in large can sizes have lots of sugar, which provides energy in the form of calories. Although calories are added to a person's diet, sugar on its own adds no nutritional value. It is claimed that adding taurine, an amino acid associated with building protein, to energy drinks makes the consumer more alert. There is no scientific evidence to support this claim. Some vitamins, for example B and glucuronolactone, are added to increase energy levels, but there is no scientific evidence to support this practice. Medicinal herbs like ginseng and gingko biloba are added to some energy drinks as it is claimed that they improve performance, but again, there is no evidence to support this.

Energy drinks are widely available and found anywhere consumers purchase beverages including drug, grocery, and convenience stores and gas stations. They are packaged with flashy labels and often placed near juices and sports drinks.

Information Found

Victor found lots of information on energy drinks in the print and broadcast media, on the Internet, and in academic literature. Professional and trade associations had information energy drinks as well as numerous government sources. Many research organizations were involved in investigating the effects of consuming energy drinks. The following is some of the information found.

Industry trade associations did not provide much guidance. The websites for the Canadian Pharmacists Association (CPhA) and Neighbourhood Pharmacy Association of Canada did not appear to have information on energy drinks that was accessible by the public.

A study of Atlantic Canadian high school students by the Propel Centre for Population Health Impact, University of Waterloo, found: the more students consumed energy drinks, the more they will suffer from depression or become addicted to alcohol or marijuana; the drinks appeal to young people because of temporary benefits, including increased alertness, improved mood, and enhanced mental and physical energy; younger teens were more likely to consume energy drinks than older teens possibly as the result of advertising designed to appeal to this age group.[3] The Canadian Beverage Association was critical of the study claiming that the findings reflect only an association and not causality.[4]

Several health organizations have warned of the dangers associated with the consumption of energy drinks by children and teens. Research presented at an American Heart Association meeting showed how energy drinks impacted cardiovascular health, including causing irregular heartbeats that might contribute to heart attacks and sudden death. Energy drinks might also be associated with high blood pressure. The Canadian Paediatric Society has warned that children and adolescents should avoid sports and energy drinks. The *Canadian Medical Association Journal* has often warned of the dangers of caffeine in energy drinks and the fact that they can pose a serious health risk to children and adolescents.

There has been frequent media mention of other research results including:

- Research has found that mixing alcohol and energy drinks increases the usage of alcohol alone.
- The boost received from energy drinks is short-lived and often accompanied with other problems.
- Regular consumption increases the possibility of eroding tooth enamel.
- Consumption of six or more energy drinks per month increases the risk of smoking cigarettes, abusing prescription drugs, and engaging in physical fights.
- Excessive levels of caffeine in drinks impair cognition.
- Energy drinks are safe if consumed in moderation along with a good diet.

The sale of energy drinks was regulated in Canada under the *Food and Drugs Act* and *Food and Drug Regulations*. On the issue of caffeine, Health Canada limited the amount to 400 mg per litre in an energy drink. Most small energy drinks containers (less than 250 ml) would have between 80 to 100 mg of caffeine and larger containers could not have more than 180 mg. Health Canada deemed that energy drinks were safe for consumption as long as no more than 400 mg of caffeine was consumed per day.

Health Canada requires caffeinated energy drink labels are include: a nutrition facts table, statement of the total caffeine content from all sources, cautionary consumption statements, warnings to children, pregnant and breastfeeding women and others sensitive to caffeine, and a statement "Do not mix with alcohol." Consumption incidents reports from industry and consumers identifying health or safety concerns related to energy drinks are to be filed with the Canadian Food Inspection Agency.

In November 2010, a Health Canada Expert Panel on Caffeinated Energy Drinks made extensive recommendations about the regulation of energy drinks. Recommendations included: energy drinks should be referred to as "stimulant drug containing drinks;" the drinks should be sold under the supervision of a pharmacist and not sold to those under 18 years; extensive labeling changes including listing of ingredients and warnings of dangers; and there should be investigations into approaches to reducing the risks from energy drink consumption.[5] For the most part, the recommendations of the Panel have not been implemented.

The Canadian Beverage Association, a trade association for non-alcoholic drink manufactures, supported the consumption of energy drinks within limits and under conditions recommended by Health Canada. The Association pointed out that coffee, tea, chocolate, caffeinated soft drinks and over the counter medications contained caffeine. In fact, a 237 ml serving (8 ounces) of coffee contained about 180 mg of caffeine. Consumers were advised to be aware of their caffeine intake and not mix energy drinks with alcohol. The Association also recommended that its members adhere to "Energy Drinks Marketing Code." The Code stated that marketing and promotional practices should be consistent with the *Food and Drug Act* and regulations. The Code specified practices relating to advertising, the sponsorship of events, and not selling energy drinks in schools. Members were to provide consumers with information of energy drinks and not promote them to children.[6]

Victor found some pharmacists had taken action on the issue. In September 2014, Graham MacKenzie, owner of Stone's Drug Store in Baddeck, N.S., announced that the store would no longer by selling soft drinks and other sugary beverages. A year later MacKenzie stated that sales had been hardly affected and that consumer reaction was positive.[7] In 2010, Murphy's Pharmacies in P.E.I. stopped selling energy drinks to persons under the age of 18 years. Murphy's sales and marketing manager stated that it was the responsible thing to do.

Possible Actions

Victor concluded that had four alternatives to addressing the issue energy drinks: do nothing, attempt to educate his customers, sell only to adults, and not to sell energy drinks at all.

Victor felt in all conscience that something had to be done and he should not ignore the issue especially since he was a health professional. If the consumption of energy drinks became a prominent issue, he could be accused of not taking action.

Educating customers about the issue was a possibility. Victor could post signs advising of the dangers of consuming energy drinks especially among young people. Also, he could make available brochures or pamphlets on the issue.

Any ban on selling energy drinks to young people would be challenging to implement. It is not clear at what age individuals can consume the drinks with less risk. A ban on the sale of the drinks children below the age of 12 years may be possible. There would be some administrative costs as identification would have to be checked. It might be appropriate to shelve the drinks behind the counter.

Lastly, Victor could decide not to sell energy drinks. There may be some financial consequences, that is, lower sales and profits. Banning the sale would bring attention to the issue in the community which may be appreciated. If he banned the sale of energy drinks, he would have to considering banning other unhealthy products containing excessive salt, fat, and sugar.

Victor wondered what he should do.

 Gabriel Resources Ltd. and the Rosia Montana Saga[8]

A saga is any very long story or history describing dramatic events or parts involving a group, place, industry, or corporation. A saga exists relating to the mining of gold and other minerals in the Rosia Montana area of Transylvania, Romania. The mine is located the scenic Apuseni Mountains in the northwestern part of Romania, 400 kilometres from the capital, Bucharest. It is Europe's largest deposit of gold and other minerals and has been mined since the second century. The Romans mined the rich gold seams and used the gold to finance their expansion. Since then, many governments in the region mined the site, including communist regimes. The government-funded mine closed in 2006 as required for Romania's entry into the European Union.[9] The gold remaining is in low grade ore that would have to be processed with cyanide. Two thousand years of mining activity have has left environmental devastation and resulted in the region's economic decline as evidenced by an 80 percent unemployment rate in the area.

Canadian mining interests became involved in the late 1990s and Gabriel Resources Ltd. (Gabriel) was launched at that time and has been involved since then. In 1999, Gabriel received a licence from the Romanian government to go ahead with a new project to mine gold and silver from the area. For over 15 years, Gabriel has been attempting to start a new mining venture but has not been successful because of lack of government cooperation and opposition from Romanian and international NGOs. Gabriel's involvement may be the last stage in the Rosia Montana mineral deposit saga.

The Company and the Project

Gabriel is a Canadian resource company listed on the Toronto Stock Exchange (GBU.TSX) and obtaining permission to develop the gold and silver project has been its focus. The project is owned through Rosia Montana Gold Corporation S.A. (RMGC) in which Gabriel holds an 80.69 percent interest. The remaining 19.31 is owned the Romanian government-owned Minvest Roşia Montană S.A. The project was estimated to cost US$1.5 billion to develop.[10]

The project is one of the largest gold deposits in Europe with an estimated 10.1 million ounces of gold and 47.6 ounces of silver. Estimates vary, but the project could contribute US$24 billion to Romanian GDP depending on mineral prices. The project would provide jobs and stimulate other economic initiatives in the area reducing poverty. It is estimated that over 7,000 direct and indirect jobs would be created, with 2,300 jobs during construction and over 880 during the life of the mine.

Gabriel planned to use state of the art technology to build the open pit mine covering 300 hectares and requiring the relocation of about 2,000 residents. The waste rock and cyanide laced sludge would be deposited in nearby valley that would serve as a tailings pond contained by a dam over 100 metres in height. The workings of the historical mines would be cleaned up and the company indicated that it would remediate the polluted regions. It also had detailed environmental plans that included the replanting of trees, the treatment of run-off water, and the re-contouring of slopes with topsail and vegetation.

Gabriel was sensitive to safeguarding Rosia Montana cultural heritage and had spent over $30 million on various efforts including the establishment of a museum. Some areas of the community would be protected zones to preserve historic structures. Archaeological finds would be preserved and protected including the several miles of the Roman mining tunnels.

The company's intention was to achieve economic, environmental, social and heritage sustainability. Gabriel's sustainability policies included commitment to the United Nations Global Compact, the OECD's Guidelines for Multinational Enterprises, and the International Cyanide Management Code.

Gabriel management believed that its plans for the Rosia Montana were supported by many local residents although a minority were opposed. The project was a major undertaking as the old operations and the surrounding environment had to be rehabilitated, a community accommodated, and a new mine built that would minimize any adverse effects of a mining operation. There were many challenges in getting approval for the project from many sources.

Chronology of Challenging Events

Unfortunately in 2000, a tailing dam at a gold recovery mine in Northern Romania collapsed and 100,000 cubic metres of cyanide laced water was released and polluted the Somes, Tisza, and Danube rivers affecting 2.5 million persons in Hungary and Romania. This ecological accident alerted many Romanians and others of the potential dangers of mining and the tailings ponds used. Various environmental NGOs became involved and pressured the Romanian government not to allow any new mines. In 2005 a documentary, *New El Dorado,* produced by a Hungarian film maker was released portraying mining projects as a curse and not an asset to the country. The documentary generated considerable interest particularly among the NGOs and financial support for opposed the project poured in from Romania and internationally.[11]

Nevertheless, Gabriel operations continued with some support from the Romanian government while the World Bank rejected a request for funding. Gabriel ran newspaper advertisements promoting the project and partly financed—but did not have editorial control over—a countering documentary, *Mine Your Own Business.* Released in 2006 and subtitled "A Documentary about the Dark Side of Environmentalism," the film interviews some of the world's poorest people about how environmental NGOs are campaigning to keep them in poverty because their way of life is thought to be quaint. It examines campaigns against large mining projects in the developing world including Rosia Montana. The documentary claims that environmentalists distort and exaggerate the risks of mining projects and in doing so prevents poor people and communities from improving their well-being.[12]

Activity continued at the mine site and three-quarters of the properties on the site were purchased. Historical restoration of some properties was completed and a museum developed. In September 2007, the Romanian government's Ministry of the Environment suspended Gabriel's environmental review or assessment. There was opposition to the review from NGOs who claimed that the company had provided false documentation. Supporters of the mine claimed this move would discourage investment and that suspending the review was an arbitrary and illegal move. There was also a court challenge by Alburnus Maior, the local NGO, and the Open Society Institute. In November 2007, the court annulled the project's archeological discharge certificate and in December workers were laid off and the land acquisition program cancelled.

In 2009, a new Romanian government was attempting to encourage foreign investment after years of Communist regimes, in particular that of dictator Nicolae Ceausescu. There was renewed hope for the project, and the new government reopened the environmental review process in 2010. In August 2011, the Romanian president supported the project and an archeological discharge permit was awarded. The historical structures were protected, but an environmental assessment would need to be done.

These initiatives were criticized by environmentalists, archaeologists, historians, and various international organizations. They believed that the mine still threatened the environment and that priceless Roman era mining galleries were being destroyed. In December 2013, MiningWatch Canada, Greenpeace, Friends of the Earth, the Council of Canadians, and Earthworks requested in an open letter that the Canadian Minister of Foreign Affairs and Members of Parliament withdraw any Canadian government support for Gabriel's Romania project.

However, the government requested a revised share of the profits through higher taxation, royalties, and dividends. It was speculated that achieving these concessions would convince more Romanians of the financial benefits of the project. It also requested that the amount of cyanide laced materials to be dumped in the tailing pond be reduced. In April 2012 the archeological zoning permit was invalidated by the Romanian court. Protests against the project continued into 2013. By September of that year, Gabriel had spent $583 million and 15 years on the project.

Some positive news did occur. The Romanian government approved the draft law relating to the concessions but this would have to receive parliamentary approval. It was speculated that parliament may reject the draft because of protests being held across country, including in Rosia Montana. About this time, parliament voted to create a special commission to review the project which would report in a few months. Meanwhile, thirty-three miners occupied the mine demanding that the project go ahead.

In November 2013, the parliamentary commission opposed the draft bill stating that such a bill should apply to all mining operations and not specifically to Gabriel. As a result of these events, Gabriel began winding down the operations of RNGC and 400 employees were suspended with three-quarters pay.

Gabriel's Challenge

In January 2015, Gabriel filed a Notice requesting that the Romanian government engage formally in a process of consultation as contemplated by bilateral investment treaties. Investment treaties are agreements regarding a country's treatment, in this case Romania, of individuals or companies from another country, in this case Gabriel from Canada. Canada has two such treaties with Romania dating from 1997 and 2011. With this Notice, Gabriel sought to initiate positive dialogue and engage formally in the process of consultation leading to an amiable resolution of the problems associated with the project. There was no response from the Romanian government.

In a press release dated July 2015, Gabriel announced that it had filed a request for arbitration before the World Bank's International Centre for Settlement of Investment Disputes (ICSID) against Romania. The ICSID is an institution established for the resolution of investment disputes and it provides facilities and services to support conciliation and arbitration. Participation is voluntary and it is not a court of law. Canada had been a member of ICSID since 2011 and Romania had been a member since 1975.[13] Gabriel claimed that Romania had breached the bilateral investment treaty obligations. The company claimed that Romania had blocked and prevented the project without due process and without compensating Gabriel for the value of its investment in the project.

In April 2019, Gabriel was still involved with the ICSID arbitration process. The saga continues.

Corporate Social Responsibility to Food Banks[14]

Phillip Veldhuis was president of Savalot Enterprises, a small, family-owned wholesale food business. The company operated in a medium-sized Canadian city and its customers included health and educational institutions, restaurants, catering groups, and service clubs. Savalot's main social responsibility initiative was supporting the local food banks. Surplus edible food items were forwarded weekly to the food banks and the company made a substantial monetary donation each year.

Phillip fully understood the need for the food banks as outlined by Food Banks Canada, a national charitable organization of Canadian food banks. Located in Toronto, its mission was "to reduce hunger in Canada by enabling an effective food bank community that addresses both the short-term need for food and longer-term solutions." Its vision was "to be the voice for the hungry in Canada," and it embraced the values of Teamwork, Transparency, and Integrity.

Every year Food Banks Canada published statistics on hunger and the usage of the food banks, and recommended solutions to hunger. Statistical highlights from a recent publication were the following:

- Each month, there are about 1.1 million visits to food banks, and 1.7 million Canadians use a food bank during a year.

- Nationally, 35.2 percent of those relying on food banks are children, 19.1 percent are single-parent households, and 6.3 percent are seniors.

- 59 percent of households using food banks are on social assistance or disability-related supports.

- According to Food Banks Canada, there are more than 550 food banks and more than 3,000 food programs in Canada.

- Use of food banks was 26 percent higher than in 2008, before the start of the global financial crisis that year.[15]

Corporations contribute millions of kilograms of food each year, and a substantial percent of Food Bank Canada's revenues come from corporate donors. It acts as a clearing house mostly for food, sending it out to food banks across the country. Community food banks have their own local sources of food and funding.

The economy had taken a downturn in the area where Savalot operated, and Phillip believed that this might be part of the reason why food bank usage had also increased in his community. It seemed that each year the local food bank was faced with an increasing demand for food.

Despite the frequency of usage and the apparent need for food banks, Phillip had been reading about the problems associated with them. Some critics argued that food banks may provide some relief but they did not really address the problems causing hunger. Even Food Banks Canada indicated that high rents and lack of affordable housing, the high rates for early learning and child care, and an inadequate Employment Insurance system forced Canadians to use food banks.

Phillip also noticed that there had been considerable criticism of the food bank approach to alleviating hunger. Letters to the editor of various newspapers claimed that some users abused the food banks and that many were too lazy to find work. Other critics claimed that hunger will never be eliminated, and to suggest that it could be if more were donated was misleading. Many experiencing hunger did not use the food banks as they were reluctant or too embarrassed to accept charity. Those who do use food banks often felt that the experience was stigmatizing, humiliating, and degrading.

Furthermore, food banks alone were not providing all the food needed and some users were still hungry. Most food banks had to ration food offerings to once a week or month, and the best that could be done was to ensure that users experienced less hunger. Food banks were criticized for not giving out the most nutritious food given the focus on canned fruits and vegetables, staples such as flour and coffee, and boxed dried food like instant soups, macaroni and cheese dinners, and dry cereals. These foods contained salt and trans-fats or other ingredients not desirable in the diets of some people.

Others pointed out that food banks had been operating for over 35 years, having been established during the recession in the 1980s in Alberta. They suggested that the problem of hunger was too big for charities alone to solve and governments would have to help out. In fact, it was suggested that the operation of food banks by charities was enabling governments to avoid their responsibility to this social issue.

Phillip was shocked when he read the comments by Elaine Power, associate professor in the School of Kinesiology and Health Studies at Queen's University about food banks and the role of corporations. In reality, food banks are somewhere to dispose of their surplus edible food they cannot sell. Furthermore, corporate-sponsored food drives are good for employee morale but do not result in alleviating hunger as much as claimed. Power emphasized that the problem of hunger is a complicated one not addressed solely by food banks, and that all are complicit in ignoring the problem. This includes corporations that benefit from their donations by displaying to society that they are good corporate citizens, and by not having to pay to dispose of the food in a landfill.[16]

Phillip felt a little guilty, because in effect his business was using food banks to dispose of food products it could not sell for one reason or another. Phillip wondered if, despite the company's best intentions, it may not be contributing much to address the underlying causes of the problem and to providing sufficient assistance to those in need.

 ## The Bread Scandal and Loblaw's Ethical Culture[17]

Karolina Vestman has been interested in Loblaw Companies Limited (Loblaw) since she worked as a cashier in their local grocery supermarket during high school. She had retained that interest during her college business studies since she is a shareholder. She had saved some money while working and decided to invest in Loblaw stock. Her father was so impressed that he doubled the money and now her 100 shares were worth $6,500 and paid a dividend.

Karolina was particularly impressed with Loblaw's extensive social responsibility initiatives described in the company's annual *Corporate Social Responsibility Report*. The report stated that the company believed in taking a responsible approach to business. In a message to stakeholders, Galen G. Weston, Chairman and Chief Executive Officer, stated, "I believe that business has both the opportunity and responsibility to have a positive effect in the community."[18]

The report described Loblaw's approach to corporate social responsibility (CSR) in detail. The main sections of the 24-page report were "Living our Purpose," describing a commitment to feeding Canada's kids, reducing food waste, and providing the best fresh and local produce possible; the "Environment," outlining reducing carbon footprint, improving energy efficiency, converting vehicles to electric, and reducing and diverting waste; "Sourcing," involving a commitment to worker safety, avoiding cotton sources that use child labour, supporting a safe and transparent supply chain, and adhering to animal welfare principles; and "Community," detailing the encouragement of wellness, supporting women's health and interests, and promoting employee diversity and inclusion.

Various targets were identified to meet the CSR initiatives and a progress summary provided. A final section described governance practices relating to CSR. The board of directors' involvement in CSR was described and mention was made of the company's Code of Conduct, CSR Committee, Supplier Code of Conduct, and the Core Values of care, ownership, respect, and excellence.[19]

With this interest in Loblaw, Karolina was surprised to learn from the media about the company's involvement in price-fixing.

The Bread Price-Fixing

In October 2017, the Competition Bureau confirmed that it was investigating price-fixing of bread products and raided the offices of several grocery stores, including Loblaw, which had alerted the Bureau to the practice in 2015. It was alleged that the price of bread had been coordinated amongst the bakeries and retail stores. Provisions 45, 46, and 48 of the *Competition Act* prohibit arrangements to reduce competition as it is not considered to be socially responsible and harms consumers and businesses. In particular, Section 45 states:

45 (1) Every person commits an offence who, with a competitor of that person with respect to a product, conspires, agrees or arranges

(a) to fix, maintain, increase or control the price for the supply of the product[20]

The Bureau states that price-fixing conspiracies are difficult to detect and prove. Penalties for price-fixing include fines up to $25 million, imprisonment to a maximum term of 14 years, or both.[21]

The possible price-fixing disclosure and investigation began in 2015. Loblaw, George Weston Limited (Loblaw's parent company, which also owned Shoppers Drug Mart and President's Choice Financial) and Weston Foods (owned by George Weston Limited) revealed their involvement in the price-fixing arrangement from 2001 until 2015 to the Competition Bureau. They had been cooperating with the Bureau since discovering the anti-competitive behaviour in March 2015. In January 2016 the Canadian Federation of Independent Grocers contacted the Competition Bureau about the possibility of price-fixing in the industry. The matter was being fully investigated but under competition legislation the companies were required to keep their cooperation confidential. Loblaw and George Weston had been granted immunity from criminal prosecution because they voluntarily disclosed the possible price-fixing arrangement.

Between 2002 and 2014, bread prices increased an average of 5.25 percent per year while the food inflation rate averaged 2.57 percent. Canada Bread Co. Ltd. and Weston Foods produced 80 percent of packaged bread in Canada, making the possibility of cartel arrangements easier. Besides Loblaw, the other retailers alleged to be involved were Walmart Canada, Sobeys Inc., Metro Inc., and Giant Tiger Stores. The price of bread increased 15 times over the 2002 to 2015 period. The two producers received a seven cent increase while the retailers got 10 cents. It was alleged that the two producers communicated directly with each other and then met individually with retailers. The retailers demanded that the producers manage the retail competition through this coordination of retail prices. The retailers agreed to boost prices on the condition that competitors did the same. The result was a maintenance of fixed pricing in the market. This arrangement was alleged, but not proven in court. The retailers agreed to cooperate with the Competition Bureau in its investigation.

Loblaw's Media Release

In a media release on December 19, 2017, entitled "George Weston and Loblaw take action to address industry-wide anti-competitive activity" Loblaw and George Weston outlined the issue, the action they had taken to address it and admitted that it should never had occurred. As a result of internal investigations, the employees involved were no longer with the companies. An enhanced compliance program had been implemented. A new independent compliance office led by a Chief Compliance Officer was established to ensure competition law compliance. All sales and marketing personnel, store managers, and senior management at Weston Bakeries, George Weston, and Loblaw had undergone intensive compliance re-training with continuing updates and monitoring taking place. Also, the companies committed to an ISO 19600 competition compliance program certification to provide independent third party validation.[22] Loblaw also announced that it was offering customers a $25 Loblaw Card, which can be used to purchase items sold in Loblaw grocery stores across Canada. This goodwill gesture was not requested by the Competition Bureau. Media and academic commentators viewed the move as a clever way of handling the crisis by admitting guilt and offering consumers some compensation.[23]

The media release was considered a good preemptive move as it allowed Loblaw and George Weston to be out in front of the issue before extensive media coverage. The companies were following a proven crisis management practice of responding quickly, apologizing, and outlining remedial actions. It was viewed as a careful, well-thought-out damage control calculation. Some viewed the release as throwing competitors under the bus and it suggested guilt by association. The timing of the announcement in December, just prior to the busy Christmas season, was questioned. Even with the announcement, the companies were still vulnerable to class action legal suits. Several emerged, but did not appear to be progressing.

Competitors' Reactions

The media release implicated competitors and the other main bread producer, Canada Bread, by suggesting an industry-wide price-fixing arrangement. Canada Bread stated that it operated with the highest ethical standards. Sobeys stated that it had no reason to believe it was involved and had not violated the *Competition Act*. Sobeys also stated that the media release implicated them in the arrangement, which was unfair, unsubstantiated, and maybe defamatory, and threatened to sue Loblaw. Metro Inc. said that it was cooperating with the Competition Bureau's investigation as well as conducting an internal investigation and had not found that it had violated the *Competition Act*. Other retailers made similar statements. However, the other retailers were on the defensive given Loblaw's exerting control through the announcement. It is not clear whether or not the other retailers were involved in the pricing arrangement; if they were, they were not admitting it.

The $25 Loblaw Card Controversy

The application for the card required providing personal information, which, in addition to the customer's name, included date of birth, residential address, and personal contact information. Verification of the application involved agreeing to allow the program administrator to contact the customer, confirming that all the information was correct, and indicating that the customer had purchased packaged bread products at a Loblaws store between January 1, 2002, and March 1, 2015. The application, cardholder agreement, program privacy policy, and instructions for completing the application was six pages long. Applications for the card had to be submitted by May 8, 2018. Loblaw estimated that 6 million customers might take advantage of the offer and that the cost would be between $75 million and $150 million.

The offer of the $25 card received mixed reaction. Some considered it an appropriate move to handle the issue or possible crisis. It was felt that the offer helped preserve Loblaw's reputation, but the move blindsided competitors and they could not react to the $25 as they hadn't admitted any guilt. There was concern about the security of the personal information, particularly email addresses. Some customers feared that the information required when applying could be used for other marketing purposes. This concern increased when some applicants were required to provide a driver's licence or utility bill as proof of residence, which they felt increased risk of identity theft. Scammers set up similar sites and customers were warned to be careful. Customers were insulted that the company did not trust them after Loblaw had taken advantage of them for 14 years. The Privacy Commissioner asked Loblaw why it was requiring additional identification. Later, many customers who had been requested to provide additional information did receive the cards. Some viewed the request as a public relations blunder and a security risk.

Competitors viewed it as a marketing tactic or window dressing as Loblaw would benefit when customers spent the $25 in Loblaw stores. The Canadian Federation of Independent Grocers viewed it as a marketing ploy to lure customers. Some commentators thought the money should be distributed through the Competition Bureau. Some customers felt that the $25 was insufficient given the years over which the price-fixing occurred.

Immunity Program

Loblaw received immunity from prosecution and would not be subject to criminal charges or penalties as it had voluntarily disclosed the practice. Karolina had not heard of immunity from prosecution. She learnt that there were "Immunity and Leniency Programs" under the *Competition Act*, administered by the Commissioner of Competition and the Director of Public Prosecutions. The purpose of the programs "is to uncover and stop criminal anti-competitive activity prohibited by the *Competition Act* and to deter others from engaging in similar behaviour." Immunity is described as "an extraordinary grant by the Crown to forego prosecution, while leniency is a discretionary decision by the Crown to recommend a reduction of the sanctions to be imposed by a court." The government believed that these programs were effective in detecting, investigating, and prosecuting criminal activity. Without the programs, cartels would go undetected.[24]

Implications of Codes of Conduct

Loblaw Companies Limited's Code of Conduct[25] included a clause to "Uphold the Law" where it stated that it took compliance with the law seriously, expected all employees to do so, and provided training to help compliance with legal obligations. Its Supplier Code of Conduct[26] contained a statement that suppliers must at all times comply with local laws and regulations but didn't appear to contain mention of price-fixing.

George Weston Limited's Code of Conduct contained a similar statement relating to compliance with the law, the reliance on employees to understand the law that applies to their work, and the participation in training. In addition, a section dealt with dealing with competitors and antitrust compliance. It stated that laws exist to ensure fair competition and that employees must comply with them. Employees were required to read the company's Competition Law Policy.[27]

Loblaw and George Weston had in place Codes that covered the possibility of a price-fixing arrangement. There is no indication as to why employees did not follow these guidelines. It appeared that these Codes might have been insufficient to prevent inappropriate behaviour. The identities of the employees who may have been whistleblowers was never disclosed. From the perspective of crisis management, Loblaw and George Weston controlled the situation quite well.

After reviewing all the media coverage and various corporate websites, Karolina had several questions:

- Why were the bread producers and retailers not caught sooner?
- Why did it take 14 years to uncover, given all the parties involved?
- Was disciplinary action taken internally by the companies other than Loblaw?
- Were Loblaw and George Weston highly responsible corporate citizens in reporting the price-fixing?
- Why are cartel arrangements so hard to detect?
- Was Loblaw fair to others?
- Were Loblaw and George Weston highly responsible corporate citizens when claiming an industry price-fixing arrangement in their media release?
- Was the Bureau's process fair?
- Are immunity programs fair to all stakeholders?
- Why did Loblaw not face some penalties? Or punishment?
- Should customers trust the bread producers or retailers?

Karolina was still deciding whether or not Loblaw was socially responsible and had the appropriate ethical culture. Of course, she could always sell her shares.

"Here's to Our Next 100 Years" and the Closing of a Plant[28]

Darrell Yasinski was a business history buff! Although a business student, he took a course in Canadian business history as an Arts elective. He was introduced to two classic books on the topic: Michael Bliss' *Northern Enterprise: Five Centuries of Canadian Business* and Graham D. Taylor and Peter A. Baskerville's *A Concise History of Business in Canada*.[29] Also, he has read several Canadian corporate histories as well as other accounts of business successes and failures.

Darrell lived in Oshawa, Ontario, the location of General Motors Canada Limited's (GM Canada) assembly plant. GM Canada was founded in 1919 with the merger of McLaughlin Motor Company and Chevrolet Motor Company of Canada, which was incorporated as a wholly owned subsidiary of General Motors Corporation. The Canadian company has produced passenger vehicles of various types, except for the period from 1942 to 1945 when it suspended automobile production to manufacture tanks, machine guns, and other military equipment. In 2002, a plant in Québec that assembled Camaros was closed. The existing Oshawa assembly plant began production in November 1953 and in the 1980s employed up to 23,000 people. At its peak production in 2007, the plant assembled 1 million units. In 2016, GM invested $400 million to upgrade the assembly line but its costs were still higher than for plants in the Southern United States and Mexico.

In 2018, the plant assembled about 330,000 Chevrolet Impala, Buick Regal, Cadillac XTS, and Chevrolet Equinox, all of them older models. It also finished Chevrolet Silverado and GMC Sierra trucks. There were about 3,000 jobs at the plant and Oshawa was the Canadian headquarters and technical centre. GM Canada also operated an engine and transmission plant in St. Catharines, Ontario, and a CAMI assembly plant in Ingersoll, Ontario. The Oshawa plant had won numerous awards for its productivity and as a desirable place to work.

Darrell was pleased to read a General Motors Canada Media Release on November 8, 2018, entitled "Here's to Our Next 100 Years: GM Canada Celebrates its 100th Anniversary."[30] The Release stated that "Our vision for the next 100 years starts with our bold 'Triple Zero' vision – achieving a world with zero crashes, zero emissions and zero congestion."

Oshawa Plant Closure

Darrell was shocked on Monday, November 25, 2018, when General Motors announced the closure of the Oshawa assembly plant. The announcement stated that General Motors was transforming its operations to achieve its vision of Zero Crashes, Zero Emissions, Zero Congestion. To accomplish this vision, the company was reducing costs and optimizing capital expenditures to achieve a cash savings of approximately $6 billion by the end of 2020. This was to be done by transforming its product development workforce and processes, investing in new and more efficient vehicles, increasing production capacity for new models, and reducing the number of employees. The Oshawa plant was part of the effort to increase plant utilization corporation-wide. This would be accomplished by closing three assembly plants (Oshawa and two in the United States). In addition, two propulsion plants in the United States would be closing.[31]

The Oshawa assembly plant employed about 3,000 people, about 2,500 of whom were unionized. In the United States, the four plant closures resulted in about 6,700 jobs being lost. It was estimated that for each job lost there were seven spin-off jobs lost, significantly increasing the economic impact on a community.

Many factors led to the closing. The closure had little to do with the Oshawa plant operations that were considered to be efficient with a highly qualified workforce. General Motors had too many plants worldwide and too many models no longer in demand. The closure was an indication that General Motors felt that the Oshawa plant was not central to their future direction. The Oshawa assembly plant was operating at one-third capacity and other plants were underutilized. Furthermore, vehicle assembly was cheaper in the Southern United States, Mexico, and other offshore locations where tax breaks were offered, labour was cheaper, and labour laws were more favourable.

General Motors was losing market share against other manufacturers. The overall vehicle market was static or maybe slightly down. Purchasing tastes were shifting as cars were not as important to consumers as in the past and increased quality and dependability prolonged vehicle life. There was a shift from the sedans that Oshawa produced to SUVs and low emission vehicles. Telecommuting workers and ride-sharing operations such as Uber and Lyft reduced the need for cars. Also, demand was increasing for electric cars requiring new technology and production plants.

Reaction to the Closure

Automobile manufacturing was the second largest industry in Canada, contributing $18 billion to the gross domestic product and $87 billion in exports, and employing 126,000 workers directly and another 500,000 indirectly. There was considerable nostalgic feeling for GM Canada due to its long presence in the community. With the closure, workers and citizens felt angry and expressed disbelief. They felt it was a callous decision and that the workers and their families were being abandoned.

There were several possible futures for the laid-off workers. About one-half were eligible to retire and some income support was available to the other half. Retraining assistance was possible, but considered inadequate and only available after employees had searched for other employment. Some pointed out the considerable grant and loan assistance available to corporations, while workers were offered limited assistance.

In hindsight, some observers pointed out that there had been warning signs for three decades in the form of a series of layoffs. At the end of the 1980s, the assembly plant produced 700,000 vehicles per year and employed 23,000. By 2018, 300,000 vehicles were being produced by about 2,500 employees.

There was considerable discussion of government involvement to keep the plant operating. The Canadian and Ontario governments had bailed out GM Canada and Chrysler in 2009 with $13.7 billion in loans secured by accepting shares. By 2014, these shares had been sold but taxpayers still lost $3.5 billion. It was argued that GM Canada had a moral obligation after all the government assistance provided in the past. This assistance had bought time but not assured jobs forever. In discussions with Prime Minister Trudeau and Premier Ford of Ontario, the company made it clear that it was not after government assistance. The automobile industry was going through a global restructuring and saving the plant was not feasible.

There was speculation that President Trump's isolationist and tariff policies influenced the decision. General Motors may have had to close the Oshawa plant as four were closed in the United States. In other words, the Oshawa plant was sacrificed since it was politically unacceptable to only close the U.S. plants. General Motors denied that the closure was a politically inspired move.

The union representing the 2,500 assembly workers was determined to fight for the plant, pressuring governments and the company. The Unifor president, Jerry Dias, proposed the allocation of a new model to be assembled at the Oshawa plant. He also proposed a 40 percent tariff on vehicles manufactured in Mexico, claiming that Mexico gave unfair subsidies and was selling vehicles below cost in Canada. In a media advertisement, Unifor claimed that "after taking nearly $11 billion from Canadians, GM wants to bail on us while expanding in Mexico." It encouraged Canadians to support the auto workers by buying only Canadian and U.S. union made vehicles.[32]

Financial analysts were pleased with the move and the price of General Motors' stock rose 7.8 percent to $38.75 on the day of the announcement.

The "Transformation Agreement"

On May 8, 2019, GM Canada and Unifor announced a "Transformation Agreement" that was designed to transition the GM assembly plant to a parts manufacturing and advanced vehicle testing facility. GM Canada would invest $170 million to change the plant to one focused on parts stamping, related sub-assembly, and other activities, and convert part of the plant to a test track for autonomous and advance technology vehicles. About 300 union jobs would be retained with the possibility of an increase in the future. To assist laid-off workers, GM Canada would offer relocations to other plants, enhance the retirement packages, open a centre for employees to plan for future career possibilities, and provide financial support for retraining. The Agreement maintained a GM Canada presence in Oshawa and kept the plant intact.[33]

An industry analyst felt that the announcement was more than a token gesture and was good news for workers and the community. Jobs in stamping operations were more secure than in assembly plants, and it was a positive signal for the plant's longevity. Credit was given to Unifor for pressuring for some jobs and Premier Doug Ford was criticized for not supporting the initiative by the union. Many workers were still concerned for their future.

The Next Few Years and the Changing Canadian Economy

Darrell thought about the Oshawa plant closure and realized that what is happening in the automobile industry had occurred before in Canada. From reading business history, Darrell had learnt that plant shutdowns, downsizing, and layoffs occur frequently as the demand for various goods and services changes both nationally and globally, new technologies alter costs, and foreign competition increases. He noted that the Oshawa economy had suffered job losses at the GM plant before, but the city had diversified into health care, retail, and education. The Canadian economy was strong and growing with over 200,000 jobs created in 2018 and unemployment at a four year low.

Furthermore, industries had to change to remain competitive and new industries were emerging. Industries will need knowledge based workers and efforts should be placed on improving educational approaches and skills training. Governments should focus on maintaining the strong social safety net, for example, by extending employment insurance benefits.

An issue is what responsibilities any corporation has when a plant closes. It must take into account social responsibilities but it also has to consider its economic sustainability. Darrell wondered whether or not the decisions made by General Motors were irresponsible or appropriate to address a changing business environment.

Just Dump It in the Lake[34]

On February 21, 2009, a "Notice of a Proclamation Exempting the Waters of Sandy Pond from Section 22 of the Navigable Waters Protection Act" appeared in the *Canada Gazette*, the official newspaper of the Government of Canada.[35] The Notice stated that "interested parties may make representations concerning the proposed proclamation within 30 days after the date of publication of this notice."[36] Those opposing the project had until March 21 to respond.

The Environment and Mining

Mining has several impacts on the environment; a major one relates to disposing or storing of waste materials or tailings after a processing or refining process. In the past, the tailings were simply put in piles, dumped in bodies of water, including the ocean, or contained in human-made holding areas or ponds. All of these approaches threatened the environment and possibly the health of surrounding residents. As a result, the industry sought better ways to dispose of the waste materials. Research suggested an approach whereby waste materials would be deposited in natural lakes, which would contain the harmful chemicals. Ideal lakes for this approach would be near the plant, have limited watershed, and be deep. This approach was preferable to constructing open holding ponds that might leak and were expensive to build and maintain.

In order to do this, some way had to be found to get around existing legislation, in particular, the *Fisheries Act*, which made it illegal to pollute fish-bearing waters.[37] However, the "Metal Mining Effluent Regulations" of the Act allowed federal bureaucrats to redefine a lake as a tailing impoundment area. To date, 16 sites have been applied for and listed in Schedule 2 of the regulations.[38]

In order for a lake to be listed, a notice must be issued exempting the lake from Section 22 (see Table 1) of the *Navigable Waters Protection Act*. An Order in Council[39] is necessary under Section 23 (see Table 1) to place the lake on Schedule 2 and allow for the dumping of waste into the body of water.

TABLE 1	Sections 22 and 23 of the *Navigable Waters Protection Act*
22. No person shall throw or deposit or cause, suffer or permit to be thrown or deposited any stone, gravel, earth, cinders, ashes or other material or rubbish that is liable to sink to the bottom in any water, any part of which is navigable or that flows into any navigable water, where there are not at least twenty fathoms of water at all times, but nothing in this section shall be construed so as to permit the throwing or depositing of any substance in any part of a navigable water where that throwing or depositing is prohibited by or under any other Act.	
R.S., c. N-19, s. 20.	
23. The Governor in Council, when it is shown to the satisfaction of the Governor in Council that the public interest would not be injuriously affected thereby, may, by proclamation, declare any rivers, streams or waters in respect of which sections 21 and 22 apply, or any parts thereof, exempt in whole or in part from the operation of those sections, and may revoke the proclamation.	
R.S., c. N-19, s. 21.	

Source: Department of Justice, Government of Canada, Navigable Waters Protection Act, Chapter N-22, R.S., C. N19, s.1. Reproduced with the permission of the Minister of Public Works and Government Services Canada, 2010.

Vale's Sandy Pond Proposal

Vale planned construction of a hydromet nickel processing plant at Long Harbour, Newfoundland and Labrador, 100 kilometres west of St. John's. Plant construction was to begin in 2009, and completed by 2012 at an estimated cost of $2.17 billion. It would employ 1,600–2,000 persons in the construction stage and about 400–450 full-time employees when in operation. The plant was intended to process 50,000 tonnes of nickel, 3,270 tonnes of copper, and 2,460 tonnes of cobalt annually from ore mined at the company's Voisey Bay mine in NL.

The facility required a disposal of tailings plan and the company decided to use Sandy Pond. About 400,000 tonnes of effluent would be dumped in the lake annually. The pond was about 6 kilometres from the plant and covered about 38 hectares. Dams would be constructed to enlarge the holding area to about 78 hectares. Vale was a signatory to the Mining Association of Canada's "Towards Sustainable Mining (TSM)" initiative.[40] The company stated that it accepted responsibility for the environment and acted responsibly.[41]

Arguments Supporting the Use of Sandy Pond

Vale said that it had seriously studied the alternatives and their environmental impact. It claimed that using Sandy Pond was the most environmentally friendly approach and stated that the Department of Fisheries and Oceans agreed. Submerging the waste prevents oxidization, which releases toxic substances. Ponds do not leak and human-made holding ponds would be much larger, requiring 180 hectares. Economically the pond made sense as costs of using the pond were $62 million versus $490 million for a human-made holding pond. Overall, using Sandy Pond was the least threat to the environment and the health of the community. Furthermore, the economic development was needed in the area of high unemployment after a phosphorus plant closed about 20 years prior.

Arguments Opposing the Use of Sandy Pond

Using lakes as dumps is an emotional issue. Environmentalists stated that Sandy Pond was a pristine lake with trout, eels, and smelt and used for local recreation. Mining Watch complained that the government was making it too easy to use lakes as industrial waste dumps and disposal sites. Moreover, there was a "hidden subsidy" to the mining industry when it managed to get around the *Fisheries Act* enabling it to reduce costs.

The controversy over Sandy Pond generated substantial public comment. Opposition to the dumping of wastes came from stakeholders such as Centre for Long Term Environmental Action NL (CLEANf/Ld), the Sierra Club of Canada, the Council of Canadians, the New Democratic Party, the Canadian Union of Public Employees, the David Suzuki Foundation, and Maude Barlow, a senior adviser on water to the United Nations.

Professor Murray's Ethical Dilemmas[42]

Everyone in their workplace, personal life, or society is confronted with ethical dilemmas from time to time. College instructors are no exception. Much has been written on teaching ethics, but little about the ethics of teaching. Yet all instructors have their personal integrity to consider and a responsibility to teach in an ethical manner. Also, they should consider the ethical implications of actions taken by colleagues, students, and themselves.

Below are incidents that present ethical dilemmas for college or university instructors. For each incident, identify what the dilemma is, the stakeholders involved, what the instructor should do, and who is harmed by or benefits from the decision. In addition, identify the ethical principle that formed the basis for the decision.

Incident #1

Professor Wayne Murray answered a knock at his door to find a young man whom he did not recognize. The young man explained that he represented a used-book company that gathered textbooks and then sold them to bookstores. These stores then resold them at prices lower than new copies, thus saving students money. He offered to purchase any "sample" or "inspection" copies of textbooks that Professor Murray had received from publishers that he did not need.

Professor Murray often received free textbooks from the publishers and had not recommended most of them for use in his courses. Such textbooks sat on his book shelves for years, were thrown out, or sometimes sent to educational institutions in developing countries. The young man was a student at the university for whom this part-time job would help him finance his education. Professor Murray was not sure what he should do.

Incident #2

Professor Murray had taught general management courses, such as strategy management, at a Canadian university for over 15 years. Despite his experience, he was still uneasy when students requested extensions to assignments or examination deferrals.

The assignments were described in detail on course outlines distributed at the first class. This was a requirement for all courses and all instructors complied with the policy. As a result, all students were aware of all assignment due dates and the dates of mid-term examinations well in advance.

Each semester, Professor Murray received several requests for extensions or deferrals. The reasons for the requests could be categorized into three types: (1) those based upon student illness or an illness or death in the student's family or close friends; (2) those based on work overload resulting from several assignments or examinations occurring at the same time; and (3) those based on the student's claim that they were busy with work and/or extracurricular activities.

The first category presented no difficulty for Professor Murray. He granted the request for extension usually without requiring documentation. But, the second and third reasons concerned him.

Professor Murray was particularly concerned about the ethical implications of the requests and of the actual granting of extensions. He was concerned about fairness and justice to students who worked to meet the deadlines. He worried about consistency in dealing with the requests and their legitimacy. He did not believe that students fully appreciated the awkward position in which these requests placed him.

Incident #3

As a professor of management, Professor Murray attempted to keep up-to-date on his area of specialization by reading selected academic journals. He felt this improved his teaching as students would be presented with recent research discoveries. He also tried to keep track of research developments so that he could use them to enhance his own research activity.

A colleague's research was in a related area and Professor Murray always read these articles out of interest and so that he could discuss the findings with his colleague. Last year, his colleague published an excellent article that tested a management theory. The article included a comprehensive six-page review of relevant literature and Professor Murray had used this review himself to prepare lecture materials. This year his colleague published another article in a different journal testing a similar theory. However, the literature review for this article included five pages from the previous article without any alterations. Furthermore, his colleague did not state that the review had been previously published.

Plagiarism was a serious problem with student assignments. Students had been warned of the seriousness of the practice and three students had been expelled for copying the writings of others without referencing them. Professor Murray was taken aback by the fact that his colleague had plagiarized, even if it was his own work.

Incident #4

Students were frequently used as subjects for professors' research projects. Such a practice was convenient for the professors as it reduced the need to recruit participants. Furthermore, students were contributing to the advancement of knowledge, which they may or may not have appreciated. Although occurring less frequently, the practice still occurred. There were college policies relating to the practice and agencies that funded research had strict policies about obtaining consent and making participation voluntary.

Professor Murray had colleagues who used students as research subjects. He had heard that some of his colleagues secretly conducted surveys in their classes without advising the administration. He thought that students should not be asked to participate in a study by their professor under any circumstances. It was difficult, if not impossible, to eliminate the real or perceived influence or power that the professor had with students. He was thinking of proposing a college policy that disallowed soliciting survey participation in the classroom setting. If faculty wanted to use students in their studies, they should advertise for them and perhaps offer incentives. The important point would be that the studies would not be associated with a particular course and classroom setting. Some of Professor Murray's colleagues felt that he was being too strict and limiting their ability to conduct research.

Incident #5

Professor Murray and his colleagues were alarmed at the reports of student cheating at colleges and universities. *Maclean's* magazine carried several stories on the subject with titles such as, "The great university cheating scandal" (Feb. 12, 2007, 32–36), "Cheating? Who us?" (Feb. 26, 2007, 41), and "Cheating on your exam? It's no big deal" (June 25, 2007, 25). There was considerable discussion of the issue and some codes of conduct were developed at his college. Students were advised of the college's policy regarding cheating and the fact that students could be expelled. From his experience and according to his colleagues, cheating continued.

One of the *Maclean's* articles stated that 44 percent of professors said that they didn't report students caught cheating. This statistic became more relevant when Professor Murray suspected a student of cheating in an examination. First of all, Professor Murray saw the student leaning over and reading other students' papers. Secondly, the same student was seen removing a piece of paper from their shirt sleeve.

Professor Murray found it awkward to do anything at the time, as approaching the student would have disrupted the examination. He thought that it was not fair to other students that this student should get away with cheating. But, he concluded that it would be difficult to prove that the cheating occurred; it would be his word against the student's. Furthermore, he did not look forward to the numerous meetings and hearings that would be involved if he accused the student of cheating.

Incident #6

In one of his courses, Professor Murray assigned several case studies which the students could purchase online from the Harvard Business School. On the day when the first case was to be discussed, he asked how many had purchased the case. About half of the students held up their hands. He then asked if the others had the case and had read it. They informed him that they had obtained the case for free from an Internet site. He was able to access the Harvard site, which provided a count of the number of sales along with the names of the students who had bought the case. About half of the students had purchased the cases. Given this situation, Professor Murray discussed in class the appropriateness of obtaining the cases and that copyright issues were involved. However, he did not mention that he had access to sales data.

Before the next class, when another case was to be discussed, Professor Murray searched the Internet and could not find the case available. He then checked the Harvard site again. The number of sales had not changed. He wondered how he should deal with this in the class. Should he tell the students he could see who had purchased the case? Then again, he was unsure of whether he should have told the students upfront that he had access to this information. He wondered what to do, and whether he should do anything at all.

Fortis and the Chalillo Dam: Balancing Economic Development and Environmental Impact[43]

Fortis Corporation

Fortis Inc. is a diversified electric utility holding company headquartered in St. John's, NL. *Fortis* is a Latin word meaning strong, powerful, and firm. [Fortis Inc. is not associated with the Fortis international banking and insurance financial firm headquartered in The Netherlands and Belgium.]

In 2001, Fortis wholly owned Newfoundland Power Inc., the principal distributor of power in Newfoundland and Labrador, Maritime Electric Company Limited, the main distributor in Prince Edward Island, and Fortis Properties, a non-utility subsidiary with investments in commercial properties in Atlantic Canada. Other financial interests included electric utilities in Ontario, New York State, the Cayman Islands, and Belize. The Belizean interests were 67 percent of Belize Electricity Limited (BEL), the only distributor of electricity in Belize, and 100 percent of Belize Electric Company Limited (BECOL), which owned a hydroelectric plant on the Macal River at Mollejon, Belize.

The Fortis operations in Belize embroiled the company in an environmental responsibility issue that consumed substantial costs, time, and energy. BEL had been owned by the Government of Belize and was the main supplier of electricity in the country. In October and November 1999, Fortis Inc. acquired 67 percent of the company for $36 million in cash. It later acquired BECOL and a proposal by this company to develop a hydroelectric project in Belize received international attention and became a sensitive issue for management.[44]

The Chalillo Project

Fortis, through BECOL, proposed construction of a dam on the Macal River in the Cayo District of western Belize at cost of about US$27.3 million. The site was located in an unpopulated wilderness area, part of which was in the Mountain Pine Ridge Forest Reserve and Chaquibul National Park. These areas covered most of the southern half of Cayo district. It would produce 7.3 MW of electricity for the Belize network and regulate the river's flow. The control over the water flow would increase the productivity and reliably of the Mollejon hydro power station downstream.

The Chalillo project included:

- a 49.5 m high by 340 m wide dam on the river,
- a reservoir with a total surface area of 9.5 km²,
- a powerhouse at the foot of the dam,
- an 18 km transmission line from the powerhouse to the Mollejon plant, and
- ancillary requirements including an access road and construction camp.[45]

There were benefits to the Belizean citizens and the country's economy. Most importantly, the project would increase electrical output and raise energy self-sufficiency. The second dam on the Macal River would increase the productivity of the existing electrical plant at Mollejon. The output from the two plants would reduce reliance on petroleum generation as diesel-fuelled generators could be closed. This would reduce greenhouse gas emissions and the possibility of oil spills.

A large portion of Belizean electrical energy was imported from Mexico under a contract that was to expire in 2008. The Mexican system experienced difficulties and it was not a stable source, resulting in power outages in Belize. The completion of the Chalillo project meant that Belize would have a more reliable and secure supply of electricity, stabilizing and possibly reducing prices. Alternative sources of energy were examined by the government and BEL including thermal options (diesel and gas turbines), biomass, Battery Energy Storage Systems, and solar and wind power. Studies by BEL determined that power generated from the hydro source was less expensive than any other. However, BEL was committed to purchasing power from a bagasse-fuelled generation facility planned by Belize Sugar Industries Limited (BSI). The facility would produce energy by burning crushed sugarcane and wood wastes from nearby sawmills.

There were other benefits to the project. The dam and reservoir would control flooding on the Macal River with significant economic, health, and safety benefits to downstream residents, many of whom lived in the river's floodplain. Also, there would be a steadier supply of water for residents especially during the dry season. Employment would be created during construction and there would be economic benefits from supplying goods and services to the project.[46]

Opposition to the Project

During 2001, criticisms and opposition were voluminous. Several Canadian print and broadcast media carried stories, there were letters to the editor in newspapers, and protest websites were established.

Numerous environmental non-governmental organizations (ENGOs) campaigned against the project, including:

- Probe International (PI)
- Natural Resources Defense Council (NRDC)
- Sierra Club of Canada
- Belize Alliance of Conservation Non-Governmental Organizations (BACONGO)
- Humber Environmental Action Group
- Humber Natural History Society
- Petitcodiac Riverkeeper
- Action Environment
- Defenders of Wildlife
- Environment Coalition of Prince Edward Island
- Falls Brook Centre

In particular, PI carried out an aggressive campaign and coordinated the protests of other ENGOs.[47] PI is an environmental advocacy group that fights to stop ill-conceived aid, trade projects, and foreign investments. It works to give citizens the tools they need to stop such projects using the rule of law, democratic processes, and honest and transparent accounting. It is a division of the Energy Probe Research Foundation, a well-known Canadian environmental and energy policy ENGO created in 1980. Its tactics include writing letters to public officials, preparing and publishing reports and articles, media releases, speech presentations, and public demonstrations.

The other main opposition came from NRDC, an environmental action group founded in 1970. Its mission is to safeguard the Earth: its people, plants, and animals, and the natural systems on which all life depends. It has offices in seven U.S. cities, staff of about 300 lawyers, scientists, and policy experts, and about 1 million members. Robert F. Kennedy, Jr., a lawyer, was the main spokesperson for NRDC on the Chalillo project.[48]

PI maintained an elaborate website in opposition to the project. Another website devoted exclusively to the Chalillo project was Stop Fortis! (no longer available), which contained extensive information on the project including photographs. Several environmental groups placed advertisements in Canadian newspapers.

The criticisms of Fortis's practices and the dam's construction are summarized in Exhibit 1. Fortis and Stanley Marshall, President and CEO, responded to this criticism. A news release was issued on November 1, 2001, "Decision to Build Hydroelectric Dam in Belize Should Reside with Belizeans." The main points made in the release were:

- Belizeans should decide on the construction of the dam.
- Contrary to information from ENGOs, the dam is economically feasible and will ensure a more stable energy supply.
- Information presented by ENGOs is misleading the media about the environmental impact of the project.
- Fortis is willing to review its business activities with stakeholders.

EXHIBIT 1	Main Criticisms of the Chalillo Project

- The threat to wildlife and plant life, especially endangered species.
- The dam would exacerbate the water quality problems downstream.
- The dam may flood Maya ruins destroying the cultural landscape.
- Limestone caves may drain the reservoir.
- The claim that the project was uneconomic and not the cheapest option. The only reason the project was viable was because BEL had a monopoly and could recover costs from captive customers.
- Fortis' unwillingness to consider alternative sources, denying consumers the right to better and cheaper electricity.
- The allegation that Fortis asked the Canadian government, through CIDA, to pay for a study justifying the project. It was claimed that the study was biased, involved too much secrecy, and failed to promote and ensure effective stakeholder consultation.
- According to environmental groups, Fortis denied them access to pertinent information and failed to consult them.
- Fortis wouldn't make its own geology studies and engineering plans public or agree to an independent panel review.
- There was insufficient information on the impact of the project.

Source: Used with permission of Probe International.

In a story in *The Telegram* on November 2, Marshall stated to a reporter, "This bombardment in the media of misleading information is putting enormous pressure on me, attacking me personally and inundating the media with lies." He also said, "Whatever we do as an electric company will impact the environment, but it's a question of how well we can manage our activities. On balance, this project is a good one. If I felt personally that we were going to threaten an endangered species and wipe it out—no. I would not propose going ahead with it."[49]

The project had consumed a lot of time, energy, and resources, and Fortis management wondered whether or not it was worth it. There might be less demanding projects that would add as much value to the company.

Endnotes

Frontmatter

1. These environments are similar to those identified by the previous domain statement of the Social Issues in Management Division, Academy of Management.

2. Academy of Management, Social Issues in Management Domain statement at http://aom.org/Divisions-and-Interest-Groups/Academy-of-Management-Division---Interest-Group-Domain-Statements.aspx#sim.

3. "About Us," International Association of Business and Society website at http://iabs.net/Home.aspx.

Chapter 1

1. Based on Pete Engardio, "Beyond the Green Corporation," *BusinessWeek*, January 29, 2007, 50–64.

2. Richard T. De George, *Competing with Integrity in International Business* (Oxford: Oxford University Press, 1993), 6.

3. ibid, 41.

4. "What is the Social License," On Common Ground Consultants Inc., and Robert Boutilier and Associates, accessed October 9, 2012, http://socialicense.com/definition.html.

5. CanTrust Index 2019, Proof Inc. website at https://www.getproof.com/thinking/the-proof-cantrust-index/?gclid=EAIaIQobChMIvPrOzJfL4wIVEz0MCh3l1QujEAAYASAAEgL3AvD_BwE accessed July 23, 2019.

6. 2019 Edelman Trust Barometer Canada, Edelman Canada at https://www.edelman.ca/sites/default/files/edelman-trust/2019-Canadian-Trust-Barometer-Edelman.pdf.

7. John H. Tory, "Integrity Tops the List for Essential Qualities of Good CEO," *The Globe and Mail*, September 2, 2002, B5.

8. Michael E. Porter and Mark R. Kramer, "Strategy and Society: The Link Between Competitive Advantage and Corporate Social Responsibility," *Harvard Business Review* 84, Issue 12 (December 2006): 83–84.

9. Len Karakowsky, Archie B. Carroll, and Ann K. Buchholz, *Business and Society: Ethics and Stakeholder Management*, Canadian Edition. Toronto: Nelson (2005) 20.

10. Thomas Donaldson and Thomas W. Dunfee, "Towards a Unified Conception of Business Ethics: Integrative Social Contract Theory," *Academy of Management Review*, April 1994, 252–253.

Chapter 2

1. Portions of this chapter are a revised and expanded version from Robert W. Sexty, "The Fundamentals of Canadian Capitalism: Theoretical and Practical Perspectives," in *Canadian Business and Society: Understanding Social and Ethical Challenges* (Scarborough, ON: Prentice-Hall Canada Inc., 1995), 37–46.

2. "The next capitalist revolution," *The Economist*, November 17, 2018, 13.

3. The first four forms listed are adapted from Christopher Farrell, "Faces of Capitalism," *BusinessWeek* (Special 1994 Bonus Issue), November 18, 1994, 19.

4. Ian Bremmer, "State Capitalism and The Crisis," *McKinsey Quarterly* (online), July 9, 2009, accessed January 2, 2016, http://www.mckinseyquarterly.com/home.aspx; and Pete Engardio, "State Capitalism," *BusinessWeek*, February 9, 2009, 39–43.

5. These views can be found at: Robert W. Tracinski, "The Moral Basis of Capitalism," The Center for the Advancement of Capitalism accessed January 2, 2016, http://www.capitalismcenter.org/Philosophy/Essays/The_Moral_Basis_of_Capitalism.htm; Devin T. Stewart, "Is Ethical Capitalism Possible?", Policy Innovations, January 21, 2009, accessed January 2, 2016, http://www.policyinnovations.org/ideas/commentary/data/000105; and Joel F. Wade, "The Moral Defense of Capitalism," *The Daily Bell*, August 8, 2011, accessed January 2, 2016, http://www.policyinnovations.org/ideas/commentary/data/000105.

Chapter 3

1. This definition is based on the work of R. Edward Freeman in *Strategic Management: A Stakeholder Approach* (Boston: Pitman, 1984), 53.

2. Freeman, *Strategic Management*, 45.

3. Ibid, 45.

4. Jack Kapica, "Pope Warns of Profitability over People," *The Globe and Mail*, May 2, 1991, A6; and George Bragues, "The Capitalist Pope," *National Post*, April 5, 2005, FP23.

5. William C. Frederick, Keith Davis, and James E. Post, *Business and Society: Corporate Strategy, Public Policy, Ethics* (New York: McGraw-Hill, 1988), Chapter 4.

6. Henry Mintzberg, *Power In and Around Organizations* (Englewood Cliffs, NJ: Prentice-Hall, Inc., 1983), chapters 4 and 9.

7. Robert Phillips, "Some Key Questions about Stakeholder Theory," *Ivey Business Journal* (online), March/April 2004.

8. Judith F. Samuelson, "How Do We Fix Executive Pay? By Looking Beyond Executives," The Aspen Institute, August 15, 2018, accessed August 27, 2018, at https://www.aspeninstitute.org/blog-posts/how-do-we-fix-executive-pay-by-looking-beyond-executives/.

9. Coro Strandberg, "The Sustainability Pay Link," *Corporate Knights*, Summer 2014 Issue, accessed May 12, 2016, http://www.corporateknights.com/channels/workplace/the-sustainability-pay-link-14018967/.

10. John Argenti, "Stakeholders: The Case Against," *Long Range Planning* 30 (1997): 442–445.

11. Andrew Campbell, "Stakeholders: The Case in Favour," *Long Range Planning* 30 (1997): 446–49.

12. Steven L. Wartick and John F. Mahon, "Toward a Substance Definition of the Corporate Issue Construct," *Business and Society*, Vol. 33, No. 3, December 1994, 308.

13. This definition is based upon one formulated by Jon Johnson, "Issues Management—What Are the Issues?" *Business Quarterly* 48 (Fall 1983): 1.

14. Steven L. Wartick and Robert E. Rude, "Issues Management: Corporate Fad or Corporate Function?" *California Management Review* 29 (1986): 132–36; and Joseph F. Coates et al., *Issues Management: How You Can Plan, Organize and Manage the Future* (Mt. Airy, MD: Lomond Publishers, Inc., 1986), 15–16.

15. Coates, *Issues Management*, 19–20.

16. Steven Fink, *Crisis Management: Planning for the Inevitable* (New York: AMACOM, 1986).

17. Ibid, 15–16.

18. Ibid, 15–16.

19. Christine M. Pearson and Ian I. Mitroff, "From Crisis Prone to Crisis Prepared: A Framework for Crisis Management," *Academy of Management Executive*, Vol. 7, No 1, 1993, 48–59.

20. Norman R. Augustine, "Managing the Crisis You Tried to Prevent," *Harvard Business Review*, November–December 1995, 147–158.

21. Ian I. Mitroff and Paul Shrivastava, "Effective Crisis Management," *The Academy of Management Executive*, Vol. 1, No. 3, 1987, 283–29; Jonathan

L. Bernstein, "The Ten Steps of Crisis Communications," *Crisisnavigator*, Vol. 11, Issue 4 (April 2010), available at http://www.crisisnavigator.org/The-Ten-Steps-of-Crisis-Communications.490.0.html; and Daniel F. Muzyka, "Communicating in a Crisis: Act with Honesty and Empathy," *The Globe and Mail*, June 9, 2008, B8.

22. Linda Stamato, "Should Business Leaders Apologize? Why, When and How an Apology Matters," *Ivey Business Journal,* July-August 2008, 1–8.

Chapter 4

1. Archie B. Carroll, *Business and Society: Ethics and Stakeholder Management* (Cincinnati, OH: South-Western Publishing, 1989), 62.

2. Edward R. Freeman, *Strategic Management: A Stakeholder Approach* (Boston: Pitman, 1984).

3. Ibid, 53.

4. Ibid, 54–64.

5. Ibid, 64–69.

6. Ibid, 69–73.

7. John M. Bryson, *Strategic Planning for Public and Nonprofit Organizations: A Guide to Strengthening and Sustaining Organizational Achievement,* revised edition (San Francisco: Jossey-Bass Publishers, 1995), 284–286.

8. Paul C. Nutt and Robert W. Backoff, *Strategic Management of Public and Third Sector Organizations: A Handbook for Leaders* (San Francisco: Jossey-Bass Publishers, 1992), 196–98; and Bryson, *Strategic Planning for Public and Nonprofit Organizations,* 285–286.

9. Grant T. Savage, Timothy W. Nix, Carlton J. Whitehead, and John D. Blair, "Strategies for Assessing and Managing Organizational Stakeholders," *Academy of Management Executive* 5(2) (1991): 61–75.

10. Freeman, *Strategic Management,* 142–144.

11. The typology can be found by entering *Diagnostic Typology of Organizational Stakeholders* into Google search.

12. Ibid, 65.

13. Ronald K. Mitchell, Bradley R. Agle, and Donna J. Wood, "Toward a Theory of Stakeholder Identification and Salience: Defining the Principle of Who and What Really Counts," *Academy of Management Review,* Vol. 22, No. 4 (1997): 853–86.

14. Ibid, 289–293.

15. Compiled from ibid, 299–304. The typology can be found at Google search

for *Stakeholder Typology: One, Two, or Three Attributes Present* images or https://www.researchgate.net/figure/Stakeholder-typology-One-two-or-three-attributes-present-Mitchell-et-al_fig1_236727192.

16. Jeff Frooman. "Stakeholder Influence Strategies," *Academy of Management Review,* Vol. 24, No. 2 (1999): 191–205.

17. Ibid, 196–197.

18. Ibid, 198.

19. Ibid, 200. A table of the influence strategies is available at https://www.stakeholdermap.com/stakeholder-influence.html.

20. Jeanne Liedtka, "Collaborating across Lines of Business for Competitive Advantage," *Academy of Management Executive Journal,* Volume 10, No. 2 (1996): 20–37.

21. Ann Svendsen, *The Stakeholder Strategy: Profiting from Collaborative Business Relationships* (San Francisco: Berrett-Koehler Publishers, 1998), 2–5.

22. Ibid, 71–184.

23. Archie B. Carroll, *Business and Society: Ethics and Stakeholder Management* (Cincinnati, OH: South-Western Publishing, 1989), 479–489; and John M. Bryson, *Strategic Planning for Public and Nonprofit Organizations* (San Francisco: Jossey-Bass Publishers, 1988).

24. Questions about Materiality and topic Boundary, https://www.globalreporting.org/standards/questions-and-feedback/materiality-and-topic-boundary/.

25. "Air Canada's Materiality Matrix," Corporate Sustainability Report 2016 entitled Citizens of the World, Air Canada, page 13 at https://www.aircanada.com/content/dam/aircanada/portal/documents/PDF/agents/en/documents/csr_2016_report_en.pdf.

Chapter 5

1. Philip V. Lewis, "Defining Business Ethics: Like Nailing Jello to a Wall," *Journal of Business Ethics* 4 (1985): 381.

2. Larue Tone Hosmer, "Strategic Planning as if Ethics Mattered," *Strategic Management Journal* 15 (1994): 23.

3. Larue Tone Hosmer, *The Ethics of Management* (Homewood, IL: Irwin, 1987), 96.

4. *An Inquiry into the Nature and Causes of the Wealth of Nations,* published in 1776. Online edition available at the Adam Smith Institute website, http://www.adamsmith.org.

5. Larue Tone Hosmer, *Moral Leadership in Business* (Burr Ridge, IL: Irwin, 1994).

6. Ian Maitland, "The Human Face of Self-Interest," *Journal of Business Ethics* 38 (2002): 3–17.

7. John Kaler, "Reasons to Be Ethical: Self-Interest and Ethical Business," *Journal of Business Ethics* 27 (2000): 161–173.

8. Ibid.

9. Anthony M. Pagano, "Criteria for Ethical Decision Making in Managerial Situations," *Proceedings* (New Orleans: National Academy of Management, 1987): 1–12.

10. Hosmer, "Strategic Planning As If Ethics Mattered," *Strategic Management Journal*, June 14, 2007.

11. Lawrence Kohlberg, "The Claim of Moral Adequacy of a Highest Stage of Moral Judgment," *The Journal of Philosophy* LXX (1973): 630–646; Lawrence Kohlberg, *Essays on Moral Development, Vol. 1: The Philosophy of Moral Development* (New York: Harper and Row, 1981); and Lawrence Kohlberg, "Stage and Sequence: The Cognitive Development Approach to Socialization," in *Handbook of Socialization Theory and Research,* D.A. Goslin, ed. (Chicago: Rand McNally, 1969), 347–480.

12. L. Kohlberg and R. Ryncarz, "Beyond Justice Reasoning: Moral Development and Consideration of a Seventh Stage," in C. Alexander and E. Langer, eds., *Higher Stages of Human Development: Perspectives on Adult Growth* (New York: Oxford University Press, 1990).

13. Linda Klebe Treviño and Michael E. Brown, "Managing to Be Ethical: Debunking Five Business Myths," *Academy of Management Executive,* Vol. 18, No. 2 (2004): 69–72, 77.

14. Mahzarin R. Banaji, Max H. Bazerman, and Dolly Chugh, "How (Un)ethical Are You?" *Harvard Business Review,* Vol. 81, Issue 12, December 2003, 56–64.

Chapter 6

1. Lisa Jones Christensen et al, "Taking Responsibility for Corporate Social Responsibility: The Role of Leaders in Creating, Implementing, Sustaining, or Avoiding Socially Responsible Behaviors," *The Academy of Management Perspectives,* 2014, Vol. 28, No. 2, 172–174.

2. Michel Dion, "Corporate Citizenship as an Ethic of Care: Corporate Values, Codes of Ethics, and Global Governance," in Jorg Andriof and Malcolm McIntosh, *Perspectives on Corporate Citizenship* (London: Greenleaf Publishing, 2002), 118–137.

3. Jack Kooten, *Strategic Management in the Public and Nonprofit Organization* (New York: Praeger, 1989), 125.

4. Lee Ginsberg and Neil Millier, "Value-Driven Management," *Business Horizons,* May/June (1992): 23–27.

5. Errol P. Mendes and Jeffrey A. Clark, "The Five Generations of Corporate Codes of Conduct and Their Impact on Corporate Social Responsibility," *Human Rights Research Centre,* University of Ottawa, accessed January 23, 2003, http://www.cdp-hrc.uottawa.ca/publicat/five.html.

6. Laura L. Nash, "Ethics without the Sermon," *Harvard Business Review,* November–December 1981, 79–89.

7. Ibid, 89.

8. Anthony M. Pagano, "Criteria for Ethical Decision Making in Managerial Situations," *Proceedings,* National Academy of Management, New Orleans (1987): 1–12.

9. This is a variation of a definition by Michael McDonald, "Ethics and Conflict of Interest," the W. Maurice Young Centre of Applied Ethics, University of British Columbia, http://www.ethics.ubc.ca/people/mcdonald/conflict.htm.

10. Kenneth Kernaghan and John W. Langford, "Conflict of Interest," chapter 6 in *The Responsible Public Servant* (Halifax: The Institute for Research on Public Policy and The Institute of Public Administration of Canada, 1990), 133–155.

11. Competition Bureau Canada, "Whistleblowing Study—Models of Whistleblowing Protection," http://www.competitionbureau.gc.ca/internet/index.cfm?itemid=1276&lg=e.

12. Ontario Securities Commission, OSC Policy 15–601 - Whistleblower Program, http://www.osc.gov.on.ca/en/SecuritiesLaw_rule_20151028_15-601_policy-whistleblower-program.htm and OSC Awards $7.5 Million to Three Whistleblowers, February 27, 2019, News Release at http://www.osc.gov.on.ca/en/NewsEvents_nr_20190227_osc-awards-to-three-whistleblowers.htm.

13. Stephen M. Kohn, "The Sarbanes-Oxley Act ('Sox'): Legal Protections for Corporate Whistleblowers," National Whistleblowing Center, http://www.whistleblowers.org/html/sarbanes-oxley.htm.

14. Steven Bavaria, "Corporate Ethics Should Start in the Boardroom," *Business Horizons,* January–February (1991): 9–19.

15. James Gillies, *Boardroom Renaissance: Power, Morality and Performance in the Modern Corporation* (Toronto: McGraw-Hill Ryerson, 1992), Chapter 8.

16. Archie B. Carroll, "The Moral Leader: Essential for Successful Corporate Citizenship," in Jorg Andriof and Malcolm McIntosh, *Perspectives on Corporate Citizenship* (London: Greenleaf Publishing, 2002), 145–150.

17. André Nijhof, Olaf Fisscher, and Jan Kees Looise, "Coercion, Guidance and Mercifulness: The Different Influences of Ethics Programs on Decision Making," *Journal of Business Ethics* 27, 1–2 (September 2000): 33–42.

18. Ibid, 35.

19. Ibid, 38.

20. Ibid, 39.

21. *Management Ethics,* Summer 2008, 66–67.

22. Max B.E. Clarkson, "Ethics and Profit: The Changing Values of Business in Society." Unpublished presentation to the Faculty of Business Administration, Memorial University of Newfoundland, St. John's (March 3, 1993).

23. Ibid.

24. Gene Laczniak, "Business Ethics: A Manager's Primer," *Business* (Georgia State University, 1983): 23–29.

25. Free Management Library, *Business Ethics: Managing Ethics in the Workplace and Social Responsibility,* http://www.managementhelp.org/ethics/ethxgde.htm#anchor33077.

26. Linda Klebe Treviño and Michael E. Brown, "Managing to Be Ethical: Debunking Five Business Myths," *Academy of Management Executive* 18, no. 2 (May 2004): 69–81.

27. Jay Barney, "Organizational culture: Can It be a Source of Sustainable Advantage," *Academy of Management Review,* II, No. 3, 656–665.

28. L. K. Treviño and K. A. Nelson, *Managing Business Ethics: Straight Talk About How to do it Right* (5th Edition) 2011, Hoboken, NJ: John Wiley & Sons, Inc., 151.

29. Mark S. Schwartz, *Business Ethics: An Ethical Decision-Making Approach,* 2017, Wiley Blackwell: Chichester, UK, 191–211.

30. Literature reviewed for this section: Trevor Cole, "Why Good People Do Bad Things," *University of Toronto Magazine,* Winter 2005, 1927; Charles D. Kerns, "Why Good Leaders Do Bad Things," *Graziadio Business Review,* Vol. 6, Issue 4 (2003), available at http://gbr.pepperdine.edu/2010/08/why-good-leaders-do-bad-things; N. Craig Smith et al., "Why Managers Fail to Do the Right Thing: An Empirical Study of Unethical and Illegal Conduct," *Business Ethics Quarterly,* Vol. 17, Issue 4 (2007): 633–667; Sunday Samson Babalola, "Determinants of Unethical Business Behaviour among Owner–Managers," *Journal of Human Values,* Vol. 15, No. 1 (January/June 2009): 61–75; and Yuri Mishima, "Why Pressure Makes Good People Do Bad Things," Network for Business Sustainability, posted May 6, 2011, available at http://www.nbs.net/csr/8536/.

31. Ethics Practitioners' Association of Canada (EPAC), "Our Competencies" at http://epac-apec.ca/who-we-are/our-competencies.

Chapter 7

1. *Guidance on Social Responsibility,* International Organization for Standardization, 2009, Section 2.1.18, http://isotc.iso.org/livelink/livelink/fetch/-8929321/8929339/8929348/3935837/3974907/ISO_DIS_26000_Guidance_on_Social_Responsibility.pdf?nodeid=8385026&vernum=-2, pp. 3–4. Additional information on ISO 26000 available at http://www.iso.org/iso/catalogue_detail?csnumber=42546.

2. ISO 26000 - Social responsibility, International Organization for Standardization, https://www.iso.org/iso-26000-social-responsibility.html.

3. Roger A. Buchholz, "Corporate Responsibility and the Good Society: From Economics to Ecology," *Business Horizons* (July/August 1991): 19.

4. Alexander Dahlsrud, "How Corporate Social Responsibility Is Defined: An Analysis of 37 Definitions," *Corporate Social Responsibility and Environmental Management* 15 (2008): 1–13.

5. Donna J. Wood, "Corporate Social Performance Revisited," *The Academy of Management Review,* Vol. 16, No. 4 (1991): 695.

6. Ibid, 695–700.

7. Stefan Schaltegger and Roger Burritt, "Business Cases and Corporate Engagement with Sustainability: Differentiating Ethical Motivations," *Journal of Business Ethics,* (2018), 147: 241–259.

8. Ibid, p. 253.

9. Ibid, pp. 253–254.

10. Ibid, pp. 253–254.

11. Ibid. p. 254.

12. Ibid, pp; 254–255.

13. Ibid, p. 255.

14. Richard J. Klonoski, "Foundational Considerations in the Corporate Social Responsibility Debate," *Business Horizons* (1991, July/August): 16.

15. Ibid, 16.

16. Archie Carroll, "The Pyramid of Corporate Social Responsibility: Toward the Moral Management of Organizational Stakeholders," *Business Horizons* (July/August 1991): 39–48.

17. Images of the pyramid are available from a "Carroll's Pyramid of CSR" Google search.

18. Ibid, 39–43.

19. Marcel van Marrewijk, "Concepts and Definitions of CSR and Corporate Sustainability: Between Agency and Communion," *Journal of Business Ethics* 44, No. 2 (2003): 102–103.

20. Peter W. Roberts and Grahame R. Dowling, "Corporate Reputation and Sustained Superior Financial Performance," *Strategic Management Journal* 23 (2002): 1077–1093.

21. The Aspen Institute, "Social Impact Management: A Definition," http://www .aspeninstitute.org/site/c.huLWJeMRKpH /b.729881/k.5FC2/Social_Impact _Management_A_Definition.htm.

22. Ibid.

23. Wayne Norman and Chris MacDonald, "Getting to the Bottom of 'Triple Bottom Line,'" *Business Ethics Quarterly,* Vol. 14, Issue 2 (2004): 243–262.

24. World Economic Forum—The Business Case for Corporate Citizenship, "Global Corporate Citizenship," http://web .worldbank.org/archive/website00818/WEB /OTHER/THE_BUSI.HTM.

25. Donna J. Wood and Jeanne M. Logsdon, "Theorising Business Citizenship," in Jörg Andriof and Malcolm McIntosh, *Perspectives on Corporate Citizenship* (London: Greenleaf Publishing, 2002), 87.

26. Dirk Matten and Andrew Crane, "Corporate Citizenship: Towards an Extended Theoretical Conceptualization," *Academy of Management Review* 30 , No. 1 (2005): 166–179.

27. Dirk Matten and Andrew Crane, "Corporate Citizenship: Towards an Extended Theoretical Conceptualization," *Academy of Management Review* 30, No. 1 (2005): 168–170.

28. Ibid, 172–173.

29. Ibid, 174.

30. Ibid, 175.

31. Wood and Logsdon, 83–103.

32. Ibid, 87.

33. Ibid.

34. Mark S. Schwartz and Archie B. Carroll, "Integrating and Unifying Competing and Complementary Frameworks: The Search for a Common Core in the Business and Society Field," *Business and Society,* Vol. 47, No. 2 (June 2008): 148–186.

35. Ibid, 168.

36. Ibid, 169.

37. Ibid, 171.

38. Ibid, 173.

39. Mark S. Schwartz and Archie B. Carroll, "Integrating and Unifying Competing and Complementary Frameworks: The Search For a Common Core in the Business and Society Field," *Business and Society*, Volume 47, Number 2, June 2008, 175.

Chapter 8

1. Statistics Canada. Table 11-10-0130-01 Summary of charitable donors

2. Minda Zetlin, "Companies Find Profit in Corporate Giving," *Management Review* (December 1990): 10.

3. John Pepin, "Venture Capitalists and Entrepreneurs Become Venture Philanthropists," http://www.evpa .eu.com/downloads/PepinArticle _VenturePhilanthropy_revised0404_pdf.pdf.

4. Elizabeth Bihl, "Sponsorship Makes Good Business Sense," *Canada Export,* Vol. 10, No. 11 (1992): 2.

5. Ibid, 2, 7.

6. Business for Social Responsibility, "Community Involvement," http://www.bsr .org/AdvisoryServices/CI.cfm.

7. Some of the report's findings are summarized. The report was published by the Conference Board of Canada on August 15, 2015, and authored by Alison Howard.

8. *Corporate Community Investment in Canada: A Profile of the Profession,* Conference Board of Canada, Ottawa, December 2017.

9. Responsible Investment and Indigenous Trusts: A Discussion Paper, National Aboriginal Trust Officers Association, Hagersville, ON, March 2018, accessed at https://www.sauder.ubc.ca/Faculty /Research_Centres/Centre_for_Social _Innovation_and_Impact_Investing /Core_Themes/Impact_Investing/~/media /Files/ISIS/Reports/Impact%20Investing %20Reports/Impact%20Investing%20in%20 the%20Indigenous%20Context%20-%20 Executive%20Summary%20-%20FINAL. ashx] on February 2, 2019.

10. "Redwashing," First Nations at http://www.firstnations.de/indian_land /misrepresented-redwashing.htm accessed on February 2, 2019.

11. "Is Giving Back Worthwhile," *Profit Magazine*, May 2014, 22.

12. Lisa Princic et al., *Engaging Small Business in Corporate Social Responsibility* (Vancouver: Canadian Business for Social Responsibility, October 2003), 13.

13. Ibid, 16.

14. This list was generated from a student assignment, "Corporate Social Responsibility and Small Business," Business 7010— Business and Society, Faculty of Business Administration, Memorial University of Newfoundland, Winter 2006.

15. Heledd Jenkins, "A Critique of Conventional CSR Theory: An SME Perspective," *Journal of General Management,* Vol. 29, No 4 (Summer 2004): 37–57.

16. "Working with Community Groups: A Guide for Small Business," Network for Business Sustainability, November 5, 2012, http://nbs.net/wp-content/uploads /SME-Resource-Community-Engagement .pdf.

17. Robert Sexty, "Small Business/ Entrepreneurship Biography of Social Responsibility & Ethics." Available from the author at rsexty@mun.ca.

18. *SMEs: The Expertise Challenge*, Network for Business Sustainability at https://nbs.net/p/how-can-businesses -develop-sustainability-expertise-7fcc26e0 -4aef-44a3-97b2-3d4803ed313c.

Chapter 9

1. For detailed results refer to "2019 Best 50: Our 18th Annual Best 50 Corporate Citizens in Canada," *Corporate Knights* website at https://www.corporateknights .com/reports/2019-best-50 and in *Corporate Knights,* Summer 2019, Vol. 18, Issue 3, 32–33, 35–37.

2. The last three points are from the "Quality, Credibility and Communications" assessment criteria used in *Corporate Sustainability Reporting in Canada,* Ottawa: Stratos Inc., December 2005, 39, http://www.stratos-sts.com/wp-content /uploads/2013/04/2005_12_CSR-Gaining -Momentum.pdf.

3. "Sustainability Practices 2018: Trends in Corporate Sustainability Reporting in North America, Europe, and Asia-Pacific," The Conference Board Inc. website at https:// www.conference-board.org/sustainability -practices/ accessed February 15, 2019.

4. C. J. Fombrun, *Reputation: Realizing Value from the Corporate Image* (Boston: Harvard Business School Press, 1996), 72.

5. Mary Choquette and Peri Turnbull, "How Corporate Social Responsibility Can Affect Your Reputation," Members' Briefing 302, Ottawa: The Conference Board of Canada, November 2000, 1–2.

6. "Public Affairs Reputation Management: Benchmarking Report," The Conference Board of Canada, September 2015.

7. John F. Mahon, "Corporate Reputation: A Research Agenda Using Strategy and Stakeholder Literature," *Business and Society* 41, 4 (December 2002): 428.

8. Dylan Minor and John Morgan, "CSR as Reputation Insurance: Primum Non Nocere," *California Management Review*, Vol. 53, Issue 2 (Spring 2011): 40–59.

9. Jay Janney and Steve Gove, "Reputation and Corporate Responsibility Aberrations, Trends, and Hypocrisy: Reactions to Firm Choices in the Stock Option Backdating Scandal," *Journal of Management Studies*, Vol. 48, No. 7 (2011): 1562–1585.

10. Andrea Stanaland and Patrick Murray, "Consumer Perceptions of the Antecedents and Consequences of Corporate Social Responsibility," *Journal of Business Ethics*, Vol. 102 (2011): 47–55.

11. Jantzi Social Index, "About the JSI," http://www.jantzisocialindex.com.

12. Dow Jones Sustainability Indexes, "Welcome to the Dow Jones Sustainability Indexes," http://www.sustainability-index.com/.

13. Sandra E. Martin, "Staff Stay at Companies with Heart," *National Post,* August 16, 2004, FP10.

14. "Building Trust: Why Transparency Must be Part of the Equation," Globescan website at https://globescan.com/building-trust-transparency-white-paper/ accessed February 15, 2019.

15. Arthur B. Laffer, Andrew Coors, and Wayne Winegarden, "Does Corporate Social Responsibility Enhance Business Profitability?" CSRWatch™/SRIWatch, http://www.csrwatch.com/Sub/Resources/csr_profitability.htm.

16. H.E. Bowman and W. Haire, "A Strategic Posture Towards Corporate Social Responsibility," *California Management Review* 18 (1975): 49–58.

17. Marc Orlitzky, Frank L. Schmidt, and Sara L. Rynes, "Corporate Social and Financial Performance: A Meta-Analysis," *Organizational Studies* 24 (2003): 403–441.

18. Joshua D. Margolis and James P. Walsh, "Misery Loves Companies: Rethinking Social Initiatives by Business," *Administrative Science Quarterly* 48 (2003): 273–278.

19. John Peloza, "Primer: Valuing Sustainability," Network for Business Sustainability accessed November 6, 2012, http://nbs.net/knowledge/business-case/valuing-sustainability/primer; and "Metrics for Valuing Business Sustainability: A Framework for Executives," Network for Business Sustainability, 2011, accessed November 6, 2012, http://nbs.net/wp-content/uploads/NBS-Executive-Report-Valuing.pdf.

20. "The National Corporate Social Responsibility Report: Managing Risks, Leveraging Opportunities,"The Conference Board of Canada, May 26, 2004 at https://www.conferenceboard.ca/e-library/abstract.aspx?did=734.

21. Canadian Centre for Ethics and Corporate Policy, "About Us," http://www.ethicscentre.ca/EN/about/.

22. Corporate Social Responsibility (CSR), An implementation Guide for Canadian Business https://www.ic.gc.ca/eic/site/csr-rse.nsf/eng/h_rs00599.html.

23. "About GRI," Global Reporting Initiative website at https://www.globalreporting.org/information/about-gri/Pages/default.aspx.

24. "About GRI," Global Reporting Initiative website at https://www.globalreporting.org/information/about-gri/Pages/default.aspx.

25. Aaron Chatterji and David Levine, "Breaking Down the Wall of Codes: Evaluating Non-Financial Performance Measurement," *California Management Review,* Vol. 48, No. 2 (2006): 29–30.

26. Ibid, 44–48.

27. Compiled from Diana McLaren, "Measuring the Good Global Citizen," *The Globe and Mail,* November 26, 2008, B18; and *CSR Trends: A Comprehensive Survey of Corporate Social Responsibility Report Trends, Benchmarks and Best Practices,* Craib Design & Communications and PricewaterhouseCoopers LLP study, http://www.craib.com/craib_public/pdf/ARTrends/CSR_TRENDS_3_LR.pdf.

28. Mary Choquette and Peri Turnbull, "How Corporate Social Responsibility Can Affect Your Reputation," Members' Briefing 302 (Ottawa: Conference Board of Canada, November 2000), 3–4.

29. Sustainability Reporting to Improve Organizational Performance, Network for Business Sustainability at https://nbs.net/p/full-report-sustainability-reporting-to-improve-organizational-performance-fca36288-5f89-428e-a4a6-57fe7e691e8c.

30. "2013 Eligibility Procedures and Accreditation Standards for Business Accreditation," *The Association to Advance Collegiate Schools of Business*, pages 5–7, accessed February 16, 2019.

31. "Making the Grade: The 2018 Better World MBA Results," *Corporate Knights: The Magazine for Clean Capitalism,* Fall 2018 Edition available at https://www.corporateknights.com/reports/2018-better-world-mba-methodology/making-the-grade-15417432/ accessed February 8, 2019.

32. *The Times Higher Education University Impact Rankings* website at https://www.timeshighereducation.com/rankings/impact/2019/overall#!/page/0/length/25/sort_by/rank/sort_order/asc/cols/undefined and https://www.timeshighereducation.com/world-university-rankings/methodology-impact-rankings-2019 accessed on April 6, 2019.

33. The Principles for Responsible Management Education (PRME), "What is PRME" at http://www.unprme.org/about-prme/index.php.

34. The Principles for Responsible Management Education (PRME), "Sharing Information on Progress (SIP)" at http://www.unprme.org/reporting/index.php.

35. The Principles for Responsible Management Education (PRME), "Become a Signatory" at http://www.unprme.org/participation/index.php.

36. Coro Strandberg, *The Future of Corporate Social Responsibility* (Vancouver: VanCity Credit Union, 2002).

37. Ibid, 5.

38. Ibid, 7–16.

39. Ibid, 17.

40. Allen L. White, *Fade, Integrate or Transform? The Future of CSR* (San Francisco: Business for Social Responsibility, 2005).

Chapter 10

1. David Heald, "Privatization, Analysing Its Appeal and Limitations," Fiscal Studies 5.1 (1984): 36.

2. Jonathan N. Goodrich, "Privatization in America," *Business Horizons* (January–February 1988): 11–17.

3. Whitehorse Mining Initiative, Natural Resources Canada website at https://www.nrcan.gc.ca/mining-materials/policy/government-canada/8698.

4. The Kimberly Process website at https://www.kimberleyprocess.com/.

5. Extractive Industries Transparency Initiative website at https://eiti.org/.

6. "Building the Canadian Advantage: A CSR Strategy for the International Extractive Sector," Natural Resources Canada website at https://www.nrcan.gc.ca/mining-materials/publications/8776.

7. https://www.international.gc.ca/trade-agreements-accords-commerciaux/topics-domaines/other-autre/csr-strat-rse.aspx?lang=eng.

8. "Voluntary Principles on Security and Human Rights" at http://www.voluntaryprinciples.org.

9. "Supporting Corporate Social Responsibility initiatives" https://www.canada.ca/en/employment-social-development/services/labour-relations/international/support.html.

10. "Responsible Business Conduct Abroad," Global Affairs Canada website at https://www.international.gc.ca/trade-agreements-accords-commerciaux/topics-domaines/other-autre/csr-rse.aspx?lang=eng.

11. "Social Responsibility," Natural Resources Canada website at https://www.nrcan.gc.ca/mining-materials/mining/responsible-mineral-development/corporate-social-responsibility/18693.

12. Jean-Pascal Gond, Nahee Kan, and Jeremy Moon, "The government of self-regulation: on the comparative dynamics of corporate social responsibility," *Economy and Society,* Volume 40, Number 4, November 2011, 640–671.

13. Corruption of Foreign Public Officials Act (S.C. 1998, c. 34) at http://laws-lois.justice.gc.ca/eng/acts/c-45.2/index.html.

14. "Integrity Framework" Public Works and Government Services Canada, http://www.tpsgc-pwgsc.gc.ca/ci-if/ci-if-eng.html; and "Principles" at http://www.tpsgc-pwgsc.gc.ca/ci-if/principes-principles-eng.htm.

15. "Government of Canada›s Integrity Regime," Public Works and Government Services Canada, http://www.tpsgc-pwgsc.gc.ca/ci-if/ci-if-eng.html; and "Government of Canada Announces Improvements to Integrity of Federal Procurement," Government of Canada, http://news.gc.ca/web/article-en.do?nid=995629.

16. "Remediation Agreements and Orders to Address Corporate Crime," Department of Justice Canada website at https://www.canada.ca/en/department-justice/news/2018/03/remediation-agreements-to-address-corporate-crime.html.

17. "Using Tax Havens to Avoid Paying Taxes Worth the Risk?," Canada Revenue Agency website at http://www.cra-arc.gc.ca/E/pub/tg/rc4507/rc4507-09e.pdf.

18. "Bay Street and Tax Havens: Curbing Corporate Canada's Addiction," Canadians for Tax Fairness," November 2017 accessed at https://www.taxfairness.ca/sites/taxfairness.ca/files/pdf/canadian_for_tax_fairness_-_tax_havens_2017_april_2018_web.pdf.

19. "Tax Information Exchange Agreements," Department of Finance Canada website https://www.fin.gc.ca/treaties-conventions/tieaaerf-eng.asp.

20. "Economic Action Plan 2015," Department of Finance, Government of Canada at http://actionplan.gc.ca/en/initiative/reducing-taxes-small-businesses#sthash.GGBi5nv7.dpuf.

21. Duanjie Chen and Jack Mintz, "Small Business Taxation: Revamping Incentives to Encourage Growth," *The School of Public Policy, University of Calgary, SPP Research Papers*, Volume 4, Issue 7, May 2011.

22. Benjamin Dachis and John Lester, "Small Business Preferences as a Barrier to Growth: Not so Tall After All," C.D. Howe Institute, Commentary No. 26, May 2015.

23. "About Us," Canadians for Tax Fairness website at http://www.taxfairness.ca/.

24. Zach Dubinsky, "Wealthy Canadians hiding up to $240B abroad, CRA says," CBC News, June 28, 2018 at https://www.cbc.ca/news/business/cra-tax-gap-foreign-holdings-1.4726983.

25. Bruce Carson, Registration of Lobbyists, *Library of Parliament Current Issue Review* (Ottawa: Supply and Services Canada. Cat. No. YM32-1/86-18-1988-05E 1988), 8.

26. "Profile," Public Affairs Association of Canada, http://www.publicaffairs.ca/whoweare/profile.shtml.

27. Based upon a definition in Donald L. Barlett and James B. Steele, "Corporate Welfare," *Time* Canadian Edition, November 9, 1998, 32.

Chapter 11

1. "What is responsible investment," Principles for Responsible Investment (PRI) at https://www.unpri.org/pri/what-is-responsible-investment.

2. Responsible Investment Association of Canada website at https://www.riacanada.ca/responsible-investment/.

3. Responsible Investment Association (Canada), Community Relations at https://www.riacanada.ca/responsible-investment/.

4. Canadian Council for Aboriginal Business, Progressive Aboriginal Relations (PAR) at https://www.ccab.com/programs/progressive-aboriginal-relations-par.]

5. National Aboriginal Trust Officers Association (NATOA) website at https://natoa.ca.

6. Mark Sevestre and Kevin Thomas, "It's time for investors to do more to advance reconciliation," *The Telegram* (St. John's, NL), April 25, 2019, B2.

7. Jon Entine, "The Myth of Social Investing: A Critique of Its Practices and Consequences for Corporate Social Performance Research," *Organization and Environment*, Vol. 16, No. 3 (September 2003): 352–368.

8. Robert K. Mueller, "Changes in the Wind in Corporate Governance," *Journal of Business Strategy* 1(4) (1981): 9.

9. *Report of the Toronto Stock Exchange, Committee on Corporate Governance in Canada* (Toronto: The Toronto Stock Exchange, 1994), 7.

10. *OECD Principles of Corporate Governance* (Paris: OECD Publications, 2004): 18–19, 32–39, http://www.oecd.org/topic/0,2686,en_2649_34813_1_1_1_1_37439,00.htm.

11. *Where Were the Directors: Guidelines for Improving Corporate Governance in Canada* (Toronto: Toronto Stock Exchange Committee on Corporate Governance in Canada, May 1994), 24. There are many definitions of independence and this one was not adopted in National Instrument 58–201.

12. "Annual Report Card 2017: Advancing Diverse Leadership on Canada's Corporate Boards," Canadian Board Diversity Council (CBDC) website at https://boarddiversity.ca/cbdc/annualreport/.

13. "Canadian Securities Regulators Release Fourth Review Regarding Women on Boards and in Executive Officer Positions," Canadian Securities Administrators Media Release, September 27, 2018, at https://www.securities-administrators.ca/aboutcsa.aspx?id=1739&terms=women%20on%20boards and a follow up release with same title dated February 28, 2019 at https://www.securities-administrators.ca/aboutcsa.aspx?id=1772.

14. Barbara Shector, "Canadian Shareholders Increasingly Aggressive on 'Say-on-Pay,' *The National Post,* May 1, 2015 accessed at http://business

.financialpost.com/news/canadian-shareholders-increasingly-aggressive-on-say-on-pay; Katy Pitch, "Say-on-Pay": Back in the Spotlight this Proxy Season," Stikeman Elliot website accessed at http://www.canadiansecuritieslaw.com/2015/05/articles/corporate-governance/sayonpay-back-in-the-spotlight-this-proxy-season/; and Darren Henderson, "Why Canada Should Adopt Mandatory Say-on-Pay," *Ivey Business Journal* accessed at http://iveybusinessjournal.com/publication/why-canada-should-adopt-mandatory-say-on-pay/.

15. "SEC Adopts Rule for Pay Ratio Disclosure," Securities and Exchange Commission website at http://www.sec.gov/news/pressrelease/2015-160.html.

16. "2015 Best Practices for Proxy Circular Disclosure," Canadian Coalition for Good Governance at http://www.ccgg.ca/site/ccgg/assets/pdf/2015_bestpractices.pdf page 5

17. "Disclosure of Corporate Governance Practices," National Instrument 58–201, https://www.osc.gov.on.ca/documents/en/Securities-Category5/rule_20050617_58-201_corp-gov-guidelines.pdf.

18. OECD Principles of Corporate Governance: 24–25.

19. Larry Colero, Crossroads Programs, Inc., "Five Questions That Directors Should Ask," University of British Columbia, The W. Maurice Young Centre for Applied Ethics, accessed November 7, 2006, http://www.ethics.ubc.ca/papers/invited/5questions.html.

20. Mark Schacter, *What Directors Need to Know about Corporate Social Responsibility* (Ottawa: Mark Schacter Consulting, 2004), 4–5, 10.

Chapter 12

1. "The gig economy," BMO Wealth Management Insight, Canadian Edition, July 2018 at https://www.bmo.com/assets/pdfs/wealth/bmo_gig_economy_report_en.pdf accessed March 6, 2019.

2. *Employment Equity Act,* 1995, C.44, s. 2.

3. *Canadian Human Rights Act,* 1986. c. 14, s. 1.

4. Canada's Best Diversity Employers 2019 at https://www.canadastop100.com/diversity/ accessed March 6, 2019.

5. There are numerous acronyms associated with this cause, including 2SLGBTQQIA representing "two-spirit, lesbian, gay, bisexual, transgender, queer, questioning, intersex and asexual.

6. "Before and after #MeToo: A look at police-reported sexual assaults in Canada," Statistics Canada Release dated November 8, 2018 accessed at https://www150.statcan.gc.ca/n1/pub/11-627-m/11-627-m2018036-eng.htm on November 12, 2018.

7. Rosemarie Tong, "Feminist Ethics," *Encyclopedia of Business Ethics and Society,* (ed.) Robert W. Kolb, (Thousand Islands, CA: Sage Publications Inc.) Online Edition 2007.

8. "Feminist Ethics: An Alternative Voice," Villanova University, MPA 8300 Leadership Ethics, accessed February 20, 2013, http://www83.homepage.villanova.edu/richard.jacobs/MPA%208300/theories/feminist.html; and Rosemarie Tong and Nancy Williams, "Feminist Ethics," *The Stanford Encyclopedia of Philosophy (Summer 2011 Edition),* (ed.) Edward N. Zalta, accessed January 21, 2013, http://plato.stanford.edu/entries/feminism-ethics.

9. Janet L. Borgerson, "On the Harmony of Feminist Ethics and Business Ethics," *Business and Society Review,* Vol. 112, No. 4 (December 2007): 477–509.

10. Hewitt & Associates, "CSR as a Driver of Employee Engagement," Canadian Business for Social Responsibility, accessed December 2012, http://cbsr.ca/blog/csr-driver-employee-engagement.

11. "Hewitt and CBSR Data Establishes Strong Relationship between Employee Engagement and Views on CSR," Press Release, Hewitt Associates, January 25, 2010.

12. Maria José Ramos, "CSR as a Driver of Employee Engagement," Canadian Business for Social Responsibility, accessed December 7, 2012, http://cbsr.ca/blog/csr-driver-employee-engagement.

13. D.M. Mayer et al., "Who Displays Ethical Leadership and Why Does It Matter? An Examination of Antecedents and Consequences of Ethical Leadership," *Academy of Management Journal,* Vol. 55, Issue 1 (February 2012): 151–171.

14. Jindeck Chun et al., "How Does Corporate Ethics Contribute to Firm Performance? The Mediating Role of Collective Organizational Commitment and Organizational Citizenship Behavior," *Journal of Management,* Vol. 20 (January 2011): 1–15.

15. C.B. Bhattacharya et al., "Listing Corporate Social Responsibility to Win the Way for Talent," *M.I.T Sloan Management Review,* Vol. 48, No. 2 (2008): 37–44.

16. Adam Grant et al., "Giving Commitment: Employee Support Programs and the Prosocial Sensemaking Process," *Academy of Management Journal* 51 (2008): 898–918.

17. Janice Obuchowski, "Searching for Meaningful Work," *National Post,* March 23, 2010, FP10.

18. "The New Normal: Sustainable Practices Your Future Employees Will Demand," Network for Business Sustainability, January 11, 2010, accessed December 7, 2012, http://nbs.net/knowledge/perspectives-from-students-on-how-organizations-can-be-more-sustainable.

19. Robert W. Sexty, "Defining Consumer Sovereignty," *Canadian Business and Society: Understanding Social and Ethical Challenges* (Scarborough, ON: Prentice-Hall Canada, 1995), 352–354.

20. "Ethical consumerism," *The Guardian,* https://www.theguardian.com/money/2001/feb/22/ethicalmoney1 accessed March 8, 2019.

21. Magdaiena Öberseder et al., "Why Don't Consumers Care About CSR? A Qualitative Study Exploring the Role of CSR in Consumption Decisions," *Journal of Business Ethics,* Vol. 104, No. 4 (2011): 449–460.

22. June Cotte and Remi Trudel, *Socially Conscious Consumerism: Executive Briefing on the Body of Knowledge,* Network for Business Sustainability, Richard Ivey School of Business, University of Western Ontario, 2009, accessed July 7, 2016, http://nbs.net/wp-content/uploads/NBS_Consumerism_Brief_2009.pdf.

23. Pat Augar et al., "Do Social Product Features Have Value to Consumers?" *International Journal of Research in Marketing,* Vol. 25, No. 3 (2008): 183–91.

24. Kendall Cox Park, "Understanding ethical consumers: willingness-to-pay by moral cause," Journal of Consumer Marketing, Volume 35, Issue 2 (2018), 157–168.

25. Michael P. Ciuchta and Jan O'Toole, "Buy Local? Organizational Identity in the Localism Movement," *Business and Society*, 2018, Vol. 57, No. 7 1481–1497.

26. "About BALLE," Business Alliance for Local Living Economies (BALLE) website at https://bealocalist.org/about/ accessed November 6, 2018.

27. "About AMIBA," American Independent Business Alliance website at https://www.amiba.net/about accessed November 6.

28. "Free exchange: Home rules," *The Economist,* November 25, 2017, 72.

29. "About SDAC," Supplier Diversity Alliance Canada at http://www .supplierdiversityalliance.ca/sdac.html accessed March 8, 2019.

30. Stephen Brammer et al., "Managing Sustainable Global Supply Chains: Frameworks and Practices," May 25, 2011, Network for Business Sustainability, http://nbs.net/wp-content/uploads/NBS-Executive -Report-Supply-Chains.pdf.

31. Fair Trade Association, accessed March 10, 2019, http://www.fairlabor.org/about -us. and http://www.fairlabor.org/our-work /labor-standards.

32. International Council of Toy Industries, accessed March 10, 2019, http://www .toy-icti.org.

33. "Sustainability Purchasing Initiative: A Study Assessing Interest in a Sustainability Purchasing Network to Grow Sustainability Purchasing in the Region," C. Easton and Associates et al, May 2005, 5.

34. "Extended Producer Responsibility," Environment Canada, https://www.ec.gc.ca /gdd-mw/default.asp?lang=En&n =FB8E9973-1.

35. Rob Shimp, "Engaging and Influencing External Stakeholders in Product Stewardship," The Conference Board, March 2018 available at https://www .conference-board.org/publications /publicationdetail.cfm?publicationid =7773.

36. "What is Life Cycle Thinking?" Life Cycle Initiative, United Nations Environment at https://www .lifecycleinitiative.org/starting-life-cycle -thinking/what-is-life-cycle-thinking/. Another source of information is "Use Life Cycle Assessment," Network of Sustainable Business website at https://nbs.net/p /use-life-cycle-assessment-to-map-your -organization-s-fu-3cb0e7a1-21e9-4580 -b6a0-4daa4e989952.

37. "What Is Fairtrade?" Fairtrade Foundation, accessed July 14, 2016, http://www.fairtrade .org.uk/en/what-is-fairtrade/faqs.

38. "About Fairtrade," Fairtrade Canada, accessed August 4, 2016, http://fairtrade.ca /sitecore/content/fairtrade/home/what-is -fairtrade?sc_lang=en.

39. Fairtrade International, accessed February 10, 2013, http://www.fairtrade .net; Fairtrade Canada, accessed February 10, 2013, http://www.fairtrade.ca; and Fair Trade U.S.A., accessed February 10, 2013, http://www.fairtradeusa.org.

40. Peter Griffiths, "Ethical Objections to Freetrade," *Journal of Business Ethics,* Vol. 105, No. 3 (2012): 357–373.

41. Tina D. Beuchelt and Manifred Zeller, "Profits and Poverty: Certification's Troubled Link for Nicaragua's Organic and Fair-Trade Coffee Producers," *Ecological Economics* 70 (2011): 1316–1324.

42. Fair Trade, Employment and Poverty Reduction Research, SOAS University of London, accessed January 20, 2016, http:// ftepr.org/about/; Signe Langdford, "The Fair Trade Dilemma," *The Globe and Mail,* June 10, 2015, L5; and "Fair Trade: Good Thing, or Bad?," *The Economist,* July 5, 2014, 72.

Chapter 13

1. Michael Edwards, "Part 1: The Case for NGOs—The Mouse That Roared," *The Globe and Mail,* January 3, 2002, A15.

2. *Partnering for Innovation: Driving Change Through Business/NGO Partnerships* (Vancouver: Canadian Business for Social Responsibility, 2005), 7–8. Also available at http://www.cbsr.ca.

3. Alan Rugman and Karl Moore, "Part 2: Are NGOs a Threat? Biting the Hand That Feeds Us," *The Globe and Mail,* January 4, 2002, A13.

4. Debora L. Spar and Lane I. LaMure, "The Power of Activism: Assessing the Impact of NGOs on Global Business," *California Management Review,* Vol. 45, No. 3 (Spring 2003): 81.

5. Ibid, 84–85.

6. Ibid, 85.

7. *Partnering for Innovation: Driving Change Through Business/NGO Partnerships* (Vancouver: Canadian Business for Social Responsibility, 2005), 3–4. Also available at http://www.cbsr.ca.

8. Ibid, 10–12.

9. Jonathan Doh, "Partnering with NGOs: The 4 Keys to Success," Network for Business Sustainability, July 19, 2012, accessed December 10, 2012, http://nbs.net /partnering-with-ngos-the-4-keys-to-success/.

10. "Working with Business," World Wildlife Fund Canada website at http:// www.wwf.ca/about_us/howwework /business/ accessed March 11, 2019.

11. Julian F. Kolbel et al., "How Media Coverage of Corporate Social Irresponsibility Increases Financial Risk," *Strategic Management Journal,* Volume 38, Issue 11, November 2017, 2266–2284.

12. Consumer Complaints," News Media Canada website at https://nmc-mic.ca /about-newspapers/press-complaints/ accessed March 8, 2019.

13. "About Us," Canadian Radio-television and Telecommunications Commission (CRTC) website at https://crtc.gc.ca/eng /acrtc/org.htm accessed March 8, 2019.

14. "About the CAB," Canadian Association of Broadcasters website at http://www.cab-acr.ca/english/about /default.shtm accessed on March 8, 2019.

15. Steven Wartick, "The Relationship Between Intensive Media Exposure and Change in Corporate Reputation," *Business and Society*, Volume 3, Issue 1, 192, 33–49.

16. 2019 Edelman Trust Barometer - Canada, p. 14 accessed at https://www .edelman.ca/sites/default/files/edelman -trust/2019-Canadian-Trust-Barometer -Edelman.pdf on March 12, 2019.

17. 2019 Edelmam Trust Barometer - Canada, pp. 13–15, accessed at https:// www.edelman.ca/sites/default/files /edelman-trust/2019-Canadian-Trust -Barometer-Edelman.pdf on March 12, 2019.

18. Edward J. Romar, "Virtue Is Good Business: Confucianism as a Practical Business Ethic," *Journal of Business Ethics,* Vol. 38 (2002): 119–131.

19. "Spiritual Capital Research Program," Metanexus Institute, http://www.metanexus .net/spiritual%5Fcapital/.

20. Peter Goodspeed, "Faith in the Marketplace," *National Post,* June 17, 2005, A1, A12.

21. William C. Symonds, "Earthly Empires: How Evangelical Churches Are Borrowing from the Business Playbook," *BusinessWeek,* May 23, 2005, 78–88.

22. Michelle Conlin, "Religion in the Workplace: The Growing Presence of Spirituality in Corporate America," *BusinessWeek,* November 1, 1999, 151–158; Ian I. Mitroff and Elizabeth A. Denton, *A Spiritual Audit of Corporate America: A Hard Look at Spirituality, Religion and Values in the Workplace* (San Francisco: Jossey-Bass Publishers, 1999); Robert A. Giacalone and Carole L. Jurkiezicz, "Right from Wrong: The Influence of Spirituality on Perceptions of Unethical Business Activities," *Journal of Business Ethics* 46 (2003): 85–97.

23. Symonds, "Earthly Empires."

24. Robert W. Sexty, Business and Education. Working Paper #02–05. Faculty of Business Administration, Memorial University of Newfoundland, St. John's, NL, 2002.

25. Ibid.

Chapter 14

1. Garrett Hardin, "The Tragedy of the Commons," *Science*, Vol. 162, December 13, 1968, 1243–1248.

2. Colin Hutchison, "Environmental Issues: The Challenge for the Chief Executive," *Long Range Planning* 25(3) (1992): 58.

3. Leanne Morrison et al., "Environmental Reporting Through an Ethical Looking Glass," *Journal of Business Ethics,* Vol. 150 (2018) 903–908.

4. Leanne Morrison *et al*, "Environmental Reporting Through an Ethical Looking Glass," *Journal of Business Ethics,* Volume 150 (2018) 903–908.

5. United Nations, *The World Commission on Environment and Development: Our Common Future* (New York: Oxford University Press, 1987).

6. *Business Strategy for Sustainable Development: Leadership and Accountability for the '90s* (Winnipeg: International Institute for Sustainable Development, 1992), 11.

7. Environment Canada, "Glossary of Terms," http://www.ec.gc.ca/default .asp?lang=En&n=7EBE5C5A-1; and Environment Canada, "What Is Acid Rain?" http://www.msc.ec.gc.ca/cd /factsheets/acidrain/index_e.cfm.

8. Environment Canada, "Glossary of Terms."

9. Environment Canada, "Stratospheric Ozone," http://www.ec.gc.ca/indicateurs -indicators/.

10. Environment Canada, "Glossary of Terms."

11. Canadian Environmental Protection Act glossary, Government of Canada https:// www.canada.ca/en/environment-climate -change/services/canadian-environmental -protection-act-registry/general-information /glossary.html#G; Canadian Environmental Protection Act, 1999 (S.C. 1999, c. 33) at https://laws-lois.justice.gc.ca/eng/acts /c-15.31/.

12. *Federal Sustainable Development Act* (S.C. 2008, c. 33) at https://laws-lois .justice.gc.ca/eng/acts/f-8.6/index.html.

13. *Bill C-69*, An Act to enact the Impact Assessment Act and the Canadian Energy Regulator Act, to amend the Navigation Protection Act and to make consequential amendments to other Acts at https://www .parl.ca/DocumentViewer/en/42-1/bill/C-69 /royal-assent.

14. Canadian Environmental Assessment Agency, Government of Canada, News release, June 21, 2019 – Ottawa, Ontario, "Better rules for major projects become law in Canada: Canada's new approach to impact assessments is designed to protect the environment and grow the economy" at https://www.canada.ca /en/environmental-assessment-agency /news/2019/06/better-rules-for-major -projects-become-law-in-canada-canadas -new-approach-to-impact-assessments-is -designed-to-protect-the-environment-and -grow-the.html.

15. Canadian Environmental Assessment Agency will become the Impact Assessment Agency of Canada at https://www.canada .ca/en/environmental-assessment-agency .html.

16. Jamie R. Hendry, "Taking Aim at Business: What Factors Lead Environmental Non-Government Organizations to Target Particular Firms?" *Business and Society*, Vol. 45, No. 1 (March 2006): 47–86.

17. Laura Jones, "A Different Kind of Environmentalist," *Fraser Forum*, April 2001, 4.

18. "When Regulation Beats Market Mechanisms," *National Post*, March 27, 2007, FP15.

19. "How Companies Can Win with Carbon Pricing," Network for Business Sustainability, August 10, 2015, accessed January 23, 2016, http://nbs.net/how -companies-can-win-with-carbon -pricing/.

20. "Update on the output-based pricing system: technical backgrounder," Government of Canada website at https:// www.canada.ca/en/services/environment /weather/climatechange/climate-action /pricing-carbon-pollution/output-based -pricing-system-technical-backgrounder .html.

21. "Shell Quest CSS Project Approved with Conditions," News Release, Energy Resources and Conservation Board, Calgary, July 10, 2012.

22. Preston Manning, "We must restore balance between the environment and the economy," *The Globe and Mail,* October 20, 2018, O11.

23. *Business Strategy for Sustainable Development: Leadership and Accountability for the '90s* (Winnipeg: International Institute for Sustainable Development, 1992), 21–24.

24. Nicole Darrnall et al., "Environmental Management Systems and Green Supply Chain Management: Complements for Sustainability," *Business Strategy and the Environment*, Vol. 17 (2008): 30–45.

25. Bruce Hofer et al., "The Competitive Determinants of a Firm's Environmental Management Activities: Evidence from US Manufacturing Industries," *Journal of Operations Management*, Vol. 30 (2012): 9–84.

26. "Measuring and Valuing Environmental Impacts: An Introductory Guide," Network for Business Sustainability, http://nbs .net/wp-content/uploads/NBS-Executive -Report-Impacts.pdf.

27. I.B. Vasi and B. King, "Social Movements, Risk Perceptions, and Economic Outcomes: The Effect of Primary and Secondary Stakeholder Activism on Firm's Perceived Environmental Risk and Financial Performance," *American Sociological Review*, Vol. 77, No. 4 (2012): 1–24.

28. OSC Staff Notice 51–716–Environmental Reporting, Ontario Securities Commission, February 29, 2008; Janet McFarland, "Clean Up Environmental Disclosure: OSC," *The Globe and Mail*, February 28, 2008, B4; and Sandra Rubin, "When OSC Goes Green, Lawyers See Red," *The Globe and Mail,* March 19, 2008, B7.

29. CSA Staff Notice 51–354 *Report on Climate Change Related Disclosure Project*, April 5, 2018, https://www.osc.gov .on.ca/en/SecuritiesLaw_csa_20180405_51 -354_disclosure-project.htm and Canadian Securities Administrators (CSA), Backgrounder: CSA Staff Notice 51–354 Report on Climate change-related Disclosure Project, https://www.osc.gov.on.ca/documents /en/Securities-Category5/csa_20180405_51 -354_backgrounder-disclosure-project.pdf.

30. Ecolabel Index, "All ecolabels in Canada," assessed at http://www .ecolabelindex.com/ecolabels/?st=country,ca March 13, 2019.

31. Nicole Darnall et al., "Third-Party Certification, Sponsorship, and Consumers' Ecolabel Use," *Journal of Business Ethics,* Vol. 150 (2018), 953– 969.

32. Michael Lucins et al., "The Sustainability Liability: Potential Negative Effects of Ethicality on Product Acceptance," *Journal of Marketing*, Vol. 74 (2010): 15–31.

33. John Peloza, "What Makes Your Consumers Go Green? It Depends on Who's Around," April 16, 2012, Network for Business Sustainability at http://nbs.net /what-makes-your-consumers-go-green-it -depends-on-whos-around/.

34. "Going Green Can Attract and Keep Employees," *The Globe and Mail*, January 19, 2008, B16.

35. Marjo Johne, "Show Us the Green, Workers Say," *The Globe and Mail*, October 10, 2007, C1, C6.

36. "SHRM Survey Asks How 'Green' Is the American Workplace," Society for Human Resource Management, Press Release, January 16, 2008.

37. Catherine Ramus and Ulrich Steger, "The Roles of Supervisory Support Behaviours and Environmental Policy in Employee 'Ecoinitiatives' at Leading-Edge European Companies," *Academy of Management Journal*, Vol. 43, No. 4 (2000): 605–626.

38. "Canada's Greenest Employers" at https://www.canadastop100.com /environmental/ accessed March 18, 2019.

39. Rebecca Walberg, "Green Careers Are Growing," *National Post*, March 23, 2010. FP9.

40. GoodWork Canada at http://www .goodworkcanada.ca/.

41. "Sustainability Reporting Guidelines— G3 Version for Public Comment," Global Reporting Initiative, Amsterdam, The Netherlands, 2006, 18–18; "Sustainability Reporting Guidelines," Global Reporting Initiative, Amsterdam, The Netherlands, 2002, 47–50.

42. "Measuring and Valuing Environmental Impacts: An Introductory Guide," Network for Business Sustainability Web site, at http://nbs.net/wp-content/uploads/NBS -Executive-Report-Impacts.pdf.

43. Leanne Morrison, *op cit*, 903–918.

44. Mark Steyn, "'Sustainable' Development? There's No Such Thing," *National Post*, September 3, 2002, A12; and Peter Foster, "Sustainability Scam," *National Post,* April 8, 2006, FP19.

45. Peter Nowak, "Few Taking Leadership Role on Environment," *National Post*, September 25, 2006, FP2.

46. Anantha K. Duraiappah, "Ecosystem Services and Human Well-Being: Do Global Findings Make Any Sense?" *BioScience*, Vol. 61, No. 1 (January 2011): 7–8; and Clara Raudsepp-Hearne et al., "The Paradox Persists: How to Resolve It," *BioScience,* Vol. 61, No. 1 (January 2011): 11–12.

47. "From a linear to a circular economy," Government of the Netherlands accessed June 26, 2018, at https://www.government .nl/topics/circular-economy/from-a-linear -to-a-circular-economy; Nathan Kunz, Kieren Mayers, and Luk N. Van Wassenhove, "Stakeholder Views on Extended Producer Responsibility and the Circular Economy," *California Management Review,* Vol. 60, Issue 3, 2018, 45–70; and Mark Esposito, Terence Tse, and Khaled Soufani, "Introducing a Circular Economy: New Thinking with New Managerial and Policy Implications," *California Management Review*, Vol. 60, Issue 3, Spring 2018, 5–19.

Chapter 15

1. John Black, "Globalization," *A Dictionary of Economics* (Oxford University Press, 2002). Oxford Reference Online, Oxford University Press, Memorial University of Newfoundland, http://www .oxfordreference.com/views/ENTRY .html?subview=Main&entry=t19.e1359.

2. Andrew Hurrell, "Globalization," *The Concise Oxford Dictionary of Politics*. Ed. Iain McLean and Alistair McMillan (Oxford University Press, 2003). Oxford Reference Online, Oxford University Press, Memorial University of Newfoundland, http://www.oxfordreference.com/views /ENTRY.html?subview=Main&entry=t86 .e554.

3. John Scott and Gordon Marshall, "Globalization," *A Dictionary of Sociology* (Oxford University Press, 2005). Oxford Reference Online, Oxford University Press, Memorial University of Newfoundland, http://www.oxfordreference.com/views /ENTRY.html?subview=Main&entry=t88 .e937.

4. "The WTO," World Trade Organization at https://www.wto.org/english/thewto_e /thewto_e.htm accessed March 18, 2019.

5. World Bank, http://www.worldbank.org/.

6. International Monetary Fund, http:// www.imf.org/.

7. "About the ILO," International Labour Organization, http://www.ilo.org/public /english/about/index.htm.

8. "About Us," World Economic Forum website at https://www.weforum.org/about /world-economic-forum accessed March 28, 2019.

9. Institute for Management Development, Country Profile-Canada at https://www .imd.org/wcc/world-competitiveness -center-rankings/world-competitiveness -ranking-2018/.

10. "Global Competitiveness Report," World Economic Forum, http://www3 .weforum.org/docs/GCR2018/05FullReport/ TheGlobalCompetitivenessReport2018.pdf.

11. "Who We Are," and "Corruption Perceptions Index 2015," Transparency International, accessed August 9, 2016, http://www.transparency.org/whoweare /organisation/faqs_on_corruption and https://www.transparency.org /cpi2015/#results-table.

12. *The Corruption of Foreign Public Officials Act: A Guide,* May 1999, Justice Laws website, http://laws-lois.justice.gc.ca /eng/acts/C-45.2/page-1.html.

13. "Canada's Enforcement of the Foreign Bribery Offence Is Lagging; Must Urgently Boost Efforts to Prosecute," OECD Newsroom at http://www.oecd.org /document/31/0,3746,en_21571361 _44315115_47443999_1_1_1_1,00 .html; "Canada: Phase 3—Report on the Application of the Convention on Combating Bribery of Foreign Public Officials in International Business Transactions," OECD, accessed August 9, 2016, https://www.oecd.org/canada /Canadaphase3reportEN.pdf; and "2009 Revised Recommendation on Combating Bribery in International Business Transactions," OECD, accessed August 9, 2016, https://www.oecd.org/daf/anti -bribery/44176910.pdf.

14. Theresa Tedesco, "Boards Must Step Up on Corporate Crime," *National Post*, January 24, 2013, FP2; and Terence Corcoran, "Rooted in Government," *National Post,* February 6, 2013, FP1, 3.

15. "OECD will follow Canadian proceedings addressing allegations of political interference in foreign bribery prosecution," OECD Anti-Corruption Division at http://www.oecd.org/corruption /oecd-will-follow-canadian-proceedings -addressing-allegations-of-political -interference-in-foreign-bribery-prosecution .htm accessed on March 20, 2019.

16. Information on TRACE International is available at http://www.traceinternational .org/.

17. Alexandra Wrage, "Corruption Interruption," *Corporate Knights,* Winter 2016, 68–69.

18. Publish What You Pay, http://www .publishwhatyoupay.org/.

19. "About Us," Canadian Centre of Excellence for Anti-Corruption (CCEAC) website at http://cceac.ca/about-us/ accessed March 22, 2019.

20. "Universal Declaration of Human Rights," United Nations, accessed August 9, 2016, http://www.un.org/en/universal -declaration-human-rights/index.html.

21. *Guiding Principles on Business and Human Rights*, United Nations Human Rights, Office of the High Commissioner, New York, 2011. Also available at https:// www.edc.ca/content/dam/edc/en/non -premium/GuidingPrinciplesBusinessHR _EN.pdf.

22. "Voluntary Principles on Security and Human Rights." at https://www .voluntaryprinciples.org/.

23. Dexter Roberts and Pete Engardio, "Secrets, Lies, and Sweatshops," *BusinessWeek*, November 27, 2006, 50–58.

24. Nicholas D. Kristof, "Fight Poverty: Build Sweatshops," *National Post*, June 7, 2006, A20; and Michael Walker, "Why the World Needs More Sweatshops," *Fraser Forum*, March 2006, 3–4.

25. Benjamin Powell, "Sweatshop Regulation: Tradeoffs and Welfare Judgements," *Journal of Business Ethics*, (2018) Vol. 151, 29–36

26. "Why Women's Rights?," Oxfam Canada at https://www.oxfam.ca/who-we-are/about-oxfam/why-womens-rights/ accessed March 21, 2019.

27. *Canadian Business and the Millennium Development Goals* (Vancouver: Canadian Business for Social Responsibility, 2005).

28. C.K. Prahalad and Stuart L. Hart, "The Fortune at the Bottom of the Pyramid," *Strategy + Business*, Issue 26, 2002.

29. C.K. Prahalad, *The Fortune at the Bottom of the Pyramid: Eradicating Poverty Through Profits*, (Upper Saddle River, NJ: Pearson Education Inc. Wharton School Publishing 2005).

30. "Bottom of the Pyramid," Aspen Institute, www.CasePlace.org.

31. "A Common Definition of Fair Trade," Fairtrade Foundation, http://www.fairtrade.org.uk/.

32. Tavia Grant, "Major World Banks Join Microfinance Revolution," *The Globe and Mail*, November 23, 2006, B11.

33. *Doing Business with the Poor: A Field Guide* (Conches-Geneva: World Business Council for Sustainable Development, 2004), 10–14.

Chapter 16

1. "About," Canadian Business for Social Responsibility website at https://www.cbsr.ca/who-we-are.

2. Do Business Like a Canadian website at https://www.dobusinesslikeacanadian.ca/values.

3. Do Business Like a Canadian website at https://www.dobusinesslikeacanadian.ca.

4. The Pledge, https://www.dobusinesslikeacanadian.ca/pledge.

5. Further discussion of the fourth sector is available at Fourth Sector, http://www.fourthsector.net/; and "The Emerging Fourth Sector," Aspen Institute, https://www.aspeninstitute.org/sites/default/files/content/docs/pubs/4th%20sector%20paper%20-%20exec%20summary%20FINAL.pdf.

6. Anadila Mahbub, "The Economy's Fourth Sector," Sustainability Law at Lewis and Clark Law School, accessed August 9, 2016, http://sustainabilityandlaw.com/2011/04/22/the-economyd-fourth-sector-by-anadila-mahbub/.

7. "10 Things New Sustainability Managers Need to Know," Network for Business Sustainability, http://nbs.net/wp-content/uploads/10-Things-for-Managers1.pdf.

8. "From Challenges to Opportunities: The 7 Sustainability Opportunities for Canadian Business," Network for Business Sustainability, accessed February 4, 2016, http://nbs.net/wp-content/uploads/NBS-2015-Opportunities-Report.pdf.

9. Andrew Valentine, "Social Enterprise: 20 Questions for Directors of Non-Profit Organizations," Chartered Professional Accountants Canada, Toronto, 2014.

10. The Social Enterprise Council of Canada (SECC) website at https://socialenterprisecouncilcanada.wordpress.com/.

11. "Benefits of Caring and Sharing," *The Times* (London), Public Agenda Section, May 24, 2005, 11

12. Paul Tracey and Neil Stott, "Social Innovation: a window on alternative ways of organizing and innovating," *Innovation: Organization & Management*, Vol. 19, No. 1, 2017, 51–60.

13. Heerad Sabeti, "The For-Benefit Enterprise," *Harvard Business Review*, November 2011, 99–104.

14. More information can be found at "What Are B Corps?" Certified B Corporation website, http://www.bcorporation.net/.

15. MaRS Centre for Impact Investing, accessed February 3, 2016, http://impactinvesting.marsdd.com/strategic-initiatives/benefit-corporation-b-corp-hub/.

16. Adapted from Steve Zimmerman and Jeanne Bell, *The Sustainability Mindset: Using the Matrix Map to Make Strategic Decisions* (San Francisco, CA: Jossey-Bass, 2015), chapters 1, 5, and 6.

17. "Defining Social Innovation," Graduate School of Business, Stanford University, accessed February 29, 2016, https://www.gsb.stanford.edu/faculty-research/centers-initiatives/csi/defining-social-innovation.

18. "Inclusive innovation: New ideas and new partnerships for stronger communities," Employment and Social Development Canada at https://www.canada.ca/en/employment-social-development/programs/social-innovation-social-finance/reports/recommendations-what-we-heard.html#h2.02 accessed March 30, 2019.

19. "Impact Investing in Canada: State of the Nation, March 2014," MaRS Centre for Impact Investing, accessed February 29, 2016, https://www.marsdd.com/mars-library/impact-investing-in-canada-state-of-the-nation/.

20. "Inclusive innovation: New ideas and new partnerships for stronger communities," Employment and Social Development Canada at https://www.canada.ca/en/employment-social-development/programs/social-innovation-social-finance/reports/recommendations-what-we-heard.html#h2.02 accessed March 30, 2019.

21. Fall Economic Statement 2018, Government of Canada at https://www.budget.gc.ca/fes-eea/2018/docs/statement-enonce/chap02-en.html accessed March 30, 2019.

22. "The Landscape for Social Impact Investing - a White Paper," Toronto Dominion Bank, March 31, 2013, accessed February 29, 2016, https://www.td.com/document/PDF/corporateresponsibility/publications/The-Landscape-for-Social-Impact-Investing-a-White-Paper-Links.pdf.

23. "The New Powers of Giving," *The Economist*, July 1, 2006, 64.

24. Naomi Buck, "Meddling Billionaires," *Corporate Knights*, accessed August 10, 2016, http://www.corporateknights.com/channels/social-enterprise/meddling-billionaires-14435064/; Joe Chidley, "The Price of Doing Good," *National Post*, December 3, 2015, FP11; and Adam Waldman, "Zuckerberg's LLC is Built for Highly Leveraged Social Change," *The Globe and Mail*, December 9, 2015, B4.

25. Paul Adler and Seok-Woo Kwon, "Social Capital: Prospects for a New Concept," *Academy of Management Review*, Vol. 27, No. 1 (2002): 17–40.

26. Scott E. Seibert, Maria L. Kraimer, and Robert C. Linden, "A Social Capital Theory of Career Success," *Academy of Management Journal*, Vol. 44, No. 2 (2001): 220.

27. Ann Svendsen, Robert G. Boutilier, and David Wheeler, *Stakeholder Relationships, Social Capital and Business Value Creation* (Toronto: The Canadian Institute of Chartered Accountants, 2003).

28. Ibid, 4.

29. Ibid, 18.

30. Ibid, 19–20.

31. Al Gore and David Blood, *Manifesto for Sustainable Capitalism*, Generation Foundation, accessed February 4, 2016, https://www.genfound.org/media/pdf-wsj -manifesto-sustainable-capitalism-14-12-11 .pdf and https://www.genfound.org/ frameworks/.

32. Michael E. Porter and Mark R. Kramer, "Strategy and Society: The Link Between Competitive Advantage and Corporate Social Responsibility," *Harvard Business Review*, Vol. 84, Issue 12 (Dec. 2006), 78–92.

33. Michael E. Porter and Mark R. Kramer, "Strategy and Society: The Link Between Competitive Advantage and Corporate Social Responsibility," *Harvard Business Review*, Vol. 84, Issue 12 (Dec. 2006), 78–92.

34. Ibid, 85.

35. Ibid, 85.

36. Ibid, 89–91.

37. Ibid, 92.

38. "Sustainability Centres," Network for Business Sustainability at https://nbs.net /sustainability-centres accessed March 29, 2019.

39. A. Wiek, L. Withycombe, and C.L. Redman, "Key Competences in Sustainability: A Reference Framework for Academic Program Development," *Sustainability Development,* 6, 203–218.

40. Andrew J. Hoffman, "Management as a Calling," *Stanford Social Innovation Review,* September 4, 2018 at https://ssir .org/articles/entry/management_as_a _calling#.

41. Coalition of Universities for Responsible Investing at https://ccuri .wordpress.com/ accessed March 30, 2019.

42. Community Based Research Canada (CBRC) at https:// communityresearchcanada.ca/ accessed March 30, 2019.

43. Canadian Alliance for Community Service-Learning, accessed August 10, 2016, http://www .communityservicelearning.ca.

44. Graduation Pledge Alliance at http:// www.graduationpledge.org/ accessed March 30 2019.

45. The MBA Oath at http://mbaoath.org/ accessed March 30, 2019.

46. Joseph Blasi and Douglas L. Kruse, "Today's youth reject capitalism, but what do they want to replace it?," *The Conversation* (Canada) posted April 4, 2018 at https://theconversation.com /todays-youth-reject-capitalism-but -what-do-they-want-to-replace-it-94247 accessed March 30, 2019; Joseph Blasi and Douglas L. Kruse, "Today's Young Adults Want to Resign Capitalism. But Into What?," *Yesmagazine* posted April 5, 2018 at https://www.yesmagazine.org /new-economy/todays-young-adults -want-to-redesign-capitalism-but-into -what-20180405; and Mark Trumbull and Eoin O'Carroll, "Faces of a new capitalism: How Millennials are embracing socialist values," The Christian Science Monitor October 11, 2018 at https://www .csmonitor.com/Business/2018/1011/Faces -of-a-new-capitalism-How-Millennials-are -embracing-socialist-values accessed March 30, 2019.

Cases

1. This is a fabricated case and the names of persons and places are fictitious. This case was prepared from public sources to provide material for classroom discussion, and it is not intended to illustrate either effective or ineffective response to a business and society managerial situation.

2. EatRight Ontario website, http://www .eatrightontario.ca/en/default.aspx.

3. "Energy Drinks Linked to Teen Health Risks," Propel Centre for Population Health Impact, University of Waterloo, March 6, 2014, https://uwaterloo.ca/propel/news /energy-drinks-linked-teen-health-risks.

4. "Energy Drinks in Canada: Know the Facts," Canadian Beverage Association, http://www.canadianbeverage.ca/wp -content/uploads/2014/01/Energy-Drink -Brochure-Layout-English-layout-Sept-23 -to-print.pdf.

5. Report of the Expert Panel on Caffeinated Energy Drinks, November 2010, Health Canada, http://www.hc-sc .gc.ca/dhp-mps/prodnatur/activit/groupe -expert-panel/report_rapport-eng.php; and "Questions and Answers: Caffeinated Energy Drinks," Health Canada, http:// www.hc-sc.gc.ca/fn-an/prodnatur/questions -caf-eng.php and http://www.hc-sc.gc.ca /fn-an/prodnatur/questions-caf-eng.php#a1.

6. Energy Drinks Marketing Code, http:// www.canadianbeverage.ca/wp-content /uploads/2013/12/CBA-Energy-drinks -Code-FINAL-English.pdf.

7. Stone's Drug Store, http://www .stonespharmasave.com/; "Press Release: Soft Drinks and Sugary Beverages," Graham's Blog, http://stonespharmasave .com/blog/?p=560; "Store Stops Selling Energy Drinks to Minors," CBC News – Prince Edward Island, http://www.cbc .ca/news/canada/prince-edward-island /store-stops-selling-energy-drinks-to -minors-1.932565.

8. This case was prepared from public sources to provide material for classroom discussion, and it is not intended to illustrate either effective or ineffective response to a business and society managerial situation.

9. Roşia Montana Gold Corporation (RMGC), accessed August 9, 2015, http:// en.rmgc.ro/index.html; and Gabriel Resources Ltd., www.gabrielresources.com/.

10. Eric Regular, "The New Romans," *Report on Business*, November 2010, 57–67.

11. *New El Dorado*, Institute of Documentary Film, accessed August 9, 2015, http://www.dokweb.net/cs/.

12. *Mine Your Own Business,* accessed August 9, 2015, www .mineyourownbusiness.org.

13. "About ICSID," International Centre for Settlement of Investment Disputes, accessed August 9, 2015, https://icsid .worldbank.org/apps/ICSIDWEB/about /Pages/default.aspx.

14. This case was prepared from public sources to provide material for classroom discussion, and it is not intended to illustrate either effective or ineffective response to a business and society managerial situation. This is a fabricated case, and the names Phillip Veldhuis and Savalot Enterprises are fictitious.

15. "2018 Impact Report," Food Banks Canada at https://www.foodbankscanada .ca/Annual-Reports.aspx and "HungerCount 2018" at https://hungercount.foodbankscanada .ca/overallfindings/ accessed April 3, 2019.

16. Views attributed to Elaine Power were contained in personal correspondence and permission was granted to use. Other information was obtained from the following: Dietitians of Canada, "Food Banks," *Practice: Exploring Members' Practice Issues,* accessed February 29, 2012, http://www.practiceblog.dietitians .ca/2010/01/food-banks.html; Jeff Nield, "Will Closing Food Banks Help End Hunger?" Tree Hugger, accessed February 29, 2012, http://www.treehugger.com /green-food/will-closing-food-banks-help -end-hunger.html; Elaine Power, "Canadian Food Banks: Obscuring the Reality of Hunger and Poverty," *Food Ethics,* Winter 2011, Vol. 6, Issue 4, 18–20; and Elaine Power, "Time to Close Our Food Banks," *The Globe and Mail,* July 25, 2011, A11.

17. This case was prepared from public sources to provide material for classroom discussion, and it is not intended to illustrate either effective or ineffective response to a business and society managerial situation. Karolina Vestman is a fictitious person.

18. Loblaw 2017 Corporate Social Responsibility Report, "Our Purpose: Live Life Well," at https://www.loblaw.ca/CSRReport.pdf, pages 2–3.

19. Loblaw 2017 Corporate Social Responsibility Report, "Our Purpose: Live Life Well," at https://www.loblaw.ca/CSRReport.pdf, pages 4–24.

20. *Competition Act* (R.S.C., 1985, c. C-34), Government of Canada at https://laws-lois.justice.gc.ca/eng/acts/c-34/page-11.html#h-20.

21. "Price-fixing," Competition Bureau Canada at https://www.competitionbureau.gc.ca/eic/site/cb-bc.nsf/eng/h_00112.html.

22. International Organization for Standardization, "ISO 19600:2014: Compliance management systems – Guidelines," at https://www.iso.org/standard/62342.html.

23. "George Weston and Loblaw take action to address industry-wide anti-competitive activity," Press Release Details, December 19, 2017, Loblaw Companies Limited at https://media.loblaw.ca/English/media-centre/press-releases/press-release-details/2017/George-Weston-and-Loblaw-take-action-to-address-industry-wide-anti-competitive-activity/default.aspx.

24. "Immunity and Leniency Programs under the *Competition Act*, Government of Canada at https://www.competitionbureau.gc.ca/eic/site/cb-bc.nsf/eng/04391.html accessed April 5, 2019.

25. Loblaw Companies Limited, Code of Conduct at https://www.loblaw.ca/content/dam/lclcorp/pdfs/Governance/LCL_Code_of_Conduct_2017_EN.pdf, page 10.

26. Loblaw Companies Limited, Supplier Code of Conduct at https://www.loblaw.ca/content/dam/lclcorp/pdfs/Responsibility/SupplierCodeOfConduct/Supplier%20Code%20of%20Conduct%20-LCL-2016.pdf.

27. George Weston Limited, Code of Conduct at http://www.weston.ca/en/pdf_en/GWL_Code_of_Conduct_EN.pdf, pages 13 and 15.

28. This case was prepared from public sources to provide material for classroom discussion, and it is not intended to

illustrate either effective or ineffective response to a business and society managerial situation. Darrell Yasinski is a fictitious person.

29. Michael Bliss, *Northern Enterprise: Five Centuries of Canadian Business*, Toronto: McClelland and Stewart, 1987, and Graham D. Taylor and Peter A. Baskerville, *A Concise History of Business in Canada*, Toronto: Oxford University Press, 1994.

30. General Motors Canada, "Here's to Our Next 100 Years: GM Canada Celebrates its 100th Anniversary," Media Release, 2018-11-08.

31. "General Motors Accelerates Transformation," Corporate Newsroom/United States, General Motors website at https://media.gm.com/media/us/en/gm/news.detail.html/content/Pages/news/us/en/2018/nov/1126-gm.html.

32. About the Campaign - Save Oshawa GM at https://www.saveoshawagm.ca/about accessed January 29, 2019.

33. "GM Canada and Unifor reach agreement to save hundreds of jobs with a C$170 million investment in Oshawa," GM Canada and Unifor joint Media Release, May 8, 2019, at https://media.gm.ca/media/ca/en/gm/oshawa_transformation_agreement.html.

34. This case was prepared from public sources to provide material for classroom discussion, and it is not intended to illustrate either effective or ineffective response to a business and society managerial situation.

35. "About Us," *Canada Gazette,* Government of Canada, http://www.gazette.gc.ca/cg-gc/about-sujet-eng.html.

36. *Canada Gazette,* Vol. 143, No. 8, February 21, 2009, accessed August 10, 2016, http://publications.gc.ca/gazette/archives/p1/2009/2009-02-21/pdf/g1-14308.pdf.

37. *Fisheries Act.* Government of Canada. R.S., c. F-14, s. 1, http://laws-lois.justice.gc.ca/eng/acts/F-14/page-1.html#s-1.

38. "Metal Mining Effluent Regulations," Environment Canada, Government of Canada, http://gazette.gc.ca/rp-pr/p1/2010/2010-05-15/html/reg1-eng.html#REF10.

39. An order in council is a notice of an administrative decision originating with the

Canadian federal cabinet and is approved by the Governor General. Orders in council can be notices of appointments or regulations or legislative orders in relation to and authorized by an existing act of parliament. Orders in council are published in the *Canada Gazette.*

40. "Towards Sustainable Mining Guiding Principles," Mining Association of Canada, http://mining.ca/towards-sustainable-mining/tsm-guiding-principles.

41. "Sustainability Management: Environment," Vale, accessed August 10, 2016, http://www.vale.com/canada/EN/aboutvale/communities/environment/Pages/Sustainable-Mining.aspx.

42. This case was prepared from public sources to provide material for classroom discussion, and it is not intended to illustrate either effective or ineffective response to a business and society managerial situation. Professor Wayne Murray is a fictional character.

43. This is a fabricated situation with background information obtained from the following. Certified General Accountants of Canada, CGA-Canada Code of Ethical Principles and Rules of Conduct, Version 2.12, June 2011, http://www.cga-canada.org/en-ca/StandardsLib/ca_ceproc.pdf. This case was prepared from public sources to provide material for classroom discussion, and it is not intended to illustrate either effective or ineffective response to a business and society managerial situation.

44. *Generating Growth 2001 Annual Report,* Fortis Inc., 10–24.

45. Information for this section was obtained from "Chalillo Hydropower Project Summary," a brochure published by Fortis Inc., Belize Electric Company Ltd., and Belize Electricity Limited, October 2001, 10.

46. Ibid, 7, 10, 15–17.

47. Probe International, accessed August 10, 2016, https://journal.probeinternational.org/2001/01/25/press-release-environmentalists-urge-newfoundland-based-fortis-corporation-abandon-hydro-scheme-belize/.

48. Natural Resources Defense Council, http://www.nrdc.org/about/.

49. Will Hilliard, "Dam Opponents Misled: Fortis," *The Telegram* (St. John's, NL), November 2, 2001, A3.

Glossary

A

Acid rain A generic term used for precipitation that contains an abnormally high concentration of sulphuric and nitric acid.

Active shareholders Those who participate in the governance to the full extent allowed by the law.

Anti-globalists Individuals and organizations that oppose globalization or are critical of it.

Audit committee Comprises members of the board of directors and oversees the internal and external accounting auditing function to ensure that financial statements accurately and appropriately represent the condition of the corporation and that regulated disclosures are made.

B

B Corporation (or B Corp) A social enterprise that operates to make profits but has a strong commitment to addressing social and environmental problems. A certification process is required in order to be eligible to receive the designation of B Corp.

Board of directors A group of individuals elected by shareholders to govern or oversee the corporation's affairs.

Boycott An act to abstain from using, buying, or dealing with a person, organization, or country as an expression of protest, usually for moral, economic, social, political, or environmental reasons.

Bribery Making questionable payments, known as bribes, to government officials to influence their decisions.

Business citizenship Includes the responsibilities of corporate citizenship on a local and national basis and extends it to a global or universal scope.

Business ethics The rules, standards, codes, or principles that provide guidelines for morally right behaviour and truthfulness in specific situations.

Business sustainable development According to the IISD, "adopting business strategies and activities that meet the needs of the enterprise and its stakeholders today while protecting, sustaining, and enhancing the human and natural resources that will be needed in the future."

Business-to-business Commercial activity where one corporation sells goods or services to another corporation rather than to consumers.

C

Cap-and-trade A system whereby governments cap total carbon emissions and then give or sell companies carbon permits that add up to the cap. Also referred to as *emissions trading*.

Capitalism An economic system that allows for private ownership of the means of production (land, labour, and capital) and assumes that economic decision making is in the hands of individuals or enterprises who make decisions expecting to earn a profit.

Carbon capture and storage (CCS) Carbon emissions are captured and injected into underground formations.

Carbon pricing When governments impose a fee on carbon: the more a company emits, the more they pay; A financial instrument that businesses and governments use to reduce carbon emissions.

Cause-related marketing The purchase of a particular product results in a donation being made by a corporation to a non-profit organization's program.

CEO pay ratio The ratio of the compensation of the corporation's chief executive officer (CEO) to the median compensation of its employees.

Charitable foundation A corporation or trust that is constituted and operated exclusively for charitable purposes.

Circular economy A circular economy is restorative and regenerative by design so materials constantly flow around a 'closed loop' system preserving value rather than being used once and then discarded.

Civil society The voluntary, community, and social organizations or institutions that contribute to the functioning of society but are usually not related to or supported by government.

Clean capitalism Based on *Corporate Knights'* definition as "an economic system that incorporates the social, economic and ecological costs (and benefits) into our marketplace activities and the prices we pay."

Climate change (global warming) According to Environment Canada, it is "the result of human activities altering the chemical composition of the atmosphere through the build-up of greenhouse gases that trap heat and reflect it back to the Earth's surface." Also referred to as *global warming*.

Code of conduct Explicitly states what appropriate behaviour is by identifying what is acceptable and unacceptable.

Code of ethics A statement of principles or values that guide behaviour by describing the general value system within which a corporation attempts to operate in a given environment.

Collaboration A meta-capability to establish and maintain relationships that allows the organization to tap into a powerful source of creative energy, a large pool of innovative ideas, and a wider network.

Commons Any resource used as though it belongs to all.

Community Investment (CI) The efforts of a corporation to help develop a community and create economic opportunities through a variety of means from donations to direct involvement in commercial undertakings.

Competition The condition in a market system in which many rival sellers seek to provide goods and services to many buyers.

Compliance officer A manager who is responsible for ensuring that all employees are familiar with the corporation's policies and codes, and government regulations and laws.

Conflict of interest A situation in which an individual has a private or personal interest that is sufficient to appear to influence the objective exercise of that individual's duties.

Conscious capitalism The reorientation of business from a single focus on profits to emphasizing integrity, higher standards of corporate behaviour, and inclusion of all stakeholders.

Consumer sovereignty The assumption existing in an economy that consumers have and exercise power over producers through the decisions they make in purchasing the goods and services provided by corporations.

Consumerism A social movement seeking to protect and augment the rights and powers of buyers in relation to sellers.

Corporate agenda The real or imagined domination of public policy or government programs by corporations or business organizations in their own best interests.

Corporate citizenship Occurs when a corporation demonstrates that it takes into account its complete impact on society and the environment as well as its economic influence.

Corporate culture A complex set of values, beliefs, assumptions, and symbols that define the way in which an organization conducts its business.

Corporate ethics programs Some combination of a statement of values, code of conduct and/or ethics, ethics training, ethics audits and consulting services, ethics officers and committees, and ethics reporting systems.

Corporate governance The processes, structures, and relationships through which the shareholders, as represented by a board of directors, oversee the activities of the corporation.

Corporate philanthropy The effort of business to contribute to society socially; manifested by donations of money or goods and services in kind.

Corporate public affairs The management function responsible for monitoring and interpreting the governmental environment of the corporation or industry, and for managing the responses necessary to protect the interests of the corporation or industry.

Corporate reputation As defined by Fombrun, "a perceptual representation of a corporation's past actions and future prospects that describes the corporation's overall appeal to all of its key constituents [stakeholders] when compared with other leading rivals."

Corporate social responsibility (CSR) The way a corporation achieves a balance among its economic, social, and environmental responsibilities in its operations so as to address shareholder and other stakeholder expectations.

Corporate social responsibility (CSR) reporting (sustainability reporting) A management function that documents the corporation's economic, ethical/social, and environmental responsibilities and initiatives, and communicates this information to relevant stakeholders. Also known as *sustainability reporting*.

Corporate sponsorship A partnership between a business sponsor and an event or a non-profit organization that is established for mutual benefit.

Corporate sustainability (CS) Corporate activities demonstrating the inclusion of social and environmental as well as economic responsibilities in business operations as they impact all stakeholders presently and in the future.

Corporate voluntarism The time and talent employees commit to community organizations with support and/or consent from employers who recognize the value of such efforts to society.

Corporate welfare Any action by municipal, provincial, or federal governments that gives a specific corporation or an entire industry a benefit not offered to others.

Corruption According to Transparency International, "the abuse of entrusted power for private gain."

Creative capitalism Places the resolution of social needs as primary instead of secondary to economic activity and performance.

Crisis A turning point, a crucial time, and a situation that has reached a critical point.

Crisis management An approach involving planning and removing much of the risk and uncertainty, allowing the corporation to achieve more control over events.

D

Deontological ethics An approach to ethics that determines goodness or rightness from examining the acts rather than from the consequences of the acts.

Deregulation The reduction of government influence or impact over the economy, allowing for a freer and more efficient marketplace.

Discrimination The preferential (or less than preferential) treatment on bases not directly related to qualifications of the job or performance on the job.

Diversity management A voluntary initiative that goes beyond what is required by law to eliminate workplace discrimination.

Dual-class stock More than one type of share or stock with different voting rights and dividend payments is issued by a single corporation.

E

Economic freedoms Exist when the business system operates with few restrictions on its activities.

Economic globalization The integration of fragmented markets into a global economy.

Economic system An arrangement using land, labour, and capital to produce, distribute, and exchange goods and services to meet the needs and wants of people in society.

Ecosystem A biological community of interacting organisms and their physical environment.

Employee engagement The emotional and intellectual commitment of an individual or group to an organization that supports building and sustaining business performance.

Employment equity The fair and equal treatment of employees.

Environmental ethic The set of values or principles that govern a corporation's practices relating to the environment.

Environmental non-governmental organizations (ENGOs) Groups that hold shared values or attitudes about the challenges confronting the natural environment and advocate for changes to improve the condition of the environment.

Equality of opportunity The assumption that all individuals or groups have an even chance at responding to some condition in society.

Ethic of caring Gives attention to specific individuals or stakeholders harmed or disadvantaged and their particular circumstances.

Ethic of justice Considers that moral decisions are based on the primacy of a single value: justice.

Ethical consumerism A form of activism where consumers buy products, goods, and services that are ethically produced and/or that are not harmful to the environment and society.

Ethical corporate culture A "slice" or "subset" of the organization's broader culture, maintained through an interplay and alignment of formal organizational systems, such as policies, leadership, authority structures, reward systems, training programs, and informal organizational systems such as peer behaviour and ethical norms.

Ethical dilemma A situation or problem where a person has to make a difficult choice between two alternatives, neither of which resolves an issue or problem in an ethically acceptable fashion.

Ethical relativism The belief that ethical answers depend on the situation and no universal standards or rules exist to guide or evaluate morality.

Ethics audit A systematic effort to discover actual or potential unethical behaviour in an organization.

Ethics committee A group, comprising directors, managers, or staff, formed to monitor ethical standards and behaviour.

Ethics of business The rules, standards, codes, or principles that provide guidance for morally appropriate behaviour in managerial decision making relating to the operation of the business enterprise's and business' relationship with society.

Ethics officer An independent manager, reporting to the board of directors or CEO, who reviews complaints or information from anyone in the organization or any stakeholder, studies the situation, and recommends action if necessary.

Extended producer responsibility From Environment Canada, it is "an environmental policy approach in which a producer's responsibility, physical and/or financial, for a product is extended to the post-consumer stage of a product's life cycle."

F

Fair trade A term commonly used to identify products that are involved with sustainability purchasing; usually focuses on the beginning of the product chain.

Feminist ethics Diverse, gender-focused approaches to ethical theory and practice.

Fiduciary duties Obligations owed by directors to shareholders that are prescribed by laws or regulations.

For-benefit (or benefit) corporation A social enterprise that aims to make profits but also has a strong commitment to addressing social and environmental problems. Also called a *benefit corporation.*

Fourth sector New organizational forms that integrate business or private, social, and public methods. Sometimes referred to as *hybrid organizations.*

Free enterprise system An economic system characterized by ownership of private property by individuals and enterprises, the profit motive, a competitive market system, and a limited involvement by government.

G

Gig economy Refers to persons whose participation in the labour force is in short-term, temporary jobs, contracts, and self-employment.

Global Reporting Initiative (GRI) A non-profit organization that works toward a sustainable global economy by providing guidance in sustainability reporting.

Globalists Individuals and organizations that support globalization.

Globalization A process of decreasing constraints on the interactions among the nations and peoples of the world.

Greed The excessive desire to acquire or possess more, especially more material wealth, than one needs or deserves.

Green marketing Selling environmentally friendly goods and services to consumers.

Greenhouse gases (GHG) Gases that absorb and trap heat in the atmosphere and cause a warming effect on Earth. Some occur naturally in the atmosphere, while others result from human activities. Greenhouse gases include carbon dioxide, water vapour, methane, nitrous oxide, ozone, chlorofluorocarbons, hydrofluorocarbons, and perfluorocarbons.

Greenwashing A form of advertising or public relations that deceptively provides the perception that a corporation's policies or practices are socially responsible.

H

Human rights The fundamental rights and freedoms to which all individuals, groups, and societies are entitled.

I

Inclusive capitalism An approach that would address "the growing inequality in the distribution of income and wealth; to unemployment especially among the young; to falling social mobility; to the 1% vs 99%; to poverty more generally and how capitalism can help to alleviate it."

Independent (or unrelated) director "A director who is free from any interest and any business or other relationship which could, or could reasonably be perceived to, materially interfere with the director's ability to act in the best interests of the corporation."

Individual rights ethic Relies on a list of agreed-upon rights for everyone that will be upheld by everyone and that becomes the basis for deciding what is right, just, or fair.

Individualism The view that the individual, and not society or a collective, is the paramount decision maker in society; assumes that the individual is inherently decent and rational.

Influence pathway Occurs where withholding and usage strategies could be performed by an ally of the stakeholder with whom the organization has a resource dependence.

Integrity The appropriateness of a corporation's behaviour and its adherence to moral guidelines acceptable to society such as honesty, fairness, and justice.

Integrity management An ethics program that combines a compliance-based and a values-based approach.

Intellectual property An umbrella term for patents, copyrights, trademarks, industrial designs, integrated circuit topographies, and plant breeders' rights.

International non-governmental organizations (INGOs) Groups that hold shared values and attitudes about the issues relating to globalization and advocate for changes to improve the conditions in developing countries.

Issue A point in question or a matter that is in dispute where different views are held of what is or what ought to be corporate performance–based management or stakeholder expectations.

Issue analysis Any effort to understand the source, nature, and extent of a question or matter in dispute facing the corporation which will result in addressing or resolving the matter.

Issue materiality A question or matter that is sufficiently important to warrant management's attention; also referred to as *sustainability materiality.*

Issues management A systematic process by which the corporation can identify, evaluate, and respond to those economic, social, and environmental issues that may impact significantly upon it.

L

Laissez-faire capitalism An economic system operating with absolute minimum interference by the government in the affairs of business. Government involvement is strictly limited to providing essential services such as police and fire protection.

Legitimacy The belief in the rightness of an institution, in this case the appropriateness of our business system to supply the goods and services wanted by Canadian society.

Legitimacy A generalized perception or assumption that the actions of an entity are desirable, proper, or appropriate within some socially constructed system of norms, values, beliefs, and definition that is based on the individual, the organization, or society.

Libel chill Occurs when a business threatens legal action if a particular article or book is published.

Life cycle thinking (LCT) Life cycle thinking (LCT) is about going beyond the traditional focus on production site and manufacturing processes to include environmental, social, and economic impacts of a product over its entire life cycle.

Lobbying All attempts to influence directly or indirectly any government activity; includes any attempt to influence legislators, their staff members, public administrators, and members of regulatory agencies.

Localism A social movement that supports economic practices oriented toward strengthening local economies and reducing reliance on nonlocal resources.

M

Management information circular The document used to communicate with shareholders.

Market environmentalism Exists where economic incentives created by the market are more effective at protecting the environment than is government intervention.

Matrix mapping A technique of categorizing an organization's stakeholders by their influence according to two variables; usually involves plotting them on a two-by-two matrix.

Microfinance The provision of financial products, such as micro-credit, micro-insurance, and savings accounts, to persons living in areas of poverty without access to banking services.

Moral capitalism Capitalism based "Principles for Business" through which "principled capitalism can flourish and sustainable and socially responsible prosperity can become the foundation for a fair, free and transparent global society."

Moral reasoning A systematic approach to thinking or reasoning through the implications of a moral problem or issue.

Moral standards The means by which individuals judge their actions and the actions of others based upon accepted behaviour in society.

Mutual fund A pool of money from many individual investors that is invested on their behalf, usually in a specific kind of investment.

N

Non-governmental organization (NGO) Any group outside of the public or private sectors that holds shared values or attitudes about an issue confronting society and advocates for change around that issue.

Non-voting shares Common shares without voting privileges.

O

Offsets (emissions-reduction credits) Credits purchased from other corporations or organizations to mitigate greenhouse gases released into the environment.

Oligopoly A type of competition where the few sellers in an industry behave similarly.

Output-based price system A carbon pricing system where instead of paying the charge on fuels that they purchase, industrial facilities in the system will face a carbon price on the portion of their emissions that are above a limit, which will be determined based on relevant output-based standards (emissions per unit of output).

Owners Those individuals or groups who have invested in a corporation in the form of equity or shares; usually referred to as shareholders.

Ozone Naturally occurring gas, formed from normal oxygen, that protects Earth by filtering out ultraviolet (UV) radiation from the sun.

P

Passive shareholders Those who do not attempt to influence the affairs of the corporation even though they have a legal right to do so.

Personal virtues ethic An individual's or corporation's behaviour is based upon being a good person or corporate citizen with traits such as courage, honesty, wisdom, temperance, courage, fidelity, integrity, and generosity.

Philanthrocapitalism According to *The Economist*, draws upon the philosophy of capitalist style objectives and criteria with an entrepreneurial spirit to get more from non-profit or social organizations.

Pluralistic society One where influence or power is decentralized by dispersing it among a variety of institutions.

Policy development institution (think tank) An organization that researches and analyzes various important social, economic, and political issues confronting society.

Political globalization The process by which world power relationships change and there is a loss of sovereignty by the state.

Power A relationship among social actors in which one social actor, A, can get another social actor, B, to do something that B would not otherwise do.

Private equity firms Firms that manage large pools of money acquired from wealthy individuals or families and big institutions such as pension and mutual funds.

Private or civil regulation A non-profit, independent organization that sets standards for responsible business practices.

Private sector That part of the economy not controlled and operated by government but run by individuals and corporations to make a profit.

Privatization According to Heald, the "strengthening of the market at the expense of the state."

Profits The excess of revenues over expenses; closely associated with competition.

Progressive capitalism A new form of capitalism that advocates for an increasing role for government in making the market system serve society, including the regulation of business to ensure competition, the realigning of the relationship between corporations and employees, and a new social contract that allows business and society to work together.

Public sector The part of the economy operated by government departments, agencies and organizations usually not to operate businesses or make profits, but to provide such things as a legal system, policing and prison services, defence organizations, transportation infrastructure, and educational and health institutions.

Public–private partnership A cooperative venture between the public and private sectors, built on the expertise of each partner, that best meets clearly defined public needs through the appropriate allocation of resources, risks, and rewards.

R

Redwashing A term to describe the deception of the general public by government and industry in trying to cover up their theft of Indigenous Peoples' lands, natural resources, and cultural riches by pretending that they are acting in the best interests of Indigenous Peoples.

Remediation agreement or deferred prosecution agreement A voluntary agreement between a government prosecutor and a corporation accused of committing an offence that establishes undertakings to avoid criminal charges.

Reputation management Any effort to enhance the corporation's image and good name; in the past, the focus of these efforts was on media and public relations and, to some extent, crisis management.

Resource dependence Exists when a stakeholder is supplying a resource and can exert some form of control over it.

Responsible corporation A business undertaking that responds to social, ethical, and environmental responsibilities in addition to its economic obligations.

Responsible enterprise system An economic system operating as a free enterprise system but incorporating the element of accountability.

Responsible investment (RI) An approach to investing that aims to incorporate environmental, social, and governance (ESG) factors into investment decisions, to better manage risk and generate sustainable, long-term returns.

Restricted shares Involve some limit on voting, for example only one vote for every 10 or 100 shares owned; sometimes called *uncommon shares*.

Right of private property The legal right to own and use economic goods, for example land and buildings.

S

Salience The degree to which managers give priority to competing stakeholder claims.

Say-on-pay The ability of shareholders to vote on the remuneration of executives.

Self-interest ethic Individuals or corporations set their own standards for judging the ethical implications of their actions; only the individual's values and standards are the basis for actions.

Self-regulation Regulation imposed by the corporation or industry and not by the government or market forces.

Self-regulatory organizations (SROs) Industry or professional groups that are delegated or designated a regulatory function including the development, use, and enforcement of standards.

Service-learning A method of teaching, learning, and reflecting, combining classroom learning with service to the community either locally or in developing countries.

Shareholder democracy The exercise of power by owners to ensure they are treated fairly and enjoy equally the privileges and duties of ownership.

Sharing economy A sustainable social and economic system involving the sharing of human and physical resources. Sometimes referred to as *peer-to-peer e-commerce*.

Slowbalisation A new term used to describe the reaction against globalization; that is, its faltering or slower growth. It was coined by Adjiedj Bakas, a Dutch trend watcher, in 2015.

Social auditing A systematic assessment that identifies, measures, evaluates, reports, and monitors the effects an enterprise has on society that are not covered in the traditional financial reports.

Social capital Any aspect of a corporation's organizational arrangements that creates value and facilitates the actions of stakeholders within and external to the corporation.

Social contract A set of two-way understandings that characterizes the relationship between two major institutions.

Social enterprise A model of business operation where some or all profits are deliberately used to further social aims.

Social entrepreneur An innovative, visionary leader of a non-profit or for-profit business with real-world problem-solving creativity and a high awareness for ethical, social, and environmental considerations.

Social entrepreneurship Involves the activities undertaken to enhance social wealth in some innovative way.

Social extrapreneurship The process of inter-organizational action that facilitates alternative combinations of ideas, peoples, places, and resources to address social challenges.

Social finance Investments intended to create a measurable social or environmental impact as well as to generate financial returns.

Social impact investing The financing of initiatives to address social and environmental challenges and that generates a financial return and measurable benefits to society.

Social impact management Defined by the Aspen Institute as "the field of inquiry at the intersection of business needs and wider societal concerns that reflects and respects the complex interdependency between the two."

Social innovation According to Graduate School of Business, Stanford University, it is "a novel solution to a social problem that is more effective, efficient, sustainable, or just than current solutions" where the "value created accrues primarily to society rather than to private individuals."

Social intrapreneurship The process of addressing social challenges from inside established organizations.

Social licence The privilege of operating in society with minimal formalized restrictions—that is, legislation, regulation, or market requirements—based on maintaining public trust by doing what is acceptable to stakeholders in the business and society relationship.

Social media Online technologies and practices that people use to share opinions, insights, experiences, and perspectives.

Social or cultural globalization The emergence of a worldwide cultural system.

Social purpose This term is being used in place of social responsibility or sustainability. It means that the corporation is responsible to society and that it is aware and concerned about the ethical, social, and environmental issues facing business and society. It means that the corporation will become involved in addressing these issues.

Social sector That part of the economy that operates privately but, unlike the private sector, operates for social purposes with no intention to make profits.

Social venture philanthropy The investment of human and financial resources by corporations in non-profit community development agencies to generate a social return instead of only a financial one.

Socialization of capitalism The process through which the business system conforms to the expectations of society resulting in desired socially responsible outcomes.

Spirituality An individual's sense of peace or purpose with him/herself and the connection to others and even nature that provides meaning to life and a sense of one's self.

Stakeholder An individual or group who can influence and/or is influenced by the achievement of an organization's purpose.

Stakeholder capitalism An economic system in which corporations accept broader obligations beyond financial ones for shareholders.

Stakeholder engagement Efforts by a corporation to understand and involve relevant individuals, groups, or organizations by considering their moral concerns in strategic and operational initiatives.

Stakeholder management capability The ability of managers to identify stakeholders and their influence, to develop the organizational practices to understand stakeholders, and to undertake direct contact with stakeholders.

Standard environmentalism Occurs when government regulation is a necessary remedy for the market's failure to provide enough environmental amenities.

State capitalism An economic system in which governments manipulate market outcomes for political and social purposes.

Statement of values A description of the beliefs, principles, and basic assumptions about what is desirable or worth striving for in an organization.

Strategic giving An attempt to rationalize the shareholder interest with corporate philanthropy where the corporation benefits directly from the funds given.

Strategic management The process through which a corporation establishes its mission and objectives, analyzes the environment and resource capabilities in order to formulate strategy, creates the organizational systems and processes needed to implement the strategy, and devises mechanisms for evaluating performance.

Supplier diversity The process of reaching out to groups not traditionally included or underrepresented in the supply chain or within the purchasing process of major corporations or governments.

Supply (or value) chain The route that a product travels from the procurement of raw materials, the transformation into intermediate goods and then final products, and the delivery to consumers through a distribution system to its ultimate disposal by the consumer.

Supranational institution An international organization that transcends national boundaries, where the member states share in decision making on particular issues pertaining to the members.

Sustainability purchasing Involves selecting goods and services which promote a healthier community and environment by considering the costs as well as the environmental and social impacts of products and services through all stages of their lifecycle: from product/service development and manufacturing through product/ service use and ultimately to the disposal of whatever remains of the product/ service at the end of its useful life.

Sustainability strategy A plan that views economic, ethical, social, and environmental responsibilities more intensively and integrates corporate social responsibility (CSR) into all facets of the corporation's operations.

Sustainable capitalism As defined by Al Gore and David Blood, an "economic system within which business and trade seek to maximise long-term value creation, accounting for all material ESG (environmental, social and governance) metrics."

Sustainable development Development ensuring that the use of resources and the impact on the environment today does not damage prospects for the use of resources or the environment by future generations.

T

Tax haven Defined by CRA as a jurisdiction with one or more of the following characteristics: no tax, or very low rates of taxation; strict bank-secrecy provisions; a lack of transparency in the operation of its tax system; and a lack of effective exchange of information with other countries.

Teleological ethics An approach to ethics that focuses on outcomes or results of actions.

Third-party certification An approval or endorsement by an organization independent of government and business after reviewing the production or provision of a good or service to ascertain whether or not the product complies with specific standards relating to such things as safety, quality, performance, or environmental responsibility.

Transfer pricing The price set for goods and services sold between legal entities of the corporation.

Triple-E (economic, ethical, and environmental) bottom line Evaluates a corporation's performance according to a summary of the economic, social, and environmental value the corporation adds or destroys.

U

Universal rules ethic Ensures that managers or corporations have the same moral obligations in morally similar situations.

Urgency The degree to which the stakeholder's claim or relationship calls for immediate attention; exists when a claim or relationship is of a time-sensitive nature and when that claim or relationship is important or critical to the stakeholder.

Usage strategies An approach in which the stakeholder continues to supply a resource but specifies how it will be used.

Utilitarian ethic Focuses on the distribution of benefits and harms to all stakeholders with the view to maximizing benefits.

V

Value judgments Subjective evaluations of what is considered important; based on how managers intuitively feel about the goodness or rightness of various goals.

Venture capital company A type of private equity firm that usually acquires part ownership of business enterprises for which they provide financial and management assistance.

Virtue ethics An approach to ethics that emphasizes the individual's character or identity and focuses on being instead of doing.

W

Waste management According to Environment Canada, it is "disposal, processing, controlling, recycling and reusing the solid, liquid, and gaseous wastes of plants, animals, humans and other organisms."

Whistleblowing An act of voluntary disclosure of inappropriate behaviour or decisions to persons in positions of authority in an organization.

Withholding strategies An approach where the stakeholder discontinues providing a resource to an organization with the intention of changing a certain behaviour.

Work ethic A code of values, or a body of moral principles, claiming that work is desirable, a natural activity, and is good in and of itself.

Worker capitalism Describes employee ownership as workers are turned into capitalists through stock ownership.

Sources

Chapter 1

- **Everyday Ethics 1.5:** "Report on Sustainability 2018," Suncor Energy Inc. at https://sustainability.suncor.com/en ?_ga=2.40167466.988145932.1557928856-996061747.1557928856 accessed May 16, 2019.
- **Case 1.1:** Sears Canada Retiree Group (SCRG) web site at https://www.scretireegroup.ca/ accessed on November 15, 2018; "A primer on Sears Canada employees' battle to protect their pensions," Benefits Canada at https://www.benefitscanada.com /news/a-primer-on-sears-canada-employees-battle-to-protect-their-pensions-117565 accessed on November 15, 2018; and William B.P. Robson, "Lesson from the Sears Disaster: Fund Pensions Properly!" November 7, 2017 C.D. Howe Institute web site November 2, 2017 at https://www.cdhowe.org/intelligence-memos/william-bp-robson-lesson-sears-disaster-fund-pensions -properly accessed November 15, 2018.
- **Case 1.2:** Léo Charbonneau, "The Cheat Checker," *University Affairs*, April 2004, 16–20; Sarah Schmidt, "Professors Using In-class Exams and Essays to Fight Plagiarists," *National Post,* March 31, 2004, A1; and Heather Sokoloff, "One in Three Students Plagiarize," *National Post,* August 30, 2003, A1.

Chapter 2

- **Everyday Ethics 2.2:** Richard Truscott, "Property Rights Are the Key to Indian Posperity," Canadian Taxpayers Federation, accessed August 20, 2012, http://taxpayer.com/commentary/property-rights-are-key-indian-prosperity; Christopher Alcantara, "Individual Property Rights on Canadian Indian Reserves: The Historical Emergence and Jurisprudence of Certificates of Possession," available at http://www2.brandonu.ca/library/cjns/23.2/cjnsv23no2_pg391–424.pdf; Tom Flanagan, Christopher Alcantara, and Andre Le Dressay, *Beyond the Indian Act: Restoring Aboriginal Property Rights*, Montreal: McGill-Queen's University Press, 2010; and Tom Flanagan and Christopher Alcantara, "Individual Property Rights on Canadian Indian Reserves," Fraser Institute, 2002, available at http://www.fraserinstitute.org/publicationdisplay .aspx?id=12290&terms=property+rights+indian.
- **Responsibility for Ethics 2.2:** "The Power of Parity: Advancing Women's Equality in Canada," McKinsey and Company, June 2017 accessed at https://www.mckinsey.com/featured-insights/gender-equality/the-power-of-parity-advancing -womens-equality-in-canada on November 20, 2018; "Fact Sheet: The Gender Wage Gap in Canada," Canadian Women's Foundation web site at https://www.canadianwomen.org/the-facts/the-wage-gap/gclid=EAIaIQobChMIiO2y4pXk3gI VxR6GCh3ZywgjEAMYAiAAEgLUL_D_BwE accessed on November 20, 2018; "Gender equality in Canada: Mainstreaming, Governance, and Budgeting," Organisation for Economic Co-operation and Development (OECD) web site at http://www.oecd.org /canada/gender-equality-in-canada-9789264301108-en.htm accessed November 20, 2018; and David Macdonald, The Double-Pane Glass Ceiling: The Gender Pay Gap at the Top of Corporate Canada, Canadian Centre for Policy Alternatives, January 2019.
- **Everyday Ethics 2.3:** "Competition Bureau checks WestJet's discount airline Swoop for predatory pricing," CBC News, CBC News, Dec 12, 2018 https://www.cbc.ca/news/business/westjet-swoop-competition-bureau-1.4942490 accessed January 2, 2019; Competition Bureau, http://www.competitionbureau.gc.ca/eic/site/cb-bc.nsf/eng/home accessed January 2, 2019; "Flair Airlines Position on Canadian Competition Bureau Announcement," The Canadian Business Journal, December 11, 2018 at http://www .cbj.ca/flair-airlines-position-on-canadian-competition-bureau-announcement/ accessed January 2, 2019; and "'David and Goliath' battle prompted predatory pricing probe into WestJet: Flair CEO," CTV News, December 12, 2018 at https://www .ctvnews.ca/business/david-and-goliath-battle-prompted-predatory-pricing-probe-into-westjet-flair-ceo-1.4214887.
- **Everyday Ethics 2.4:** Income data from 2017 Consolidated Financial Statements in the banks' Annual Reports; and Bank Accountability Campaign, Democracy Watch web site at https://democracywatch.ca/campaigns/bank-accountability-campaign/ accessed November 16, 2018.
- **Responsibility for Ethics 2.3:** Work Ethic of the Millennials. Sources: "Generation Uphill," Special Report, *The Economist*, January 23, 2016, 1–12; Colby Cosh, "Millennials not actually inferior," *National Post*, October 26, 2017, A11; and "Debunking the Millennial Myth," *The Globe and Mail*, November 21, 2018, B5.
- **Everyday Ethics 2.5:** Megan Grant, "Where Does The Word "Boycott" Come From? It All Started With a 19th Century Englishman — VIDEO," December 14, 2016, Bustle web site at https://www.bustle.com/articles/200191-where-does-the -word-boycott-come-from-it-all-started-with-a-19th-century-englishman-video accessed November 20, 2018; Ethical Consumer, Boycotts List at https://www.ethicalconsumer.org/ethicalcampaigns/boycotts accessed November 20,2018; Michael Livingston, "Here's when boycotts have worked — and when they haven't," *Los Angeles Times*, March 01, 2018 accessed at http://www .latimes.com/nation/la-na-boycotts-history-20180228-htmlstory.html on November 20, 2018; Tijs Broek et al, "The Effect of Online Protests and Firm Responses on Shareholder and Consumer Evaluation," *Journal of Business Ethics*, December 2017, Volume 146, Issue 2, 279–294; and Alan Tomhave and Mark Vopat, "The Business of Boycotting: Having Your Chicken and Eating It Too," *Journal of Business Ethics*, September 2018, Volume 152, Issue 1, 123–132.
- **Everyday Ethics 2.6:** "'Greed is Good,' Again," *The Telegram* (St. John's, NL), April 29, 2009, B4; "Recession Won't make Gekko Blush in Sequel," *National Post*, April 30, 2009, A1; and Terence Corcoran, "In Hollywood, War and Wall St. are Both Hell," *National Post*, March 23, 2010, FP15.

- **Case 2.1:** Access Canada web site at http://www.accesscopyright.ca/ accessed on November 20, 2018; Fair Dealing Copyright Act (R.S.C., 1985, c. C-42) accessed at https://laws-lois.justice.gc.ca/eng/acts/c-42/ on November 20, 2018; Free Dealing Guidelines, Universities Canada web site at http://www.cmec.ca/docs/copyright/Fair_Dealing_Guidelines_EN.pdf accessed November 20, 2018; and 8 Facts About Canadian Copyright Law, Copyrightlaws.com web site at https://www.copyrightlaws.com/8-facts-about-canadian-copyright-law/ accessed November 20, 2018.

Chapter 3

- **Responsibility for Ethics 3.2:** The Chartered Professional Accountants of Canada (CPA Canada) web site at https://www.cpacanada.ca/; Chartered Professional Accountants of British Columbia (CPABC) web site at https://www.bccpa.ca/; and the CPABC Code—June 2015 accessed at https://www.bccpa.ca/CpaBc/media/CPABC/Members/Regulatory/Governing%20Documents/CPABC-Code-of-Professional-Conduct-FINAL-(June-23-2015).pdf.
- **Everyday Ethics 3.3:** David Macdonald, *Mint Condition: CEO Pay in Canada,* Canadian Centre for Policy Alternatives, Ottawa, ON. January 2019; and Hugh Macdonald, *Staying Power: CEO Pay in Canada*, Canadian Centre for Policy Alternatives, Ottawa, ON. January 2016.
- **Figure 3.2:** Based on description in Chapter 3 of Steven Fink, *Crisis Management: Planning for the Inevitable* (New York: AMACOM, 1986), 20–28.

Chapter 4

- **Responsibility for Ethics 4.1:** Google search for "jobs in stakeholder relations in Canada" and included job sites such as Careerjet, Workopolis, and Indeed Canada.
- **Figure 4.1:** Based on Paul C. Nutt and Robert W. Backoff, *Strategic Management of Public and Third Sector Organizations: A Handbook for Leaders* (San Francisco: Jossey-Bass Publishers, 1992), 191; and John M. Bryson, *Strategic Planning for Public and Nonprofit Organizations: A Guide to Strengthening and Sustaining Organizational Achievement,* revised edition (San Francisco: Jossey-Bass Publishers, 1995), 284.
- **Power/Dynamism Matrix:** Adapted from A. Mendelow, *Proceedings of 2nd International Conference on Information Systems,* Cambridge, MA, 1981; and from Gerry Johnson and Kevan Scholes, *Exploring Corporate Strategy: Text and Cases,* Third Edition (London: Prentice Hall International, 1993), 175–176.
- **Power/Interest Matrix:** Adapted from A. Mendelow, *Proceedings of 2nd International Conference on Information Systems,* Cambridge, MA, 1981; and from Gerry Johnson and Kevan Scholes, *Exploring Corporate Strategy: Text and Cases,* Third Edition (London: Prentice Hall International, 1993), 176–177.
- **Hendry's Stakeholder Influence Strategies:** Reference: Jamie R. Hendry, "Stakeholder Influence Strategies," *Journal of Business Ethics,* 2005, Volume 61, 75–99.
- **Den Hond and de Bakker's Ideologically Motivated Activism:** Reference: Frank den Hond and Frank G. A. de Bakker, "Ideologically Motivated Activism: How Activist Groups Influence Corporate Social Change Activities," *Academy of Management Review,* 2007, Volume 32, No. 3, 901–924. The typology is from page 911.

Chapter 5

- **Table 5.1:** Summarized from Larue Tone Hosmer, "Strategic Planning as if Ethics Mattered," *Strategic Management Journal,* Vol. 15 (1994): 22–24.
- **Responsibility for Ethics 5.2:** The Ayn Rand Institute, https://www.aynrand.org/?pagename=index; and The Ayn Rand Institute Canada, http://aynrandinstitute.ca, accessed April 3, 2019.
- **Everyday Ethics 5.1:** USADA, "Report on proceedings under the World Anti-Doping Code and the USADA Protocol: Reasoned decision of the United States Anti-Doping Agency on disqualification and ineligibility," Mark Gollom, "Did Lance Armstrong redeem or incriminate himself? Armstrong did a poor job of rehabilitating his image, experts say," CBC News, January 18, 2013, accessed January 20, 2013; NBC News, "Lance Armstrong steps down from Livestrong, loses Nike, Bud contracts," accessed January 20, 2013; Nick Hoult, "Lance Armstrong says he is 'fall guy' for cycling's problems, *The Telegraph*, accessed January 20, 2013; and "Times Topics: Lance Armstrong," *The New York Times*, February 7, 2013, accessed February 20, 2013.
- **Responsibility for Ethics 5.1:** "The Council of Better Business Bureaus, Inc. Copyright 2016. Council of Better Business Bureaus, Inc., 3033 Wilson Blvd., 6th Floor, Arlington, VA 22201, www.bbb.org."
- **Everyday Ethics 5.2:** "Community Involvement," Raymond James Ltd. web site at https://www.raymondjames.ca/about-us/community-involvement/community-stories accessed April 3, 2019.

Chapter 6

- **Everyday Ethics 6.2:** Compiled from Manulife, "Code of Business Conduct and Ethics" https://www.manulife.com/en/about/corporate-governance.html (under "You may also be interested in...") accessed January 28, 2019. Listing from Table of Contents and quotation from page 5.

- **Table 6.3:** Kenneth Kernaghan and John W. Langford, "Conflict of Interest," Chapter 6 in *The Responsible Public Servant* (Halifax: The Institute for Research on Public Policy and The Institute of Public Administration of Canada, 1990), 133–155; and Michael McDonald, "Ethics and Conflict of Interest," The W. Maurice Young Centre of Applied Ethics, University of British Columbia.

- **Responsibility for Ethics 6.1:** Based on Ethics Practitioners' Association of Canada web site, accessed January 28, 2019, http://epac-apec.ca/.

- **Everyday Ethics 6.5:** Based on "Code of Business Conduct and Ethics," Barrick Gold Corporation, pages 19–26, accessed January 28, 2019, https://barrick.q4cdn.com/788666289/files/governance/Barrick-Code-of-Business-Conduct-and-Ethics.pdf.

- **Case 6.2:** "Subway Worker Fired for Feeding Fire Victims," Cnews, canoe.ca, June 11, 2010, accessed February 23, 2012, http://cnews.canoe.ca/CNEWS/Canada/2010/06/11/14355351.html?cid=rssnewscanada; CTV News, June 10, 2010, http://www.ctv.ca/CTVNews/TopStories/20100610/ns-subway-firing-100610, accessed February 23, 2012; "Fired Subway Worker Doesn't Want to Work There Anymore," CTV News, June 11, 2010, accessed August 12, 2016, http://www.ctvnews.ca/fired-subway-worker-doesn-t-want-to-work-there-anymore-1.521608; "Nova Scotia Quiznos Offers Job to Submarine Samaritan Fired by Rival Chain," *National Post,* June 12, 2010, A12; Roger Taylor, "Fired Sandwich Artist Back on Job with Competitor," *The ChronicleHerald.ca,* June 12, 2010, accessed June 21, 2010, http://thechronicleherald.ca/Business/1186991.html; and Mark Harden, "Quiznos Franchisee Rescues Canada's Hoagie Hero," *Denver Business Journal,* June 15, 2010, accessed August 12, 2016, http://www.bizjournals.com/denver/blog/broadway_17th/2010/06/quiznos_franchisee_helps_out_canadas_hoagie_hero.html.

Chapter 7

- **What would you do if...?:** Adapted from *Volkswagen Sustainability Report,* accessed January 6, 2016, http://www.volkswagenag.com/content/vwcorp/content/en/sustainability_and_responsibility.html; Corporate Responsibility, accessed January 6, 2016, http://en.volkswagen.com/en/company/responsibility/corporate-responsibility.html; and "Volkswagen is Giving Back at Camp Oochigeas," accessed January 6, 2016, http://www.vw.ca/en/corporate/vw-cares.html.

- **Table 7.1:** Compiled from Christine Shropshire and Amy J. Hillman, "A Longitudinal Study of Significant Change in Stakeholder Management," *Business & Society,* Volume 46, Number 1, March 2007, 68–74.

- **Everyday Ethics 7.2:** "BMO Commits $10 Million to United Way; CEO Darryl White Brings Together GTA Business Leaders to Tackle Economic Disparity in Communities," News release September 21, 2018 assessed at https://newsroom.bmo.com/2018-09-20-BMO-Commits-10-Million-to-United-Way-CEO-Darryl-White-Brings-Together-GTA-Business-Leaders-to-Tackle-Economic-Disparity-in-Communities.

- **Everyday Ethics 7.4:** Adapted from Imperial Oil Limited, "Corporate Citizenship Highlights 2016," accessed January 31, 2019, https://www.imperialoil.ca/en-ca/community/corporate-citizenship-highlights/2016-highlights/2016-highlights.

- **Case 7.1:** Shoppers Drug Mart Inc., "Growing Women's Health," accessed July 19, 2016, http://www.shoppersloveyou.ca/events/growing-womens-health-1026; and The Governor General of Canada, His Excellency the Right Honourable David Johnston, accessed July 19, 2016, http://www.gg.ca/document.aspx?id=15397.

- **Case 7.2:** TD Grade One Book Giveaway at https://www.td.com/corporate-responsibility/reads.jsp?cm_sp=cMEREAD000-001/ accessed January 31, 2019; Canadian Children's Book Centre accessed January 31, 2019, http://bookcentre.ca/about; and Tristan Hopper, "School Spurn Free Books over Bank Logo: Keep Eye on The Prize, and The Prize is Children's Literacy," *National Post,* November 13, 2013, A1.

Chapter 8

- **Table 8.2:** Compiled from the December 2003 issue of Canadian Business for Social Responsibility's *Good Company Newsletter,* and other sources.

- **Responsibility for Ethics 8.1:** METRO web site, "Update: Corporate Responsibility 2018 (for the 2017 fiscal year) at https://corpo.metro.ca/userfiles/file/PDF/Responsabilite_entreprise/2018/2018_CSR_report.pdf accessed February 6, 2019.

- **Everyday Ethics 8.1** "We are Committed to Our Community," 18 Asset Management web site at https://18assetmanagement.com/our-company/in-the-community; "Community Funding," BlueShore Financial web site at https://www.blueshorefinancial.com/AboutUs/OurCommunity/CommunityFunding; "Charitable Grants Report 2017Canada," GlaxoSmithKline Inc. web site at https://ca.gsk.com/media/1393398/charitable-grants-report-2017.pdf; "Charities We Support," Smith's Funeral Homes web site at http://www.smithsfh.com/Charities_We_Support_921993.html; and "Supporting Our Community," Corporate Responsibility Report 2017–2018, Woodbine Entertainment Group web site at https://woodbine.com/wp-content/uploads/WEG-Corporate-Responsibility-Report-2017-18.pdf. All accessed February 5, 2019.

- **Responsibility for Ethics 8.2:** Imagine Canada web site at http://www.imaginecanada.ca/ accessed February 2, 2019; "Canada's top-rated charities 2019," *Money Sense Magazine* at https://www.moneysense.ca/save/financial-planning/canadas-top-rated-charities-2019-overview/ accessed February 5, 2019; Charity Intelligence Canada web site at https://www.charityintelligence.ca/about-ci accessed February 3, 2019; and Better Business Bureau (BBB) Canada, "Give org.," at https://www.bbb.org/us/storage/0/Shared%20Documents/Standards%20for%20Charity%20Accountability.pdf accessed February 6, 2019.

- **Everyday Ethics 8.2:** Compiled from Philanthropic Foundations Canada, https://pfc.ca/resources/canadian-foundation-facts/; The J.W. McConnell Family Foundation, https://mcconnellfoundation.ca/about/; The Birks Family Foundation, http://www.birksfamilyfoundation.ca/ and the Donner Canadian Foundation, https://www.donnerfoundation.org//. All accessed February 4, 2019.

- **Everyday Ethics 8.3:** Based on Social Ventures Partners Calgary, http://www.socialventurepartners.org/calgary/, accessed February 5, 2019.

- **Everyday Ethics 8.4:** "Team Depot," The Home Depot web site at https://www.homedepot.ca/en/home/corporate-information/our-community/the-home-depot-canada-foundation/how-we-help/team-depot.html; PWC Canada, Corporate Responsibility Highlights 2018, "Community engagement," https://www.pwc.com/ca/en/corporate-responsibility/publications/P501338-CR-FY18-Highlights-final.pdf; IGM Financial, "Community Service," at https://www.igmfinancial.com/en/corporate-responsibilty/ourcommunity/communityservice; Westjet, "WestJetters Caring for Our Community" at https://www.westjet.com/en-ca/about-us/community-investment/caring-community; and Capital Power Corporation, "Employee Giving" at https://www.capitalpower.com/community/community/Pages/EmployeeCommunitySupport.aspx. All accessed February 4, 2019.

- **Table 8.3:** Based on Peter M. Brophey, "Corporate Voluntarism: Putting Something Back," *Canadian Business Review* (Spring 1987); Julie Traves, "What Goes Around . . . Corporate Volunteering Boosts the Bottom Line," *Canadian Business,* January 31–February 13, 2005, 67–68; and Shirley Won, "Doing Good Helps You Do Well at Work," *The Globe and Mail,* January 19, 2005, C1.

- **Everyday Ethics 8.5:** Adapted from IBM, "Corporate Service Corps," at http://www.ibm.com/ibm/responsibility/corporateservicecorps/programdetails.htm accessed February 8, 2019; and Uniterra, Leave for Change® http://uniterra.ca/en/volunteering/corporate-volunteering accessed on January 9, 2019.

- **Everyday Ethics 8.6:** "Community Support," Kent Building Supplies web site at https://kent.ca/community-support; "Corporate Sponsorships," Kruger Inc. web site at https://www.kruger.com/corporate-responsibility/in-the-community/; "Sponsorships and Community," SportChek web site at https://www.sportchek.ca/help-desk/corporate-information/sponsorships---community.html; "National Sponsorships," Tim Hortons web site at https://www.timhortons.com/ca/en/corporate/national-sponsorship.php; and "Sponsorships," SaskTel web site at https://www.sasktel.com/about-us/Community/Sponsorships. All accessed on February 8, 2019.

- **Responsibility for Ethics 8.3:** Imagine Canada, "Caring Company Program," http://www.imaginecanada.ca/our-programs/caring-company-program accessed January 6, 2016.

- **Table 8.4:** Compiled and adapted from Heledd Jenkins, "A Critique of Conventional CSR Theory: An SME Perspective," *Journal of General Management*, Vol. 29, No 4, Summer 2004, Table 3: Divergence in CSR Theory for Large and Small Organizations, page 51.

- **Everyday Ethics 8.7:** "Indigenous Peoples," AltaGas Ltd. web site at https://www.altagas.ca/responsibility/indigenous-peoples; "First Nations: Building Strong Working Relationships," Canfor Corporation web site at https://www.canfor.com/responsibility/first-nations; "Hudbay 2018 Annual and CSR Report," HudBay Minerals at https://s1.q4cdn.com/305438552/files/2018/en/_doc/Hudbay_2018_Annual_CSR_Report.pdf, pages 41 and 53; "Hydro-Québec and Indigenous Communities Partners For Over 40 Years," Hydro-Québec at http://www.hydroquebec.com/data/a-propos/pdf/partnership-indigenous-communities-2017g422a.pdf; and "Our Responsibility: Aboriginal Relations," Pembina Pipeline Corporation web site at http://www.pembina.com/our-responsibility/aboriginal-relations/. All web sites accessed on July 4, 2019.

- **Everyday Ethics 8.8:** Citigrow web site at http://www.citigrow.ca/ accessed February 8, 2019.

- **Case 8.1:** Beer, Wine, Spirits Producers' Commitments, accessed January 15, 2016, http://www.producerscommitments.org/; "Our Sustainability & Responsibility Strategy," Diageo plc, accessed January 15, 2016, http://www.diageo.com/en-row/csr/sustainability/Pages/default.aspx; and "Responsible Consumption," Molson Coors Brewing Company, accessed January 15, 2016, http://www.molsoncoors.com/en/responsibility/what-matters-to-us/alcohol-responsibility.

- **Case 8.2:** Marjorie Polycarpe, "Re-examining Workplace Giving Programs," Inside Corporate Philanthropy (December 31, 2003); Tara Weiss, "Giving at the Office Without Going Broke," *Forbes*, June 22, 2006, accessed August 16, 2016, http://www.forbes.com/2006/06/22/business-basics-donation-cs_tw_0622officegifts.html; David Aston, "'Tis the Season to be Inundated," *The Globe and Mail*, November 14, 2007, C1–C2; and Jennifer Myers, "Giving Spirit Untarnished by Recession," *The Globe and Mail*, November 28, 2009, B17.

Chapter 9

- **Everyday Ethics 9.1:** "Sustainability Overview," Maple Leaf Foods web site at https://www.mapleleaffoods.com/sustainability /overview/ accessed February 15, 2019, and "2017 Sustainability Report," Maple Leaf Foods web site at https://www.mapleleaffoods .com/wp-content/uploads/2018/07/MLF_2017SustainabilityReport.pdf accessed February 15, 2019.

- **Responsibility for Ethics 9.1:** Adapted from Sustainalytics, Jantzi, accessed February 11, 2019, http://www.sustainalytics.com /JSI.

- **Everyday Ethics 9.2:** Compiled from "Building the Economy for Everyone," Corporate Social Responsibility Report 2017, Scotiabank at https://www.scotiabank.com/corp/downloads/Scotiabank_CSR_Report_2017_ENG.pdf accessed February 15, 2019.

- **Table 9.1:** Global Reporting Initiative (GRI) Standards. GRI is an independent international organization that has pioneered sustainability reporting since 1997. GRI helps businesses and governments worldwide understand and communicate their impact on critical sustainability issues such as climate change, human rights, governance and social well-being. This enables real action to create social, environmental and economic benefits for everyone. The GRI Sustainability Reporting Standards are developed with true multi-stakeholder contributions and rooted in the public interest.

- **Table 9.2:** Based on Coro Strandberg, *The Future of Corporate Social Responsibility* (Vancouver: VanCity Credit Union, September 2002), 6. Available at http://corostrandberg.com/wp-content/uploads/2002/12/future-of-csr.pdf.

- **Case 9.1:** "About," Innovative Medicines Canada web site at http://innovativemedicines.ca/about/; "Voluntary Disclosure of Payments," Innovative Medicines Canada web site at http://innovativemedicines.ca/ethics/voluntary-disclosure-of-payments/; Joel Lexchin, "What Big Pharma pays your doctor," *The Conversation*, July 4, 2018 at https://theconversation.com/what-big -pharma-pays-your-doctor-99431; and Open Pharma web site at http://open-pharma.org/. All accessed on February 16, 2019.

Chapter 10

- **Responsibility for Ethics 10.3:** The Canadian Real Estate Association, The Realtor® Code at https://www.crea.ca/wp-content /uploads/2016/03/The-REALTOR-Code.pdf.

- **Everyday Ethics 10.1:** "Earls restaurant moves to Humane Certified beef—what is it and is it healthier?" Global News, April 28, 2016 accessed at http://globalnews.ca/news/2668722/earls-restaurant-moves-to-humane-certified-beef-what-is-it-and-is-it-healthier/; "Earls Beef Controversy Ends With Restaurant Backing Down," Huff Post, 05/04/2016 accessed at http://www.huffingtonpost.ca/2016/05/04 /what-s-the-beef-earls-restaurants-will-serve-canadian-beef-again_n_9838956.html; "Earls meat decision gives much to chew on: Questions arise about what 'Certified Humane' means," CBC News, May 1, 2016 accessed at http://www.cbc.ca/news/canada /saskatoon/beef-certified-humane-canada-1.3558451; and Earls Kitchen + Bar accessed at https://earls.ca/.

- **Everyday Ethics 10.2:** "Corporate Social Responsibility Annual Report," Export Development Corporation web site accessed at https://www.edc.ca/en/about-us/corporate/corporate-social-responsibility.html; "2017 Corporate Responsibility Highlights Report," Toronto Hydro web site accessed at http://www.torontohydro.com/sites/electricsystem/corporateresponsibility/Pages /default.aspx; "Responsibility," Liquor Control Board of Ontario web site accessed at http://www.lcbo.com/content/lcbo/en /responsibility.html#.XHBSfa1YbIU;and 2017 Social Responsibility Report, Canada Post web site accessed at https://www .canadapost.ca/assets/pdf/aboutus/2017_csrreport_en.pdf.

- **Everyday Ethics 10.3:** Adapted from "Ethics & Compliance Timeline," SNC-Lavalin, accessed July 24, 2016, http://www .snclavalin.com/en/ethics-compliance-timeline; *Corruption of Foreign Public Officials Act* (S.C. 1998, c. 34), http://laws-lois .justice.gc.ca/eng/acts/c-45.2/index.html; Theresa Tedesco, "SNC Vows to Fight Charges," *National Post,* Feb. 20, 2015, A1, A3; Drew Hasselback, "SNC-Lavalin Charges Reveal the Teeth in Canada's New Anti-bribery Law," *National Post,* Feb. 19, 2015, Online edition at http://business.financialpost.com/legal-post/snc-lavalin-charges-reveal-the-teeth-in-canadas-new-anti-bribery -law.; and Nicolas Van Praet, "SNC-Lavalin hearing begins for fraud, bribery allegations," *The Globe and Mail,* 30 Oct. 2018, B3.

- **Everyday Ethics 10.4:** Adapted from John W. Warnock, "Cameco Uses Dummy Corporation to Avoid Taxes," Saturday, June 1, 2013, accessed January 19, 2016, http://johnwwarnock.blogspot.ca/2013/06/cameco-uses-dummy-corporation-to-avoid.html; CBC News Saskatchewan,"Ottawa Accuses Cameco of Multi-Million Dollar Tax Dodge," September 19, 2013, accessed January 19, 2016, http:// www.cbc.ca/news/canada/saskatchewan/ottawa-accuses-cameco-of-multi-million-dollar-tax-dodge-1.1860079; and "CRA appeals $2.2B tax bill dispute decision that ruled in favour of uranium giant Cameco," CBC News, October 26, 2018 at https://www.cbc.ca /news/canada/saskatoon/cra-appeals-2-2b-tax-bill-dispute-decision-that-ruled-in-favour-of-uranium-giant-cameco-1.4879410 accessed February 24, 2019.

- **Everyday Ethics 10.5:** Adapted from "Code of Ethics and Business Conduct," Bombardier, accessed February 26, 2019, http://www.bombardier.com/content/dam/Websites/bombardiercom/supporting-documents/BInc/Bombardier-code-of-ethics -currentversion-en.pdf, p. 19; and "Code of Ethics and Business Conduct," Rspsol Canada web site at https://www.repsol.ca /imagenes/repsolporca/en/CodeofEthicsandBusinessConduct_tcm24-74685.pdf, p. 23 accessed February 26, 2019.

- **Responsibility of Ethics 10.5:** Adapted from Office of the Commissioner of Lobbying of Canada, accessed January 14, 2016, https://ocl-cal.gc.ca/eic/site/012.nsf/eng/h_00008.html.
- **Case 10.1:** "Alcohol," Canadian Centre on Substance Use and Addiction, The University of Victoria web site at http://www.ccdus.ca/Eng/topics/alcohol/Pages/default.aspx; "Health Canada-funded study examines attitudes, opinions and behaviours related to alcohol use," News Release #17-097, May 5, 2017 Government of Yukon web site at http://www.gov.yk.ca/news/17-097.html; "Alcohol warning labels about cancer risk a Canadian first," February 28, 2018, Canadian Centre on Substance Use and Addiction, The University of Victoria web site at https://www.uvic.ca/research/centres/cisur/about/news/current/alcohol-warning-labels-about-cancer-risk-a-canadian-first.php; and "Northern Territories Alcohol Study to resume," News Release #18-027, February 15, 2018 Government of Yukon web site at http://www.gov.yk.ca/news/18-027.html. All accessed on February 22, 2019.

Chapter 11

- **Responsibility for Ethics 11.1:** Compiled by the author from *Management Information* and *Proxy Circulars*.
- **Everyday Ethics 11.1:** Based on Mountain Equipment Co-op, http://www.mec.ca; and Vancouver City Savings Credit Union, https://www.vancity.com.
- **Responsibility for Ethics 11.3:** Adapted from Jantzi Social Index accessed March 1, 2019, http://www.sustainalytics.com/JSI; S&P/TSX Renewable Energy and Clean Technology Index (CAD) accessed March 2, 2019 at https://ca.spindices.com/indices/equity/sp-tsx-renewable-energy-and-clean-technology-index; Dow Jones Sustainability Indexes, accessed March 1, 2019, http://www.sustainability-index.com/; and "FTSE4Good Index Series," accessed March 1, 2019, https://www.ftse.com/products/indices/ftse4good.
- **Responsibility for Ethics 11.5:** Compiled by the author from Management Information and Proxy Circulars.
- **Responsibility for Ethics 11.6:** "About CCGG," Canadian Coalition for Good Governance, accessed March 7, 2019, https://www.ccgg.ca/index.cfm?pagepath=About_CCGG&id=17564
- **Responsibility for Ethics 11.7:** Adapted from Canadian Board Diversity Council, accessed March 1, 2019, http://www.boarddiversity.ca; 30% Club Canada, accessed March 1, 2019, http://30percentclub.org/; Catalyst Canada, accessed March 1, 2019, http://www.catalyst.org/regions/canada; and "About OnBoard Canada," OnBoard Canada, accessed March 1, 2019, https://onboardcanada.ca/about/.
- **Responsibility for Ethics 11.8:** Adapted from "Disclosure of Corporate Governance Practices," National Instrument 58-101, Ontario Securities Commission, accessed March 1, 2019, https://www.osc.gov.on.ca/documents/en/Securities-Category5/ni_20160329_58-101_unofficial-consolidation.pdf.
- **Responsibility for Ethics 11.9:** Adapted from "Board Games: The 17th Annual Corporate Governance Ranking" *The Globe and Mail,* 26 November 2018, 10, and "Board Shareholder Confidence Index," Clarkson Centre for Business Ethics and Board Effectiveness, University of Toronto at http://www.rotman.utoronto.ca/FacultyAndResearch/ResearchCentres/ClarksonCentreforBoardEffectiveness/BoardShareholderConfidenceIndex.
- **Responsibility for Ethics 11.10:** Adapted from National Instrument 58–101, "Disclosure of Corporate Governance Practices, Clause 5," http://www.osc.gov.on.ca/en/14198.htm.
- **Case 11.1:** Adapted from Stuart Weinberg, "In Advisors We Trust, Though Not Always Wisely," *The Globe and Mail*, October 21, 2006, B13; Gordon Pape, "Wanted: One Impartial Financial Planner," *CARP Magazine*, June 2007, 52; Jonathan Cheveau, "Giving CFPs More Respect," *National Post*, June 10, 2008, FP15; Doug Steiner, "A Moral Gauge," *Report on Business*, January 2009, 23; and Hugh Anderson, "Investors Need Better Information," *National Post*, October 30, 2007, FP6.
- **Case 11.2:** Inter Pipeline Ltd. web site at http://www.interpipeline.com/; "Sustainability Report 2017" at http://www.interpipeline.com/files/pdf/sustainability/Inter%20Pipeline%20Sustainability%20Report.pdf; "Sustainability Summary Statistics" at http://www.interpipeline.com/files/Sustainabiility%20Summary%20Sheet%202018.pdf; and "2017 Annual Report," at http://www.interpipeline.com/files/pdf/investorrelations/2018/2017%20Annual%20Report.pdf. All accessed February 27, 2019.

Chapter 12

- **Responsibility for Ethics 12.1:** Best Employers in Canada 2019, accessed March 8, 2019, https://archive.macleans.ca/article/2018/12/1/best-employers-in-canada-2019; Canada's Best Employers 2018—Small and Medium Sized Companies, accessed March 9, 2019, https://www.canadianbusiness.com/lists-and-rankings/best-jobs/best-employers/small-medium-employers-2018; and Canada's Top 100 Employers, accessed March 8, 2019, https://www.canadastop100.com/national/.
- **Responsibility for Ethics 12.2:** Adapted from "PIPEDA fair information principles," The Office of the Privacy Commissioner of Canada accessed March 8, 2019, https://www.priv.gc.ca/en/privacy-topics/privacy-laws-in-canada/the-personal-information-protection-and-electronic-documents-act-pipeda/p_principle/.
- **Everyday Ethics 12.1:** Corporate Overview, BCE Inc. at http://www.bce.ca/; "Diversity and inclusion," *BCE Inc. 2017 Corporate Responsibility Report*, 26–29. at http://www.bce.ca/responsibility/corporate-responsibility/2017-cr

-report/2017-csr-report.pdf; and *Canada's Best Diversity Employers 2019* https://www.canadastop100.com/diversity/. All accessed March 6, 2019.

- **Everyday Ethics 12.2:** Adapted from Dawn Iacobucci, Kent Grayson and Amy Ostrom, "Customer Satisfaction Fables," *Sloan Management Review,* Summer 1994, 93–96; Tom Sorell, "The Customer Is Not Always Right," *Journal of Business Ethics,* Volume 13, 1994, 913–914.

- **Responsibility for Ethics 12.5:** Adapted from "Our Legislation," Competition Bureau of Canada accessed March 8, 2019, http://www.competitionbureau.gc.ca/eic/site/cb-bc.nsf/eng/h_00125.html.

- **Everyday Ethics 12.3:** Adapted from "Supplier Code of Business Conduct," Canadian Tire Corporation, Limited, accessed March 8, 2019, https://s22.q4cdn.com/405442328/files/doc_downloads/ethical/CTC-Supplier-Code-of-Conduct-July-4-2012.pdf.

- **Responsibility for Ethics 12.7:** Adapted from Supply Chain Management Association (SCMA) at https://scma.com/en/about-scma and https://scma.com/en/education-accreditation accessed March 9, 2019.

- **Responsibility for Ethics 12.8:** Adapted from "Our Organization," Competition Bureau of Canada accessed March 8, 2019, https://competitionbureau.gc.ca/eic/site/cb-bc.nsf/eng/h_00148.html; and *The Competition Act,* accessed March 8, 2019, https://www.laws.justice.gc.ca/eng/acts/C-34/index.html.

- **Responsibility for Ethics 12.10:** Adapted from BuySmart Network, accessed March 13, 2019, https://www.buysmartbc.com/.

- **Responsibility for Ethics 12.11:** Adapted from Ethical Trading Initiative, accessed March 10, 2019, https://www.ethicaltrade.org/about-eti and https://www.ethicaltrade.org/eti-base-code.

Chapter 13

- **Responsibility for Ethics 13.3:** "Newspapers and Recycling," News Media Canada at https://nmc-mic.ca/public-affairs/newspapers-and-recycling/ and "Newspapers and the Environment: What You Need to Know," News Media Canada at https://nmc-mic.ca/sites/default/files/Newspapers-%20A%20Green%20Choice%202011.pdf on March 11, 2019.

- **Everyday Ethics 13.3:** Compiled from Policy Development Institutions (Think Tanks).

- **Responsibility for Ethics 13.5:** Adapted from "Vocation of the Business Leader: A Reflection," Pontifical Council for Justice and Peace, The Vatican, March 30, 2012, accessed March 9, 2019, https://www.stthomas.edu/media/catholicstudies/center/ryan/publications/publicationpdfs/vocationofthebusinessleaderpdf/PontificalCouncil_4.pdf.

- **Responsibility for Ethics 13.6:** Adapted from Corporate Chaplains Canada, accessed March 10, 2019, http://chaplains.ca/; and "About Workplace Centre," Workplace Centre for Spiritual and Ethical Development accessed March 11, 2019, http://workplacecentre.org/about-us.

- **Everyday Ethics 13.4:** Monique Potvin Kent et al. "Food and beverage marketing in primary and secondary schools in Canada," BMC Public Health (2019) 19:114 at https://ruor.uottawa.ca/bitstream/10393/38780/1/12889_2019_Article_6441.pdf and "The Ottawa Principles," Stop Marketing to Children Coalition at https://stopmarketingtokids.ca/the-ottawa-principles/.

- **Case 13.1:** Indian Resource Council web page at http://irccanada.ca/; Stephen Buffalo,"We are First Nations that support pipelines, when pipelines support First Nations," *National Post*, September 13, 2018 at https://business.financialpost.com/opinion/we-are-first-nations-that-support-pipelines-when-pipelines-support-first-nations accessed March 14, 2019; Martin Olszynski "Federal Court of Appeal Quashes Trans Mountain Pipeline Approval: The Good, the Bad, and the Ugly," Faculty of Law, University of Calgary, ABLawg.ca posted on September 6, 2018 at https://ablawg.ca/2018/09/06/federal-court-of-appeal-quashes-trans-mountain-pipeline-approval-the-good-the-bad-and-the-ugly/; and Ashifa Kassam, "First Nations group proposes oil pipeline that protects indigenous rights," *The Guardian*, September 8, 2018 accessed at https://www.theguardian.com/world/2018/sep/08/canada-oil-pipeline-first-nations-proposal-indigenous-rights on March 15, 2019.

- **Case 13.2:** Adapted from SLAPP "Defamation and SLAPPs," Canadian Internet Policy and Public Interest Clinic, University of Ottawa, http://www.cippic.ca/en/defamation-and-slapps; "Awards and Recognition," and "About Us" at Resolute Forest Products web site https://www.pfresolu.com/Awards_and_Recognition/ and https://www.pfresolu.com/About_Us/ accessed March 12, 2019; Terence Corcoran, "SLAPP setback for Greenpeace," *National Post*, July 16, 2014, FP9, and "Resolute Loses Most of Lawsuit Against Groups in the U.S." *National Post*, January 23, 2019, FP12.

Chapter 14

- **What would you do if...?:** Lisa Gosselin, "Which Salmon Should I Buy?" accessed March 15, 2012, https://ca.news.yahoo.com/which-salmon-should-i-buy-.html; "Farmed vs. Wild Salmon—Which is Better?" ctvbc.ca, March 4, 2010, accessed March 21, 2012, http://www.ctvbc.ctv.ca/servlet/an/local/CTVNews/20100219/bc_ctv_investigates_food_fish_100219/20100304; David Cox, "Farmed vs Wild Salmon? A Comparison," Fish Vet Group, accessed March 30, 2012, http://www.thefishsite.com/articles/107/farmed-vs-wild-salmon-a-comparison; Wild Salmon vs. Farmed Raised: Which is Better?" Pays to Live Green, accessed March 30, 2012, http://www.paystolivegreen.com/2009/02/wild-salmon-vs-farmed-raised-which-is-better; Joseph Schwartz, "Wild versus Farmed Salmon: The Pros and Cons," *Medical News Today*, December 26, 2005, accessed March 30, 2012, http://www.medicalnewstoday.com/releases/35370.php; and "What's New and Beneficial about Salmon" The World's Healthiest Foods, accessed August 26, http://www.whfoods.com/genpage.php?tname=foodspice&dbid=104.

- **Responsibility for Ethics 14.2:** "About Evergreen," Evergreen at "About Friends of the Earth Canada," Evergreen at https://www.evergreen.ca/about/; Friends of the Earth Canada at https://foecanada.org/en/about/; "About Us," Environmental Defence Canada at https://environmentaldefence.ca/about-us/; "About," Canadian Parks and Wilderness Society (CPAWS) at http://cpaws.org/about; "About Us," David Suzuki Foundation at https://davidsuzuki.org/about/. All accessed on March 15, 2019.

- **Everyday Ethics 14.1:** Adapted from RBC Blue Water Project™, Royal Bank of Canada, accessed March 20, 2019, http://www.rbc.com/community-sustainability/environment/rbc-blue-water/index.html.

- **Everyday Ethics 14.2:** "Offset Your Carbon Footprint by Planting Trees," Tree Canada at https://treecanada.ca/reforestation-carbon-offsetting/carbon-offsetting; "Welcome," coolaction.com at http://www.coolaction.com/index.htm; and "Our Story," Bullfrog Power at https://www.bullfrogpower.com/our-story. All accessed March 15, 2019.

- **Everyday Ethics 14.3:** *Carbon Disclosure Project* at https://www.cdp.net/en and CDP Canada Report 2017, November 2017 at https://b8f65cb373b1b7b15feb-c70d8ead6ced550b4d987d7c03fcdd1d.ssl.cf3.rackcdn.com/cms/reports/documents/000/002/859/original/Canada-edition-climate-change-report-2017.pdf?1511193746 accessed March 18, 2019.

- **Everyday Ethics 14.4:** Adapted from Canada Green Building Council, https://www.cagbc.org/.

- **Responsibility for Ethics 14.4:** Adapted from *Common Environmental Labels and Claims in Canada*, Office of Consumer Affairs (OCA), Government of Canada, http://www.ic.gc.ca/eic/site/oca-bc.nsf/eng/ca02523.html accessed March 20, 2019.

- **Everyday Ethics 14.5:** Adapted from Jake MacDonald, "Field of Dreams," *Canadian Geographic Magazine*, April 2014, 44–48; "The First Straw: Why Print on Wheat Paper," "Little Startup on the Prairie," and "Woody's Paper Trail," *Corporate Knights*, November 2013, 6, 54–58 and 60–62; and "Prairie Pulp & Paper gets foothold in U.S.," Association Manitoba News and Media at https://www.biomb.ca/news/246/article-246 accessed March 18, 2019.

- **Responsibility for Ethics 14.5:** Based on "About Us," Ceres web site http://www.ceres.org/about-us; "All About ISO," International Organization for Standardization web site at https://www.iso.org/about-us.html; and "About IISD," International Institute for Sustainable Development web site at https://www.iisd.org/about/about-iisd.

- **Responsibility for Ethics 14.6:** Adapted from Bjørn Lomborg web site at https://www.lomborg.com/ accessed March 17 2019; and Copenhagen Consensus Center web site at https://www.copenhagenconsensus.com/?ID=1626 accessed August 18, 2019.

- **Responsibility for Ethics 14.7:** Circular Economy Leadership Coalition (CELC) web site at http://circulareconomyleaders.ca/index.html; "A Circular Economy For Plastics in Canada: A bold vision for less waste and more value," Smart Prosperity Institute, February 2019 at http://circulareconomyleaders.ca/downloads/A_Circular_Economy_for_Plastics_in_Canada.pdf; "Rethinking plastic packaging—towards a more circular economy," Unilever Canada at https://www.unilever.com/sustainable-living/reducing-environmental-impact/waste-and-packaging/rethinking-plastic-packaging/#244-421040; and "Circular & Climate Positive," IKEA Canada at https://www.ikea.com/ms/en_CA/this-is-ikea/people-and-planet/index.html. Accessed March 14, 2019.

- **Case 14.1:** "Consumer Corner: Canadian Pet Market Outlook, 2014," Alberta Agriculture and Forestry, accessed January 2, 2016, http://www1.agric.gov.ab.ca/$department/deptdocs.nsf/all/sis14914; "Latest Canadian Pet Population Figures Released," Released February 12, 2015, Canadian Animal Health Institute, accessed January 2, 2016, https://www.canadianveterinarians.net/documents/canadian-pet-population-figures-cahi-2014; The Pet Industry Joint Advisory Council—Canada, accessed January 2, 2016, http://www.pijaccanada.com/en/default.aspx; Canadian Animal Health Institute accessed January 2, 2016, http://www.cahi-icsa.ca/; Katrina Clarke, "Animal Magnetism: Young Professionals Looking for Companionship Aren't Getting Hitched—They're Getting Pets," *National Post*, July 19, 2014, A9; Garry Marr, "Doing the Math on Your Cute, but Costly, Best Friend," *National Post*, September 11, 2013, FP6; E. Paul Cherniack and Ariella R. Cherniack, *Canadian Medical Association Journal*, July 14, 2015, 187 (10), 715–716; and "Dog-Dazed," CBC/Radio Canada, accessed January 2, 2016, http://www.cbc.ca/doczone/episodes/dog-dazed. "Dog-Dazed" also is available on YouTube at https://www.youtube.com/watch?v=E-F9Co_oFZc.

- **Case 14.2:** Adapted from MovieReviewIntelligence, "Dr. Seuss's The Lorax Movie Reviews," http://moviereviewintelligence.com/movie-reviews/dr_seuss_the_lorax/, accessed December 12, 2012; Rotten Tomatoes, "The Lorax Movie Reviews," http://rottentomatoes.com/m/the_lorax/reviews, accessed December 12, 2012; and Martin Morrow, "A Dr., a Lorax and a timely message," *The Globe and Mail*, December 19, 2017, A12.

Chapter 15

- **What would you do if...?:** "2011 Intellectual Property (IP) Crime Statistics," Royal Canadian Mounted Police, accessed August 9, 2016, http://www.rcmp-grc.gc.ca/fep-pelf/ipr-dpi/report-rapport-2012-eng.htm; and *Report on Counterfeiting and Piracy in Canada: A Road Map for Change*, Canadian Anti-Counterfeiting Network, accessed August 9, 2016, http://cacn.ca/wp-content/uploads/2013/09/Roadmap_for_Change.pdf and http://cacn.ca/wp-content/uploads/2013/09/CACN-Report-on-counterfeiting-Executive-Update-nov-2011.pdf.

- **Responsibility for Ethics 15.2:** Adapted from "About CorpWatch" at https://corpwatch.org/node/4?id=11314 accessed March 18, 2019; "Who We Are," Oxfam International at https://www.oxfam.org/en/about:// accessed March 18, 2019; "Who We Are," Amnesty International at https://www.amnesty.org/en/who-we-are/, accessed March 18, 2019; and "About Us," Greenpeace International at https://www.greenpeace.org/international/explore/about/ accessed March 18, 2019.

- **Everyday Ethics 15.1:** "Decoding Environmental Logos," Domtar Corporation web site at https://www.domtar.com/sites/default/files/2018-05/SustainabilityDeciphered-Infographic_1920X1080_0.pdf accessed March 20, 2019.
- **Responsibility for Ethics 15.3:** Adapted from "Principles of Business," Caux Round Table,http://www.cauxroundtable.org/principles; "Guidelines for Multinational Enterprises," Organisation for Economic Co-operation and Development (OECD) at http://www.oecd.org/corporate/mne/; "Principles for Global Corporate Responsibility: Benchmarks for Measuring Business Performance" at https://www.bench-marks.org/; "About The Equator Principles," The Equator Principles Association at https://equator-principles.com/about/; and "The Principles for Responsible Investment" at https://www.unpri.org/pri/what-are-the-principles-for-responsible-investment.
- **Table 15.2:** Compiled from Corruption Perceptions Index 2018, Transparency International at https://www.transparency.org/cpi2018 accessed March 20, 2019.
- **Responsibility for Ethics 15.4:** Adapted from Extractive Industries Transparency Initiative at www.eiti.org. accessed March 20, 2019
- **Everyday Ethics 15.3:** "Working Together for a Sustainable Future: Sustainable Development Summary Report 2017," Agnico Eagle Mines Limited at https://s21.q4cdn.com/374334112/files/doc_downloads/2018/11344_SD-Summary_2017_EN.pdf, page 14, accessed March 21, 2019.
- **Everyday Ethics 15.4:** Compiled from "Code of Conduct for Suppliers," Reitmans (Canada) Limited at http://content.reitmanscanadalimited.com/pdf/code_of_conduct.pdf?_ga=2.129238212.932506600.1553002699-214190148.1553002699 accessed March 20, 2019.
- **Everyday Ethics 15.5:** Adapted from "An Economy for the 1%," Oxfam Canada, January 17, 2016 at https://www.oxfam.ca/publication/an-economy-for-the-1/ accessed March 20, 2019.
- **Everyday Ethics 15.6:** Adapted from "Face Value: Macro Credit," *The Economist*, October 21, 2006, 78; Nobel Prize.org, "The Nobel Peace Prize 2006," http://nobelprize.org/nobel_prizes/peace/laureates/2006/index.html; and Grameen Bank, http://www.grameen-info.org accessed March 20, 2019.
- **Case 15.1:** "Swept Aside: An Investigation into Human Rights Abuse at Kinross Gold's Morro do Ouro Mine," Above Ground, December 11, 2017 at https://aboveground.ngo/swept-aside-report-kinross-gold-morro-ouro/; "Responsible Mining at Paracatu," Kinross Gold Corporation at https://s2.q4cdn.com/496390694/files/doc_downloads/2018/CSR_Reports/CSR_Paracatu_v3.pdf; "Brazil: NGOs allege that Morro do Ouro gold mine violated land, environmental & cultural rights, including right to FPIC; it includes comments and rejoinder from the NGOs, Kinross & Export Dev.," Business & Human Rights Resource Centre at https://www.business-humanrights.org/en/brazil-justi%C3%A7a-global-fed-quilombola-do-est-de-mg-n%E2%80%99golo-and-above-ground-accuse-kinross-export-dev-canada-of-human-rights-abuses-it-includes-comments-from-the-institutions; and Operations—Paracatu, Brazil, Kinross Gold Corporation at https://www.kinross.com/operations/default.aspx#americas-paracatu.
- **Case 15.2:** Adapted from Steve Hamm and Nandini Lakshman, "Widening Aisles for Indian Shoppers," *BusinessWeek*, April 30, 2007, 44; Rajesh Mahapatra, "Wal-Mart Taps into Booming Indian Market," *The Globe and Mail*, August 7, 2007, B8; Anuj Choppa, "Retail Giants Push India's Shopkeepers to the Brink," *The Globe and Mail,* October 30, 2007, B17; "India Retreats on Retail Reform," *The Globe and Mail*, December 8, 2011, p. B8; and Brad Stone and Saritha Rai, "A Package to India," Bloomberg *BusinessWeek*, October 22, 2018, 42–47.

Chapter 16

- **What would you do if...?:** Our Purpose, Mission and Values," Canadian Business for Social Responsibility web site at https://www.cbsr.ca/who-we-are. Used with permission from CBSR.
- **Everyday Ethics 16.1:** St. John's Bakery at http://www.stjohnsbakery.com; Cleaning Solution at http://www.cleaningsolution.ca; Internet Café at https://www.nlhhn.org/cafe.htm; EthniCity at http://centrefornewcomers.ca/ethnicity-catering; and Just Us! Coffee at https://www.justuscoffee.com/.
- **Everyday Ethics 16.2:** Adapted from Enactus web site at http://enactus.org/ and https://enactus.org/country/canada/ accessed March 30, 2019. Used with permission.
- **Everyday Ethics 16.3:** Compiled from Bullfrog Power, accessed August 9, 2016, www.bullfrogpower.com/our-story/; Salt Spring Coffee, accessed February 3, 2016, www.saltspringcoffee.com; PeaceWorks, accessed February 3, 2016, peaceworks.ca/about-us; Enviro-Stewards, accessed February 3, 2016, www.enviro-stewards.com/; "About," Animikii Inc. web site at https://www.animikii.com/ accessed March 22, 2019; and "About," Business Development Bank of Canada at https://www.bdc.ca/en/about/who-we-are/pages/default.aspx accesseed on March 25, 2019.
- **Everyday Ethics 16.4:** Adapted from Centre for Social Innovation web site at https://socialinnovation.org/ accessed March 26, 2019, and The McConnell Foundation at https://mcconnellfoundation.ca/about/purpose/ and http://mcconnellfoundation.ca/en/programs/social-innovation-fund accessed March 26, 2019.
- **Responsibility for Ethics 16.2** Adapted from Principles for Responsible Management Education (PRME) at http://www.unprme.org/about-prme/the-six-principles.php accessed March 30, 2019.

- **Everyday Ethics 16.6:** "Making the grade," *Corporate Knights,* Fall 2018 Issue, November 9, 2018 accessed at https://www.corporateknights.com/magazines/2018-better-world-mba-issue/making-the-grade-15417432/ on January 2, 2019.

- **Case 16.1:** Adapted from Jason Markusoff, "If You Build It, He Will Come," *Maclean's Magazine*, October 19, 2015, 56–57; "Spinning Spinoffs," *The Telegram* (St. John's, NL), September 24, 2014, A6; "No Public Money for Saddledome 2.0," *National Post*, November 14, 2014, A16; "A Monument to Government Waste," *National Post*, January 29, 2015, A8; and Jen Gerson, "Nenshi's re-election is a win for every city blackmailed by a sports team," *National Post*, October 17, 2018 at https://nationalpost.com/opinion/jen-gerson-neshis-re-election-a-win-for-every-city-blackmailed-by-a-sports-team.

- **Case 16.2:** Airbnb: "Advantages and Disadvantages," Investopedia at https://www.investopedia.com/articles/personal-finance/032814/pros-and-cons-using-airbnb.asp; "11 Pros And Cons Of Using AirBnB You Need To Know," BaldThoughts.com at https://baldthoughts.boardingarea.com/2018/02/pro-cons-airbnb; and "Explore Airbnb," Airbnb Inc. web site at https://www.airbnb.com/. All accessed on March 25, 2019.

- **Table 16.3:** Marc Stears and Imogen Parker, "Responsible capitalism and behavioural change: Evaluating the Social Business Trust and planning for the future," Institute for Public Policy Research, December 2012 at https://www.ippr.org/files/images/media/files/publication/2012/12/responsible-capitalism_Dec2012_9999.pdf.

  "About Us," *Corporate Knights: The Magazine for Clean Capitalism,* https://www.corporateknights.com/us/about-us/.

  "Learn What We Do," Conscious Capitalism®, at https://www.consciouscapitalism.org/learn-what-we-do. John Mackey, founder and co-CEO of Whole Foods Market, is the leading business proponent of conscious capitalism.

  "About," Caux Round Table for Moral Capitalism at http://www.cauxroundtable.org/.

  Barbara Kiviat and Bill Gates, "Making Capitalism More Creative," *Time* (online edition), July 31, 2008, http://content.time.com/time/magazine/article/0,9171,1828417,00.html.

  Coalition for Inclusive Capitalism at https://www.inc-cap.com/.

- **Responsibility for Ethics 15.5:** Source: Adapted from United Nations Sustainable Development Goals, accessed March 24, 2019, https://www.un.org/sustainabledevelopment/blog/2016/08/sdgs-egovernance/.

Index